Mudrās

in Buddhist and Hindu Practices

— An Iconographic Consideration —

by

Fredrick W. Bunce

Professor Emeritus of Art

Indiana State University

D.K. Printworld (P) Ltd.

New Delhi

Mudrās

in Buddhist and Hindu Practices

Cataloging in Publication Data — DK
[Courtesy: D.K. Agencies (P) Ltd. <docinfo@dkagencies.com>]

Bunce, Fredrick W. (Fredrick William), 1935-
Mudrās in Buddhist and Hindu practices : an iconographic consideration / by Fredrick W. Bunce.
p. cm.
Includes bibliographical references (p.)
ISBN 13: 9788124603123
ISBN 10: 812460312X

1. Mudrās (Buddhism) — Encyclopedias. 2. Mudrās (Hinduism) — Encyclopedias. 3. Gesture — Encyclopedias. 4. Idols and images — Encyclopedias. I. Title.

DDC 704.948 943 21

ISBN 13: 978-81-246-0312-3
ISBN 10: 81-246-0312-X
First Published in India in 2005
Second impression in 2009

Published and printed by:
D.K. Printworld (P) Ltd.
Regd. office : *"Sri Kunj,"* F-52, Bali Nagar,
Ramesh Nagar Metro Stn., New Delhi - 110 015
Phones : (011) 2545 3975; 2546 6019; *Fax* : (011) 2546 5926
E-mail: dkprintworld@vsnl.net
Web: www.dkprintworld.com

Cataloging in Publication Data — DK
[Courtesy: D.K. Agencies (P) Ltd. <docinfo@dkagencies.com>]

Bunce, Fredrick W. (Fredrick William), 1935-
Mudrās in Buddhist and Hindu practices : an iconographic consideration / by Fredrick W. Bunce.
p. cm.
Includes bibliographical references (p.)
ISBN 13: 9788124603123
ISBN 10: 812460312X

1. Mudrās (Buddhism) — Encyclopedias. 2. Mudrās (Hinduism) — Encyclopedias. 3. Gesture — Encyclopedias. 4. Idols and images — Encyclopedias. I. Title.

DDC 704.948 943 21

ISBN 13: 978-81-246-0312-3
ISBN 10: 81-246-0312-X
First Published in India in 2005
Second impression in 2009

Published and printed by:
D.K. Printworld (P) Ltd.
Regd. office : *"Sri Kunj,"* F-52, Bali Nagar,
Ramesh Nagar Metro Stn., New Delhi - 110 015
Phones : (011) 2545 3975; 2546 6019; *Fax* : (011) 2546 5926
E-mail: dkprintworld@vsnl.net
Web: www.dkprintworld.com

Contents

List of Figures

List of Figures

List of Figures

List of Figures

List of Figures

List of Figures

List of Figures

List of Figures

List of Figures

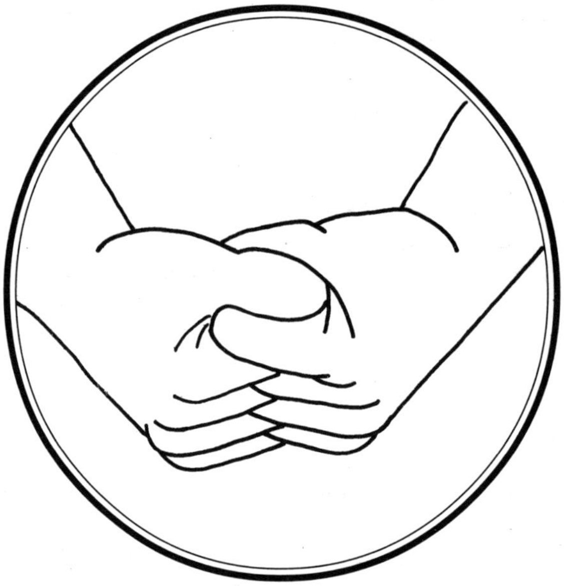

User's Guide

User's Guide

1.
General

Since this is a compilation, the information is as it appears within the various sources--both visual and verbal. Within the purview of the sources, the variations are also noted. Since there may be a number of mudras which do not appear within this compilation, please, realize that this is not a "sin of commission," rather one of unintended omission.

The Headwords appear under their English transliteral phonetic equivalent.

In general, this compilation is arranged in the following sequence:

Headwords,
Language origins, variations and other language terms,
Descriptions,
Sources, and
Figures, if appropriate.

These entries are followed by:

Bibliography,
Descriptive Terms' Designations,
Mudra List.

1.1
Transliterations

The Languages utilized in this compilation are not represented by their unique scripts, rather they are presented in their "English transliteral phonetic equivalent" forms, which refers to those terms (**headwords**) which are presented in an English phonetic form--e.g., *chatur* as opposed to *catur*. Whereas the phrase "Indic (Chinese, Pali or Tibetan, etc.) transliteral equivalent" refers to those terms (**headwords**) which are presented with the proper diacritical marks or other transliteral equivalent forms--e.g., *chih-ch'ṃan-yin* as opposed to *chih-ch'uan-yin*. The exception is Tibetan (See: below).

1.1.1
Language Transliterations

The **language transliterations** used in this compilation are:

Chin. = Chinese: The English **transliteral phonetic equivalent** used herein is that of the Wade-Giles, rather than the Pinyin as the former is that which is found in the sources;

Eng. = English: English terms are only utilized in **headwords** when the source(s) use it and do not include the appropriate **transliteral equivalents;**

Ind. = Indic: Represents the various related languages of the sub-continent--e.g., Sanskrit, Hindi, Tamil, etc.--in all cases the English **transliteral phonetic equivalent** is used in the **headwords;**

Jap. = Japanese: The English **transliteral phonetic equivalent** is used in the **headwords;**

Pali = Generally Pali is the formal language of Thai Theravada Buddhism and is used infrequently in this compilation;

Thai = The English **transliteral phonetic equivalent** of Thai terms is used in the **headwords;**

Tib. = Tibetan: The **transliteral equivalents** used are those of A. von Staḷl-Holstein and S. C. Das, English **transliteral phonetic equivalent** are not utilized.

2.
Individual Entries/ Headwords

2.1
Word order

The individual entries are alphabetical, according to the Roman/English alphabet, including the Tibetan language transliterations, therefore--e.g., *hKhor-lo* appears under "H" rather then "K."

2.2 Transliteral Variations

In addition, the inter-changeable use of the letters "v" and "w" or, in some instances "b" and "v" found within the Sanskrit are presented as found within the particular source--e.g., *deva/dewa*, etc.

3. Language Origin, Variation(s) and Other Language(s) Parenthesis

3.1 language origin

Following the **headword** immediately within the parenthesis will be found the **language origin**.

3.2 transliteral equivalent

A *mudra's* primary entry (**headword**) and description, within this compilation, will be found generally following the **transliteral equivalent** form. However, if there is no language **transliteral equivalent** noted, it will appear as found in the text cited, in English. This language **transliteral equivalent** will be found within the parenthesis directly following each primary entry (**headword**)--e.g., **chandra-mriga mudra** -- (Ind.: *candra-mṛga-mudrā*) ; or **pang phratabreakhanan** -- (Thai: *pang phratabreakhanan*; Indic: *abhaya-katyavalaṁbita mudrā*); or **hora no-in (mudra)** -- (Jap.: *hora no-in* [*mudra*]; Ind.: *śaṅkha mudrā*). See: **11. Sample Entry** below.

3.3 Diacritical Marks

The diacritical marks that are frequently used in the presentation of transliterated Indic languages are omitted in the **headwords**. The Indic transliteral equivalent does appear within the **Language Origin[s] and Other Language(s) Parenthesis** (See: **12. Sample Entry** below) following each appropriate **headword.** In the **Mudra List** at the rear of this study, diacritical marks are not employed.

However, since this is a compilation of terms from various sources, the spellings of the *mudras* are as they appear therein. As such, in some cases, the 's' presents a problem. That is, whether the Indic is 's' or 'ṣ' or 's' is in some cases not noted--e.g., HS does not indicate the diacritical marks of any of the primary 'S' and the internal 's.'

The **phonetic transliterations** employed are as follows:

c	=	ch (as in church)
ṛ	=	ri (as in rich)
ṣ	=	sh (as in shine)
ś	=	sh (as in sheet [retroflex])

3.4 Headword transliteral variations

One scholar may present the transliteral spelling of a *mudra* one way whereas another may indicate a variation--e.g., *mukha* or *mukham*--generally, one spelling variation will be employed. However, if there are significant variations, they will appear after the Indic **transliteral equivalent** following the abbreviation "aka" (also known as).

3.5 Headword other term(s)

A number of *mudras* are known by another term or terms within a particular language. When these **headword other term(s)** are single or double, they will appear within the **Language Origin and Variation(s) Parenthesis** following the Indic **transliteral equivalent** and preceded by the abbreviation "aka."

3.6
Headword translated or other applied terms

Numerous headwords often refer to a specific thing or action. Where these are known they will appear in a separate parentheses and within quotes, following the **Language Origin, Variation(s) and Other Language(s) Parenthesis**.

4.
Mudra Description

Following the **Language Origin, Variation(s) and other Language(s) Parentheses** will appear a descriptive passage of varying lengths. The **Mudra Description** may include:

4.1
Relation to other languages or *mudras*,

4.2
Type of *mudra*--i.e., deity centered, Tantric centered, etc., and

4.3
Verbal description of the *mudra*.

5.
Source(s) Parenthesis

The **source(s)** from which the information presented in each entry has been compiled will appear within parentheses as initials at the end of each entry. The initials are also found below under Initial **Abbreviations** and the complete entry will be found in the **Bibliography:** See: **11. Example Entry**, and **5.1 Initial Abbreviations**, below. This abbreviation will be followed by a number which refers to the page from which the material was gleaned--e.g., (GDe 66)--i.e., Gauri Devi, *Esoteric Mudras of Japan: etc.*, p. 66.

5.1
Initial Abbreviations List

The following are identifying initial abbreviations which appear in parentheses after each entry, where applicable. Full bibliographic information is to be found in the Bibliography.

AAv Arthur Avalon, Shakta and Shakti.
ACG Ananda Coomaraswamy and Gopala Kristnayya Duggirala, *The Mirror of Gesture.*
AGe Alice Getty, *The Gods of Northern Buddhism*: etc.
AKG Antoinette K. Gordon, *The Iconography of Tibetan Lamaism.*
AMK Ajit Mookerjee and Madhu Khanna, *The Tantric Way: Art, Science, Ritual.*
AMo Ajit Mookerjee, *Ritual Art of India.*
BBh Benoytosh Bhattacharyya, *The Indian Buddhist Iconography Mainly Based on the Seadhatermalea and other Cognate Tantric Texts of Ritual.*
BCO Blanche Christine Olschak, *Mystic Art of Ancient Tibet.*
BNS B. N. Sharma, *Iconographic Parallelism in India and Nepal.*
CSi C. Sivaramamurti, *The Art of India*
DRN Damrong Rajanubhab, (Prince), *Monuments of the Buddha in Siam.*
EDS E. Dale Saunders, *Mudra: A Study of Symbolic Gestures in Japanese Buddhist Sculpture.*
ERJ Eva Rudy Jansen, *The Book of Buddhas.*
ERJ II Eva Rudy Jansen, *The Book of Hindu Imagery.*
GDe Gauri Devi, *Esoteric Mudras of Japan: etc.*
GLi G. Liebert, *Iconographic dictionary of the Indian Religions.*
HKS H. Krishna Sastri. *South-Indian Images of Gods and Goddesses.*
HZi H. Zimmer, ed. by J. Campbell. *The Art of Indian Asia.*
JDo John Dowson, *A Classical Dictionary of Hindu Mythology.*
JBo Jean Boisselier, *The Heritage of Thai Sculpture.*
KDe Keshav Dev, *Mudra Vigyan: A Way of Life.*

KIM K.I. Matics, *A History of Wat Phra Chetuphon and its Buddha Images.*

KVa Kapila Vatsyayan, *Indian Classical Dance.*

LCB Lokesh Chandra and Fredrick W. Bunce, *360 Buddhas, Bodhisattvas and Other Deities: The "Chu Fo P'u-sa Sheng Hsiang Tsan" a Unique Pantheon.*

LCS Lokesh Chandra and Sharada Rani, *Mudras in Japan: etc.*

MiS Michael Saso, *Homa Rites and Mandala Meditation in Tendai Buddhism.*

MJS M. and J. Stutley, *A Dictionary of Hinduism.*

MMR Marylin M. Rhie and Robert A. F. Thurman, *Wisdom and Compassion, the Sacred Art of Tibet.*

MSD M.C. Subhadradis Diskul, *Art in Thailand: A Brief History.*

ODD Oxford University Press, *Oxford-Duden Pictorial Thai and English Dictionary.*

OFr O. Frankfurter, "The Attitudes of the Buddha," *Journal of the Siam Society.*

PBa P. Banerjee, et al. *Buddhist Iconography.*

PSa Prem Saran, Tantra, *Hedonism in Indian Culture.*

PSS (Phra) Suradej Sutthi, *Translation of Thai pang (mudras).*

RKP R. K. Poduval, *Administrative Report of the Archeological Department.*

RLM Rambavan A. Mishra, & Lalbihasri Mishra, *Nityakarma-Pujaprakasha.*

RNW Réne de Nebesky-Wojkowitz, *Oracles and Demons of Tibet: The Cult and Iconography of the Tibetan Protective Deities.*

RSG Ramesh S. Gupte, *Iconography of the Hindus, Buddhists and Jains.*

SBa Stephen Batchelor, *The Tibetan Guide.*

SBe Stephan Beyer, *The Cult of Tara: Magic and Ritual in Tibet.*

SVB Steve Van Beek and Luca Invernizzi Tettoni, *The Arts of Thailand.*

TGR T. A. Gopinatha Rao, *Elements of Hindu Iconography.*

6. Figures

The **Figures** are drawn reproductions of the described *mudras*, and are identified by the appropriate and corresponding **Figure #, Mudra Title (headword)**.

The drawn **Figures** within this compilation are of two types and are so noted after the **Mudra Title (headword):**

6.1 "as seen by the holder"

refers to the point of view as seen by the eyes of the one holding the *mudra.*

6.2 "as seen by another"

refers to the point of view as seen by the eyes of an observer, another person, other than the one holding the *mudra*, and generally, in front, or in rare instances to the side of the one holding the *mudra.*

7. Bibliography

The **Bibliography** includes those specific sources cited in the text within the **Source(s) Parenthesis** as well as corollary material related to this compilation.

8. Appendix A: Descriptive Terms' Designations

Due to the numerous and often confusing terms employed which are related to the verbal description of *mudras*, the following computer generated drawings along with specific descriptive terms and/or phrases are included. These terms are those utilized within the descriptions within this compilation and appear following the **Bibliography**.

9. Appendix B: Thai Postures of the Lord Buddha

The **Thai Postures of the Lord Buddha**, follow the **Descriptive Terms' Designations**. They are those ordered by Chakri King, Rama III (Phra Nangklao) from the Prince Patriarch Paramanujita Jinorasa (Somtej Phra Paramanujit), are included as there are 'new' positions established and they assume major importance in Southeast Asia.

10. Appendix C: Mudra List

An aplhabetized **Mudra List** is included of all the *mudras* (**headwords**) within the compilation. Diacritical marks are not employed in the **Mudrā List**.

11. Sample Entry

abhaya mudra III[(2.1)] -- (Ind.:[(3.1)] *abhaya-mudrā*[(3.2)] aka *abhayamdada mudrā,*[(3.5)] *śaṇtida mudrā;*[(3.5)] Eng.:[(3.1)] restraining the waters *mudra;*[(3.5)] Chin.:[(3.1)] *shih-wu-wei-yin;*[(3.5)] Jap.:[(3.1)] *semui-in;*[(3.5)] Tib.:[(3.1)] *jigs-med phyag-rgya*[(3.5)])[(3)] A *mudra*, a ritual hand pose, a seal, which is common to the Theravada Buddhist tradition in Thailand.[(4.1)] One of forty *mudras* and *asanas* compiled by the Prince Patriarch Paramanujita Jinorasa and established during the reign of Rama III as being acceptable for the depiction of images of The Lord Buddha--i.e., "restraining the waters" the fourteenth of the forty attitudes noted.[3][(4.2)] This *abhaya-mudra* is a combined (Ind.: *saṁyutta*) form, held by both hands. In this form the hands are raised, fingers and thumbs extended upwards and together, relaxed, slightly cupped, palm facing outward and generally on a line level with the chest or shoulders. Thus formed, the hands are held at either side of the shoulders.[(4.3)] The figure is standing in this pose. It is related to the *abhaya mudra I.* See: *abhaya-abhaya mudra.* (BBh[(5.1)] 189, JBo[(5.1)])[(5)] (See: **Figure 3**)[(6)]

abhaya mudra IV[(2.1)] -- (Ind.:[(3.1)] *abhaya-mudrā*[(3.2)])[(3)] A *mudra*, a ritual hand pose, a seal, a *mudra* which is common to yogic tradition, particularly the *Yoga Tatva Mudra Vigyan* form,[(4.1)] and is held by a devotee or practitioner. This *abhaya-mudra* is a combined (Ind.: *saṁyutta*) form, held by both hands. It is utilized for sacrifice, fearlessness and courage.[(4.2)] This *mudra* is formed by both hands in the deity-centered *vitarka-mudra* -- i.e., palm facing outwards, tips of the thumb and index finger touch, middle, ring and little fingers are relaxed and point upwards--held at shoulder level and to either side of the body.[4][(4.3)] (KDe[(5.1)] 32)[(5)] (See: **Figure 4**)[(6)]

Preface
&
Introduction

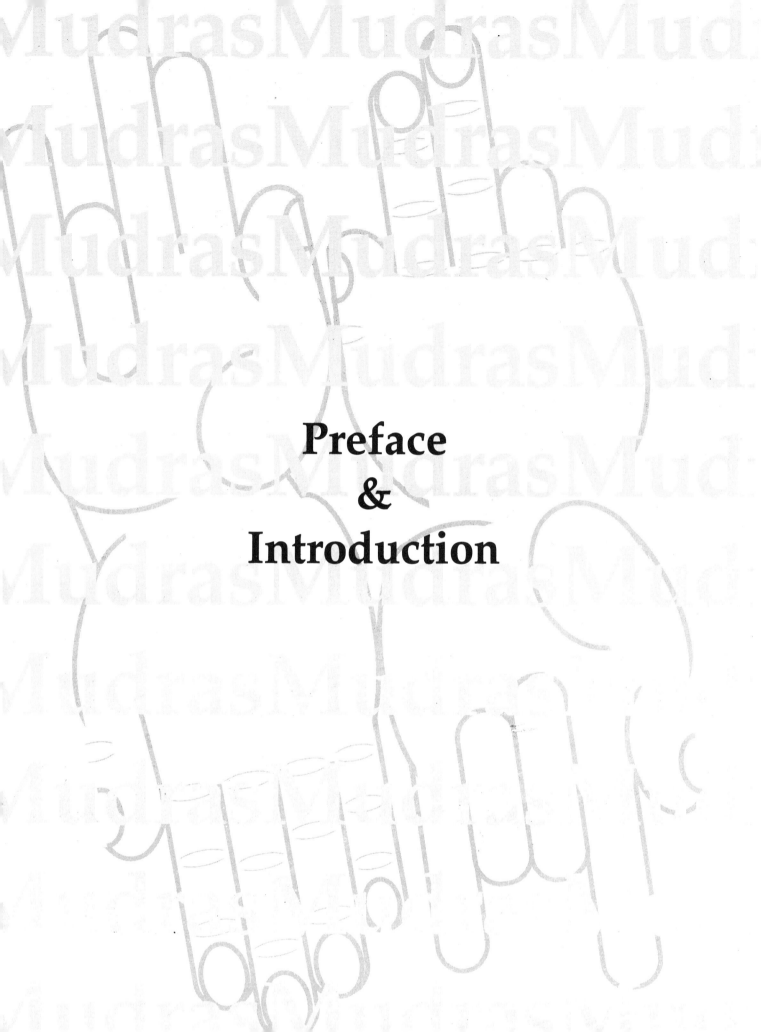

Preface

The genesis of this compilation has come from three works which the author had previously published--i.e., *An Encyclopaedia of Buddhist Deities, Demigods, Godlings, Saints and Demons: With Special Focus on Iconographic Attributes.*; *A Dictionary of Buddhist and Hindu Iconography--Illustrated--Objects, Devices, Concepts, Rites and Related Terms*; and *An Encyclopaedia of Hindu Deities, Demigods, Godlings Demons and Heroes: With Special Focus on Iconographic Attributes*. It was noted that there were a number of *mudra* which were specifically assigned to the deities of the two pantheons. Also, a number of these *mudras* were identical to those practiced by Tibetan, Chinese and Japanese Buddhist (*Vajrayana, Mantrayana*) traditions and held or formed by a devotee or priest during various rites, as well as various *yogic* and dramatic practices. Identical, but frequently with different terms or names. It was decided to compile the hundreds of *mudra*--i.e., deity centered, rite centered, *yogic* centered and dramatic centered--in one volume and to illustrate each.

In so doing, it is to be noted that there are numerous citations. Some may feel that the notes are inordinate in their profusion. However, they were included so that the reader may easily: refer to the proper locations, become aware of the varied interpretations of a number of *mudra*, and be made aware of clarifying additions made by the author.

It was decided to illustrate the *mudras* with drawings for ease of identification. Each unique *mudra* is illustrated by an individual drawing. The drawings are generally drawn from the perspective of the one holding the *mudra*, except in those instances where it was deemed more illustrative to draw the *mudra* from the viewer's standpoint.

F.W. Bunce

Introduction

From the mundane to the esoteric, from the sacred to the profane, from the religious to the secular, symbols, iconographs, have been part of the human repertoire since time in memorium. Some of the earliest elements of iconography are to be seen in pertoglyphs and paintings preserved on the walls of caves. Whatever humankind has touched or made can be seen as a symbol.

Symbols of wealth and power may be the most ostentatious--from an emerald necklace to a Rolls Royce, or a villa on the Riviera. Conspicuous consumption sets one group part from another, the "haves" from the "have nots," the wealthy from the less wealthy or poor. Symbols of rank may be viewed in various circumstances--e.g., the cut and shape of an academic hood worn during formal ceremonies, the shape, size and adornment of the coronets of peers worn during a coronation; and in Southeast Asia the wearing of yellow clothing has been and still is reserved for royalty (sultans) and their immediate family. There are symbols which have been associated with vocation--e.g., a needle and thread with a tailor, or a hammer and saw with a carpenter. A flat brimmed, high crown bowler-like hat identifies Peruvian Indians, or a full feathered headdress with feathered trailer signifies members of the Sioux Tribe. all are symbols of belonging and affiliation.

These secular symbols and the myriad others have been overshadowed by religious symbols. This is particularly true in the visual arts.

There are a number of iconographic features associated with both Buddhist and Hindu deities with rather precise, technical meanings and/or descriptions. Terms which apply when the deities are represented in either two- or three-dimensional forms. For example: the term *vajra* (Ind.; Tib.: *rdor-rje*) refers to a diamond or adamantine scepter which is symbolic of indestructibility and the wisdom which destroys passion. Its form is rather precise, allowing for regional variations. The same is true of a stupa (Ind.[1]: *caitya*; Tib.: *mcod-rten*) which is an architectural form that is synonymous with Buddhism; or a trident (Ind.: *triśūla*; Tib.: *rtse-gsum*) which is more often seen in Hindu iconography. The various devices with characteristics unique to their practices are, indeed numerous and sometimes rather complicated.

Iconic attributes are not limited to objects held or worn, but also apply to bodily forms as well. Among the most important of these traits are the positions--i.e., ritual positions--held by the hand(s) of the various deities--i.e., *mudras* or *hastas*.[2]

Mudras, or hand positions are not the sole province of either the Hindu (Brahmanic) or Buddhist religions. In Christianity hand positions are often a telling feature of the Deity or of a saint. Frequently the Lord Christ is shown with his right hand raised, his index and middle fingers extended upwards, his ring and little fingers folded into the palm and the thumb overlapping the latter two. This is known as a symbol of grace or benediction or of forgiveness. Likewise, a female saint may be depicted with their hands crossed over her breasts. This is particularly true of martyrs. That hand position signifies resignation and the acceptance of the will of God. Also, this latter position is often seen to be held by the body of a deceased in the Christian tradition. The meaning is the same--acceptance of God's will.

Very often Buddhist and Hindu *mudras* indicate the character of the deity and in most cases they are a great aid in identifying the particular deity in question. In addition, a number of the *mudras*--i.e., *Tantric mudras*--are held by the devotees and/or the priests/lamas who are participating in a specific ceremony.

For the casual observer or devotee the presentation in either two- or three-dimensional form of a deity, whether Buddhist or Hindu, is important. The various technical terms that are applied to the deity are, in most cases, of little interest to these casual spectators. For the student/researcher of religious practices, these technical/descriptive terms began assume some tangible and/or iconic importance.

Mudras can be arranged into four subcategories--i.e., 1) those which are generally held or depicted in the representation of deities, demigods, godlings, demons and heroes, both Buddhist and Hindu, 2) those which are associated with particular *tantric* worship, particularly of Japanese, Chinese and Tibetan *Vajrayana* or *Mantrayana* rites, 3) those which are associated with *yogic* meditational practices, and 4) those which are associated with dramatic practices, including dance. There are a number of *mudras* which are unique to or are strictly deity-centered--e.g., *dharmacakra-mudra* or *vajrahumkara-mudra*--others are similar or identical with deity-centered *mudras*, but with different titles or names--e.g., *pataka-mudra* (*abhaya-mudra*) or the drama oriented *suchi-mudra*[3] (*tarjani-mudra*)--and still others which are unique to *tantric*, *yogic* and dramatic practices. The first category, those associated with specific deities, is rather finite--amounting to a few score positions. It is within the category of *tantric* rites, particularly as practiced in Japan, that hand positions multiply to the hundreds.

Within these four subcategories the *mudras* may be further delineated into single hand (Ind.: *asamyutta*) and combined (Ind.: *samyutta*)or two-handed *mudras*. Single hand, "static" positions predominates within the first--i.e., the deity centered--group. That is not to say that *mudras* involving both hands, combined *mudras*, do not form an important part within this category.[4] When one merely considers the possible variations of a single fist the myriad of possible *mudras* is truly staggering--e.g., 1) fist with thumb placed on the third phalange of the index finger, 2) fist with thumb placed on the second phalange of the index finger, 3) fist with thumb placed on the first phalange of the index finger, 4) fist with thumb folded inside the fingers, 5) fist with thumb folded inside the fingers and the index finger curled so that its nail rests on the second phalanges of the thumb, etc., etc., etc. Among the latter three categories single hand *mudras* do exist and are of some importance. However, within these categories the combined-form *mudras* proliferates. In *tantric, yogic* and dramatic practices, *mudras* are formed and movement is frequently required to fulfill the tenets of the particular *mudra*--i.e., within the rites of *Tendai* Buddhism of Japan the"*Hak-Ken: Mudra* for sending off the Vision" requires a triple "flicking motion" of the index fingers.[5]

In considering just two works--i.e., Lokesh Chandra and Sharada Rani, *Mudras in Japan: etc.* and Gauri Devi, *Esoteric Mudras of Japan: etc.*--1,811 separate illustrations needed to be considered. A large number were repeated. In the case of the "*vajranjali-mudra*," it was duplicated one-hundred-seventeen times in the two works. A system was needed to facilitate the ease of identification of these 1,811 illustrations. They may be grouped into approximately 430 different and distinct *mudras*.[6] This identification system involved first: single, double or combination *mudras* and their variations. Single hand *mudras* are: 1) fist-type *mudras*: those in which three or more fingers (including the thumb) are brought into or in close proximity with the palm, 2) open hand-type *mudras*: those in which two or less fingers (including the thumb) are brought into or in close proximity with the palm, and 3) others: single hand *mudras* which to not conform to the two variations noted above. Double or combination hand *mudras* are: 1) inner fist-type *mudras* ("Inner Bonds Fist" [Jap.: *naibaku ken-in*]): in which three or more fingers (including the thumb) are interlaced and are folded into the palm of the hand, 2) outer fist-type *mudras* ("Outer Bonds Fist" [Jap.: *gebaku ken-in*]): in which three or more fingers (including the thumb) are interlaced and rest on the back of the hand, 3) *anjali*-type *mudras*: where hands are brought together, palm towards palm, the fingers are extended upwards and tips generally touch or are in close proximity, 4) *stupa*-type mudras: similar to the *anjali*-type except, the thumbs rest together and point upwards, and the tips of the forefingers touch the tips of the thumbs in various manners (i.e., tips-to-tips, tips of the index fingers in front of the tips of the thumbs, or tips of the index fingers behind of the tips of the thumbs), 5) *dhyana*-type *mudras*: where one hand rests upon the other, the fingers generally extended in some manner, and 6) others: double or combination-type *mudras* which to not conform to the five double variations noted above.

There are numerous English sources which in part deal with these myriad iconic features in greater or lesser detail. There are, on the other hand, isolated studies which are quite detailed.[7] For the student/researcher these sources become quite important, particularly if he or she is not acquainted or fluent in the languages of the numerous prime sources--e.g., Sanskrit, Tibetan, Japanese, Chinese, Mongolian, etc. Clarity of description assumes the level of a prime concern.

Discrepancies within the descriptive passages become highly problematical. It becomes obvious in consulting the various sources available that there is, if not a discrepancy or confusion, at least some variation(s) which exists between the written term and the visualized or drawn *mudras* and/or *asanas*. When confronting the term "*abhaya mudra*" most sources recognize one form of this pose.[8] However, the term "*anjali mudra*" brings forth seemingly insoluble conundrums--i.e., there are described and/or shown three distinct forms which are related only through the use of the descriptive terms "salutation," "greeting," or "worship." Another problematical pose is the *vyakhyana mudra*. It is described as similar or another name for: the *dharmachakra mudra*, the *chin mudra*, or the *vitarka mudra*. Such problems are not isolated to the various *mudras*. In a similar manner, this apparent confusion or discrepancy also can be seen in *asanas*. The *asana* known as *ardhaparyankasana* is seen by some as a seated position while others view it as a standing position. Even the pose known as *alidhasana*, which is generally seen as a standing pose related to shooting a bow and arrow, is by one source named as a seated posture!

There were a number of problems which arose in the process of this compilation. Numerous descriptions found in A. Coomaraswamy, *The Mirror of Gesture*, were ambiguous and confusing. The importance of this work is not to be discounted, however, there are a number of confusing descriptions. Nonetheless, problems with the descriptions were plentiful--e.g., regarding *mudras* entitled: "*Aviddha-vakra* (swinging curve): . . . *Pataka* hands are shown with grace and with (movement of) the elbows" or "*Nitamba* (buttocks): *Pataka* hands face upwards, turned over, (extended from) the shoulder to the buttocks." In supplying a clear verbal description the "usage(s)" were taken into account and certain "leaps of faith" had to be made. These interpretational descriptions are duly noted. In the two works which display hundreds of esoteric Japanese *Mantrayana mudras*--i.e., Gauri Devi, *Esoteric Mudras of Japan: etc.*, and Lokesh Chandra and Sharada Rani, *Mudras in Japan: etc.*--numerous *mudras* were not entitled--e.g., LCS, pp., 64 #1.32, 116 #2,175, 174# 3.144-3.146, etc.--while there were *mudras* which bore titles that described their particular use during the various rites (in many cases there was conflict)--e.g., GDe, p. 166, "*Mudra* of *Ratna Bodhisattva* (i.e. of *Vajraratna*)," and the identical *mudra* on p. 178, "*Mudra* of *Arya Avalokitesvara*, no.2," and again the identical *mudra* in LCS, p. 114, # 2.167, "*Vajraraksa bodhisattva*," and still further,the identical *mudra* on p. 259, # 4.180 "*Mudra* of the edict of gods on earth." In none of these last four *mudras* was the gesture given either a Japanese or Indic name! Luckily, the *mudra* is virtually identical to the *uttarabodhi* noted and illustrated in a number of sources.[9]

Finally, a number of sources, particularly secondary sources, possess apparent errors which cannot be attributed to the prime source, but to lack of adequate proofing. The publication: *Mudra Vigyan -- A Way of Life*, indicates a number of spelling errors or un-noted variations--e.g., "*sinhakrant*" (p. 53), "*shinghakrant*" (p.86) and "*singhakrant*" (p. 108) all for the same *mudra*; "*veragya*" (pp. 27 & 108) and "*veiragya*" (p. 88).[10] To say that any publication is without typographical or proofing error would be vain, however, every effort should be made to present as consistent a work as possible.

Further, there are forty *mudras* established during the reign of Rama III as being acceptable for the depiction of images of The Lord Buddha.[11] These *mudras* do not necessarily find referents to traditional Hindu or *Mahayana* Buddhist *mudras*. Further, in many cases, the mudras find no referents to Indic terms. How then are they to be categorized and/or entitled?

This study, this compilation, therefore, utilizes as its parameters those studies which have gone before, particularly sources in English. A number of works assume major importance--e.g., Lokesh Chandra and Sharada Rani, *Mudras in Japan: etc.*; and Gauri Devi, *Esoteric Mudras of Japan: etc.*--if nothing else, because of the sheer mass of information contained.[12] Others, consulted are for popular consumption, but offer important or rarely seen *mudras*.[13]

In addition, where there are variations, they too, are listed. There are two additional categories which are to be found herein-- 1) "descriptive terms" which have been assigned to the forty *mudras* compiled by the Prince Patriarch Paramanujita Jinorasa (Paramanuchit Chinorot), and 2) "assigned terms" from the fifty-seven *mudras* illustrated in: Stephan Beyer, *The Cult of Tara: Magic and Ritual in Tibet*.

Other problems are found in both GDe and LCS in which *mudras* are presented which are associated with different deities and for which no common name is given--e.g., *Sachittotpada-Bodhisattva mudra* or *Dharmachakra-pravartana-bodhisattva-varga-mudra*.

A number of the drawings in the two above cited works were ill-conceived, poorly drawn--e.g., LCS, p. 113, #2.161 in which the left hand is shown with a thumb and five fingers! This, of course, is not the fault of the authors. However the presentation of such images, especially those in which careful delineation of the various fingers is not possible, does place the viewer/reader in a quandary.

Finally, all this being said, in such a compilation, errors may, inadvertently occur. For those errors and/or omissions the author apologizes and invites any correction or addition.

Mudrās

(Hastas)

-- A --

abhaya mudra I -- (Ind.: *abhaya-mudrā* aka *abhayamdada mudrā, śāntida mudrā*; Chin.: *shih-wu-wei-yin*; Jap.: *semui-in*; Tib.: *jigs-med phyag-rgya*) A *mudra*, a ritual hand pose, a seal, which is common to both the Buddhist and Hindu traditions and is depicted or held by a deity. Also, a *tantric mudra* which is common to the Japanese and Chinese Buddhist (*Vajrayana, Mantrayana*) tradition and is held or formed by a devotee or priest. It may be accompanied by a *mantra*. The *abhaya-mudra I*[1] is a single (Ind.: *asaṁyutta*) form, held by one hand. It de-notes the action of pacification--e.g., 1) the transmission of protection against harm, generally of a spiritual nature, although it is seen or believed by some to extend to physical protection; or 2) the granting the condition of being without fear ('fear not'), the imparting of calm or reassurance to the spirit (soul). It frequently is a *mudra* held by fierce deities whose fierceness and enmity is directed towards enemies of the faith--in such an instance the *mudra* is directed to the disciple who falls under the protection of the deity. The form of this *mudra* is generally held by the right hand:[2] the hand is raised, fingers and thumb extended and together, relaxed, slightly cupped, palm facing forward and generally on a line level with the chest. In the case of a deity with multiple hands and arms, this *mudra* is usually held by the principle (front) hand which underlines its importance of use. (AGe, AKG 20, BBh 189, GDe 161, JBo, LCS 222, MJS 1, RSG 3) (See: **Figure 1**)

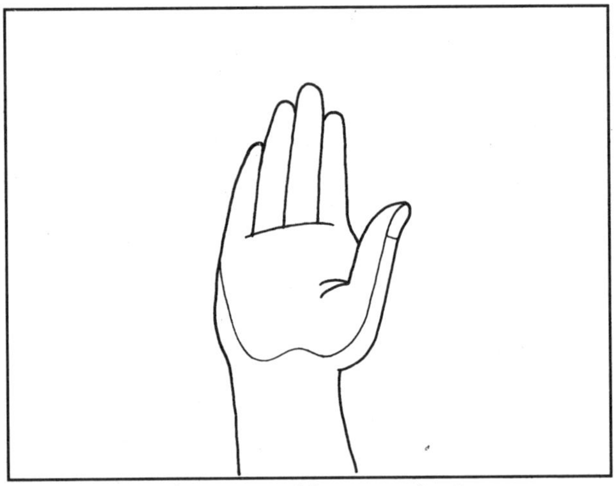

Figure 1 -- abhaya mudra I
(as seen by another)

abhaya mudra II -- (Ind.: *abhaya-mudrā* aka *abhayamdada mudrā, śāntida mudrā*; Chin.: *shih-wu-wei-yin*; Jap.: *semui-in*; Tib.: *jigs-med phyag-rgya*) A *mudra*, a ritual hand pose, a seal, which is common to the Theravada Buddhist tradition in Thailand. This *abhaya-mudra* is a single (Ind.: *asaṁyutta*) form, held by one hand. It denotes warning or halting someone. The form of this *mudra* is generally held by the left hand: the hand is raised, fingers and thumb extended and together, relaxed, slightly cupped, palm facing forward

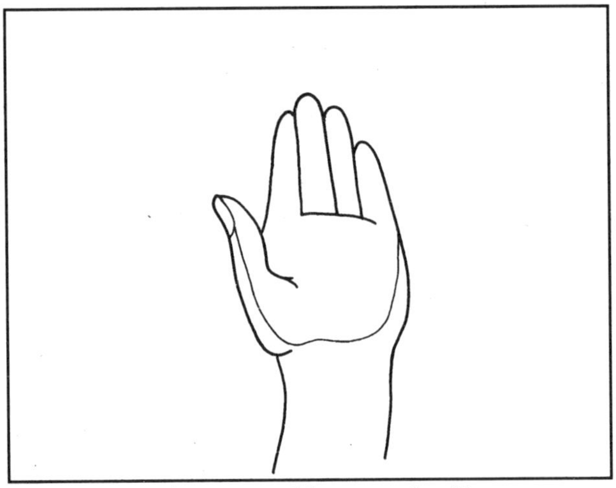

Figure 2 -- abhaya mudra II
(as seen by another)

and generally on a line level with the chest. (BBh 189, JBo) (See: **Figure 2**)

abhaya mudra III -- (Ind.: *abhaya-mudrā* aka *abhayamdada mudrā, śāntida mudrā*; Eng.: restraining the waters *mudra*; Chin.: *shih-wu-wei-yin*; Jap.: *semui-in*; Tib.: *jigs-med phyag-rgya*) A *mudra*, a ritual hand pose, a seal, which is common to the Theravada Buddhist tradition in Thailand. One of forty *mudras* and *asanas* compiled by the Prince Patriarch Paramanujita Jinorasa and established during the reign of Rama III as being acceptable for the depiction of images of The Lord Buddha--i.e., "restraining the waters" the fourteenth of the forty attitudes noted.[3] This *abhaya-mudra* is a combined (Ind.: *saṁyutta*) form, held by both hands. In this form the hands are raised, fingers and thumbs extended upwards and together, relaxed, slightly cupped, palm facing forward and generally on a line level with the chest or shoulders. Thus formed, the hands are held at either side of the shoulders. The figure is standing in this pose. It is related to the *abhaya mudra I*. (See: *abhaya-abhaya mudra*) (BBh 189, JBo) (See: **Figure 3**)

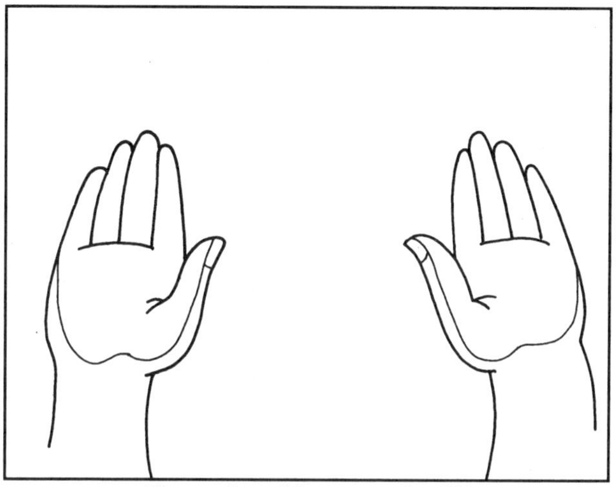

Figure 3 -- abhaya mudra III
(as seen by another)

abhaya mudra IV -- (Ind.: *abhaya-mudrā*) A *mudra*, a ritual hand pose, a seal, a *mudra* which is common to yogic tradition, particularly the *Yoga Tatva Mudra Vigyan* form, and is held by a devotee or practitioner. This *abhaya-mudra* is a combined (Ind.: *saṁyutta*) form, held by both hands. It is utilized for sacrifice, fearlessness and courage. This *mudra* is formed by both hands in the deity-centered *vitarka-mudra*--i.e., palm facing forward, tips of the thumb and index finger touch, middle, ring and little fingers are relaxed and point upwards--held at shoulder level and to either side of the body.[4] (KDe 32) (See: **Figure 4**)

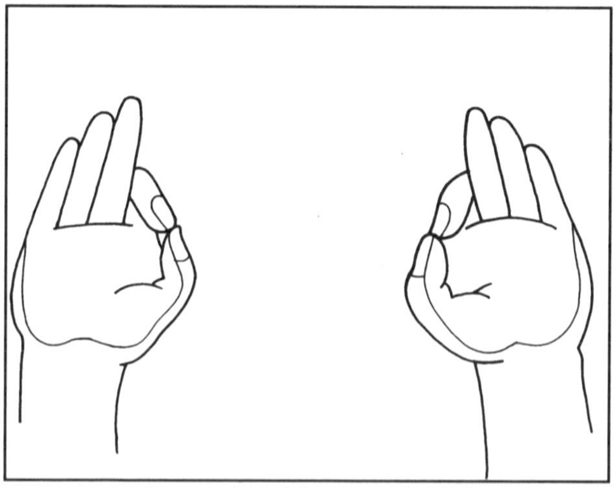

Figure 4 -- abhaya mudra IV
(as seen by another)

abhaya-abhaya mudra -- (Ind.: *abhaya-abhaya-mudrā*; Eng: restraining the waters *mudra*; Thai: *pang ham-samut*) This is a descriptive term for the Thai, *pang ham-samut*.[5] (See: *abhaya-mudra III*) (DRN 36, JBo)

abhaya-dhyana mudra -- (Ind.: *abhaya-dhyāna-mudrā*; Eng.: restraining *Mara mudra*; Thai: *pang harm-marn*) This is a descriptive term.[6] (See: *pang harm-marn*) (DRN 37, JBo, PSS, ODD 680)

abhaya-katyavalambita mudra -- (Ind.: *abhaya-kaṭyāvalambita-mudrā*; Eng.: traveling by boat *mudra*; Thai: *pang phratabreakhanan*) This is a descriptive term.[7] (See: *pang phratabreakhanan*) (DRN 36, JBo 205)

abhaya-lolahasta mudra I -- (Ind.: *abhaya-lolahasta-mudrā*; Eng.: restraining the kinsmen *mudra*; Thai: pang ODD #33) This is a descriptive term.[8] (See: pang ODD #33) (DRN 36, JBo 205, ODD 680)

abhayamdada mudra -- (Ind.: *abhayamdada-mudrā* aka *abhaya mudra*; Jap.: *semui-in*) A variant term applied to *abhaya mudra I*. See: *abhaya mudra I*. (EDS 55)

Figure 5 -- abhisheka mudra
(as seen by the holder)

abhisheka mudra -- (Ind.: *abhiṣeka-mudrā* aka *abhiṣeka[ṇa] mudra*; Chin.: *kuan-ting-yin*; Jap.: *kanjo-in*) A *mudra*, a ritual hand pose, a seal, which is common to both the Buddhist and Hindu traditions. It denotes consecration through the annointing of water via a conch shell (Ind.: *śaṅkha*). It is related to the *kshepana mudra* and the *uttarabodhi mudra*. Generally, the anointing is of a sacred image rather than a person. The *abhisheka mudra* is a combined (Ind.: *saṁyutta*) form, held by both hands. The hands are in mirror image and formed by: middle, ring and little fingers are folded into the palm, the index finger is extended and the thumb lays against the index finger. So formed the two hands are brought together, thumbs touching along their length, the upper phalanges of the index fingers are pressed together and the knuckles of the middle, ring and little fingers touch. The index fingers point upward. This *mudra* is held chest high. Although *abhisheka* refers to a conch shell, the form of the hands, thus held, is more reminiscent of a bottle with a long neck utilized in certain rites to sprinkle water. The *abhisheka mudra* is related to the *kshepana mudra* in as much as both are involved in unction. (EDS 111, MJS 1) (See: **Figure 5**)

Figure 6 -- abhisheka-guhya mudra
(as seen by the holder)

abhisheka-guhya mudra -- (Ind.: *abhiṣeka-guhya-mudrā*) A *mudra*, a ritual hand pose, a seal, a *tantric mudra* which is common to the Japanese Buddhist (*Vajrayana, Mantrayana*) tradition and is held or formed by a devotee or priest. It may be accompanied by a *mantra*. The *abhisheka-guhya mudra* is a combined (Ind.: *saṁyutta*) form, held by both hands. This *mudra* is formed by: palms face each other, middle, ring and little fingers are interlaced with fingers inside the loose 'fist,' thumbs touch each other along their outer edge, index fingers extend upwards slightly curled and the tips touch. (LCS 239) (See: **Figure 6**)

abhisheka(na) mudra -- (Ind.: *abhiṣekana-mudrā* aka *abhiṣeka mudra*) A variant (spelling) of *abhisheka mudra*. See: *abhisheka mudra*. (EDS 111)

accepting the bundle of grass mudra -- (Eng.; Thai: *pang sungrabyaka*; Ind.: *añcita-lolahasta mudrā*) The English descriptive phrase for the Thai: *pang sungrabyaka*. See: *pang sungrabyaka*. (DRN 35, JBo, PSS)

accepting the rice-gruel offering mudra -- (Eng.; Ind.: *añcita-añcita mudrā I*; Thai: *pang sung rabmathupayas*) The English descriptive phrase for the Thai: *pang sung rabmathupayas*. See: *pang sung rabmathupayas*. (DRN 35, JBo, PSS)

Achala-agni mudra -- (Ind.: *Acala-agni-mudrā*) A *mudra*, a ritual hand pose, a seal, a *tantric mudra* which is common to the Japanese Buddhist (*Vajrayana, Mantrayana*) tradition and is held or formed by a devotee or priest during the rites of *Garbhadhatu Mandala, Vajradhatu Mandala, Homa Rites* and other rites. It may be accompanied by a *mantra*. The *Achala-agni mudra*[9] is a combined (Ind.: *saṁyutta*) form, held by both hands. It denotes fire, flame or combustion. This *mudra* is formed by: palms face backwards, thumbs folded into palms, middle and ring fingers folded over thumbs, index fingers extend, little fingers flex at first and second knuckles. Thus formed the tips of the index fingers and the second phalanges of the little fingers touch. (GDe 38) (See: **Figure 7**)

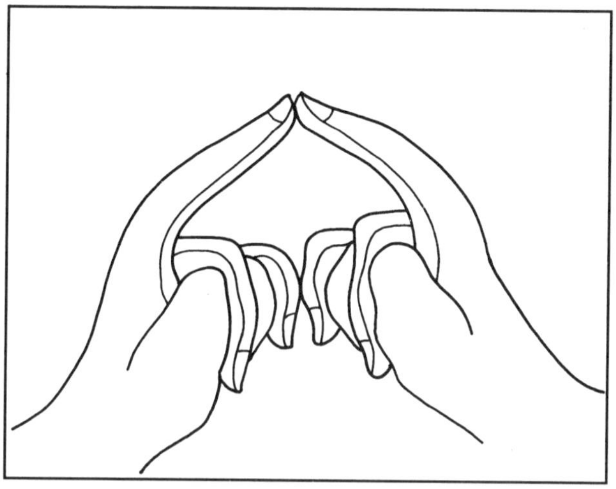

Figure 7 -- Achala-agni mudra
(as seen by the holder)

adamantine posture -- (Eng.; Chin.: *an-shan-yin, ch'u-ti-yin*; Ind.: *bhasparśa mudrā, bhūmiśparśa mudrā, bhūmisparśana mudrā, bhūmisparśa mudrā, bhūsparś mudrā, bhūsparśa mudrā, māravijaya mudrā*; Jap.: *anzan-in* [*mudra*], *sokuchi-in* [*mudra*]; Thai: *manwichai* [*mudra*), *pang maravichai*, (*pang*) *sadung-man*) The English descriptive phrase for *bhumisparsha mudra*. See: *bhumisparsha mudra*. (DRN 37, JBo)

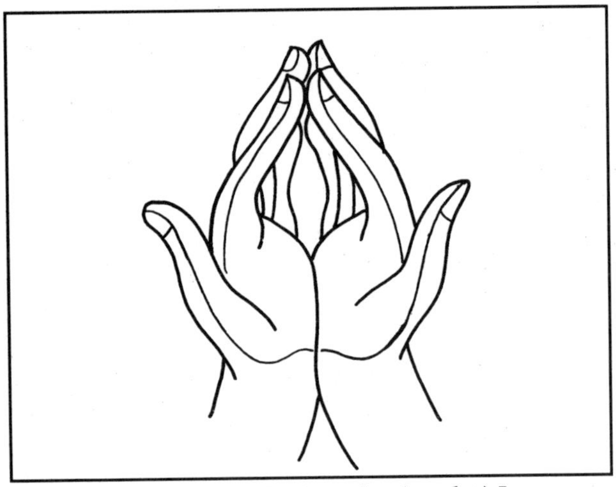

Figure 8 -- adara gassho (mudra) I
(as seen by the holder)

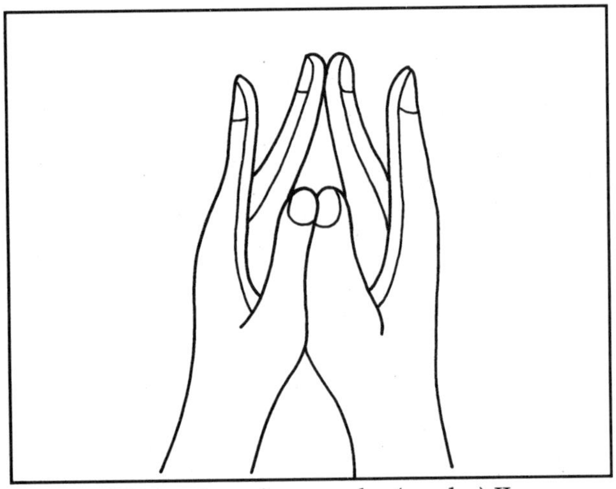

Figure 9 -- adara gassho (mudra) II
(as seen by the holder)

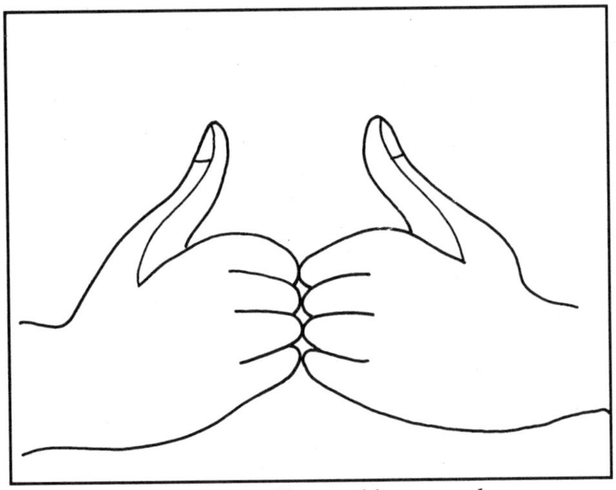

Figure 10 -- adho-mukham mudra
(as seen by another)

adara gassho (mudra) I -- (Jap.: *adara gassho* [*mudrā*]; Ind.: *ādhāra mudrā*) A *mudra*, a ritual hand pose, a seal, a *tantric mudra* which is common to the Japanese Buddhist (*Vajrayana, Mantrayana*) tradition and is held or formed by a devotee or priest. It may be accompanied by a *mantra*. Specifically one of the twelve, elemental "hand clasps" (Jap. *junigosho* or *junigassho*). The *adara gassho (mudra) I* is a combined (Ind.: *saṁyutta*) form, held by both hands. The form is held: palms face the midline, outside edges of palms touching their whole length, the tips of the fingers touch, are cupped and the thumbs extend outward. This *mudra* represents the holding of water. (EDS 41) (See: Figure 8)

adara gassho (mudra) II -- (Jap.: *adara gasshō* [*mudrā*]; Ind.: *ādhāra mudrā*) A *mudra*, a ritual hand pose, a seal, a *tantric mudra* which is common to the Japanese Buddhist (*Vajrayana, Mantrayana*) tradition and is held or formed by a devotee or priest. It may be accompanied by a *mantra*. Specifically one of the twelve, elemental "hand clasps" (Jap. *junigosho* or *junigassho*). The *adara gassho (mudra) II* is a combined (Ind.: *saṁyutta*) form, held by both hands. The form is held: palms face the midline, slightly separated, the tips of the middle fingers and the thumbs touch the index, ring and little fingers splay outward slightly. Thus formed the fingers and thumbs point downwards. This *mudra* represents the "covering hands facing downwards."[10] (EDS 42) (See: **Figure 9**)

adhara mudra I -- (Ind.: *ādhāra mudrā*; Jap.: *adara gassho* [*mudra*]) The Indic term for *adara gassho* [*mudra*] *I*. See: *adara gassho* [*mudra*] *I*. (EDS 41)

adhara mudra II -- (Ind.: *ādhāra mudrā*; Jap.: *adara gassho* [*mudra*]) The Indic term for *adara gassho* [*mudra*] *II*. See: *adara gassho* [*mudra*] *II*. (EDS 42)

adho-mukham mudra -- (Ind.: *adho-mukham-mudrā*) A *mudra*, a ritual hand pose, a seal, a *mudra* which is common to yogic tradition, particularly the *Yoga Tatva Mudra Vigyan* form, and is held by a devotee or practitioner. The *adho-mukham mudra* is a combined (Ind.: *saṁyutta*) form, held by both hands. It is one of the twenty-four *mudras* held before the *Gayatri Jap* of the thirty-two total *Gayatri mudras*.[11] It is utilized for all sickness, especially cancer. This *mudra* is formed by: palms facing downwards, index, middle, ring and little fingers together and curled towards the palm, thumb extends upwards. Thus formed, the backs of the fingers touch along the first and second phalanges, and the mudra is held waist high. (KDe 82, RLM 72) (See: **Figure 10**)

adhishthana mudra -- (Ind.: *adhiṣṭhāna-mudrā*) A *mudra*, a ritual hand pose, ā seal, a *tantric mudra* which is common to the Japanese Buddhist (*Vajrayana, Mantrayana*) tradition and is held or formed by a devotee or priest during various rites. It may be accompanied by a *mantra*. The *adhishthana mudra*[12] is a combined (Ind.: *saṁyutta*) form, held by both hands. It denotes an offering. This *mudra* is formed by: right palm facing forward, index, middle, ring fingers extend upwards, tip of the thumb touches the tip of the curled little finger; left palm facing the midline, hand is fisted, thumb outside, resting against the index finger and holds a rosary. (LCS 58) (See: **Figure 11**)

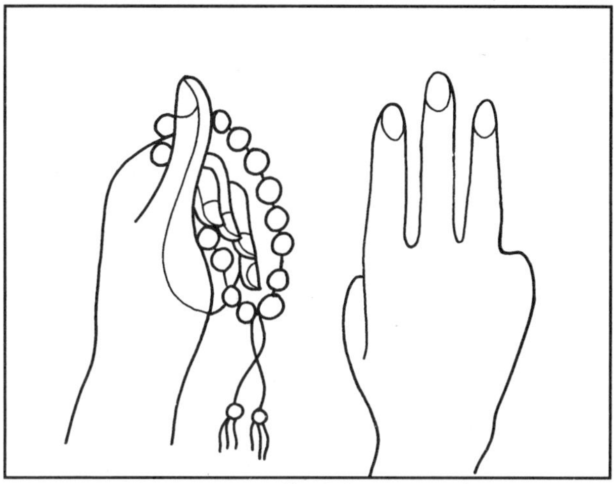

Figure 11 -- adhishthana mudra
(as seen by the holder)

adho-mushti-mukula mudra -- (Ind.: *adho-muṣṭi-mukula-mudrā*) A hand pose, a seal, a dramatic (Ind.: *natya*) *mudra* or gesture (Ind.: *darpaṇa*) held or formed by a performer, dancer or actor. The *adho-mushti-mukula mudra* is a combined (Ind.: *saṁyutta*) form, held by both hands. This *mudra* is formed by: the palms face the midline, the middle, ring and little fingers fold into the palm, the tips of the thumbs touch the tips of the curled index fingers, forming a circle. Thus formed, the circled thumbs and index fingers are inter-linked. (ACG 49) (See: **Figure 12**)

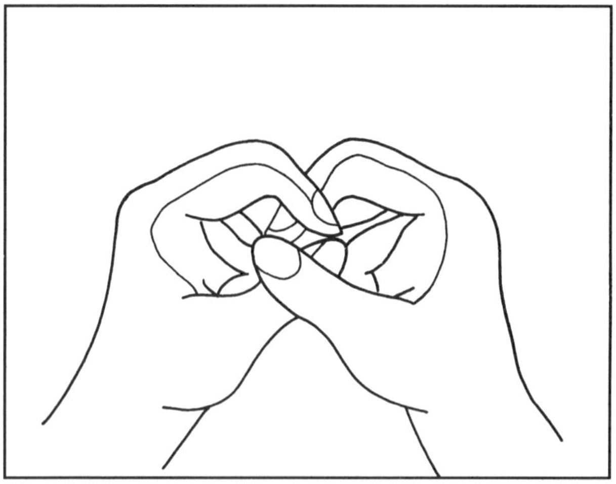

Figure 12 -- adho-mushti-mukula mudra
(as seen by the holder)

agni-chakra mudra -- (Ind.: *agni-cakra-mudrā*) A *mudra*, a ritual hand pose, a seal, a *tantric mudra* which is common to the Japanese Buddhist (*Vajrayana, Mantrayana*) tradition and is held or formed by a devotee or priest during the rites of the *Garbhadhatu Mandala*. It may be accompanied by a *mantra*. The *agni-chakra mudra* is a combined (Ind.: *saṁyutta*) form, held by both hands. This *mudra* is formed by: palms face the midline, index extended straight upwards, middle, ring and little fingers folded into the palm, thumb covering the second phalanges of the middle finger. Thus formed the two hands are brought together, the second phalanges

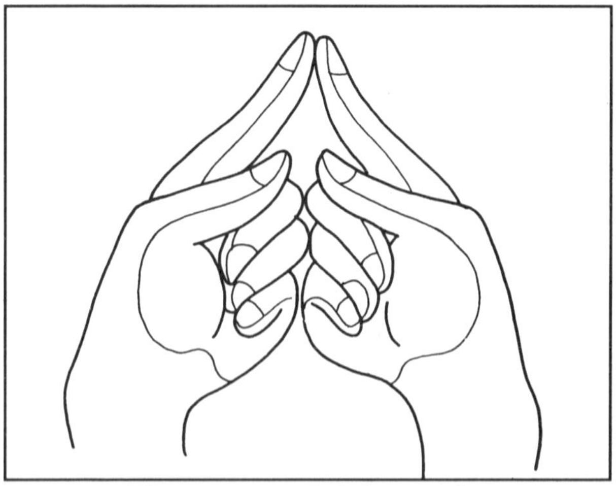

Figure 13 -- agni-chakra mudra
(as seen by the holder)

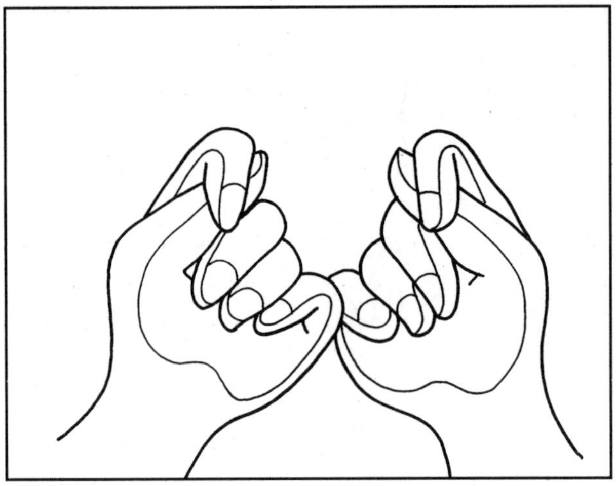

Figure 14 -- agni-chakra-shamana mudra I
(as seen by the holder)

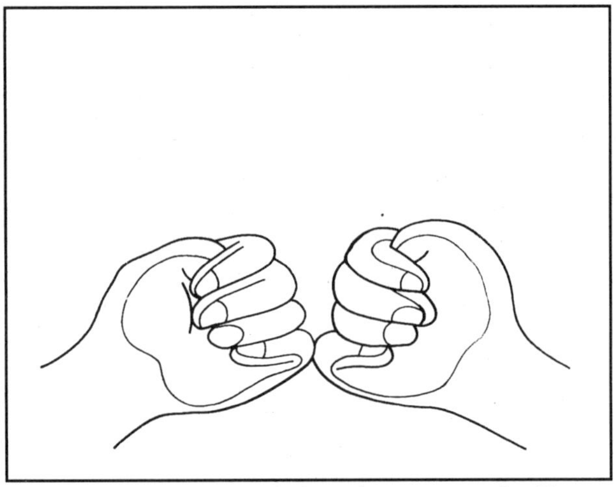

Figure 15 -- agni-chakra-shamana mudra II
(as seen by the holder)

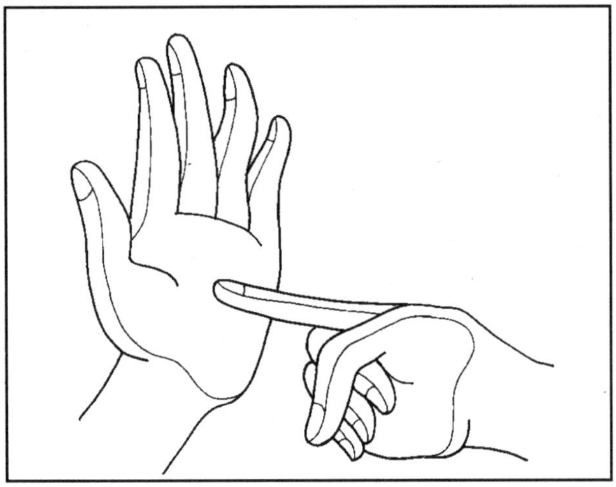

Figure 16 -- agni-jvala mudra
(as seen by the holder)

of the middle, ring and little fingers touching along their length and the tips of the index fingers meet. (LCS 148) (See: **Figure 13**)

agni-chakra-shamana mudra I -- (Ind.: *agni-cakra-śamana-mudrā*) A *mudra*, a ritual hand pose, a seal, a *tantric mudra* which is common to the Japanese Buddhist (*Vajrayana, Mantrayana*) tradition and is held or formed by a devotee or priest. It may be accompanied by a *mantra*. The *agni-chakra-shamana mudra I* is a combined (Ind.: *saṁyutta*) form, held by both hands. This *mudra* is formed by: palms facing backwards, finger folded into the palm, the thumbs are inserted between the index and middle fingers. Thus formed the two "fists" are brought together and touch along the outside edge of the palms. (GDe 334, LCS 265) (See: **Figure 14**)

agni-chakra-shamana mudra II -- (Ind.: *agni-cakra-śamana-mudrā*) A *mudra*, a ritual hand pose, a seal, a *tantric mudra* which is common to the Japanese Buddhist (*Vajrayana, Mantrayana*) tradition and is held or formed by a devotee or priest. It may be accompanied by a *mantra*. The *agni-chakra-shamana mudra II* is a combined (Ind.: *saṁyutta*) form, held by both hands. This *mudra* is formed by: palms facing upwards, finger folded into the palm, the thumbs are inserted between the index and middle fingers. Thus formed the two "fists" are brought together and touch along the third knuckles of both hands. (LCS 210) (See: **Figure 15**)

agni-jvala mudra -- (Ind.: *agni-jvālā-mudrā*) ("flame") A *mudra*, a ritual hand pose, a seal, a *tantric mudra* which is common to the Japanese Buddhist (*Vajrayana, Mantrayana*) tradition and is held or formed by a devotee or priest during various rites. It may be accompanied by a *mantra*. The *agni-jvala mudra* is a combined (Ind.: *saṁyutta*) form, held by both hands. This *mudra* is formed by: left palm faces midline, thumb and fingers extended upwards, right palm faces downwards, middle, ring and little fingers folded into palm, thumb folded over fingers, index finger extends towards midline and tip touches left palm. (GDe 333, LCS 210) (See: **Figure 16**)

agni-shala mudra -- (Ind.: *agni-śālā-mudrā* aka *vajra-jvālā mudrā*) A *mudra*, a ritual hand pose, a seal, a *tantric* *mudra* which is common to the Japanese Buddhist (*Vajrayana, Mantrayana*) tradition and is held or formed by a devotee or priest. It may be accompanied by a *mantra*. The *agni-shala mudra* is a combined (Ind.: *saṁyutta*) form, held by both hands. This *mudra* is formed by: palms facing upwards, thumbs and fingers extended towards the midline and are separated, thumbs separated from fingers, but parallel. Thus formed the right hand rests on the upturned left, the tips of the thumbs touch. This *mudra* is similar to the *dhyana mudra*. (LCS 64) (See: **Figure 17**)

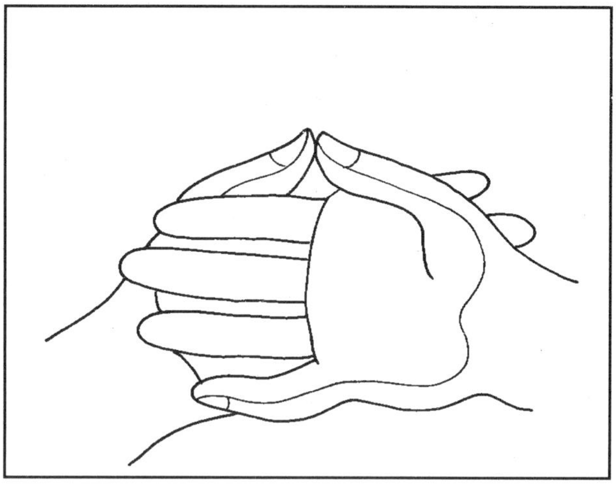

Figure 17 -- agni-shala mudra
(as seen by the holder)

agraja mudra -- (Ind.: *agraja-mudrā*) ("*mudra* of the elder brother") A *mudra*, a ritual hand pose, a seal, a *tantric mudra* which is common to the Japanese Buddhist (*Vajrayana, Mantrayana*) tradition and is held or formed by a devotee or priest during the rites of *Garbhadhatu Mandala*. It may be accompanied by a *mantra*. The *agraja mudra* is a combined (Ind.: *saṁyutta*) form, held by both hands. This *mudra* is formed by: right palm facing downwards, thumbs and fingers extended towards the midline; left palm facing upwards, thumbs and fingers extended towards the midline. Thus formed the right hand rests on the upturned left. This *mudra* resembles the *dhyana mudra* and is opposite to the *anuja mudra*. (LCS 181) (See: **Figure 18**)

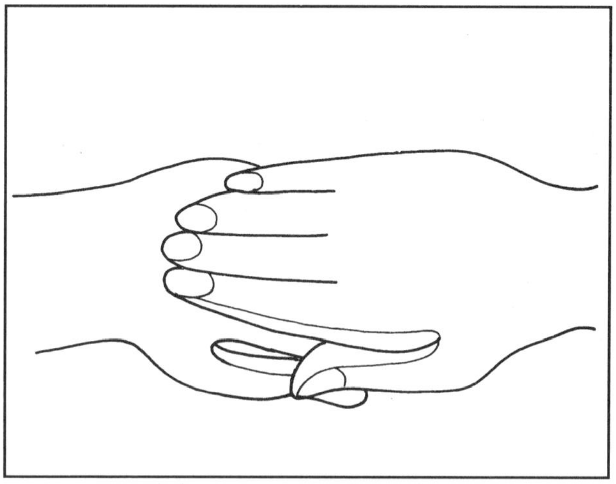

Figure 18 -- agraja mudra
(as seen by the holder)

ahayavarada mudra -- (Ind.: *ahāyavarada-mudrā*) A *mudra*, a ritual hand pose, a seal, which is common to both the Buddhist and Hindu traditions although not generally depicted in two or three dimensional works as it requires motion and/or time. It denotes the calling or beckoning of one for the purpose of bestowing a boon. Therefore, it is related to the *varada mudra*, as the name suggests. The *ahayavarada mudra* is a single (Ind.: *asamyutta*) form, held by one hand and requires movement. The form is: fingers and thumb are extended and together, relaxed, slightly cupped, palm facing forward and downward at approximately 45°, away from the body and generally at the level of the chest. Thus held, the fingers are repeatedly brought into the palm and then extended back out in a relatively rapid motion.[13] (MJS 4) (See: **Figure 19**)

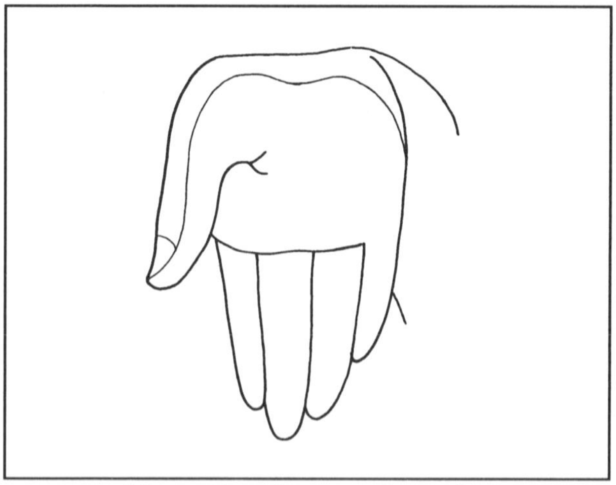

Figure 19 -- ahayavarada mudra
(as seen by another)

ahayavarada-dhyana mudra -- (Ind.: *ahāyavarada-dhyāna-mudrā*; Eng.: bestowing ordination *mudra*; Thai:

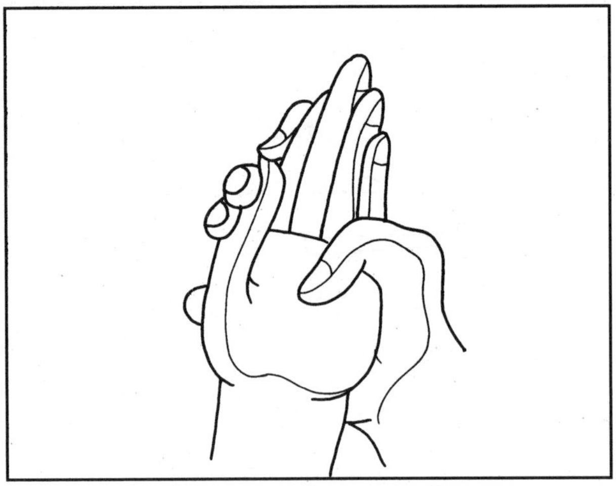

Figure 20 -- ahvana mudra
(as seen by the holder)

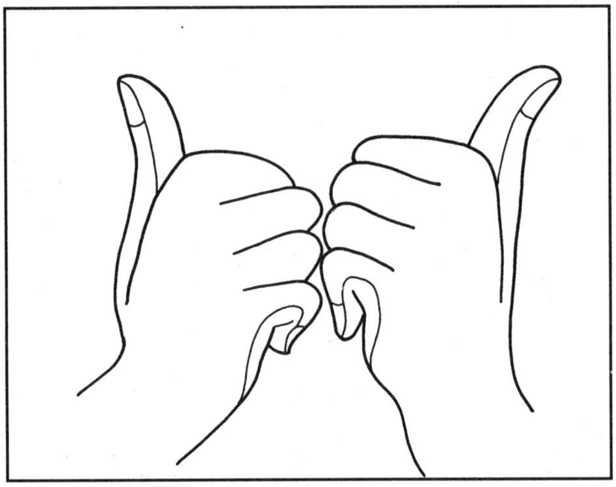

Figure 21 -- aja-mukha mudra
(as seen by another)

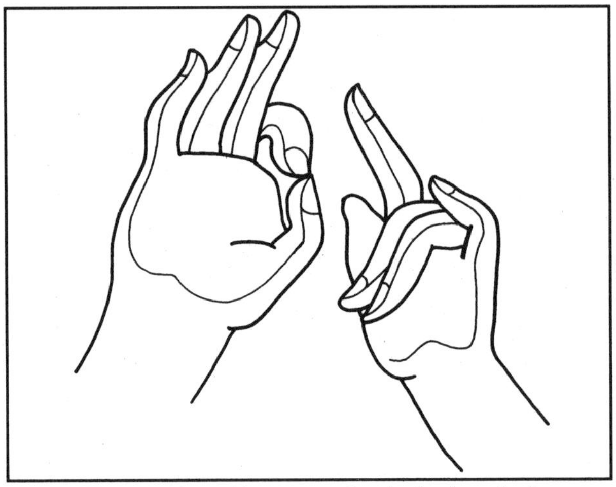

Figure 22 -- Ajanta temborin-in (mudra)
(as seen by another)

pang phratarn-ehibhikkhu) This is a descriptive term.[14] (See: *pang phratarn-ehibhikkhu*) (DRN 36, JBo)

ahayavarada-kataka mudra -- (Ind.: *ahāyavarada-kataka-mudrā* aka *ahāyavarada-jñāna mudrā*; Eng.: contemplating the corpse or reflecting on worldly impermanence; Thai: *pang plong-kammathan*) This is a descriptive term.[15] (See: *pang plong-kammathan*) (DRN 36, JBo 204)

ahayavarada-jnana mudra -- (Ind.: *ahāyavarada-jñāna-mudrā* aka *ahayavarada-kaṭaka mudrā*; Eng.: contemplating the corpse or reflecting on worldly impermanence; Thai: *pang plong-kammathan*) This is a descriptive term.[16] (See: *pang plong-kammathan*) (DRN 36, JBo 204)

ahvana mudra -- (Ind.: *āhvāna-mudrā*) A *mudra*, a ritual hand pose, a seal, a *tantric mudra* which is common to the Japanese Buddhist (*Vajrayana, Mantrayana*) tradition and is held or formed by a devotee or priest. It may be accompanied by a *mantra* and denotes evocation. The *ahvana mudra* is a combined (Ind.: *saṁyutta*) form, held by both hands. This *mudra* is formed by: left palm in front of the chest and rotated so that the palm faces left, fingers and thumb extended upwards; right hand grasps the left, palm against the back of the left, fingers curling around the thumb of the left and right thumb curling around the base of the little finger of the left hand. (GDe 398, LCS 278) (See: **Figure 20**)

aja-mukha mudra -- (Ind.: *aja-mukha-mudrā*) ("goat head") A hand pose, a seal, a dramatic (Ind.: *nāṭya*) mudra or gesture (Ind.: *darpaṇa*) held or formed by a performer, dancer or actor. It denotes an animal, in this case a goat head. The *aja-mukha mudra* is a combined (Ind.: *saṁyutta*) form, held by both hands. This *mudra* is formed by: palms facing mid-line, fingers brought into the palms forming a fist, thumbs extends upwards. Thus formed the hands are brought in contact along the second phalanges. (ACG 50) (See: **Figure 21**)

Ajanta temborin-in (mudra) -- (Jap.: *Ajaṇṭa* [Ind.] *temborin-in* aka *temborin-in* [*mudrā*]; Ind.: *dharmacakra mudra*) A *mudra*, a ritual hand pose, a seal, which is common to the Japanese Buddhist tradition.[17] A variant term and form applied to the *temborin-in* (*mudra*) and a variation of the *dharmachakra mudra*. It denotes the turning of the wheel of the law. The *Ajanta temborin-in (mudra)* is a combined (Ind.: *saṁyutta*) form, held by both hands. The form is indicated by: the right hand resembling the *vitarka mudra* except the tips of the thumb and index finger are not touching; the left hand is held in a relaxed pose, palm towards the midline, index finger extended upwards, middle, ring and little fingers curve loosely towards the palm (not fisted as in the *tarjani mudra*) with the thumb extended upwards. The tip of the left index finger is parallel to tip of the thumb of the right hand and they are held at chest level. (EDS 94) (See: **Figure 22**)

akasha-jala mudra -- (Ind.: *ākāśa-mudrā*] aka *vajra-jala mudra*; Jap.: *kongo mo-in* [*mudra*]) A variant term applied to *vajra-jala mudra*. Also, the Indic term for *kongo mo-in (mudra)*. See: *vajra-jala mudra*; see: *kongo mo-in (mudra)*. (LCS 63)

akka-in (mudra) -- (Jap.: *akka-in* [*mudrā*]; Ind.: *argha mudrā*) ("water") A *mudra*, a ritual hand pose, a seal, a *tantric mudra* which is common to the Japanese Buddhist (*Vajrayana, Mantrayana*) tradition and is held or formed by a devotee or priest during the rites of *Garbhadhatu Mandala, Vajradhatu Mandala, Homa Rites* and other rites. It may be accompanied by a *mantra*. The *akka-in (mudra)* is a combined (Ind.: *saṁyutta*) form, held by both hands. It denotes washing away impurities. This *mudra* is formed by: palms facing backwards, thumbs folded into the palms, fingers folded over the thumbs. Thus formed, the "fists" are brought together, the little fingers almost touch. (GDe 42) (See: **Figure 23**)

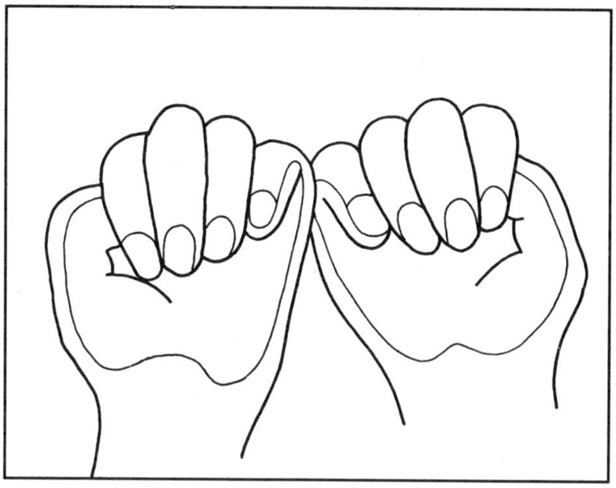

Figure 23 -- akka-in (mudra)
(as seen by the holder)

akshata mudra -- (Ind.: *akṣata-mudrā* aka *patra mudra*) A variant term applied to *patra mudra*. See: *patra mudra*. (GDe 15, LCS 155 & 193)

ala-padma mudra -- (Ind.: *ala-padma-mudrā* aka *sola-padma mudra*) A variant term applied to *sola-padma mudra*. See: *sola-padma mudra*. (ACG 34)

alapallava mudra -- (Ind.: *alapallava-mudrā* aka *anchita mudra*) A *mudra*, a ritual hand pose, a seal, which is common to the Hindu tradition, especially to the *chaturam* dance pose of the Lord *Shiva*. The form is similar to the *anchita mudra* and characterized as: "that pose of the hand in which the fingers are kept separated and all turn towards the palm. . . ."[18] See: *anchita mudra.* (TGR 267)

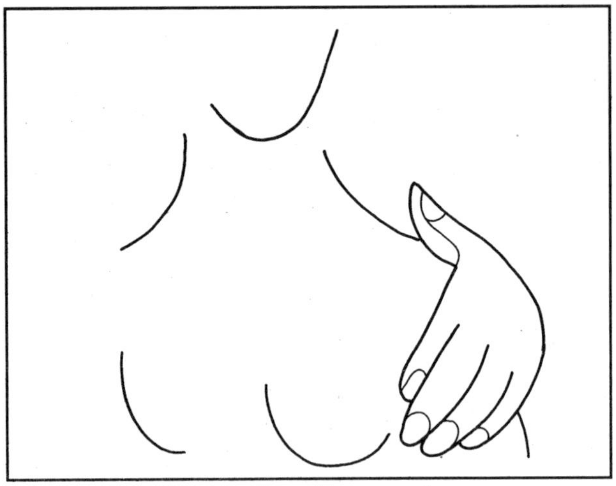

Figure 24 -- alinga mudra
(as seen by another)

alinga mudra -- (Ind.: *āliṅga-mudrā* aka *alingana mudra*) A *mudra*, a ritual hand pose, a seal, which is common to the Hindu tradition, especially to the *Alingana-murti* (*Chandrashekharamurti*) of the Lord *Shiva.* It denotes affection and/or attachment for the consort of the one who holds this *mudra*. The *alinga mudra* is a single (Ind.: *asaṁyutta*) form, held by one hand. The form is generally the extension of the left arm around the back (shoulders) of the consort (female) with the hands clasping the upper arm (deltoid area). Variations show the left hand resting usually on the consorts left shoulder, or fondling the left breast, or clasping the consort's side below the left breast. Frequently this *mudra* is applied in association with: *Shiva* & *Parvati* (*Alingana-murti*), although the action may be applied to other major gods with their goddess/consorts. (BNS, JDo, TGR 123) (See: **Figure 24**)

alingana mudra -- (Ind.: *āliṅgana-mudrā* aka *alinga mudra*) A variant term for *alinga mudra.* See: *alinga mudra.* (TGR 123)

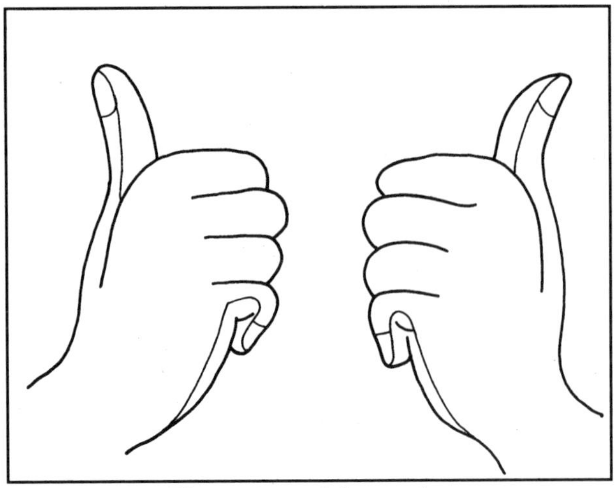

Figure 25 -- aloke mudra
(as seen by another)

aloke mudra -- (Ind.: *āloke-mudrā*) This is an assigned term.[19] A *mudra*, a ritual hand pose, a seal, which is common to the Buddhist (*Vajrayana*) tradition, a *tantric mudra*. It denotes lamps, particularly small yak-butter lamps (Ind.: *āloke*), which are one of the five 'gifts' or 'outer offerings' proffered to a divine guest--the other four being: flowers, incense, perfume and food--during the early stages worship, particularly as associated with the worship of the powerful *Vajrayana* goddess, *Tara.* The *aloke mudra* is a combined (Ind.: *saṁyutta*) form, held by both hands. The form is identical for both hands in mirror-pose--the fists are clenched in front of the chest, palms turned backwards towards the chest, knuckles up and thumbs extend upwards resembling the wicks or flame of lamps. The *mantra* associated with this mudra is: "*OM Guru-sarva-Tathagata aloke puja-megha-samudra-spharana-samaye HUM.*"[20] (SBe 147) (See: **Figure 25**)

amalaka mudra -- (Ind.: *āmalaka-mudrā*) A hand pose, a seal, a dramatic (Ind.: *nāṭya*) *mudra* or gesture (Ind.: *darpana*) held or formed by a performer, dancer or actor. It denotes the *amalaka* tree. The *mudra* employed is the *samyama-nayaka mudra*. See: *samyama-nayaka mudra*. (ACG 49)

Ambarisha mudra -- (Ind.: *Ambarīṣa-mudrā*) A hand pose, a seal, a dramatic (Ind.: *nāṭya*) *mudra* or gesture (Ind.: *darpaṇa*) held or formed by a performer, dancer or actor. The *Ambarisha mudra* is a single (Ind.: *asaṁyutta*) form, held by one hand. It denotes *Ambarisha*, one of a number of famous rulers or heroes. The *mudra* employed is identical in form to the *kartari mudra*. See: *kartari mudra*. (ACG 47)

Amida-butsu seppo-in (mudra) I -- (Jap.: *Amida-butsu seppō-in* [*mudrā*] aka *an-i-in*) A *mudra*, a ritual hand pose, a seal, which is common to the Japanese Buddhist tradition, is a variant of the *an-i-in* (*mudra*) and assigned to the "Esoteric *Amida*." It is noted as applicable to: "Middle Class: Lower Life."[21] The *Amida-butsu seppo-in* (*mudra*) *I* is a combined (Ind.: *saṁyutta*) form, held by both hands. The form is identical in both hands: palms face forward, the first phalanges of the thumb touches the first phalanges of the index finger, the middle finger curls towards the palm, the ring finger curls slightly towards the palm, the little finger extends upward. Thus formed the hands are brought close together, but not touching and the *mudra* is held in front of the chest. (EDS 74) (See: **Figure 26**)

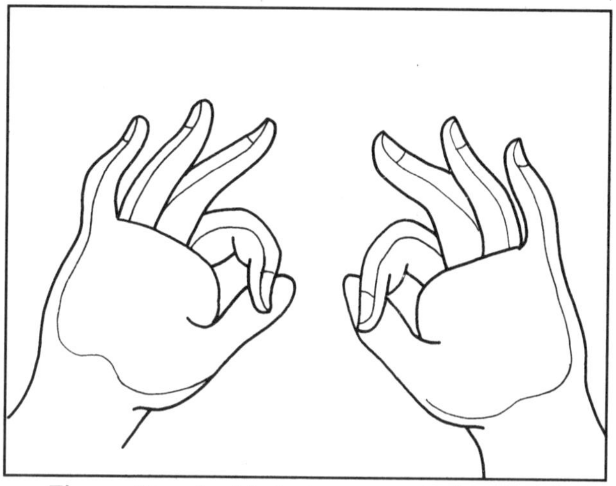

Figure 26 -- Amida-butsu seppo-in (mudra) I
(as seen by another)

Amida-butsu seppo-in (mudra) II -- (Jap.: *Amida-butsu seppō-in* [*mudrā*] aka *an-i-in*) A *mudra*, a ritual hand pose, a seal, which is common to the Japanese Buddhist tradition, is a variant of the *an-i-in* (*mudra*) and assigned to the "Esoteric *Amida*."[22] It is noted as applicable to: "Middle Class: Middle Life."[23] The *Amida-butsu seppo-in* (*mudra*) *II* is a combined (Ind.: *saṁyutta*) form, held by both hands. The form is identical in both hands: palms face forward, the first phalanges of the thumb touches the first phalanges of the middle finger, the index finger curls towards the palm, the ring finger curls slightly towards the palm, the little finger extends upward. Thus formed the hands are brought close together, but not touching and the *mudra* is held in front of the chest. (EDS 74) (See: **Figure 27**)

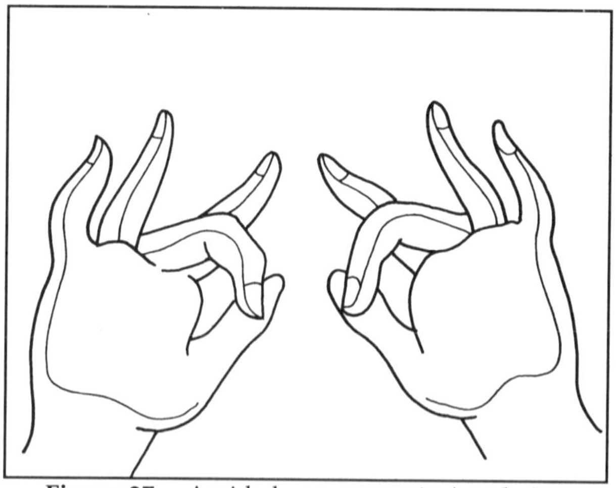

Figure 27 -- Amida-butsu seppo-in (mudra) II
(as seen by another)

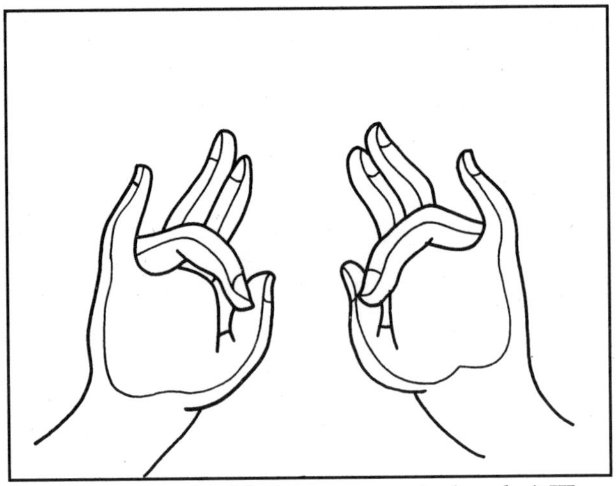

Figure 28 -- Amida-butsu seppo-in (mudra) III
(as seen by another)

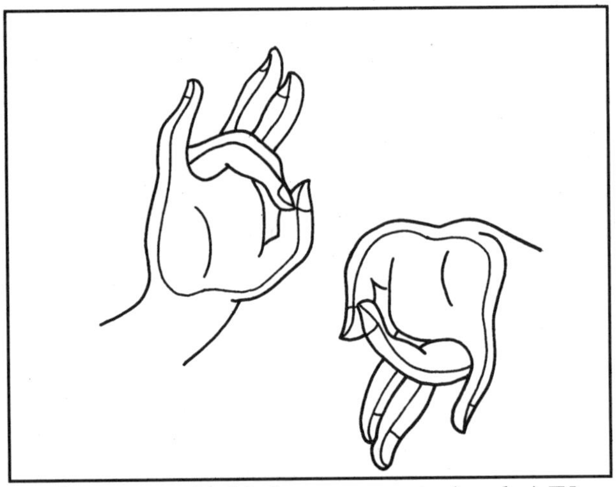

Figure 29 -- Amida-butsu seppo-in (mudra) IV
(as seen by another)

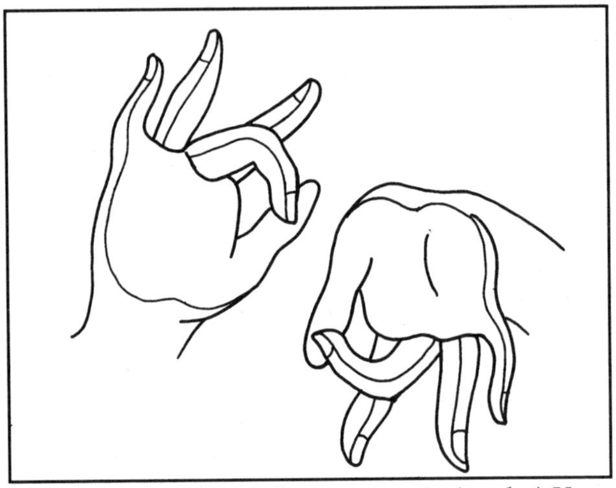

Figure 30 -- Amida-butsu seppo-in (mudra) V
(as seen by another)

Amida-butsu seppo-in (mudra) III -- (Jap.: *Amida-butsu seppō-in* [*mudrā*] aka *an-i-in*) A *mudra,* a ritual hand pose, a seal, which is common to the Japanese Buddhist tradition, is a variant of the *an-i-in* (*mudra*) and assigned to the "Esoteric *Amida.*" It is noted as applicable to: "Middle Class: Upper Life."[24] The *Amida-butsu seppo-in* (*mudra*) *III* is a combined (Ind.: *saṁyutta*) form, held by both hands. The form is identical in both hands: palms face forward, the first phalanges of the thumb touches the first phalanges of the ring finger, the index finger curls towards the palm, the middle finger curls slightly towards the palm, the little finger extends upward. Thus formed the hands are brought close together, but not touching and the *mudra* is held in front of the chest. (EDS 74) (See: **Figure 28**)

Amida-butsu seppo-in (mudra) IV -- (Jap.: *Amida-butsu seppō-in* [*mudrā*] aka *an-i-in*) A *mudra,* a ritual hand pose, a seal, which is common to the Japanese Buddhist tradition, is a variant of the *an-i-in* (*mudra*) and assigned to the "Esoteric *Amida.*" It is noted as applicable to: "Lower Class: Lower Life."[25] The *Amida-butsu seppo-in* (*mudra*) *IV* is a combined (Ind.: *saṁyutta*) form, held by both hands. The form is identical in both hands: palms face forward, the first phalanges of the thumb touches the first phalanges of the ring finger, the index finger curls towards the palm, the middle finger curls slightly towards the palm, the little finger extends upwards (right hand). Thus formed the right hand's fingers point upwards, the left hand's fingers point downwards and the *mudra* is held in front of the trunk. (EDS 74) (See: **Figure 29**)

Amida-butsu seppo-in (mudra) V -- (Jap.: *Amida-butsu seppō-in* [*mudrā*] aka *an-i-in*) A *mudra,* a ritual hand pose, a seal, which is common to the Japanese Buddhist tradition, is a variant of the *an-i-in* (*mudra*) and assigned to the "Esoteric *Amida.*" It is noted as applicable to: "Middle Class: Middle Life."[26] The *Amida-butsu seppo-in* (*mudra*) *V* is a combined (Ind.: *saṁyutta*) form, held by both hands. The form is identical in both hands: palms face forward, the first phalanges of the thumb touches the first phalanges of the middle finger, the index finger curls towards the palm, the ring finger curls slightly towards the palm, the little finger extends upwards (right hand). Thus formed the right hand's fingers point upwards, the left hand's fingers point downwards and the *mudra* is held in front of the trunk. (EDS 74) (See: **Figure 30**)

Amida-butsu seppo-in (mudra) VI -- (Jap.: *Amida-butsu seppō-in* [*mudrā*] aka *an-i-in*) A *mudra*, a ritual hand pose, a seal, which is common to the Japanese Buddhist tradition, is a variant of the *an-i-in* (*mudra*) and assigned to the "Esoteric *Amida*." It is noted as applicable to: "Middle Class: Upper Life."[27] The *Amida-butsu seppo-in* (*mudra*) *VI* is a combined (Ind.: *saṁyutta*) form, held by both hands. The form is identical in both hands: palms face forward, the first phalanges of the thumb touches the first phalanges of the index finger, the middle curls towards the palm, the ring finger curls slightly towards the palm, the little finger extends upwards (right hand). Thus formed the right hand's fingers point upwards, the left hand's fingers point downwards and the *mudra* is held in front of the trunk. (EDS 74) (See: **Figure 31**)

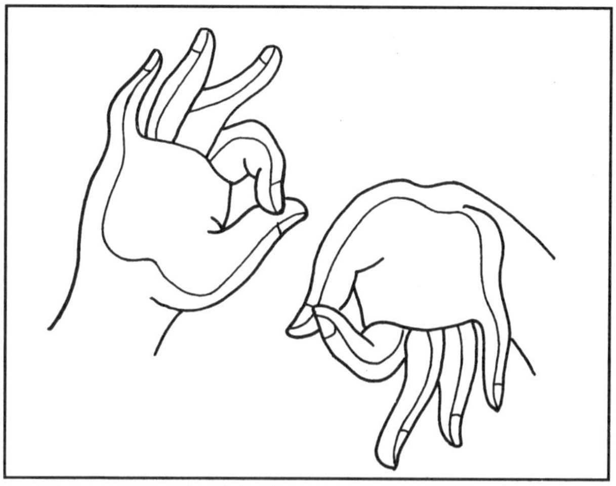

Figure 31 -- Amida-butsu seppo-in (mudra) VI
(as seen by another)

anchita mudra -- (Ind.: *añcita-mudrā* aka *alapallava mudra*) A *mudra*, a ritual hand pose, a seal, which is more common to the Hindu tradition. It is called the "bent" or "cupped hand."[28] The *anchita mudra* is a single (Ind.: *asaṁyutta*) form, held by one hand. The form may be held in either hand: palm upwards, fingers cupped somewhat, the thumb slightly bent towards the fingertips, fingers oriented outward. Thus formed the hand is generally held at waist level. (MJS 8) (See: **Figure 32**)

anchita-ahayavarada mudra -- (Ind.: *añcita-ahāyavarada-mudrā* aka *gandhararattha mudra;* Thai: *pang khor-phon*) This is a descriptive term.[29] A variant term for *gandhararattha mudra*. See: *gandhararattha mudra*. (DRN 37, JBo 205, MSD, SVB)

anchita-anchita mudra I -- (Ind..: *añcita-añcita-mudrā;* Eng.: accepting the rice-gruel offering; Thai: *pang sung rabmathupayas*) This is a descriptive term.[30] See: *pang sung rabmathupayas*. (DRN 35, JBo 204, PSS)

anchita-anchita mudra II -- (Ind..: *añcita-añcita-mudrā;* Eng.: carrying the alms bowl *mudra;* Thai: *pang uhm-bhatr*) This is a descriptive term.[31] (See: *pang uhm-bhatr*) (DRN 36, JBo 205, ODD 680, PSS)

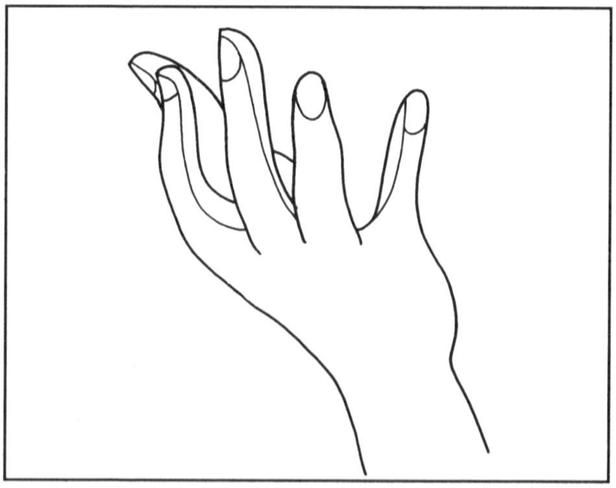

Figure 32 -- anchita mudra
(as seen by another)

anchita-dhyana mudra -- (Ind.: *añcita-dhyāna-mudrā;* Eng.: eating the myrobalan fruit *mudra;* Thai: *pang chan-samor*) This is a descriptive term.[32] (See: *pang chan-samor*) (DRN 36, OFr 13, JBo 204, PSS)

anchita-katyavalambita mudra -- (Ind.: *kaṭyāvalambita-mudrā;* Eng.: setting the dish afloat *mudra;* Thai: *pang loy tard*) This is a descriptive term.[33] See: *pang loy tard.* (DRN 35, JBo 204, OFr 6, PSS, ODD 680)

anchita-lolahasta mudra -- (Ind.: *añcita-lolahasta-mudrā;* Ind.: *anchita-lolahasta mudra;* Thai: *pang sungrabyaka*) This is a descriptive term.[34] See: *pang sungrabyaka*). (DRN 35, JBo 204, ODD 680, OFr 7, PSS)

anchita-nidratahasta mudra I -- (Ind.: *añcita-nidrātahasta-mudrā;* Eng.: receiving the mango *mudra;* Thai: *pang rab-pholmamuang*) This is a descriptive term.[35] See: *pang rab-pholmamuang*. (DRN 37, JBo 205, ODD 680, OFr 22, PSS)

anchita-nidratahasta mudra II -- (Ind.: *añcita-nidrātahasta-mudrā;* Eng.: in the *Palelayaka* forest *mudra;* Thai: *pang palelai*) This is a descriptive term.[36] See: *pang palelai.* (DRN 36, JBo 205, ODD 680, OFr 28, PSS)

Angarakha mudra -- (Ind.: *Aṅgārakha-mudrā*) A hand pose, a seal, a dramatic (Ind.: *nāṭya*) *mudra* or gesture (Ind.: *darpaṇa*) held or formed by a performer, dancer or actor. The *Angarakha mudra* is a combined (Ind.: *saṁyutta*) form, held by both hands. It denotes Mars, one of the nine planets (Ind.: *navagraha*). This *mudra* is formed by: right palm faces the midline, the fingers are fisted, the thumb lies over the first phalanges of the fingers; left palm faces forward, the index finger and the thumb point upwards, together, the middle, ring and little fingers are folded into the palm. (ACG 46) (See: **Figure 33**)

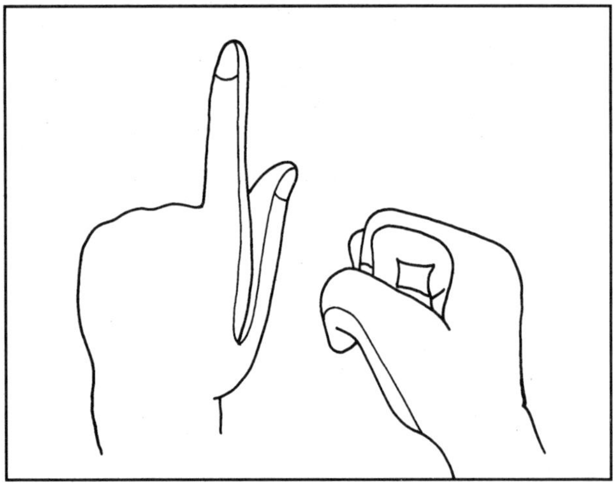

Figure 33 -- Angarakha mudra
(as seen by the holder)

an-i-in (mudra) -- (Jap.: *an-i-in* [*mudrā*]; Chin.: *an-wei-yin;* Ind.: *vitarka mudrā*) A *mudra*, a ritual hand pose, a seal, a *tantric mudra* which is common to the Japanese and Chinese Buddhist (*Vajrayana, Mantrayana*) tradition and is held or formed by a devotee or priest. It may be accompanied by a *mantra*. It denotes the act of presenting a homily, and additionally represents the act of spiritual or theological disputation The *an-i-in* (*mudra*) is a combined (Ind.: *saṁyutta*) form, held by both hands. This *mudra* is formed by: right hand is held cupped--similar to the *anchita mudra*--level with waist (resting on the right thigh if seated), palm upward, fingers forward. The left hand is held at shoulder height, palm facing forward, the index finger is flexed, the outer edge of the phalange's tip rests against the thumb's first phalange's pad, the middle, ring and little fingers are extended upwards. In intent, it is related to the *vitarka mudra*, although its form differs considerably. The 'cupped' right hand may be so placed as to hold sacred scriptures during disputation.[37] (EDS 66) (See: **Figure 34**)

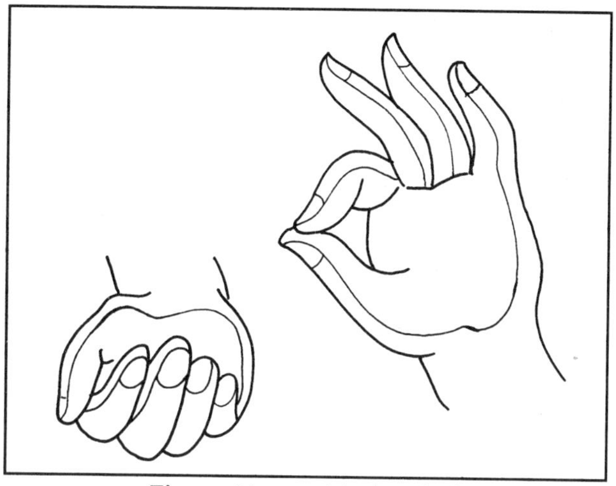

Figure 34 -- an-i-in (mudra)
(as seen by another)

an-i-shoshu-in (mudra) -- (Jap.: *an-i-shoshu-in* [*mudrā*]; Chin.: *an-wei she-ch'u yin*) A *mudra*, a ritual hand pose, a seal, a *tantric mudra* which is common to the Japanese and Chinese Buddhist (*Vajrayana, Mantrayana*) tradition and is held or formed by a devotee or priest. It may be accompanied by a *mantra* and is a variant of the *an-i-in* (*mudra*). It denotes the act of calming and gathering as well as welcoming one to Paradise. The *an-i-shoshu-in* (*mudra*) is a combined (Ind.: *saṁyutta*) form, held by both hands. This *mudra* is formed by: right hand is held slightly cupped--similar to the *anchita mudra*--level with waist, palm towards midline, fingers forward. The left hand is held in the same manner as the left hand of the *an-i-in* (*mudra*). In intent, it is related to the *abhaya mudra*, although its form is considerably different. The 'cupped' right hand, so rotated may be viewed as a gesture of 'appeasement.'[38] (EDS 69) (See: **Figure 35**)

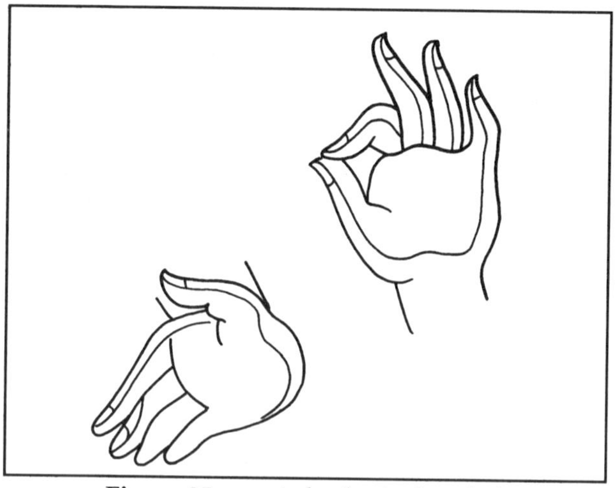

Figure 35 -- an-i-shoshu-in (mudra)
(as seen by another)

anjali mudra I -- (Ind.: *añjali-mudrā* aka *anjalikarma mudra, padmanjali mudra, samputanjali mudra, sarvarajendra mudra, vajra-anjalikarma mudra*; Chin.: *chin-kang ho-chang*; Jap.: *kongo-gassho, nebina-gassho*) A *mudra*, a ritual hand pose, a seal, which is common to both the Buddhist and Hindu traditions and is depicted or held by a deity. It is noted by some as indicating greeting or salutation.[39] However, others view it as a pose of adoration or worship.[40] It is also a dramatic (Ind.: *nāṭya*) *mudra* or gesture (Ind.: *darpaṇa*) held or formed by a performer, dancer or actor. The *anjali mudra* is a combined (Ind.: *saṁyutta*) form, held by both hands. This *mudra* is formed by: both hands brought together, palm to palm, fingers extended upwards, slightly

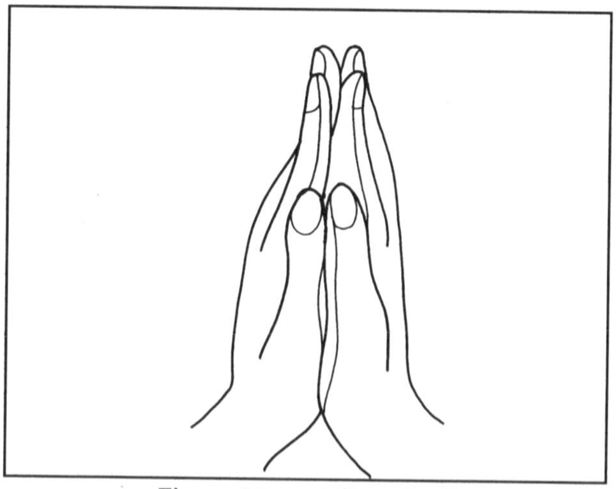

Figure 36 -- anjali mudra I
(as seen by the holder)

cupped and held with the tips of the fingers at the level of the chin.[41] (ACG 39, BBh 189, EDS 41, ERJ II 23, MJS 9, TGR 16) (See: **Figure 36**)

anjali mudra II -- (Ind.: *añjali-mudrā* aka *adhara mudra*[42]; Jap.: *adara-gassho*) A *mudra*, a ritual hand pose, a seal, which is common to the Buddhist tradition and is depicted or held by a deity. Also, a tantric *mudra* which is common to the Japanese Buddhist (*Vajrayana, Mantrayana*) tradition and is held or formed by a devotee or priest. It may be accompanied by a *mantra*. It is noted by one source as indicating a salutation.[43] The *anjali mudra* is a combined (Ind.: *saṁyutta*) form, held by both hands. This *mudra* is formed by: hands are brought together, fingers extended forwards (parallel to the ground), outer edge of palms and little fingers touch, while thus held the hands are slightly rotated open or cupped and held at chest level as if in anticipation of receiving some small object(s). This *mudra* is similar to the *patra mudra*. (EDS 41, RSG 3, AKG 20) (See: **Figure 37**)

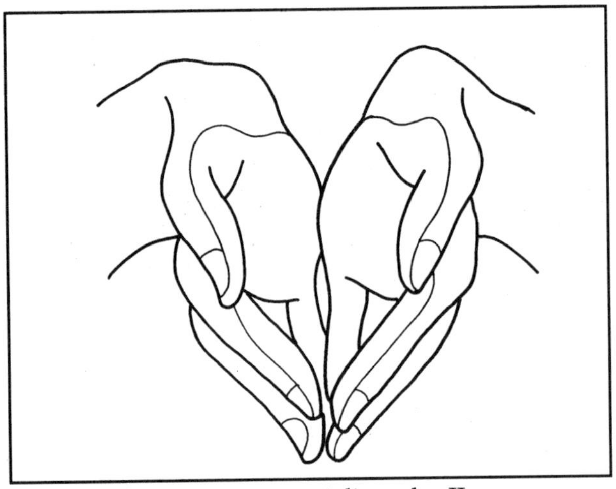

Figure 37 -- anjali mudra II
(as seen by another)

anjali mudra III -- (Ind.: *añjali-mudrā*) A *mudra*, a ritual hand pose, a seal, which is more common to the Buddhist tradition, particularly to the *Vajrayana* practice, and employed infrequently in the Hindu tradition. It denotes greeting or salutation.[44] The *anjali mudra III* is a combined (Ind.: *saṁyutta*) form, held by both hands. The form involves hands: held above the head, palms upwards, heels of the palms touching, fingers are extended, slightly separated and curved gently upwards. This *mudra*, thus formed, frequently is utilized to hold an image--e.g., the *tantric* form of *Avalokiteshvara* holds an image of *Amitabha* in this pose. (AGe, AKG 20. GDe 140) (See: **Figure 38**)

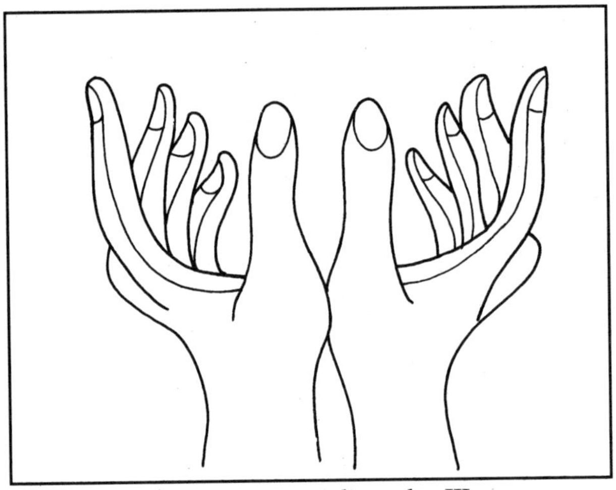

Figure 38 -- anjali mudra III
(as seen by the holder)

anjalikarma mudra -- (Ind.: *añjalikarma-mudrā* aka *anjali mudra, vajra-anjalikarma mudra*; Jap.: *kongo-gassho* [*mudra*], *sashu-gassho* [*mudra*]) A variant term applied to *anjali mudra*. See: *anjali mudra*. (EDS 76)

ankusha mudra -- (Ind.: *āṅkuśa-mudrā*) A *mudra*, a ritual hand pose, a seal, a *tantric mudra* which is common to the Japanese Buddhist (*Vajrayana, Mantrayana*) tradition and is held or formed by a devotee or priest during the rites of *Garbhadhatu Mandala, Vajradhatu*

Mandala, Homa Rites and other rites. It may be accompanied by a *mantra*. The *ankusha mudra* is a combined (Ind.: *saṁyutta*) form, held by both hands. This *mudra* is formed by: palms face each other, fingers and thumbs are interlaced with fingers and thumb inside (palm-side) the 'fist' (Jap.: *naibaku ken-in* [*mudra*]), the index finger of the right hand is erect, bending slightly over the fist. (GDe 146, LCS 144) (See: **Figure 39**)

an-shan-yin (mudra) -- (Chin.: *an-shan-yin* [*mudrā*]; Jap.: *anzan-in* [*mudra*]) The Chinese term for *anzan-in* (*mudra*). See: *anzan-in* (*mudra*). (EDS 81)

anuchitta mudra -- (Ind.: *anucitta-mudrā*) A *mudra*, a ritual hand pose, a seal, a *tantric mudra* which is common to the Japanese Buddhist (*Vajrayana, Mantrayana*) tradition and is held or formed by a devotee or priest in the performance of various rites. It may be accompanied by a *mantra*. The *anuchitta mudra* is a combined (Ind.: *saṁyutta*) form, held by both hands. This *mudra* is formed by: palms of both hands brought together but not touching, middle and little fingers are interlaced, index and ring fingers curl and touch the opposite at the tips, thumbs touch along their outer edges. (GDe 225, LCS 238) (See: **Figure 40**)

anuja mudra -- (Ind.: *anuja-mudrā*) ("*mudra* of the younger brother") A *mudra*, a ritual hand pose, a seal, a *tantric mudra* which is common to the Japanese Buddhist (*Vajrayana, Mantrayana*) tradition and is held or formed by a devotee or priest during the rites of *Garbhadhatu Mandala*. It may be accompanied by a *mantra*. The *anuja mudra* is a combined (Ind.: *saṁyutta*) form, held by both hands. This *mudra* is formed by: right palm facing down ward, thumbs and fingers extended towards the midline; left palm facing downwards, thumbs and fingers extended towards the midline. Thus formed the left hand rests on the downturned right. This *mudra* resembles the *dhyana mudra* and the *bihararieisata gassho* (*mudra*) It is opposite to the *agraja mudra*. (LCS 181) (See: **Figure 41**)

an-wei she-ch'u-yin (mudra) -- (Chin.; Jap.: *an-i-shoshu-iñ* [*mudrā*]) The Chinese term for *an-i-shoshu-in*. See: *an-i-shoshu-in*. (EDS 69)

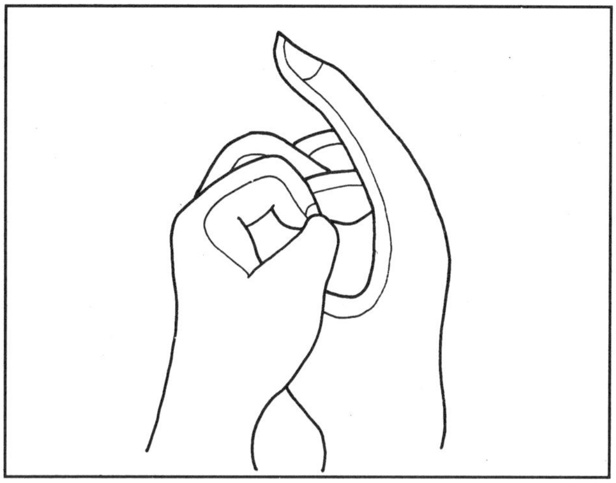

Figure 39 -- ankusha mudra
(as seen by the holder)

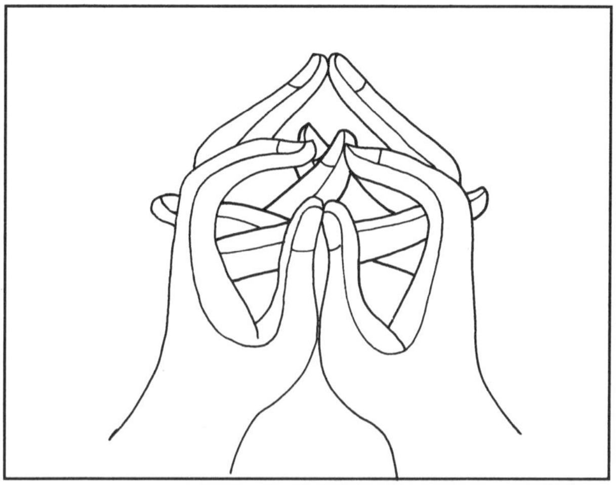

Figure 40 -- anuchitta mudra
(as seen by the holder)

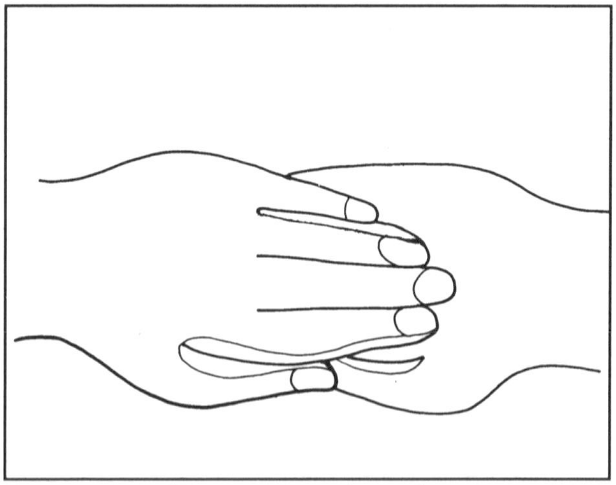

Figure 41 -- anuja mudra
(as seen by the holder)

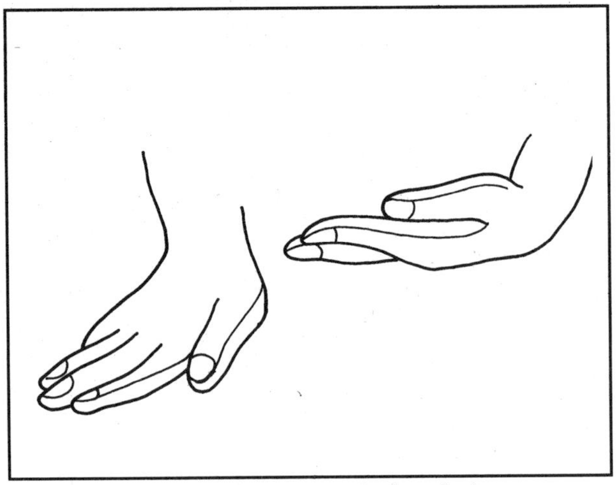

Figure 42 -- anzan-in (mudra)
(as seen by another)

Figure 43 -- apan mudra
(as seen by another)

Figure 44 -- apan-vayu mudra
(as seen by another)

an-wei-yin (mudra) -- (Chin.; Jap.: *an-i-in* [*mudrā*]) The Chinese term for the Japanese *an-i-in*. See: *an-i-in*. (EDS 66)

anzan-in (mudra) -- (Jap.: *anzan-in* [*mudrā*], aka *sokuchi-in* (*mudra*); Chin.: *an-shan-yin, ch'u-ti-yin*; Eng.: *adamantine posture*; Ind.: *bhasparśa mudrā, bhūmisparśa mudrā, bhūmisparśana mudrā, bhūmisparśa mudrā, bhūsparś mudrā, bhusparśa mudrā, māravijaya mudrā*; Thai: *manwichai* [*mudra*], *pang maravichai*, [*pang*] *sadung-man*) A *mudra*, a ritual hand pose, a seal, a *tantric mudra* which is common to the Japanese and Chinese Buddhist (*Vajrayana, Mantrayana*) tradition and is held or formed by a devotee or priest. It may be accompanied by a *mantra*. It is a variation of the *sokuchi-in* (*mudra*). It denotes the dominion over the earth and the vanquishing of its demons.[45] It is related to 'calling the earth to witness' (Ind.: *bhūmisparśa*). The form is generally displayed by the standing Lord Buddha, although it may also be held by the seated figure The *anzan-in* (*mudra*) is a combined (Ind.: *saṁyutta*) form, held by both hands. This *mudra* is formed by: the right hand is held palm down, parallel with the ground, fingers extended, while the left hand is held waist high, palm up, similar to the *dhyana mudra*. It is one of a number of variations on the *sokuchi-in* (*bhumisparsha mudra*) to be found in Japanese Buddhist iconography. (EDS 81) (See: **Figure 42**)

apan mudra -- (Ind.: *apāna-mudrā*) A *mudra*, a ritual hand pose, a seal, a mudra which is common to yogic tradition, particularly the *Yoga Tatva Mudra Vigyan* form, and is held by a devotee or practitioner. The *apan mudra* is a single (Ind.: *asaṁyutta*) form, held by one hand. It is utilized for bodily purification. This *mudra* is formed by: the palm facing forward, the index and little fingers extended straight upwards, the middle and ring fingers bent, together towards the palm and the tip of the thumb touching the tips of the middle and ring fingers. This *mudra* resembles the *karana mudra*. (KDe 56-59) (See: **Figure 43**)

apan-vayu mudra -- (Ind.: *apāna-vāyu-mudrās* aka *Mrit-Sanjivani mudra*) A *mudra*, a ritual hand pose, a seal, a *mudra* which is common to yogic tradition, particularly the *Yoga Tatva Mudra Vigyan* form, and is held by a devotee or practitioner. The *apan-vayu mudra* is a single (Ind.: *asaṁyutta*) form, held by one hand. It is utilized for the heart and the pulse. This *mudra* is formed by: the palm facing forward, the index finger folded tightly into the palm, the middle and ring fingers curled towards the palm, the little finger straight upwards, and the tip of the thumb touching the tips of the middle and ring fingers. (KDe 131) (See: **Figure 44**)

arala mudra I -- (Ind.: *arāla-mudrā*) A *mudra*, a ritual hand pose, a seal, which is common to the Hindu tradition and is depicted or held by a deity. The *arala mudra* is a single (Ind.: *asaṁyutta*) form, held by one hand. It denotes a bird and further may symbolize culpability or even the imbibing of poison. The form is generally shown with the arm extended to the side or the hand at shoulder height, palm downward, fingers extended, except the index finger which points downward. This *mudra* is similar to the *pataka mudra*.[46] (MJS 10) (See: **Figure 45**)

arala mudra II -- (Ind.: *arāla-mudrā*) ("bent") A hand pose, a seal, a dramatic (Ind.: *nāṭya*) *mudra* or gesture (Ind.: *darpaṇa*) held or formed by a performer, dancer or actor. The *arala mudra* is a single (Ind.: *asaṁyutta*) form, held by one hand. It denotes the imbibing of poison. This *mudra* is formed by: the *pataka mudra* (middle, ring and little fingers extend upwards and together), except the thumb curls tightly and the index finger also curls towards the palm, the palm faces forward away from the body.[47] (KVa 134 [8]) (See: **Figure 46**)

arala mudra III -- (Ind.: *arāla-mudrā*) ("bent") A hand pose, a seal, a dramatic (Ind.: *nāṭya*) *mudra* or gesture (Ind.: *darpaṇa*) held or formed by a performer, dancer or actor. The *arala mudra* is a single (Ind.: *asaṁyutta*) form, a variation held by one hand. It denotes the imbibing of poison. This *mudra* is formed by: the *pataka mudra* (thumb, middle, ring and little fingers extend upwards and together), except the index finger curls towards the palm, the palm faces forward away from the body. (ACG 29-30) (See: **Figure 47**)

arala-kataka-mukha mudra -- (Ind.: *arāla-kaṭaka-mukha-mudrā*) A hand pose, a seal, a dramatic (Ind.: *natya*) *mudra* or gesture (Ind.: *darpaṇa*) held or formed by a performer, dancer or actor. The *arala-kataka-mukha*

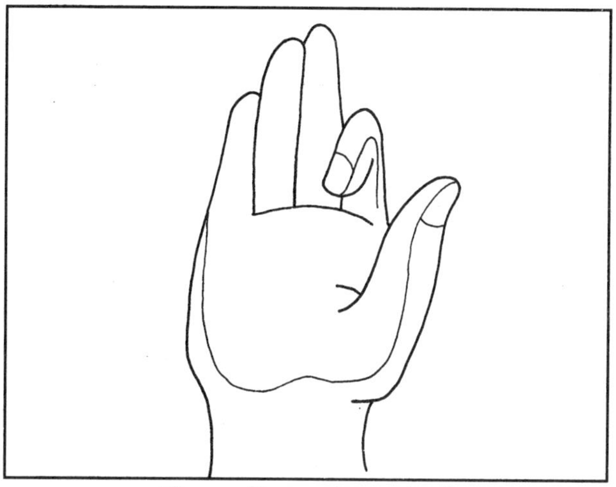

Figure 45 -- arala mudra I
(as seen by another)

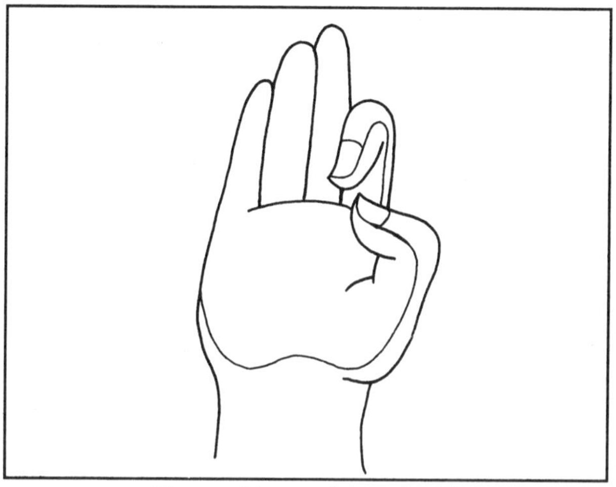

Figure 46 -- arala mudra II
(as seen by another)

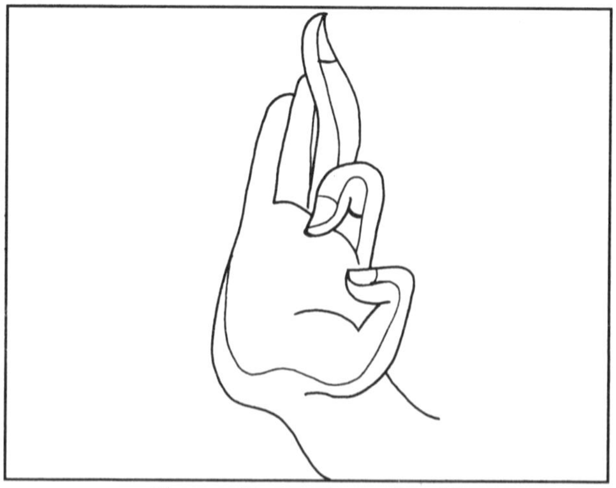

Figure 47 -- arala mudra III
(as seen by another)

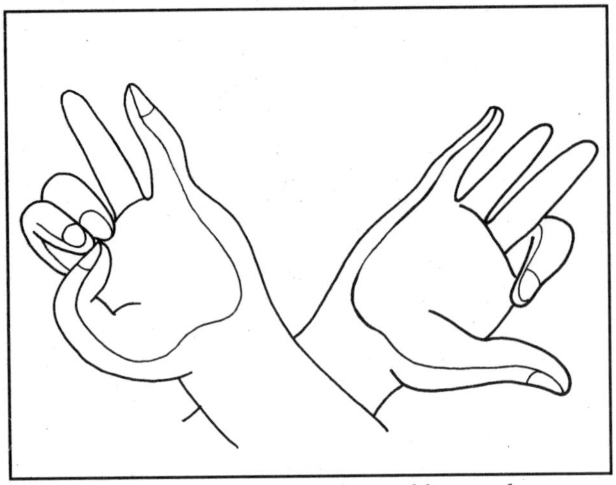

Figure 48 -- arala-kataka-mukha mudra
(as seen by another)

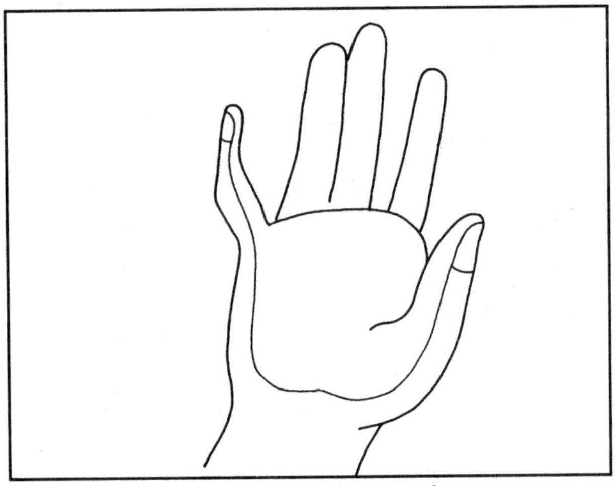

Figure 49 -- archita mudra
(as seen by another)

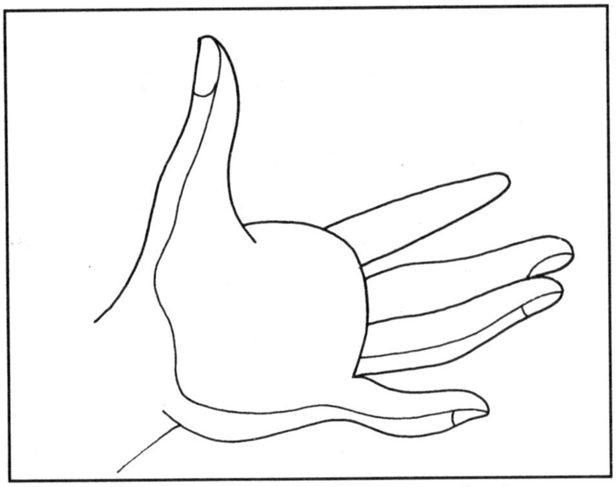

Figure 50 -- ardhachandra mudra I
(as seen by another)

mudra is a combined (Ind.: *saṁyutta*) form, held by both hands. It denotes anxiety and dismay. This *mudra* is formed by: right palm faces forwards, middle, ring and little fingers extend upwards and together, thumb curls tightly and the index finger also curls towards the palm; left palm faces forwards, the index finger curls over the tip of the thumb and the middle finger folds into the palm, the ring and little fingers curve slightly towards the palm progressively. Thus formed, the hands cross at the wrists. (ACG 43) (See: **Figure 48**)

archita mudra -- (Ind.: *arcita-mudrā*) A *mudra*, a ritual hand pose, a seal, which is common to the Hindu tradition and *Shiva-Nataraja Chaturam*.[48] It denotes a greeting or salutation. The *archita mudra* is a single (Ind.: *asaṁyutta*) form, held by one hand. The form is generally shown with the right hand held at chest or shoulder height, palm forward, fingers extended upward in a relaxed manner. This *mudra* is similar in form to the *ahayavarada mudra*. (RSG 63) (See: **Figure 49**)

ardhachandra mudra I -- (Ind.: *ardhacandra-mudrā*) A *mudra*, a ritual hand pose, a seal, which is more common to the Hindu tradition than the Buddhist and is depicted or held by a deity. It is a pose which is used to hold an object, generally a bowl which may contain fire--e.g., as with the *Shiva-Nataraja Katisama*. The *ardhachandra mudra I* is a single (Ind.: *asaṁyutta*) form, held by the left hand. The form is represented by the hand: palm upwards and fingers slightly cupped resembling a crescent or half moon (Ind.: *ardhacandra*),[49] the thumb is at right angle to the fingers, and similarly bent. In form it appears related to the *anchita mudra*. (ERJ II 25, MJS 10, RSG 63) (See: **Figure 50**)

ardhachandra mudra II -- (Ind.: *ardhacandra-mudrā*) ("half moon") A hand pose, a seal, a dramatic (Ind.: *nāṭya*) *mudra* or gesture (Ind.: *darpaṇa*) held or formed by a performer, dancer or actor. The *ardhachandra mudra II* is a single (Ind.: *asaṁyutta*) form, held by one hand. It denotes the moon, consecrating an image, prayer, etc.[50] This *mudra* is formed by: fingers extended, together and pointing upwards, relaxed, the thumb extends away from the fingers, palm facing forward and generally on a line level with the chest. (ACG 29, KVa 134 [7]) (See: **Figure 51**)

ardha-chatura mudra -- (Ind.: *ardha-catura-mudrā*) A hand pose, a seal, a dramatic (Ind.: *nāṭya*) *mudra* or gesture (Ind.: *darpaṇa*) held or formed by a performer, dancer or actor noted in ACG but without description.[51] (ACG 44)

ardha-mukha mudra -- (Ind.: *ardha-mukha-mudrā*) A *mudra*, a ritual hand pose, a seal, a dramatic (Ind.: *nāṭya*) *mudra* or gesture (Ind.: *darpaṇa*) held or formed by a performer, dancer or actor. The *ardha-mukha mudra* is a single (Ind.: *asaṁyutta*) form, held by one hand.This mudra is formed by: either hand, palm generally faces forward, index, midlle,and little fingers are folded into the palm, the tip of the thumb touches the tip of the ring finger. (ACG 49) (See: **Figure 52**)

ardha-mukula mudra -- (Ind.: *ardha-mukula-mudrā*) A hand pose, a seal, a dramatic (Ind.: *nāṭya*) *mudra* or gesture (Ind.: *darpaṇa*) held or formed by a performer, dancer or actor noted in ACG but without description.[52] (ACG 44)

ardhanjali mudra -- (Ind.: *ardhañjali-mudrā*) A *mudra*, a ritual hand pose, a seal, which is more common to the Hindu tradition than the Buddhist. It is a pose which is used as a sign of blessing, benediction or may be used as one of greeting or worship. The *ardhanjali mudra* is a single (Ind.: *asaṁyutta*) form, held by one hand. The form is held at chest level along the vertical mid-line, fingers extended upwards, slightly cupped and palm facing towards the midline. It is similar to the benedictory pose held by Christian liturgical priests. (BNS, MJS 11) (See: **Figure 53**)

ardhanjali-dhyana mudra -- (Ind.: *ardhañjali-dhyāna-mudrā*; Eng.: making a gift of hair *mudra*; Thai: *pang phra-keit-tatu*) This is a descriptive term.[53] See: *pang phra-keit-tatu*. (DRN 36, JBo 205, ODD 680, OFr 15, PSS)

ardha-pataka mudra -- (Ind.: *ardha-pātaka-mudrā* or *ardha-patākā-mudrā*) ("half flag") A *mudra*, a ritual hand pose, a seal, which is common to both the Buddhist and Hindu traditions and is depicted or held by a deity. Also, a hand pose, a seal, a dramatic (Ind.: *nāṭya*) *mudra* or gesture (Ind.: *darpaṇa*) held or formed by a performer, dancer or actor. The *ardhapataka mudra* is a

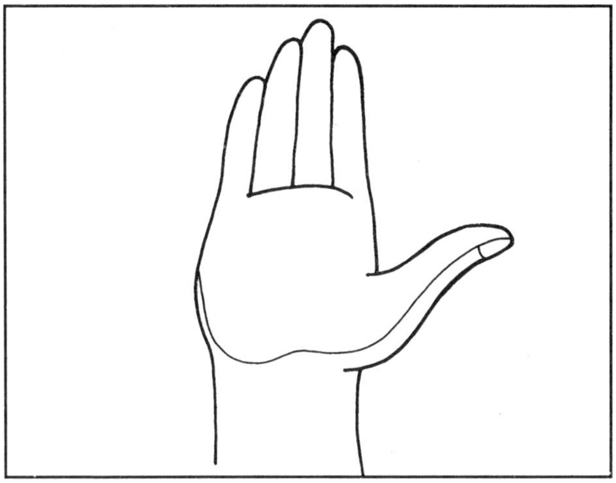

Figure 51 -- ardhachandra mudra II
(as seen by another)

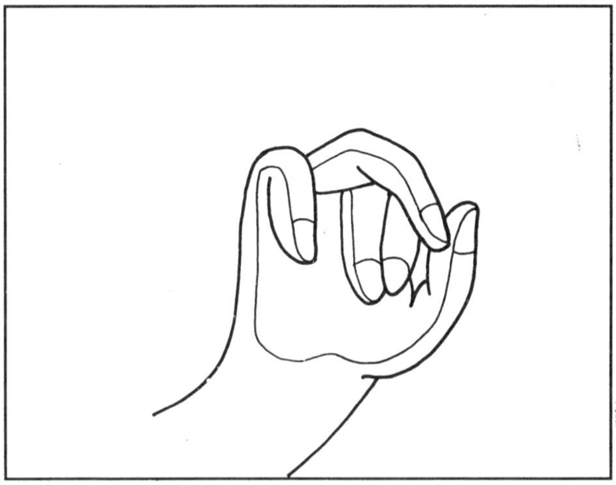

Figure 52 -- ardha-mukha mudra
(as seen by another)

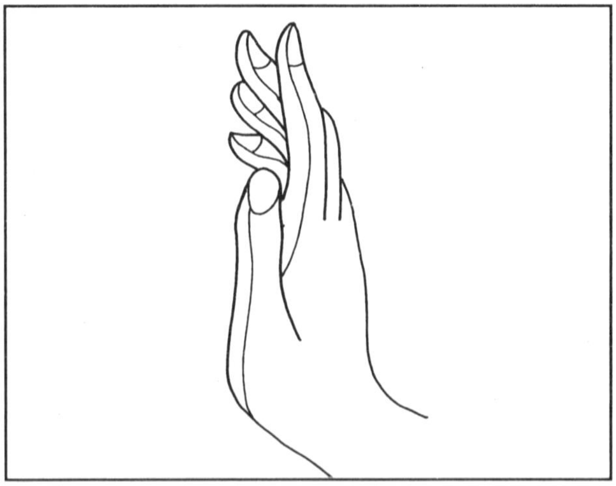

Figure 53 -- ardhanjali mudra
(as seen by the holder)

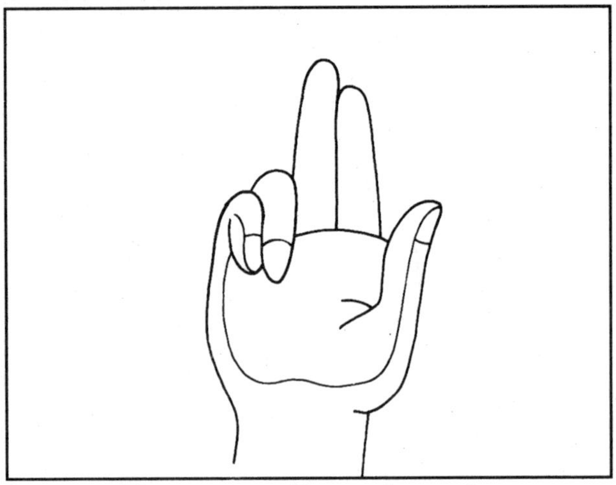

Figure 54 -- ardha-pataka mudra
(as seen by the holder)

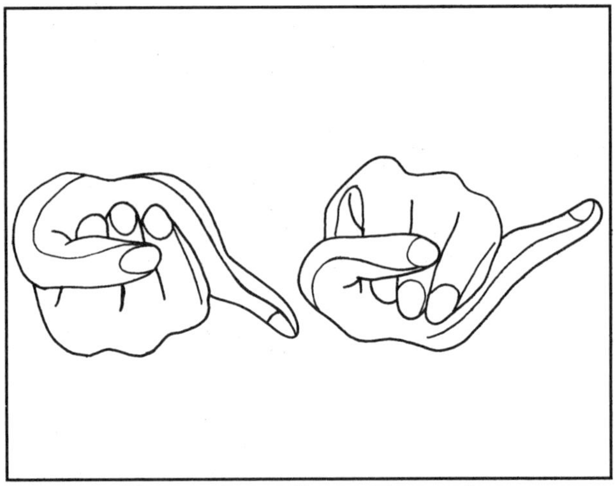

Figure 55 -- ardha-rechita mudra
(as seen by another)

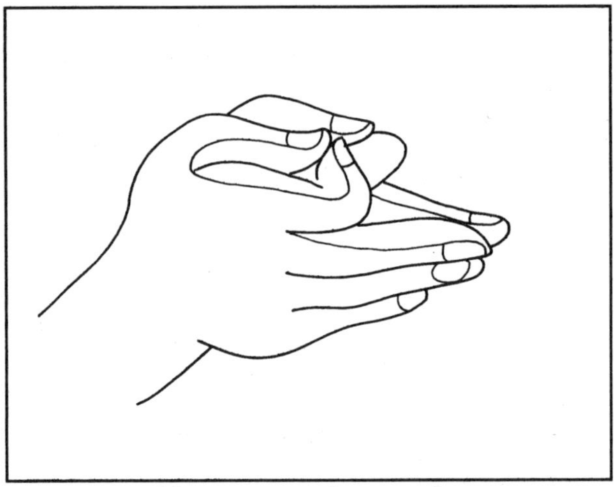

Figure 56 -- argham mudra
(as seen by another)

single (Ind.: *asaṁyutta*) form, held by one hand. It denotes: a dagger, knife, flag, etc.[54] The *mudra* is formed by: the hand raised, index, middle fingers and thumb extended, together and pointing upwards, ring and little fingers bent towards the palm, palm facing forward and generally on a line level with the chest. It is similar to the *kartari-hasta* except the tips of the thumb and ring fingers do not touch. (ACG 28, JDo, KVa 134 [3], MJS 11) (See: **Figure 54**)

ardha-rechita mudra -- (Ind.: *ardha-recita-mudrā*) A hand pose, a seal, a dramatic (Ind.: *nāṭya*) *mudra* or gesture (Ind.: *darpaṇa*) held or formed by a performer, dancer or actor. The *ardha-rechita mudra* is a combined (Ind.: *saṁyutta*) form, held by both hands. It denotes invitation, giving gifts and concealing actions. This *mudra* is formed by: right palm face upwards, the index, middle and ring fingers curl towards the palm, the thumb rests along the curled index finger, the little finger is straight and pointing forwards; left palm face downwards, the index, middle and ring fingers curl towards the palm, the thumb rests along the curled index finger, the little finger is straight and pointing forwards. Thus formed the hands are held in front of the trunk, close, but not touching. (ACG 43) (See: **Figure 55**)

argham mudra -- (Ind.: *argham-mudrā*) This is an assigned term.[55] A *mudra*, a ritual hand pose, a seal, which is common to the Buddhist (*Vajrayana*) tradition, a *tantric mudra*. It denotes 'water for the face,' which is one of the two 'waters' or 'outer offerings' proffered to a divine guest--the other one being: water for the feet--during the early stages worship, particularly as associated with the worship of the powerful *Vajrayana* goddess, *Tara*. The *argham mudra* is a combined (Ind.: *saṁyutta*) form, held by both hands. The form is in mirror-pose--the tips of the thumb and the index finger touch, the other three fingers are extended, thus formed, the two hands are brought tightly together, palms and fingers of both hands as one. The extended fingers are pointed away from the body and the *mudra* is held near the chest, just below the chin. The *mantra* associated with this *mudra* is: "*OM Guru-sarva-Tathagata pravara-satkara-mahasatkara-maha-argham Praticcha HUM SVAHA.*"[56] (SBe 147) (See: **Figure 56**)

argha mudra -- (Ind.: *argha-mudrā*]; Jap.: *akka-in* [*mudra*]) The Indic term for *akka-in* (*mudra*). See: *akka-in* (*mudra*). (GDe 42)

Arjuna mudra I -- (Ind.: *Arjuna-mudrā*) A hand pose, a seal, a dramatic (Ind.: *nāṭya*) *mudra* or gesture (Ind.: *darpaṇa*) held or formed by a performer, dancer or actor. The *Arjuna mudra* is a combined (Ind.: *saṁyutta*) form, held by both hands. It denotes *Arjuna*, one of a number of famous rulers or heroes. The *mudras* employed are two *tripitaka mudras* held level with the shoulder and moved forward and backwards, alternately. See: *tripitaka mudra*. (ACG 47) (See: **Figure 57**)

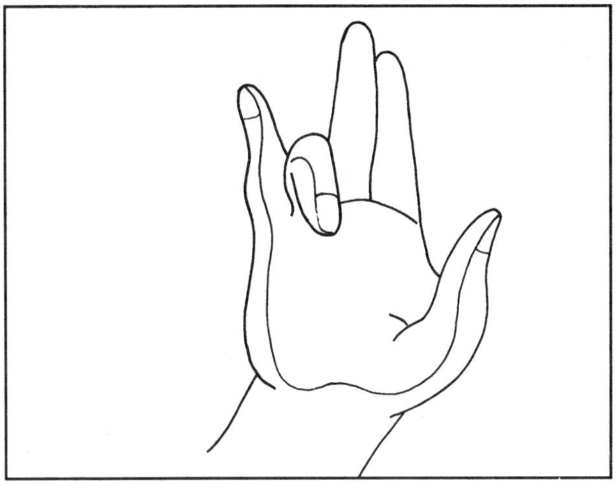

Figure 57 -- Arjuna mudra I
(as seen by another)

arjuna mudra II -- (Ind.: *arjuna-mudrā*) A hand pose, a seal, a dramatic (Ind.: *nāṭya*) *mudra* or gesture (Ind.: *darpaṇa*) held or formed by a performer, dancer or actor. It denotes the *arjuna* tree. The *mudra* employed is identical in form to the *simha-mukha mudra*. See: *simha-mukha mudra*. (ACG 48)

ashcharya mudra -- (Ind.: *āścarya-mudrā* aka *vismaya mudra*) A variant term applied to *vismaya mudra*. See: *vismaya mudra*. (MJS 12)

ashoka mudra -- (Ind.: *aśoka-mudrā*) A hand pose, a seal, a dramatic (Ind.: *nāṭya*) *mudra* or gesture (Ind.: *darpaṇa*) held or formed by a performer, dancer or actor. It denotes the *ashoka* tree. The *ashoka* mudra is a combined (Ind.: *saṁyutta*) form, held by both hands. The *mudra* is: the hands are raised, fingers and thumbs extended, together and pointing upwards, relaxed, slightly cupped, palms facing forward. Thus formed the hands are crossed at the wrists, generally level with the chest and moving too and fro. (See: *pataka mudra*) (ACG 49) (See: **Figure 58**)

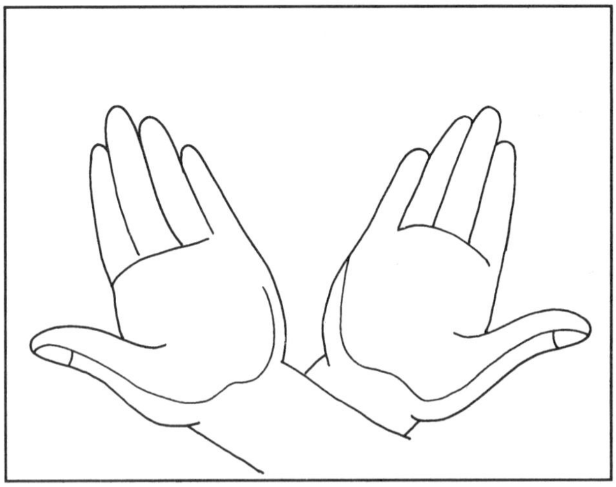

Figure 58 -- ashoka mudra
(as seen by another)

ashta-dala-padma mudra -- (Ind.: *aṣṭa-dala-padma-mudrā*) ("eight petal lotus") A *mudra*, a ritual hand pose, a seal, a *tantric mudra* which is common to the Japanese Buddhist (*Vajrayana, Mantrayana*) tradition and is held or formed by a devotee or priest during the rites of *Garbhadhatu Mandala, Vajradhatu Mandala, Homa Rites* and other rites. It may be accompanied by a *mantra*. The *ashta-dala-padma mudra* is a combined (Ind.: *saṁyutta*) form, held by both hands. It denotes "per-

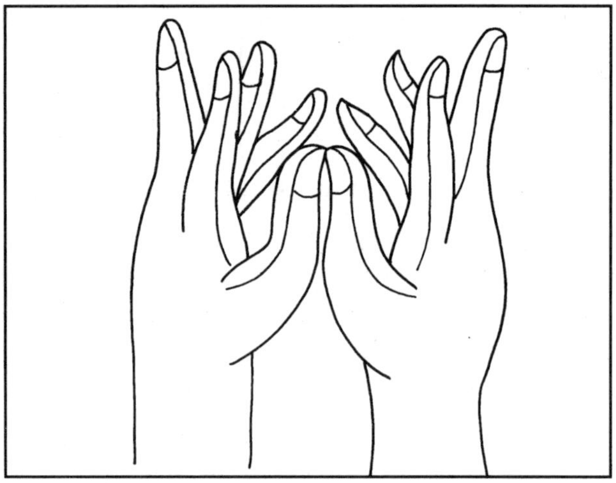

Figure 59 -- ashta-dala-padma mudra
(as seen by the holder)

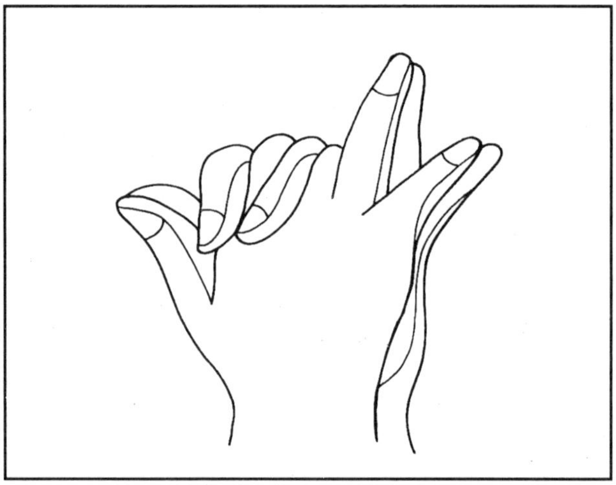

Figure 60 -- ashva-ratna mudra
(as seen by another)

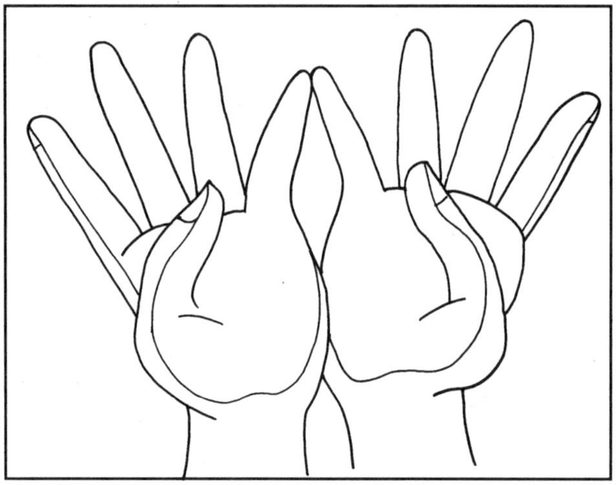

Figure 61 -- avahana mudra
(as seen by the holder)

fect beatitude and the satisfaction of all desires."[57] This *mudra* is formed by: palms facing midline, fingers and thumbs slightly splayed and pointing upwards. Thus formed, the hands are brought together, thumbs, heels of the hands, and tips of the little fingers touch forming a hollow space. (GDe 21, LCS 1.4) (See: **Figure 59**)

ashva-ratna mudra -- (Ind.: *aśva-ratna-mudrā*) This is an assigned term.[58] A *mudra*, a ritual hand pose, a seal, which is common to the Buddhist (*Vajrayana*) tradition, a *tantric mudra*. It denotes the gift of a precious horse (Tib.: *rtam-mchog*) associated with the *saptaratna* (Tib.: *rgyal-srid sna-bdun*) or seven gems of sovereignty (Tib.: *nor-bu-chab-bdun*), also referred to as the 'space vast treasury,' particularly as it is associated with the worship of the powerful *Vajrayana* goddess, *Tara*. The *ashva-ratna mudra* is a combined (Ind.: *saṁyutta*) form, held by both hands. The form is in mirror-pose: the basis is the interlaced fingers, however, the thumbs are side-by-side (not interlaced), and the ring and little fingers, likewise are not interlaced, but rest against their counterparts along their whole length, and they are separated--i.e., the ring and little fingers are splayed. The mantra associated with this mudra is: "*OM Ashva-ratna Praticcha HUM SVAHA*."[59] (SBe 152) (See: **Figure 60**)

ashvattha mudra -- (Ind.: *aśvattha-mudrā*) A hand pose, a seal, a dramatic (Ind.: *nāṭya*) *mudra* or gesture (Ind.: *darpaṇa*) held or formed by a performer, dancer or actor. It denotes the *ashvattha* or *pipal* tree. The *mudra* employed is the *alapadma mudra* with fingers waving. See: *alapadma mudra*. (ACG 48)

avahana mudra -- (Ind.: *āvāhana-mudrā*) A *mudra*, a ritual hand pose, a seal, which is common to the Hindu tradition. It denotes invocation or supplication. The *avahana mudra* is a combined (Ind.: *saṁyutta*) form, held by both hands. The form is identical for both hands--the fingers are splayed, thumbs touching the lowest phalanges of the ring finger and the hands are joined along the outer edge of the little finger and palm which faces upwards. It appears to be similar or a variation of *anjali mudra II*. (AMo, MJS 15) (See: **Figure 61**)

avahani mudra -- (Ind.: *āvāhanī-mudrā* aka *avahana mudra*) A variant (spelling) of *avahana mudra*. See: *avahana mudra*. (AMo)

avahittha mudra -- (Ind.: *avahitta-mudrā*) A hand pose, a seal, a dramatic (Ind.: *nāṭya*) *mudra* or gesture (Ind.: *darpana*) held or formed by a performer, dancer or actor. The *avahittha mudra* is a combined (Ind.: *saṁyutta*) form, held by both hands. It denotes debility, wasting of the body, etc.[60] This *mudra* is formed by: palms face forward, thumbs, middle and little fingers extend upwards, index and ring fingers curve towards the palms. Thus formed the hands are held against the chest, close, but not touching. (ACG 41) (See: **Figure 62**)

aviddha-vakra mudra -- (Ind.: *āviddha-vakra-mudrā*) A hand pose, a seal, a dramatic (Ind.: *nāṭya*) *mudra* or gesture (Ind.: *darpaṇa*) held or formed by a performer, dancer or actor. The *aviddha-vakra mudra* is a combined (Ind.: *saṁyutta*) form, held by both hands. It denotes slenderness, difference, folk dances, etc.[61] This *mudra* is formed by: palms facing forward, fingers and thumbs together and extended upwards. Thus formed, the hands are close, but not touching, held a short distance in front of the chest and the elbows are held slightly away from the body.[62] (ACG 42) (See: **Figure 63**)

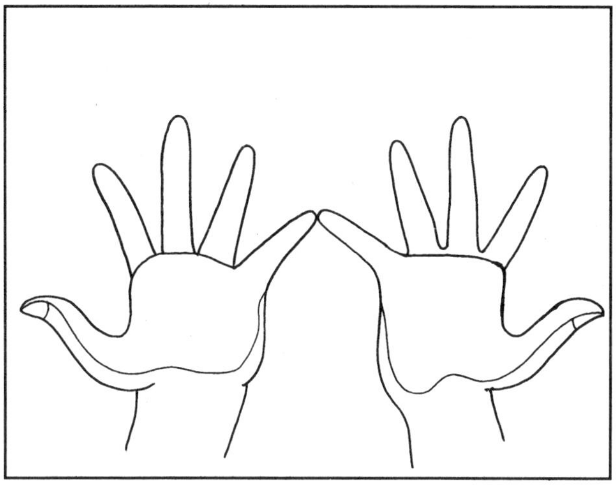

Figure 62 -- avahittha mudra
(as seen by the holder)

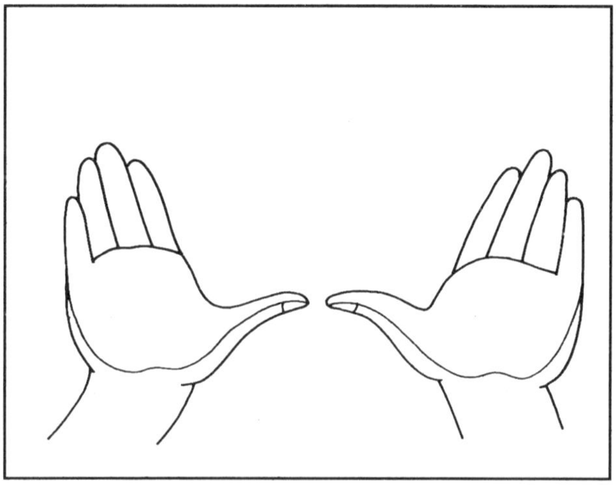

Figure 63 -- aviddha-vakra mudra
(as seen by another)

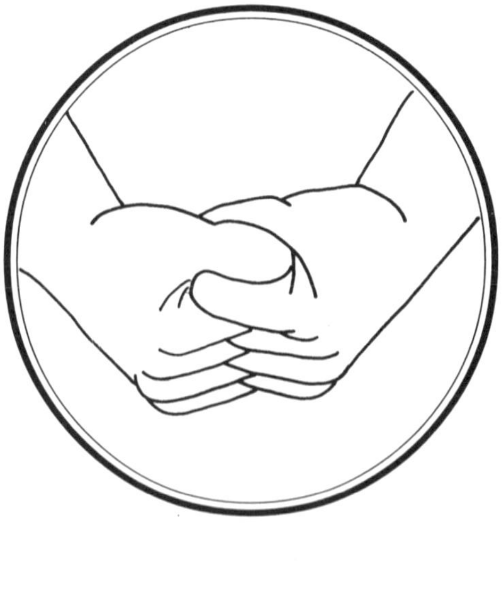

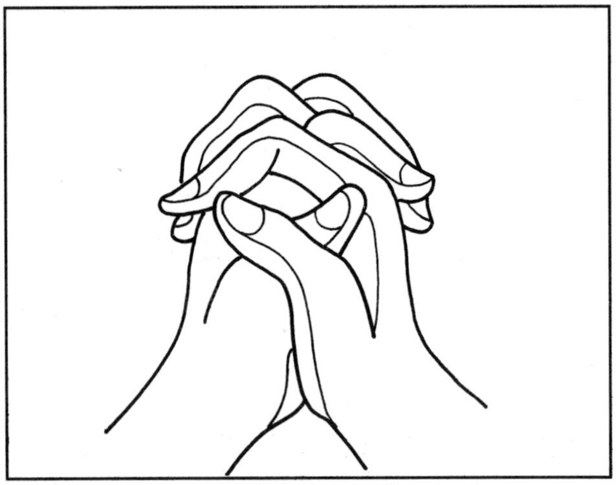

Figure 64 -- bahya-bandha mudra
(as seen by the holder)

Figure 65 -- baka mudra
(as seen by another)

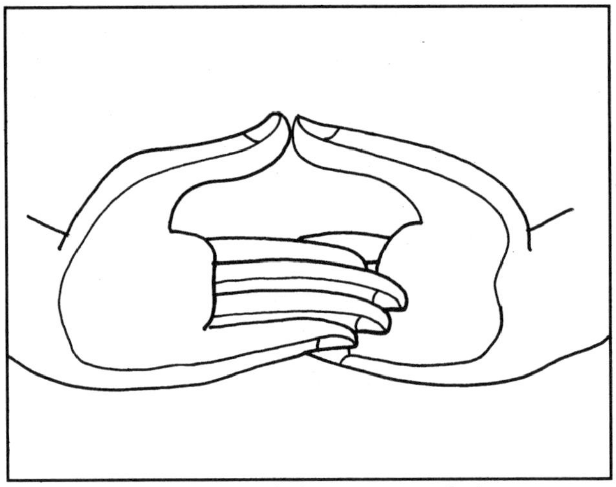

Figure 66 -- baku jo in (mudra)
(as seen by the holder)

-- B --

bahya-bandha mudra -- (Ind.: *bāhya-bandha-mudrā*) A *mudra*, a ritual hand pose, a seal, a *tantric mudra* which is common to the Japanese Buddhist (*Vajrayana, Mantrayana*) tradition and is held or formed by a devotee or priest during the rites of the *Vajradhatu Mandala*. It may be accompanied by a *mantra*. The *bahya-bandha mudra* is a combined (Ind.: *saṁyutta*) form, held by both hands. This *mudra* is formed by: hands are brought together, palm to palm, the fingers and thumbs are interlaced on top, and thumbs cross, right over left. This *mudra* is similar to the *granthitam mudra*. (LCS 119) (See: **Figure 64**)

baka mudra -- (Ind.: *baka-mudrā*) A hand pose, a seal, a dramatic (Ind.: *nāṭya*) *mudra* or gesture (Ind.: *darpaṇa*) held or formed by a performer, dancer or actor. It denotes a bird, in this case a crane. The *baka mudra*[1] is a single (Ind.: *asaṁyutta*) form, held by one hand. This *mudra* is formed by: the first phalanges of the thumb and index finger are brought together and extended, the middle, ring arch upwards, and little finger touches palm. (ACG 50) (See: **Figure 65**)

baku jo in (mudra) -- (Jap.: *baku jō in* [*mudrā*]) A *mudra*, a ritual hand pose, a seal, a *tantric mudra* which is common to the Japanese Buddhist (*Vajrayana, Mantrayana*) tradition and is held or formed by a devotee or priest during the rites of the *Vajradhatu Mandala*. It may be accompanied by a *mantra*. The *baku jo in* (*mudra*) is a combined (Ind.: *saṁyutta*) form, held by both hands. This *mudra* is formed by: hands brought together, palms upwards, fingers interlaced inside (palm-side) at the second phalanges of the fingers, tips of the thumbs arch over and touch. This *mudra* is similar to the *jo-in mudra*. (GDe 67) (See: **Figure 66**)

Balaramavatara mudra -- (Ind.: *Balarāmāvatāra-mudrā*) A hand pose, a seal, a dramatic (Ind.: *nāṭya*) *mudra* or gesture (Ind.: *darpaṇa*) held or formed by a performer, dancer or actor. The *Balaramavatara mudra* is a combined (Ind.: *saṁyutta*) form, held by both hands. It denotes *Rama*, the strong one, one of the ten *avatars* (Ind.: *dashavatara*) of the Lord *Vishnu* This *mudra* is formed by: right palm facing outward, fingers and thumb extended, together and pointing upwards, relaxed, slightly cupped; left palm faces the midline, the fingers are fisted, the thumb lies over the first phalanges of the fingers. (ACG 46) (See: **Figure 67**)

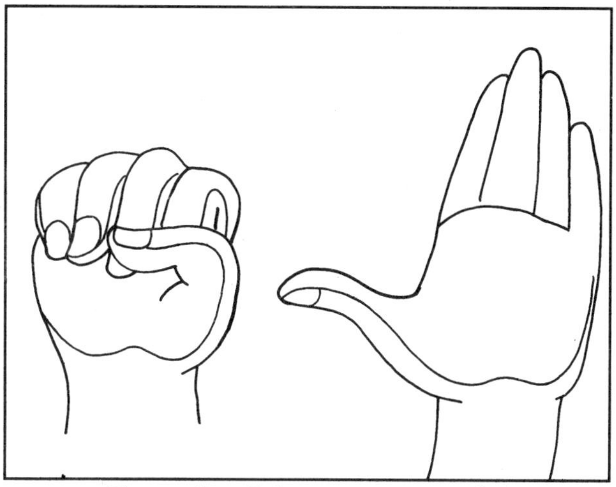

Figure 67 -- Balaramavatara mudra
(as seen by another)

BAM mudra -- (Ind.: *BĀM-mudrā*) This is an assigned term.[2] A *mudra*, a ritual hand pose, a seal, which is common to the Buddhist (*Vajrayana*) tradition, a *tantric mudra*. It denotes "to bind," and is the third syllable of a four syllable invocatory *mantra* particularly as associated with the invocation ceremony attached to the worship of the powerful *Vajrayana* goddess, *Tara*. The *BAM mudra* is a combined (Ind.: *saṁyutta*) form, held by both hands. This *mudra* is identical to both hands--the tips of the middle and ring fingers touch the last phalanges of the thumb which is curled towards the palm, the index and little fingers extend upward. Thus formed the tips of the index and little fingers touch, and the *mudra* is held just below the level of the chin, in front of the chest. The *mantra* associated with this mudra is: "*Jah Hum* **BAM** *Hoh*."[3] (SBe 102) (See: **Figure 68**)

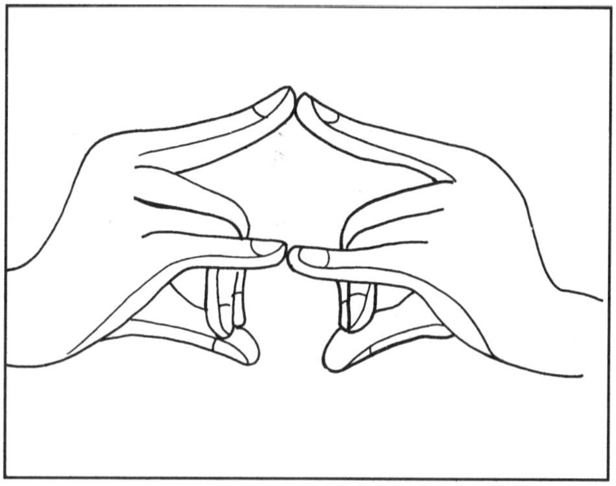

Figure 68 -- BAM mudra
(as seen by another)

bana mudra -- (Ind.: *bāṇa-mudrā*) A *mudra*, a ritual hand pose, a seal, a *tantric mudra* which is common to the Japanese Buddhist (*Vajrayana, Mantrayana*) tradition and is held or formed by a devotee or priest during the rites of *Vajradhatu Mandala*. It may be accompanied by a *mantra*. The *bana mudra* is a combined (Ind.: *saṁyutta*) form, held by both hands. This *mudra* is formed by: first interlacing the fingers to the back of the hand, the tips of the little fingers and the thumbs touch, and the middle fingers are curled inward (towards the palm) touching the opposite along the first and second phalanges. Thus formed, the palms are frequently turned backward, facing the waist. (LCS 85) (See: **Figure 69**)

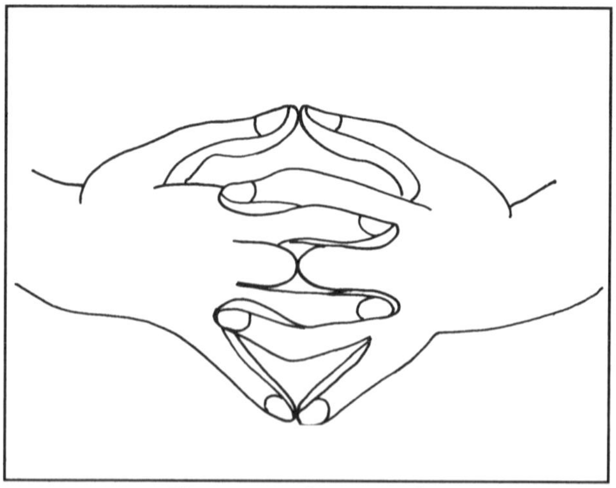

Figure 69 -- bana mudra
(as seen by another)

basara-un-kongo-in (mudra) I -- (Ind.: *basara-un-kongō-in* [*mudrā*]; Chin.: *chuan-yueh-lo-hung chin-kang-yin*; Ind.: *vajrahumkara mudra*) A *mudra*, a ritual hand pose, a seal,

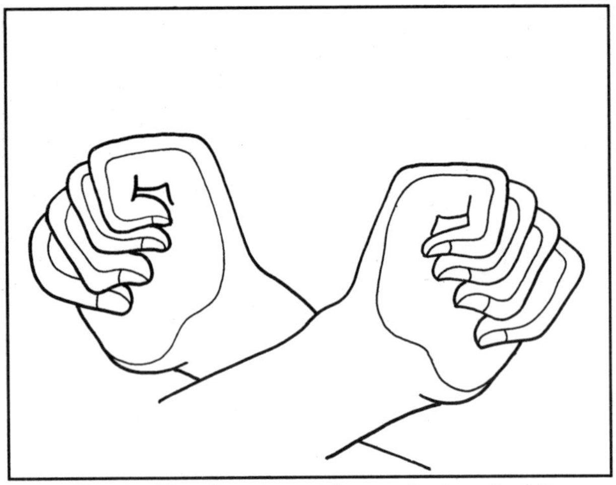

Figure 70 -- basara-un-kongo-in (mudra) I
(as seen by another)

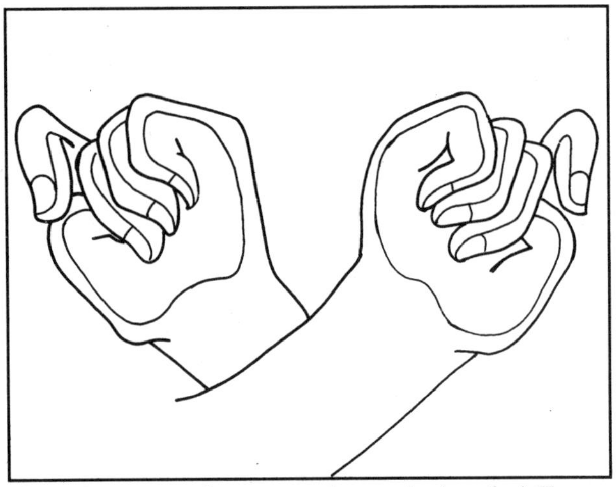

Figure 71 -- basara-un-kongo-in (mudra) II
(as seen by 0000)

a *tantric mudra* which is common to the Japanese and Chinese Buddhist (*Vajrayana, Mantrayana*) tradition and is held or formed by a devotee or priest. It may be accompanied by a *mantra*. It denotes adamantine strength and anger; as well as knowledge which destroys passion and the truth of the law.[4] The *basara-un-kongo-in* (*mudra*) is a combined (Ind.: *saṁyutta*) form, held by both hands. This *mudra* is formed by: the fingers and thumb form a tight fist, the thumb is covered by the fingers, palm facing outward, the hands (arms) are crossed at the wrist with the right hand in front (the left closest to the body), thus formed the *mudra* is held in front of the chest. (EDS 114, GDe 244) (See: **Figure 70**)

basara-un-kongo-in (mudra) II -- (Ind.: *basara-un-kongō-in* [*mudrā*]; Chin.: *chuan-yueh-lo-hung chin-kang-yin*; Ind.: *vajrahumkara mudra*) A *mudra*, a ritual hand pose, a seal, a *tantric mudra* which is common to the Japanese and Chinese Buddhist (*Vajrayana, Mantrayana*) tradition and is held or formed by a devotee or priest. It may be accompanied by a *mantra*. The *basara-un-kongo-in* (*mudra*) *II* is a combined (Ind.: *saṁyutta*) form, held by both hands. This *mudra* is formed by: palms facing outward, the middle, ring and little fingers and thumbs form a tight fist, the thumbs are covered by the three fingers, the index fingers are flexed inwards with their tips resting on the second phalanges of the thumbs. Thus formed, the hands (arms) are crossed at the wrist with the right hand in front (the left closest to the body), thus formed the *mudra* is held in front of the chest. (LCS 243) (See: **Figure 71**)

bathing mudra -- (Eng.; Ind.: *jñāna-lolahasta mudrā*; Thai: *pang song-nam-phon*) The English descriptive phrase for the Thai: *pang song-nam-phon*. See: *pang song-nam-phon*. (DRN 36, JBo 205, OFr 30, PSS)

bdud-rtsi thabs-sbyor phyag-rgya (mudra) -- (Tib.; Indic.: *vajra-amṛta-kuṇḍali mudrā*) The Tibetan transliteral term for *vajra-amrita-kundali mudra*. See: *vajra-amrita-kundali mudra*. (SBe 347)

bestowing ordination mudra -- (Eng.; Ind.: *ahāyavarada-dhyāna mudrā*; Thai: *pang phratarn-ehibhikkhu*) The English descriptive phrase for the Thai *pang phratarn-ehibhikkhu*. See: *ahayavarada-dhyana mudra*. (DRN 36, JBo)

Bhagiratha mudra -- (Ind.: *Bhagīratha-mudrā*) A hand pose, a seal, a dramatic (Ind.: *nāṭya*) *mudra* or gesture (Ind.: *darpaṇa*) held or formed by a performer, dancer or actor. The *Bhagiratha mudra* is a combined (Ind.: *saṁyutta*) form, held by both hands. It denotes *Bhagiratha*, one of a number of famous rulers or heroes. The *mudra* employed is identical in form to the *ardhachandra mudra*. See: *ardhachandra mudra*. (ACG 47)

bhartri mudra -- (Ind.: *bhartr̥-mudrā*) A hand pose, a seal, a dramatic (Ind.: *nāṭya*) *mudra* or gesture (Ind.: *darpaṇa*) held or formed by a performer, dancer or actor. The *bhartri mudra* is a combined (Ind.: *saṁyutta*) form, held by both hands. One of eleven *mudras* representing "relationships" and one which denotes the husband. This *mudra* is formed by: right palm faces mid-line, fingers brought into the palm forming a fist, thumb extends upwards; left palm faces forwards, the first phalanges of the thumb and index finger are touching and extended, the middle, ring and little fingers are separated, straight and pointing upwards. (ACG 45) (See: **Figure 72**)

Figure 72 -- bhartri mudra
(as seen by the holder)

bhartri-bhratri mudra -- (Ind.: *bhartr̥-bhratr̥-mudrā*) A hand pose, a seal, a dramatic (Ind.: *nāṭya*) *mudra* or gesture (Ind.: *darpaṇa*) held or formed by a performer, dancer or actor. The *bhartri-bhratri mudra* is a combined (Ind.: *saṁyutta*) form, held by both hands. One of eleven mudras representing "relationships" and one which denotes brother-in-law. This *mudra* is formed by: right palm faces outward, index, middle fingers and thumb extended, pointing upwards, the index and middle fingers are slightly separated, ring and little fingers bent towards the palm; left palm faces mid-line, fingers brought into the palm forming a fist, thumb extends upwards. (ACG 45) (See: **Figure 73**)

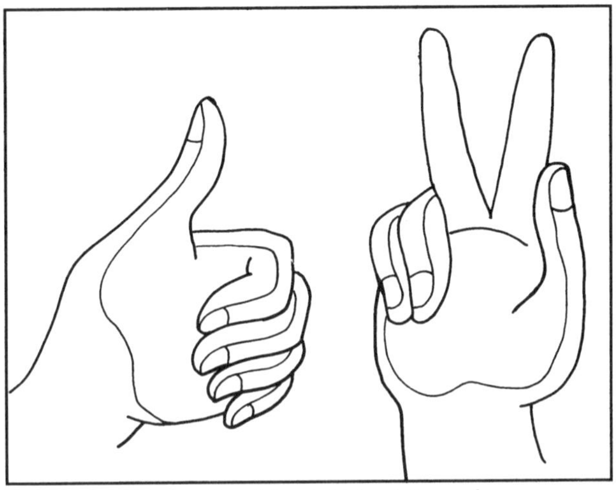

Figure 73 -- bhartri-bhratri mudra
(as seen by the holder)

bhasparsha mudra -- (Ind.: *bhasparśa-mudrā* aka *bhūmisparśa mudrā, bhūmisparśana mudrā, bhūmiśparśa mudrā, bhūsparś mudrā, bhūsparśa mudrā, māravijaya mudrā*; Chin.: *an-shan-yin, ch'u-ti-yin*; Eng.: *adamantine posture*; Jap.: *anzan-in* [*mudra*], *sokuchi-in* [*mudra*]; Thai: *manwichai* [*mudra*], *pang maravichai*, [*pang*] *sadung-man*)

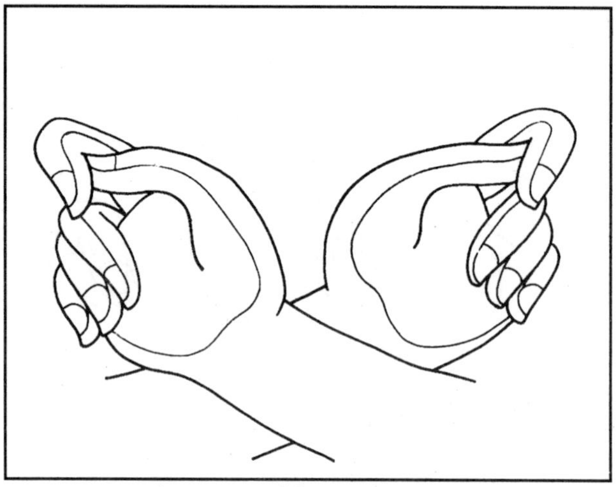

Figure 74 -- bherunda mudra
(as seen by the holder)

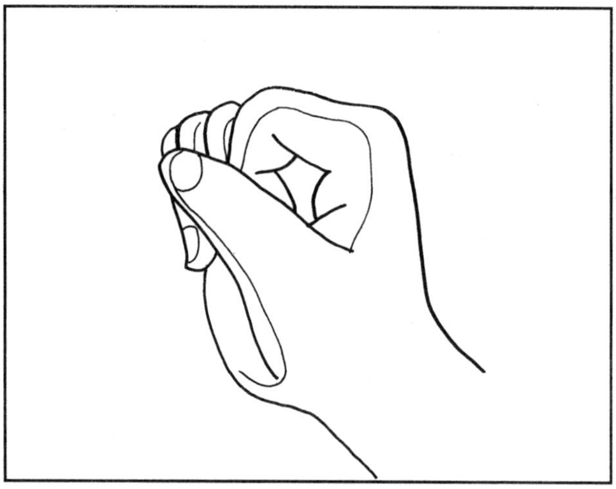

Figure 75 -- Bhima mudra
(as seen by the holder)

Figure 76 -- bhinnanjali mudra
(as seen by the holder)

A variant (spelling) of *bhumisparsha mudra*. See: *bhumisparsha mudra*. (AKG, EDS, RSG)

bherunda mudra -- (Ind.: *bheruṇḍa-mudra*) A hand pose, a seal, a dramatic (Ind.: *nāṭya*) *mudra* or gesture (Ind.: *darpaṇa*) held or formed by a performer, dancer or actor. The *bherunda mudra* is a combined (Ind.: *saṁyutta*) form, held by both hands. It denotes a pair of *bherundas*. This *mudra* is formed by: palms face the midline, the middle, ring and little fingers fold into the palm, the "pad" of the thumb touches the third phalanges of the middle fingers, the index fingers curl over the tops of the thumbs, Thus formed the hands are brought together so that the wrists of the two hands cross. (ACG 41) (See: **Figure 74**)

Bhima mudra -- (Ind.: *Bhīma-mudrā*) A hand pose, a seal, a dramatic (Ind.: *nāṭya*) *mudra* or gesture (Ind.: *darpaṇa*) held or formed by a performer, dancer or actor. The *Bhima mudra* is a single (Ind.: *asaṁyutta*) form, held by one hand. It denotes *Bhima*, one of a number of famous rulers or heroes. This *mudra* is formed by: palm faces the midline, the fingers are fisted, the thumb lies over the second phalanges of the fingers. So formed the the hand is held level with the chest and moved forward and backward. (See: *mushti mudra*) (ACG 47) (See: **Figure 75**)

Bhimarathi mudra -- (Ind.: *Bhīmarathī-mudrā*) A hand pose, a seal, a dramatic (Ind.: *nāṭya*) *mudra* or gesture (Ind.: *darpaṇa*) held or formed by a performer, dancer or actor. It denotes the *Bhimarathi*, one of the famous rivers of India. The *mudra* employed is identical in form to the *arala mudra*. See: *arala mudra*. (ACG 48)

bhinnanjali mudra -- (Ind.: *bhinnāñjali-mudrā*) A hand pose, a seal, a dramatic (Ind.: *nāṭya*) *mudra* or gesture (Ind.: *darpaṇa*) held or formed by a performer, dancer or actor. It denotes an animal, in this case an ass. The *bhinnanjali mudra* is a combined (Ind.: *saṁyutta*) form, held by both hands. This *mudra* is formed by: both hands brought close together, index fingers are slightly flexed and touch at their tips, middle, ring and little fingers extended upwards, slightly cupped and the thumbs together. (ACG 50) (See: **Figure 76**)

bhramara mudra -- (Ind.: *bhramara-mudrā*) A *mudra*, a ritual hand pose, a seal, which is common to the Hindu tradition and is depicted or held by a deity. The *bhramara mudra* is a single (Ind.: *asaṁyutta*) form, held by one hand. It may denote any one of four things: 1) a call for silence, 2) a bee (Ind.: *bhramara*), 3) a crane, or 4) sexual union.[5] This *mudra* is formed by: the tip of the middle finger touches the joint between the first and middle phalanges of the thumb, the index finger curls, the ring and little fingers are extended upwards, and splayed. It is not to be confused with the *vitarka mudra*. (ACG 35-36, MJS 22) (See: **Figure 77**)

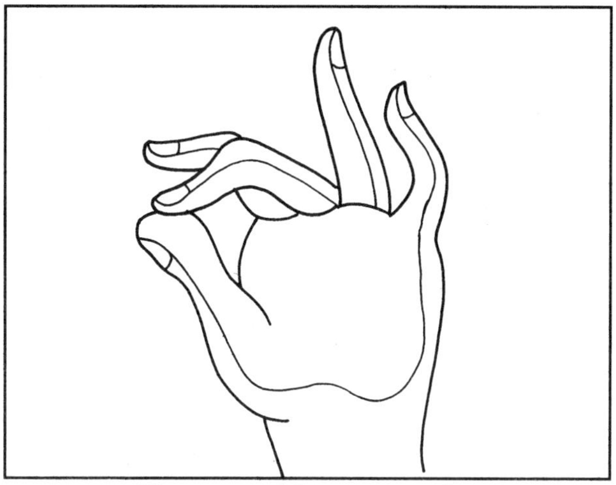

Figure 77 -- bhramara mudra
(as seen by another)

bhuddhashramana mudra -- (Ind.: *bhuddhaśramaṇa-mudrā* aka *buddhashramana mudrā*) A variant (spelling) of *buddhashramana mudra*. See: *buddhashramana mudra*. (RSG 3)

bhumi-bandha mudra -- (Ind.: *bhūmi-bandha-mudrā*] aka *vajra-bandha mudra*) A variant term applied to *vajra-bandha mudra* See: *vajra-bandha mudra*. (LCS 135)

bhumishparsha mudra -- (Ind.: *bhūmiśparśa-mudrā* aka *bhasparśa mudrā, bhūmisparśana mudrā, bhūmisparsha mudrā, bhūsparś mudrā, bhūsparśa mudrā, māravijaya mudra*; Chin.: *an-shan-yin, ch'u-ti-yin*; Eng.: *adamantine posture*; Jap.: *anzan-in* [*mudra*], *sokuchi-in* [*mudra*]; Thai: *manwichai* [*mudra*], *pang maravichai*, [*pang*] *sadung-man*) A variant (spelling) of *bhumisparsha mudra*. See: *bhumisparsha mudra*. (BBh 190)

bhumishparshana mudra -- (Ind.: *bhūmisparśana-mudrā* aka *bhasparśa mudrā, bhūmisparśa mudrā, bhūmisparśa mudrā, bhūsparś mudrā, bhūsparśa mudrā, māravijaya mudrā*; Chin.: *an-shan-yin, ch'u-ti-yin*; Eng.: *adamantine posture*; Jap.: *anzan-in* [*mudra*], *sokuchi-in* [*mudra*]; Thai: *manwichai* [*mudra*], *pang maravichai*, [*pang*] *sadung-man*) A variant (spelling) of *bhumisparsha mudra*. See: *bhumisparsha mudra*. (BBh 190)

bhumisparsha mudra -- (Ind.: *bhūmisparśa-mudrā* aka *bhasparśa mudrā, bhūmishparśa mudrā, bhūmisparśana mudrā, bhūsparś mudrā, bhūsparśa mudrā, māravijaya mudra*; Chin.: *an-shan-yin, ch'u-ti-yin*; Eng.: *adamantine posture*; Jap.: *anzan-in* [*mudra*], *sokuchi-in* [*mudra*]; Thai: *manwichai* [*mudra*], *pang maravichai*, [*pang*] *sadung-man*) A *mudra*, a ritual hand pose, a seal, which is common

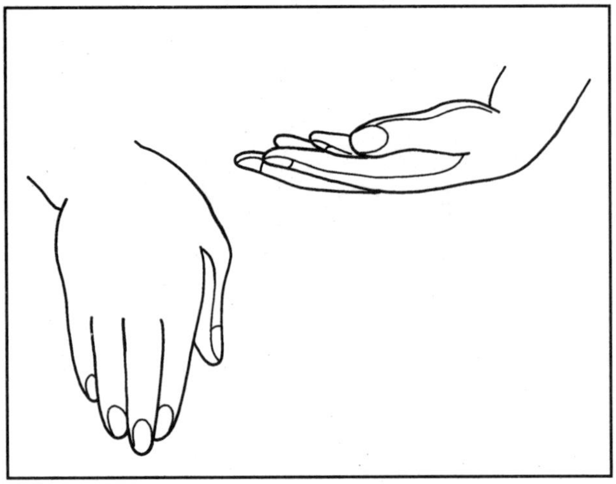

Figure 78 -- bhumisparsha mudra
(as seen by another)

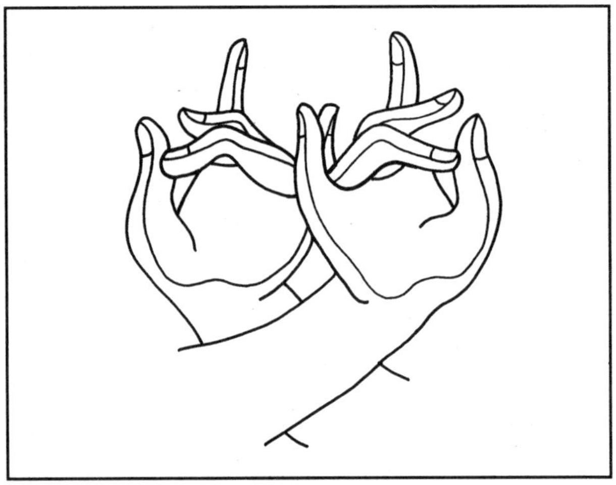

Figure 79 -- bhutadamara mudra
(as seen by another)

to the Buddhist traditions throughout Asia. It denotes the calling the earth to witness the defect of evil (forces) as represented by *Mara*, by the Lord Buddha which was accomplished during the forty day meditation under the *bodhi* tree. It is also one of forty Thai Buddhist *mudras* and *asanas* compiled by the Prince Patriarch Paramanujita Jinorasa and established during the reign of Rama III as being acceptable for the depiction of images of The Lord Buddha--i.e., "subduing *Mara*" the fifth of the forty attitudes noted.[6] The *bhumisparsha mudra* is a combined (Ind.: *saṁyutta*) form, held by both hands. The form is different for both hands and held while the Lord Buddha is seated in meditation--the right forearm rest upon the right thigh, the hand is relaxed and bends at the wrist, fingers pointing downward (frequently touching the ground), palm facing backward; the relaxed left hand rests in the lap, palm facing upwards (*dhyana mudra*). The *mudra* is particularly popular amongst the *Theravada* Buddhist of Thailand, Myanmar and Sri Lanka. See also: *abhaya-varada mudra*. (AKG 20, BBh 190, BCO 214, EDS 80, JBo 204, RSG 3) (See: **Figure 78**)

bhushparsha mudra -- (Ind.: *bhūsparśa-mudrā* aka *bhasparśa mudrā, bhūmiśparśa mudrā, bhūmisparśana mudrā, bhūmisparśa mudrā, bhusparś mudrā, māravijaya mudrā*; Chin.: *an-shan-yin, ch'u-ti-yin*; Eng.: adamantine posture; Jap.: *anzan-in* [*mudra*], *sokuchi-in* [*mudra*]; Thai: *manwichai* [*mudra*], *pang maravichai*, [*pang*] *sadung-man*) A variant (spelling) of *bhumisparsha mudra*. See: *bhumisparsha mudra*. (BBh 190)

bhutadamara mudra -- (Ind.: *bhūtaḍāmara-mudrā* aka *trailokyavijaya mudrā*) A *mudra*, a ritual hand pose, a seal, which is common to the Buddhist tradition. It denotes the inspiration of awe or amazement and in some cases the warding off of evil.[7] The *bhutadamara mudra* is a combined (Ind.: *saṁyutta*) form, held by both hands. This *mudra* is formed by--palms facing outwards, index and little fingers extend upwards, ring fingers curl into the palms, middle fingers curl somewhat towards the palm, tips of thumbs are brought close to the tips of the middle fingers, but do not touch. Thus formed the hands (arms) are crossed at the wrist with the right hand in front (the left closest to the body), and the *mudra* is held in front of the chest. This *mudra* is generally ascribed to *Vajrapani* who is also known as *Bhutadamaravajrapani*. See: *trailokyavijaya mudra II*. (AKG 20, BCO, 206 RSG 5) (See: **Figure 79**)

bihararieisata gassho (mudra) -- (Jap.: *bihararieisata gasshō* [*mudrā*] aka *hanjakugoshochaku gassho* (*mudra*); Ind.: *viparyasta mudra*) A *mudra*, a ritual hand pose, a seal, a *tantric mudra* which is common to the Japanese Buddhist (*Vajrayana*, *Mantrayana*) tradition and is held or formed by a devotee or priest. It may be accompanied by a *mantra*. Specifically one of the twelve, elemental "hand clasps" (Jap. *junigosho* or *junigassho*). The *bihararieisata gassho* (*mudra*) is a combined (Ind.: *saṁyutta*) form, held by both hands. This *mudra* is formed by: the right hand is relaxed, palm upwards, and rests on the left hand; the left hand is relaxed, palm downwards, and rests on the lap or in front of waist.[8] This *mudra* is similar to the *anuja mudra*. (EDS 42) (See: **Figure 80**)

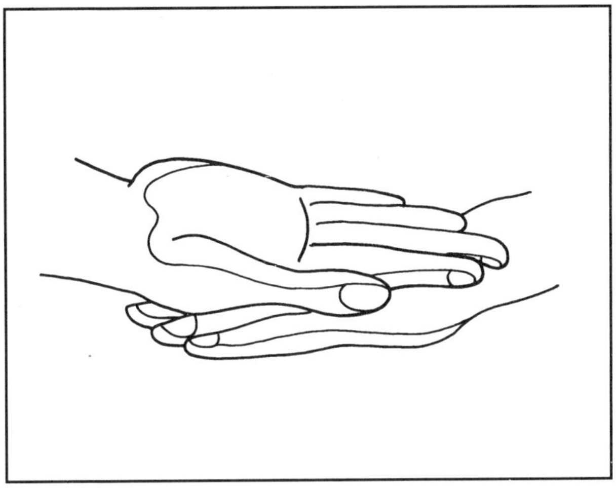

Figure 80 -- bihararieisata gassho (mudra)
(as seen by another)

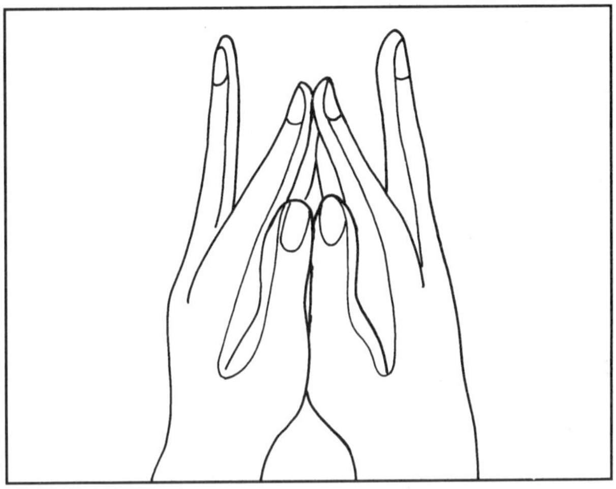

Figure 81 -- boda gassho (mudra)
(as seen by the holder)

Biroshana-in (mudra) -- (Jap.: *Biroshana-in* [*mudrā*] aka *mushofushi-in* [*mudra*], *butsubu sotoba-in* [*mudra*], *dai sotoba-in* [*mudra*], *hen hokkai mushofushi-in* [*mudra*], *mushofushi to-in* [*mudra*], *rito-in* [*mudra*]; Chin.: *wu-so-pu-chih-yin*; Ind.: *stupa mudra*) ("the *mudra* of *Vairochana*") A variant term applied to *mushofushi-in* (*mudra*). See: *mushofushi-in* (*mudra*). (EDS 115)

biroshananyoraidaimyochi-in (mudra) -- (Ind.: *biroṣananyoraidaimyōci-in* [*mudrā*] aka *bodaiindo-daiichichi-in* [*mudra*], *chi ken-in* [*mudra*], *nometsu-mumyokokuan-in* [*mudra*]:Chin.: *Chih-ch'ṃan-yin* (*mudra*); Ind.: *vajra mudrā*, *jñāna mudrā*, *bodhaśrī mudrā*) A variant term applied to *chi ken-in* (*mudra*). It means "*mudra* of the great and marvelous Knowledge of *Vairoc(h)ana*."[9] See: *chi ken-in* (*mudra*) (EDS 102)

boda gassho (mudra) -- (Jap.: *boda gasshō* [*mudrā*] aka *mi be renge gassho* [*mudra*]; Ind.: *puna mudrā*) The Japanese term for *puna mudra*. A *mudra*, a ritual hand pose, a seal, which is common to the Japanese Buddhist tradition. Specifically one of the twelve, elemental "hand clasps" (Jap. *junigosho* or *junigassho*). The *boda gassho* (*mudra*) is a combined (Ind.: *saṁyutta*) form, held by both hands. This *mudra* is formed by: the hands are brought together, heel-of-palm to heel-of-palm, fingers extended upwards, thumbs, index and little fingers tips touch the opposite, middle and ring fingers flare outwards forming an open-cup-form. This *mudra* is referred to as the "newly opening lotus"[10] (See: *puna mudra*) (EDS 40) (See: **Figure 81**)

bodaiindodaiichichi-in (mudra) -- (Ind.: *bodaiindōdaiichichi-in* [*mudrā*] aka *chi ken-in* [*mudra*], *nometsumumyokokuan-in* [*mudra*], *biroshananyoraidaimyochi-in* [*mudra*]; Chin.: *Chih-ch'ṃan-yin* (*mudra*); Ind.: *vajra mudra, jnana mudra, bodhashri mudra*) A variant term applied to *chi ken-in* (*mudra*). It means "first Knowledge *mudra* which conducts souls to enlightenment."[11] See: *chi ken-in* (*mudra*). (EDS 102)

bodhashri mudra -- (Ind.: *bodhaśrī-mudrā* aka Ind.: *vajra mudrā, jñāna mudrā;* Chin.: *chih-ch'ṃan-yin* [*mudra*]; Jap.: *biroshananyoraidaimyochi-in* [*mudra*]; *bodai-indodaiichichi-in* [*mudra*], *chi ken-in* [*mudra*], *nometsumumyokokuan-in* [*mudra*]) A variant term applied to *chi ken-in* (*mudra*). See: *chi ken-in* (*mudra*). (EDS 102)

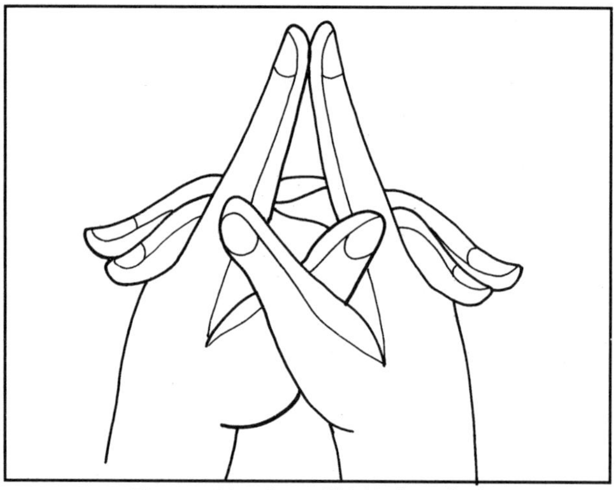

Figure 82 -- bon jiki-in (mudra)
(as seen by the holder)

bon jiki-in (mudra) -- (Jap.: *bon jiki-in* [*mudrā*]; Ind.: *uttarabodhi mudrā*[?], *kṣepaṇa mudrā*[?]) A *mudra*, a ritual hand pose, a seal, a *tantric mudra* which is common to the Japanese Buddhist (*Vajrayana, Mantrayana*) tradition and is held or formed by a devotee or priest during the rites of the *Vajradhatu Mandala*. It may be accompanied by a *mantra*. The *bon jiki-in* (*mudra*)[12] is a combined (Ind.: *saṁyutta*) form, held by both hands. This *mudra* is formed by: palm to palm, all fingers and thumbs interlace except the index fingers which point upwards or outwards. Thus formed the *mudra* is held at chest level, or above the head. In form it is similar to the *uttarabodhi* and *kshepana mudras*. (GDe 85) (See: **Figure 82**)

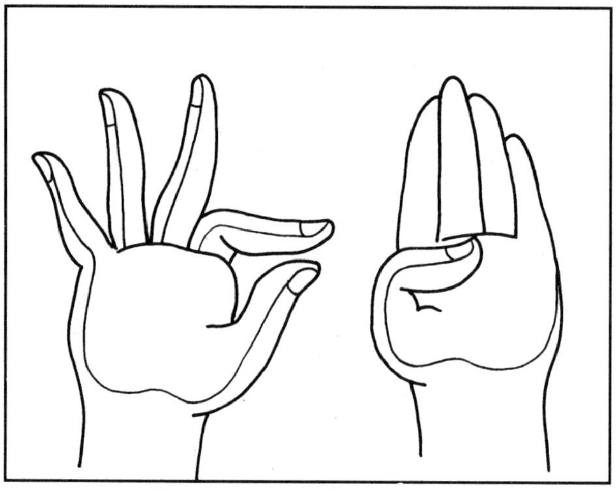

Figure 83 -- Brahma mudra
(as seen by another)

Brahma mudra -- (Ind.: *Brahmā-mudrā*) A hand pose, a seal, a dramatic (Ind.: *nāṭya*) *mudra* or gesture (Ind.: *darpaṇa*) held or formed by a performer, dancer or actor which denotes a specific deity. The *Brahma mudra* is a combined (Ind.: *saṁyutta*) form, held by both hands. It denotes the Lord *Brahma*.[13] This *mudra* is formed by: right palm faces forwards, the first phalanges of the thumb and index finger are touching and extended, the middle, ring and little fingers are separated, straight and pointing upwards; left palm facing forwards, the fingers, together and extended upwards, the little finger is separated slightly, the tip of the thumb crosses the palm and touches the base of the ring finger. Thus formed the hands are held at shoulder level. (ACG 45) (See: **Figure 83**)

Brahmana mudra -- (Ind.: *Brāhmaṇa-mudrā*) A hand pose, a seal, a dramatic (Ind.: *nāṭya*) *mudra* or gesture (Ind.: *darpaṇa*) held or formed by a performer, dancer or actor. The *Brahmana mudra* is a combined (Ind.: *saṁyutta*) form, held by both hands. It denotes the *Brahmanas*, one of the four castes. This *mudra* requires movement and is formed by: right palm faces mid-line, fingers brought into the palm forming a fist, thumb extends upwards, so formed the right hand moves "to and fro;" left palm faces mid-line, fingers brought into the palm forming a fist, thumb extends upwards. (ACG 46) (See: **Figure 84**)

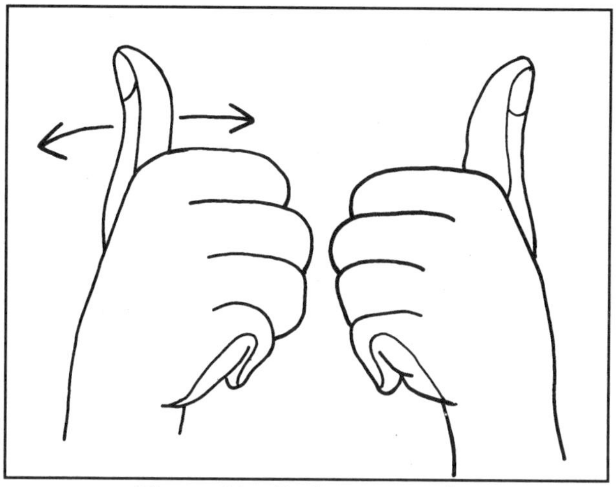

Figure 84 -- Brahmana mudra
(as seen by another)

brahmokta-shuktunda mudra -- (Ind.: *brahmokta-śuktuṇḍa-mudrā*) A hand pose, a seal, a dramatic (Ind.: *nāṭya*) *mudra* or gesture (Ind.: *darpaṇa*) held or formed by a performer, dancer or actor noted in ACG but without description.[14] (ACG 44)

Brihaspati mudra -- (Ind.: *Bṛhaspati-mudrā*) A hand pose, a seal, a dramatic (Ind.: *nāṭya*) *mudra* or gesture (Ind.: *darpaṇa*) held or formed by a performer, dancer or actor. The *Brihaspati mudra* is a combined (Ind.: *saṁyutta*) form, held by both hands. It denotes Jupiter, one of the nine planets (Ind.: *navagraha*). This *mudra* is formed by: right palm faces mid-line, fingers brought into the palm forming a fist, thumb extends upwards; left palm faces mid-line, fingers brought into the palm forming a fist, thumb extends upwards. Thus formed they are held at chest level and somewhat apart. (ACG 46) (See: **Figure 85**)

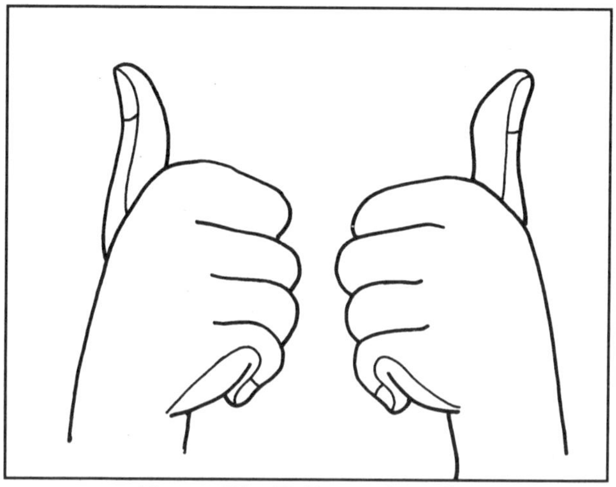

Figure 85 -- Brihaspati mudra
(as seen by another)

bu bosatsu-in (mudra) -- (Jap.: *bu bosatsu-in* [*mudrā*]; Ind.: *nritya mudra*) ("*Bodhisattva* of dance") A *mudra*, a ritual hand pose, a seal, a *tantric mudra* which is common to the Japanese Buddhist (*Vajrayana, Mantrayana*) tradition and is held or formed by a devotee or priest during the rites of *Vajradhatu Mandala, Homa Rites* and other rites. It may be accompanied by a *mantra*. The *bu bosatsu-in*[15] (*mudra*) is a combined (Ind.: *saṁyutta*) form, held by both hands. It denotes the offering of dance. This *mudra* is identical for both

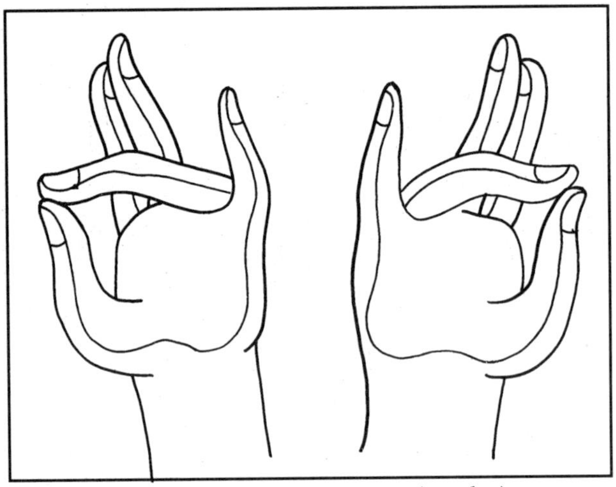
Figure 86 -- bu bosatsu-in (mudra)
(as seen by the holder)

Figure 87 -- Buddhalochani mudra
(as seen by the holder)

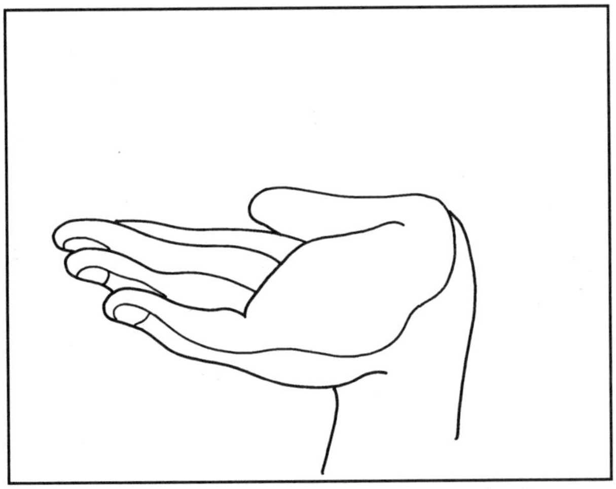
Figure 88 -- buddhashramana mudra I
(as seen by the holder)

hands: palms facing the body and slightly apart, ring fingers folded towards the palms, thumbs folded towards the palm and touching the ring fingers' tip, index, middle and little fingers are erect and pointed upwards. (GDe 79) (See: **Figure 86**)

Buddhalochani mudra -- (Ind.: *Buddhalocanī-mudrā*) A *mudra*, a ritual hand pose, a seal, a *tantric mudra* which is common to the Japanese Buddhist (*Vajrayana, Mantrayana*) tradition and is held or formed by a devotee or priest during various rites in which a deity is acknowledged. It is a *mudra* which is associated with the deity *Buddhalochani*. It may be accompanied by a *mantra*. The *Buddhalochani mudra*[16] is a combined (Ind.: *saṁyutta*) form, held by both hands. It denotes *Buddhalochani*. This *mudra* is formed by: palms brought close, thumbs extend upwards and touch along their length, index fingers are flexed at their first two knuckles, their first phalanges behind the first phalanges of the thumb, middle, ring and little fingers extend and interlace at their first phalanges. (LCS 215) (See: **Figure 87**)

buddhapatra mudra -- (Ind.: *buddhapātra-mudrā*; Chin.: *fo-puo-yin*; Jap.: *buppatsu-in*) The Indic term for *buppatsu-in*. See: *buppatsu-in*. (EDS 113)

buddhashramana mudra I -- (Ind.: *buddhaśramaṇa-mudrā* aka *bhuddhashramana mudra*; Tib.: *myang-hdas phyag-rgya*) A *mudra*, a ritual hand pose, a seal, which is more common to the Buddhist tradition, seen infrequently within the Hindu practice. It denotes another form of greeting or salutation and may also refer to citing the *Tathagata*.[17] The *buddhashramana mudra I* is a single (Ind.: *asaṁyutta*) form, held by one hand. This *mudra* is usually held by the right hand--palm facing upwards, fingers extended, wrist rotated so that the fingers point outward from the front of the body, and held at the level of the head. (AKG 20, BCO, RSG 3) (See: **Figure 88**)

buddhashramana mudra II -- (Ind.: *buddhaśramaṇa-mudrā* aka *paritrān-āsaya-mati mudrā*; Tib.: *myang-hdas phyag-rgya*) A *mudra*, a ritual hand pose, a seal, which is common to the Buddhist tradition. It is referred to as a symbol of renunciation[18] or as the rejection of earthly possessions. It is often referred to as: the Gesture of Renunciation, or the Gesture Beyond Mercy, or the Great Gesture of *Nirvana*. Also, a *tantric mudra* which is common to the Japanese and Chinese Buddhist (*Vajrayana, Mantrayana*) tradition and is held or formed by a devotee or priest. It may be accompanied by a *mantra*. The *buddhashramana mudra II* is a single (Ind.: *asaṁyutta*) form, held by one hand. This *mudra* is formed by the right hand: fingers together pointing outward or away from the body towards the right and palm facing downward. Thus formed the arm is fully extended downward and hand held away from the body of the holder. (BCO 206, GDe 278) (See: **Figure 89**)

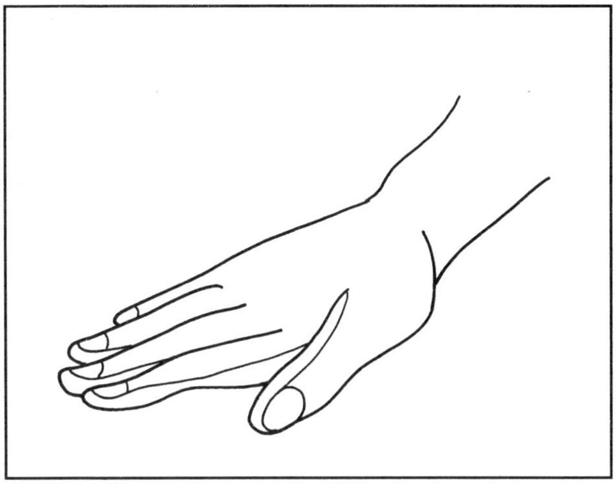

Figure 89 -- buddhashramana mudra II
(as seen by another)

buddhashramana-dhyana mudra -- (Ind.: *buddha-śramaṇa-dhyāna-mudrā*; Eng.: making the four alms bowls into one *mudra*; Thai: *pang phra-sarnbhatr*) This is a descriptive term.[19] See: *pang phrasarnbhatr*. (DRN 36, JBo 204, ODD 680, OFr 14, PSS)

Budha mudra -- (Ind.: *Budha-mudrā*) A hand pose, a seal, a dramatic (Ind.: *nāṭya*) *mudra* or gesture (Ind.: *darpaṇa*) held or formed by a performer, dancer or actor. The *Budha mudra* is a combined (Ind.: *saṁyutta*) form, held by both hands. It denotes Mercury, one of the nine planets (Ind.: *navagraha*). This *mudra* is formed by: palm facing outward, right fingers and thumb extended, together and pointing upwards, relaxed, slightly cupped; left palm faces the midline, the fingers are fisted, the thumb lies over the first phalanges of the fingers and twisted ("askew"). (ACG 46) (See: **Figure 90**)

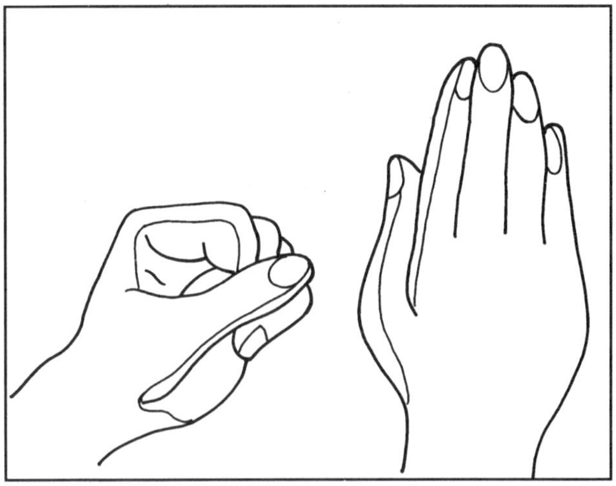

Figure 90 -- Budha mudra
(as seen by the holder)

buku-in (mudra) -- (Ind.: *buku-in* [*mudrā*]) A *mudra*, a ritual hand pose, a seal, a *tantric mudra* which is common to the Japanese Buddhist (*Vajrayana, Mantrayana*) tradition and is held or formed by a devotee or priest during various rites. It may be accompanied by a *mantra*. The *buku-in* (*mudra*)[20] is a combined (Ind.: *saṁyutta*) form, held by both hands. This *mudra* is formed by: right palm facing downwards, fingers and thumb to together and extended out, left grasps the robe in the *padma-mushti* (*mudra*). (GDe 414) (See: **Figure 91**)

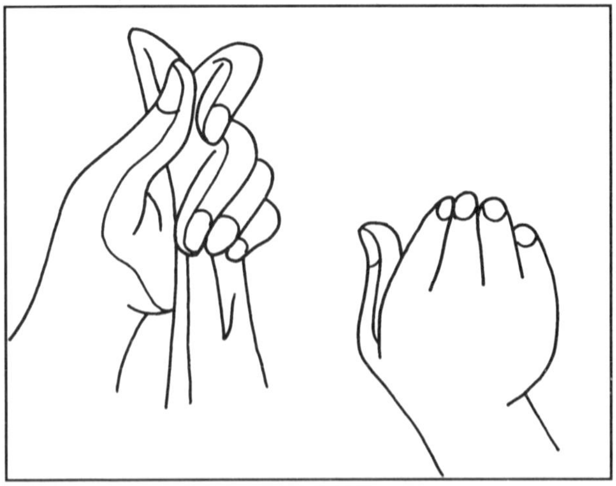

Figure 91 -- buku-in (mudra)
(as seen by the holder)

bu mo-in (mudra) -- (Jap.: *bu mō-in* [*mudrā*]) ("the mother of classes") A *mudra*, a ritual hand pose, a seal,

Figure 92 -- bu mo-in (mudra)
(as seen by the holder)

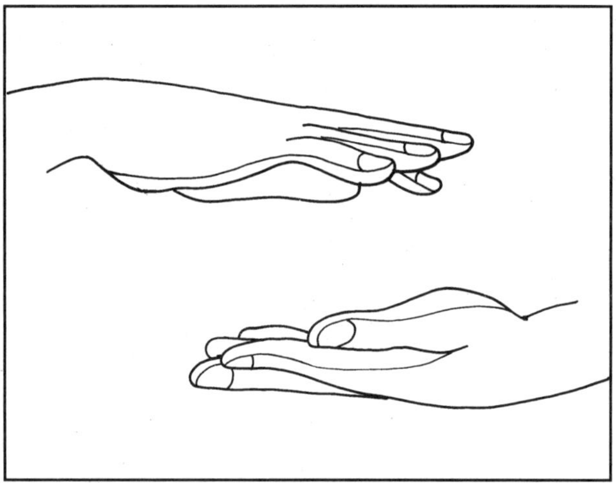

Figure 93 -- buppatsu-in (mudra)
(as seen by another)

Figure 94 -- butsu bu sammaya-in (mudra)
(as seen by the holder)

a *tantric mudra* which is common to the Japanese Buddhist (*Vajrayana, Mantrayana*) tradition and is held or formed by a devotee or priest during the rites of *Garbhadhatu Mandala, Vajradhatu Mandala, Homa Rites* and other rites. It may be accompanied by a *mantra*. The *bu mo-in* (*mudra*) is a combined (Ind.: *saṁyutta*) form, held by both hands. It denotes the five eyes of the *Buddha*. This *mudra* is formed by: palms face midline and are close, thumbs extend upwards and touch along their outside edges, middle and ring fingers extend and their tips touch, index fingers curl and their tips touch the first knuckle of the middle fingers, little fingers extend straight upwards. (GDe 51) (See: **Figure 92**)

buppatsu-in (mudra) -- (Jap.: *buppatsu-in* [*mudrā*]; Chin.: *fo-puo-yin*; Ind.: *buddhapatra mudra*) A *mudra*, a ritual hand pose, a seal, a *tantric mudra* which is common to the Japanese Buddhist (*Vajrayana, Mantrayana*) tradition and is held or formed by a devotee or priest. It may be accompanied by a *mantra*. It denotes the Lord *Buddha* as a mendicant and that the one who holds this *mudra* is the receptacle of the Law (Ind.: *Dharma*). The *buppatsu-in* (*mudra*) is a combined (Ind.: *saṁyutta*) form, held by both hands. This *mudra* is formed by: left hand is held palm upwards, fingers extended, relaxed, slightly cupped and at the level of the navel; the right hand is similarly held, but palm facing downwards and slightly above the left hand. This *mudra* is only held by the Lord Buddha in a seated position. (EDS 113) (See: **Figure 93**)

butsu bu sammaya-in (mudra) -- (Jap.: *butsu bu sammaya-in* [*mudrā*]) ("the *sammaya* of the *Buddha* group") A *mudra*, a ritual hand pose, a seal, a *tantric mudra* which is common to the Japanese Buddhist (*Vajrayana, Mantrayana*) tradition and is held or formed by a devotee or priest during the *Eighteen-Step Rites*. It may be accompanied by a *mantra*. The *butsu bu sammaya-in*[21] (*mudra*) is a combined (Ind.: *saṁyutta*) form, held by both hands. It denotes the group of Buddhas.[22] This *mudra* is formed by: the hands brought together along their outer edge forming a hollow, little fingers touching along their length, middle, and ring fingers touch at their tips, index fingers curl slightly and their tips touch the back of the middle finger's second phalanges, thumbs curl slightly and their tips touch the base of the index fingers. (GDe 97) (See: **Figure 94**)

butsubu sotoba-in (mudra) -- (Jap.: *butsubu sotoba-in* [*mudrā*] aka *mushofushi-in* [*mudra*], *Biroshana-in* [*mudra*], *dai sotoba-in* [*mudra*], *hen hokkai mushofushi-in* [*mudra*], *mushofushi to-in* [*mudra*], *rito-in* [*mudra*]; Chin.: *wu-so-pu-chih-yin*; Ind.: *stupā mudrā*) ("*stupa mudra* of the Buddha area") A variant term applied to *mushofushi-in* (*mudra*). See: *mushofushi-in* (*mudra*). (EDS 115)

bu zo-in (mudra) -- (Jap.: *bu zō-in* [*mudrā*]) ("respectfully escorting back") A *mudra*, a ritual hand pose, a seal, a *tantric mudra* which is common to the Japanese Buddhist (*Vajrayana, Mantrayana*) tradition and is held or formed by a devotee or priest during the rites of *Garbhadhatu Mandala, Vajradhatu Mandala, Homa Rites* and other rites. It may be accompanied by a *mantra*. The *bu zo-in* (*mudra*) is a combined (Ind.: *saṁyutta*) form, held by both hands. It denotes the seeing off the deities from the temple. This *mudra* is formed by: palms face midline and are close, thumbs cross, index, ring and little fingers interlace on the back of the hands, middle fingers extend upwards and their tips touch. (GDe 53, LCS 72) (See: **Figure 95**)

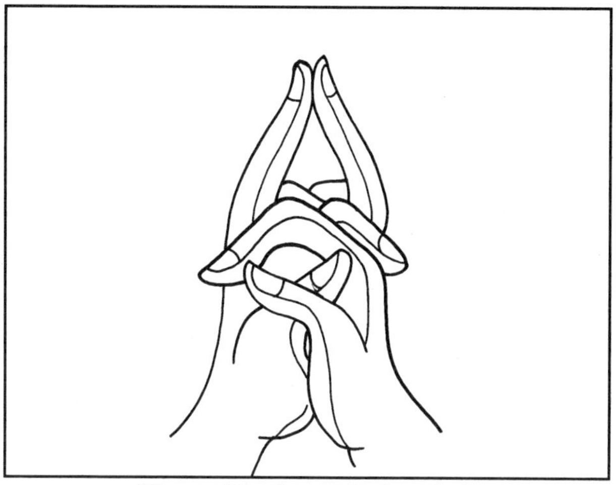

Figure 95 -- bu zo-in (mudra)
(as seen by the holder)

bya-lding phyag-rgya (mudra) -- (Tib.; Indic.: *sarva-buddha-bodhisattvanam mudra*) The Tibetan transliteral term for *sarva-buddha-bodhisattvanam mudra*. See: *sarva-buddha-bodhisattvanam mudra*. (SBe 347)

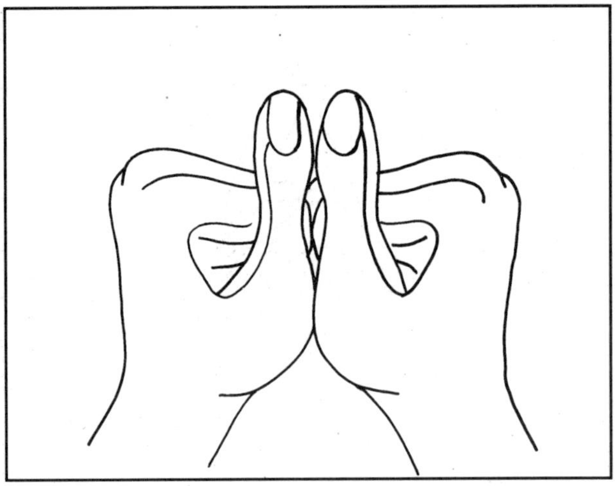
Figure 96 -- chaga mudra
(as seen by the holder)

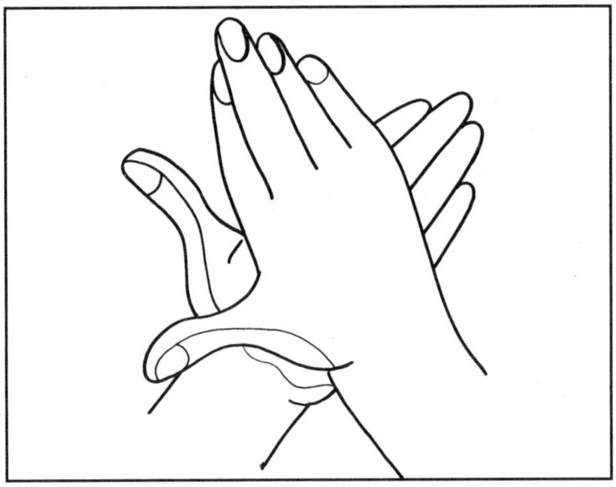
Figure 97 -- chakra mudra I
(as seen by the holder)

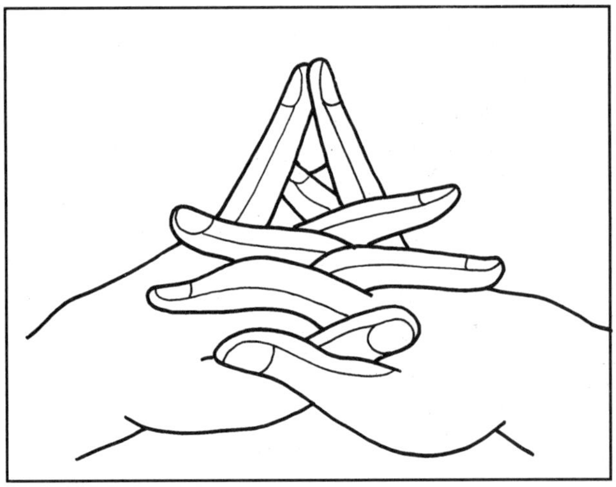
Figure 98 -- chakra mudra II
(as seen by the holder)

-- C --

calling down the rain mudra -- (Eng.; Ind.: *añcita-ahāyavarada mudrā, gandhararatta mudrā;* Thai: *pang khor-phon*) The English descriptive phrase for the Thai: *pang khor-phon*. See: *pang khor-phon*. (DRN 37, JBo, MSD 38, SVB)

carrying the alms bowl mudra -- (Eng.; Ind.: *añcita-añcita mudrā;* Thai: *pang uhm-bhatr*) The English descriptive phrase for the Thai: *pang uhm-bhatr*. See: *pang uhm-bhatr*. (PSS, DRN 36, JBo, ODD 680)

chaga mudra -- (Ind.: *caga-mudrā*) A hand pose, a seal, a dramatic (Ind.: *nāṭya*) *mudra* or gesture (Ind.: *darpaṇa*) held or formed by a performer, dancer or actor. It denotes an animal, in this case a goat. The *chaga mudra*[1] is a combined (Ind.: *saṁyutta*) form, held by both hands. This *mudra* is similar to the *shikhara mudra* and formed by: palms faces mid-line, fingers brought into the palm forming a fist, thumbs extends upwards. Thus formed both hands are brought together, palm facing palm. (ACG 50) (See: **Figure 96**)

chakra mudra I -- (Ind.: *cakra-mudrā*) A hand pose, a seal, a dramatic (Ind.: *nāṭya*) *mudra* or gesture (Ind.: *darpaṇa*) held or formed by a performer, dancer or actor. This *mudra* denotes a discus. The *chakra mudra* is a combined (Ind.: *saṁutta*) form, held by both hands. This *mudra* is formed by: right palm facing downwards and rotated 45° to the left, fingers extended, together and pointing outwards parallel to the ground, the thumb extends away from the fingers; left palm facing upwards and rotated 45° to the right, fingers extended, together and pointing outwards, relaxed, the thumb extends away from the fingers. Thus formed, the palms are brought together and rotated a quarter turn so that the fingers of one hand are oriented 90° from those of the other. (ACG 41) (See: **Figure 97**)

chakra mudra II -- (Ind.: *cakra-mudrā*) A *mudra*, a ritual hand pose, a seal, a *tantric mudra* which is common to the Japanese Buddhist (*Vajrayana, Mantrayana*) tradition and is held or formed by a devotee or priest. It may be accompanied by a *mantra*. The *chakra mudra*[2] is a combined (Ind.: *saṁyutta*) form, held by both hands. This *mudra* is formed by: first loosely interlacing the fingers and thumbs of both hands on top, the ring fingers extend upward or outward and touch at their tips. (GDe 298, LCS 256) (See: **Figure 98**)

chakra-ratna mudra -- (Ind.: *cakra-ratna-mudrā*) This is an assigned term.[3] A *mudra*, a ritual hand pose, a seal, which is common to the Buddhist (*Vajrayana*) tradition, a *tantric mudra*. It denotes the gift of a precious wheel (Tib.: *hkhor-lo*) associated with the *saptaratna* (Tib.: *rgyal-srid sna-bdun*) or seven gems of sovereignty (Tib.: *nor-bu-chab-bdun*), also referred to as the 'space vast treasury,' particularly as it is associated with the worship of the powerful *Vajrayana* goddess, *Tara*. The *chakra-ratna mudra* is a combined (Ind.: *saṁyutta*) form, held by both hands. This *mudra* is formed by--the right hand: palm upwards, fingers extended, pointed outward; the left palm downward, fingers extended, touching the right palm or slightly above it, and at a 90° angle to the right hand. The *mantra* associated with this mudra is: "*OM Cakra-ratna Praticcha HUM SVAHA*."[4] (SBe 152) (See: **Figure 99**)

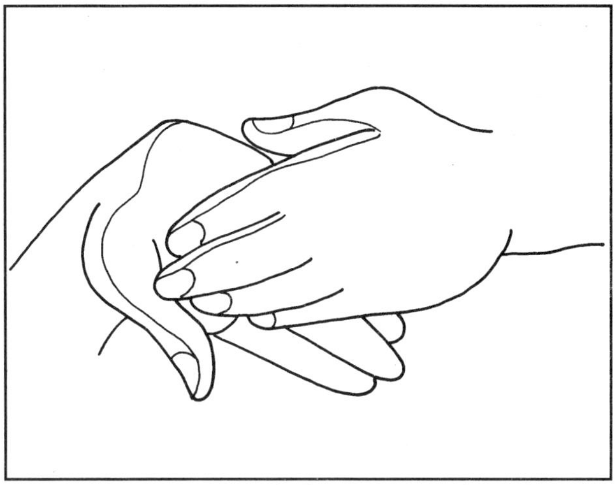

Figure 99 -- chakra-ratna mudra
(as seen by another)

chakravaka mudra -- (Ind.: *cakravāka-mudrā*) A hand pose, a seal, a dramatic (Ind.: *nāṭya*) *mudra* or gesture (Ind.: *darpaṇa*) held or formed by a performer, dancer or actor. It denotes a bird. The *chakravaka mudra* is a single (Ind.: *asaṁyutta*) form, held by one hand. This *mudra* is formed by: the palm turned upwards, the thumb and fingers are stretched far apart, stiff; so formed, the little finger is at 90° to the palm and the ring finger is at 45° to the palm and shaken or fluttered. It is similar to the *sola-padma mudra*. (ACG 50) (See: **Figure 100**)

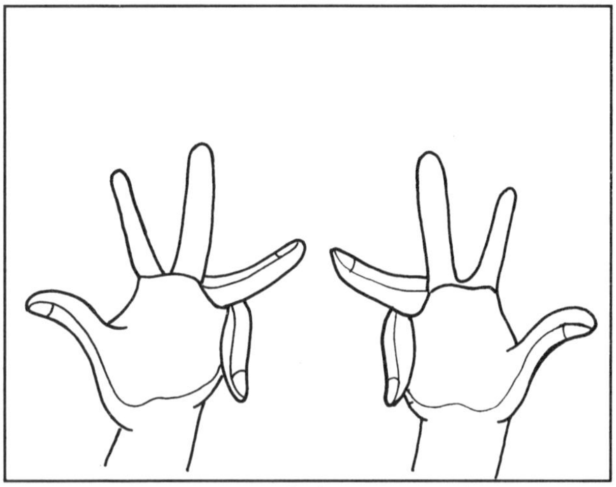

Figure 100 -- chakravaka mudra
(as seen by the holder)

chakravartin mudra -- (Ind.: *cakravartin-mudrā*) A *mudra*, a ritual hand pose, a seal, a *tantric mudra* which is common to the Japanese Buddhist (*Vajrayana, Mantrayana*) tradition and is held or formed by a devotee or priest during various rites in which a deity is acknowledged. It is a *mudra* which is associated with the *chakravartin*. It may be accompanied by a *mantra*.

Figure 101 -- chakravartin mudra
(as seen by the holder)

Figure 102 -- chakshur mudra
(as seen by the holder)

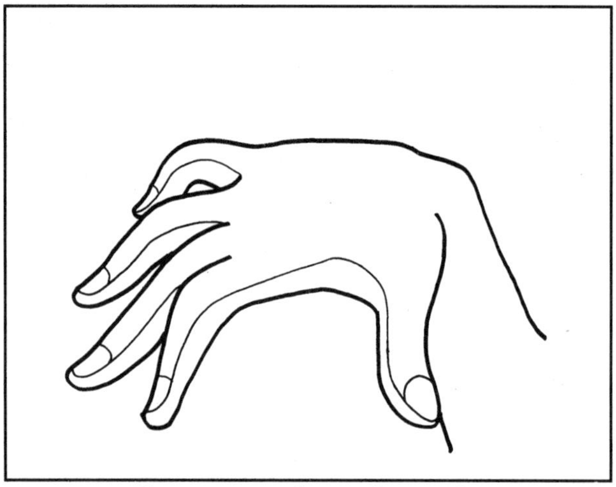

Figure 103 -- champaka mudra
(as seen by another)

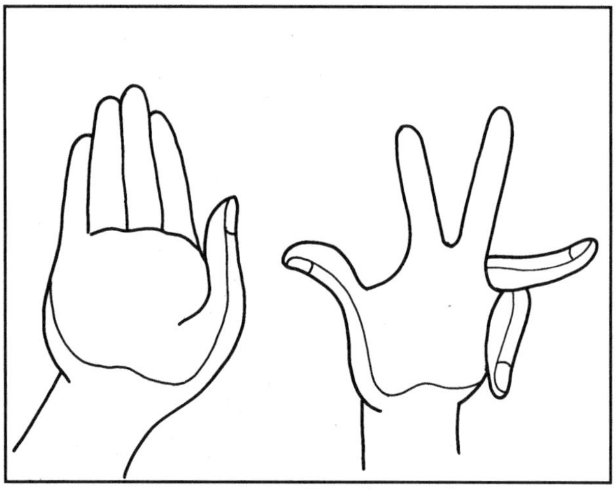

Figure 104 -- Chandra mudra
(as seen by another)

The *chakravartin* (*mudra*)[5] is a combined (Ind.: *saṁyutta*) form, held by both hands. It denotes a universal ruler. This *mudra* is formed by: the palms brought close, the thumbs extend upwards and touch along their outer edges, index fingers flex at their second knuckle, their tips touching the tips of the thumbs, middle and little fingers fold into the palms, ring fingers extend and touch at their tips. (LCS 215) (See: **Figure 101**)

chakshur mudra -- (Ind.: *cakṣur-mudrā* aka *mūla-guhya-mudrā*) A *mudra*, a ritual hand pose, a seal, a *tantric mudra* which is common to the Japanese Buddhist (*Vajrayana, Mantrayana*) tradition and is held or formed by a devotee or priest during the rites of *Garbhadhatu Mandala, Vajradhatu Mandala, Homa Rites* and other rites. It may be accompanied by a *mantra*. The *chakshur mudra* is a combined (Ind.: *saṁyutta*) form, held by both hands. It denotes eyes. This *mudra* is formed by: palms face each other, middle, ring and little fingers, and thumbs are interlaced with fingers and thumbs inside (palm-side) the 'fist,' index fingers extend upwards and touch at their tips. It resembles the *uttarabodhi mudra* except the fingers and thumbs are on the inside. (GDe 328, LCS 208) (See: **Figure 102**)

champaka mudra -- (Ind.: *campaka-mudrā*) A hand pose, a seal, a dramatic (Ind.: *nāṭya*) *mudra* or gesture (Ind.: *darpaṇa*) held or formed by a performer, dancer or actor. It denotes the *champaka* tree. The *champaka mudra* is a single (Ind.: *asaṁyutta*) form, held by one hand. This *mudra* is formed generally in the right hand, and by: palm downwards, the thumb, index, middle and little fingers are cupped slightly as in the *padmakosha mudra*, ring finger is bent and rests in the palm and extended. See: *padmakosha mudra*. (ACG 49) (See: **Figure 103**)

chandra mudra -- (Ind.: *candra-mudrā*) A hand pose, a seal, a dramatic (Ind.: *nāṭya*) *mudra* or gesture (Ind.: *darpaṇa*) held or formed by a performer, dancer or actor. The *chandra mudra* is a combined (Ind.: *saṁyutta*) form, held by both hands. It denotes the moon, one of the nine planets (Ind.: *navagraha*). This *mudra* is formed by: right palm facing outward, fingers and thumb extended, together and pointing upwards, relaxed, slightly cupped; left palm turned upwards, the thumb and fingers are stretched far apart, stiff; so formed, the little finger is at 90° to the palm and the ring finger is at 45° to the palm. (ACG 46) (See: **Figure 104**)

chandrakala mudra I -- (Ind.: *candrakāla-mudrā*) A *mudra*, a ritual hand pose, a seal, which is generally common to the Hindu tradition and is depicted or held by a deity. The *chandrakala mudra* is a single (Ind.: *asaṁyutta*) form, held by one hand. It denotes the crescent moon and, therefore, it represents the Lord *Shiva*, as well as representing the tusks of a boar. This *mudra* is formed by: the index, middle and ring fingers folded into the palm, the thumb and little fingers are extended. (MJS 30) (See: **Figure 105**)

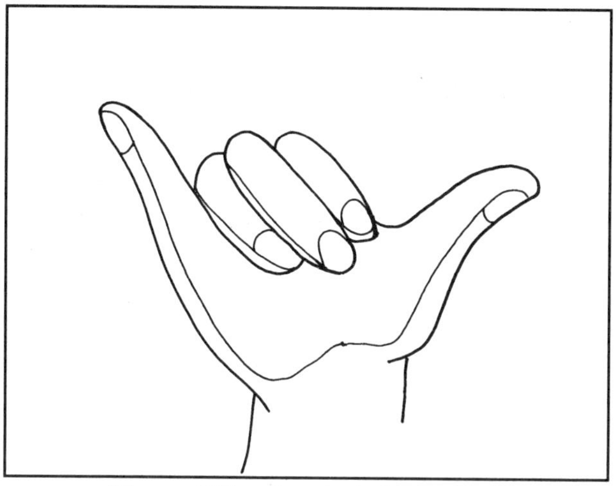

Figure 105 -- chandrakala mudra I
(as seen by another)

chandrakala mudra II -- (Ind.: *candrakāla-mudrā*) A hand pose, a seal, a dramatic (Ind.: *nāṭya*) *mudra* or gesture (Ind.: *darpaṇa*) held or formed by a performer, dancer or actor. The *chandrakala mudra* is a single (Ind.: *asaṁyutta*) form, held by one hand. It denotes the crescent moon. This *mudra* is a variation[6] and formed by: the middle, ring and little fingers folded into the palm, the thumb and index fingers are extended, straight and separated. It is similar to the *suchi mudra*. (ACG 32) (See: **Figure 106**)

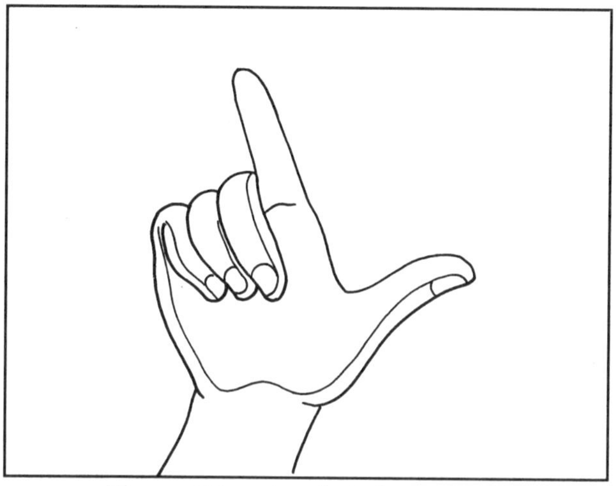

Figure 106 -- chandrakala mudra II
(as seen by another)

chandra-mriga mudra -- (Ind.: *candra-mṛga-mudrā*) A hand pose, a seal, a dramatic (Ind.: *nāṭya*) *mudra* or gesture (Ind.: *darpaṇa*) held or formed by a performer, dancer or actor, particularly when denoting a 'porcupine deer.' The *chandra-mriga mudra* is a single (Ind.: *asaṁyutta*) form, held by one hand. This *mudra* is formed by: palm faces forward, middle and third fingers are straight and bend at the third knuckle towards the palm, they touch the tip of the thumb, the index and the little fingers extend upwards. (ACG 49) (See: **Figure 107**)

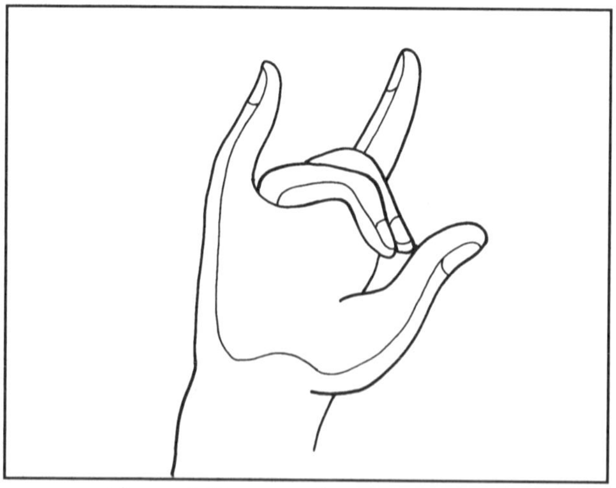

Figure 107 -- chandra-mriga mudra
(as seen by another)

chapetadana mudra -- (Ind.: *capeṭadāna-mudrā*) A *mudra*, a ritual hand pose, a seal, which is most common to the Buddhist tradition, although it infrequently appears within Hindu practice. It denotes warning or threatening. The *chapetadana mudra* is a single (Ind.: *asaṁyutta*) form, held by one hand. The form is similar to the *abhaya mudra*: palm faces forward, fingers extended upwards. Thus formed the hand is held shoulder high, even with the head, or higher and a little to the side as if about to deliver a slap. It is more aggressive in intent than the *tarjani mudra* and is rarely seen.[7] (BBh 189) (See: **Figure 108**)

chaturahasta mudra -- (Ind.: *caturhasta-mudrā*) A *mudrā*, a ritual hand pose, a seal, which is common to the Hindu tradition. It denotes a crafty enemy or a panderer as the *mudra* represents a jackal. The *chaturahasta mudra*[8] is a single (Ind.: *asaṁyutta*) form, held by one hand. This *mudra* is formed by--palm facing downwards, little finger extended upwards, index, middle and ring fingers held at 90° to the little finger, thumb touching the middle finger, and generally held at shoulder level. This *mudra* is generally held by the Lord *Shiva* in the *Chaturatandava*[9] form. (MJS 30) (See: **Figure 109**)

chatura mudra I -- (Ind.: *catura-mudrā*) A *mudra*, a ritual hand pose, a seal, which is generally common to the Hindu tradition and is depicted or held by a deity. The *chatura mudra* is a single (Ind.: *asaṁyutta*) form, held by one hand. The form is held by a single hand, generally the right hand--palm facing forward, fingers and thumb upwards, hand cupped, and held between the waist and shoulders. This pose is identified as being held in the lower right hand of *Shiva-Nataraja Chaturam*.[10] It is to be noted that this *mudra* appears similar to the *abhaya mudra*, however,the intent of this pose is not noted in the source. (RSG 63) (See: **Figure 110**)

chatura mudra II -- (Ind.: *catura-mudrā*) A *mudra*, a ritual hand pose, a seal, which is generally common to the Hindu tradition and is depicted or held by a deity. The *chatura mudra* is a single (Ind.: *asaṁyutta*) form, held by one hand. The form is held by a single hand, generally the right hand--palm facing forward, little finger points upwards, index, middle and ring fingers at right angle to the little finger, thumb touches the middle of the three. This pose is identified as being held by *Shiva-Nataraja Chaturam*.[11] It is to be noted that this *mudra* appears similar to the *vyaghra mudra*, but the intent of this pose is not noted in the source. See: *vyaghra mudra*. (TGR 167) (See: **Figure 111**)

chatura mudra III -- (Ind.: *catura-mudrā*) A hand pose, a seal, a dramatic (Ind.: *nāṭya*) *mudra* or gesture (Ind.:

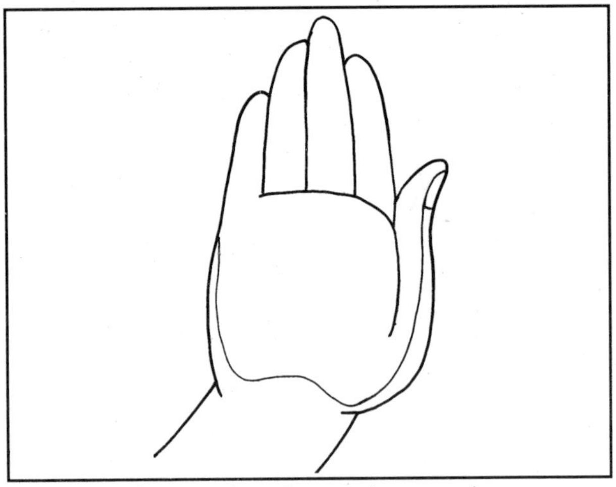

Figure 108 -- chapetadana mudra
(as seen by another)

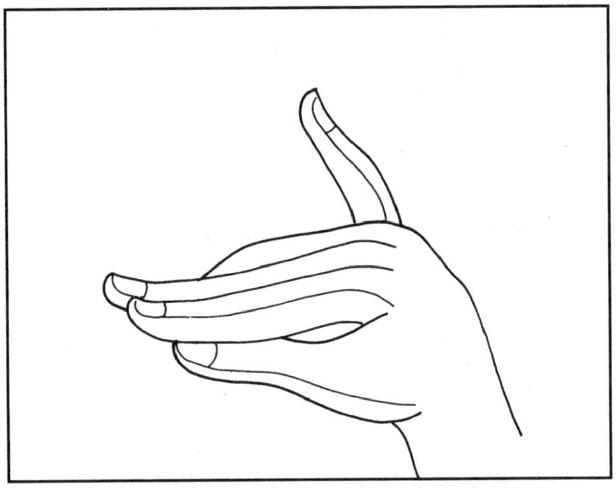

Figure 109 -- chaturahasta mudra
(as seen by another)

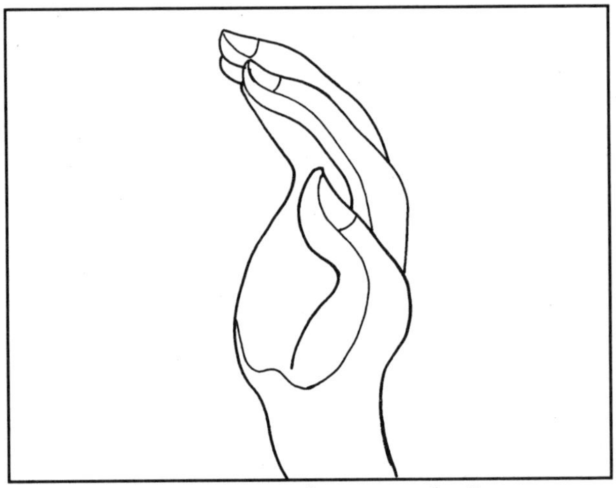

Figure 110 -- chatura mudra I
(as seen by the holder)

darpaṇa) held or formed by a performer, dancer or actor. The *chatura mudra* is a single (Ind.: *asaṁyutta*) form, held by one hand. It denotes sorrow, the difference of caste, etc.[12] This *mudra* is a variation and formed by: the palm facing forwards, the fingers, together and extended upwards, the little finger is separated slightly, the tip of the thumb crosses the palm and touches the base of the ring finger. (ACG 35, KVa 136 [28]) (See: **Figure 112**)

chaturashra mudra -- (Ind.: *caturaśra-mudrā*) A hand pose, a seal, a dramatic (Ind.: *nāṭya*) *mudra* or gesture (Ind.: *darpaṇa*) held or formed by a performer, dancer or actor. The *chaturashra mudra* is a combined (Ind.: *saṁyutta*) form, held by both hands. It denotes churning, milking, tying the bodice, etc.[13] This *mudra* is formed by: the hands are raised, fingers and thumbs extended, together and pointing upwards, relaxed, slightly cupped, palms facing outward and generally on a line level with the chest. Thus formed the hands are close together, but not touching. (ACG 42) (See: **Figure 113**)

chatur-dig-bandha mudra -- (Ind.: *catur-dig-bandha-mudrā* aka *vajravali mudra*; Jap.: *kongo cho-in* [*mudra*]) ("the *vajra* wall" or "the *vajra* fence") A *mudra*, a ritual hand pose, a seal, a *tantric mudra* which is common to the Japanese Buddhist (*Vajrayana, Mantrayana*) tradition and is held or formed by a devotee or priest during the *Eighteen-step Rite*. It may be accompanied by a *mantra*. The *chatur-dig-bandha mudra*[14] is a combined (Ind.: *saṁyutta*) form, held by both hands. It denotes enclosing of the sacred precincts. This *mudra* is formed by: palms facing upwards, the four fingers splayed, index and little fingers touch at their tips, thumbs rest along the index fingers, tips of the splayed middle fingers rest between the bases of the opposite index and middle fingers, tips of the splayed ring fingers rest between the bases of the opposite ring and little fingers, the right middle and ring fingers are on top of the left middle and ring fingers. The "crossed" middle and ring fingers form two "X's." (GDe 103, LCS 61) (See: **Figure 114**)

chatur-mukham mudra -- (Ind.: *catur-mukham-mudrā*) A *mudra*, a ritual hand pose, a seal, a *mudra* which is

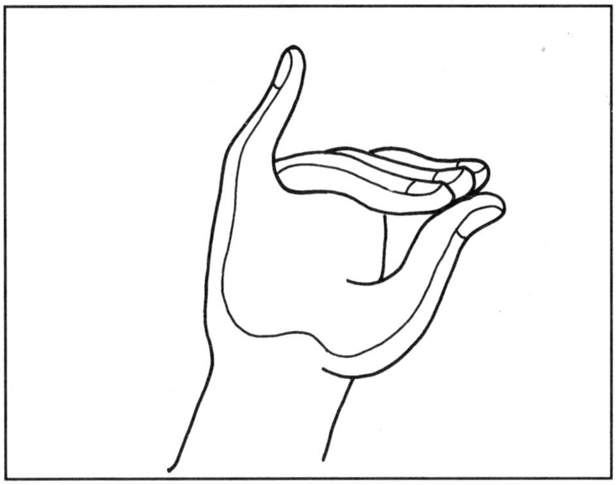

Figure 111 -- chatura mudra II
(as seen by another)

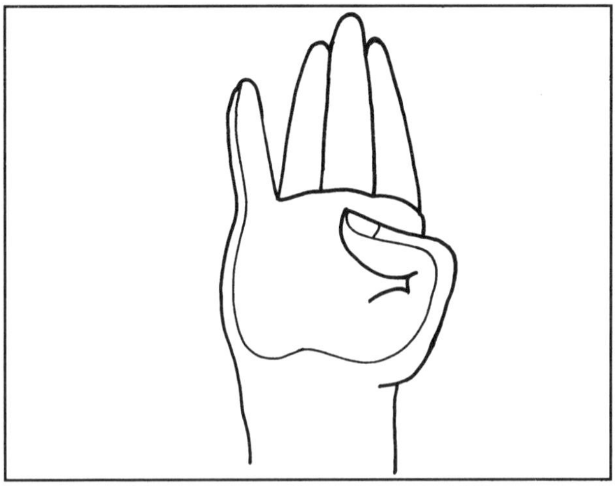

Figure 112 -- chatura mudra III
(as seen by another)

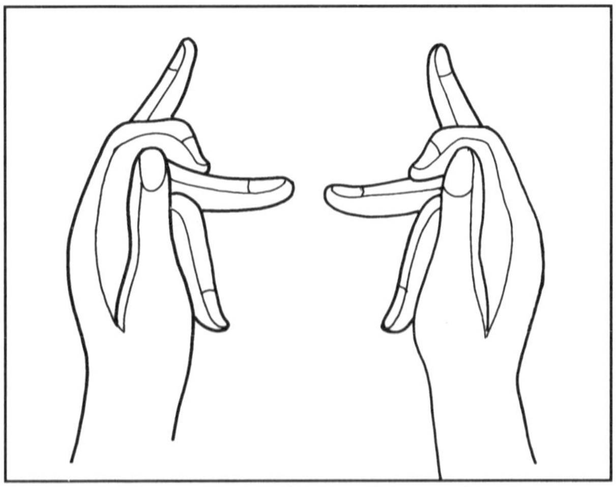

Figure 113 -- chaturashra mudra
(as seen by the holder)

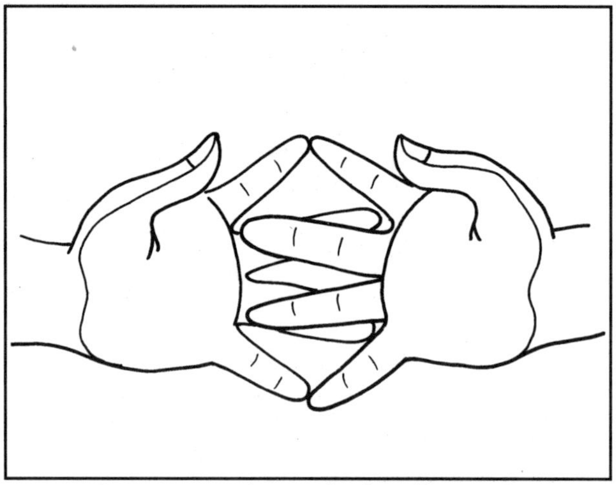

Figure 114 -- chatur-dig-bandha mudra
(as seen by the holder)

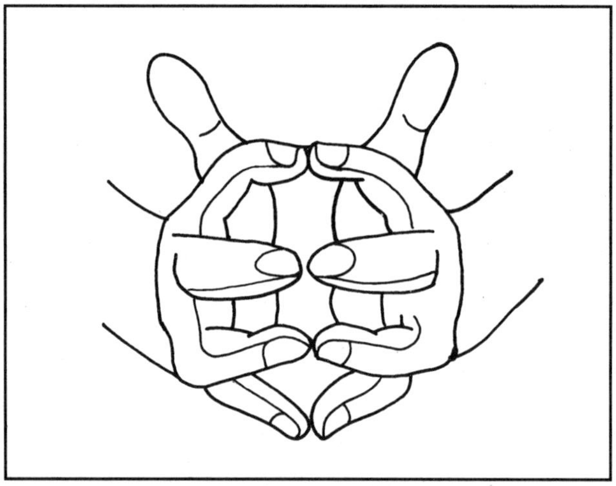

Figure 115 -- chatur-mukham mudra
(as seen by another)

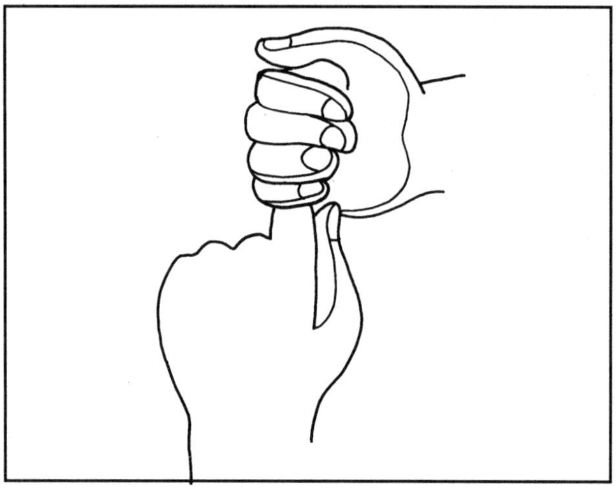

Figure 116 -- chi ken-in (mudra) I
(as seen by the holder)

common to yogic tradition, particularly the *Yoga Tatva Mudra Vigyan* form, and is held by a devotee or practitioner. The *catur-mukham mudra* is a combined (Ind.: *saṁyutta*) form, held by both hands. It is one of the twenty-four *mudras* held before the *Gayatri Jap* of the thirty-two total *Gayatri mudras.*[15] It is utilized for all sickness, especially cancer. This *mudra* is formed by: palms facing midline, fingers splayed and parallel to the ground, tips of index, middle, ring and little fingers touch, thumb extends upwards. Thus formed, the *mudra* is held waist high. (KDe 81, RLM 72) (See: **Figure 115**)

chhu tshong mo khiu keu-yin (mudra) -- (Chin.: *chhu tshong mo khiu keu-yin* [*mudrā*]; Jap.: *jo zu ma ko ku-in* [*mudra*]) The Chinese term for *jo zu ma ko ku-in* (*mudra*). See: *jo zu ma ko ku-in* (*mudra*). (GDe 105)

chih-ch'ṃan-yin (mudra) -- (Chin.: *chih-ch'ṃan-yin* [*mudrā*]; Ind.: *vajra mudrā, jñāna mudrā, bodhaśrī mudrā*; Jap.: *bodaiindodaiichichi-in* [*mudra*], *chi ken-in* [*mudra*], *nometsumumyokokuan-in* [*mudra*], *biroshananyoraidaimyochi-in* [*mudra*]) The Chinese term for *chi ken-in* (*mudra*). See: *chi ken-in* (*mudra*). (EDS 102)

chi ken-in (mudra) I -- (Jap.: *chi ken-in* [*mudrā*] aka *biroshananyoraidaimyochi-in* [*mudra*], *bodaiindo-daiichichi-in* [*mudra*], *nometsumumyokokuan-in* [*mudra*]; Chin.: *chih-ch'ṃan-yin* (*mudra*); Ind.: *vajra mudrā, jñāna mudrā, bodhaśrī mudrā*) A *mudra,* a ritual hand pose, a seal, a *tantric mudra* which is common to the Japanese and Chinese Buddhist (*Vajrayana, Mantrayana*) tradition and is held or formed by a devotee or priest. It may be accompanied by a *mantra*. It denotes adamantine knowledge derived from *Vairochana*. The *chi ken-in* (*mudra*) is a combined (Ind.: *saṁyutta*) form, held by both hands. This *mudra* is formed by: the left hand is fisted, thumb enclosed, index finger pointing upward, palm facing forward, and held level with the navel; the right hand is fisted, thumb exposed (See: *kongo ken-in*), palm facing chest, and the little finger and the subsequent fingers are curled around the first phalanges of the left hand ectended index finger.[16] (EDS 102) (See: **Figure 116**)

chi ken-in (mudra) II -- (Jap.: *chi ken-in* [*mudrā*] Ind.: *jnana-mushti mudra*)A *mudra*, a ritual hand pose, a seal, a *tantric mudra* which is common to the Japanese Buddhist (*Vajrayana, Mantrayana*) tradition and is held or formed by a devotee or priest during various rites. It may be accompanied by a *mantra*. The *chi ken-in* (*mudra*) *II* (Ind.: *jñāna-muṣṭi mudrā*) is a combined (Ind.: *saṁyutta*) form, held by both hands. This *mudra* is formed by: left palm facing forward, hand fisted, thumb enclosed, index finger pointing upward, held level with the navel; the right hand is fisted, thumb curled inside the fingers, palm facing midline, and the little finger and the subsequent fingers are curled around the first phalanges of the left hand. (GDe 139, LCS 61) (See: **Figure 117**)

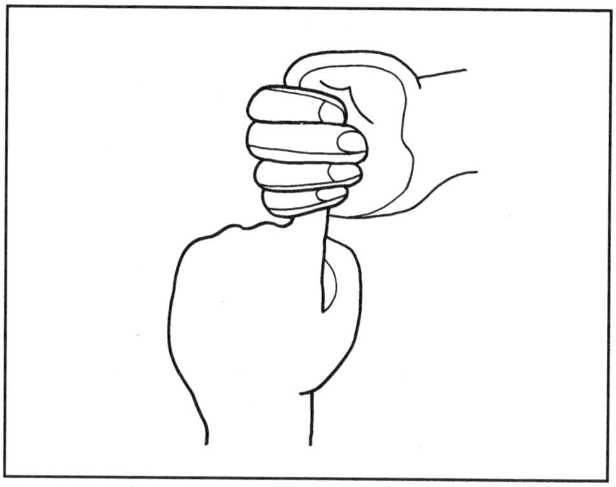

Figure 117 -- chi ken-in (mudra) II
(as seen by the holder)

chiku cho sho-in (mudra) -- (Jap.: *chiku chō shō-in* [*mudrā*]) ("*mudra* of invitation to the constellations") A *mudra*, a ritual hand pose, a seal, a *tantric mudra* which is common to the Japanese Buddhist (*Vajrayana, Mantrayana*) tradition and is held or formed by a devotee or priest during the rites of *Homa* and other rites. It may be accompanied by a *mantra*. The *chiku cho sho-in* (*mudra*) is a combined (Ind.: *saṁyutta*) form, held by both hands. It denotes an invitation to the twenty-eight constellations (Ind.: *nakṣatras*).[17] This *mudra* is formed by: the left hand, palm facing upwards thumb folded into the palm, index, middle, ring and little fingers folded over the thumb; right palm faces forward, ring and little fingers folded into the palm, thumb folded over the ring and little fingers, index and middle fingers extend straight upward. Thus formed, the left hand rests on the left thigh and the right is held in front of the chest. (GDe 93) (See: **Figure 118**)

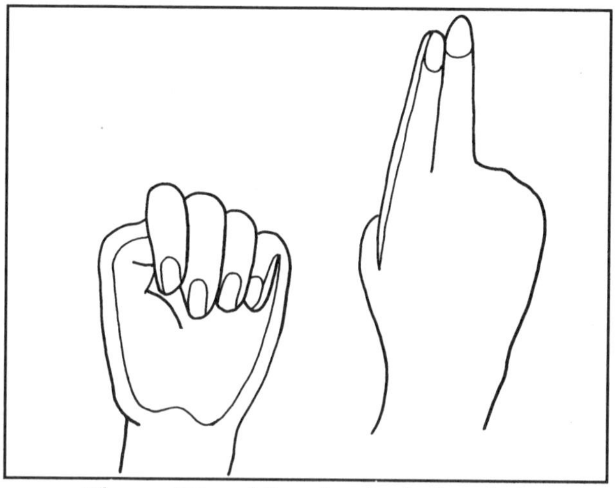

Figure 118 -- chiku cho sho-in (mudra)
(as seen by the holder)

chin mudra I -- (Ind.: *cin-mudrā* aka *sandarśana mudrā, vyākhyāna mudrā*[18]) A *mudra*, a ritual hand pose, a seal, which is most common to the Hindu tradition. It denotes disclosure or revelation of the Absolute One. The *chin mudra I* is a single (Ind.: *asaṁyutta*) form, held by one hand. This *mudra* is formed by--palm facing upwards, tips of the thumb and index finger touch, middle, ring and little fingers are relaxed and point out parallel with the ground. This *mudra* is not to be confused with the *vitarka mudra*. See: *vyakhyana mudra*. (MJS 32) (See: **Figure 119**)

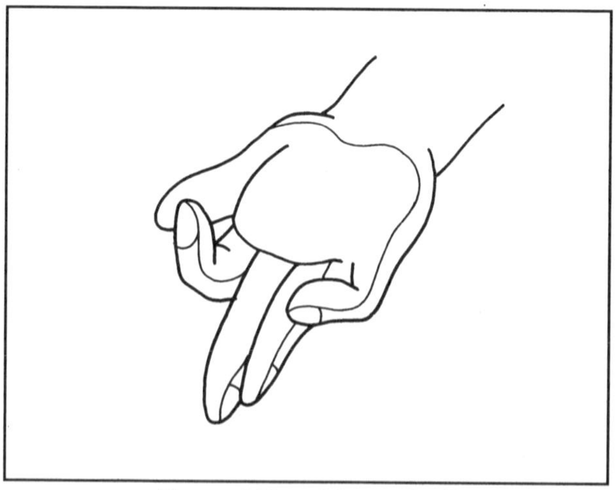

Figure 119 -- chin mudra I
(as seen by another)

chin mudra II -- (Ind.: *cin-mudrā* aka *sandarśana mudrā, vyākhyāna mudrā*) A *mudra*, a ritual hand pose, a seal,

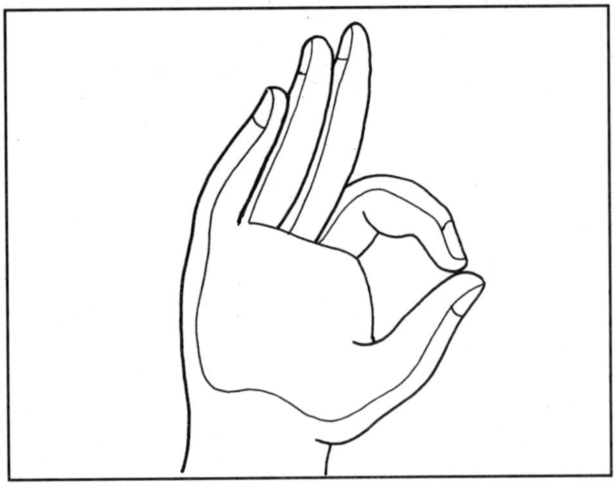

Figure 120 -- chin mudra II
(as seen by another)

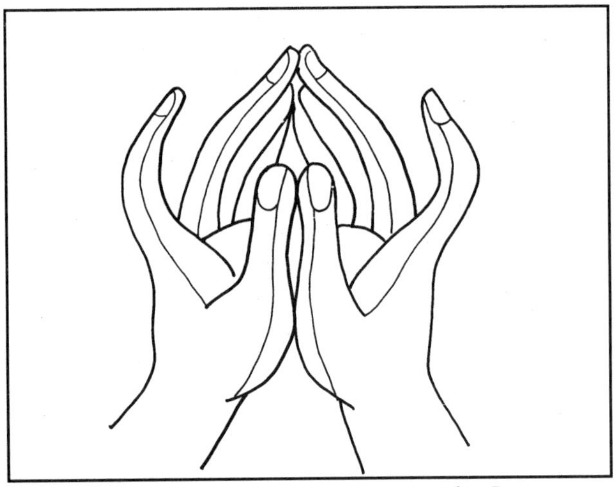

Figure 121 -- chintamani mudra I
(as seen by the holder)

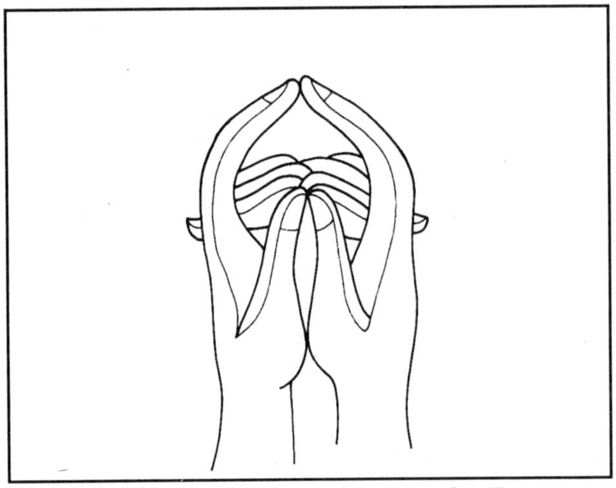

Figure 122 -- chintamani mudra II
(as seen by the holder)

which is most common to the Hindu tradition. It denotes disclosure or revelation of the Absolute One. The *chin mudra II* is a single (Ind.: *asaṁyutta*) form, held by one hand. This *mudra* is formed by--palm facing forward, tips of the thumb and index finger touch, middle, ring and little fingers are relaxed and point downward.[19] (RSG 3) (See: **Figure 120**)

chin-kang ho-chang (mudra) -- (Chin.; Jap.: *kongo-gassho* [*mudrā*]) The Chinese term for *kongo-gassho* (*mudra*). See: *kongo-gassho* (*mudra*). (EDS 76)

chintamani mudra I -- (Ind.: *cintāmaṇi-mudrā*; Jap.: *nyo-i-shu-in*) ("the precious wish-bestowing stone") A *mudra*, a ritual hand pose, a seal, a *tantric mudra* which is common to the Japanese Buddhist (*Vajrayana, Mantrayana*) tradition and is held or formed by a devotee or priest during the rites of *Garbhadhatu Mandala, Vajradhatu Mandala, Homa Rites* and other rites. It may be accompanied by a *mantra*. The *chintamani mudra I* is a combined (Ind.: *saṁyutta*) form, held by both hands. It denotes the joys and satisfactions procured through the right way. This *mudra* is identical for both hands and is formed by: palms facing midline and are separated, thumbs touch along their outer edges, middle, ring and little fingers touch at their tips, index fingers curve slightly and press against the second phalanges of the middle fingers. (GDe 31) (See: **Figure 121**)

chintamani mudra II -- (Ind.: *cintāmaṇi-mudrā*) ("the precious wish-bestowing stone") A *mudra*, a ritual hand pose, a seal, a *tantric mudra* which is common to the Japanese Buddhist (*Vajrayana, Mantrayana*) tradition and is held or formed by a devotee or priest during the rites of *Garbhadhatu Mandala, Vajradhatu Mandala, Homa Rites* and other rites. It may be accompanied by a *mantra*. The *chintamani mudra II* is a combined (Ind.: *saṁyutta*) form, held by both hands, and is a variation of *chintamani mudra I*. This *mudra* is formed by: palms facing midline, thumbs extend upwards and touch along their outer edges, index fingers curve, arch over, their tips touching, middle, ring and little fingers interlace over the back of the opposite hands. (GDe 300, LCS 257) (See: **Figure 122**)

chintamani mudra III -- (Ind.: *cintāmaṇi-mudrā*) ("the precious wish-bestowing stone") A *mudra*, a ritual hand pose, a seal, a *tantric mudra* which is common to the Japanese Buddhist (*Vajrayana, Mantrayana*) tradition and is held or formed by a devotee or priest during the rites of *Garbhadhatu Mandala, Vajradhatu Mandala, Homa Rites* and other rites. It may be accompanied by a *mantra*. The *chintamani mudra III* is a combined (Ind.: *saṁyutta*) form, held by both hands, and is a variation of *chintamani mudra I*. This *mudra* is formed by: palms facing midline, thumbs crossed, index fingers curve, arch over, their tips touching, middle, ring and little fingers interlace at their tips. (GDe 284, LCS 253) (See: **Figure 123**)

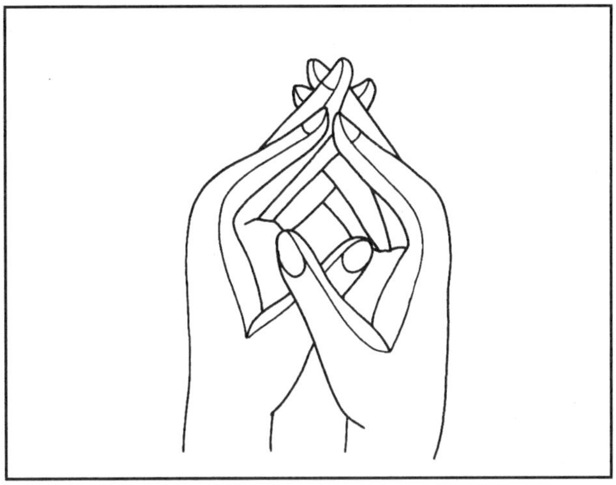

Figure 123 -- chintamani mudra III
(as seen by the holder)

chintamani mudra IV -- (Ind.: *cintāmaṇi-mudrā*) ("the precious wish-bestowing stone") A *mudra*, a ritual hand pose, a seal, a *tantric mudra* which is common to the Japanese Buddhist (*Vajrayana, Mantrayana*) tradition and is held or formed by a devotee or priest during the rites of *Garbhadhatu Mandala, Vajradhatu Mandala, Homa Rites* and other rites. It may be accompanied by a *mantra*. The *chintamani mudra IV*[20] is a combined (Ind.: *saṁyutta*) form, held by both hands, and is a variation of *chintamani mudra I*. It denotes protection and acceptance of sacred teachings. This *mudra* is formed by: palms facing midline, thumbs cross, index, ring and little fingers interlace over the back of the opposite hands, middle fingers curve slightly and arch over their tips touching. (GDe 69) (See: **Figure 124**)

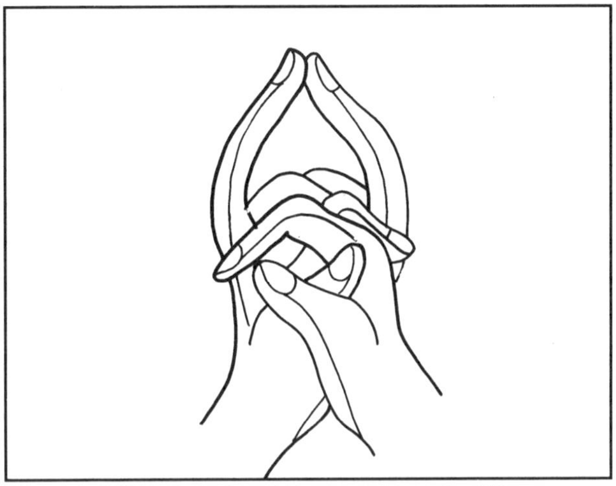

Figure 124 -- chintamani mudra IV
(as seen by the holder)

chintamani mudra V -- (Ind.: *cintāmaṇi-mudrā*) ("the precious wish-bestowing stone") A *mudra*, a ritual hand pose, a seal, a *tantric mudra* which is common to the Japanese Buddhist (*Vajrayana, Mantrayana*) tradition and is held or formed by a devotee or priest during various rites. It may be accompanied by a *mantra*. The *chintamani mudra V* is a combined (Ind.: *saṁyutta*) form, held by both hands, and is a variation of *chintamani mudra I*. This *mudra* is formed by: palms facing midline, thumbs extend upwards and touch, index middle and ring fingers curve, arch over, close, but not touching, little fingers touch at their tips. (GDe 223) (See: **Figure 125**)

Figure 125 -- chintamani mudra V
(as seen by the holder)

chitta mudra -- (Ind.: *citta-mudrā* aka *ratna-ghaṭa mudrā*) A variant term applied to *ratna-ghata mudra*. See: *ratna-ghata mudra*. (GDe 330)

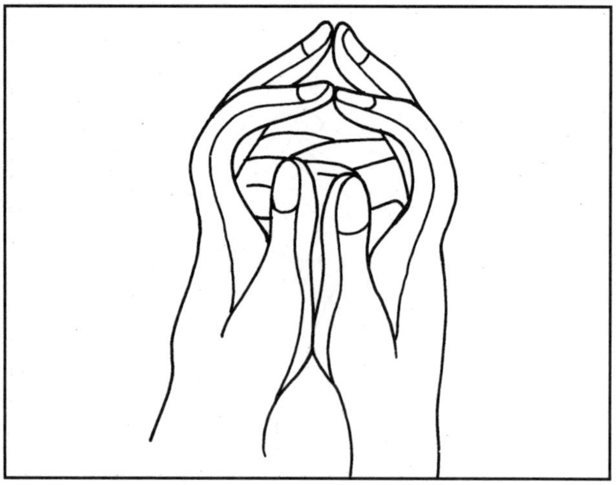

Figure 126 -- chitta-guhya mudra
(as seen by the holder)

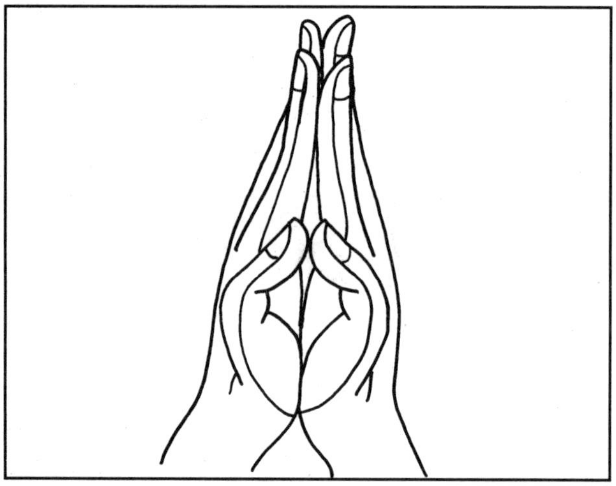

Figure 127 -- cho butsu fu-in (mudra)
(as seen by the holder)

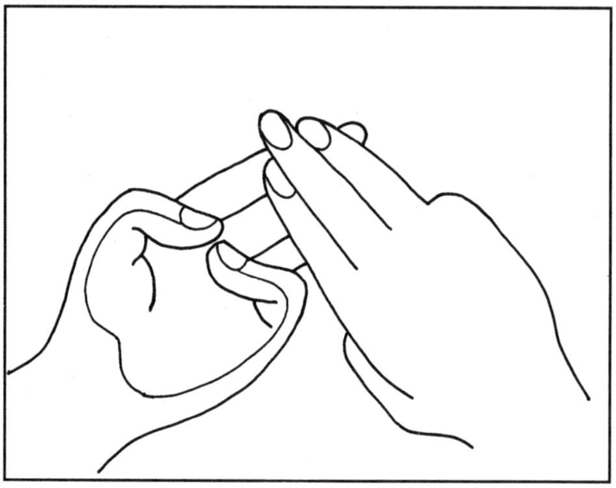

Figure 128 -- cho kongo renge-in (mudra)
(as seen by the holder)

chitta-guhya mudra -- (Jap.: *citta-guhya-mudrā*) A *mudra*, a ritual hand pose, a seal, a *tantric mudra* which is common to the Japanese Buddhist (*Vajrayana, Mantrayana*) tradition and is held or formed by a devotee or priest during the rites of *Garbhadhatu Mandala, Vajradhatu Mandala, Homa Rites* and other rites. It may be accompanied by a *mantra*. The *chitta-guhya mudra* is a combined (Ind.: *saṁyutta*) form, held by both hands. This *mudra* is formed by: palms facing midline, thumbs extended upwards and touching along their length, index and middle fingers extend upward, curve slightly and touch at their tips, ring and little fingers interlace, straight over the top. (GDe 224, LCS 69) (See: **Figure 126**)

cho butsu fu-in (mudra) -- (Jap.: *chō butsu fu-in* [*mudrā*] aka *se-ten cho sho no-in*) ("the Buddhas and men are one") A *mudra*, a ritual hand pose, a seal, a *tantric mudra* which is common to the Japanese Buddhist (*Vajrayana, Mantrayana*) tradition and is held or formed by a devotee or priest during the rites of *Garbhadhatu Mandala, Vajradhatu Mandala, Homa Rites* and other rites. It may be accompanied by a *mantra*. The *cho butsu fu-in* (*mudra*) is a combined (Ind.: *saṁyutta*) form, held by both hands. It denotes a request for entry as well as an energizing *mudra*. This *mudra* is similar to the *anjali mudra* and is formed by: palms brought together, fingers together, extending upwards and touching their counterparts, thumbs are flexed and the tips touch the third knuckles of the index fingers. Thus formed, the *mudra* is held at the level of the chest. (GDe 3) (See: **Figure 127**)

cho kongo renge-in (mudra) -- (Jap.: *chō kongō renge-in* [*mudrā*]) A *mudra*, a ritual hand pose, a seal, a *tantric mudra* which is common to the Japanese Buddhist (*Vajrayana, Mantrayana*) tradition and is held or formed by a devotee or priest during the rites of *Garbhadhatu Mandala, Vajradhatu Mandala, Homa Rites* and other rites. It may be accompanied by a *mantra*. The *cho jo kongo-in*[21] (*mudra*) is a combined (Ind.: *saṁyutta*) form, held by both hands. This *mudra* is identical for both hands and is formed by: little fingers folded into the palms, thumbs folded into the palms and over the little fingers, index, middle and ring fingers extend. Thus formed, the left palm faces downwards, the right palm faces upwards, the index, middle and ring fingers of the left hand rest on the index, middle and ring fingers of the right hand at right angles. (GDe 67) (See: **Figure 128**)

cho nen ju-in (mudra) -- (Jap.: *chō nen ju-in* [*mudrā*]) ("the true meditation of recitation") A *mudra*, a ritual hand pose, a seal, a *tantric mudra* which is common to the Japanese Buddhist (*Vajrayana, Mantrayana*) tradition and is held or formed by a devotee or priest during the rites of *Garbhadhatu Mandala, Vajradhatu Mandala, Homa Rites* and other rites. It may be accompanied by a *mantra*. The *cho nen ju-in* (*mudra*) is a combined (Ind.: *saṁyutta*) form, held by both hands. It denotes true meditation. This *mudra* is identical for both hands and is formed by: thumbs touching the tips of the curled ring fingers, the index fingers are erect, the tips of the middle and little fingers touch their counterparts. (GDe 50) (See: **Figure 129**)

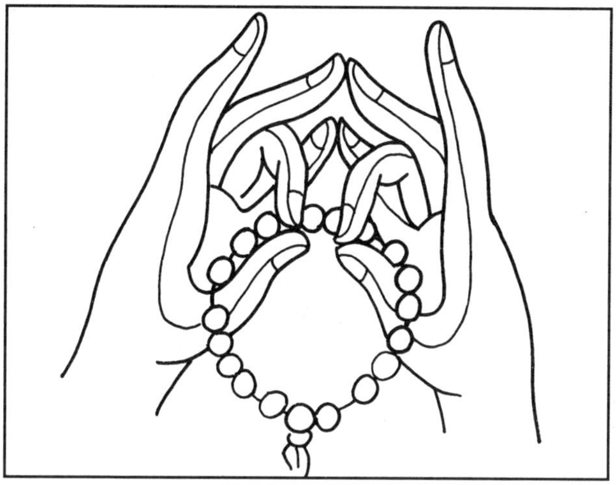

Figure 129 -- cho nen ju-in (mudra)
(as seen by the holder)

chonmukhmukham mudra I -- (Ind.: *chonmukhmukham-mudrā* aka *unmukhonmukham mudrā*) A *mudra*, a ritual hand pose, a seal, a mudra which is common to yogic tradition, particularly the *Yoga Tatva Mudra Vigyan* form, and is held by a devotee or practitioner. The *chonmukhmukham mudra*[22] is a combined (Ind.: *saṁyutta*) form, held by both hands. It is one of the twenty-four *mudras* held before the *Gayatri Jap* of the thirty-two total *Gayatri mudras*.[23] It is utilized for all sickness, especially cancer. This *mudra* is formed by: right palm faces upwards, the tips of the fingers and thumb are brought together, touching, pointing upwards; left palm faces downwards, the tips of the fingers and thumb are brought together, touching, pointing downwards. Thus formed, the tips of the fingers of the two hands meet and the *mudra* is held chest high and the hands may be reversed. (KDe 84 & 107) (See: **Figure 130**)

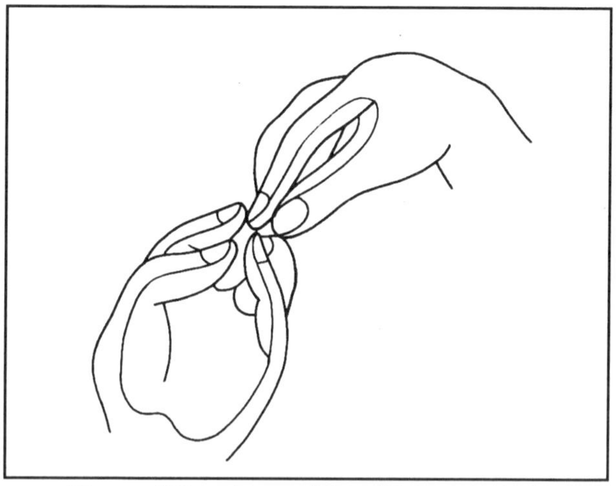

Figure 130 -- chonmukhmukham mudra I
(as seen by the holder)

chonmukhmukham mudra II -- (Ind.: *chonmukhmukham-mudrā*) A *mudra*, a ritual hand pose, a seal, a *mudra* which is common to yogic tradition, particularly the *Yoga Tatva Mudra Vigyan* form, and is held by a devotee or practitioner. The *chonmukhmukham mudra II* is a combined (Ind.: *saṁyutta*) form, held by both hands. It is one of the twenty-four *mudras* held before the *Gayatri Jap* of the thirty-two total *Gayatri mudras*.[24]

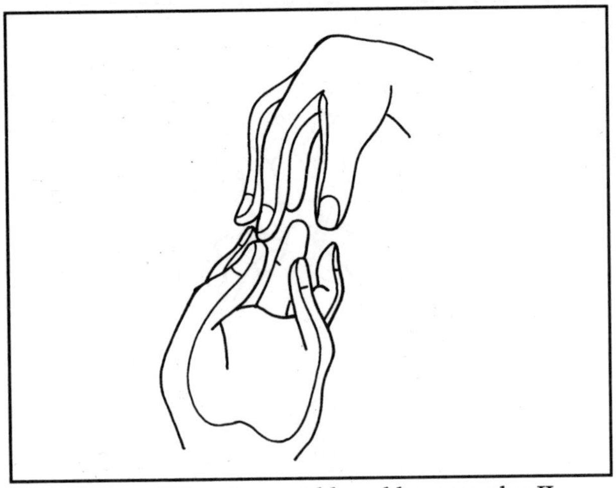

Figure 131 -- chonmukhmukham mudra II
(as seen by the holder)

Figure 132 -- cho zai-in (mudra)
(as seen by the holder)

It is utilized for all sickness, especially cancer. This *mudra* is formed by: right palm faces downwards, the tips of the fingers and thumb are brought together, touching, pointing upwards; left palm faces upwards, the tips of the fingers and thumb are brought together, touching, pointing downwards. Thus formed, the tips of the fingers of the two hands meet and the *mudra* is held chest high and the hands may be reversed. (KDe 84 & 107) (See: **Figure 131**)

choosing the chief disciples mudra -- (Eng.; Ind.: *tarjanī (II)-dhyāna mudrā*; Thai: *pang thong-tang-etatakkasatarn*) The English descriptive phrase for the Thai *pang thong-tang-etatakkasatarn*. See: *pang thong-tang-etatakkasatarn*. (DRN 37, JBo 205, ODD 680, OFr 18, PSS)

chos-dbying rnam-dag phyag-rgya (mudra) -- (Tib.; Indic.: *sarva-dharmah mudrā*) The Tibetan transliteral term for *sarva-dharmah mudra*. See: *sarva-dharmah mudra*. (SBe 347)

chos-sbyin phyag-rgya -- (Tib.; Indic.: *vitarka mudrā*) The Tibetan transliteral term for *vitarka mudrā*. See: *vitarks mudra*. (BCO 217)

cho zai-in (mudra) -- (Jap.: *chō zai-in* [*mudrā*]) A *mudra*, a ritual hand pose, a seal, a *tantric mudra* which is common to the Japanese Buddhist (*Vajrayana, Mantrayana*) tradition and is held or formed by a devotee or priest during the rites of *Vajradhatu Mandala*. It may be accompanied by a *mantra*. The *cho zai-in*[25] (*mudra*) is a combined (Ind.: *saṁyutta*) form, held by both hands. It denotes calling together crimes which are to be destroyed. This *mudra* is formed by: palms facing midline and close, thumbs crossed, index fingers curled at their first two joints and touching their nails, middle fingers extended and touch at their tips, ring and little fingers interlaced and folded their tips touching the third knuckle of their counterpart. (GDe 66) (See: **Figure 132**)

chuan-fa-lun-yin (mudra) -- (Chin.; Jap.: *temborin-in*) The Chinese term for *temborin-in* (*mudra*). See: *temborin-in* (*mudra*). (EDS 94)

chuan-yṃeh-lo-hung chin-kang-yin (mudra) -- (Chin.; Jap.: *basara-un-kongo-in*) The Chinese term for *basara-un-kongo-in* (*mudra*). See: *basara-un-kongo-in* (*mudra*). (EDS 114)

ch'u-ti-yin (mudra) -- (Chin.; Jap.: *sokuchi-in*) The Chinese term for *sokuchi-in* (*mudra*). See: *sokuchi-in* (*mudra*). (EDS 80)

contemplating the approach of his death mudra -- (Eng.; Ind.: *jñāna-nidratahasta mudrā*; Thai: *pang plong-aryusangkharn*) The English descriptive phrase for the Thai *pang plong-aryusangkharn*. See: *pang plong-aryusangkharn*. (DRN 36, JBo 204, ODD 279, OFr 34, PSS)

contemplating the corpse mudra -- (Eng. aka reflecting on worldly impermanence; Ind.: *ahāyavarada-jñāna mudrā, ahāyavarada-kaṭaka mudra*; Thai: *pang plong-kammathan*) An English descriptive phrase for the Thai *pang plong-kammathan*. See: *pang plong-kammathan*. (DRN 36, JBo)

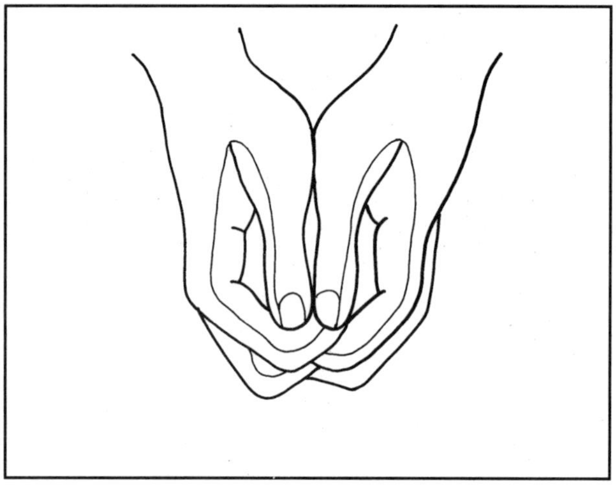

Figure 133 -- dai kai-in (mudra)
(as seen by another)

-- D --

dai kai-in (mudra) -- (Jap.: *dai kai-in* [*mudrā*]) ("the great ocean") A *mudra*, a ritual hand pose, a seal, a *tantric mudra* which is common to the Japanese Buddhist (*Vajrayana, Mantrayana*) tradition and is held or formed by a devotee or priest during the rites of *Garbhadhatu Mandala, Vajradhatu Mandala, Homa Rites* and other rites. It may be accompanied by a *mantra*. The *dai kai-in*[1] (*mudra*) is a combined (Ind.: *saṁyutta*) form, held by both hands. It denotes the purification and sanctification of the temple precincts. This *mudra* is formed by: palms facing the midline and close, thumbs side by side and touching, fingers are interlaced inwards. Thus formed the hands are rotated downward so that the fingers are oriented towards the ground. (GDe 33) (See: **Figure 133**)

dai sotoba-in (mudra) -- (Jap.: *dai sotoba-in* [*mudrā*] aka *mushofushi-in* [*mudra*], *Biroshana-in* [*mudra*], *butsubu sotoba-in* [*mudra*], *hen hokkai mushofushi-in* [*mudra*], *mushofushi to-in* [*mudra*], *rito-in* [*mudra*]; Chin.: *wu-so-pu-chih-yin*; Ind.: *stūpa mudrā*) ("great *stūpa mudrā*") A variant term applied to *mushofushi-in* (*mudra*). See: *mushofushi-in* (*mudra*). (EDS 115)

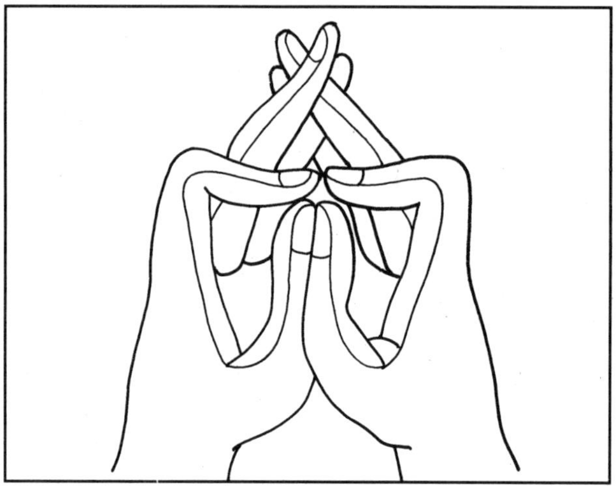

Figure 134 -- dai ye-to no-in (mudra)
(as seen by the holder)

dai ye-to no-in (mudra) -- (Jap.: *dai ye-to no-in* [*mudrā*]) ("the sword of great knowledge") A *mudra*, a ritual hand pose, a seal, a *tantric mudra* which is common to the Japanese Buddhist (*Vajrayana, Mantrayana*) tradition and is held or formed by a devotee or priest during the rites of *Garbhadhatu Mandala, Vajradhatu Mandala, Homa Rites* and other rites. It may be accompanied by a *mantra*. The *dai ye-to no-in* (*mudra*)[2] is a combined (Ind.: *saṁyutta*) form, held by both hands. It denotes protection from and the annihilation of sins. This *mudra* is formed by: the palms touch at the 'heels,' middle, ring and little fingers extend and cross at their tips, a narrow space is left between the hands, the index fingers bend at the second joint and their tips touch, the thumbs touch along their outer length and their tips rest on the tips of the joining index fingers. (GDe 22, LCS 195) (See: **Figure 134**)

damaru mudra -- (Ind.: *ḍamaru-mudrā* aka *ḍamaruhasta* [*mudrā*]) A variant term applied to *damaruhasta* (*mudra*). See: *damaruhasta* (*mudra*). (ERJ II, 25)

damaruhasta (mudra) -- (Ind.: *ḍamaruhasta* [*mudrā*] aka *ḍamaru mudrā*) A *mudra*, a ritual hand pose, a seal, which is common to the *Vajrayana* Buddhist and Hindu traditions. This *mudra*, similar to the *karana mudra*, is that pose taken when holding a *damaru*. The *damaruhasta* (*mudra*) is a single (Ind.: *asaṁyutta*) form, held by one hand. This *mudra* is formed by: palm facing forward, index and little fingers extended upwards, middle and ring folded into the palm, the thumb holds the tips of the middle and ring fingers in place, and the narrow (middle) section of the *damaru* fits between the index and little fingers.[3] (MJS 35) (See: **Figure 135**)

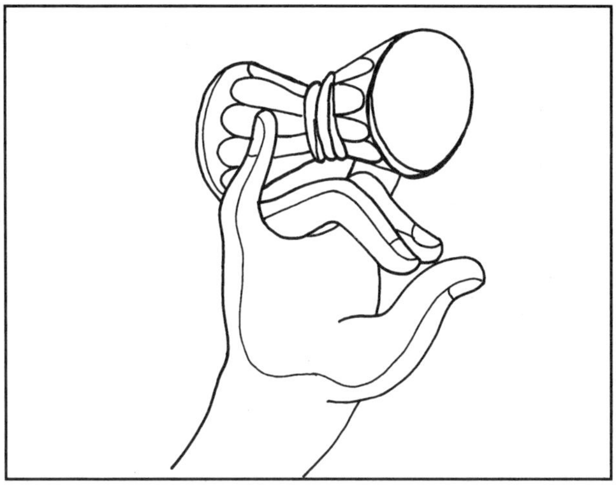

Figure 135 -- damaruhasta (mudra)
(as seen by another)

dampati mudra -- (Ind.: *dampati-mudrā*) A hand pose, a seal, a dramatic (Ind.: *nāṭya*) *mudra* or gesture (Ind.: *darpaṇa*) held or formed by a performer, dancer or actor. The *dampati mudra* is a combined (Ind.: *saṁyutta*) form, held by both hands. One of eleven *mudras* representing "relationships" and one which denotes husband and wife. This *mudra* is formed by: right palm faces forward, index, middle and ring fingers curl at their first and second joints (towards the palm), the thumb is extended outward, and the little fingers extend upwards; left palm faces mid-line, fingers brought into the palm forming a fist, thumb extends upwards.[4] (ACG 44) (See: **Figure 136**)

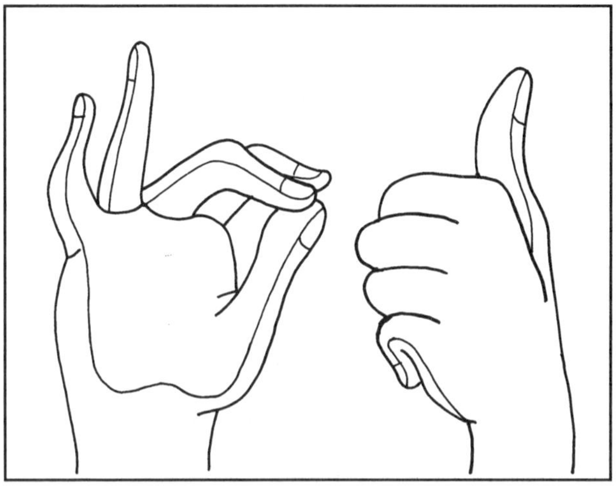

Figure 136 -- dampati mudra
(as seen by another)

dana mudra -- (Ind.: *dāna-mudrā* aka *varada mudrā*) A variant term applied to *varada mudra*. See: *varada mudra*. (MJS 35)

danda mudra -- (Ind.: *daṇḍa-mudrā* aka *daṇḍa*[*hasta*]-*mudrā*) A *mudra*, a ritual hand pose, a seal, which is common to the Hindu tradition. It denotes strength and the ability to distribute discipline or punishment. The intent of this *mudra* is similar to the *chapetadana mudra*. The *danda mudra* is a single (Ind.: *asaṁyutta*) form, held by one hand. The form is held by not only the hand, but involves the whole arm as well: the arm

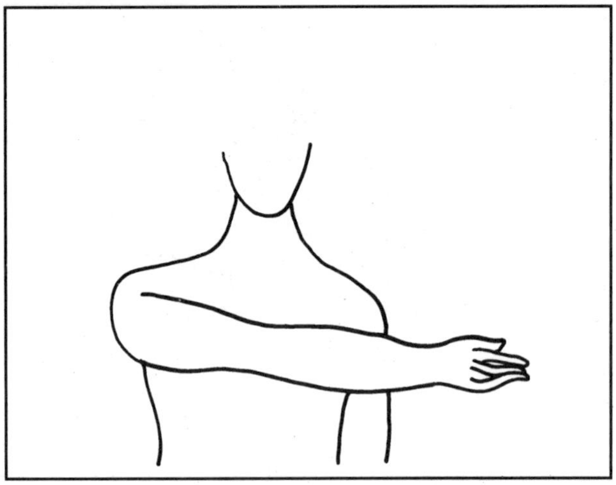

Figure 137 -- danda mudra
(as seen by another)

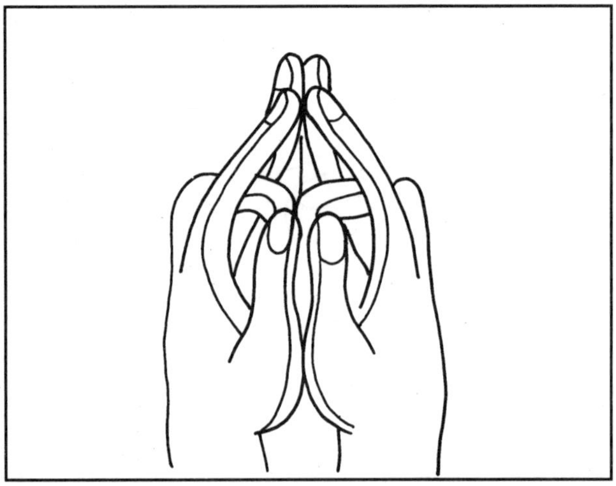

Figure 138 -- Dharani-Avalokiteshvara mudra
(as seen by the holder)

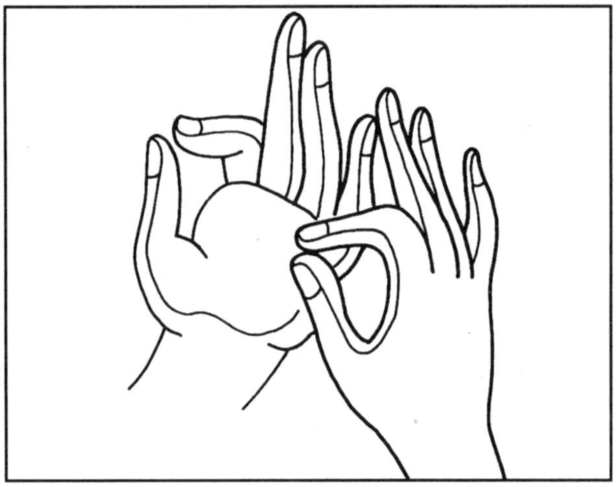

Figure 139 -- dharmachakra mudra
(as seen by the holder)

and hand are held straight and stiffly (rod-like) across the body, generally the palm faces downward. Thus held, the hand may be on a parallel with the waist or shoulder or raised above the head. It is similar to the *gaja(hasta) mudra* except while the former is stiff and straight, the latter is relaxed and graceful. (MJS 35) (See: **Figure 137**)

danda[hasta] mudra -- (Ind.: *daṇḍa[hasta]-mudrā* aka *daṇḍa mudrā*) A variant term applied to *danda mudra*. See: *danda mudra*. (MJS 35)

dbang-sgyur 'khor-lo'i phyag-rgya (mudra) -- (Tib.; Indic.: *samanta-buddhanam mudra*) The Tibetan transliteral term for *samanta-buddhanam mudra*. See: *samanta-buddhanam mudra*. (SBe 347)

Dharani-Avalokiteshvara mudra -- (Ind.: *Dhāraṇī-Avalokiteśvara-mudrā*) A *mudra*, a ritual hand pose, a seal, a *tantric mudra* which is common to the Japanese Buddhist (*Vajrayana, Mantrayana*) tradition and is held or formed by a devotee or priest during the rites of *Garbhadhatu Mandala* and other rites. It may be accompanied by a *mantra*. The *Dharani-Avalokiteshvara mudra*[5] is a combined (Ind.: *saṁyutta*) form, held by both hands. This *mudra* is formed by: palms face midline, thumbs extend upwards and touch along their length, index, ring and little fingers touch at their tips, middle fingers fold into the palm. (LCS 152) (See: **Figure 138**)

dharmachakra mudra -- (Ind.: *dharmacakra-mudrā* aka *dharmacakra-pravartana mudrā, vyākhyāna mudrā*; Chin.: *chuan-fa-lun-yin*; Jap.: *temborin-in*; Tib.: *chos-hkhor phyag-rgya*) A *mudra*, a ritual hand pose, a seal, which is common to the Buddhist tradition. It denotes preaching by setting the wheel of the law into motion. The *dharmachakra mudra* is a combined (Ind.: *saṁyutta*) form, held by both hands. This *mudra* is formed by: the tip of the thumb and the index finger touch, the middle, ring and little fingers are extended, both hands hold the same pose, however the two palms face each other but do not touch, left palm faces the midline and is slightly lower, while the right faces outward. Thus formed, the *mudra* is held at chest level. This *mudra* is generally associated with the Lord *Buddha*, but also *Vairochana* and *Maitreya*. (RSG 3, AKG 20, BCO 145, BBh 192) (See: **Figure 139**)

dharmachakra-pravartana mudra -- (Ind.: *dharmacakra-pravartana-mudrā* aka *dharma-cakra-mudrā;* Chin.: *chuan-fa-lun-yin;* Jap.: *temborin-in* [*mudra*]) ("the revolving of the *Dharma* wheel") A *mudra*, a ritual hand pose, a seal, a *tantric mudra* which is common to the Japanese Buddhist (*Vajrayana, Mantrayana*) tradition and is held or formed by a devotee or priest during the rites of *Garbhadhatu Mandala, Vajradhatu Mandala, Homa Rites* and other rites. It may be accompanied by a *mantra*. The *dharmachakra-pravartana mudra*[6] is a combined (Ind.: *saṁyutta*) form, held by both hands. It denotes the establishing of the law. This *mudra* is formed by: placing the hand back-to-back, left palm faces right, right palm faces left, the fingers intertwine, the left thumb is brought to the right palm and the right thumb touches the left thumb. (EDS 95, GDe 33, LCS 160, MMR 391) (See: **Figure 140**)

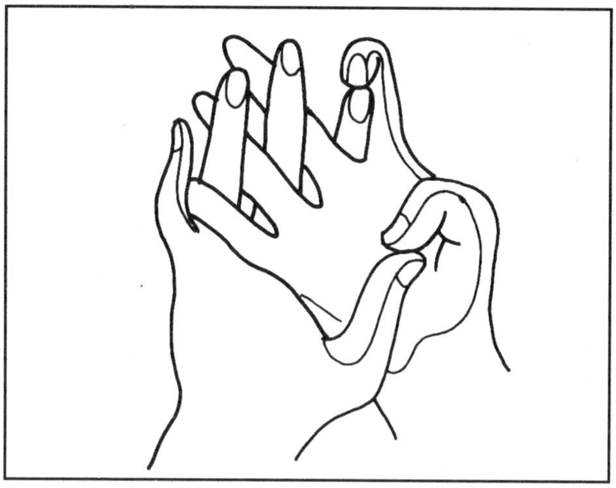

Figure 140 -- dharmachakra-pravartana mudra
(as seen by the holder)

dharmachakra-pravartana-bodhisattva-varga-mudra -- (Ind.: *dharmacakra-pravartana-bodhisattva-varga-mudrā* aka *Sacittotpada-Bodhisattva mudrā*) A *mudra*, a ritual hand pose, a seal, a *tantric mudra* which is common to the Japanese Buddhist (*Vajrayana, Mantrayana*) tradition and is held or formed by a devotee or priest during the rites of *Garbhadhatu Mandala, Vajradhatu Mandala, Homa Rites* and other rites. It may be accompanied by a *mantra*. The *dharmachakra-pravartana-bodhisattva-varga-mudra* is a combined (Ind.: *saṁyutta*) form, held by both hands. This *mudra* is identical for both hands and formed by: palms facing midline, middle, ring and little fingers curl toward the palm, thumb touched first phalanges of the middle finger, index fingers extend upwards, flex at the first and second joints. Thus formed, the two hands are brought quite close, but do not touch. (GDe 197, LCS 231) (See: **Figure 141**)

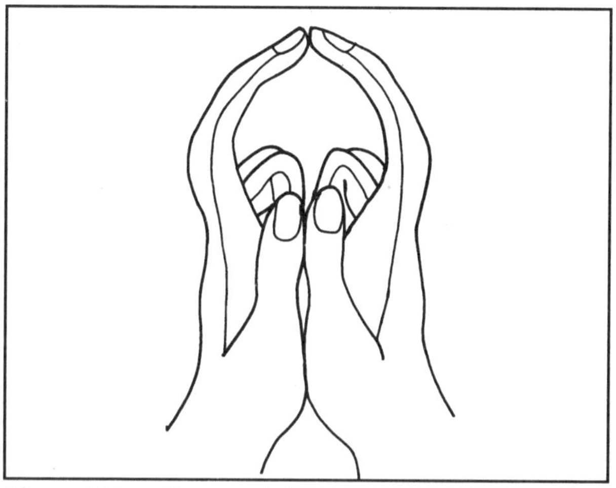

Figure 141 -- dharmachakra-pravartana-bodhisattva-varga-mudra (as seen by the holder)

dharma-pravartana mudra -- (Ind.: *dharma-pravartana-mudrā*) A *mudra*, a ritual hand pose, a seal, a *tantric mudra* which is common to the Japanese Buddhist (*Vajrayana, Mantrayana*) tradition and is held or formed by a devotee or priest during the rites of the *Vajradhatu Mandala* and other rites. It may be accompanied by a *mantra*. The *dharma-pravartana mudra*[7] is a combined (Ind.: *saṁyutta*) form, held by both hands. It denotes 'putting the Law into motion,' and, therefore related

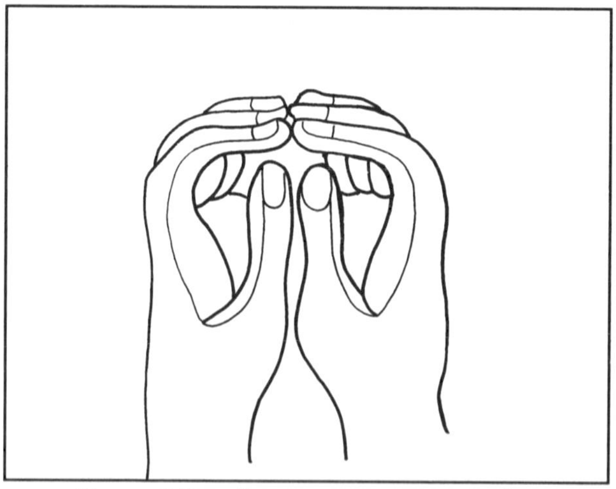

Figure 142 -- dharma-pravartana mudra
(as seen by the holder)

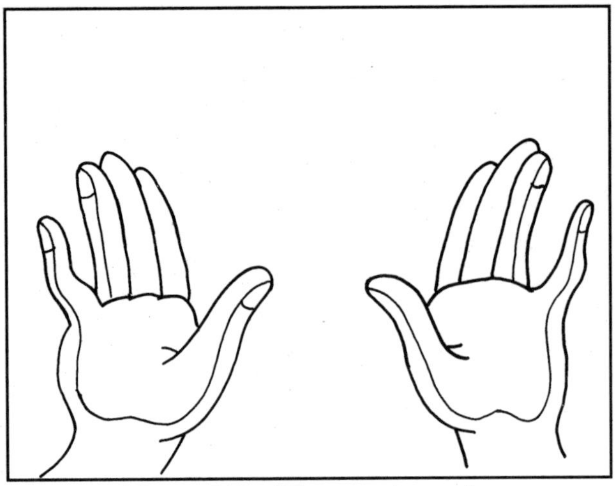

Figure 143 -- Dharmaraja mudra
(as seen by another)

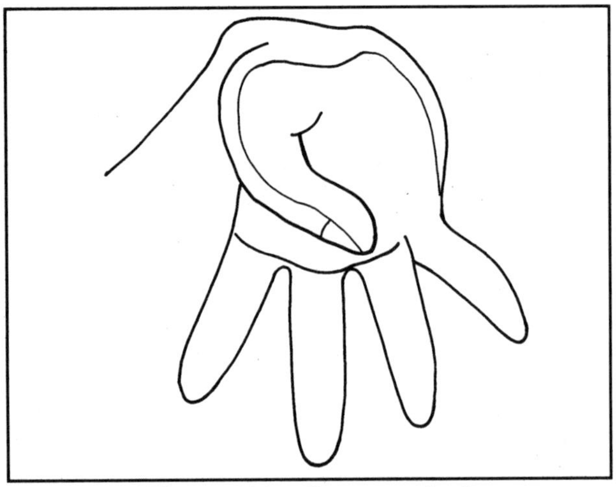

Figure 144 -- dhenu mudra I
(as seen by another)

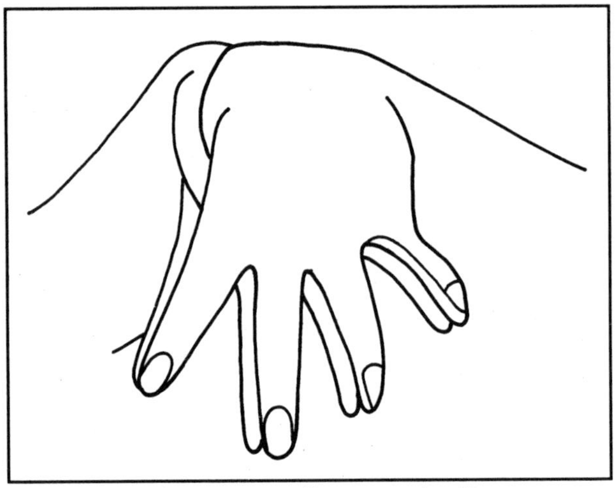

Figure 145 -- dhenu mudra II
(as seen by another)

to the *dharmachakra mudra*. This *mudra* is formed by: palms facing midline, thumbs extended upwards and touching along their length, fingers arch and touch at their very tips. (LCS 125) (See: **Figure 142**)

Dharmaraja mudra -- (Ind.: *Dharmarāja-mudrā*) A hand pose, a seal, a dramatic (Ind.: *nāṭya*) *mudra* or gesture (Ind.: *darpaṇa*) held or formed by a performer, dancer or actor. The *Dharmaraja mudra* is a combined (Ind.: *saṁyutta*) form, held by both hands. It denotes *Dharmaraja*, one of a number of famous rulers or heroes, in this case "the king of the Law (Ind.: *dharma*)." The *mudra* if formed by: palms face forwards, fingers and thumbs extended, together and pointing upwards, relaxed, slightly cupped. Thus formed the hands are held, somewhat to the side, level with the shoulders and waved. The *mudra* is similar to the *pataka mudras*. (ACG 47) (See: **Figure 143**)

dhenu mudra I -- (Ind.: *dhenu-mudrā*) A *mudra*, a ritual hand pose, a seal, which is common to the Hindu tradition. It denotes a cows udder, the four great and sacred rivers, and therefore, sanctification. The *dhenu mudra I* is a single (Ind.: *asaṁyutta*) form, held by one hand. This *mudra* is formed by: palm facing forward, fingers splayed and pointing downward, thumb folded into the palm, and is generally held at waist level. See: *sankirna mudra*. (MJS 39) (See: **Figure 144**)

dhenu mudra II -- (Ind.: *dhenu-mudrā*) A *mudra*, a ritual hand pose, a seal, which is common to the Hindu tradition. It denotes a cows udder, the four great and sacred rivers, and therefore, sanctification. The *dhenu mudra II*[8] is a combined (Ind.: *saṁyutta*) form, held by both hands. This *mudra* is formed by: palms together, fingers splayed and pointing downward, thumb folded into the palm, and is generally held at waist level. This *mudra* is not associated with a deity, but is formed by a celebrant during a purification ritual. (MJS 39) (See: **Figure 145**)

Dhritarashtra mudra -- (Jap.: *Dhṛtarāṣṭra-mudrā*) A *mudra*, a ritual hand pose, a seal, a *tantric mudra* which is common to the Japanese Buddhist (*Vajrayana, Mantrayana*) tradition and is held or formed by a devotee or priest during the rites of *Garbhadhatu Mandala* and other rites. It may be accompanied by a *mantra*.

The *Dhritarashtra mudra* is a combined (Ind.: *saṁyutta*) form, held by both hands. This *mudra* is identical for both hands and is formed by: palms face backward, middle, ring and little fingers fold into palms, thumbs touches the middle fingers, index fingers extend straight and parallel to the ground. Thus formed the hands cross, back of right hand touches heel of left palm. (LCS 175) (See: **Figure 146**)

dhupa mudra I -- (Ind.: *dhūpa-mudrā*) This is an assigned term.[9] A *mudra*, a ritual hand pose, a seal, which is common to the Buddhist (*Vajrayana*) tradition, a *tantric mudra*. It denotes incense, which is one of the five 'gifts' or 'outer offerings' proffered to a divine guest--the other four being: flowers, lamps, perfume and food--during the early stages worship, particularly as associated with the worship of the powerful *Vajrayana* goddess, *Tara*. The *dhupa mudra I* is a combined (Ind.: *saṁyutta*) form, held by both hands. This *mudra* is identical for both hands which are used simultaneously in mirror-pose: the palm faces the midline, the middle, ring and little fingers are fisted, the index finger points downward, both hands thus formed are brought close together and held below the chin. The *mantra* associated with this mudra is: "*OM Guru-sarva-Tathagata Dhupe Puja-megha-samudra-spharana-samaye HUM.*"[10] (SBe 147) (See: **Figure 147**)

dhupa mudra II -- (Jap.: *dhūpa-mudrā*) A *mudra*, a ritual hand pose, a seal, a *tantric mudra* which is common to the Japanese Buddhist (*Vajrayana, Mantrayana*) tradition and is held or formed by a devotee or priest during the rites of *Garbhadhatu Mandala* and other rites. It may be accompanied by a mantra. The *dhupa mudra II*[11] is a combined (Ind.: *saṁyutta*) form, held by both hands. This *mudra* is formed by: palms facing outwards (left to left & right ti right), thumbs splayed, fingers extend upwards. Thus formed the outer tips (nails) of the fingers touch. (LCS 186) (See: **Figure 148**)

dhupa mudra III -- (Ind.: *dhūpa-mudrā*; Jap.: *sho ko-in* [*mudra*]) The Indic term for *sho ko-in* (*mudra*). See: *sho ko-in* (*mudra*). (GDe 47)

dhyana mudra I -- (Ind.: *dhyāna-mudrā* aka *dhyānahasta mudrā, samādhi mudrā, yoga mudrā*; Chin.: *ting-yin* [*mudra*]; Jap.: *jo-in* [*mudra*]; Thai: *pang phra-nang*; Tib.:

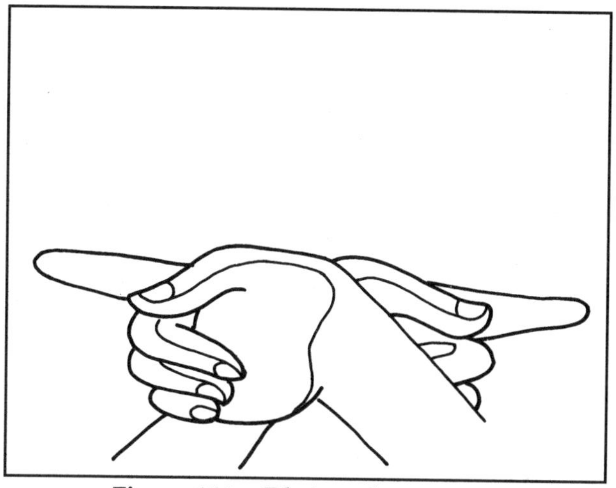

Figure 146 -- Dhritarashtra mudra
(as seen by the holder)

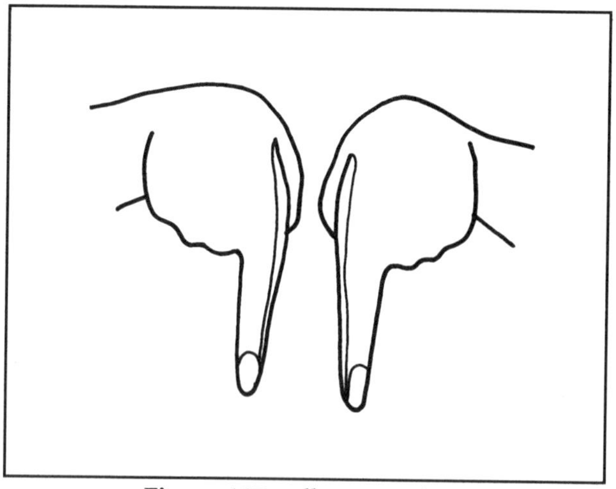

Figure 147 -- dhupa mudra I
(as seen by another)

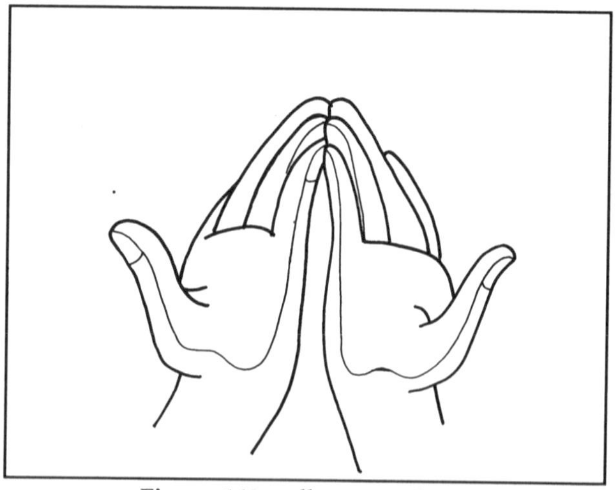

Figure 148 -- dhupa mudra II
(as seen by the holder)

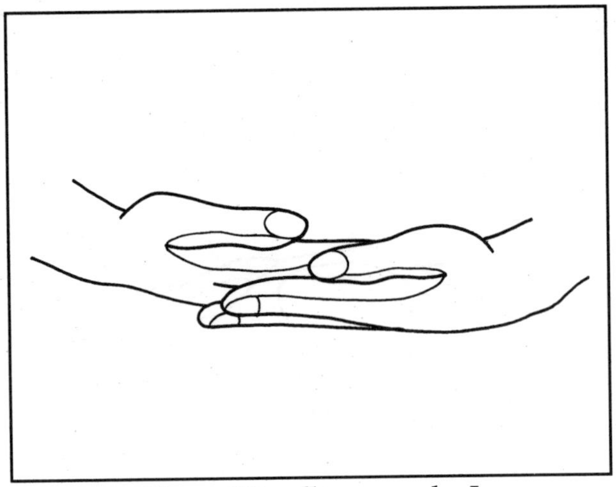

Figure 149 -- dhyana mudra I
(as seen by another)

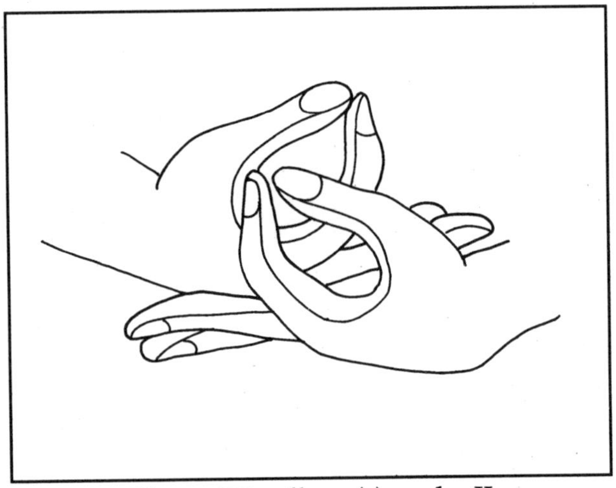

Figure 150 -- dhyan(a) mudra II
(as seen by another)

bsam-gtan phyag-rgya) A *mudra*, a ritual hand pose, a seal, which is common to both the Buddhist and Hindu traditions. It denotes a state of meditation or concentration and is held by a variety of figures: deities, *bodhisattvas, arhats, bhaktas*, etc. It is one of forty Thai Buddhist *mudras* and *asanas* compiled by the Prince Patriarch Paramanujita Jinorasa and established during the reign of Rama III as being acceptable for the depiction of images of The Lord Buddha--i.e., "meditating" the sixth of the forty attitudes noted.[12] The *dhyana mudra I* is a combined (Ind.: *saṁyutta*) form, held by both hands. This *mudra* is formed by: the hands (both the right and left) are relaxed, palms upward, the right hand rests in the left hand. The hands thusly formed rest in the lap or on the folded legs. Although the term *dhyana mudra* applies to both hands, it may also apply to a single hand which is resting, palm upwards in the lap, generally the left. (AKG 20, BBh 192, BCO 218, ERJ, ERJ II 23, MJS 40, MMR 391, RSG 3) (See: **Figure 149**)

dhyan(a) mudra II -- (Ind.: *dhyān[a]-mudrā*) A *mudra*, a ritual hand pose, a seal, a *mudra* which is common to yogic tradition, particularly the *Yoga Tatva Mudra Vigyan* form, and is held by a devotee or practitioner. The *dhyan(a) mudra* is a combined (Ind.: *saṁyutta*) form, held by both hands. It is utilized for peace and tranquility. This *mudra* is identical for both hands and is formed by: palms upwards, tips of the thumbs and index finger touch, middle, ring and little fingers are relaxed and point towards the midline. The individual hands resemble the *vitarka mudra*. Thus formed the left hand rests in the lap, palm upwards and the right hand rests in the left hand, palm also upwards. (KDe 35) (See: **Figure 150**)

dhyanahasta mudra -- (Ind.: *dhyānahasta-mudrā* aka *dhyāna mudrā, samādhi mudrā, yoga mudrā*; Chin.: *ting-yin* [*mudra*]; Jap.: *jo-in* [*mudra*]; Thai: *pang phra-nang*; Tib.: *bsam-gtan phyag-rgya*) A variant Indic term which is applied to *dhyana mudra*. See: *dhyana mudra*. (MJS 40)

dhyana-nidratahasta mudra -- (Ind.: *dhyāna-nidrātahasta-mudrā*; Eng.: receiving the offering of water mudra; Thai: **pang ODD #20**) This is a descriptive term.[13] See: **pang ODD #20**. (DRN 36, JBo 205, ODD 678, OFr 23, PSS)

diamond fist (mudra) -- (Eng.; Ind.: *vajra-mudrā;* Jap.: *kongo ken-in* [*mudra*]) The English term applied to *kongo ken-in* (*mudra*) *I.* See: *kongo ken-in* (*mudra*) *I.* (EDS 39)

Dilipa mudra -- (Ind.: *Dilīpa-mudrā*) A hand pose, a seal, a dramatic (Ind.: *nāṭya*) *mudra* or gesture (Ind.: *darpaṇa*) held or formed by a performer, dancer or actor. The *Dilipa mudra* is a single (Ind.: *asaṁyutta*) form, held by one hand. It denotes *Dilipa*, one of a number of famous rulers or heroes. The *mudra* employed is identical in form to the *pataka mudra.* See: *pataka mudra.* (ACG 47)

dipa mudra -- (Ind.: *dīpa-mudrā;* Jap.: *to myo-in* [*mudra*]) The Indic term for *to myo-in* (*mudra*). See: *to myo-in* (*mudra*). (GDe 47)

discoursing on the decrepitude of old age mudra -- (Eng.; Ind.: *nidrātahasta-nidrātahasta mudrā;* Thai: *pang song-picharanacharatham*) The English descriptive phrase for the Thai: *pang song-picharanacharatham.* See: *pang song-picharanacharatham.* (DRN 37, JBo, PSS, ODD 680)

dola(hasta) mudra -- (Ind.: *ḍola*[*hasta*]*-mudrā* aka *gaja*[*hasta*] *mudrā*) A variant term applied to *gaja*[*hasta*] *mudra.* See: *gaja*[*hasta*] *mudra.* (MJS 41)

dola mudra -- (Ind.: *ḍola-mudrā*) ("the swing") A hand pose, a seal, a dramatic (Ind.: *nāṭya*) *mudra* or gesture (Ind.: *darpaṇa*) held or formed by a performer, dancer or actor. The *dola mudra* is a combined (Ind.: *saṁyutta*) form, held by both hands. This *mudra* is formed by: palms face midline, fingers and thumbs extended downwards. Thus formed the hands are held at the side or against the thighs. It is similar to the *katyavalambita mudra*, but held with two hands. (ACG 40) (See: **Figure 151**)

dvi-mukham mudra -- (Ind.: *dvi-mukham-mudrā*) ("two heads") A *mudra*, a ritual hand pose, a seal, a *mudra* which is common to yogic tradition, particularly the *Yoga Tatva Mudra Vigyan* form, and is held by a devotee or practitioner. The *dvi-mukham mudra* is a combined (Ind.: *saṁyutta*) form, held by both hands. It is one of the twenty-four *mudras* held before the *Gayatri*

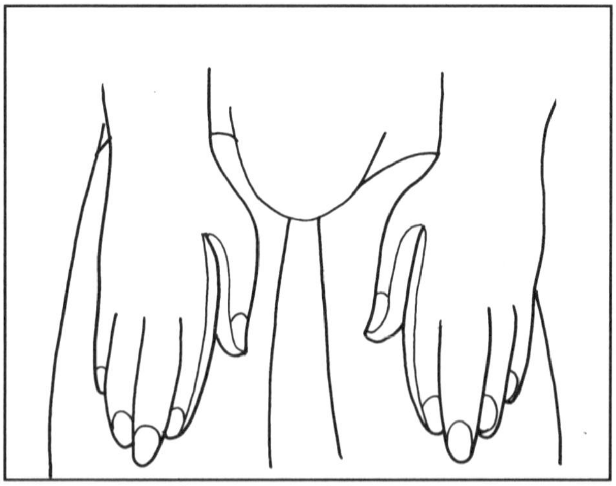

Figure 151 -- dola mudra
(as seen by another)

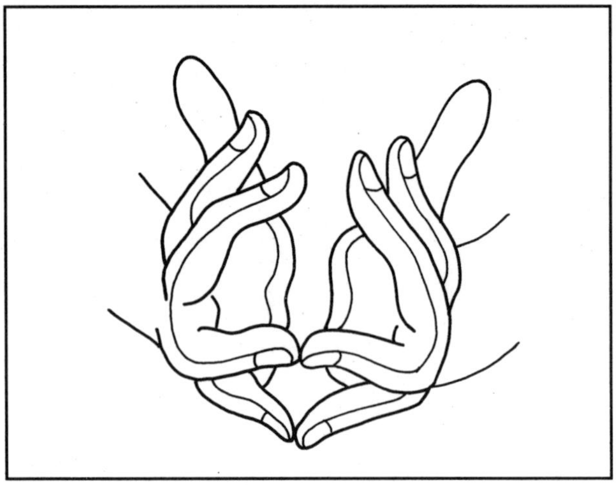

Figure 152 -- dvi-mukham mudra
(as seen by another)

Jap of the thirty-two total *Gayatri mudras*.[14] It is utilized for all sickness, especially cancer. This *mudra* is formed by: palms facing midline, fingers splayed and oriented forward, parallel to the ground, tips of ring and little fingers touch, thumb extends upwards. Thus formed, the *mudra* is held waist high. (KDe 81, RLM 70) (See: **Figure 152**)

dvirada mudra -- (Ind.: *dvirada-mudrā*) A hand pose, a seal, a dramatic (Ind.: *nāṭya*) *mudra* or gesture (Ind.: *darpaṇa*) held or formed by a performer, dancer or actor noted in ACG but without description. (ACG 44)

-- E --

eating the myrobalan fruit mudra -- (Eng.; Ind.: *añcita-dhyāna mudrā;* Thai: *pang chan-samor*) The English descriptive term.[1] for the Thai: *pang chan-samor*. See: *pang chan-samor*. (DRN 36, OFr 13, JBo 204, PSS)

eating the rice gruel mudra -- (Eng.; Ind.: *varada-dhyāna mudra;* Thai: ***pang ODD #6***) The English descriptive term.[2] for the Thai: ***pang ODD #6***. See: ***pang ODD #6***. (DRN 37, JBo 205, ODD 680, PSS)

elephant glance mudra -- (Eng.: aka *looking back at the city of Vaisali;*[3] Ind.: *jnana-lolahasta mudra;* Thai: *pang nakawalok*) The English descriptive phrase for the Thai: *pang nakawalok*. See: *pang nakawalok*. (DRN 36, JBo 205, ODD 680, OFr 35, PSS)

expounding the constituent elements mudra -- (Eng.; Ind.: *nidrātahasta-vitarka mudrā;* Thai: ***pang ODD #53***) The English descriptive term.[4] for the Thai ***pang ODD #53*** . See: ***pang ODD #53***. (PSS, DRN 37, JBo, ODD 680)

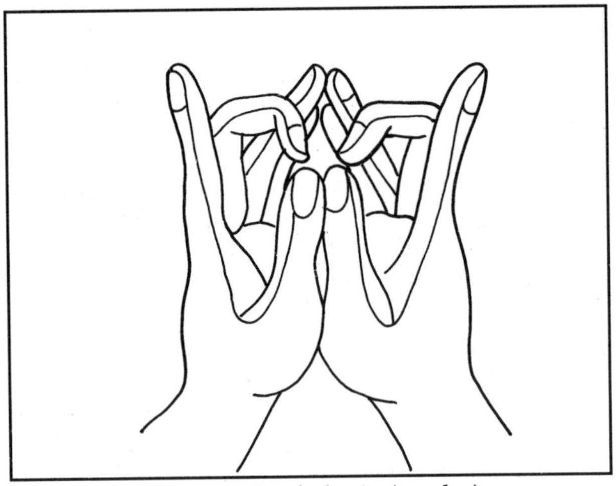

Figure 153 -- fu ko-in (mudra)
(as seen by the holder)

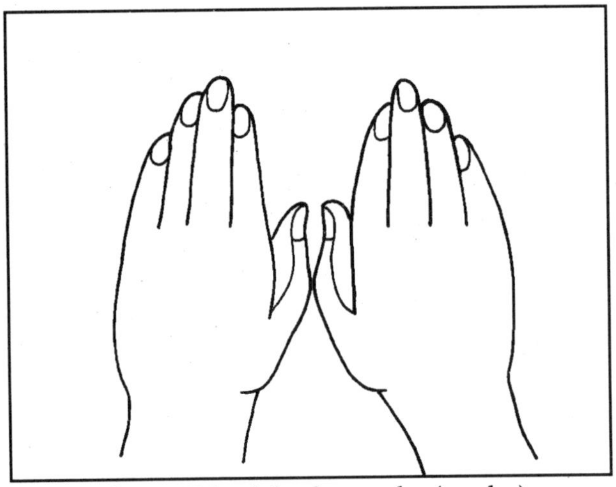

Figure 154 -- fukushu gassho (mudra)
(as seen by the holder)

-- F --

fo-puo-yin (mudra) -- (Chin.: *fo-puo-yin* [*mudrā*]; Ind.: *buddhapātra mudrā*; Jap.: *buppatsu-in* [*mudra*]) The Chinese term for *buppatsu-in* (*mudra*). See: *buppatsu-in* (*mudra*). (EDS 113)

fu ko-in (mudra) -- (Jap.: *fu kō-in* [*mudrā*]) ("the eternal light") A *mudra*, a ritual hand pose, a seal, a *tantric mudra* which is common to the Japanese Buddhist (*Vajrayana, Mantrayana*) tradition and is held or formed by a devotee or priest during the rites of *Garbhadhatu Mandala*. It may be accompanied by a *mantra*. The *fu ko-in* (*mudra*)[1] is a combined (Ind.: *saṁyutta*) form, held by both hands. It denotes the light that is never extinguished. This *mudra* is formed by: the palms facing the midline and close, the thumbs folded into the palms, the index fingers extended and straight, the middle fingers curled at the first two knuckles, the tips of the ring and little fingers touch. (GDe 27) (See: **Figure 153**)

fukushu gassho (mudra) -- (Jap.: *fukushu gasshō* [*mudrā*]) A *mudra*, a ritual hand pose, a seal, which is common to the Japanese Buddhist tradition. Specifically one of the twelve, elemental "hand clasps" (Jap. *junigosho* or *junigassho*). The *fukushu gassho* (*mudra*) is a combined (Ind.: *saṁyutta*) form, held by both hands. This *mudra* is formed by: the palms face downward, the fingers are slightly splayed and point forward. Thus held the thumbs of the two hands touch along their length. This *mudra* represents the "clasp of the covering hands."[2] (EDS 40) (See: **Figure 154**)

fu ku-yo-in (mudra) -- (Jap.: *fu ku-yō-in* [*mudrā*]) ("the universal offering") A *mudra*, a ritual hand pose, a seal, a *tantric mudra* which is common to the Japanese Buddhist (*Vajrayana, Mantrayana*) tradition and is held or formed by a devotee or priest during the rites of *Vajradhatu Mandala, Homa Rites* and other rites. It may be accompanied by a *mantra*. The *fu ku-yo-in*[3] (*mudra*) is a combined (Ind.: *saṁyutta*) form, held by both hands. This *mudra* is formed by: palms facing the midline, thumbs together, middle, ring and little fingers interlace at their tips, index fingers are erect, flexing at their first and second joints and tips touching. (GDe 80) (See: **Figure 155**)

funnu ken-in (mudra) -- (Jap.: *funnu ken-in* [*mudrā*]; Ind.: *krodha mudrā*) ("anger fist") A *mudra*, a ritual hand pose, a seal, a *tantric mudra* which is common to the Japanese Buddhist (*Vajrayana, Mantrayana*) tradition and is held or formed by a devotee or priest during the rites of *Garbhadhatu Mandala, Vajradhatu Mandala, Homa Rites* and other rites. It may be accompanied by a *mantra*. The *funnu ken-in* (*mudra*) is a single (Ind.: *asaṁyutta*) form, held by one hand. It denotes anger. This *mudra* is formed by: palm facing forward, thumb folded into the palm, middle and ring fingers folded over the thumb, index and little fingers extend straight upwards. (EDS 39) (See: **Figure 156**)

fu tsu ku yo-in (mudra) -- (Ind.: *fu tsu ku yō-in* [*mudrā*]) ("fill with decorations") A *mudra*, a ritual hand pose, a seal, a *tantric mudra* which is common to the Japanese Buddhist (*Vajrayana, Mantrayana*) tradition and is held or formed by a devotee or priest during the rites of *Garbhadhatu Mandala, Vajradhatu Mandala, Homa Rites* and other rites. It may be accompanied by a *mantra*. The *fu tsu ku yo-in*[4] (*mudra*) is a combined (Ind.: *saṁyutta*) form, held by both hands. It denotes the universal offering. This *mudra* is formed by: palms facing the midline and close, thumbs extended upward and touching along their length, index fingers arched and touch at their tips, middle fingers folded and interlaced on the outside, ring and little fingers touch at their tips. (GDe 35) (See: **Figure 157**)

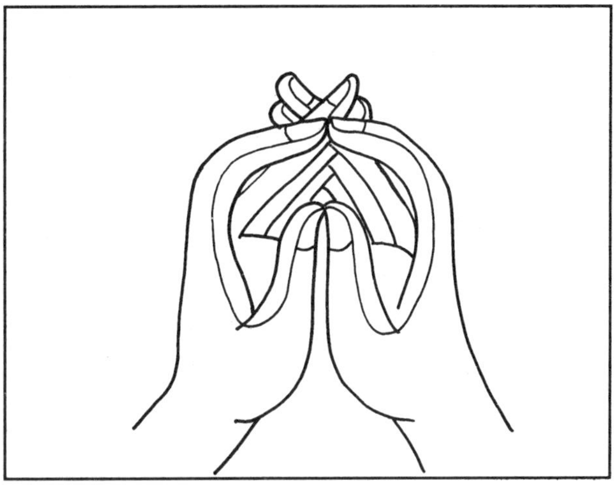

Figure 155 -- fu ku-yo-in (mudra)
(as seen by the holder)

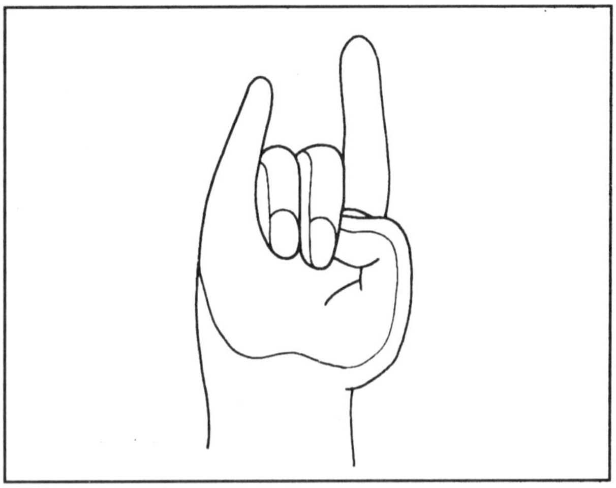

Figure 156 -- funnu ken-in (mudra)
(as seen by another)

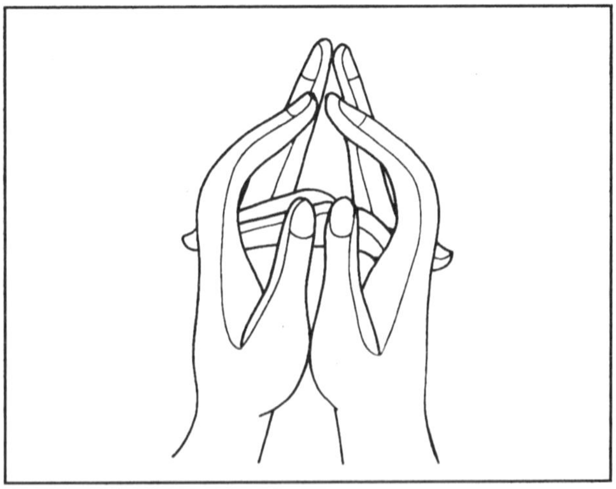

Figure 157 -- fu tsu ku yo-in (mudra)
(as seen by the holder)

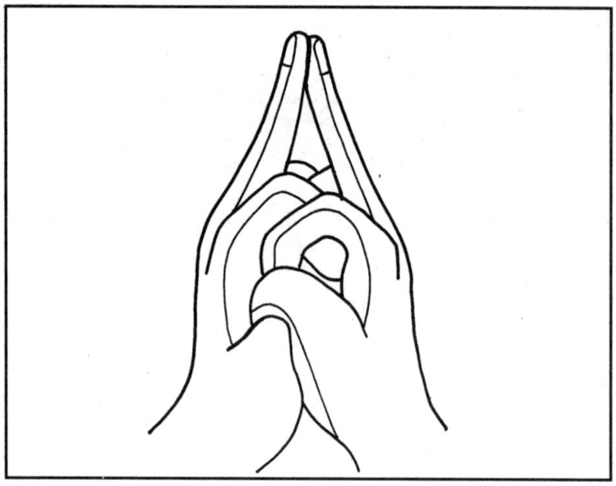

Figure 158 -- gada mudra
(as seen by the holder)

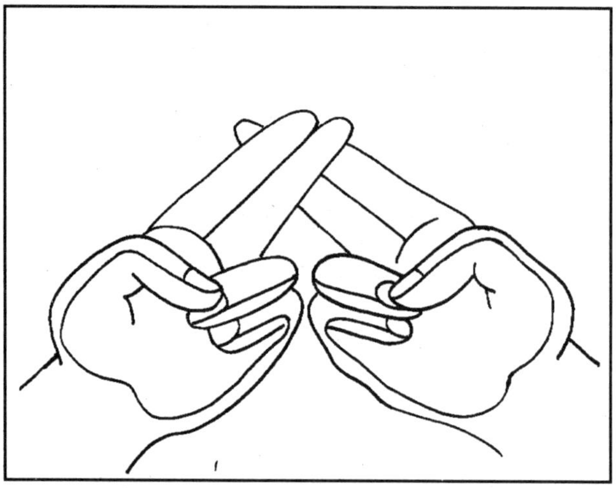

Figure 159 -- Gaganaganja mudra I
(as seen by the holder)

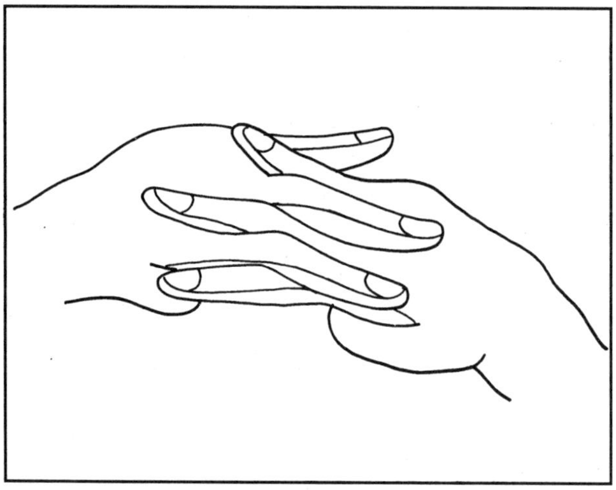

Figure 160 -- Gaganaganja mudra II
(as seen by the holder)

-- G --

gada mudra -- (Ind.: *gadā-mudrā*) A *mudra*, a ritual hand pose, a seal, which is common to the Hindu Tantric tradition. It denotes the mace and power. The *gada mudra* is a combined (Ind.: *saṁyutta*) form, held by both hands. This *mudra* is formed by: the fingers and thumbs of both hands are interlaced inwards, towards the palms, except the middle fingers which extend upwards, touching at their tips. (AMK 141) (See: **Figure 158**)

Gaganaganja mudra I -- (Jap.: *Gaganagañja-mudrā*) A *mudra*, a ritual hand pose, a seal, a *tantric mudra* which is common to the Japanese Buddhist (*Vajrayana, Mantrayana*) tradition and is held or formed by a devotee or priest during various rites. It may be accompanied by a *mantra*. The *Gaganaganja mudra* is a combined (Ind.: *saṁyutta*) form, held by both hands. It denotes the *bodhisattva Gaganaganja*. This *mudra* is formed by: palms facing backward, ring and little fingers folded into the palms, thumbs folded over the two fingers, index and middle fingers extend and together. Thus formed the extended index and middle fingers are crossed at their tips, right fingers over left. (GDe 198) (See: **Figure 159**)

Gaganaganja mudra II -- (Ind.: *Gaganagañja-mudrā*) A *mudra*, a ritual hand pose, a seal, a *tantric mudra* which is common to the Japanese Buddhist (*Vajrayana, Mantrayana*) tradition and is held or formed by a devotee or priest during various rites. It may be accompanied by a *mantra*. The *Gaganaganja mudra* is a combined (Ind.: *saṁyutta*) form, held by both hands. It denotes the *bodhisattva Gaganaganja*. This *mudra* is formed by: palms facing downward, little fingers and thumbs folded into the palm,[1] index, middle and ring fingers are straight and interlaced on top. (GDe 199) (See: **Figure 160**)

gaja mudra -- (Ind.: *gaja-mudrā* aka *gaja[hasta] mudrā*) A variant term applied to *gaja(hasta) mudra*. See: *gaja(hasta) mudra*. (BNS, JDo)

gaja(hasta) mudra -- (Ind.: *gaja[hasta]-mudrā* aka *ḍola[hasta] mudrā, gaja mudrā*) A *mudra*, a ritual hand pose, a seal, which is common to the Hindu tradition. It denotes the trunk of an elephant and power. It is a pose that is frequently found in dancing figures, particularly *Shiva-Nataraja* and other *Nrittamurtis* forms. However, this *mudra* is viewed by some as a purely aesthetic pose--i.e., without iconic import or meaning.[2] The *gaja(hasta) mudra* is a single (Ind.: *asaṁyutta*) form, held by one hand. This *mudra* is formed by: left arm crosses the front of the body, there is a slight bend at the elbow and wrist, the hand is relaxed, palm downward, and the pose assumes a graceful movement.[3] The *gaja(hasta) mudra* is at times equated with the *danda mudra*.[4] (HKS 271, MJS 44, RSG 3) (See: **Figure 161**)

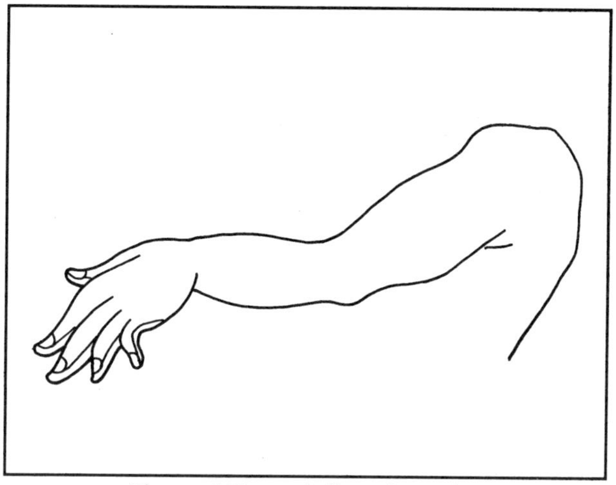

Figure 161 -- gaja(hasta) mudra
(as seen by another)

gajadanta mudra -- (Ind.: *gajadanta-mudrā*) ("the elephant's tusk") A hand pose, a seal, a dramatic (Ind.: *natya*) *mudra* or gesture (Ind.: *darpaṇa*) held or formed by a performer, dancer or actor. The *gajadanta mudra* is a combined (Ind.: *saṁyutta*) form, held by both hands. It denotes grasping a pillar, lifting anything heavy, etc.[5] This *mudra* is formed by: the palms facing forwards, the thumbs are against the index fingers' base, the index, middle, ring and little fingers curl, half-way towards the palms. Thus formed the forearms are crossed close to the elbows. (ACG 42) (See: **Figure 162**)

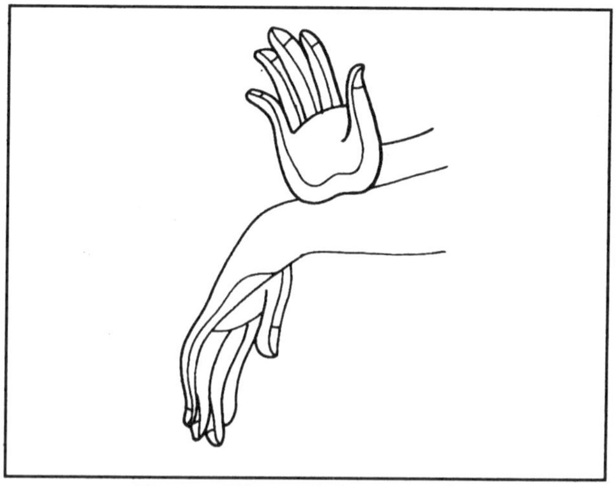

Figure 162 -- gajadanta mudra
(as seen by another)

gandha mudra I -- (Ind.: *gandha-mudrā*, aka *gandhe*) This is an assigned term.[6] A *mudra*, a ritual hand pose, a seal, which is common to the Buddhist (*Vajrayana*) tradition, a *tantric mudra*. It denotes perfume, which is one of the five 'gifts' or 'outer offerings' proffered to a divine guest--the other four being: flowers, incense, lamps and food--during the early stages worship, particularly as associated with the worship of the powerful *Vajrayana* goddess, *Tara*. The *gandha mudra I* is a combined (Ind.: *saṁyutta*) form, held by both hands. This *mudra* is formed by hands in mirror-pose: the hand, palm facing downwards, is fisted, thusly formed both are brought close together, but not touching. This *mudra* he held in front of the body, below the chin. The *mantra* associated with this mudra is: "*OM Guru-sarva-Tathagata Gandhe puja-megha-samudra-spharana-samaye HUM*."[7] (SBe 147) (See: **Figure 163**)

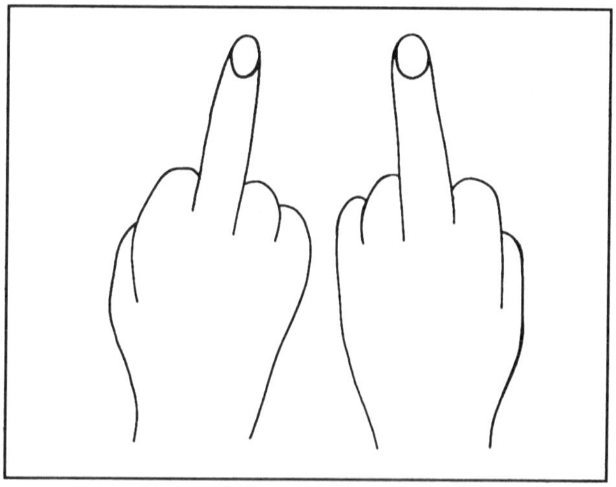

Figure 163 -- gandha mudra I
(as seen by another)

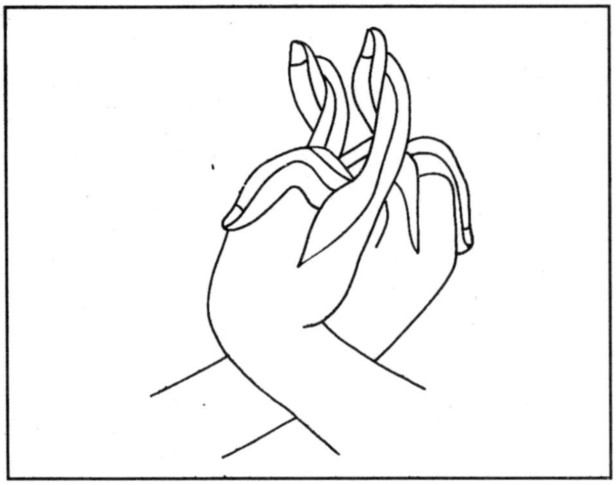

Figure 164 -- gandha mudra II
(as seen by the holder)

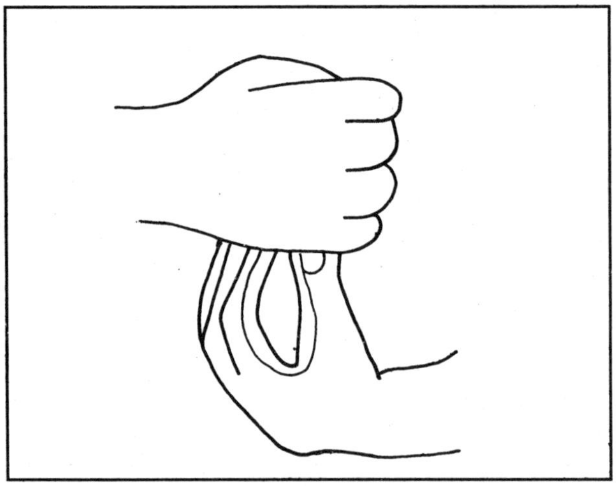

Figure 165 -- gandharan temborin-in (mudra)
(as seen by another)

gandha mudra II -- (Ind.: *gandha-mudrā*) A *mudra*, a ritual hand pose, a seal, a *tantric mudra* which is common to the Japanese Buddhist (*Vajrayana, Mantrayana*) tradition and is held or formed by a devotee or priest during various rites. It may be accompanied by a *mantra*. The *gandha mudra* is a combined (Ind.: *saṁyutta*) form, held by both hands. It denotes "smell." This *mudra* is formed by: right palm faces left, left palm faces right, thumbs folded into the palms, middle and ring fingers folded over the thumbs, index and little fingers extend and curl. Thus formed, the back of the right hand is crossed over rests against the back of the left hand, and the index and little fingers "hook." (GDe 451) (See: **Figure 164**)

gandha mudra III -- (Ind.: *gandha-mudrā*; Jap.: *zu ko-in* [*mudra*]) The Indic term for *zu ko-in* (*mudra*). See: *zu ko-in* (*mudra*). (GDe 46)

gandharan temborin-in (mudra) -- (Jap.: *gandhāran tembōrin-in* [*mudra*] aka *temborin-in*) A *mudra*, a ritual hand pose, a seal, which is common to the Japanese Buddhist tradition. It is related to the *temborin-in*[8] (*mudra*) (Ind.: *dharmacakra mudrā*) being a variation of the same. The *gandharan temborin-in* (*mudra*) is a combined (Ind.: *saṁyutta*) form, held by both hands. This *mudra* is formed by: the right hand is loosely fisted, palm facing the midline; the palm of the left hand faces upwards, the tips of the thumb and index finger touch and the other fingers curl towards the palm, and the tips of the thumb and the index finger are inserted into the bottom of the loosely fisted right hand. The *mudra* is held at waist level. (EDS 94) (See: **Figure 165**)

gandhararattha mudra -- (Ind.: *gandhāraraṭṭha-mudrā* aka *añcita-ahāyavarada mudrā*; Thai: *pang khor-phon*) A *mudra*, a ritual hand pose, a seal, which is common to the Thai Buddhist tradition. One of forty *mudras* and *asanas* compiled by the Prince Patriarch Paramanujita Jinorasa and established during the reign of Rama III as being acceptable for the depiction of images of The Lord *Buddha*--i.e., "*gandhararattha mudra*" or "calling down the rain" the twenty-seventh of the forty attitudes noted.[9] The *gandhararattha mudra* is a combined (Ind.: *saṁyutta*) form, held by both hands. This *mudra* is formed by: the right palm upwards, fingers cupped somewhat, the thumb slightly bent towards the fingertips, fingers oriented outward resting on the corresponding thigh or knee; the left is similar to the *abhaya mudra* in that the fingers and thumb are extended upwards and together, relaxed, slightly cupped, palm facing forward and downward at approximately 45°, away from the body and generally at the level of the chest. (DRN 37, JBo, MSD, ODD 680, SVB) (See: **Figure 166**)

gandharva-raja mudra -- (Ind.: *gandharva-rāja-mudrā*) A *mudra*, a ritual hand pose, a seal, a *tantric mudra* which is common to the Japanese Buddhist (*Vajrayana, Mantrayana*) tradition and is held or formed by a devotee or priest during various rites. It may be accompanied by a *mantra*. The *gandharva mudra* is a combined (Ind.: *saṁyutta*) form, held by both hands. This *mudra* is formed by: palms face each other, index, middle and ring fingers and thumbs are interlaced with fingers and thumbs inside (palm-side), little fingers extend upwards, but do not touch. (GDe 324, LCS 176) (See: **Figure 167**)

Ganga mudra -- (Ind.: *gaṅgā-mudrā* aka *tāmracūḍa mudrā*) A hand pose, a seal, a dramatic (Ind.: *nāṭya*) *mudra* or gesture (Ind.: *darpaṇa*) held or formed by a performer, dancer or actor. It denotes the river Ganges, one of the famous rivers of India. The *mudra* employed is identical in form to the *tamrachuda mudra*. See: *tamrachuda mudra*. (ACG 48)

gardabha mudra -- (Ind.: *gardabha-mudrā*) A hand pose, a seal, a dramatic (Ind.: *nāṭya*) *mudra* or gesture (Ind.: *darpaṇa*) held or formed by a performer, dancer or actor. It denotes an animal, in this case a mule. The *gardabha mudra*[10] is a combined (Ind.: *saṁyutta*) form, held by both hands. This *mudra* is formed by: palm facing forwards, the thumb is against the index finger's base which extends upwards, the middle, ring and little fingers curl, half-way towards the palm. Thus formed, the hands are crossed at the wrist. It is similar to the *naga-bandha mudra*. (ACG 49) (See: **Figure 168**)

garuda mudra -- (Ind.: *garuḍa-mudrā*) ("the *garuda*") A *mudra*, a ritual hand pose, a seal, a *tantric mudra* which is common to the Japanese Buddhist (*Vajrayana*,

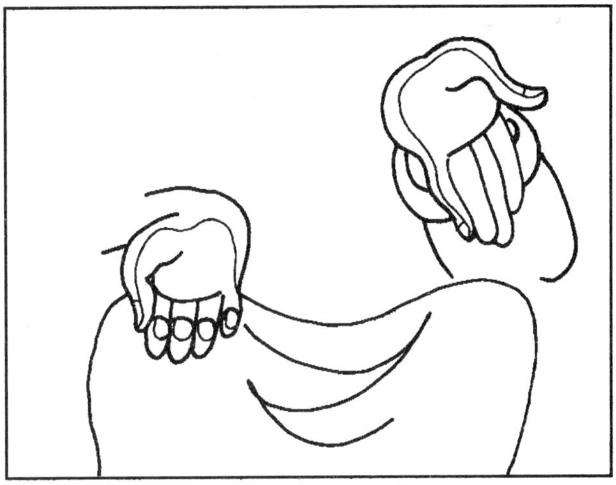

Figure 166-- gandhararattha mudra
(as seen by another)

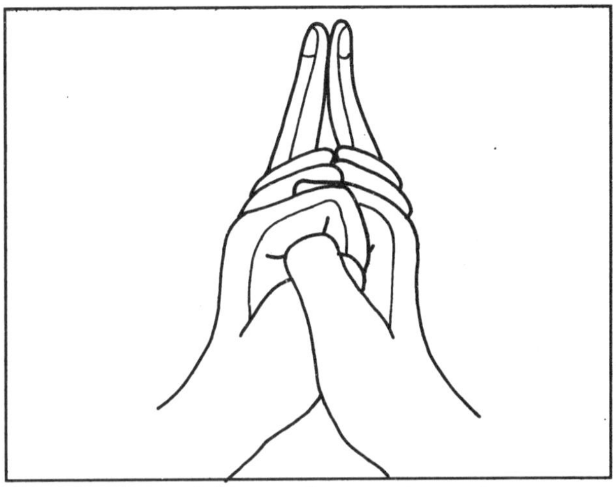

Figure 167-- gandharva-raja mudra
(as seen by the holder)

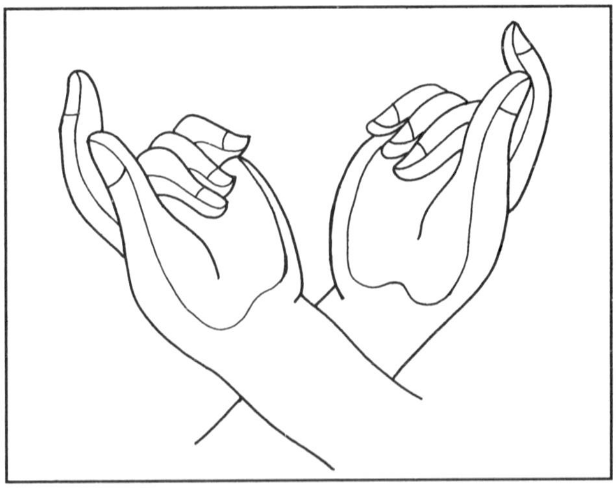

Figure 168-- gardabha mudra
(as seen by another)

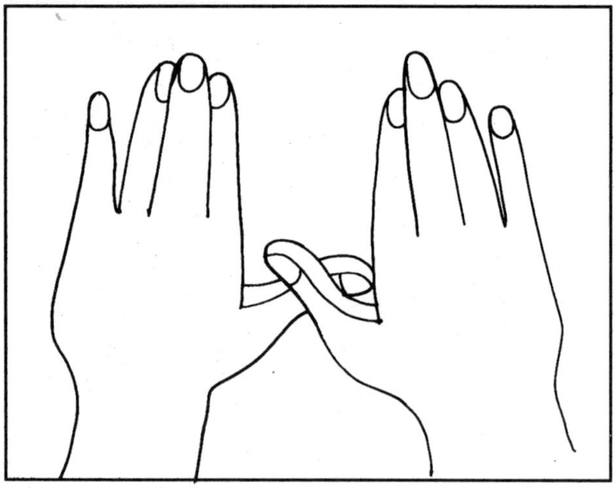

Figure 169 -- garuda mudra
(as seen by the holder)

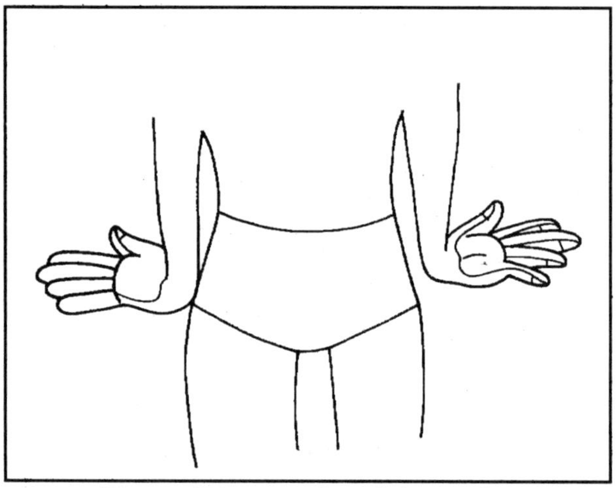

Figure 170 -- garuda-paksha mudra
(as seen by another)

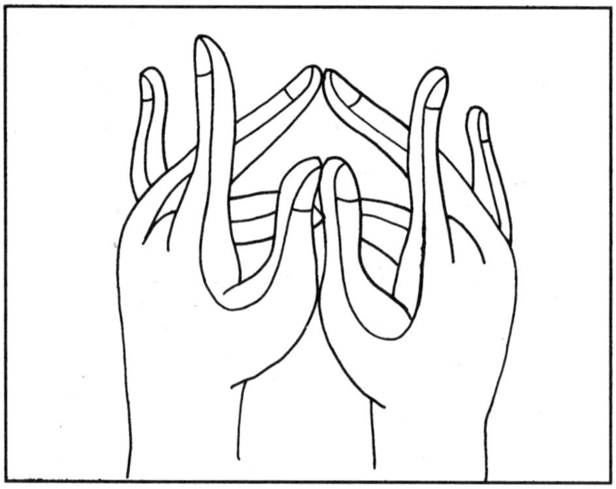

Figure 171 -- gebaku goko (gassho) mudra
(as seen by the holder)

Mantrayana) tradition and is held or formed by a devotee or priest during the rites of *Garbhadhatu Mandala, Vajradhatu Mandala, Homa Rites* and other rites. It may be accompanied by a *mantra*. Also, a dramatic (Ind.: *nāṭya*) *mudra* or gesture (Ind.: *darpaṇa*) held or formed by a performer, dancer or actor. The *garuda mudra* is a combined (Ind.: *saṁyutta*) form, held by both hands. It denotes the *garuda*, the *vahana* of the Lord *Vishnu*. This *mudra* is formed by: palms facing outward, fingers are slightly splayed, thumbs cross, right "hooks" over left. (ACG 41, GDe 181, LCS 100) (See: **Figure 169**)

garuda-paksha mudra -- (Ind.: *garuḍa-pakṣa-mudrā*) ("*Garuda's* wing") A hand pose, a seal, a dramatic (Ind.: *nāṭya*) *mudra* or gesture (Ind.: *darpaṇa*) held or formed by a performer, dancer or actor. The *garuda-paksha mudra* is a combined (Ind.: *saṁyutta*) form, held by both hands. It denotes superiority. This *mudra* is formed by: palms face upwards, fingers extended, together and pointing outwards, the thumbs extends away from the fingers. Thus formed the bent wrists are held against the hips, elbows bent. (ACG 43) (See: **Figure 170**)

gazing at the bodhi tree mudra -- (Eng.: Thai: *pang tavainetr*; Ind.: *hastasvastika mudrā*) The English descriptive phrase for the Thai *pang tavainetr*. The *mudra* (Thai: *pang*) is related to the *hastasvastika mudra*. See: *pang tavainetr*; see also: *hastasvastika mudra II*. (DRN 35, JBo, PSS)

ge baku goko (gassho) mudra -- (Jap.: *ge baku gokō* [*gasshō*] *mudrā*) ("five-pronged *vajra*") A *mudra*, a ritual hand pose, a seal, a *tantric mudra* which is common to the Japanese Buddhist (*Vajrayana, Mantrayana*) tradition and is held or formed by a devotee or priest during the rites of *Garbhadhatu Mandala, Vajradhatu Mandala, Homa Rites* and others. It may be accompanied by a *mantra*. The *ge baku goko* (*gassho*) *mudra* is a combined (Ind.: *saṁyutta*) form, held by both hands. It denotes a five-pronged *vajra*[11] and sanctification. This *mudra* is formed by: the palms brought together, thumbs extending upwards and together, index fingers extending upwards and separated, middle fingers touching at their tips, ring fingers folded on top and little fingers touching along their length. Thus formed the *mudra* is generally held at chest level. (GDe 16, LCS

169) (See: **Figure 171**)

gebaku ken-in (mudra) I -- (Jap.: *gebaku ken-in* [*mudra*] aka *kengo baku-in, kongo baku-in, shizaige ken-in* (*mudra*); Chin.: *wai-fu ch'ṃan-yin;* Ind.: *granthitam mudrā*) A *mudra*, a ritual hand pose, a seal, a *tantric mudra* which is common to the Japanese and Chinese Buddhist (*Vajrayana, Mantrayana*) tradition and is held or formed by a devotee or priest. It may be accompanied by a *mantra*. It denotes the "outer bonds fist" (one of the "Six Types of Fists") and is posed during contemplation on the moon disc.[12] The form is composed of both hands: the two hands are brought together, palm to palm, the fingers and thumbs are interlaced, the left thumb over the right and so forth, the fingers resting on the back of the hand (resembling the clasped hands of one offering a prayer and synonymous with the Christian west). This *mudra* is held in front of the chest. (EDS 119, GDe 8, LCS 117) (See: **Figure 172**)

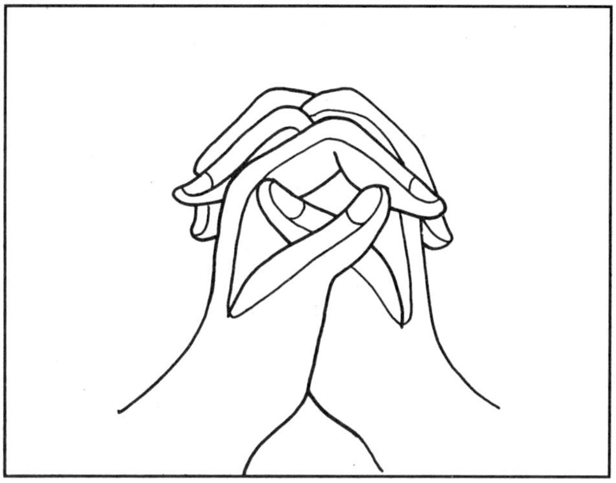

Figure 172 -- gebaku ken-in (mudra) I
(as seen by the holder)

gebaku ken-in (mudra) II -- (Jap.: *gebaku ken-in* [*mudrā*], aka *kongo baku-in* [*mudra*]; Ind.: *granthitam mudrā*) A *mudra*, a ritual hand pose, a seal, a *tantric mudra* which is common to the Japanese Buddhist (*Vajrayana, Mantrayana*) tradition and is held or formed by a devotee or priest during the rites of *Garbhadhatu Mandala, Vajradhatu Mandala, Homa Rites* and other rites. It may be accompanied by a *mantra*. The *gebaku ken-in*[13] (*mudra*) *II* is a combined (Ind.: *saṁyutta*) form, held by both hands. It denotes purity and generosity. This *mudra* is formed by: two hands are brought together, palm to palm, the fingers are interlaced and resting on the back of the hand, the thumbs are crossed. (GDe 61, LCS 121) (See: **Figure 173**)

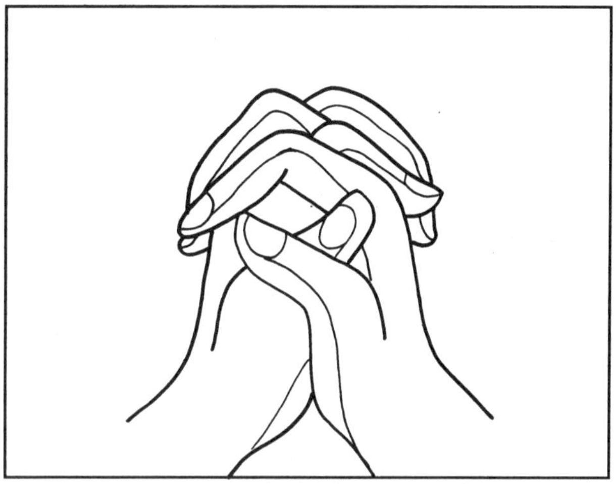

Figure 173 -- gebaku ken-in (mudra) II
(as seen by the holder)

gebaku ken-in (mudra) III -- (Jap.: *gebaku ken-in* [*mudrā*]; Ind.: *granthitaṁ mudrā*) A variant *mudra*, which is common to the Japanese Buddhist (*Vajrayana, Mantrayana*) tradition and is held or formed by a devotee or priest during the rites of *Garbhadhatu Mandala, Vajradhatu Mandala, Homa Rites* and other rites. It may be accompanied by a *mantra*. The *gebaku ken-in* (*mudra*) *III* is a combined (Ind.: *saṁyutta*) form, held by both hands. It denotes the summoning of the knowledge of *Buddha*. This *mudra* is formed by: the two hands are brought together, palm to palm, the fingers are inter-

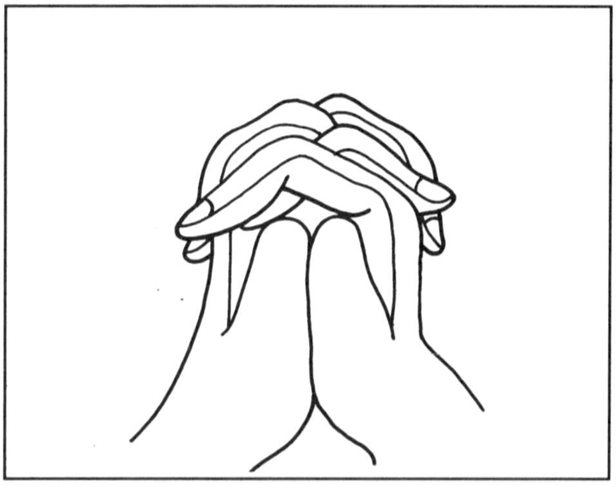

Figure 174 -- gebaku ken-in (mudra) III
(as seen by the holder)

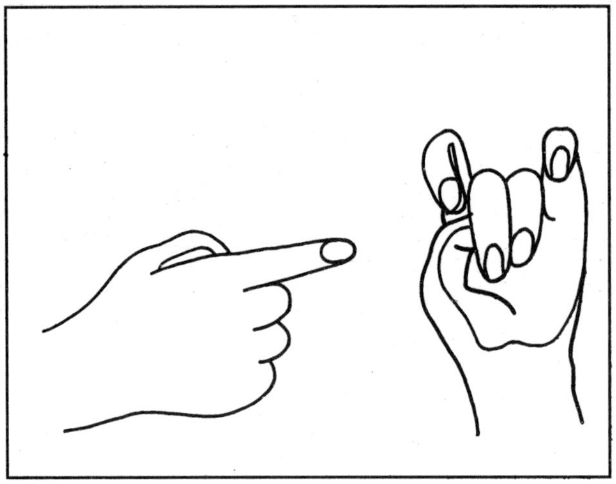

Figure 175 -- ge-in (mudra) I
(as seen by another)

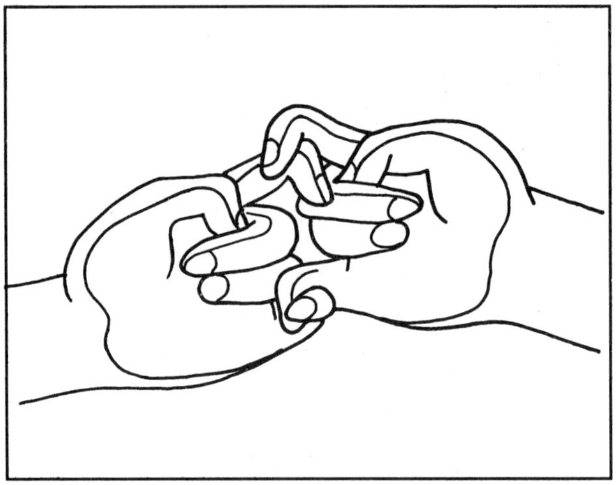

Figure 176 -- ge-in (mudra) II
(as seen by the holder)

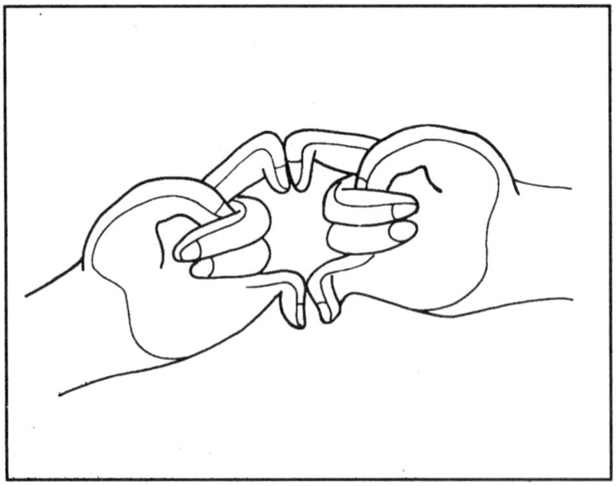

Figure 177 -- ge-in (mudra) III
(as seen by the holder)

laced, the fingers resting on the back of the hand, the thumbs are folded inside the fist. (GDe 62, LCS 118) (See: **Figure 174**)

ge-in (mudra) I -- (Jap.: *ge-in* [*mudrā*]) ("the teeth") A *mudra*, a ritual hand pose, a seal, a *tantric mudra* which is common to the Japanese Buddhist (*Vajrayana, Mantrayana*) tradition and is held or formed by a devotee or priest during the rites of *Garbhadhatu Mandala*. It may be accompanied by a *mantra*. The ge-*in* (*mudra*) is a single (Ind.: *asaṁyutta*) form, held by one hand. It denotes the destroying of enemies of religion. This *mudra* is formed by: palm generally facing forward, thumb folded into the palm, middle and ring fingers folded over the thumb, index and little fingers curl at their first two knuckles, third phalanges remains erect (upward). (GDe 46) (See: **Figure 175**)

ge-in (mudra) II -- (Jap.: *ge-in* [*mudrā*]; Ind.: *krodha mudrā, vajramuṣṭi mudrā*) A *mudra*, a ritual hand pose, a seal, a *tantric mudra* which is common to the Japanese Buddhist (*Vajrayana, Mantrayana*) tradition and is held or formed by a devotee or priest during various rites It may be accompanied by a *mantra*. The *ge-in* (*mudra*) *II*[14] is a combined (Ind.: *saṁyutta*) form, held by both hands. This *mudra* is formed by: palm faces backwards, thumb folded into the palm, middle and ring fingers fold over thumb, index and little fingers first and second phalanges curl tightly, third phalanges remains erect (upward). Thus formed the curled index and little fingers "hook" together at the first and second phalanges. (GDe 75, LCS 62) (See: **Figure 176**)

ge-in (mudra) III -- (Jap.: *ge-in* [*mudrā*]; Ind.: *krodha mudrā, vajramuṣṭi mudrā*) A *mudra*, a ritual hand pose, a seal, a *tantric mudra* which is common to the Japanese Buddhist (*Vajrayana, Mantrayana*) tradition and is held or formed by a devotee or priest during various rites It may be accompanied by a *mantra*. The *ge-in* (*mudra*) *III*[15] is a combined (Ind.: *saṁyutta*) form, held by both hands. This *mudra* is formed by: palms faces backwards, thumbs folded into the palm, middle and ring fingers fold over thumb, first and second phalanges of the index and little fingers curl tightly, third phalanges remains erect (upward). Thus formed the two hands are brought together so that the second phalanges of the index and little fingers touch. (GDe 37) (See: **Figure 177**)

ge-in (mudra) IV -- (Jap.: *ge-in* [*mudrā*]; Ind.: *krodha mudrā, vajramuṣṭi mudrā*) A *mudra*, a ritual hand pose, a seal, a *tantric mudra* which is common to the Japanese Buddhist (*Vajrayana, Mantrayana*) tradition and is held or formed by a devotee or priest during various rites It may be accompanied by a *mantra*. The *ge-in (mudra) IV*[16] is a combined (Ind.: *saṁyutta*) form, held by both hands. This *mudra* is formed by: palms faces outwards, thumbs folded into the palm, middle and ring fingers fold over thumb, first and second phalanges of the index and little fingers curl. Hands cross at the wrist. (GDe 63 & 64) (See: **Figure 178**)

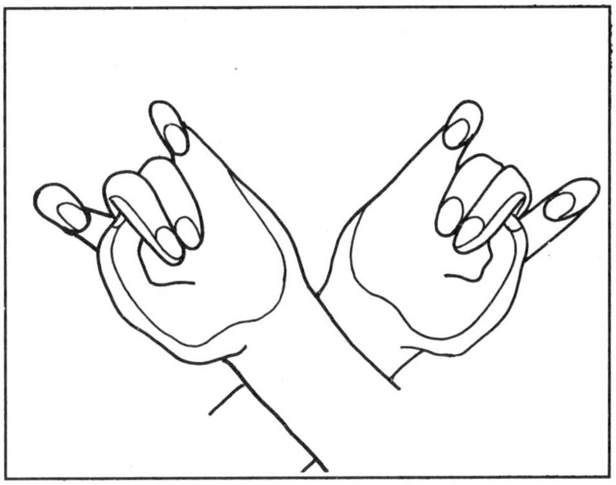

Figure 178 -- ge-in (mudra) IV
(as seen by another)

ge kai-in (mudra) -- (Jap.: *ge kai-in* [*mudrā*]) A *mudra*, a ritual hand pose, a seal, a *tantric mudra* which is common to the Japanese Buddhist (*Vajrayana, Mantrayana*) tradition and is held or formed by a devotee or priest during the rites of *Garbhadhatu Mandala, Vajradhatu Mandala, Homa Rites* and other rites. It may be accompanied by a *mantra*. The *ge kai-in* (*mudra*)[17] is a combined (Ind.: *saṁyutta*) form, held by both hands. It denotes the liberation of the world from the demons. This *mudra* is formed by: palm facing forward, thumb folded into the palm, middle and ring fingers folded over the thumb, index extends straight and little fingers curl at their first two knuckles. Thus formed, the hands are crossed at the wrists, left in front of the right and the little fingers "hook." (GDe 85) (See: **Figure 179**)

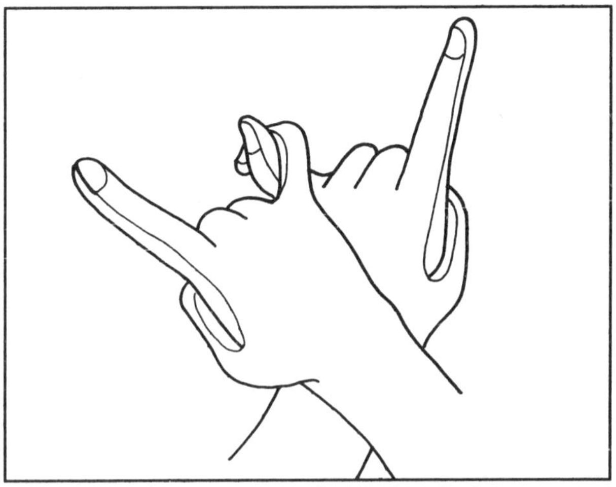

Figure 179 -- ge kai-in (mudra)
(as seen by the holder)

ghanta mudra -- (Ind.: *ghaṇṭā-mudrā*; Jap.: *rei-in* [*mudra*]) The Indic term for *rei-in* (*mudra*). See: *rei-in* (*mudra*). (GDe 41)

ghanta-vadana mudra -- (Ind.: *ghaṇṭā-vadanā-mudrā*) ("ringing the bell") A *mudra*, a ritual hand pose, a seal, a *tantric mudra* which is common to the Japanese Buddhist (*Vajrayana, Mantrayana*) tradition and is held or formed by a devotee or priest during the rites of *Garbhadhatu Mandala, Vajradhatu Mandala, Homa Rites* and other rites. It may be accompanied by a *mantra*. The *zu ko-in* (*mudra*) is a combined (Ind.: *saṁyutta*) form, held by both hands. It denotes the anointing of deities, a form of worship. This *mudra* is formed by:

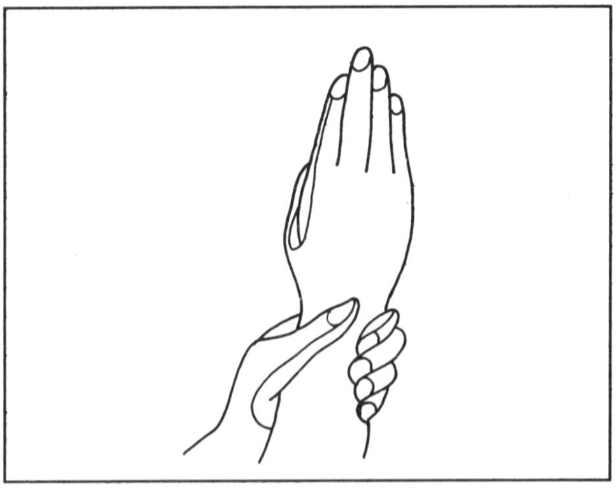

Figure 180 -- ghanta-vadana mudra
(as seen by the holder)

Figure 181 -- go buku-in (mudra)
(as seen by the holder)

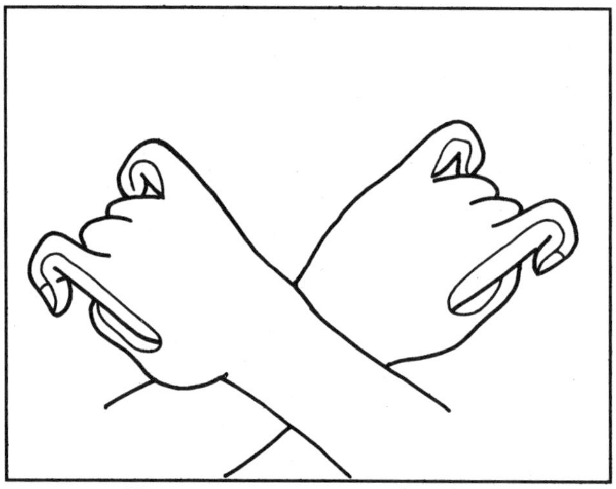

Figure 182 -- go-san-ze (mudra)
(as seen by the holder)

right palm facing forward, fingers and thumb extending upwards, left hand grasps the right forearm below the wrist, fingers curling around the arm on the outward side, thumb curled on the inward side. (LCS 66) (See: **Figure 180**)

girika mudra -- (Ind.: *girikā-mudrā*) A hand pose, a seal, a dramatic (Ind.: *nāṭya*) *mudra* or gesture (Ind.: *darpaṇa*) held or formed by a performer, dancer or actor. It denotes an animal, in this case a mole (?). The *girika mudra*[18] is a single (Ind.: *asaṁyutta*) form, held by one hand. This *mudra* is identical to the *khadga-mukula mudra*. See: *khadga-mukula mudra*. (ACG 49)

go buku-in (mudra) -- (Jap.: *gō buku-in* [*mudrā*]) A *mudra*, a ritual hand pose, a seal, a *tantric mudra* which is common to the Japanese Buddhist (*Vajrayana, Mantrayana*) tradition and is held or formed by a devotee or priest during various rites. It may be accompanied by a *mantra*. The *go buku-in* (*mudra*) is a combined (Ind.: *saṁyutta*) form, held by both hands. This *mudra* is formed by: palms facing midline, thumbs extended upwards and touching along their length, index fingers extend upwards, middle fingers are folded and interlace on top, ring fingers touch at their tips, little fingers fold inward (towards the palms). (GDe 399) (See: **Figure 181**)

godhika mudra -- (Ind.: *godhika-mudrā*) A hand pose, a seal, a dramatic (Ind.: *nāṭya*) *mudra* or gesture (Ind.: *darpaṇa*) held or formed by a performer, dancer or actor. It denotes an animal, in this case an iguana. The *godhika mudra*[19] is a single (Ind.: *asaṁyutta*) form, held by one hand. This *mudra* is identical to the *tala-pataka mudra*. See: *tala-pataka mudra*. (ACG 49)

go-san-ze (mudra) -- (Jap.: *go-san-ze* [*mudrā*]) ("vanquishing the three lives") A *mudra*, a ritual hand pose, a seal, a *tantric mudra* which is common to the Japanese Buddhist (*Vajrayana, Mantrayana*) tradition and is held or formed by a devotee or priest during the rites of *Garbhadhatu Mandala, Vajradhatu Mandala, Homa Rites* and other rites. It may be accompanied by a mantra. The *go-san-ze* (*mudra*) is a combined (Ind.: *saṁyutta*) form, held by both hands. It denotes the deity *Trailokyavijaya* (Jap.: *Gosanze*). This *mudra* is identical in both hands and is formed by: palm facing forward, thumb folded into the palm, middle and ring fingers folded over the thumb, index and little fingers curl at their first two knuckles. Thus formed, the hands are crossed at the wrists, left in front of the right. (GDe 63) (See: **Figure 182**)

granthitam mudra -- (Ind.: *granthitam-mudrā*; Chin.: *wai-fu ch'ṃan-yin*; Jap.: *gebaku ken-in* [*mudra*], *shizaige ken-in* [*mudra*]) A variant term applied to *gebaku ken-in* (*mudra*). A *mudra*, a ritual hand pose, a seal, a *mudra* which is common to yogic tradition, particularly the *Yoga Tatva Mudra Vigyan* form, and is held by a devotee or practitioner. It is one of the thirty-two *Gayatri mudras*.[20] It is utilized for all sickness, especially cancer. It is identical in form to the *gebaku ken-in* (*mudra*). (KDe 84. RLM 73)

gshegs-gsol phyag-rgya (mudra) -- (Tib.; Indic: *supratiṣṭha mudrā*) The Tibetan transliteral term for *supratishtha mudra*. See: *supratishtha mudra*. (SBe 224)

gyan mudra -- (Ind.: *gyān-mudrā* aka *jñānam mudrā*) A *mudra*, a ritual hand pose, a seal, a *mudra* which is common to yogic tradition, particularly the *Yoga Tatva Mudra Vigyan* form, and is held by a devotee or practitioner. The *gyan mudra* is a single (Ind.: *asaṁyutta*) form, held by one hand. It is utilized for increasing brain activity. It is also one of the eight *mudras* held after the *Gayatri Jap* of the thirty-two total *Gayatri mudras*.[21] This *mudra* is formed by: palm facing forward, tips of the thumb and index finger touch, middle, ring and little fingers are relaxed, slightly separated and point upwards. This *mudra* is similar to the *vitarka mudra*. (KDe 22) (See: **Figure 183**)

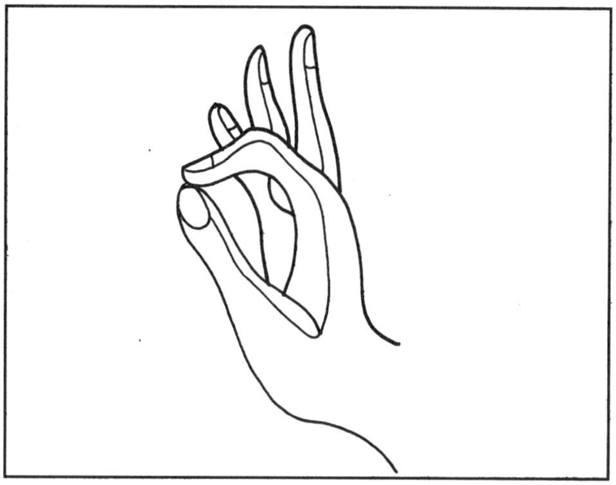

Figure 183 -- gyan mudra
(as seen by the holder)

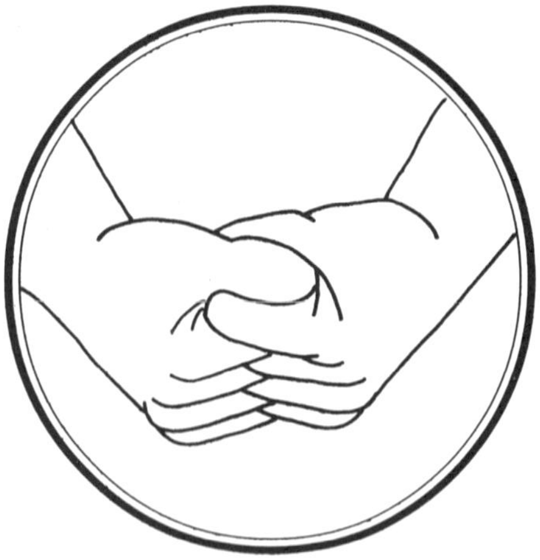

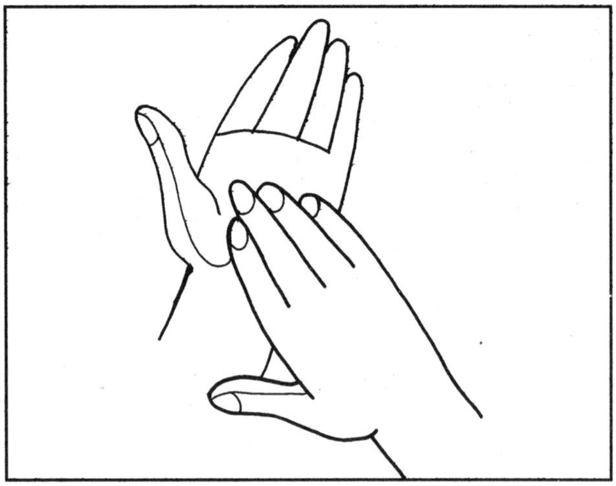

Figure 184 -- haku sho-in (mudra) I
(as seen by the holder)

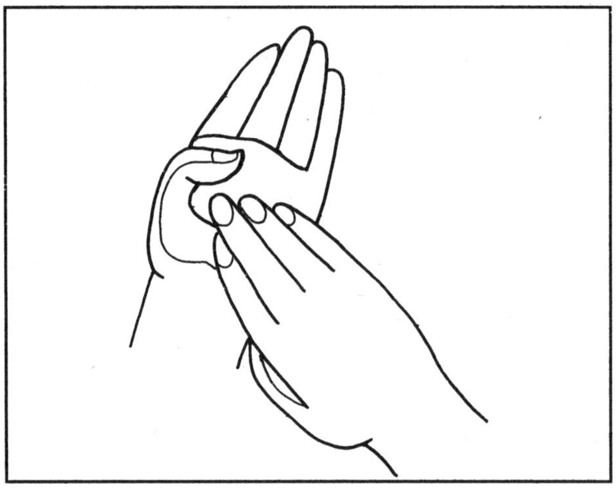

Figure 185 -- haku sho-in (mudra) II
(as seen by the holder)

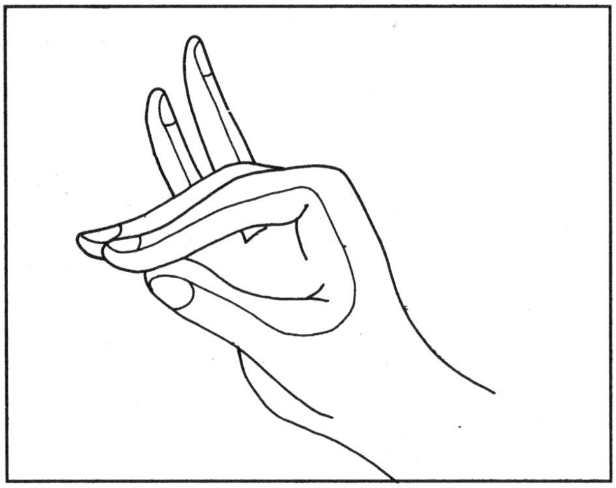

Figure 186 -- hamsa mudra
(as seen by the holder)

-- H --

hachiu-in (mudra) -- (Jap.: *hachiu-in* [*mudrā*]; Ind.: *kavaca mudrā*) The Japanese term for *kavacha mudra*. See: *kavacha mudra*. (GDe 72)

haku sho-in (mudra) I -- (Jap.: *haku shō-in* [*mudrā*]) ("clapping") A *mudra*, a ritual hand pose, a seal, a *tantric mudra* which is common to the Japanese Buddhist (*Vajrayana, Mantrayana*) tradition and is held or formed by a devotee or priest during the rites of *Garbhadhatu Mandala, Vajradhatu Mandala, Homa Rites* and other rites. It may be accompanied by a *mantra*. The *haku sho-in* (*mudra*)[1] is a combined (Ind.: *saṁyutta*) form, held by both hands. It denotes praise of attendant deities and is also used to frighten away malevolent spirits. This *mudra* is formed by: palms facing midline, fingers and thumbs extended upwards. Thus formed the two hands are shown close, but not touching. This is a *mudra* of action and the two hands are brought sharply together, clapping. (GDe 7, LCS 72) (See: **Figure 184**)

haku sho-in (mudra) II -- (Jap.: *haku shō-in* [*mudrā*]) ("clapping") A *mudra*, a ritual hand pose, a seal, a *tantric mudra* which is common to the Japanese Buddhist (*Vajrayana, Mantrayana*) tradition and is held or formed by a devotee or priest during the rites of *Garbhadhatu Mandala, Vajradhatu Mandala, Homa Rites* and other rites. It may be accompanied by a *mantra*. The *haku sho-in* (*mudra*) *II* is a combined (Ind.: *saṁyutta*) form, held by both hands. The *mudra* is identical to the *haku sho-in* (*mudra*) *I* except that the thumbs are folded into the palm. (LCS 67) (See: **Figure 185**)

hamsa mudra -- (Ind.: *haṁsa-mudrā*) ("the swan") A *mudra*, a ritual hand pose, a seal, which is common to the Hindu tradition and is depicted or held by a deity. The *hamsa mudra* is a single (Ind.: *asaṁyutta*) form, held by one hand. It denotes the ceremonial thread of marriage, the rite of initiation, and a drop of water. The *hamsa mudra* is a single (Ind.: *asaṁyutta*) form, held by one hand. This *mudra* is formed by: the palm faces forward, the first phalanges of the thumb, index and middle finger are brought together and extended, the ring and little finger arch upwards.[2] Thus formed, it is said to resemble the head of a goose (Ind.: *haṁsa*). This *mudra* may also be employed in holding a garland. It is related to the *hamsasya mudra*. (ACG 36, MJS 53) (See: **Figure 186**)

hamsa-paksha mudra I -- (Ind.: *haṁsa-pakṣa-mudrā* aka *haṁsasya mudrā*) ("the swan feather") A hand pose, a seal, a dramatic (Ind.: *nāṭya*) *mudra* or gesture (Ind.: *darpaṇa*) held or formed by a performer, dancer or actor. The *hamsa-paksha mudra* is a single (Ind.: *asaṁyutta*) form, held by one hand. It denotes restraining, gathering, etc.[3] This *mudra* is formed by: palm faces forwards, the index, middle and ring fingers curl towards the palm, the thumb rests along the curled index finger, pointing upward, the little finger is straight and pointing upwards. (ACG 36) (See: **Figure 187**)

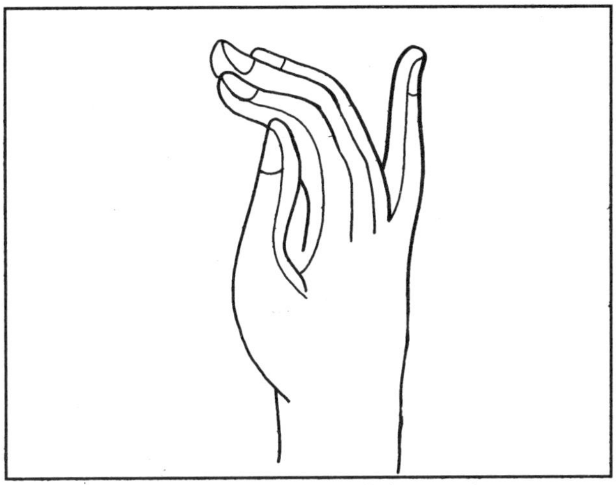

Figure 187 -- hamsa-paksha mudra I
(as seen by the holder)

hamsa-paksha mudra II-- (Ind.: *haṁsa-pakṣa-mudrā* aka *haṁsasya mudrā*) ("the swan feather") A hand pose, a seal, a dramatic (Ind.: *nāṭya*) *mudra* or gesture (Ind.: *darpaṇa*) held or formed by a performer, dancer or actor. The *hamsa-paksha mudra* is a single (Ind.: *asaṁyutta*) form, held by one hand. This *mudra* is a variation and formed by: palm faces forwards, the index, middle and ring fingers curl into the palm, the thumb rests along the curled index finger, pointing upward, the little finger is straight and pointing upwards. This *mudra* resembles the *sarpashirsha mudra*. (KVa 136 [27]) (See: **Figure 188**)

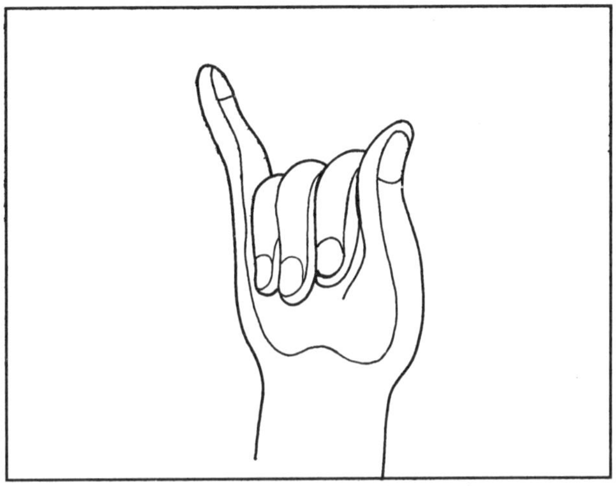

Figure 188 -- hamsa-paksha mudra II
(as seen by another)

hamsasya mudra I -- (Ind.: *haṁsasya-mudrā*) ("the swan face") A hand pose, a seal, a dramatic (Ind.: *nāṭya*) *mudra* or gesture (Ind.: *darpaṇa*) held or formed by a performer, dancer or actor. The *hamsasya mudra I* is a single (Ind.: *asaṁyutta*) form, held by one hand. It denotes marriage, initiation, etc.[4] This *mudra* is formed by: palm faces forwards, the first phalanges of the thumb and index finger are touching and extended, the middle, ring and little fingers are separated, straight and pointing upwards. (ACG 36, KVa 135 [21]) (See: **Figure 189**)

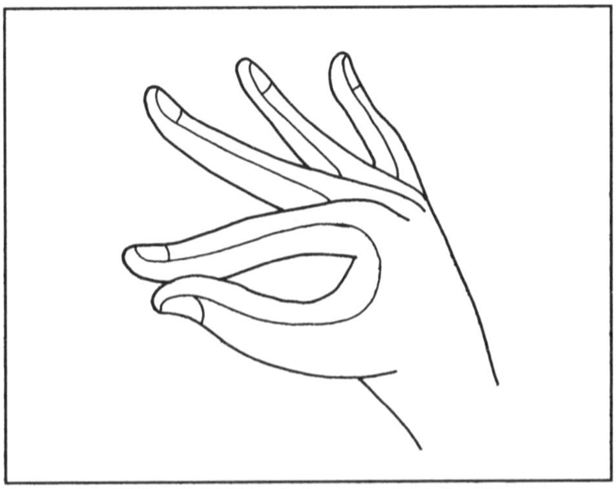

Figure 189 -- hamsasya mudra I
(as seen by the holder)

hamsasya mudra II -- (Ind.: *haṁsasya-mudrā* aka *haṁsa-pakṣa mudrā*. A variant term applied to *hamsa-paksha mudra*. See: *hamsa-paksha mudra* (KVa 136 [27])

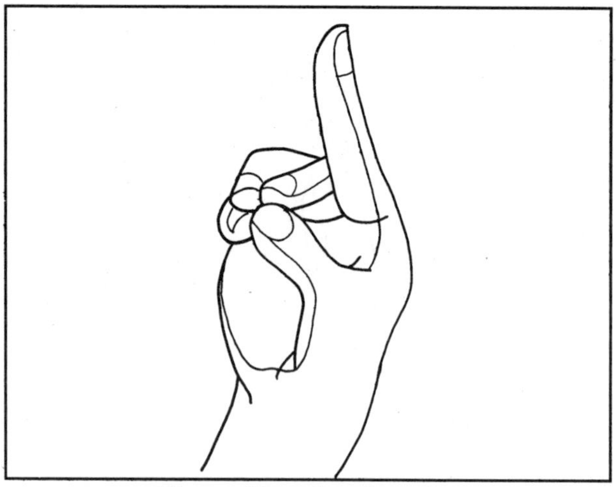

Figure 190 -- hansi mudra
(as seen by the holder)

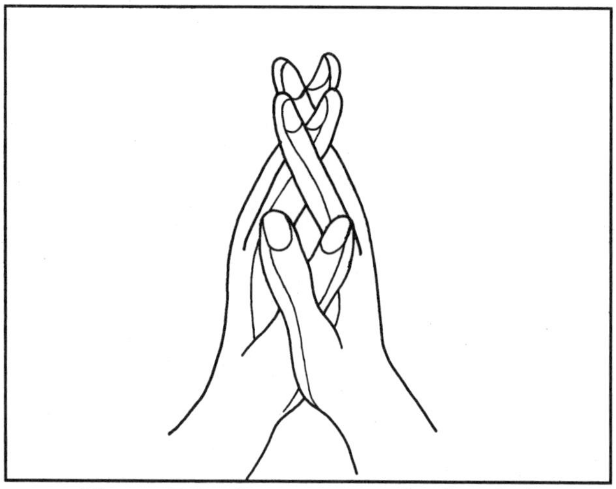

Figure 191 -- haranama gassho (mudra)
(as seen by the holder)

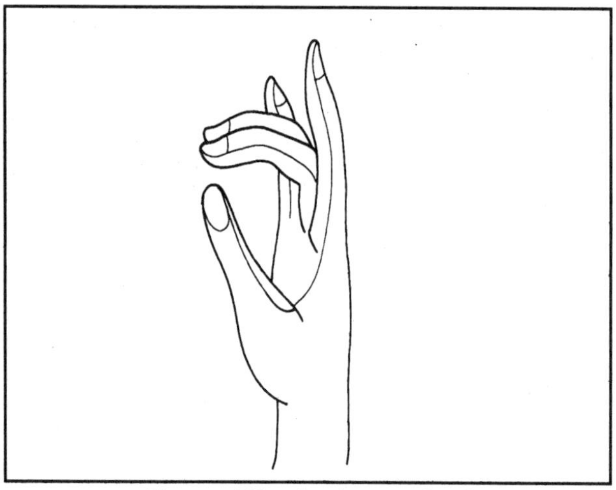

Figure 192 -- harina mudra I
(as seen by the holder)

hanjakugoshochaku gassho (mudra) -- (Jap.: *hanjakugoshochaku gassho* (*mudra*) aka *bihararieisata gassho* [*mudra*]; Ind.: *viparyasta mudrā*) A variant term applied to *bihararieisata gassho* (*mudra*).[5] See: *bihararieisata gassho* (*mudra*). (EDS 213)

hansi mudra -- (Ind.: *hansī-mudrā*) A *mudra*, a ritual hand pose, a seal, a *mudra* which is common to yogic tradition, particularly the *Yoga Tatva Mudra Vigyan* form, and is held by a devotee or practitioner. The *hansi mudra* is a single (Ind.: *asaṁyutta*) form, held by one hand. It is utilized for peace and restorative needs. This *mudra* is formed by: palm forward, the tips of the middle, ring and little fingers touch the tip of the thumb, the index finger extends straight upwards. It resembles the *tarjani mudra*. (KDe 64) (See: **Figure 190**)

haranama gassho (mudra) -- (Jap.: *haranama gasshō* [*mudrā*]; Ind.: *praṇāma mudra*) A *mudra*, a ritual hand pose, a seal, which is common to the Japanese Buddhist tradition. Specifically one of the twelve, elemental "hand clasps" (Jap. *junigosho* or *junigassho*). The *haranama gassho* (*mudra*) is a combined (Ind.: *saṁyutta*) form, held by both hands. This *mudra* is formed by: palm to palm, the fingers of the right overlap (interlock) with those of the left at the first phalanges, the thumbs similarly overlap. This is known as the "clasp of refuge."[6] See also *kongo-gassho*. (EDS 41) (See: **Figure 191**)

harina mudra I -- (Ind.: *hariṇa-mudrā*) A *mudra*, a ritual hand pose, a seal, which is common to the Hindu tradition. Its form, as the name would indicate denotes an antelope or deer. The *harina mudra* I is a single (Ind.: *asaṁyutta*) form, held by one hand. This *mudra* is formed by: the palm faces forward, the tip of the thumb touches the tips of the middle and ring fingers (forming a circle), the index and the little fingers point upwards. (RSG 3) (See: **Figure 192**)

harina mudra II -- (Ind.: *hariṇa-mudrā*) A hand pose, a seal, a dramatic (Ind.: *nāṭya*) *mudra* or gesture (Ind.: *darpaṇa*) held or formed by a performer, dancer or actor. It denotes an animal, in this case an antelope. The *harin mudra*[7] is a single (Ind.: *asaṁyutta*) form, held by one hand. This *mudra* is identical to the *mriga-shirsha mudra*. See: *mriga-shirsha mudra*. (ACG 49)

Harishchandra mudra -- (Ind.: *Hariścandra-mudrā*) A hand pose, a seal, a dramatic (Ind.: *nāṭya*) *mudra* or gesture (Ind.: *darpaṇa*) held or formed by a performer, dancer or actor. The *Harishchandra mudra* is a single (Ind.: *asaṁyutta*) form, held by one hand. It denotes *Harishchandra*, one of a number of famous rulers or heroes. The *mudra* employed is identical in form to the *shukatunda mudra*. See: *shukatunda mudra*. (ACG 47)

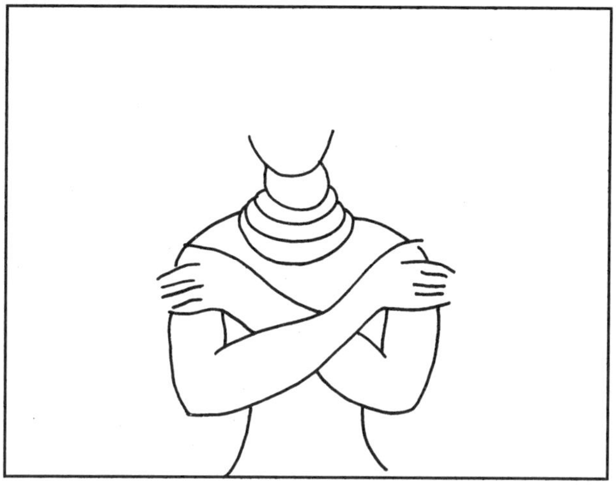

Figure 193 -- hastasvastika mudra I
(as seen by another)

hastasvastika mudra I -- (Ind.: *hastasvastika-mudrā*) A *mudra*, a ritual hand pose, a seal, which is common to the Hindu tradition. It denotes subservience or surrender to a superior deity as well as the acceptance of the inevitable and involves the arms as well. The *hastasvastika mudra I* is a combined (Ind.: *saṁyutta*) form, held by both hands. This *mudra* is formed by: palms the midline, fingers and thumbs extended and resting on the opposite upper arm, the right forearm is crossed over the left forearm. It is related to the Thai *pang tavainetr*. (ERJ II 24, MJS 55) (See: **Figure 193**)

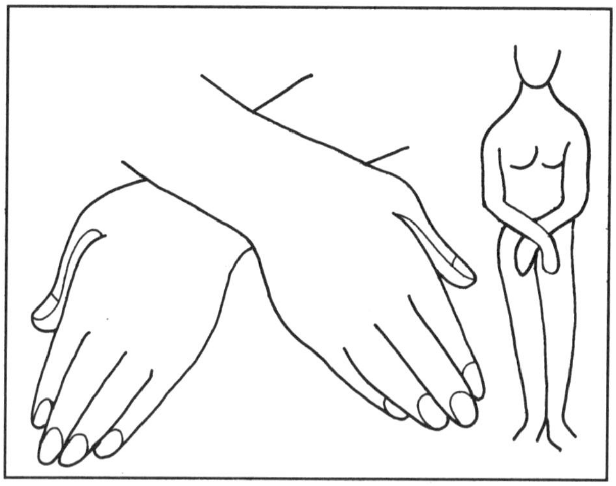

Figure 194 -- hastasvastika mudra II
(as seen by another)

hastasvastika mudra II -- (Ind.: *hastasvastika-mudrā;* Thai: *pang tavainetr*) This is a descriptive term.[8] A *mudra*, a ritual hand pose, a seal, which is common to the Thai Buddhist tradition. One of forty *mudras* and *asanas* compiled by the Prince Patriarch Paramanujita Jinorasa and established during the reign of Rama III as being acceptable for the depiction of images of The Lord *Buddha*--i.e., "gazing at the *bodhi* tree *mudra*" the seventh of the forty attitudes noted.[9] The *hastasvastika mudra II* is a combined (Ind.: *saṁyutta*) form, held by both hands. This *mudra* is formed by: the right hand crosses over the left at the wrist, both palms face backwards, fingers and thumbs extended downwards. The *mudra* is thus held in front of the groin and the figure is standing.[10] (DRN 35, JBo) (See: **Figure 194**)

hastasvastika mudra III -- (Indic: *hastasvastika-mudrā*) This is a descriptive term.[11] A *mudra*, a ritual hand pose, a seal, which is common to the Thai Buddhist tradition. One of forty *mudras* and *asanas* compiled by the Prince Patriarch Paramanujita Jinorasa and established during the reign of Rama III as being acceptable for the depiction of images of The Lord *Buddha*--i.e., "on the jeweled walkway" the eighth of the forty attitudes noted.[12] The *hastasvastika mudra III* is a combined (Ind.:

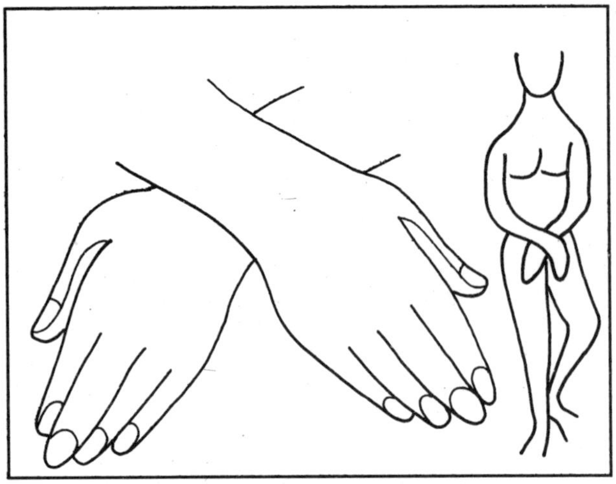

Figure 195 -- hastasvastika mudra III
(as seen by another)

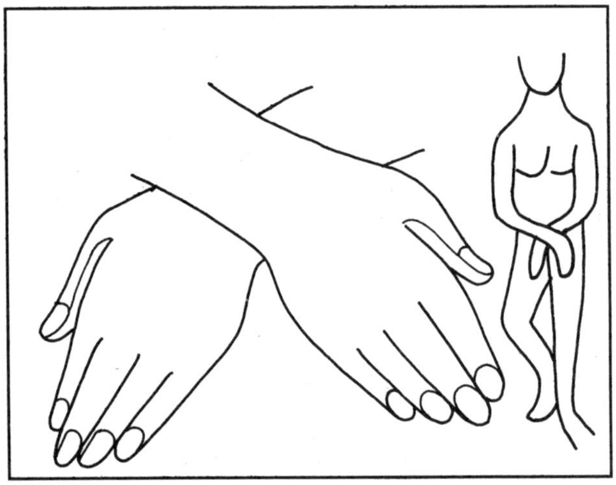

Figure 196 -- hastasvastika mudra IV
(as seen by another)

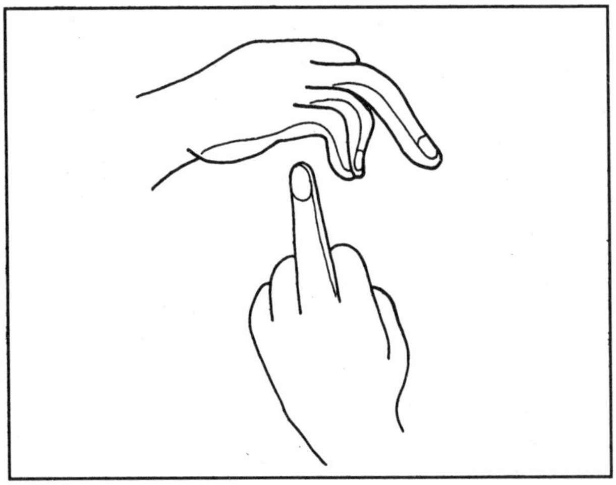

Figure 197 -- hasti-ratna mudra
(as seen by another)

saṁyutta) form, held by both hands. This *mudra* is formed by: the right hand crosses over the left at the wrist, both palms face backwards, fingers and thumbs extended downwards. The *mudra* is thus held in front of the groin and the figure is standing on right foot with the left is positioned as if striding.[13] (DRN 35, JBo) (See: **Figure 195**)

hastasvastika mudra IV -- (Indic: *hastasvastika-mudrā*; Thai: *pang phraditthanroy-phrabuddhabatr*) This is a descriptive term.[14] A *mudra*, a ritual hand pose, a seal, which is common to the Thai Buddhist tradition. One of forty *mudras* and *asanas* compiled by the Prince Patriarch Paramanujita Jinorasa and established during the reign of Rama III as being acceptable for the depiction of images of The Lord *Buddha*--i.e., "stamping his footprint in the ground" the thirty-first of the forty attitudes noted.[15] The *hastasvastika mudra IV* is a combined (Ind.: *saṁyutta*) form, held by both hands. This *mudra* is formed by: the right hand crosses over the left at the wrist, both palms face backwards, fingers and thumbs extended downwards. The *mudra* is thus held in front of the groin and the figure is standing on left foot with the right raised as if stepping.[16] (DRN 37, JBo, PSS, ODD 780) (See: **Figure 196**)

hasti-ratna mudra -- (Ind.: *hasti-ratna-mudrā*) This is an assigned term.[17] A *mudra*, a ritual hand pose, a seal, which is common to the Buddhist (*Vajrayana*) tradition, a *tantric mudra*. It denotes the gift of a precious elephant (Tib.: *glang-po*) associated with the *saptaratna* (Tib.: *rgyal-srid sna-bdun*) or seven gems of sovereignty (Tib.: *nor-bu-chab-bdun*), also referred to as the 'space vast treasury,' particularly as it is associated with the worship of the powerful *Vajrayana* goddess, *Tara*. The *hasti-ratna mudra* is a combined (Ind.: *saṁyutta*) form, held by both hands. This *mudra* is formed by--the right hand: palm facing downwards, thumb, index, ring and little fingers are 'cupped,' the middle finger arches out and downwards; the left hand is slightly below, palm facing left, thumb, index, ring and fourth fingers are fisted, the middle finger extends upwards, pointing towards the right cupped palm.[18] The *mudra* is held: right hand at chin level. The *mantra* associated with this *mudra* is: "*OM Hasti-ratna Praticcha HUM SVAHA.*"[19] (SBe 152) (See: **Figure 197**)

Hayagriva mudra I -- (Ind.: *Hayagrīvā-mudrā*) A *mudra*, a ritual hand pose, a seal, a *tantric mudra* which is common to the Japanese Buddhist (*Vajrayana, Mantrayana*) tradition and is held or formed by a devotee or priest during the *Eighteen Rites*. It may be accompanied by a *mantra*. The *Hayagriva mudra*[20] I is a combined (Ind.: *saṁyutta*) form, held by both hands. It denotes the horse faced deity. This *mudra* is formed by: palms face midline, index and ring fingers are folded into the palms and they are brought together, middle and little fingers extend upwards and the touch their opposites at the tip, thumbs extend upward, side by side. (LCS 63) (See: **Figure 198**)

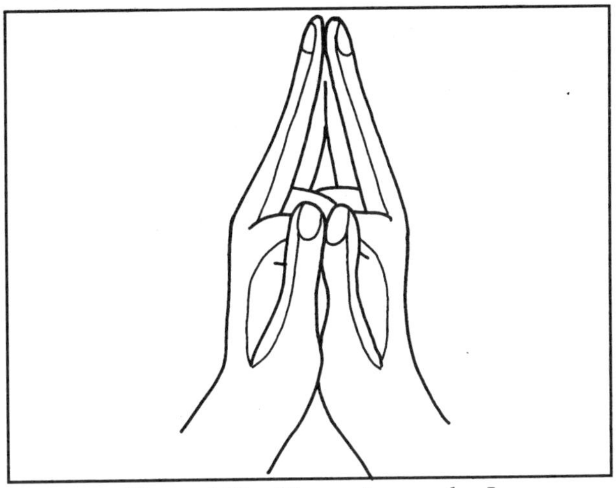

Figure 198 -- Hayagriva mudra I
(as seen by the holder)

Hayagriva mudra II -- (Ind.: *Hayagrīvā-mudrā*) A *mudra*, a ritual hand pose, a seal, a *tantric mudra* which is common to the Japanese Buddhist (*Vajrayana, Mantrayana*) tradition and is held or formed by a devotee or priest during various rites. It may be accompanied by a *mantra*. The *Hayagriva mudra II* is a combined (Ind.: *saṁyutta*) form, held by both hands. This *mudra* is formed by: palms facing midline and touching, thumbs extend upward and touch, middle and little fingers extend and touch at their tips, index fingers curls at first two knuckles and touch along the back of the first phalanges, ring fingers curl inward towards the palm. (GDe 217) (See: **Figure 199**)

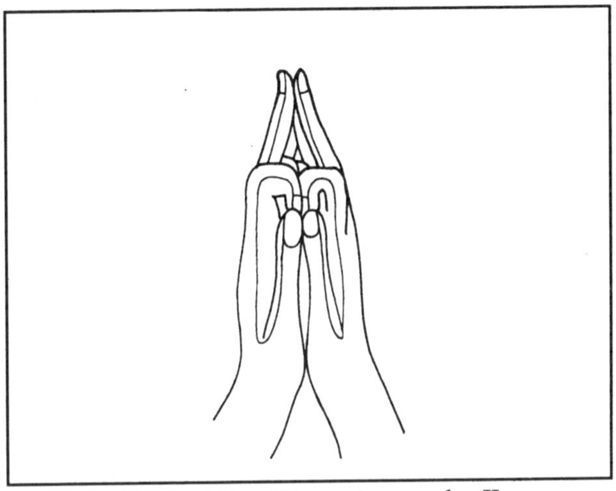

Figure 199 -- Hayagriva mudra II
(as seen by the holder)

hemanta mudra -- (Ind.: *hemanta-mudrā*) ("winter *mudra*") A *mudra*, a ritual hand pose, a seal, a *tantric mudra* which is common to the Japanese Buddhist (*Vajrayana, Mantrayana*) tradition and is held or formed by a devotee or priest during various rites. It may be accompanied by a *mantra*. The *hemanta mudra* is a combined (Ind.: *saṁyutta*) form, held by both hands. It denotes winter. This *mudra* is formed by: palms face the midline, fingers thumbs and fingers extend upwards, slightly splayed and curled. Thus formed the hands are close, each are slightly rotated inwards and held chest level. (GDe 448) (See: **Figure 200**)

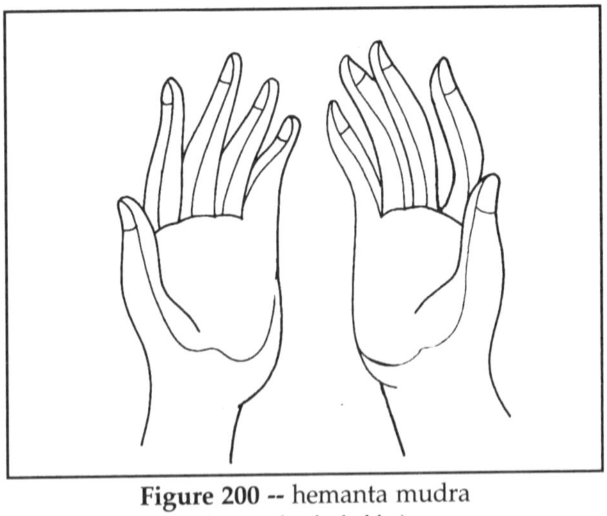

Figure 200 -- hemanta mudra
(as seen by the holder)

hen hokkai mushofushi-in (mudra) -- (Jap.: *hen hokkai mushofushi-in* [*mudrā*] aka *mushofushi-in* [*mudra*], *Biroshana-in* [*mudra*], *butsubu sotoba-in* [*mudra*], *dai sotoba-in* [*mudra*], *mushofushi to-in* [*mudra*], *rito-in* [*mudra*]; Chin.: *wu-so-pu-chih-yin*; Ind.: *stūpa mudrā*)

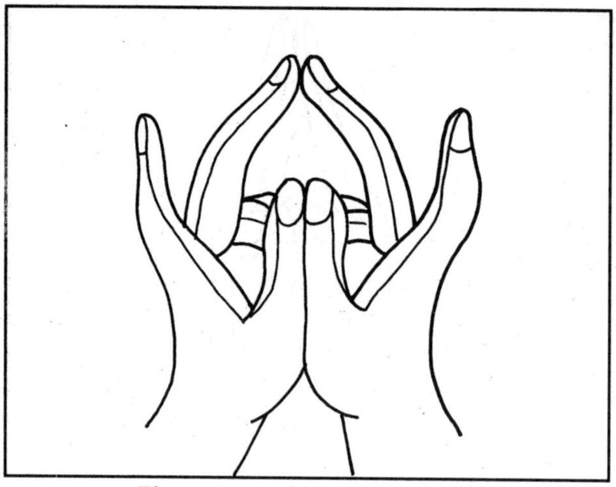

Figure 201 -- hi ko-in (mudra)
(as seen by the holder)

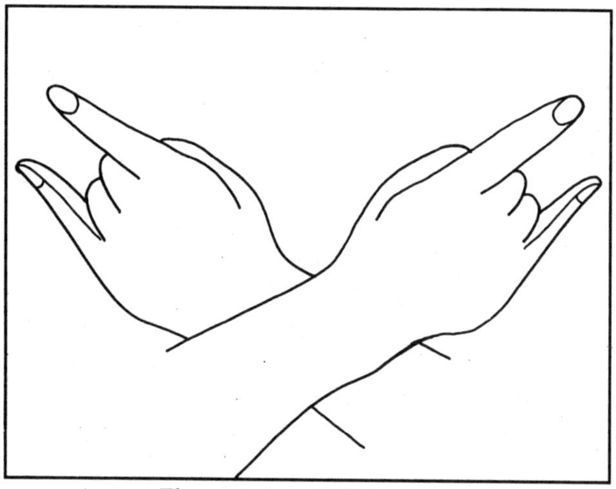

Figure 202 -- HOH mudra
(as seen by another)

("*mudra* which reaches all the essence worlds") A variant term applied to *mushofushi-in* (*mudra*). See: *mushofushi-in* (*mudra*). (EDS 115)

hi ko-in (mudra) -- (Jap.: *hi kō-in* [*mudrā*]) ("putting on the armor") A *mudra*, a ritual hand pose, a seal, a *tantric mudra* which is common to the Japanese Buddhist (*Vajrayana, Mantrayana*) tradition and is held or formed by a devotee or priest during the rites of *Garbhadhatu Mandala* and other rites. It may be accompanied by a *mantra*. The *hi ko-in* (*mudra*)[21] is a combined (Ind.: *saṁyutta*) form, held by both hands. It denotes the donning of armor. This *mudra* is formed by: palms facing midline and are separated, thumbs touch along their outer edges, middle fingers touch at their tips, ring and little fingers fold in between the palms, index fingers are erect but curve slightly. (GDe 5) (See: **Figure 201**)

hintala mudra -- (Jap.: *hīntāla-mudrā*) A hand pose, a seal, a dramatic (Ind.: *nāṭya*) *mudra* or gesture (Ind.: *darpaṇa*) held or formed by a performer, dancer or actor. It denotes the *hintala* tree. The *mudra* employed is identical in form to the *kartari-mukha mudra*. See: *kartari-mukha mudra*. (ACG 48)

HOH mudra -- (Ind.: *HOḤ-mudrā*) This is an assigned term.[22] A *mudra*, a ritual hand pose, a seal, which is common to the Buddhist (*Vajrayana*) tradition, a *tantric mudra*. It denotes "to dissolve," and is the last syllable of a four syllable invocatory *mantra* particularly as associated with the invocation ceremony attached to the worship of the powerful *Vajrayana* goddess, *Tara*. The HOH mudra is a combined (Ind.: *saṁyutta*) form, held by both hands. This *mudra* is identical to both hands--the palms face the midline, the tips of the middle and ring fingers touch the last phalanges of the thumb which is curled towards the palm, the index and little fingers extend upward, thus formed the left hand is closest to the body and the right hand crosses over the left at the points of the wrists, and the *mudra* is held just below the level of the chin, in front of the chest. The *mantra* associated with this *mudra* is: "*Jah Hum Bam HOH*."[23] (SBe 102) (See: **Figure 202**)

hokai sho-in (mudra) -- (Jap.: *hōkai shō-in* [*mudrā*] aka *kayen sho-in* [*mudra*]) A variant term applied to *kayen sho-in* (*mudra*). See: *kayen sho-in* (*mudra*). (GDe 16)

honzon bu jo no-in (mudra) -- (Jap.: *honzon bu jō no-in* [*mudrā*]) ("receiving the principle deity") A *mudra*, a ritual hand pose, a seal, a *tantric mudra* which is common to the Japanese Buddhist (*Vajrayana, Mantrayana*) tradition and is held or formed by a devotee or priest during the rites of *Garbhadhatu Mandala, Vajradhatu Mandala, Homa Rites* and other rites. It may be accompanied by a *mantra*. The *honzon bu jo no-in* (*mudra*)[24] is a combined (Ind.: *saṁyutta*) form, held by both hands. This *mudra* is formed by: palms face each other, fingers and thumbs are interlaced with fingers and thumb inside (palm-side) the fist, except the right index finger which is curled gently over the other, enclosed index finger. (GDe 93) (See: **Figure 203**)

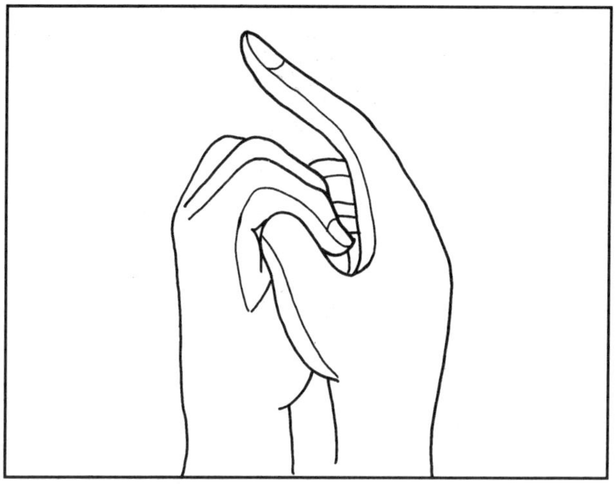

Figure 203 -- honzon bu jo no-in (mudra)
(as seen by the holder)

hora no-in (mudra) -- (Jap.: *hora no-in* [*mudrā*]; Ind.: *śaṅkha mudrā*) ("the conch") A *mudra*, a ritual hand pose, a seal, a *tantric mudra* which is common to the Japanese Buddhist (*Vajrayana, Mantrayana*) tradition and is held or formed by a devotee or priest during the rites of *Garbhadhatu Mandala, Vajradhatu Mandala, Homa Rites* and other rites. It may be accompanied by a *mantra*. The *hora no-in* (*mudra*) is a combined (Ind.: *saṁyutta*) form, held by both hands. It denotes transmission of orders and the calling of the faithful. This *mudra* is formed by both hands, identically: palms face the midline, thumbs touch along their length, index fingers curl, their tips touching the outside first knuckles of the thumbs, middle, ring and little fingers touch at their tips. (GDe 22) (See: **Figure 204**)

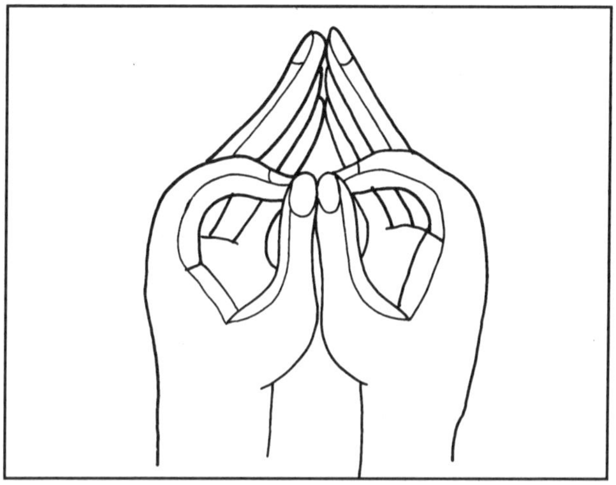

Figure 204 -- hora no-in (mudra)
(as seen by the holder)

horyuji temborin-in (mudra) -- (Jap.: *hōryūji tembōrin-in* [*mudrā*]) A *mudra*, a ritual hand pose, a seal, which is common to the Japanese Buddhist tradition and a variation on the *temborin-in* (*mudra*). It denotes preaching and the 'turning of the wheel of the law.' The *mudra* is held in both hands: the right palm faces forwards, the tips of the thumb and the index finger touch, the other three fingers arch upwards; the left palm faces upwards and slightly to the midline, the tips of the thumb and the middle finger touch, the index, ring and little fingers arch upwards. Thus held, the left hand is lower that the right and slightly in front (that is, away

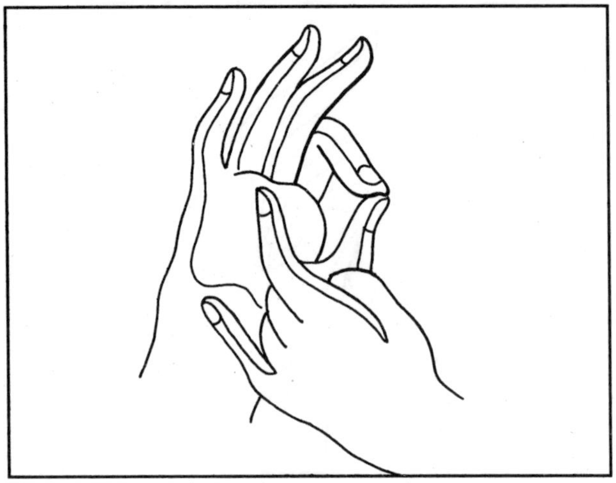

Figure 205 -- horyuji temborin-in (mudra)
(as seen by another)

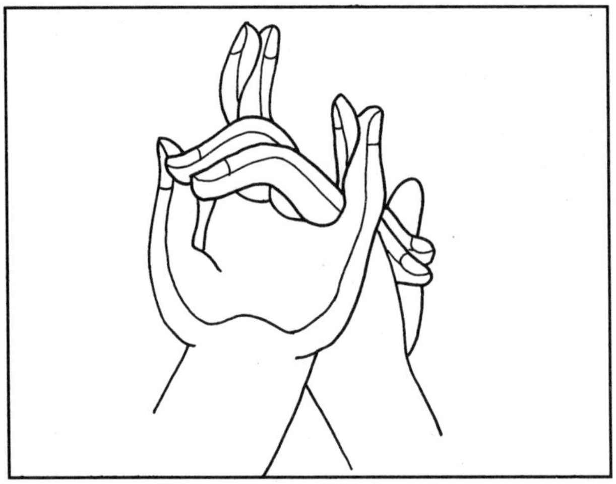

Figure 206 -- HUM mudra
(as seen by the holder)

from the chest), the tips of the touching thumbs and fingers of each hand are close together but not touching one another. (EDS 95) (See: **Figure 205**)

HUM mudra -- (Ind.: *HŪṀ-mudrā*) This is an assigned term.[25] A *mudra*, a ritual hand pose, a seal, which is common to the Buddhist (*Vajrayana*) tradition, a *tantric mudra*. It denotes "to absorb," and is the second syllable of a four syllable invocatory *mantra* particularly as associated with the invocation ceremony attached to the worship of the powerful *Vajrayana* goddess, *Tara*. The *HUM mudra* is a combined (Ind.: *saṁyutta*) form, held by both hands. This *mudra* is identical to both hands--the palms face forwards, the tips of the middle and ring fingers touch the last phalanges of the thumb which is curled towards the palm, the index and little fingers extend upward, thus formed the left hand crosses over (in front of) the right at the points of the wrists, the index and little fingers cross their counterparts--the left little finger first phalanges in front of the right little finger first phalanges, and the left index finger first phalanges in front of the right index finger first phalanges. The *mudra* is held just below the level of the chin, in front of the chest. The *mantra* associated with this *mudra* is: "*Jah **HUM** Bam Hoh*."[26] (SBe 102) (See: **Figure 206**)

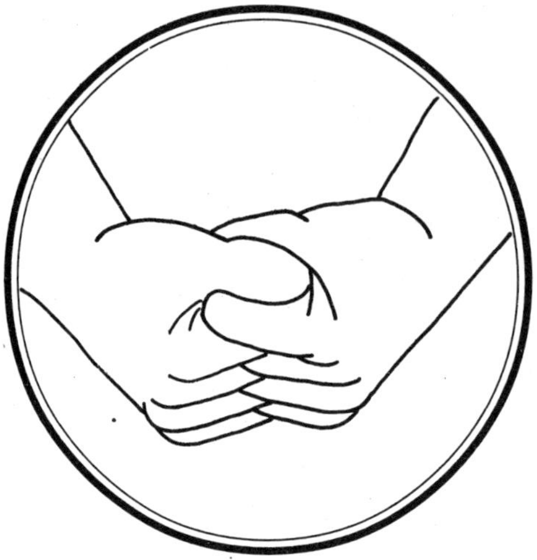

-- I --

Indra mudra -- (Ind.: *Indra-mudrā*) A hand pose, a seal, a dramatic (Ind.: *nāṭya*) *mudra* or gesture (Ind.: *darpaṇa*) held or formed by a performer, dancer or actor which denotes a specific deity. The *Indra mudra* is a combined (Ind.: *saṁyutta*) form, held by both hands. It denotes the deity *Indra*. This *mudra* is formed by: right palm faces forward, index, middle and little fingers and thumb extended, together and pointing upwards, ring finger is bent towards the palm; left palm faces forward, index, middle and little fingers and thumb extended, together and pointing upwards, ring finger is bent towards the palm. Thus formed the hands are crossed at the wrist at chest level. (ACG 45) (See: **Figure 207**)

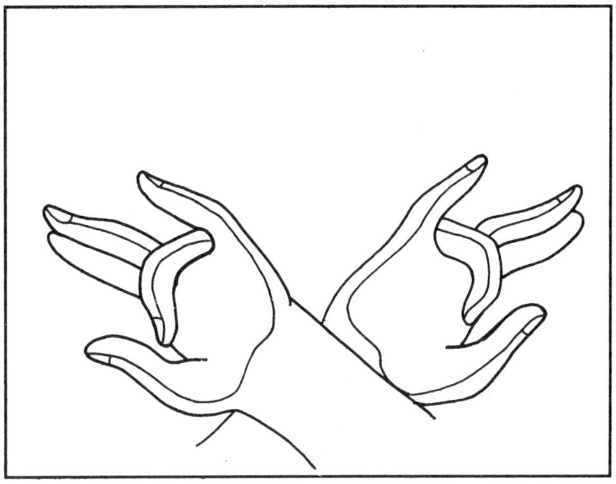

Figure 207 -- Indra mudra
(as seen by another)

in the Palelayaka forest mudra -- (Eng.; Indic: *añcita-nidrātahasta mudrā*; Thai: *pang palelai*) The English descriptive phrase for the Thai *pang palelai*. See: *pang palelai*. (DRN 36, JBo 205, ODD 680, OFr 28, PSS)

ishtaprada mudra -- (Ind.: *iṣṭaprada-mudrā* aka *varada mudrā*) A variant term applied to *varada mudra*. See: *varada mudra* (MJS 58)

Ishvara mudra -- (Ind.: *Īśvara-mudrā*) A *mudra*, a ritual hand pose, a seal, a *tantric mudra* which is common to the Japanese Buddhist (*Vajrayana, Mantrayana*) tradition and is held or formed by a devotee or priest during various rites. It may be accompanied by a *mantra*. The *Ishvara mudra*[1] is a combined (Ind.: *saṁyutta*) form, held by both hands. This *mudra* is formed by: palms together, thumbs, index and little fingers extend upward and touch along their length, middle and ring fingers interlace on top of the hands. (GDe 461, LCS 184) (See: **Figure 208**)

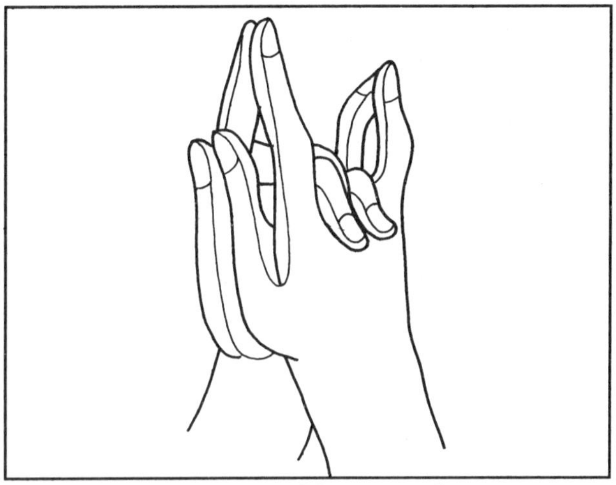

Figure 208 -- Ishvara mudra
(as seen by the holder)

issai ho byo do kai go (mudra) -- (Jap.: *issai hō byo dō kai go* [*mudra*]; Eng.: 'great *mudra* for the conversion of things') A *mudra*, a ritual hand pose, a seal, a *tantric mudra* which is common to the Japanese Buddhist (*Vajrayana, Mantrayana*) tradition and is held or formed by a devotee or priest during the rites of *Garbhadhatu*

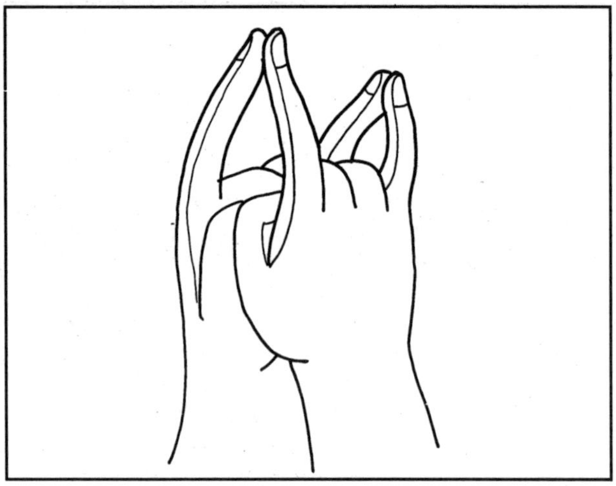

Figure 209-- issai ho byo do kai go (mudra)
(as seen by the holder)

Mandala, Vajradhatu Mandala, Homa Rites and other rites. It may be accompanied by a *mantra*. The *issai ho byo do kai go (mudra)*[2] is a combined (Ind.: *saṁyutta*) form, held by both hands. It denotes the equality and homogeneity of the Law (Ind.: *dharma*). This *mudra* is formed by: palms facing midline and close, thumbs and ring fingers folded into palms, index, middle and little fingers extend upwards and touch along their length. (GDe 31, LCS 155) (See: **Figure 209**)

-- J --

JAH mudra -- (Ind.: *JAḤ-mudrā*) This is an assigned term.[1] A *mudra*, a ritual hand pose, a seal, which is common to the Buddhist (*Vajrayana*) tradition, a *tantric mudra*. It denotes "to summons," and is the first syllable of a four syllable invocatory mantra particularly as associated with the invocation ceremony attached to the worship of the powerful *Vajrayana* goddess, *Tara*. The *JAH mudra* is a combined (Ind.: *saṁyutta*) form, held by both hands. This *mudra* is formed by--the right palm faces forwards, the tips of the middle and ring fingers touch the last phalanges of the thumb which is curled towards the palm, the index and little fingers extend upward, thus formed the left palm faces the midline and is in front of the right hand, the tip of the left hand's little finger touches the first phalanges of the index finger of the right hand. The *mudra* is held just below the level of the chin, in front of the chest. The *mantra* associated with this mudra is: "***JAH** Hum Bam Hoh.*"[2] (SBe 102) (See: **Figure 210**)

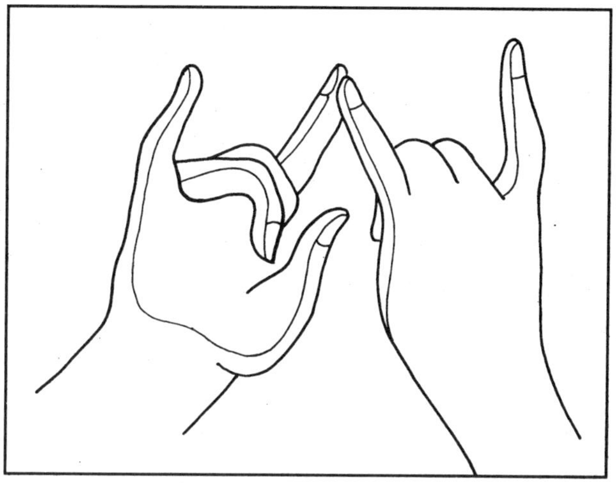

Figure 210 -- JAH mudra
(as seen by another)

jambu mudra -- (Ind.: *jambū-mudrā*) A hand pose, a seal, a dramatic (Ind.: *natya*) mudra or gesture (Ind.: *darpaṇa*) held or formed by a performer, dancer or actor. It denotes the *jambu* or rose-apple tree. The *mudra* employed is identical in form to the *ardha-pataka mudra*. See: *ardha-pataka mudra*. (ACG 49)

jigs-med phyag-rgya -- (Tib.; Ind.: *abhaya mudrā*) The Tibetan term for *abhaya mudra*. See: *abhaya mudra*. (BCO 215)

ji ketsu-in (mudra) -- (Jap.: *ji ketsu-in* [*mudrā*]; Ind.: *vajra-bandha mudra*) The Japanese term for *vajra-bandha mudra*. See: *vajra-bandha mudra*. (GDe 103)

jo kongo-in (mudra) -- (Jap.: *jo kongō-in* [*mudrā*] aka *jo renge-in* [*mudra*]) A variant term applied to *jo renge-in (mudra)*. See: *jo renge-in (mudra)*. (GDe 67)

jo renge-in (mudra) -- (Jap.: *jō renge-in* [*mudrā*] aka *jo kongo-in* [*mudra*]) A *mudra*, a ritual hand pose, a seal, a *tantric mudra* which is common to the Japanese Bud-

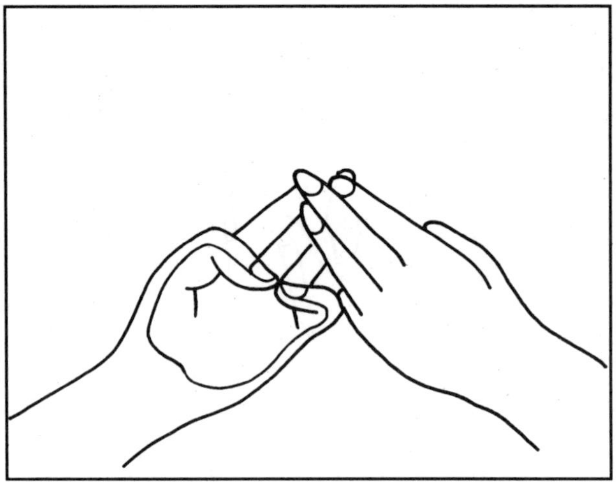

Figure 211 -- jo renge-in (mudra)
(as seen by the holder)

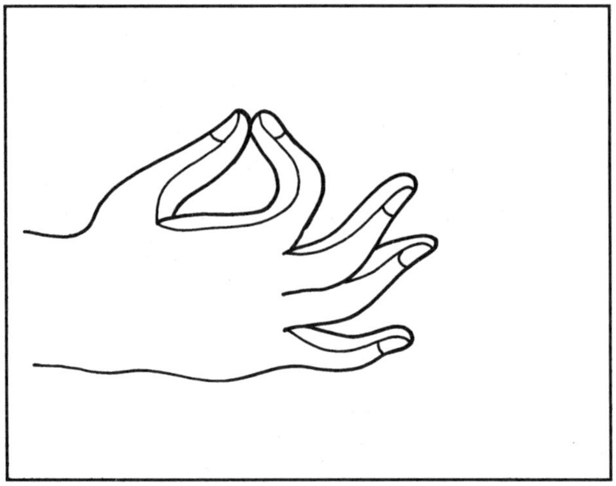

Figure 212 -- jnana mudra I
(as seen by another)

dhist (*Vajrayana, Mantrayana*) tradition and is held or formed by a devotee or priest during the rites of *Garbhadhatu Mandala, Vajradhatu Mandala, Homa Rites* and other rites. It may be accompanied by a *mantra*. The *jo kongo-in*[3] (*mudra*) is a combined (Ind.: *saṁyutta*) form, held by both hands. This *mudra* is identical for both hands and is formed by: little fingers folded into the palms, thumbs folded into the palms and over the little fingers, index, middle and ring fingers extend. Thus formed, the left palm faces upwards, the right palm faces downwards, the index, middle and ring fingers of the right hand rest on the index, middle and ring fingers of the left hand at right angles. (GDe 67) (See: **Figure 211**)

jnanam mudra -- (Ind.: *jñānam-mudrā* aka *gyān mudrā*) A variant term applied to *gyan mudra*. Also, a variant spelling for *jnana mudra*. See: *gyan mudra*; see also: *jnana mudra*. (RLM 77)

jnana mudra I -- (Ind.: *jñāna-mudrā* aka *jñānam mudrā*) A *mudra*, a ritual hand pose, a seal, which is common to the Hindu tradition. It denotes irrefutable spiritual knowledge of the Absolute One and purity. The *jnana mudra I* is a single (Ind.: *asaṁyutta*) form, held by one hand. This *mudra* is formed by the right hand: the palm is turned backwards, the tips of the thumb and the index finger touch, the other fingers are relaxed and extend to the left. Thus formed, the *mudra* is held against the middle of the chest. This *mudra* is not to be confused with the *vitarka mudra*. (HKS 271, MJS 60, RSG 3, TGR 17) (See: **Figure 212**)

jnana mudra II -- (Ind.: *jñāna-mudrā* aka *vajra mudrā, bodhaśrī mudrā*; Chin.: *chih-ch'ṃan-yin* [*mudra*]; Jap.: biroshananyoraidaimyochi-in [*mudra*]; *bodaiindo-daiichichi-in* [*mudra*], *chi ken-in* [*mudra*], *nometsu-mumyokokuan-in* [*mudra*]) A variant term applied to *chi ken-in* (*mudra*). This *mudra* is, in form, vastly different from the *chi ken-in* (*mudra*). See: *chi ken-in* (*mudra*). (EDS 102)

jnana-avalokite mudra -- (Ind.: *jñāna-avalokite-mudrā*; Tib.: *ye-shes skar-mda'i phyag-rgya*) This is an assigned term.[4] A *mudra*, a ritual hand pose, a seal, which is common to the Buddhist (*Vajrayana*) tradition, a *tantric* *mudra*. It is the fifth gesture of six of the *ma-mo-mdos mudras*. It denotes the 'comet of knowledge,' particularly as associated with the white *gtor-ma* (sacrificial cake) offering and the presentation of the thread cross (Tib.: *ma-mo-mdos* or *ma-mdos*) as part of the worship of the powerful *Vajrayana* goddess, *Tara*. The form is held with both hands: the right hand assumes the *tarjani mudra*, palm towards the midline, index finger pointing left; the left hand is below and assumes a form identical to the *dhyana mudra*. Thus formed the *mudra* is held above the waist. The *mantra* associated with this mudra is: "*OM Jnana-avalokite Samanta-spharana-rashmi-bhava-samaya-mahamani Duru Duru Hridaya-jvalani HUM*."[5] (SBe 347) (See: **Figure 213**)

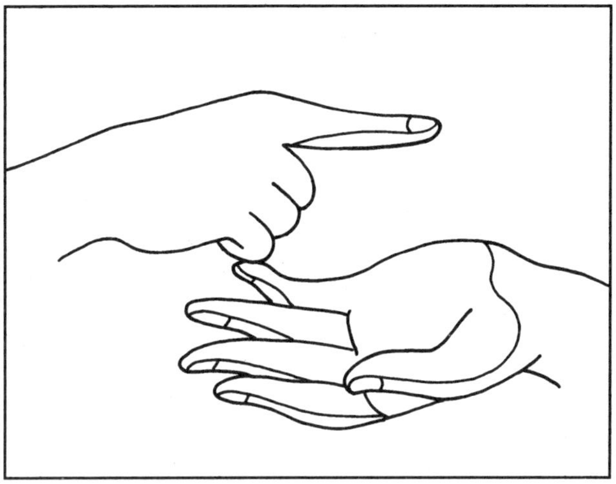

Figure 213 -- jnana-avalokite mudra
(as seen by another)

jnana-jnana mudra I -- (Indic: *jñāna-jñāna-mudrā*; Eng.: performing austerities *mudra*; Thai: *pang tukkarakiriya*) This is a descriptive term.[6] See: *pang tukkarakiriya*, (DRN 35, JBo 204, PSS)

jnana-jnana mudra II -- (Indic: *jñāna-jñana-mudrā*; Thai: *pang ram-pueng*) This is a descriptive term.[7] See: *pang ram-pueng*. (DRN 37, JBo 205, ODD 279, OFr 16, PSS)

jnana-lolahasta mudra I -- (Ind.: *jñāna-lolahasta-mudrā*; Eng.: bathing *mudra*; Thai: *pang song-nam-phon*) This is a descriptive term.[8] See: *pang song-nam-phon*. (DRN 36, JBo 205, OFr 30, PSS)

jnana-lolahasta mudra II -- (Indic: *jñāna-lolahasta-mudrā*; Eng.: elephant glance *mudra* or looking back at the city of *Vaisali mudra*; Thai: *pang nakawalok*) This is a descriptive term.[9] See: *pang nakawalok*. (DRN 36, JBo 205, ODD 680, OFr 35, PSS)

jnana-mushti mudra -- (Ind.: *jñana-muṣṭi-mudrā* aka *tathāgata-muṣṭi mudrā*; Jap.: *chi ken-in* (*mudra*) *II*, *nyorai ken-in*) A variant term applied to *chi ken-in* (*mudra*) *II*. See: *chi ken-in* (*mudra*) *II*. (EDS 40, GDe 139, LCS 61)

jnana-nidratahasta mudra -- (Indic: *jñāna-nidrātahasta-mudrā*; Eng.: contemplating the approach of his death *mudra*; Thai: *pang plong-aryu-sangkharn*) This is a descriptive term.[10] See: *pang plong-aryu-sangkharn*. (DRN 36, JBo 204, ODD 279, OFr 34, PSS)

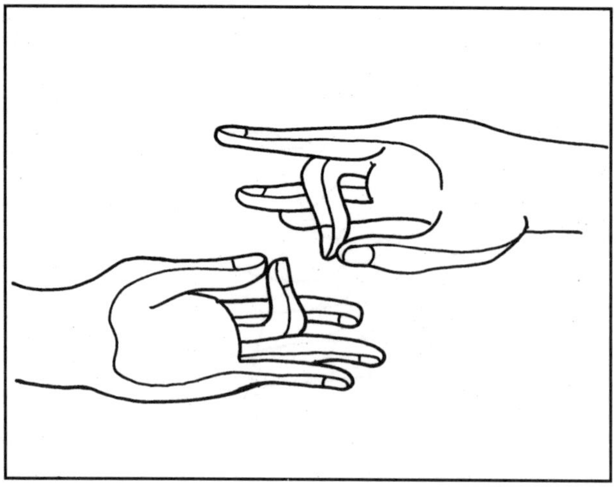

Figure 214 -- jnana-shri mudra
(as seen by the holder)

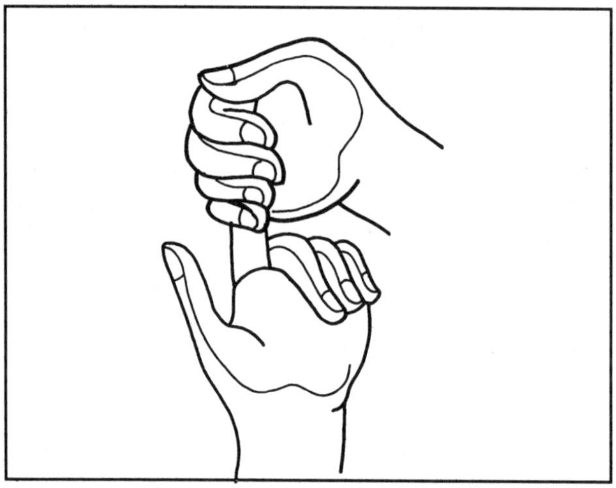

Figure 215 -- jnyana mudra
(as seen by the holder)

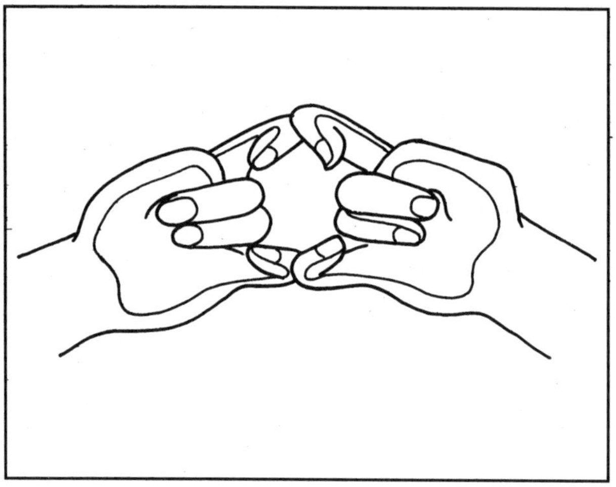

Figure 216 -- jo fudo-in (mudra)
(as seen by the holder)

jnana-shri mudra -- (Ind.: *jñāna-śrī-mudrā*) A *mudra*, a ritual hand pose, a seal, a *tantric mudra* which is common to the Japanese Buddhist (*Vajrayana, Mantrayana*) tradition and is held or formed by a devotee or priest during the rites of *Garbhadhatu Mandala, Vajradhatu Mandala, Homa Rites* and other rites. It may be accompanied by a *mantra*. The *jnana-shri mudra* is a combined (Ind.: *saṁyutta*) form, held by both hands. This *mudra* is formed by: right palm facing downwards, index, ring and little fingers extended straight towards the midline, middle finger and thumb curl and touch at their tips (similar to the *karana mudra*); left palm facing upwards, index, ring and little fingers extended straight towards the midline, middle finger and thumb curl and touch at their tips. Thus formed the left hand is slightly below the right hand. (GDe 123, LCS 213) (See: **Figure 214**)

jnyana mudra -- (Ind.: *jñāna-mudrā* aka *vajra mudrā*) A mudra, a ritual hand pose, a seal, which is common to the Buddhist (*Vajrayana*) tradition. It is represents "the unity of all things in the context of ultimate reality."[11] The *jnyana mudra* is a combined (Ind.: *saṁyutta*) form, held by both hands. This *mudra* is formed by: the left hand assumes the *tarjani mudra*, index finger pointing upwards; the right hand forms a fist over the upward extended index finger. Thus formed the *mudra* is held chest high. It is identical to the Japanese *Tathagata* "fist." (MMR 348) (See: **Figure 215**)

jo fudo-in (mudra) -- (Jap.: *jō fudō-in* [*mudrā*]) ("to become *Achala*") A *mudra*, a ritual hand pose, a seal, a *tantric mudra* which is common to the Japanese Buddhist (*Vajrayana, Mantrayana*) tradition and is held or formed by a devotee or priest during the rites of *Garbhadhatu Mandala*. It may be accompanied by a *mantra*. The *jo fudo-in*[12] (*mudra*) is a combined (Ind.: *saṁyutta*) form, held by both hands. This *mudra* is formed by: palms facing the midline, thumbs folded into the palm, middle and little fingers fold over the thumbs, index and little fingers extend and curl at their first and second knuckles. So formed the second phalanges of the index and little fingers touch their counterparts. (GDe 37) (See: **Figure 216**)

jo-in (mudra) I -- (Jap.: *jō-in-mudrā*; Chin.: *ting-yin* [*mudra*]; Ind.: *dhyāna mudrā, dhyanahasta mudrā, samādhi* *mudrā, yoga mudrā;* Thai: *pang phra-nang;* Tib.: *bsam-gtan phyag-rgya*) A *mudra*, a ritual hand pose, a seal, which is common to the Japanese and Chinese Buddhist traditions. Also, a *tantric mudra* which is common to the Japanese Buddhist (*Vajrayana, Mantrayana*) tradition and is held or formed by a devotee or priest during the rites of *Garbhadhatu Mandala, Vajradhatu Mandala, Homa Rites* and other rites. It may be accompanied by a *mantra*. The *jo-in* (*mudra*) possesses a number of variations: Type A: Variant 1, Variant 2; Type B: Variant 1, Variant 2; and Type C: Variant 1, Variant 2 and Variant 3.[13] It denotes meditation and related to the *dhyana mudra*. The *jo-in* (*mudra*) *I* is a combined (Ind.: *saṁyutta*) form, held by both hands. This *mudra* (Type A: Variant 1) is formed by: palms facing upwards, fingers and thumb together, extended and relaxed, thus formed, the right hand rests upon the left hand, and the *mudra* is held in the lap. (EDS 85) (See: **Figure 217**)

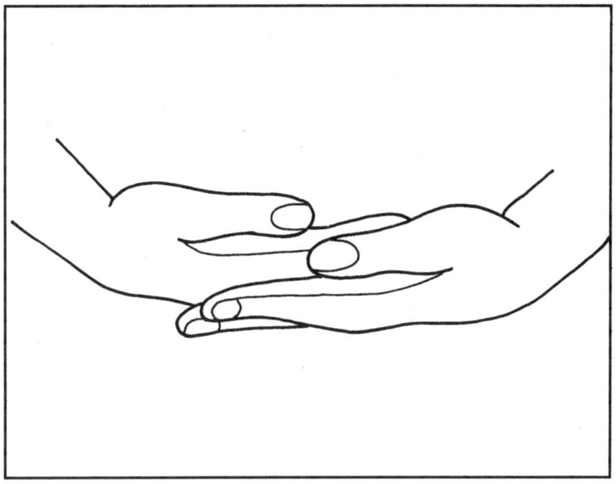

Figure 217 -- jo-in (mudra) I
(as seen by another)

jo-in (mudra) II -- (Jap.: *jō-in-mudrā;* Chin.: *ting-yin* [*mudra*]; Ind.: *dhyāna mudrā, dhyānahasta mudrā, samādhi mudrā, yoga mudrā;* Thai: *pang phra-nang;* Tib.: *bsam-gtan phyag-rgya*) A *mudra*, a ritual hand pose, a seal, which is common to the Japanese and Chinese Buddhist traditions. Also, a *tantric mudra* which is common to the Japanese Buddhist (*Vajrayana, Mantrayana*) tradition and is held or formed by a devotee or priest during the rites of *Garbhadhatu Mandala, Vajradhatu Mandala, Homa Rites* and other rites. It may be accompanied by a *mantra*. A variation of *jo-in* (*mudra*) known as Type A: Variant 2. The *jo-in* (*mudra*) *II* is a combined (Ind.: *saṁyutta*) form, held by both hands. This *mudra* (Type A: Variant 2) is formed by: palms facing upwards, fingers and thumb together, extended and relaxed, thus formed, the right hand rests upon the left hand at approximately 45°, and the *mudra* is held in the lap. (EDS 86) (See: **Figure 218**)

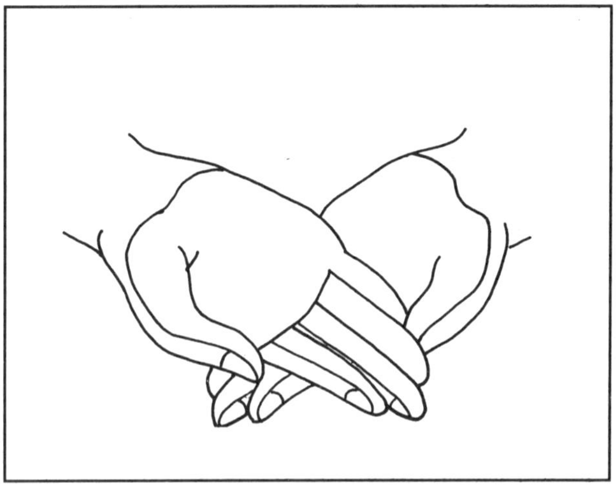

Figure 218 -- jo-in (mudra) II
(as seen by another)

jo-in (mudra) III -- (Jap.: *jō-in-mudrā;* Chin.: *ting-yin* [*mudra*]; Ind.: *dhyāna mudrā, dhyānahasta mudrā, samādhi mudrā, yoga mudrā;* Thai: *pang phra-nang;* Tib.: *bsam-gtan phyag-rgya*) A *mudra*, a ritual hand pose, a seal, which is common to the Japanese and Chinese Buddhist traditions. Also, a *tantric mudra* which is common to the Japanese Buddhist (*Vajrayana, Mantrayana*) tradition and is held or formed by a devotee or priest during

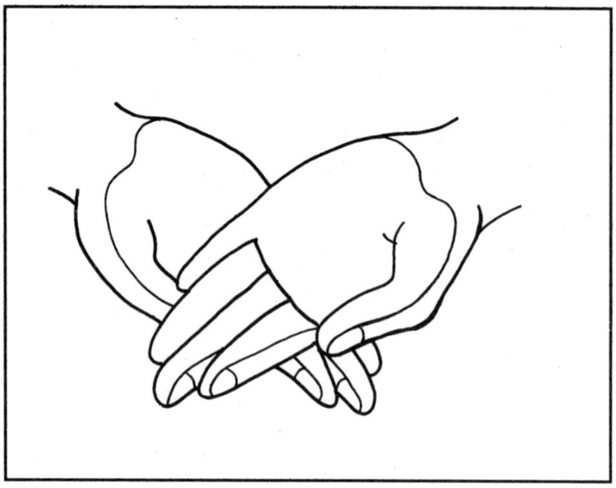

Figure 219 -- jo-in (mudra) III
(as seen by another)

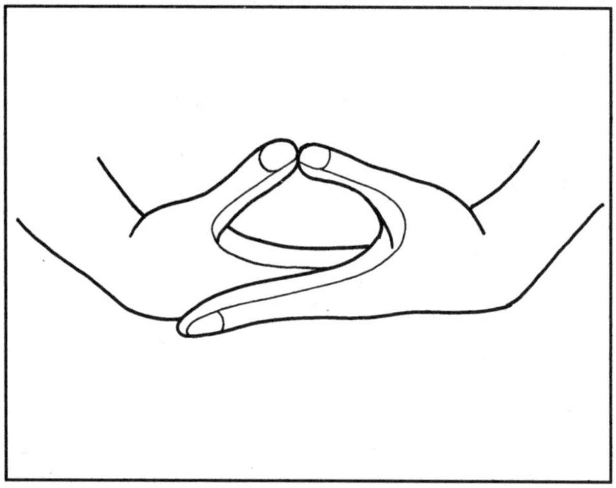

Figure 220 -- jo-in (mudra) IV
(as seen by another)

the rites of *Garbhadhatu Mandala, Vajradhatu Mandala, Homa Rites* and other rites. It may be accompanied by a *mantra.* A variation of *jo-in* (*mudra*) known as Type A: Variant 2. The *jo-in* (*mudra*) *III* is a combined (Ind.: *saṁyutta*) form, held by both hands. This *mudra* (Type A: Variant 2), the opposite to the one immediately above, is formed by: palms facing upwards, fingers and thumb together, extended and relaxed, thus formed, the left hand rests upon the right hand at approximately 45°, and the *mudra* is held in the lap. (EDS 86) (See: **Figure 219**)

jo-in (mudra) IV -- (Jap.: *jō-in-mudrā;* Chin.: *ting-yin* [*mudra*]; Ind.: *dhyāna mudrā, dhyānahasta mudrā, samādhi mudrā, yoga mudrā;* Thai: *pang phra-nang;* Tib.: *bsam-gtan phyag-rgya*) A *mudra,* a ritual hand pose, a seal, which is common to the Japanese and Chinese Buddhist traditions. Also, a *tantric mudra* which is common to the Japanese Buddhist (*Vajrayana, Mantrayana*) tradition and is held or formed by a devotee or priest during the rites of *Garbhadhatu Mandala, Vajradhatu Mandala, Homa Rites* and other rites. It may be accompanied by a *mantra.* A variation of *jo-in* (*mudra*) known as Type B: Variant 1.[14] The *jo-in* (*mudra*) *IV* is a combined (Ind.: *saṁyutta*) form, held by both hands. This *mudra* (Type B: Variant 1) is formed by: palms facing upwards, fingers together, extended and relaxed, the tips of the thumbs are raised at approximately 45°, and the tips of the thumbs touch forming a triangle with the fingers, thus formed, the right hand rests upon the left hand, and the *mudra* is held in the lap. (EDS 86) (See: **Figure 220**)

jo-in (mudra) V -- (Jap.: *jō-in-mudrā;* Chin.: *ting-yin* [*mudra*]; Ind.: *dhyāna mudrā, dhyānahasta mudrā, samādhi mudrā, yoga mudrā;* Thai: *pang phra-nang;* Tib.: *bsam-gtan phyag-rgya*) A *mudra,* a ritual hand pose, a seal, which is common to the Japanese and Chinese Buddhist traditions. Also, a *tantric mudra* which is common to the Japanese Buddhist (*Vajrayana, Mantrayana*) tradition and is held or formed by a devotee or priest during the rites of *Garbhadhatu Mandala, Vajradhatu Mandala, Homa Rites* and other rites. It may be accompanied by a *mantra.* A variation of *jo-in* (*mudra*) known as Type B: Variant 1.[15] The *jo-in* (*mudra*) *V* is a combined (Ind.: *saṁyutta*) form, held by both hands. This *mudra* (Type

B: Variant 1) is formed by: palms facing upwards, fingers together, extended and relaxed, the thumbs are raised at approximately 45°, and the tips of the thumbs touch forming a triangle with the fingers, thus formed, the left hand rests upon the right hand, and the *mudra* is held in the lap. (EDS 86) (See: **Figure 221**)

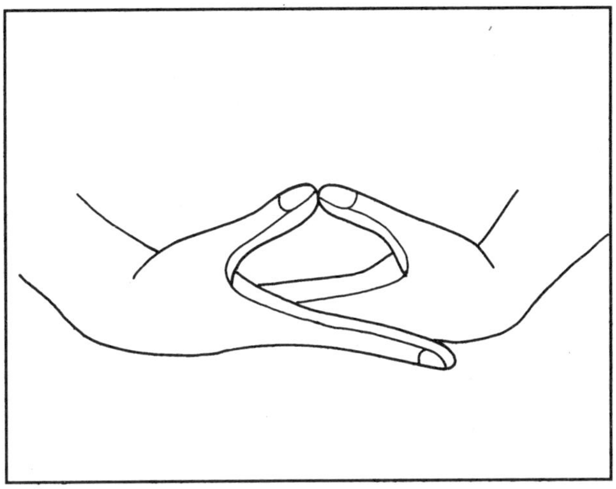

Figure 221 -- jo-in (mudra) V
(as seen by another)

jo-in (mudra) VI -- (Jap.: *jō-in-mudrā;* Chin.: *ting-yin* [*mudra*]; Ind.: *dhyāna mudrā, dhyānahasta mudrā, samādhi mudrā, yoga mudrā;* Thai: *pang phra-nang;* Tib.: *bsam-gtan phyag-rgya*) A *mudra,* a ritual hand pose, a seal, which is common to the Japanese and Chinese Buddhist traditions. Also, a *tantric mudra* which is common to the Japanese Buddhist (*Vajrayana, Mantrayana*) tradition and is held or formed by a devotee or priest during the rites of *Garbhadhatu Mandala, Vajradhatu Mandala, Homa Rites* and other rites. It may be accompanied by a mantra. A *mudra,* a ritual hand pose, a seal, which is common to the Japanese Buddhist tradition. A variation of *jo-in* (*mudra*) known as Type C: Variant 1.[16] The *jo-in* (*mudra*) *VI* is a combined (Ind.: *saṁyutta*) form, held by both hands. This *mudra* (Type C: Variant 1) is formed by: the left hand rests on the right, palms facing upwards, the first and second phalanges of the index fingers touch along their back surface (pointing upwards), the tip of the thumbs touch the tip of the respective index fingers, the middle, ring and little fingers are extended, and the *mudra* is held in the lap. (EDS 86) (See: **Figure 222**)

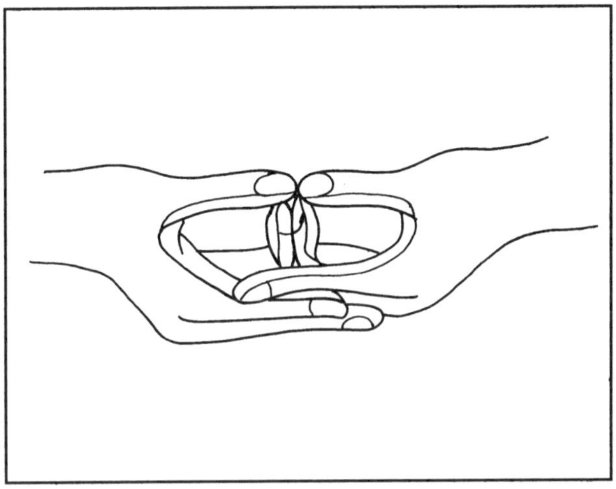

Figure 222-- jo-in (mudra) VI
(as seen by another)

jo-in (mudra) VII -- (Jap.: *jō-in-mudrā;* Chin.: *ting-yin* [*mudra*]; Ind.: *dhyāna mudrā, dhyānahasta mudrā, samādhi mudrā, yoga mudrā;* Thai: *pang phra-nang;* Tib.: *bsam-gtan phyag-rgya*) A *mudra,* a ritual hand pose, a seal, which is common to the Japanese and Chinese Buddhist traditions. Also, a *tantric mudra* which is common to the Japanese Buddhist (*Vajrayana, Mantrayana*) tradition and is held or formed by a devotee or priest during the rites of *Garbhadhatu Mandala, Vajradhatu Mandala, Homa Rites* and other rites. It may be accompanied by a *mantra.* A *mudra,* a ritual hand pose, a seal, which is common to the Japanese Buddhist tradition. A variation of *jo-in* (*mudra*) known as Type C: Variant 2. The *jo-in* (*mudra*) *VII* is a combined (Ind.: *saṁyutta*) form, held by both hands. This *mudra* (Type C: Variant 2) is formed by: the left hand rests on the right, palms fac-

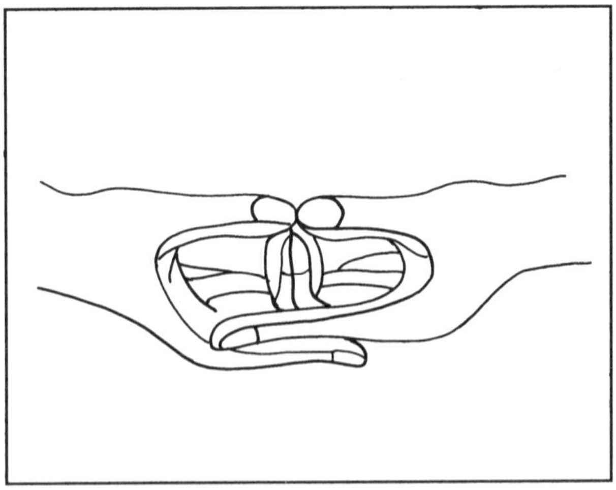

Figure 223 -- jo-in (mudra) VII
(as seen by another)

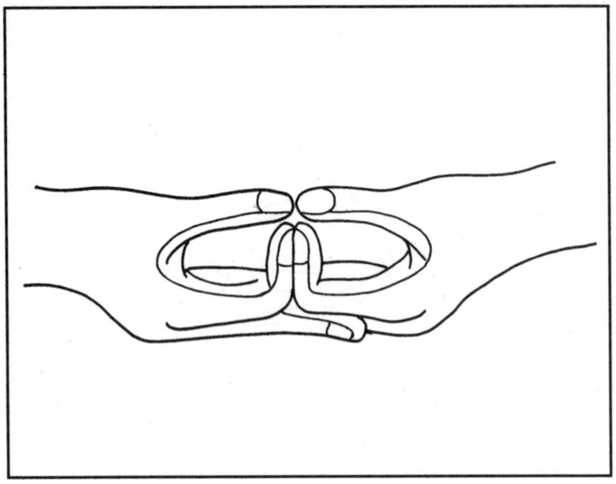

Figure 224 -- jo-in (mudra) VIII
(as seen by another)

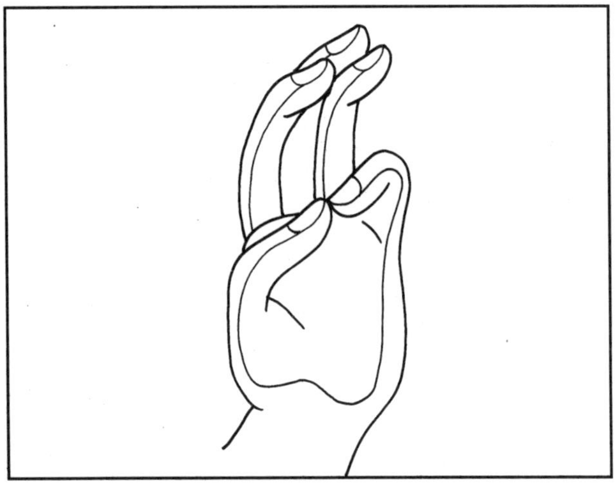

Figure 225 -- jo zu ma ko ku-in (mudra)
(as seen by another)

ing upwards, the first and second phalanges of the middle fingers touch along their back surface (pointing upwards), the tip of the thumbs touch the tip of the respective middle fingers, the index, ring and little fingers are extended, and the *mudra* is held in the lap. (EDS 86) (See: **Figure 223**)

jo-in (mudra) VIII -- (Jap.: *jō-in-mudrā*; Chin.: *ting-yin* [*mudra*]; Ind.: *dhyāna mudrā, dhyānahasta mudrā, samādhi mudrā, yoga mudrā*; Thai: *pang phra-nang*; Tib.: *bsam-gtan phyag-rgya*) A *mudra*, a ritual hand pose, a seal, which is common to the Japanese and Chinese Buddhist traditions. Also, a *tantric mudra* which is common to the Japanese Buddhist (*Vajrayana, Mantrayana*) tradition and is held or formed by a devotee or priest during the rites of *Garbhadhatu Mandala, Vajradhatu Mandala, Homa Rites* and other rites. It may be accompanied by a *mantra*. A *mudra*, a ritual hand pose, a seal, which is common to the Japanese Buddhist tradition. A variation of *jo-in* (*mudra*) known as Type C: Variant 3. The *jo-in* (*mudra*) *VIII* is a combined (Ind.: *saṁyutta*) form, held by both hands. This *mudra* (Type C: Variant 3) is formed by: the left hand rests on the right, palms facing upwards, the first and second phalanges of the ring fingers touch along their back surface (pointing upwards), the tip of the thumbs touch the tip of the respective ring fingers, the index, middle and little fingers are extended, and the *mudra* is held in the lap. (EDS 86) (See: **Figure 224**)

jo zu ma ko ku-in (mudra) -- (Jap.: *jō zu ma ko ku-in* [*mudrā*]) ("the expulsion of the demons and the purification of impurities") A *mudra*, a ritual hand pose, a seal, a *tantric mudra* which is common to the Japanese Buddhist (*Vajrayana, Mantrayana*) tradition and is held or formed by a devotee or priest during the *Eighteen-step Rites*. It may be accompanied by a *mantra*. The *jo zu ma ko ku-in*[17] (*mudra*) is a single (Ind.: *asaṁyutta*) form, held by one hand. It denotes double purification. This *mudra* is formed by: left palm generally faces forward, thumb and little figure curl towards the palm and their tips touch, index, middle and ring fingers extend upward and flex at their first knuckles.[18] (GDe 106) (See: **Figure 225**)

ju-ni kushi ji shin-in (mudra) -- (Jap.: *ju-ni kushi ji shin-in* [*mudrā*]; Ind.: *mahā-bana mudrā*) A *mudra*, a ritual hand pose, a seal, a *tantric mudra* which is common to the Japanese Buddhist (*Vajrayana, Mantrayana*) tradition and is held or formed by a devotee or priest during the rites of *Garbhadhatu Mandala, Vajradhatu Mandala, Homa Rites* and other rites. It may be accompanied by a *mantra*. The ju-*ni kushi ji shin-in* (*mudra*) is a combined (Ind.: *saṁyutta*) form, held by both hands. It denotes purification of the whole body. This *mudra* is formed by: palms oriented downwards, tips of the thumbs and little fingers touch, index and middle fingers rest on the backs of the opposite hands, middle fingers point downward flexing at their second knuckles and touching along the first and second phalanges of both. (GDe 17, LCS 126) (See: **Figure 226**)

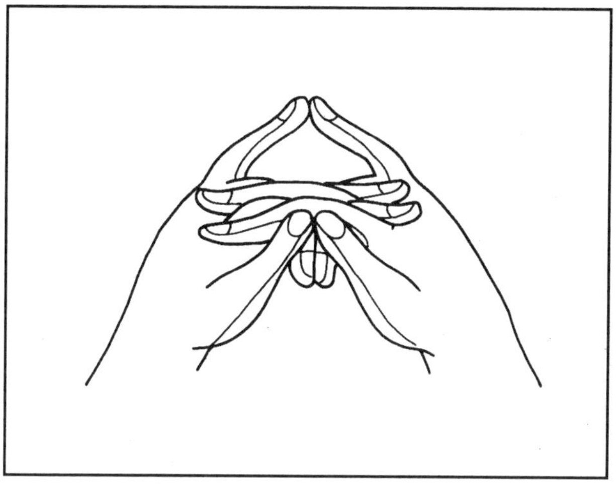

Figure 226 -- ju-ni kushi ji shin-in (mudra)
(as seen by the holder)

jyeshta-bhratri mudra -- (Ind.: *jyeṣṭa-bhrātṛ-mudrā*) A hand pose, a seal, a dramatic (Ind.: *nāṭya*) *mudra* or gesture (Ind.: *darpaṇa*) held or formed by a performer, dancer or actor. The *jyeshta-bhratri mudra* is a combined (Ind.: *saṁyutta*) form, held by both hands. One of eleven mudras representing "relationships" and one which denotes older brother. This *mudra* is formed by: right palm facing outwards, tips of the thumb and ring finger touch and extend outwards, the index and middle fingers are straight and slightly separated, the little fingers is slightly bent; left palm facing the midline, tips of the thumb and ring finger touch and extend inwards, the index and middle fingers are straight and slightly separated, the little fingers is slightly bent. (ACG 45) (See: **Figure 227**)

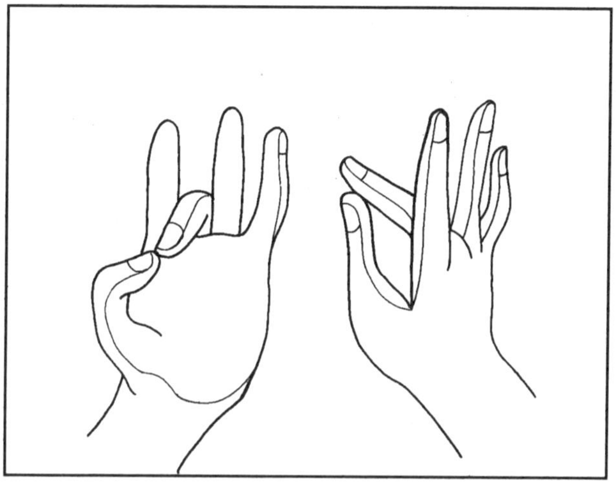

Figure 227 -- jyeshta-bhratri mudra
(as seen by the holder)

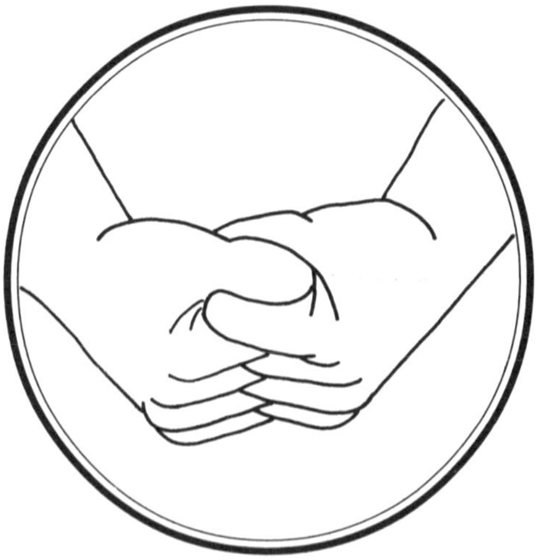

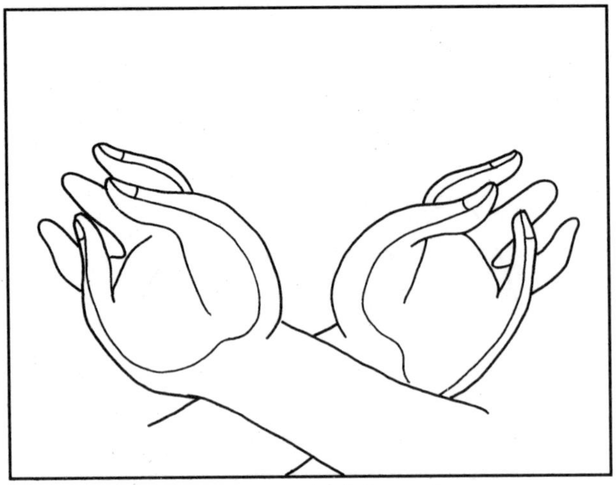

Figure 228 -- kadali mudra
(as seen by the holder)

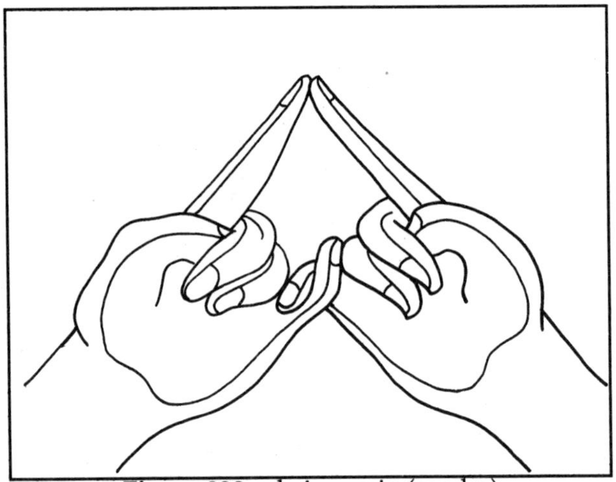

Figure 229 -- kai mon-in (mudra)
(as seen by the holder)

-- K --

kacchapa mudra -- (Ind.: *kaccapa-mudrā* aka *kaśyapa mudrā*) A variant (spelling) of *kashyapa mudra*. See: *kashyapa mudra*. (GLi, MJS 62)

kadali mudra -- (Ind.: *kadalī-mudrā*) A hand pose, a seal, a dramatic (Ind.: *nāṭya*) *mudra* or gesture (Ind.: *darpaṇa*) held or formed by a performer, dancer or actor. It denotes the *kadali* tree. The *kadali mudra* is a combined (Ind.: *saṁyutta*) form, held by both hands. This *mudra* is formed by: palms face forwards, the tips of the fingers and thumbs are brought together, but not necessarily touching, pointing forwards. Thus formed, the hands cross at the wrist, extended in front of chest and fingers move.[1] See: *mukula mudra* . (ACG 48) (See: **Figure 228**)

kai mon-in (mudra) -- (Jap.: *kai mon-in* [*mudrā*]) ("opening the gate") A *mudra*, a ritual hand pose, a seal, a *tantric mudra* which is common to the Japanese Buddhist (*Vajrayana, Mantrayana*) tradition and is held or formed by a devotee or priest during the rites of *Garbhadhatu Mandala, Vajradhatu Mandala, Homa Rites* and other rites. It may be accompanied by a *mantra*. The *kai mon-in* (*mudra*) is a combined (Ind.: *saṁyutta*) form, held by both hands. It denotes the opening of the "gates" of the *mandala*. This *mudra* is identical for both hand and is formed by: folding the middle and ring fingers into the palms, folding the thumbs over the middle and ring fingers, index finger extends, little finger extends and forms a "hook" by flexing the first two phalanges. Thus formed the palms face the midline, the tips of the index fingers touch and the little fingers' hook." (GDe 75, LCS 59) (See: **Figure 229**)

ka-in (mudra) -- (Jap.: *ka-in* [*mudrā*]) ("the wall of flames") A *mudra*, a ritual hand pose, a seal, a *tantric mudra* which is common to the Japanese Buddhist (*Vajrayana, Mantrayana*) tradition and is held or formed by a devotee or priest during the *Eighteen-step Rites*. It may be accompanied by a *mantra*. The *ka-in* (*mudra*) is a combined (Ind.: *saṁyutta*) form, held by both hands. It denotes the expulsion and frightening of the malevolent spirits from the sacred precincts. This *mudra* is formed by: palms facing generally the midline, fingers and thumbs extending upward, hands are slightly cupped. Thus formed the right hand rests in the left at approximately a 30° angle.[2] (GDe 106) (See: **Figure 230**)

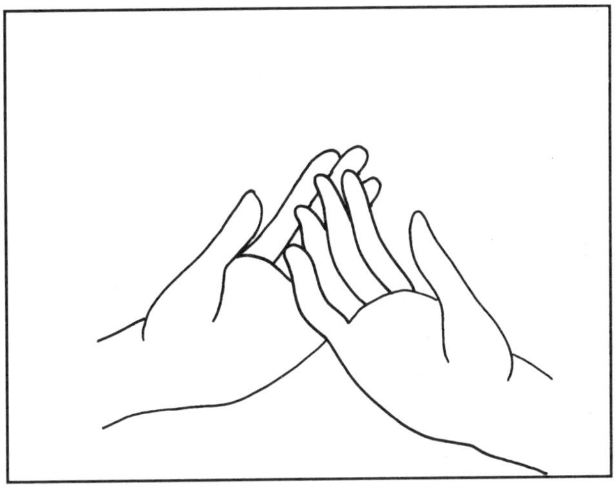

Figure 230 -- ka-in (mudra)
(as seen by the holder)

kai shin-in (mudra) -- (Jap.: *kai shin-in* [*mudrā*]) ("opening the spirit") A *mudra*, a ritual hand pose, a seal, a *tantric mudra* which is common to the Japanese Buddhist (*Vajrayana, Mantrayana*) tradition and is held or formed by a devotee or priest during the rites of *Garbhadhatu Mandala, Vajradhatu Mandala, Homa Rites* and other rites. It may be accompanied by a *mantra*. The *kai shin-in*[3] (*mudra*) is a combined (Ind.: *saṁyutta*) form, held by both hands. It denotes the opening of the spirit of the devotee. This *mudra* is formed by: palms face downward, fingers are slightly separated and point towards the midline, the tips of the thumbs and fingers of both hands interlace. (GDe 62) (See: **Figure 231**)

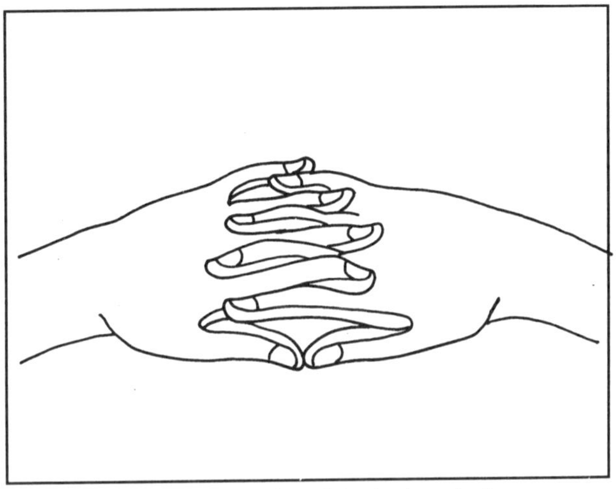

Figure 231 -- kai shin-in (mudra)
(as seen by the holder)

kaji ko sui-in (mudra) -- (Jap.: *kaji kō sui-in* [*mudrā*]) ("consecrating the perfumed water") A *mudra*, a ritual hand pose, a seal, a *tantric mudra* which is common to the Japanese Buddhist (*Vajrayana, Mantrayana*) tradition and is held or formed by a devotee or priest during the rites of *Garbhadhatu Mandala and Vajradhatu Mandala Rites*. It may be accompanied by a *mantra*. The *kaji ko sui-in* (*mudra*)[4] is a single (Ind.: *asaṁyutta*) form, held by one hand. It denotes the sanctification of perfumed libation. This *mudra* is structured by: the right hand forming a lotus fist (Ind.: *padma muṣṭi*; Jap.: *renge ken-in*) and holding in that fist a single-pronged *vajra* (Jap.: *do ko*). (GDe 6) (See: **Figure 232**)

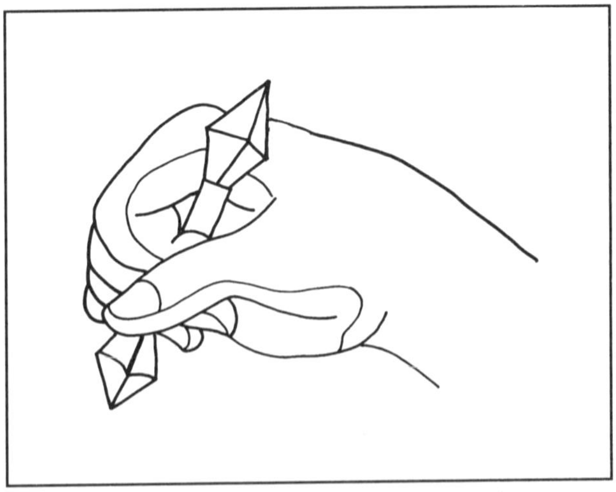

Figure 232 -- kaji ko sui-in (mudra)
(as seen by the holder)

kaka mudra -- (Ind.: *kāka-mudrā*) A hand pose, a seal, a dramatic (Ind.: *nāṭya*) *mudra* or gesture (Ind.: *darpana*) held or formed by a performer, dancer or actor. It denotes a bird, in this case a crow. The *kaka mudra*[5] is a combined (Ind.: *saṁyutta*) form, held by both hands. This *mudra* is identical in form to the *samdamsa-mukula mudra*. See: *samdamsa-mukula mudra*. (ACG 50)

Kalkiavatara mudra -- (Ind.: *Kalkiavatāra-mudrā*) A hand pose, a seal, a dramatic (Ind.: *nāṭya*) *mudra* or gesture (Ind.: *darpaṇa*) held or formed by a performer,

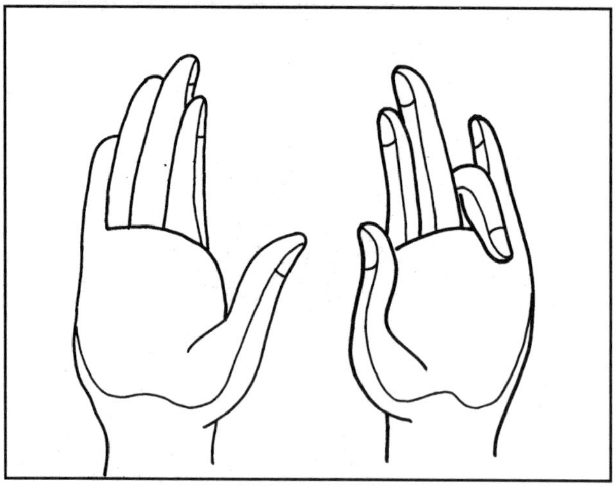

Figure 233 -- Kalkiavatara mudra
(as seen by another)

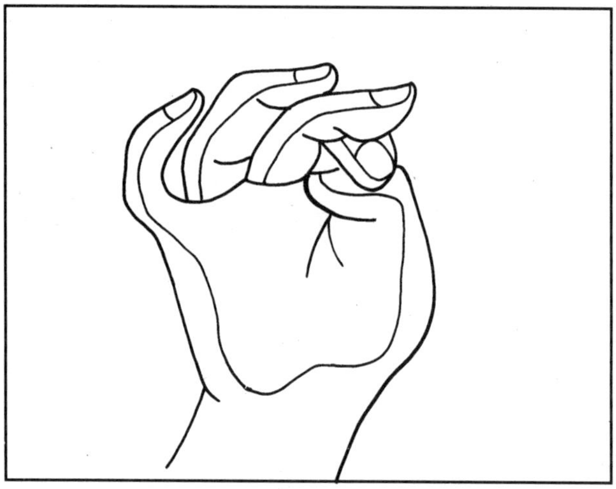

Figure 234 -- kamjayi mudra
(as seen by another)

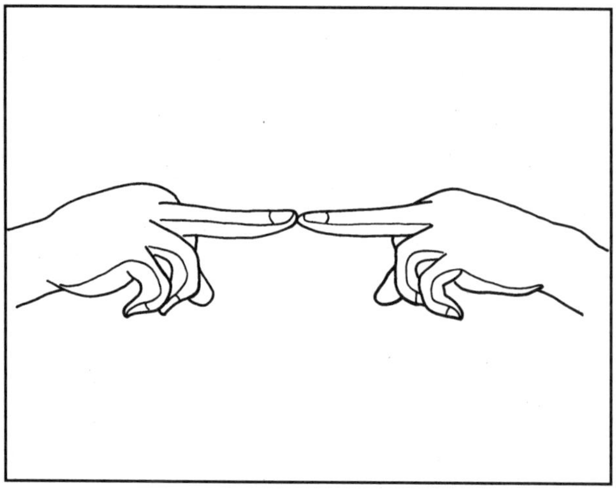

Figure 235 -- kanaka-matsya mudra
(as seen by another)

dancer or actor. The *Kalkiavatara mudra* is a combined (Ind.: *saṁyutta*) form, held by both hands. It denotes *Kalki*, one of the ten *avatars* (Ind.: *daśavātāra*) of the Lord *Vishnu* This *mudra* is formed by: right palm facing forward, fingers and thumb extended, together and pointing upwards, relaxed, slightly cupped; left palm facing forward, index, middle and little fingers and thumb extended, together and pointing upwards, ring finger is bent towards the palm. (ACG 46) (See: **Figure 233**)

kamala mudra -- (Ind.: *kamala mudrā*; Jap.: *kumma(n)ra gassho [mudra]*) The Indic term for *kumma(n)ra gassho (mudra)*. See: *kumma(n)ra gassho (mudra)*. (EDS 40)

kamjayi mudra -- (Ind.: *kāmjayī-mudrā*) A *mudra*, a ritual hand pose, a seal, a *mudra* which is common to yogic tradition, particularly the *Yoga Tatva Mudra Vigyan* form, and is held by a devotee or practitioner. The *kamjayi mudra* is a single (Ind.: *asaṁyutta*) form, held by one hand. It is utilized for repressing sexual urges. This *mudra* is formed by: right palm faces the midline, index finger curls behind and rests on the knuckle below the nail of the thumb, the middle finger curls behind and rests behind the second knuckle of the index finger, the ring finger curls behind and rests behind the second knuckle of the middle finger, the little finger curls behind and rests behind the second knuckle of the ring finger. So formed, the *mudra* is held chest high. (KDe 100) (See: **Figure 234**)

kanaka-matsya mudra -- (Ind.: *kanaka-matsya-mudrā*) This is an assigned term.[6] A *mudra*, a ritual hand pose, a seal, which is common to the Buddhist (*Vajrayana*) tradition, a *tantric mudra*. It denotes the golden fish (Tib.: *gser-gyi nya*), one of eight signs of good fortune (Indic: *aṣṭa-maṅgala*, Tib.: *bkra-shis rtags-brgyad*), an 'outer offering'--the other seven being: the knot, wheel, lotus, victory banner, umbrella, treasure vase and conch shell--which is proffered to a divine guest during worship, particularly as associated with the ceremonies of the powerful *Vajrayana* goddess, *Tara*. The form is held by both hands in mirror-pose: the palms face downwards, the hand is loosely fisted, the middle finger extends forward and touches the tip of the other middle finger so posed. The *mudra* is held at chin level. The *mantra* associated with this *mudra* is: "OM

Kanaka-matsya Praticcha SVAHA."[7] (SBe 155) (See: **Figure 235**)

kandanjali mudra -- (Ind.: *kaṇḍañjāli-mudrā*) A hand pose, a seal, a dramatic (Ind.: *nāṭya*) *mudra* or gesture (Ind.: *darpaṇa*) held or formed by a performer, dancer or actor. The *kandanjali mudra* represents a camel and is a combined (Ind.: *saṁyutta*) form, held by both hands. This *mudra* is formed by: both hands brought close together, palm to palm, fingers extended upwards, slightly cupped, the thumbs together and move up and down. (ACG 50) (See: **Figure 236**)

kanishtha-bhratri mudra -- (Ind.: *kaniṣṭha-bhrātr-mudrā*) A hand pose, a seal, a dramatic (Ind.: *nāṭya*) *mudra* or gesture (Ind.: *darpaṇa*) held or formed by a performer, dancer or actor. The *kanishtha-bhratri mudra* is a combined (Ind.: *saṁyutta*) form, held by both hands. One of eleven *mudras* representing "relationships" and one which denotes young brother. This *mudra* is formed by: right palm facing inwards, tips of the thumb and ring finger touch and extend forwards, the index and middle fingers are straight and slightly separated, the little fingers is slightly bent; left palm faces the outward, tips of the thumb and ring finger touch and extend inwards, the index and middle fingers are straight and slightly separated, the little fingers is slightly bent. (ACG 45) (See: **Figure 237**)

kanjo-in (mudra) -- (Jap.: *kanjo-in* [*mudrā*]; Chin.: *kuan-ting-yin*; Ind.: *abhiṣeka*[*na*] *mudrā*) A *mudra*, a ritual hand pose, a seal, which is common to the Buddhist *Mahayana* and *Vajrayana* Japanese and Chinese Buddhist traditions. Also, a *tantric mudra* which is common to the Japanese and Chinese Buddhist (*Vajrayana, Mantrayana*) tradition and is held or formed by a devotee or priest. It may be accompanied by a *mantra*. It denotes the ceremony of anointing. The *kanjo-in* (*mudra*) is a combined (Ind.: *saṁyutta*) form, held by both hands. This *mudra* is formed in mirror image: middle, ring and little fingers are folded into the palm, the index finger is extended and the thumb lays against the index finger. So formed the two hands are brought together, thumbs touching along their length, the upper phalanges of the index fingers are pressed together and the middle, ring and little fingers are intermeshed in-

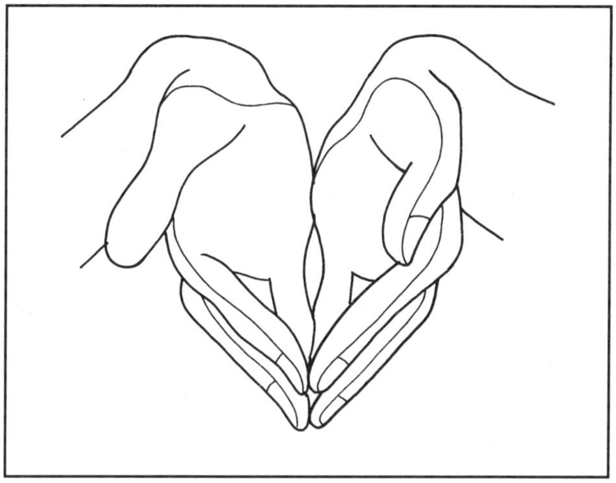

Figure 236 -- kandanjali mudra
(as seen by another)

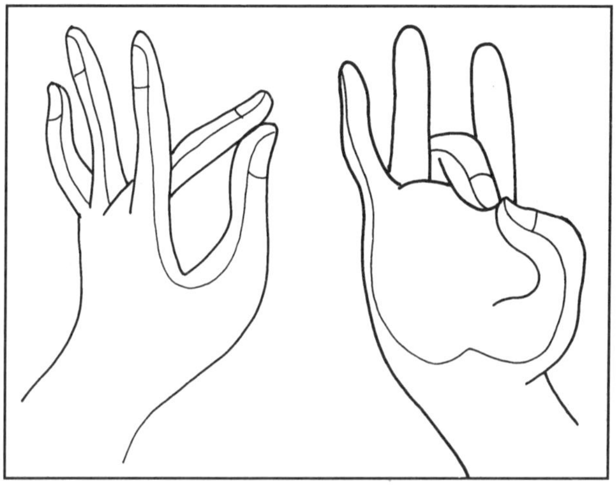

Figure 237 -- kanishtha-bhratri mudra
(as seen by another)

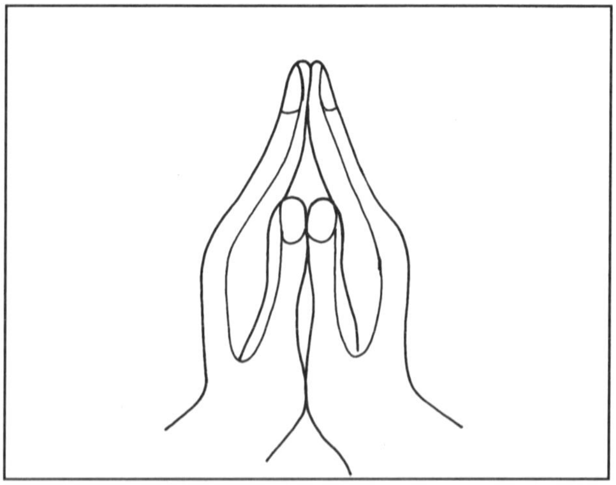

Figure 238 -- kanjo-in (mudra)
(as seen by the holder)

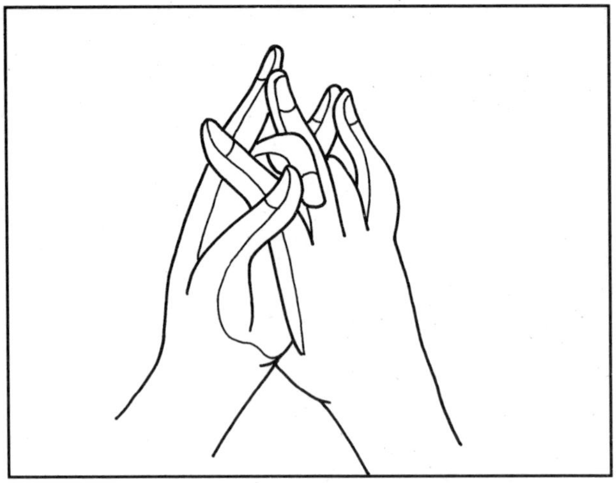

Figure 239 -- kanshukuden-in (mudra)
(as seen by the holder)

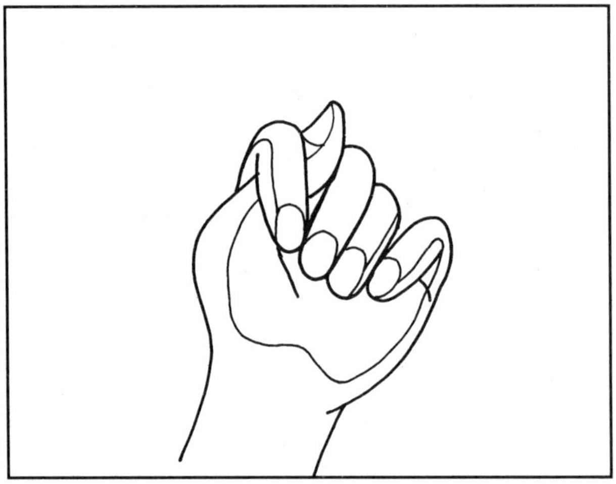

Figure 240 -- kapittha mudra I
(as seen by another)

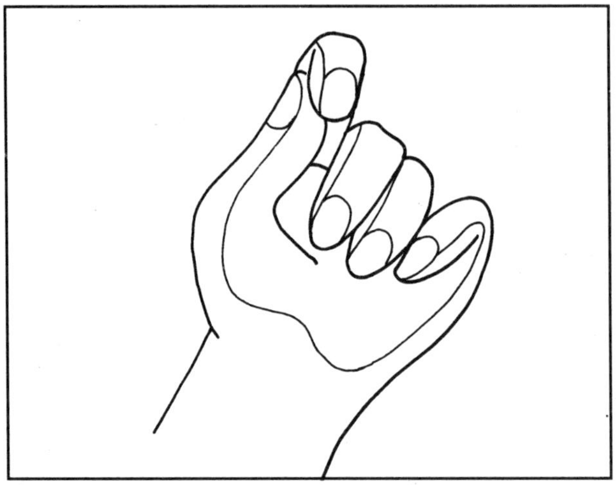

Figure 241 -- kapittha mudra II
(as seen by the holder)

side. The index fingers point upward. This *mudra* is held chest high. (EDS 111, LCS 154) (See: **Figure 238**)

kanshukuden-in (mudra) -- (Jap.: *kanshukuden-in* [*mudrā*]) A *mudra*, a ritual hand pose, a seal, a *tantric mudra* which is common to the Japanese Buddhist (*Vajrayana, Mantrayana*) tradition and is held or formed by a devotee or priest. It may be accompanied by a *mantra*. The *kanshukuden-in* (*mudra*) is a combined (Ind.: *saṁyutta*) form, held by both hands. It denotes the *Shadakshara-sutra*. This *mudra* is formed by: palms facing midline, left thumb-tip touches tip of curled middle finger, index and little fingers extend upward, ring finger is curled; right thumb, index, middle and little fingers extend upwards, ring finger curls. Thus formed, the right thumb is placed behind the outside edge of the left palm, the right index finger is inserted through the circle formed by the left thumb and middle finger, the tip of the right middle finger crosses the tip of the left index finger and the tips of both little fingers cross. (GDe 209) (See: **Figure 239**)

kapittha mudra I -- (Ind.: *kapittha-mudrā*) ("elephant apple") A *mudra*, a ritual hand pose, a seal, which is common to the Hindu tradition and is depicted or held by a deity. The *kapittha mudra* is a single (Ind.: *asaṁyutta*) form, held by one hand. It represents the offering of incense, a wood-apple ("elephant apple") and sexual union.[8] The *kapittha mudra I* is a single (Ind.: *asaṁyutta*) form, held by one hand. This *mudra* is formed usually by the left: the hand is fisted, the thumb is inserted between the index and middle fingers so formed. It is similar in form to the *kashyapa mudra* and represents the female sexual organ. It is the feminine counterpart of the *shikhara mudra*. (GLi 127, MJS 68) (See: **Figure 240**)

kapittha mudra II -- (Ind.: *kapittha-mudrā*) ("elephant apple") A hand pose, a seal, a dramatic (Ind.: *nāṭya*) *mudra* or gesture (Ind.: *darpaṇa*) held or formed by a performer, dancer or actor. The *kapittha mudra II* is a single (Ind.: *asaṁyutta*) form, held by one hand. It denotes milking cows, offering incense, etc.[9] This *mudra* is a variation formed by: first assuming the *mushti mudra* (palm faces the midline, the fingers are fisted, the thumb lies over the first phalanges of the fingers) except the index finger curls over the top of the thumb. (ACG 31, KVa 135 [13 & 14]) (See: **Figure 241**)

kapittha mudra III -- (Ind.: *kapittha-mudrā*) A hand pose, a seal, a dramatic (Ind.: *nāṭya*) *mudra* or gesture (Ind.: *darpaṇa*) held or formed by a performer, dancer or actor. It denotes the *kapittha* or elephant-apple tree. The *kapittha mudra III* is a combined (Ind.: *saṁyutta*) form, held by both hands. This *mudra* is formed by: palms turned upwards, thumbs and fingers are stretched far apart, stiff; so formed, the little fingers are at 90° to the palms and the ring fingers are at 45° to the palms. Thus formed, the hands cross at the wrists. (ACG 49) (See: **Figure 242**)

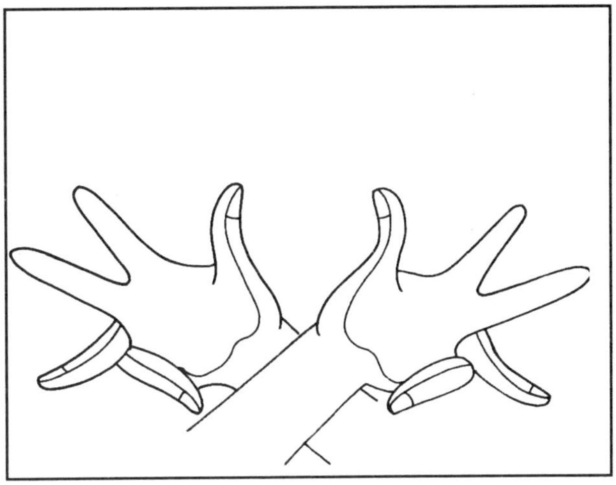

Figure 242 -- kapittha mudra III
(as seen by the holder)

kapota mudra I -- (Ind.: *kapota-mudrā*) ("the dove") A hand pose, a seal, a dramatic (Ind.: *nāṭya*) *mudra* or gesture (Ind.: *darpaṇa*) held or formed by a performer, dancer or actor. The *kapota mudra* is a combined (Ind.: *saṁyutta*) form, held by both hands. It denotes taking an oath and acquiescence. This *mudra* is formed by: palms facing the midline, fingers and thumbs extended upwards. Thus formed the hands are brought together along the outer edge of the palms and little fingers and rotated "open" somewhat so as to form a hollow space. It is similar in form although not in orientation to the *patra mudra*. (ACG 39) (See: **Figure 243**)

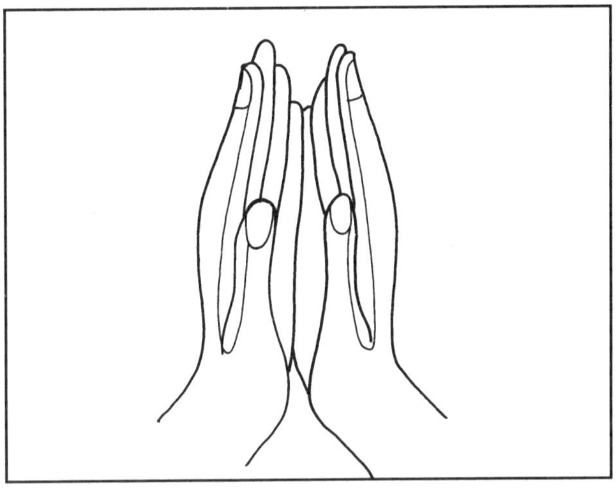

Figure 243 -- kapota mudra I
(as seen by the holder)

kapota mudra II -- (Ind.: *kapota-mudrā*) A hand pose, a seal, a dramatic (Ind.: *nāṭya*) *mudra* or gesture (Ind.: *darpaṇa*) held or formed by a performer, dancer or actor. It denotes a bird, in this case a pigeon with a speckled neck. The *kapota mudra*[10] is a combined (Ind.: *saṁyutta*) form, held by both hands. This *mudra* is formed by the *kapota mudra I*, fluttered, mimicking the flight of a bird (Ind.: *punkhita*). (ACG 50)

karana mudra I -- (Ind.: *karaṇa-mudrā*) A *mudra*, a ritual hand pose, a seal, which is common to both the Buddhist and Hindu traditions. It is employed in dance[11] and also seen as casting out demons.[12] The dance form is held in one hand: the palm faces outward, index and little fingers are erect and parallel to the ground, middle and ring fingers folded into the palm, the thumb is placed over the middle and ring fingers. This *mudra* is held to the side, generally extended outwards, however, it may be held with the fingers pointing upward.[13]

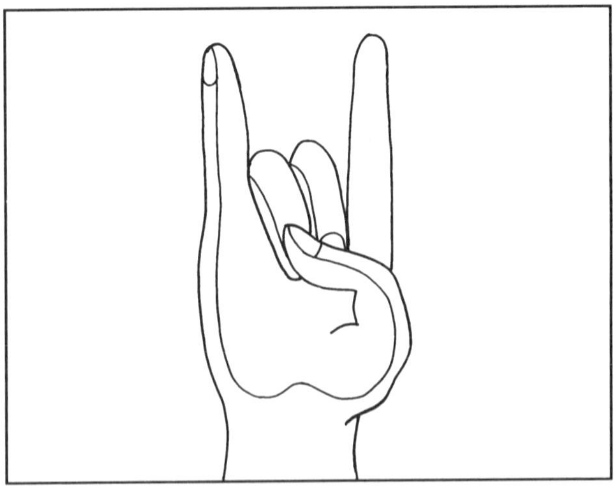

Figure 244 -- karana mudra I
(as seen by another)

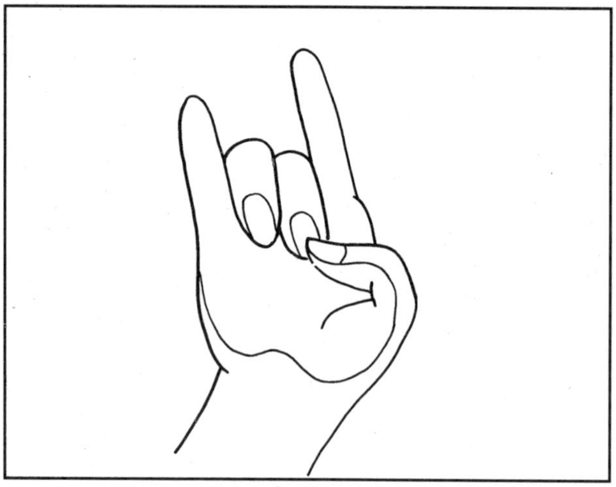
Figure 245 -- karana mudra II
(as seen by another)

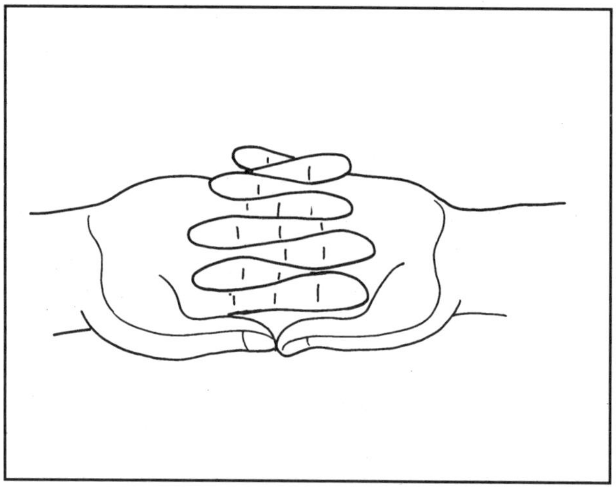
Figure 246 -- karkata mudra
(as seen by another)

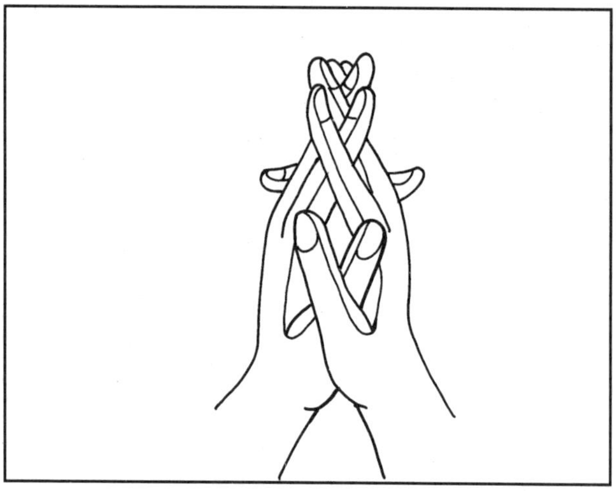
Figure 247 -- Karma-Akashagarbha mudra
(as seen by the holder)

It is to be noted that the *karana mudra* is similar in form to the *damaruhasta* (*mudra*). (AKG 20, BBh 193, BCO 154, MJS 68, RSG 7) (See: **Figure 244**)

karana mudra II -- (Ind.: *karaṇa-mudrā*) A *mudra*, a ritual hand pose, a seal, which is common to the Buddhist (*Vajrayana*) tradition, a *tantric mudra*. It is a single hand pose, a seal which denotes awe and/or amazement. The *karana mudra II* is a single (Ind.: *asaṁyutta*) form, held by one hand. This *mudra* is formed by: the middle and ring fingers curl towards the palm, the pad of the thumb touches the tip of the middle finger, the index and little fingers extend upwards, palm faces outwards, so formed the hand is held chest high.[14] (RSG 7) (See: **Figure 245**)

karihasta (mudra) -- (Ind.: *karihasta* [*mudrā*]) A *mudra*, a ritual hand pose, a seal, which is common to the Hindu tradition. A variant term applied to *gajahasta mudra*. See: *gajahasta mudra*. (JDo, BNS, MJS 69)

karkata mudra -- (Ind.: *karkaṭa-mudrā*) ("the crab") A hand pose, a seal, a dramatic (Ind.: *nāṭya*) *mudra* or gesture (Ind.: *darpaṇa*) held or formed by a performer, dancer or actor. The *karkata mudra* is a combined (Ind.: *saṁyutta*) form, held by both hands. It denotes a group, amorous feelings, bending a tree limb, etc.[15] This *mudra* is formed by: palms together, forming a fist by interlacing the fingers similar to the *granthitam mudra*, the elbows are extended outwards and the interlaced hands are rotates so the that palms face outward, fingers on the inward side. (ACG 39) (See: **Figure 246**)

Karma-Akashagarbha mudra -- (Ind.: *Karma-Ākāśagarbha-mudrā*) A *mudra*, a ritual hand pose, a seal, a *tantric mudra* which is common to the Japanese Buddhist (*Vajrayana, Mantrayana*) tradition and is held or formed by a devotee or priest during various rites in which a deity is acknowledged. It is a *mudra* which is associated with the deity *Karma-Akashagarbha*. It may be accompanied by a *mantra*. The *Karma-Akashagarbha mudra*[16] is a combined (Ind.: *saṁyutta*) form, held by both hands. This *mudra* is formed by: palms facing midline and close, thumbs crossed, right over left, index, middle and ring fingers interlace at their tips, little fingers interlace and fold over the back of the hands. (LCS 248) (See: **Figure 247**)

kartari (hasta) mudra -- (Ind.: *kartarī(hasta)-mudrā*) A *mudra*, a ritual hand pose, a seal, which is common to both the Buddhist and Hindu traditions and is depicted or held by a deity. The *kartari(hasta) mudra* is a single (Ind.: *asaṁyutta*) form, held by one hand. It denotes antagonism and death. This *mudra* is formed by: the palm faces forward the index and middle fingers are erect and separated slightly, the little finger is bent, the ring fingers bends towards the palm and the tip of the thumb touches the tip of the ring finger. The *mudra* thus held is often employed in displaying iconic devices. It is similar to the *kartari-mukha mudra* except the tips of the thumb and ring fingers in the latter do not touch. (ERJ II 25, MJS 69, RSG 3) (See: **Figure 248**)

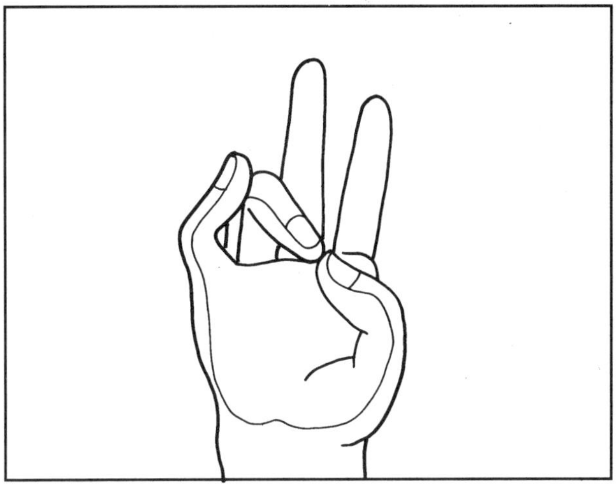

Figure 248 -- kartari (hasta) mudra
(as seen by another)

kartari-danda mudra -- (Ind.: *kartarī-daṇḍa-mudrā*) A hand pose, a seal, a dramatic (Ind.: *nāṭya*) *mudra* or gesture (Ind.: *darpaṇa*) held or formed by a performer, dancer or actor. It denotes a *dundupha* (Ind.). The *kartari-danda mudra* is a combined (Ind.: *saṁyutta*) form, held by both hands. This *mudra* is formed by: the right palm faces upwards, the index and middle fingers are extended outwards and separated slightly, the little finger is bent, the ring fingers bends towards the palm and the tip of the thumb touches the tip of the ring finger, and is placed on the left forearm; the left palm faces the midline, the fingers curve in towards the palm and the tip of the thumb touches the tip of the index finger. (ACG 51) (See: **Figure 249**)

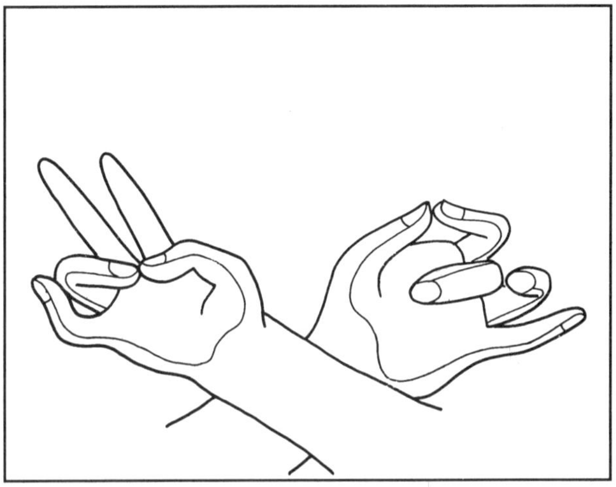

Figure 249 -- kartari-danda mudra
(as seen by the holder)

kartari-mukha mudra I -- (Ind.: *kartarī-mukha-mudrā*) ("arrow shaft face") A hand pose, a seal, a dramatic (Ind.: *nāṭya*) *mudra* or gesture (Ind.: *darpaṇa*) held or formed by a performer, dancer or actor. The *kartari-mukha-mudra* is a single (Ind.: *asaṁyutta*) form, held by one hand. It denotes: opposition, disagreement, death, etc.[17] This *mudra* is formed by: the hand raised, index, middle fingers and thumb extended, pointing upwards, the index and middle fingers are slightly separated, ring and little fingers bent towards the palm, palm facing outward and generally on a line level with the chest.[18] It is similar to the *kartari(hasta) mudra* except the tips of the thumb and ring fingers do not touch. (ACG 28-29, GDe 379, KVa 134 [4 & 5]) (See: **Figure 250**)

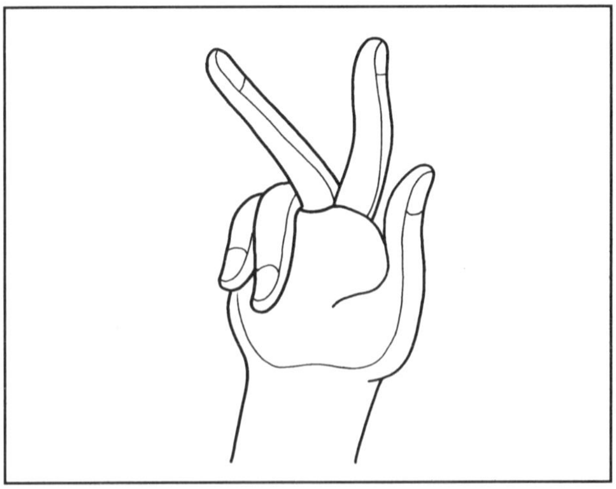

Figure 250 -- kartari-mukha mudra I
(as seen by another)

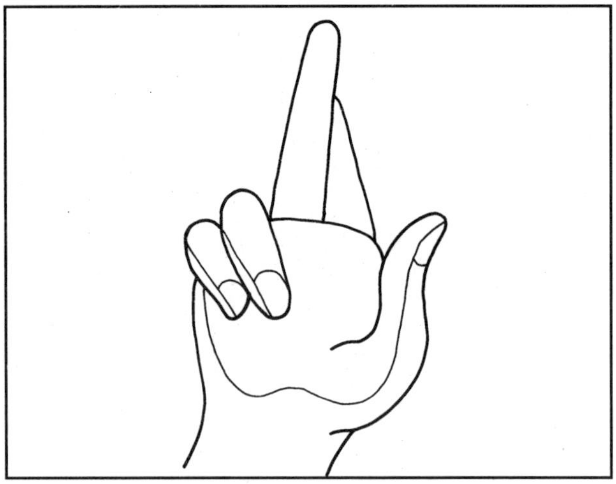

Figure 251 -- kartari-mukha mudra II
(as seen by another)

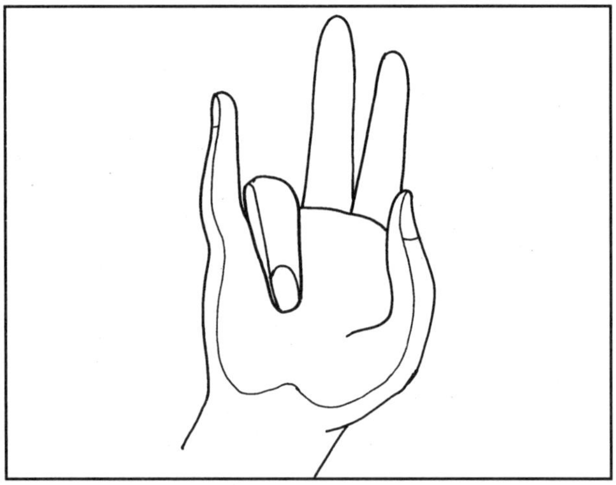

Figure 252 -- kartari-mukha mudra III
(as seen by another)

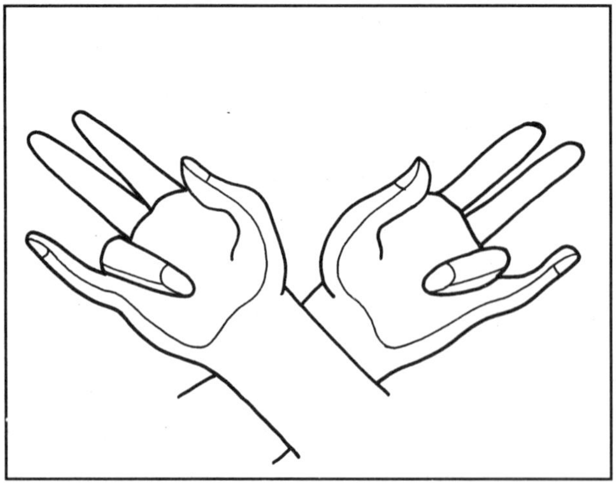

Figure 253 -- kartari-svastika mudra
(as seen by the holder)

kartari-mukha mudra II -- (Ind.: *kartarī-mukha-mudrā*) ("arrow shaft face") A hand pose, a seal, a dramatic (Ind.: *nāṭya*) *mudra* or gesture (Ind.: *darpaṇa*) held or formed by a performer, dancer or actor. The *kartari-mukha-mudra* is a single (Ind.: *asaṁyutta*) form, held by one hand. This *mudra* is a variation and formed by: the hand raised, index, middle fingers and thumb extended, pointing upwards, the index and middle fingers are slightly separated and the index finger crosses behind the middle finger, but does not touch it, ring and little fingers bent towards the palm, palm facing outward and generally on a line level with the chest. (KVa 134 [5]) (See: **Figure 251**)

kartari-mukha mudra III -- (Ind.: *kartarī-mukha-mudrā*) ("arrow shaft face") A hand pose, a seal, a dramatic (Ind.: *nāṭya*) *mudra* or gesture (Ind.: *darpaṇa*) held or formed by a performer, dancer or actor. The *kartari-mukha-mudra* is a single (Ind.: *asaṁyutta*) form, held by one hand. This *mudra* is a variation[19] formed by: the hand raised, index, middle and little fingers extended, pointing upwards, ring finger folded into the palm, the thumb bends slightly inwards, the index and middle fingers are slightly separated, palm facing outward and generally on a line level with the chest. (ACG 28-29 & Plate XI-C) (See: **Figure 252**)

kartari-svastika mudra -- (Ind.: *kartarī-svastika-mudrā*) ("crossed arrow shafts") A hand pose, a seal, a dramatic (Ind.: *nāṭya*) *mudra* or gesture (Ind.: *darpaṇa*) held or formed by a performer, dancer or actor. The *kartari-svastika mudra* is a combined (Ind.: *saṁyutta*) form, held by both hands. It denotes trees or the summit of a hill. This *mudra* is formed by: hand raised, index, middle and little fingers extended, pointing upwards, ring finger folded into the palm, the thumb bends slightly inwards, the index and middle fingers are slightly separated, palm facing outward. Thus formed by each hand, they are crossed at the wrists. (ACG 40) (See: **Figure 253**)

Karttivirya mudra -- (Ind.: *Kārttīvrya-mudrā*) A hand pose, a seal, a dramatic (Ind.: *nāṭya*) *mudra* or gesture (Ind.: *darpaṇa*) held or formed by a performer, dancer or actor. The *Karttivirya mudra* is a combined (Ind.:

saṁyutta) form, held by both hands. It denotes *Karttivirya*, one of a number of famous rulers or heroes. The *mudras* employed are two *pataka mudras* held level with the shoulder. See: *pataka mudras*. (ACG 47) (See: **Figure 254**)

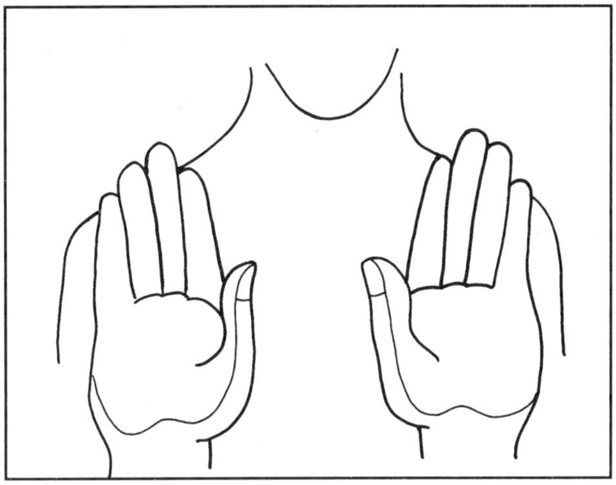

Figure 254 -- Karttivirya mudra
(as seen by another)

kashyapa mudra -- (Ind.: *kaśyapa-mudrā* aka *kacchapa mudrā*) A *mudra*, a ritual hand pose, a seal, which is common to the Hindu tradition. It denotes the *linga* with the *yoni* and is referred to as the 'turtle *mudra*.' The *kashyapa mudra* is a single (Ind.: *asaṁyutta*) form, held by one hand. This *mudra* is formed usually by the left: the hand is fisted, the thumb is inserted between the middle and ring fingers so formed. It is similar in form to the *kapittha mudra*. (GLi, MJS 70) (See: **Figure 255**)

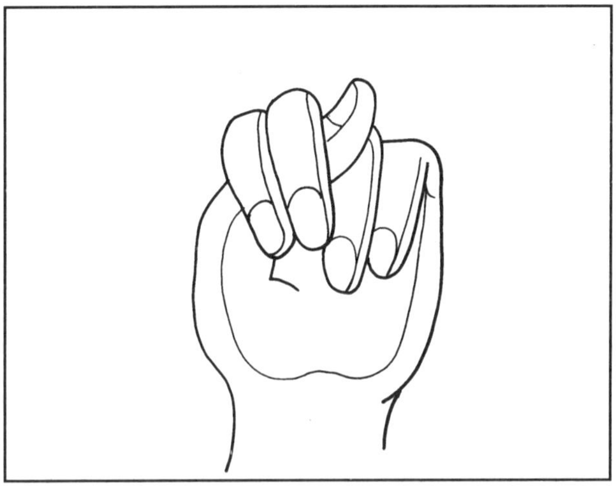

Figure 255 -- kashyapa mudra
(as seen by another)

kataka mudra I -- (Ind.: *kaṭaka-mudrā* aka *siṁha-karṇa mudrā*) A *mudra*, a ritual hand pose, a seal, which is common to the Hindu tradition, but less common in the Buddhist practice and is viewed as one of the *mudras* which are purely aesthetic--i.e., having no iconic meaning.[20] The *kataka mudra I* is a single (Ind.: *asaṁyutta*) form, held by one hand. This *mudra* is formed by: the palm faces the midline, the fingers curve in towards the palm and the tip of the thumb touches the tip of the index finger.[21] The *mudra* so formed is frequently utilized by feminine deities to hold flower offerings proffered by devotees. (HKS 272, RSG 3, TGR 14) (See: **Figure 256**)

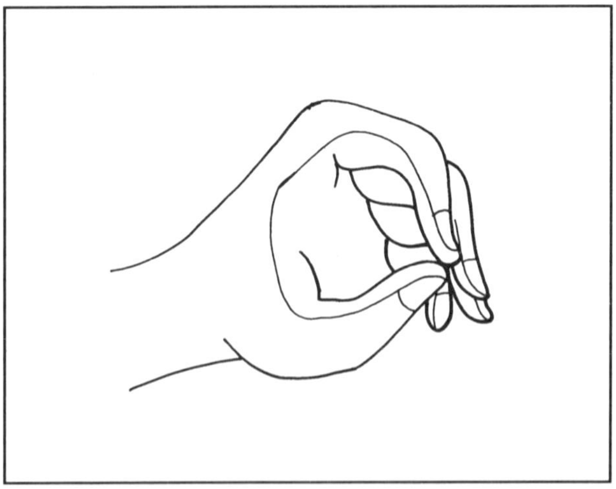

Figure 256 -- kataka mudra I
(as seen by the holder)

kataka mudra II -- (Ind.: *kaṭaka-mudrā* aka *siṁha-karṇa mudrā*) A *mudra*, a ritual hand pose, a seal, which is common to the Hindu tradition, but less common in the Buddhist practice and is depicted or held by a deity. The *kataka mudra II* is a single (Ind.: *asaṁyutta*) form, held by one hand. This *mudra*, a variation, is formed by: the palm faces the midline, the fingers curve in towards the palm and the tips of the fingers touch the thumb. The *mudra* so formed is frequently utilized by feminine deities to hold flower offerings proffered by devotees. (TGR 15) (See: **Figure 257**)

kataka mudra III -- (Ind.: *kaṭaka-mudrā* aka *siṁha-karṇa mudrā*) A hand pose, a seal, a dramatic (Ind.: *nāṭya*) *mudra* or gesture (Ind.: *darpaṇa*) held or formed by a performer, dancer or actor. The *kataka mudra III* is a

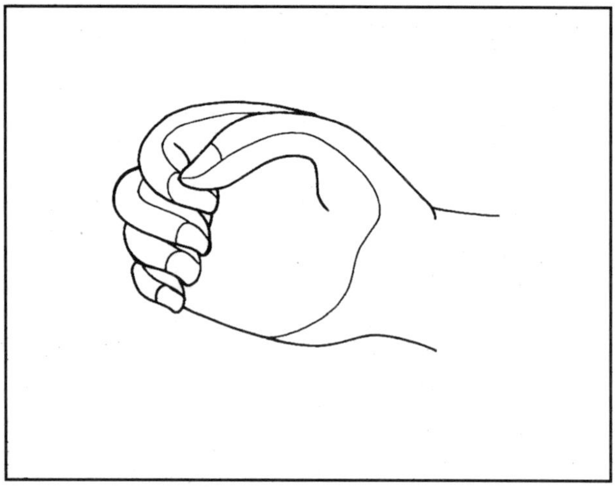

Figure 257 -- kataka mudra II
(as seen by the holder)

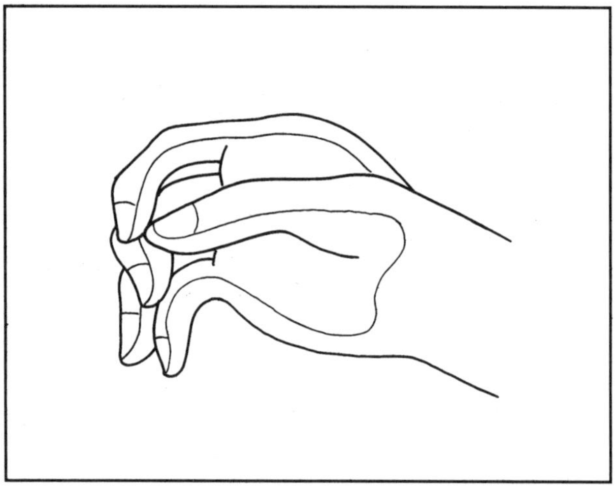

Figure 258 -- kataka mudra III
(as seen by the holder)

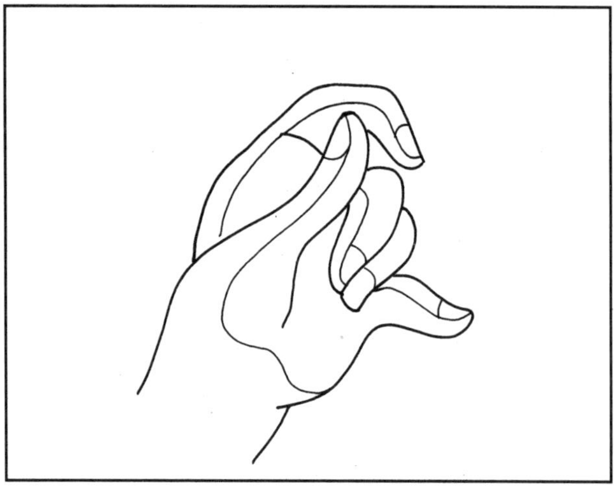

Figure 259 -- kataka mudra IV
(as seen by the holder)

single (Ind.: *asaṁyutta*) form, held by one hand. This *mudra*, a variation, is formed by: palm faces midline, the index and middle fingers curve and their tips touch the thumb, the ring and the little fingers also curve towards the palm. (ACG 31-32) (See: **Figure 258**)

kataka mudra IV -- (Ind.: *kaṭaka-mudrā* aka *kaṭaka-mukha*) ("opening in a link") A hand pose, a seal, a dramatic (Ind.: *nāṭya*) *mudra* or gesture (Ind.: *darpaṇa*) held or formed by a performer, dancer or actor. The *kataka mudra IV* is a single (Ind.: *asaṁyutta*) form, held by one hand. This *mudra*, a variation, is formed by: the palm faces outwards, the tip of the index finger touches the thumb, the middle, ring and little fingers also curve towards the palm progressively. (ACG 31-32 Plate XI-A, RSG 3 & 7 [right]) (See: **Figure 259**)

kataka mudra V -- (Ind.: *kaṭaka-mudrā* aka *kaṭaka-mukha*) ("opening in a link") A hand pose, a seal, a dramatic (Ind.: *nāṭya*) *mudra* or gesture (Ind.: *darpaṇa*) held or formed by a performer, dancer or actor. The *kataka mudra V* is a single (Ind.: *asaṁyutta*) form, held by one hand. This *mudra*, a variation, is formed by: the palm faces outwards, the index finger curls over the tip of the thumb and the middle finger folds into the palm, the ring and little fingers curve slightly towards the palm progressively. (ACG 31-32, KVa 134 [6, 15, 16]) (See: **Figure 260**)

kataka mudra VI -- (Ind.: *kaṭaka-mudrā* aka *kaṭaka-mukha*) ("opening in a link") A *mudra*, a ritual hand pose, a seal, a *tantric mudra* which is common to the Japanese and Chinese Buddhist (*Vajrayana, Mantrayana*) tradition and is held or formed by a devotee or priest. It may be accompanied by a *mantra*. The *kataka mudra VI* is a single (Ind.: *asaṁyutta*) form, held by one hand. This *mudra*, a variation, is formed by: the palm faces outwards, the index and middle fingers curl towards the palm, the thumb curls toward the palm and its tip touches the tips of the index and middle fingers, the ring and little fingers extend upwards. (GDE 281, ACG 31) (See: **Figure 261**)

kataka-mukha mudra -- (Ind.: *kaṭaka-mukha-mudrā* aka *kaṭaka mudrā*) A variant term applied to *kataka mudra*. See: *kataka mudra*. (ACG 31)

kataka-vardhana mudra -- (Ind.: *kaṭaka-vardhana-mudrā*) ("increasing link") A hand pose, a seal, a dramatic (Ind.: *nāṭya*) *mudra* or gesture (Ind.: *darpaṇa*) held or formed by a performer, dancer or actor. The *kataka-vardhana mudra* is a combined (Ind.: *saṁyutta*) form, held by both hands. It denotes coronation, marriage, religious ritual, etc.[22] This *mudra* is formed by: the palm faces outwards, the index finger curls over the tip of the thumb and the middle finger folds into the palm, the ring and little fingers curve slightly towards the palm progressively. Thus formed by each hand, they are crossed at the wrists. (ACG 40) (See: **Figure 262**)

kati mudra -- (Ind.: *kaṭi-mudrā*) A *mudra*, a ritual hand pose, a seal, which is quite common to the Hindu tradition. It denotes relaxation or informality. The *kati mudra* is a single (Ind.: *asaṁyutta*) form, held by one hand. This *mudra* is formed usually by the left: the arm is relaxed, hangs loosely at the side, the hand rests on the hip (just below the waiṣt), fingers to the front, thumb to the back, the thumb may also rest along side of the fingers.[23] It is similar, but not identical to the *katyavalambita mudra*. (MJS 70, RSG 3) (See: **Figure 263**)

katiga mudra -- (Ind.: *kaṭiga-mudrā*) A *mudra*, a ritual hand pose, a seal, which is quite common to the Hindu tradition. It denotes relaxation or informality. The *katiga mudra* is a single (Ind.: *asaṁyutta*) form, held by one hand. This *mudra* is formed by left hand: the arm is relaxed, the hand rests on the waist, fingers to the front, thumb to the back, the thumb may also rest along side the fingers. It is related to the *kati, katisamsthita, katyavalambita mudras*. (HKS 272) (See: **Figure 264**)

katisamsthita mudra -- (Ind.: *kaṭisaṁsthita-mudrā* aka *katyāvalambita mudrā*) A variant term applied to *katyavalambita mudrā*. See: *katyavalambita mudra*. (MJS 70)

katyavalambita mudra -- (Ind.: *kaṭyāvalambita-mudrā* aka *kaṭisaṁsthita mudrā*) A *mudra*, a ritual hand pose, a seal, which is quite common to the Hindu tradition. It denotes relaxation or informality. The *katyavalambita mudra* is a single (Ind.: *asaṁyutta*) form, held by one hand. This *mudrā* is formed frequently by the left hand: the arm is relaxed, hangs down at the side, the hand

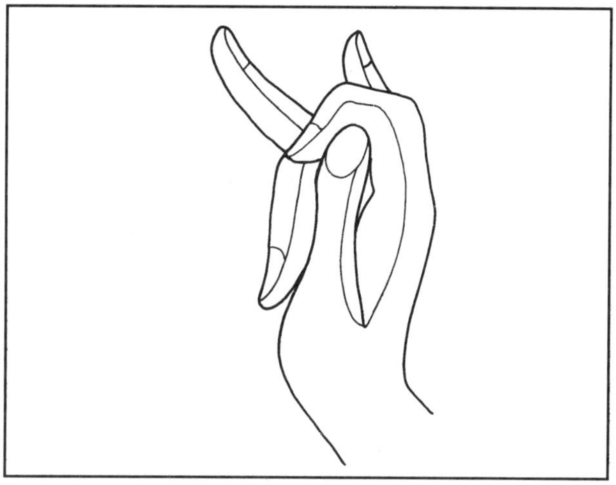

Figure 260 -- kataka mudra V
(as seen by the holder)

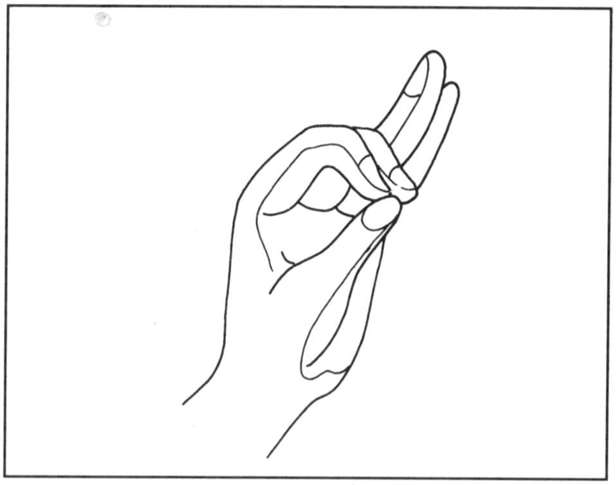

Figure 261 -- kataka mudra VI
(as seen by the holder)

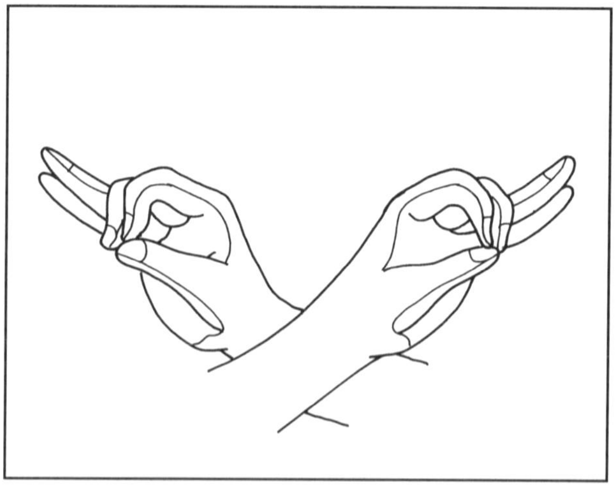

Figure 262 -- kataka-vardhana mudra
(as seen by the holder)

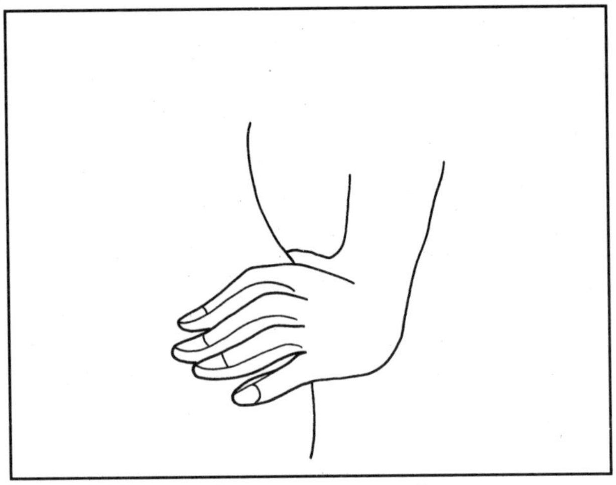

Figure 263 -- kati mudra
(as seen by another)

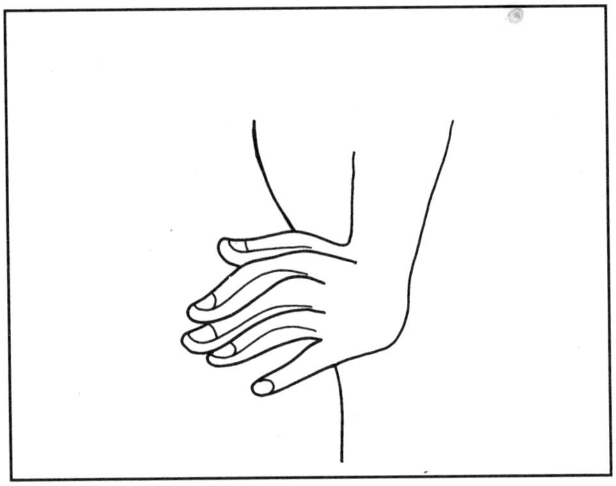

Figure 264 -- katiga mudra
(as seen by another)

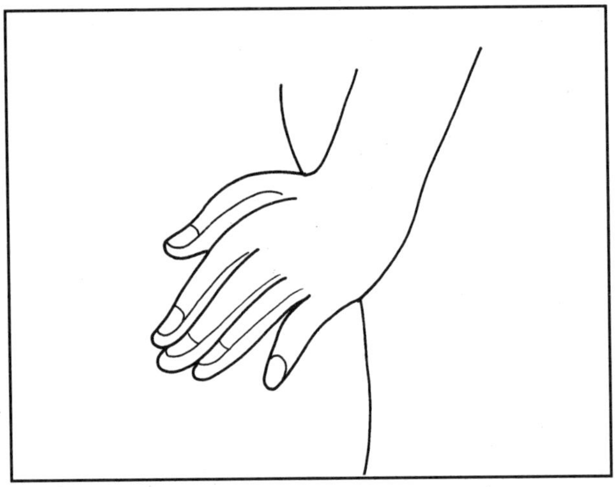

Figure 265 -- katyavalambita mudra
(as seen by another)

rests on the "loins" (thigh), fingers to the front, thumb rests along side the fingers.[24] (MJS 70, RSG 3, TGR 14) (See: **Figure 265**)

kavacha mudra I -- (Ind.: *kavaca-mudrā* aka *kāya-kavaca mudrā*; Jap.: *hachiu-in*) A *mudra*, a ritual hand pose, a seal, a *tantric mudra* which is common to the Japanese Buddhist (*Vajrayana, Mantrayana*) tradition and is held or formed by a devotee or priest during the rites of *Garbhadhatu Mandala, Vajradhatu Mandala, Homa Rites* and other rites. It may be accompanied by a *mantra*. The *kavacha mudra* is a combined (Ind.: *saṁyutta*) form, held by both hands. It denotes protection and acceptance of sacred teachings. This *mudra* is identical for both hands and is formed by: palms facing midline and are separated, thumbs touch along their outer edges, middle, ring and little fingers touch at their tips, index fingers are erect but curve slightly. (GDe 27, LCS 89) (See: **Figure 266**)

kavacha mudra II -- (Ind.: *kavaca-mudrā*) ("armor *mudra*") A *mudra*, a ritual hand pose, a seal, a *tantric mudra* which is common to the Japanese Buddhist (*Vajrayana, Mantrayana*) tradition and is held or formed by a devotee or priest during various rites. It may be accompanied by a *mantra*. The *kavacha mudra* is a combined (Ind.: *saṁyutta*) form, held by both hands. It denotes protection. This *mudra* is formed by: palms facing midline, thumbs, index, middle and little fingers extended upwards, ring fingers touch at their tips. (GDe 331) (See: **Figure 267**)

Kaveri mudra -- (Ind.: *Kāverī-mudrā*) A hand pose, a seal, a dramatic (Ind.: *nāṭya*) *mudra* or gesture (Ind.: *darpaṇa*) held or formed by a performer, dancer or actor. It denotes the *Kaveri*, one of the famous rivers of India. The *mudra* employed is identical in form to the *chatura mudra*. See: *chatura mudra*. (ACG 48)

kaya-kavacha mudra -- (Ind.: *kāya-kavaca-mudrā* aka *kavaca mudrā*) A variant term applied to *kavacha mudra*. See: *kavacha mudra*. (LCS 74)

kayen sho-in (mudra) -- (Jap.: *kayen shō-in* (*mudra*) aka *hokai sho-in* [*mudra*]) ("production of the flame") A *mudra*, a ritual hand pose, a seal, a *tantric mudra* which is common to the Japanese Buddhist (*Vajrayana*,

Mantrayana) tradition and is held or formed by a devotee or priest during the rites of *Garbhadhatu Mandala, Vajradhatu Mandala, Homa Rites* and other rites. It may be accompanied by a *mantra*. The *kayen sho-in (mudra)*[25] is a combined (Ind.: *saṁyutta*) form, held by both hands. It denotes the flame that destroys all impurities. This *mudra* is formed by: folding the thumb into the palm, the index finger is extended straight, the middle, ring and little fingers are folded over the thumb into the palm. So formed the hands are brought together, the tips of the index fingers touching as well as the second knuckles of the middle, ring and little fingers of both hands. (GDe 55) (See: **Figure 268**)

ke bosatsu-in (mudra) -- (Jap.: *ke bosatsu-in* [*mudrā*]; Ind.: *pushpa mudra*) ("the *Bodhisattva* of flowers") A *mudra*, a ritual hand pose, a seal, a *tantric mudra* which is common to the Japanese Buddhist (*Vajrayana, Mantrayana*) tradition and is held or formed by a devotee or priest during the rites of *Vajradhatu Mandala, Homa Rites* and other rites. It may be accompanied by a *mantra*. The *ke bosatsu-in*[26] (*mudra*) is a combined (Ind.: *saṁyutta*) form, held by both hands. It denotes the offering of flowers. This *mudra* is formed by: palms face upwards, fingers and thumbs extended and slightly "cupped." Thus formed the hands are so held that the finger tips are close together, but not touching their counterparts. (GDe 79) (See: **Figure 269**)

ke man-in (mudra) -- (Jap.: *ke man-in* [*mudrā*]; Ind.: *puṣpa-mālā mudrā*) The Japanese term for *pushpa-mala mudra*. See: *pushpa-mala mudra*. (GDe 47)

kengo baku-in mudra -- (Jap.: *kengo baku-in* [*mudrā*] aka *gebaku ken-in, kongo baku-in, shizaige ken-in* (*mudra*); Chin.: *wai-fu ch'ṃan-yin*; Ind.: *granthitam mudrā*) A variant term applied to *gebaku ken-in* (*mudra*). See: *gebaku ken-in* (*mudra*). (EDS 119)

kenji(sshin)-gassho (mudra) -- (Jap.: *kenji*[*sshin*]-*gassho* [*mudrā*] aka *kongo-gassho, kimyo-gassho*; Ind.: *añjali mudrā*) A *mudra*, a ritual hand pose, a seal, which is common in the Japanese Buddhist tradition. It denotes adoration, devotion or worship. The form as well as intent is similar to the *anjali mudra I*, being a variation of the same. This pose, a variation on the *kongo-gassho*,

Figure 266 -- kavacha mudra I
(as seen by the holder)

Figure 267 -- kavacha mudra II
(as seen by the holder)

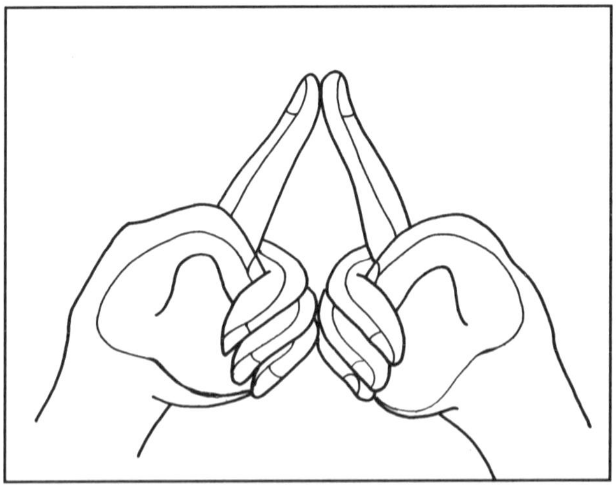

Figure 268 -- kayen sho-in (mudra)
(as seen by the holder)

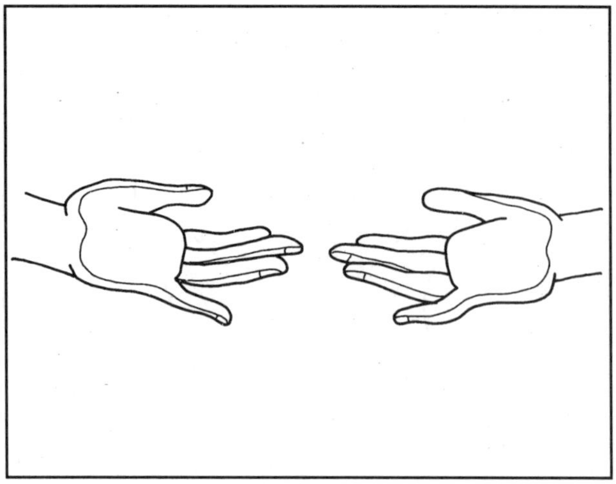

Figure 269 -- ke bosatsu-in (mudra)
(as seen by the holder)

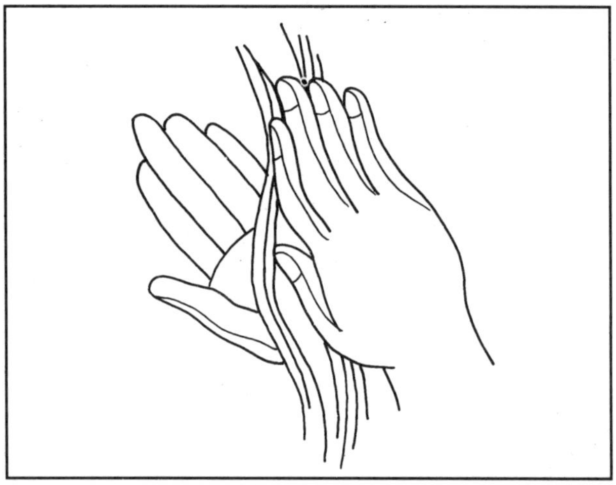

Figure 270 -- kesha-bandha mudra
(as seen by another)

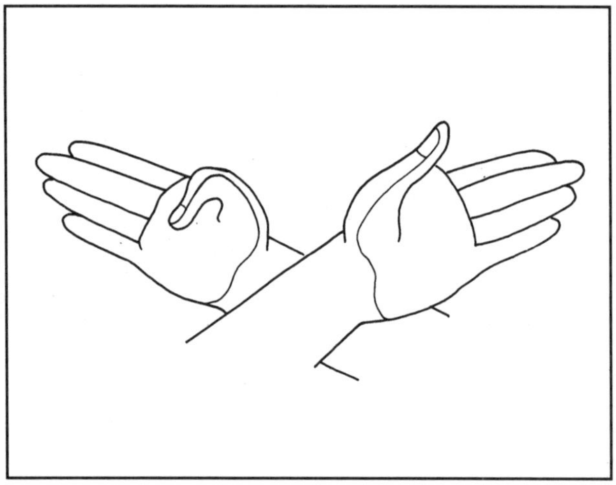

Figure 271 -- ketaki mudra
(as seen by the holder)

is identical to the *anjali mudra I*. See: *anjali mudra I*. (EDS 76)

kenjisshin-gassho (mudra) -- (Jap.: *kenjisshin-gasshō* [*mudrā*] aka *nebina gassho* [*mudra*]) A variant term applied to *nebina gassho* (*mudra*). See: *nebina gassho* (*mudra*). (EDS 77)

kenro kongo ken-in (mudra) -- (Jap.:*kenro kongō ken-in* [*mudrā*] aka *kongo ken-in*) ("adamantine fist") A variant term applied to *kongo ken-in*. See: *kongo ken-in*. (EDS 102)

kesha-bandha mudra -- (Ind.: *keśa-bandha-mudrā*) ("tying the hair") A hand pose, a seal, a dramatic (Ind.: *nāṭya*) *mudra* or gesture (Ind.: *darpaṇa*) held or formed by a performer, dancer or actor. The *kesha-bandha mudra* is a combined (Ind.: *saṁyutta*) form, held by both hands. This *mudra* is formed by: palm towards the midline, fingers and thumb extended, together and pointing backwards, relaxed, slightly cupped. Thus formed the hands are placed at the back of the head. (ACG 43) (See: **Figure 270**)

ketaki mudra -- (Ind.: *ketakī-mudrā*) A hand pose, a seal, a dramatic (Ind.: *nāṭya*) *mudra* or gesture (Ind.: *darpaṇa*) held or formed by a performer, dancer or actor. It denotes the *ketaki* or screw-pine tree. The *ketaki mudra* is a combined (Ind.: *saṁyutta*) form, held by both hands. This *mudra* is formed by: right palm faces outwards, fingers and thumb extended, together and pointing upwards, relaxed, slightly cupped; left palm facing forwards, the fingers, together and extended upwards, the little finger is separated slightly, the tip of the thumb crosses the palm and touches the base of the ring finger. Thus formed, the hands are crossed at wrists. (ACG 49) (See: **Figure 271**)

Ketu mudra -- (Ind.: *Ketu-mudrā*) A hand pose, a seal, a dramatic (Ind.: *nāṭya*) *mudra* or gesture (Ind.: *darpaṇa*) held or formed by a performer, dancer or actor. The *Ketu mudra* is a combined (Ind.: *saṁyutta*) form, held by both hands. It denotes the descending node of the moon, one of the nine planets (Ind.: *navagraha*). This *mudra* is formed by: right palm facing outward, index, middle fingers and thumb extended, together and pointing upwards, ring and little fingers bent towards the palm; left palm faces outwards, the index finger and the thumb point upwards, together, the middle, ring and little fingers are folded into the palm. (ACG 46) (See: **Figure 272**)

khadga mudra I -- (Ind.: *khaḍga-mudrā*) ("the sword") A *mudra*, a ritual hand pose, a seal, a *tantric mudra* which is common to the Japanese Buddhist (*Vajrayana, Mantrayana*) tradition and is held or formed by a devotee or priest during the rites of *Garbhadhatu Mandala, Vajradhatu Mandala, Homa Rites* and other rites. It may be accompanied by a *mantra*. The *khadga mudra*[27] is a single (Ind.: *asaṁyutta*) form, held by one hand. It denotes protection from the enemies of religion. This *mudra* is formed by: palm facing midline or outward, ring and little fingers folded into the palm, thumb folded over the ring and little fingers, index and middle fingers extend straight upward. (GDe 39) (See: **Figure 273**)

khadga mudra II -- (Ind.: *khaḍga-mudrā*) ("[drawing] the sword") A *mudra*, a ritual hand pose, a seal, a *tantric mudra* which is common to the Japanese Buddhist (*Vajrayana, Mantrayana*) tradition and is held or formed by a devotee or priest during the rites of *Garbhadhatu Mandala, Vajradhatu Mandala, Homa Rites* and other rites. It may be accompanied by a *mantra*. The *khadga mudra II*[28] is a combined (Ind.: *saṁyutta*) form, held by both hands. It denotes protection from the enemies of religion. This *mudra* is virtually identical for both hands and is formed by: ring and little fingers folded into the palm, thumb folded over the ring and little fingers, index and middle fingers extend straight. Thus formed, the left hand faces the midline, index and middle fingers point upwards, the right faces outwards, and the index and middle fingers of the right hand are inserted under the folded thumb, ring and little fingers of the left hand--i.e., resembling a sword in its scabbard. (GDe 336, LCS 222) (See: **Figure 274**)

khadga mudra III -- (Ind.: *khaḍga-mudrā*) A *mudra*, a ritual hand pose, a seal, a *tantric mudra* which is common to the Japanese Buddhist (*Vajrayana, Mantrayana*) tradition and is held or formed by a devotee or priest during the rites of *Garbhadhatu Mandala, Vajradhatu Mandala, Homa Rites* and other rites. It may be accompanied by a *mantra*. The *khadga mudra III* is a combined

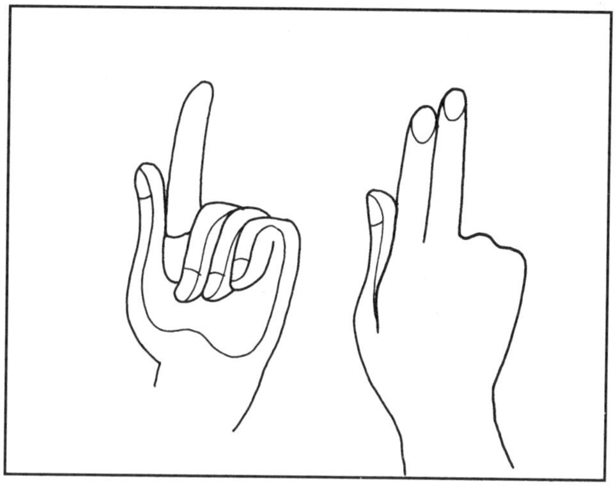

Figure 272 -- Ketu mudra
(as seen by the holder)

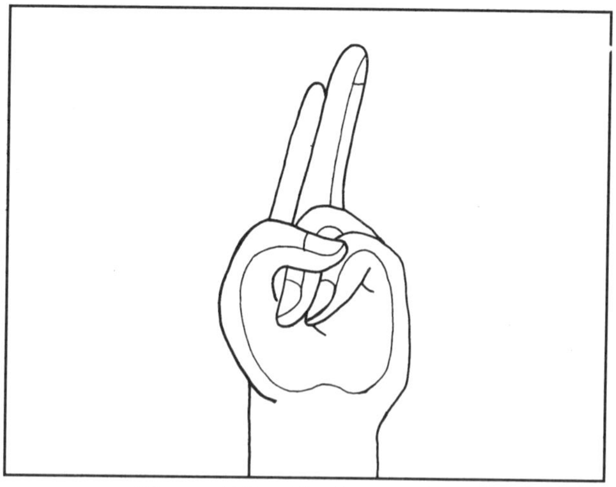

Figure 273 -- khadga mudra I
(as seen by the holder)

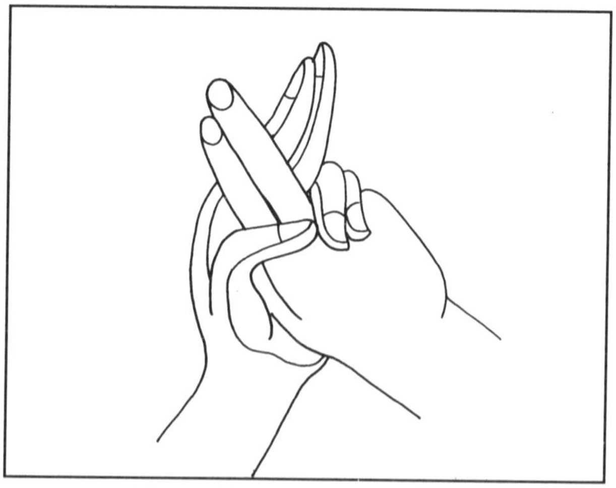

Figure 274 -- khadga mudra II
(as seen by the holder)

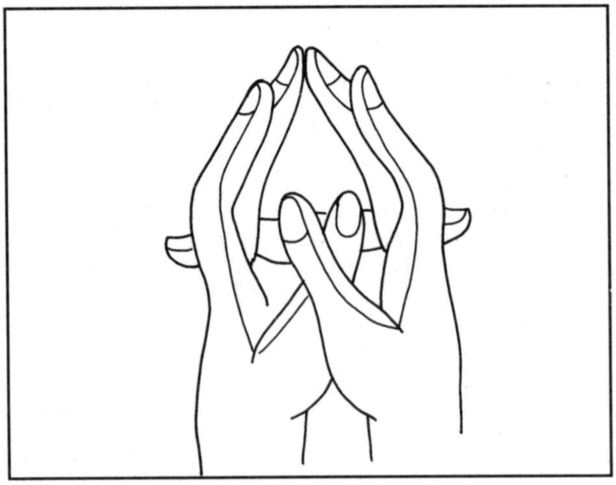

Figure 275 -- khadga mudra III
(as seen by the holder)

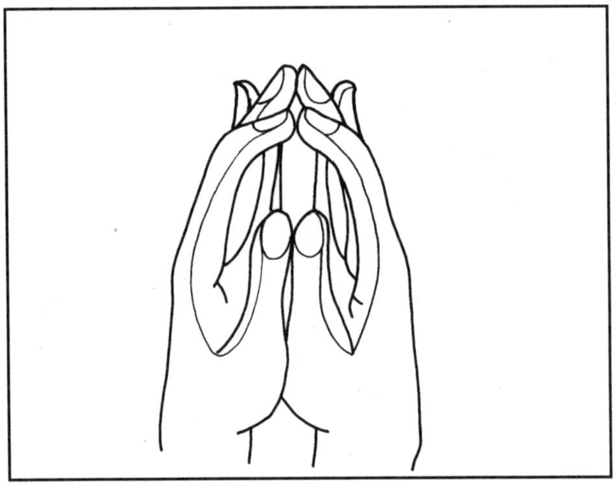

Figure 276 -- khadga mudra IV
(as seen by the holder)

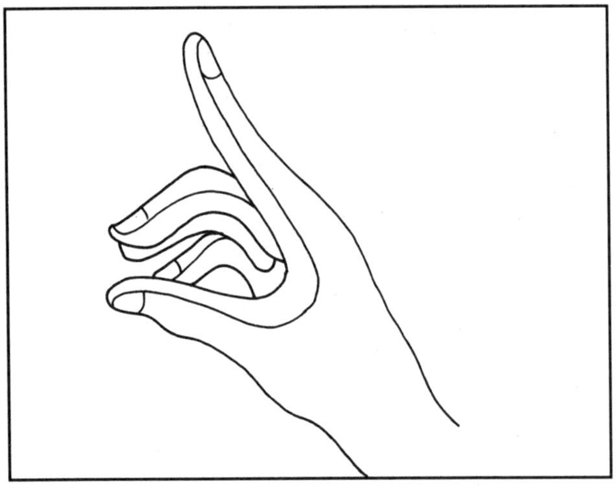

Figure 277 -- khadga-mukula mudra
(as seen by the holder)

(Ind.: *saṁyutta*) form, held by both hands. It denotes *Maha-Vairochana*. This *mudra* is formed by: palms facing midline and close, thumbs crossed, index fingers pressed against middle fingers, middle fingers curl at their first two knuckles and touch at their tips, ring and little fingers fold and interlace touching the backs of the opposite hands.[29] (GDe 68) (See: **Figure 275**)

khadga mudra IV -- (Ind.: *khaḍga-mudrā*) A *mudra*, a ritual hand pose, a seal, a *tantric mudra* which is common to the Japanese Buddhist (*Vajrayana, Mantrayana*) tradition and is held or formed by a devotee or priest during various rites. It may be accompanied by a *mantra*. The *khadga mudra IV* is a combined (Ind.: *saṁyutta*) form, held by both hands, and a variation of the *khadga mudras*. It denotes a sword. This *mudra* is formed by: palms facing midline and very close thumbs extend upwards and touch, middle, ring and little fingers touch at their tips, index fingers extend upwards, flex at the first knuckle touch at their tips. (GDe 213, LCS 129) (See: **Figure 276**)

khadga-mukula mudra -- (Ind.: *khaḍga-mukula-mudrā*) A hand pose, a seal, a dramatic (Ind.: *nāṭya*) *mudra* or gesture (Ind.: *darpaṇa*) held or formed by a performer, dancer or actor. The *khadga-mukula mudra* is a single (Ind.: *asaṁyutta*) form, held by one hand. This *mudra* is formed by: palm faces outwards, the index finger extends upwards and moves to and fro, the tips of the middle, ring and little fingers and thumb are brought together, but not necessarily touching, pointing forwards. (ACG 49) (See: **Figure 277**)

khadga-ratna mudra -- (Ind.: *khaḍga-ratna-mudrā*) This is an assigned term.[30] A *mudra*, a ritual hand pose, a seal, which is common to the Buddhist (*Vajrayana*) tradition, a *tantric mudra*. It denotes the gift of a precious sword--but here meaning: 'precious general' (Tib.: *dmag-dpon rin-chen*)--which is associated with the *saptaratna* (Tib.: *rgyal-srid sna-bdun*) or seven gems of sovereignty (Tib.: *nor-bu-chab-bdun*), also referred to as the 'space vast treasury,' particularly as it is associated with the worship of the powerful *Vajrayana* goddess, *Tara*. The *khadga-ratna mudra* is a combined (Ind.: *saṁyutta*) form, held by both hands. This *mudra* is in mirror-pose: right palm faces the midline, index and middle fingers extend to the left, ring and little fingers are folded towards the palm, the thumb touches the outer phalanges of the ring and little fingers; the left hand is similarly posed, however it points to the right and slightly downwards. The *mudra* so formed is held just below the chin. The *mantra* associated with this *mudra* is: "*OM Khadga-ratna Praticcha HUM SVAHA.*"[31] (SBe 152) (See: **Figure 278**)

khadira mudra -- (Ind.: *khadira-mudrā*) A hand pose, a seal, a dramatic (Ind.: *nāṭya*) mudra or gesture (Ind.: *darpaṇa*) held or formed by a performer, dancer or actor. It denotes the *khadira* tree. The *mudra* employed is identical in form to the *tamrachuda mudra* facing downwards. See: *tamrachuda mudra*. (ACG 49)

khanda-chatura mudra -- (Ind.: *khaṇḍa-catura-mudrā*) A hand pose, a seal, a dramatic (Ind.: *nāṭya*) *mudra* or gesture (Ind.: *darpaṇa*) held or formed by a performer, dancer or actor noted in ACG but without description. (ACG 44)

khanda-mukula mudra -- (Ind.: *khaṇḍa-mukula-mudrā*) A hand pose, a seal, a dramatic (Ind.: *nāṭya*) *mudra* or gesture (Ind.: *darpaṇa*) held or formed by a performer, dancer or actor. The *khanda-mukula mudra* is a single (Ind.: *asaṁyutta*) form, held by one hand. This *mudra* is formed by: palm faces outwards, the index finger extends upwards, the tips of the middle, ring and little fingers and thumb are brought together, but not necessarily touching, pointing forwards. (ACG 49) (See: **Figure 279**)

khatva mudra -- (Ind.: *khaṭvā-mudrā*) ("the bed") A hand pose, a seal, a dramatic (Ind.: *nāṭya*) *mudra* or gesture (Ind.: *darpaṇa*) held or formed by a performer, dancer or actor. The *khatva mudra*[32] is a combined (Ind.: *saṁyutta*) form, held by both hands. This *mudra* is formed by: palms face upwards, middle and ring fingers fold straight towards the palm, thumbs touch the second knuckles of these two fingers, index and little fingers extend straight downwards. Thus formed the tips of the middle and ring fingers of both hands touch their counterparts. (ACG 41) (See: **Figure 280**)

kia-yin (mudra) -- (Chin. *kia-yin* [*mudrā*]; Jap.: *ko-in*, *myosenden-in*; Ind.: *kavaca mudrā*) The Chinese term for *kavacha mudra*. See: *kavaca mudrā*. (GDe 5)

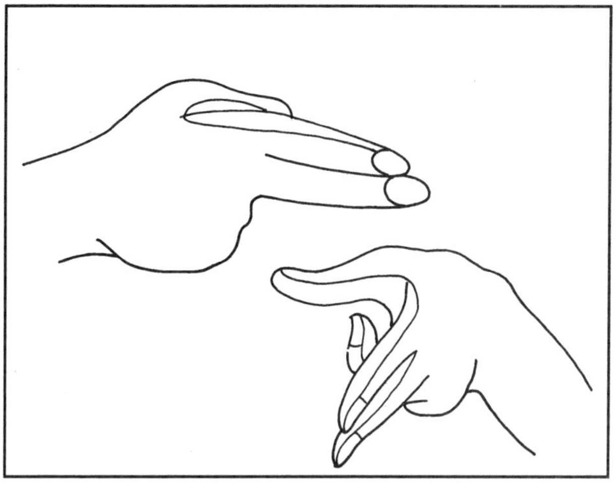

Figure 278 -- khadga-ratna mudra
(as seen by another)

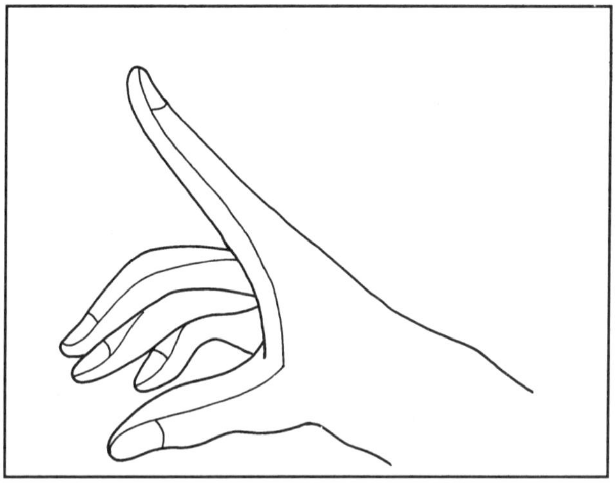

Figure 279 -- khanda-mukula mudra
(as seen by the holder)

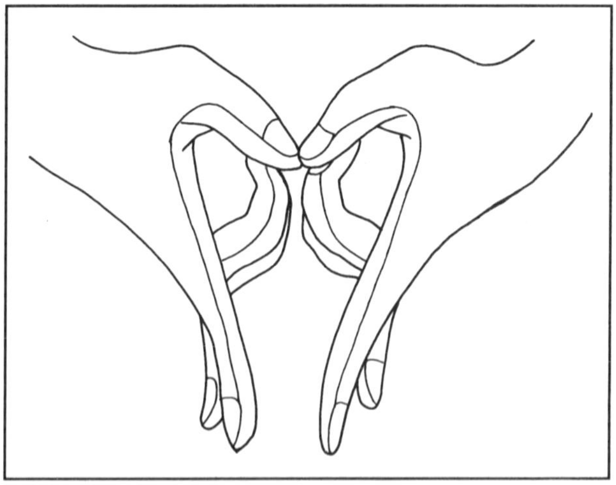

Figure 280 -- khatva mudra
(as seen by another)

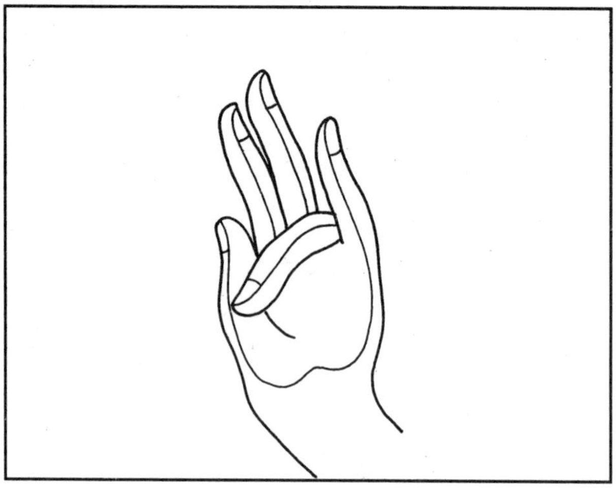

Figure 281 -- kichijo-in (mudra)
(as seen by another)

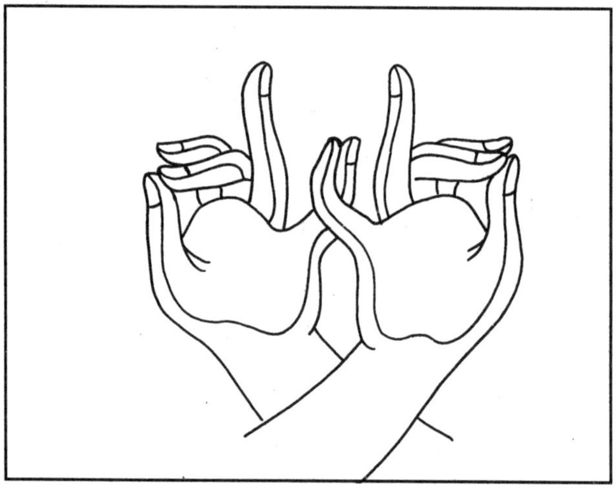

Figure 282 -- kilaka mudra
(as seen by another)

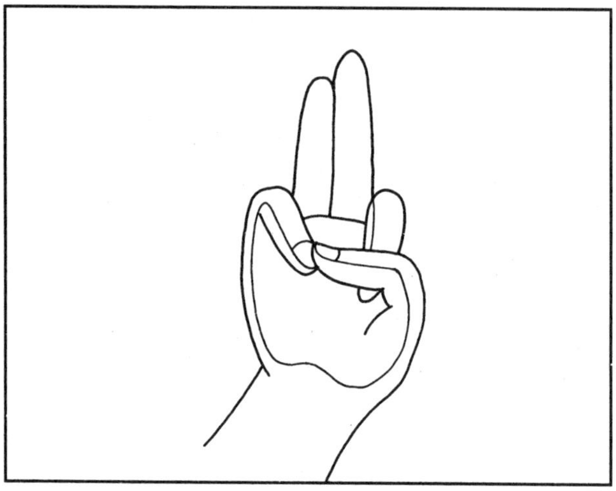

Figure 283 -- kimbei-in (mudra)
(as seen by another)

kichijo-in (mudra) -- (Jap.: *kichijō-in* [*mudrā*]) A *mudra*, a ritual hand pose, a seal, which is common to the Buddhist tradition, particularly in Japan and China and is a variant of the *an-i-in* (*mudra*). It denotes good fortune.[33] The *kichijo-in* (*mudra*) is a single (Ind.: *asaṁyutta*) form, held by one hand.[34] This *mudra* is formed by: the palm faces outwards the index, middle and little fingers are erect, the ring fingers bends towards the palm and the tip of the thumb touches the tip of the ring finger. Thus formed, it is similar to the *kartari mudra*. (EDS 71) (See: **Figure 281**)

kilaka mudra -- (Ind.: *kīlaka-mudrā*) ("the bond") A hand pose, a seal, a dramatic (Ind.: *nāṭya*) *mudra* or gesture (Ind.: *darpaṇa*) held or formed by a performer, dancer or actor. The *kilaka mudra*[35] is a combined (Ind.: *saṁyutta*) form, held by both hands. It denotes affection. This *mudra* is formed by: palms face forward, index and middle fingers curl towards the palms and they are touched by the tips of the thumbs, the ring fingers extend upwards, little fingers curled. Thus formed, the right crosses over the left, crossing at the wrist and the little fingers hook together. (ACG 41) (See: **Figure 282**)

kimbei-in (mudra) -- (Jap.: *kimbei-in* [*mudrā*]) A *mudra*, a ritual hand pose, a seal, a *tantric mudra* which is common to the Japanese Buddhist (*Vajrayana, Mantrayana*) tradition and is held or formed by a devotee or priest during the rites of *Garbhadhatu Mandala*. It may be accompanied by a *mantra*. The *kimbei-in* (*mudra*) is a single (Ind.: *asaṁyutta*) form, held by one hand. It denotes the eyes of compassion. This *mudra* is formed by: palm facing outward, index and little fingers folded into the palm, thumb folded over the index and little fingers, middle and ring fingers extended upwards. (GDe 25) (See: **Figure 283**)

kimyo-gassho (mudra) -- (Jap.: *kimyō-gassho* [*mudrā*] aka *kongo-gassho, kenji(sshin)-gassho*; Ind.: *añjali mudrā*) A *mudra*, a ritual hand pose, a seal, which is common in the Japanese Buddhist tradition. It denotes adoration, devotion or worship. The form as well as intent is similar to the *añjali mudrā I*, being a variation of the same. The *kimyo-gassho* (*mudra*) is a combined (Ind.:

saṁ-yutta) form, held by both hands. The pose, a variation on the *kongo-gassho*, is formed by: bring the hands together, palm to palm, fingers extended, the first phalanges of the middle fingers cross slightly (side by side) with right over left, and the tip of the left thumb rests over the tip of the right. (EDS 76) (See: **Figure 284**)

ko-in (mudra) -- (Jap.: *kō-in* [*mudrā*] aka *myosenden-in* [*mudra*]; Ind.: *kavaca mudrā*) The *ko-in*[36] (*mudra*) is the Japanese term for *kavacha mudra*. See: *kavacha mudra*. (GDe 5)

kongo baku-in (mudra) -- (Jap.: *kongō baku-in* [*mudrā*] aka *gebaku ken-in, kengo baku-in, shizaige ken-in* (*mudra*); Chin.: *wai-fu ch'ṃan-yin*; Ind.: *granthitam mudrā*) A variant term applied to *gebaku ken-in* (*mudra*). See: *gebaku ken-in* (*mudra*). (EDS 119, GDe 61)

kongo cho-in (mudra) -- (Jap.: *kongō chō-in* [*mudrā*]; Ind.: *chatur-dig-bandha mudra*) The Japanese term for *chatur-dig-bandha mudra*. See: *chatur-dig-bandha mudra*. (GDe 103)

kongo-gassho (mudra) -- (Jap.: *kongō-gassho* [*mudrā*] aka *kenji(sshin)-gassho, kimyo-gassho*; Ind.: *añjali mudrā*) The Japanese term and variation for *anjali mudra*. A *mudra*, a ritual hand pose, a seal, which is common in the Japanese Buddhist tradition. It denotes adoration, devotion or worship. The *kongo-gassho* (*mudra*) is a combined (Ind.: *saṁyutta*) form, held by both hands. The form as well as intent is similar to the *anjali mudra I*, being a variation of the same. Both hands are brought together, palm to palm, fingers extended upwards, slightly cupped, the fingers and thumb interlock at the first phalanges only and right thumb over left thumb. Thus formed the pose is held at chest level. (EDS 76) (See: **Figure 285**)

kongo-karuma bosatsu-in (mudra) -- (Jap.: *kongō-karuma bosatsu-in* [*mudrā*]; Ind.: *vajrakarma mudrā, vajrahuṁkāra mudrā, vajrahuṅkāra mudrā*) The Japanese term for *vajrakarma mudra* See: *vajrakarma mudra*. (GDe 91)

kongo-ken-in (mudra) I -- (Jap.: *kongō ken-in* [*mudrā*]; Ind.: *vajrahuṁkāra mudrā*) A *mudra*, a ritual hand pose,

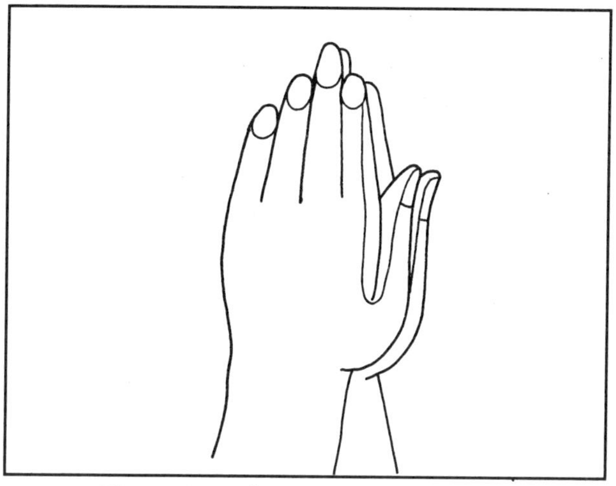

Figure 284 -- kimyo-gassho (mudra)
(as seen by another)

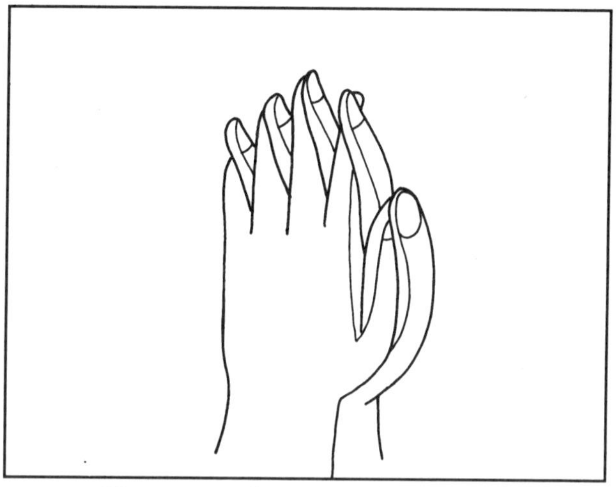

Figure 285 -- kongo-gassho (mudra)
(as seen by another)

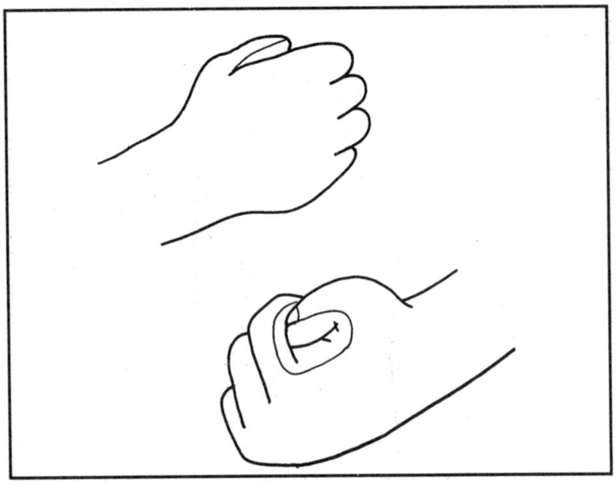

Figure 286 -- kongo-ken-in (mudra) I
(as seen by another)

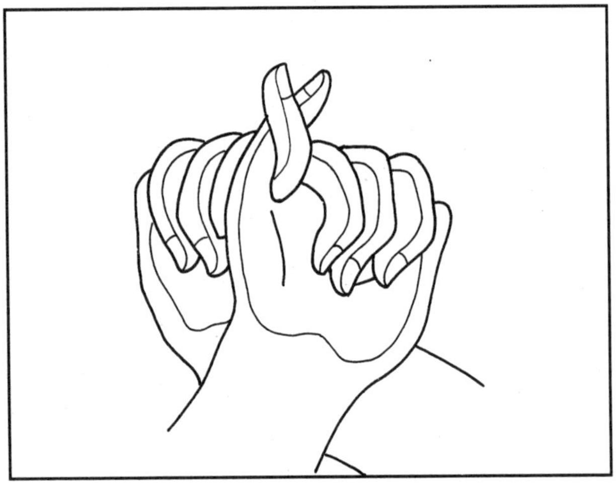

Figure 287 -- kongo-ken-in (mudra) II
(as seen by another)

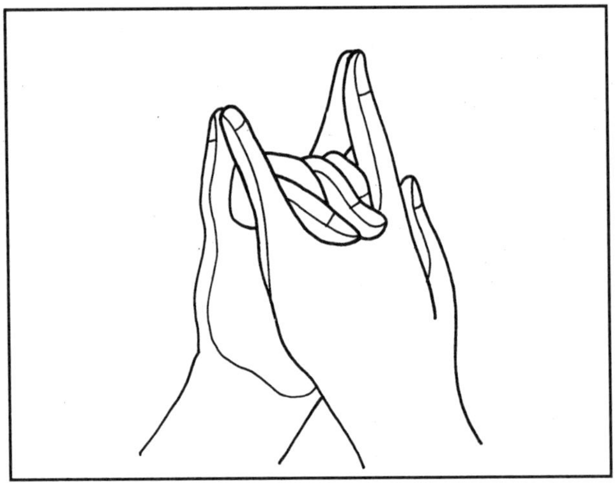

Figure 288 -- kongo mo-in (mudra)
(as seen by another)

a seal, which is common to the Japanese Buddhist tradition. It denotes adamantine strength and awesome anger. The *kongo-ken-in (mudra) I* is a combined (Ind.: *saṁyutta*) form, held by both hands. This *mudra* is identical for both hands--the fingers and thumb form a tight fist, the thumb is covered by the fingers, palm facing midline. Thus formed, the right hand is held at chest level and the left is below at waist level. the *kongo-ken-in (mudra)* is a variation of the *basara-un-kongo-in (mudra)*. (EDS 114) (See: **Figure 286**)

kongo-ken-in (mudra) II -- (Jap.: *kongō ken-in [mudrā]*; Ind.: *vajrahuṁkāra mudrā*) A *mudra*, a ritual hand pose, a seal, which is common to the Japanese Buddhist tradition. It denotes adamantine strength and awesome anger. The *kongo-ken-in (mudra) II* is a combined (Ind.: *saṁyutta*) form, held by both hands. This *mudra* is identical for both hands--palms face outward, thumbs folded into the palms, index, middle and ring fingers fold over thumbs forming a fist, the little fingers flex at their first two knuckles. Thus formed, the right hand crosses over the left and the little fingers hook. (EDS 114) (See: **Figure 287**)

kongo ken-in (mudra) III -- (Jap.; *kongō ken-in [mudrā]*; Ind. : *vajra-muṣṭi [mudrā]*) The Japanese term for *vajra-mushti (mudra)*. See: *vajra-mushti (mudra)*. (EDS 102)

kongo mo-in (mudra) -- (Jap.: *kongō mō-in [mudrā]*; Ind.: *ākāśa-jala mudrā, vajra-jala mudrā*) A *mudra*, a ritual hand pose, a seal, a *tantric mudra* which is common to the Japanese Buddhist (*Vajrayana, Mantrayana*) tradition and is held or formed by a devotee or priest during the *Eighteen-step Rite*. It may be accompanied by a *mantra*. The *kongo mo-in (mudra)* is a combined (Ind.: *saṁyutta*) form, held by both hands. It denotes the protection of the sacred precincts. This *mudra* is formed by: palms facing downwards, middle and ring fingers interlace on top (the back of the hand), index and little fingers are straight and point slightly upwards, their tips touch, thumbs rest against the index fingers. (GDe 106, LCS 63) (See: **Figure 288**)

kongo rin-in (mudra) -- (Jap.: *kongō rin-in [mudrā]*) ("the great wheel") A *mudra*, a ritual hand pose, a seal, a *tantric mudra* which is common to the Japanese Buddhist (*Vajrayana, Mantrayana*) tradition and is held or formed by a devotee or priest during the rites of *Garbhadhatu Mandala, Vajradhatu Mandala, Homa Rites* and other rites. It may be accompanied by a *mantra*. The *kongo rin-in* (*mudra*)[37] is a combined (Ind.: *saṁyutta*) form, held by both hands. It denotes the strength of faith. This *mudra* is formed by: palms facing the midline, thumbs folded into the palms, middle and ring fingers folded over the thumbs (forming the *funnu ken-in*), the extended index and little fingers are curled at the first two knuckles and are "hooked" with their counterparts. (GDe 75) (See: **Figure 289**)

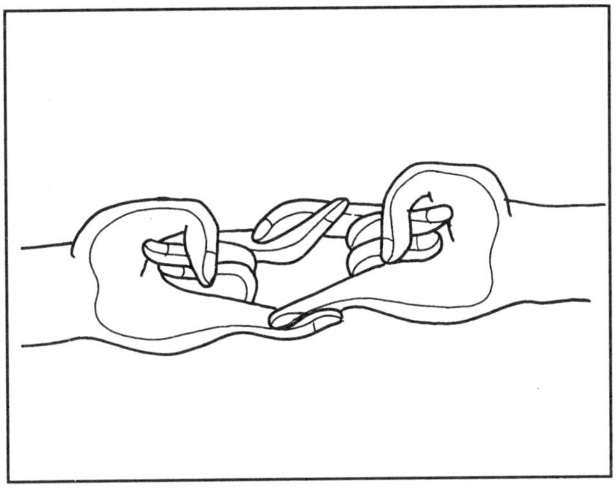

Figure 289 -- kongo rin-in (mudra)
(as seen by the holder)

ko taku(-in) (mudra) -- (Jap.: *kō taku*[*-in*] [*mudrā*]) ("the brilliant light") A *mudra*, a ritual hand pose, a seal, a *tantric mudra* which is common to the Japanese Buddhist (*Vajrayana, Mantrayana*) tradition and is held or formed by a devotee or priest during the rites of the *Garbhadhatu Mandala* and *Vajradhatu Mandala*. It may be accompanied by a *mantra*. The *ko taku(-in)* (*mudra*)[38] is a combined (Ind.: *saṁyutta*) form, held by both hands. It denotes a trident and the extinguishing of impediments. This *mudra* is formed by: little fingers folded into the palms, thumbs folded into the palms and pressing down the little fingers, the index, middle and ring fingers are erect and together. Thus formed the left is held perpendicular to the earth, palm facing outwards, the three fingers of the right hand are placed against the left elbow. (GDe 8) (See: **Figure 290**)

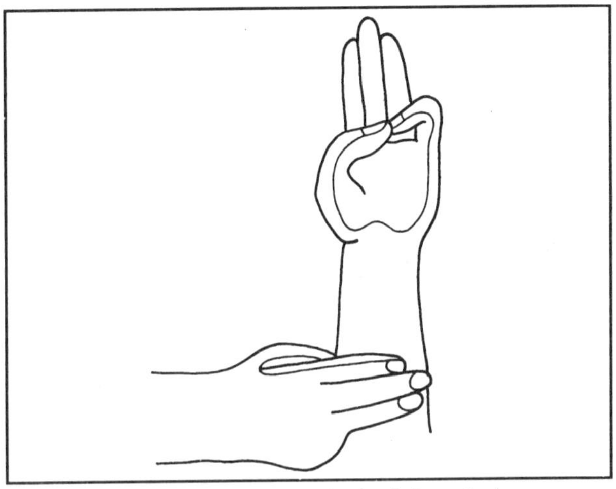

Figure 290 -- ko taku(-in) (mudra)
(as seen by another)

krishna-mriga mudra -- (Ind.: *kṛṣṇa-mṛga-mudrā*) A hand pose, a seal, a dramatic (Ind.: *nāṭya*) *mudra* or gesture (Ind.: *darpaṇa*) held or formed by a performer, dancer or actor. It denotes an animal, in this case a black antelope. The *krishna-mriga mudra*[39] is a single (Ind.: *asaṁyutta*) form, held by one hand. This *mudra* is identical to the *mushti-mriga mudra*. (See: *mushti-mriga mudra*) (ACG 49)

Krishnavatara mudra -- (Ind.: *Kṛṣṇāvatāra-mudrā*) A hand pose, a seal, a dramatic (Ind.: *nāṭya*) *mudra* or gesture (Ind.: *darpaṇa*) held or formed by a performer, dancer or actor. The *Krishnavatara mudra* is a combined (Ind.: *saṁyutta*) form, held by both hands. It denotes *Krishna*, one of the ten *avatars* (Ind.: *daśāvatāras*) of the Lord *Vishnu* This *mudra* is formed by: right palm faces the midline, index, middle and ring fingers curl at their first and second joints (towards the palm), the thumb

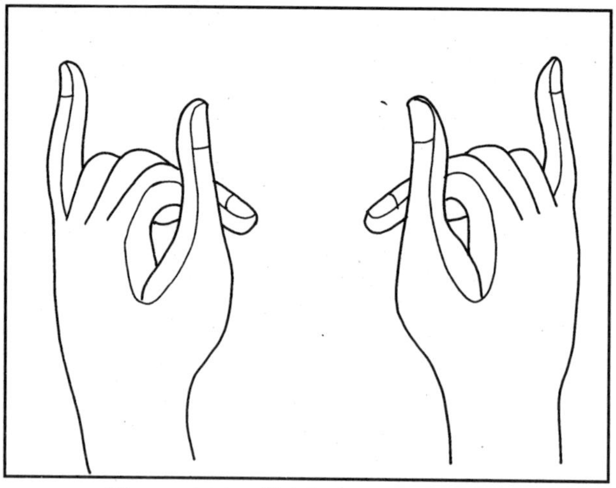

Figure 291 -- Krishnavatara mudra
(as seen by the holder)

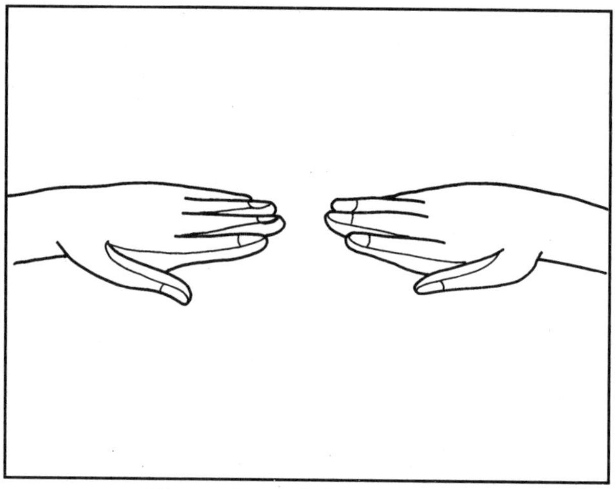

Figure 292 -- kshanti mudra
(as seen by the holder)

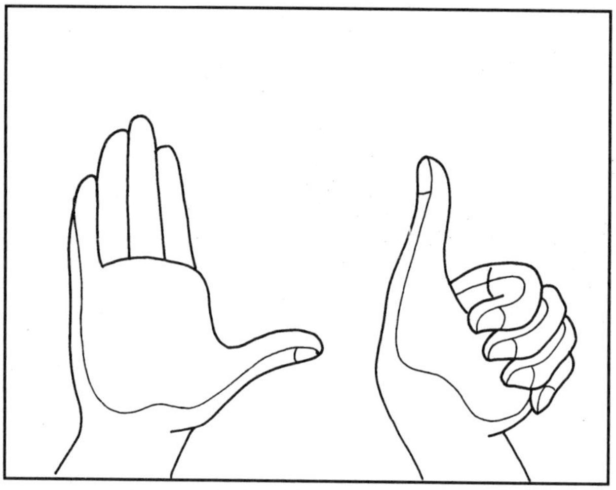

Figure 293 -- Kshattriya mudra
(as seen by another)

is extended inward, and the little fingers extend upwards; left palm faces the midline, index, middle and ring fingers curl at their first and second joints (towards the palm), the thumb is extended upwards, and the little fingers extend upwards. Thus formed the hands are held at shoulder level. (ACG 46) (See: **Figure 291**)

Krishnaveri mudra -- (Ind.: *Kṛṣṇāverī-mudrā* aka *siṁha-mukha mudrā*) A hand pose, a seal, a dramatic (Ind.: *nāṭya*) mudra or gesture (Ind.: *darpaṇa*) held or formed by a performer, dancer or actor. It denotes the river *Krishnaveri*, one of the famous rivers of India. The *mudra* employed is identical in form to the *simha-mukha mudra*. (See: *simha-mukha mudra*) (ACG 48)

krodha mudra -- (Ind.: *krodha-mudrā*]; Eng.: anger *mudra*; Jap.: *funnu ken-in* [*mudra*]) The Indic[40] term for *funnu ken-in* (*mudra*). See: *funnu ken-in* (*mudra*). (EDS)

kshanti mudra -- (Ind.: *kṣānti-mudrā*) ("patience") A *mudra*, a ritual hand pose, a seal, a *tantric mudra* which is common to the Japanese Buddhist (*Vajrayana*, *Mantrayana*) tradition and is held or formed by a devotee or priest during the rites of *Vajradhatu Mandala* and other rites. It may be accompanied by a *mantra*. The *kshanti mudra*[41] is a combined (Ind.: *saṁyutta*) form, held by both hands. It denotes patience. This *mudra* is formed by: palms facing downwards, thumbs and fingers extended towards the midline. Thus formed the tips of the extended fingers are brought close, but the two hands do not touch. (LCS 124) (See: **Figure 292**)

Kshattriya mudra -- (Ind.: *Kṣattriya-mudrā*) A hand pose, a seal, a dramatic (Ind.: *nāṭya*) *mudra* or gesture (Ind.: *darpaṇa*) held or formed by a performer, dancer or actor. The *Kshattriya mudra* is a combined (Ind.: *saṁyutta*) form, held by both hands. It denotes the *Kshattriyas*, one of the four castes. This *mudra* requires movement and is formed by: right palm faces mid-line, fingers brought into the palm forming a fist, thumb extends upwards; left palm faces mid-line, fingers brought into the palm forming a fist, thumb extends upwards, so formed the left hand moves "to and fro." (ACG 47) (See: **Figure 293**)

kshepana mudra I -- (Ind.: *kṣepaṇa-mudrā*) A *mudra*, a ritual hand pose, a seal, which is common to the *Mahayana* Buddhist tradition. It denotes the sprinkling of *amrita*, the ambrosia of immortality. The *kshepana mudra I* is a combined (Ind.: *saṁyutta*) form, held by both hands. This *mudra* is formed by: palms together, index fingers touching along their inner surface and extended, thumb, middle, ring and little fingers are interlaced with the left thumb over the right. Thus formed, the index fingers point downward and the mudra is held at waist level. The form of the *kshepana mudra* is related to the *uttarabodhi mudra*, although the position is opposite. (AKG 22, ERJ 9, RSG 3) (See: **Figure 294**)

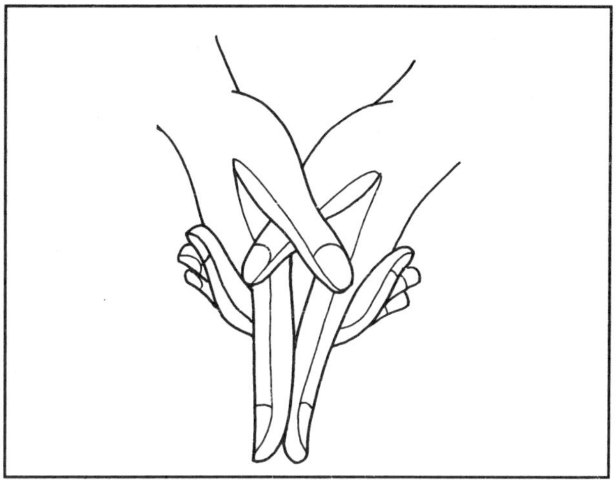

Figure 294 -- kshepana mudra I
(as seen by another)

kshepana mudra II -- (Ind.: *kṣepaṇa-mudrā*) A *mudra*, a ritual hand pose, a seal, which is common to the *Mahayana* Buddhist tradition. It denotes the sprinkling of *amrita*, the ambrosia of immortality. The *kshepana mudra II*[42] is a combined (Ind.: *saṁyutta*) form, held by both hands. This *mudra* is formed by: palms together, fingers and thumbs touch along their inner surfaces and extend, the fingers point downward and the *mudra* is held at waist level. (BBh 193) (See: **Figure 295**)

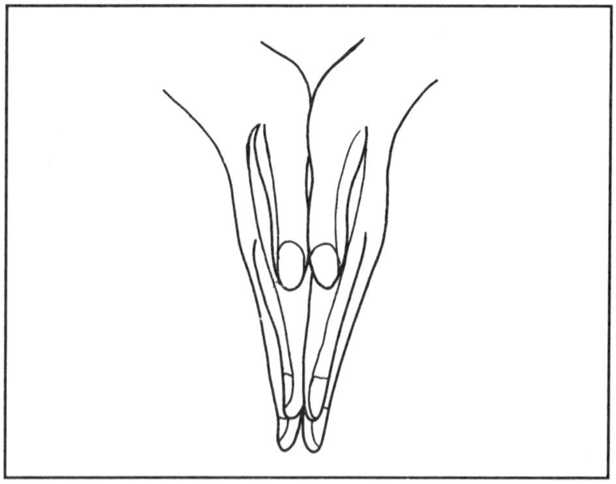

Figure 295 -- kshepana mudra II
(as seen by another)

Kshitigarbha mudra -- (Ind.: *Kṣitigarbha-mudrā*) A *mudra*, a ritual hand pose, a seal, a *tantric mudra* which is common to the Japanese Buddhist (*Vajrayana, Mantrayana*) tradition and is held or formed by a devotee or priest during the rites of *Garbhadhatu Mandala, Vajradhatu Mandala, Homa Rites* and other rites. It may be accompanied by a *mantra*. The *Kshitigarbha mudra* is a combined (Ind.: *saṁyutta*) form, held by both hands. This *mudra* is formed by: the palms facing the midline, thumbs extended upwards and touching along their length, index and middle fingers interlace and are folded into the palms, ring and little fingers extend upward and touch at their tips. (GDe 303, LCS 257) (See: **Figure 296**)

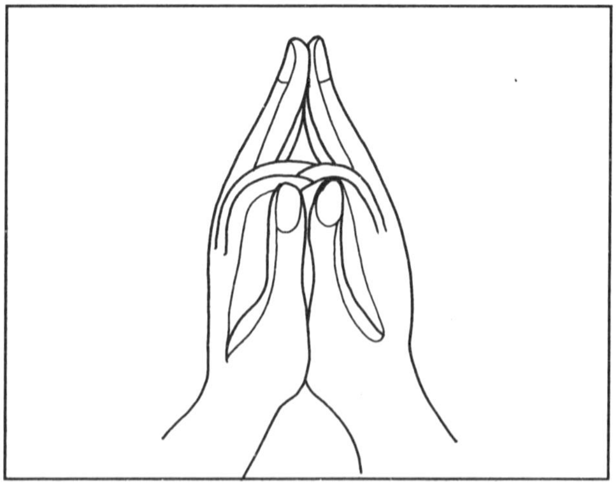

Figure 296 -- Kshitigarbha mudra
(as seen by the holder)

kuan butsu kai ye-in (mudra) -- (Jap.: *kuan butsu kai ye-in* [*mudrā*]) A *mudra*, a ritual hand pose, a seal, a *tantric mudra* which is common to the Japanese Buddhist (*Vajrayana, Mantrayana*) tradition and is held or formed by a devotee or priest during the rites of *Garbhadhatu Mandala, Vajradhatu Mandala, Homa Rites* and other rites. It may be accompanied by a *mantra*.

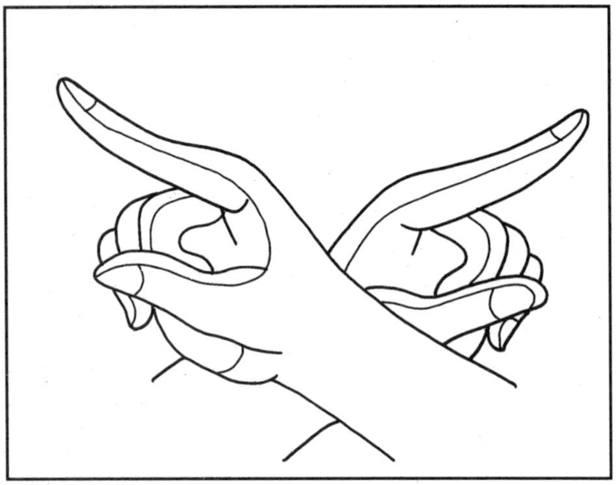

Figure 297 -- kuan butsu kai ye-in (mudra)
(as seen by the holder)

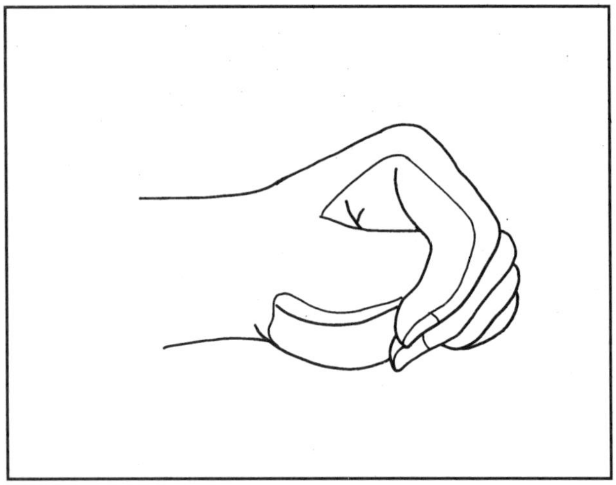

Figure 298 -- kuken (mudra)
(as seen by the holder)

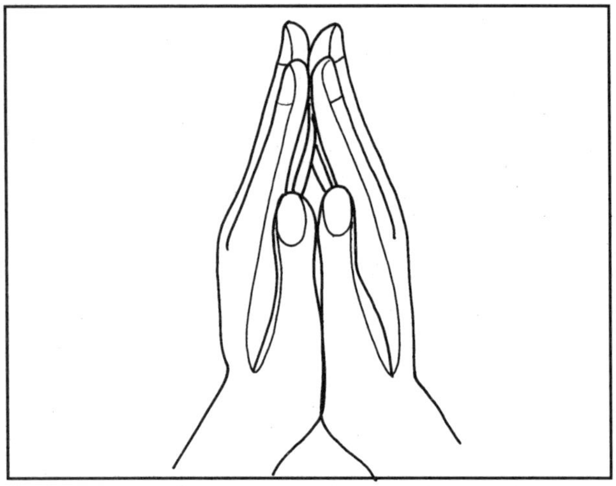

Figure 299 -- kumma(n)ra gassho (mudra)
(as seen by the holder)

The *kuan butsu kai ye-in* (*mudra*) is a combined (Ind.: *saṁyutta*) form, held by both hands. This *mudra* is formed by: palms facing midline, middle, ring and little fingers fold into the palm, thumb folds over the three fingers index finger extends straight. Thus formed the hands are crossed at the wrists, right over left. (GDe 76) (See: **Figure 297**)

kuan-ting-yin (mudra) -- (Chin.: *kuan-ting-yin* [*mudrā*]; Jap.: *kanjo-in* [*mudra*]) The Chinese term for *kanjo-in* (*mudra*). See: *kanjo-in* (*mudra*). (EDS 111)

kuken (mudra) -- (Jap.: *kūken* [*mudrā*]) A *mudra*, a ritual hand pose, a seal, a "fist" form which is common to the Japanese Buddhist tradition. It denotes the "Fist of Void."[43] The *kuken* (*mudra*) is a single (Ind.: *asaṁyutta*) form, held by one hand. This *mudra* is usually formed by the left hand: palm facing downwards, fingers are fisted, thumb inside fist. (EDS 117) (See: **Figure 298**)

kukkuta mudra -- (Ind.: *kukkuṭa-mudrā*) A hand pose, a seal, a dramatic (Ind.: *nāṭya*) *mudra* or gesture (Ind.: *darpaṇa*) held or formed by a performer, dancer or actor. It denotes a bird, in this case a rooster. The *kukkuta mudra*[44] is a single (Ind.: *asaṁyutta*) form, held by one hand. This *mudra* is identical to the *bhramara mudra*. (See: *bhramara mudra*) (ACG 50)

kumma(n)ra gassho (mudra) -- (Jap.: *kumma(n)ra gasshō* [*mudrā*]; Ind.: *kamala* [?] *mudrā*) A *mudra*, a ritual hand pose, a seal, which is common to the Japanese Buddhist tradition. Specifically one of the twelve, elemental "hand clasps" (Jap. *junigosho* or *junigassho*). The *kumma(n)ra gassho* (*mudra*) is a combined (Ind.: *saṁyutta*) form, held by both hands. This *mudra* is formed by: the hands are brought together, palms inwards, fingers extended upwards, there is definite cupping of the hands. This *mudra* is referred to as the clasp of the lotus bud. (EDS 40) (See: **Figure 299**)

kunda-dhvaja mudra -- (Ind.: *kunda-dhvaja-mudrā*) This is an assigned term.[45] A *mudra*, a ritual hand pose, a seal, which is common to the Buddhist (*Vajrayana*) tradition, a *tantric mudra*. It denotes the victory banner (Tib.: *mchog-gyi rgyal-mtshan*), one of eight signs of good fortune (Indic: *aṣṭa-maṅgala*, Tib.: *bkra-shis rtags-brgyad*), an 'outer offering'--the other seven being: the knot, wheel, lotus, golden fish, umbrella, treasure vase and conch shell--which is proffered to a divine guest during worship, particularly as associated with the ceremonies of the powerful *Vajrayana* goddess, *Tara*. The *kunda-dhvaja mudra* is a combined (Ind.: *saṁyutta*) form, held by both hands. This *mudra* is formed by both hands in mirror-pose: the palm faces inwards, the fingers are fisted, thumb extends up, the right hand over the left and the first phalanges of the thumb of the left is grasped by the fisted right. The *mudra* thus formed is held at chest level. The *mantra* associated with this *mudra* is: "*OM Kunda-dhvaja Praticcha SVAHA*."[46] (SBe 155) (See: **Figure 300**)

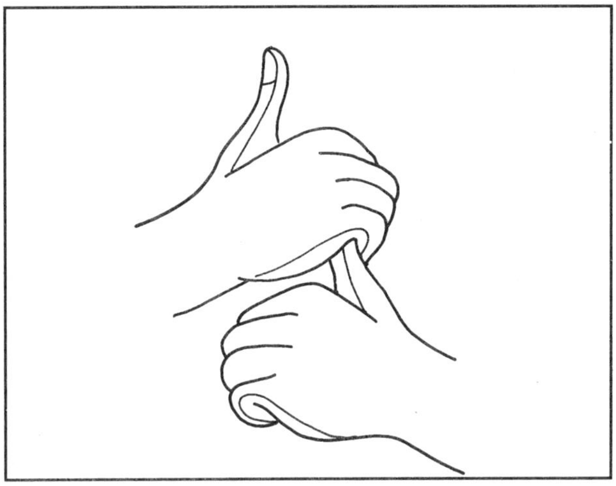

Figure 300 -- kunda-dhvaja mudra
(as seen by another)

kurma mudra I -- (Ind.: *kūrma-mudrā*) A *mudra*, a ritual hand pose, a seal, a *tantric mudra* which is common to the Hindu Buddhist (*Vajrayana, Mantrayana*) tradition and is held or formed by a devotee or priest. It may be accompanied by a *mantra*. It denotes the containment of life's breath. The *kurma mudra* is a single (Ind.: *asaṁyutta*) form, held by one hand. This *mudra* is formed by: the palm faces the midline, the fingers fold into the palm around flowers, thumb up. Thus formed the *mudra* is held at waist level. It is similar to the *kataka mudra*. (HZi 319, MJS 77) (See: **Figure 301**)

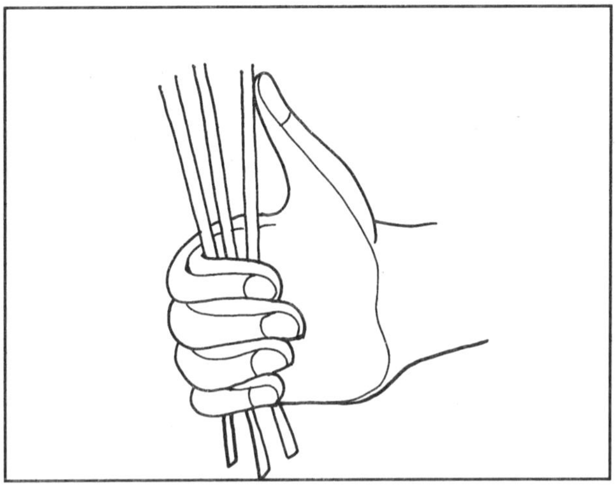

Figure 301 -- kurma mudra I
(as seen by the holder)

kurma mudra II -- (Ind.: *kūrma-mudrā*) A *mudra*, a ritual hand pose, a seal, a *mudra* which is common to yogic tradition, particularly the *Yoga Tatva Mudra Vigyan* form, and is held by a devotee or practitioner. The *kurma mudra*[47] is a combined (Ind.: *saṁyutta*) form, held by both hands. It is one of the twenty-four *mudras* held before the *Gayatri Jap* of the thirty-two total *Gayatri mudras*.[48] It is utilized for all sickness, especially cancer. This *mudra* is formed by: right palm facing downwards, index and little fingers extended straight outwards, middle and ring fingers folded into the palm; left palm facing upwards, index finger extended straight towards the midline and parallel to the ground, thumb extends at right angle to the index finger, middle, ring and little fingers are folded into the palm. Thus formed, the right hand is over the left, the tip of the right index finger touches the tip of the left thumb, and the tip of the right little finger touches the tip of the left index finger. It is one of the four *Gayatri mudras* which make reference to the Lord *Vishnu's* first five (animal) *avatars*. (KDe 86, RLM 74) (See: **Figure 302**)

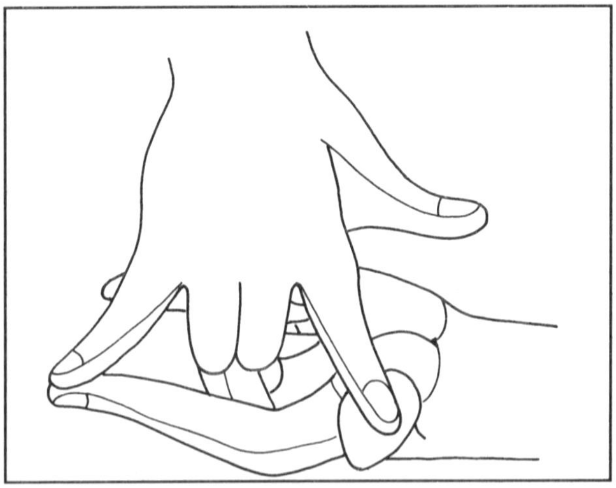

Figure 302 -- kurma mudra II
(as seen by another)

kurma mudra III -- (Ind.: *kūrma-mudrā*) A hand pose, a seal, a dramatic (Ind.: *nāṭya*) mudra or gesture (Ind.: *darpaṇa*) held or formed by a performer, dancer or actor. The *kurma mudra* is a combined (Ind.: *saṁyutta*) form, held by both hands. It denotes the tortoise avatar of the Lord *Vishnu*. This *mudra* is formed by: right palm facing downwards and rotated 45° to the left, index, middle and ring fingers curl towards the palm, little finger extends outwards, the thumb extends away from the fingers; left palm facing upwards and rotated 45° to the right, index, middle and ring fingers curl towards the palm, little finger extends outwards, the thumb extends away from the fingers. Thus formed, the hands are brought together and the curled fingers of the right rest in the palm of the left. (ACG 41) (See: **Figure 303**)

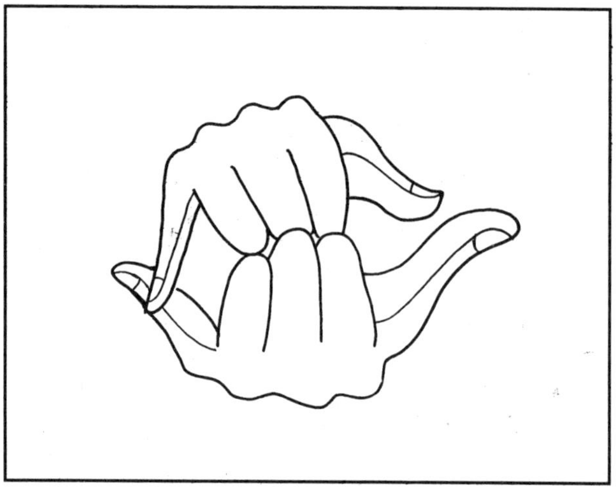

Figure 303 -- kurma mudra III
(as seen by another)

Kurmavatara mudra -- (Ind.: *Kūrmāvatāra-mudrā*) A hand pose, a seal, a dramatic (Ind.: *nāṭya*) *mudra* or gesture (Ind.: *darpaṇa*) held or formed by a performer, dancer or actor. The *Kurmavatara mudra* is a combined (Ind.: *saṁyutta*) form, held by both hands. It denotes the tortoise *avatar*, one of the ten early human/animal composite *avatars* (Ind.: *daśāvatāra*) of the Lord *Vishnu*. This *mudra* requires movement and is formed by both hands held: palms face the midline, the fingers fold into the palms, thumbs up, and held at a level with the shoulders. It is then formed by both hands held: palms facing outward, index, middle and little fingers and thumbs extend, together and pointing upwards, ring fingers are bent towards the palms. (ACG 46) (See: **Figure 304**)

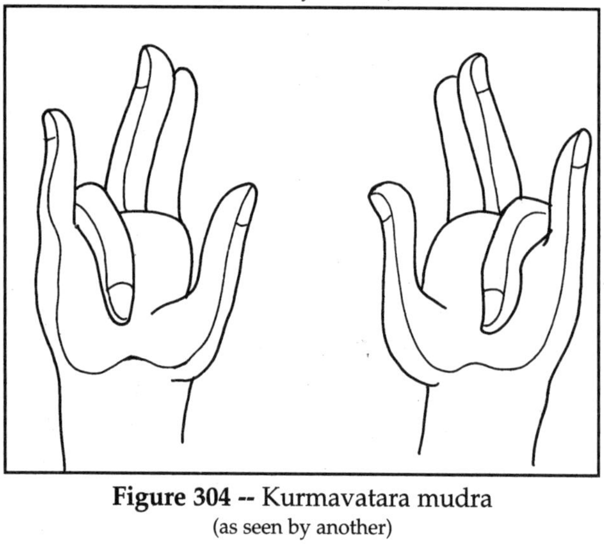

Figure 304 -- Kurmavatara mudra
(as seen by another)

kurpara mudra I -- (Ind.: *kūrpara-mudrā*) A *mudra*, a ritual hand pose, a seal, which is common to the Hindu traditions. It is a *mudra* held by the Lord *Shiva*.[49] The *kurpara mudra* I is a single (Ind.: *asaṁyutta*) form, held by one hand. This *mudra* is formed by: the right arm is slightly flexed at the elbow, the palm rests, in a relaxed manner, on the head of *Nandi*, the bull *vahana* of the Lord *Shiva*. The bull is a symbol of physical excess unbridled passion. This *mudra* may indicate the subduing of such animal passions. (HKS 267) (See: **Figure 305**)

kurpara mudra II -- (Ind.: *kūrpara-mudrā*) A *mudra*, a ritual hand pose, a seal, which is common to the Hindu traditions. It is a *mudra* held by the Lord *Shiva*. The *kurpara mudra II* is a single (Ind.: *asaṁyutta*) form, held by one hand. This *mudra* is formed by the left hand: the arm is slightly flexed at the elbow which rests on the head of *Nandi*, the palm rests, the hand droops down in a relaxed manner. (MJS 78) (See: **Figure 306**)

kurpara-kurpara mudra -- (Ind.: *kūrpara-kurparā-mudra*); Eng.: traveling by boat; Thai: *pang phratabrea-khanan*) This is a descriptive term.[50] (See: *pang phratabrea-khanan*) (OFr 27, #24)

kuruvaka mudra -- (Ind.: *kuruvaka-mudrā*) A hand pose, a seal, a dramatic (Ind.: *nāṭya*) *mudra* or gesture (Ind.: *darpaṇa*) held or formed by a performer, dancer or actor. It denotes the *kuruvaka* tree. The *kuruvaka mudra* is a combined (Ind.: *saṁyutta*) form, held by both hands. This *mudra* is formed by: the right hand raised, index, middle and little fingers and thumb extended, together and pointing upwards, ring finger is bent towards the palm, palm facing outward and generally on a line level with the chest; the left palm faces outwards the index and middle fingers are erect and separated slightly, the little finger is bent, the ring fingers bends towards the palm and the tip of the thumb touches the tip of the ring finger. (ACG 49) (See: **Figure 307**)

kushala mudra -- (Ind.: *kuśala-mudrā*) A hand pose, a seal, a dramatic (Ind.: *nāṭya*) *mudra* or gesture (Ind.: *darpaṇa*) held or formed by a performer, dancer or actor which is noted in ACG but without description. (ACG 44)

Kuvera mudra -- (Ind.: *Kuvera-mudrā*) A hand pose, a seal, a dramatic (Ind.: *nāṭya*) *mudra* or gesture (Ind.: *darpaṇa*) held or formed by a performer, dancer or actor which denotes a specific deity. The *Kuvera mudra* is a combined (Ind.: *saṁyutta*) form, held by both hands. It denotes the popular deity of wealth, *Kuvera*. *Kuvera* is indeed a very interesting deity who transcends sectarianism and is to be found in both the Hindu and the Buddhist (*Mahayana* & *Vajrayana*) pantheons. He is related to or is a form of *Vaishravana* and also one of the Eight Masters of Direction. This *mudra* is formed

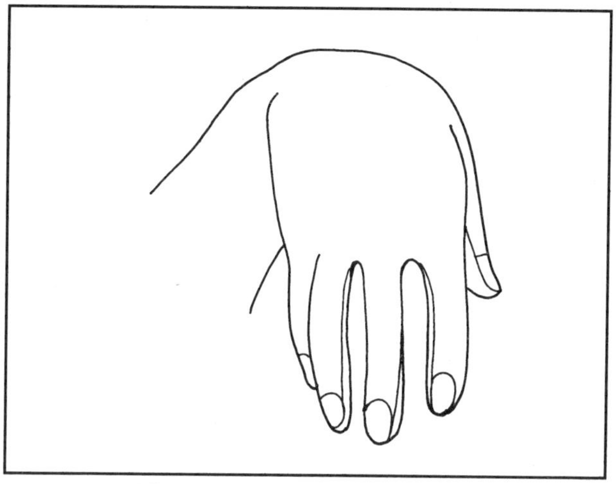

Figure 305 -- kurpara mudra I
(as seen by another)

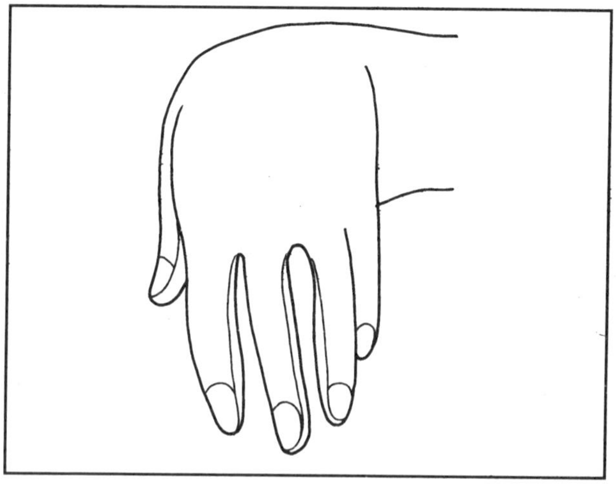

Figure 306 -- kurpara mudra II
(as seen by another)

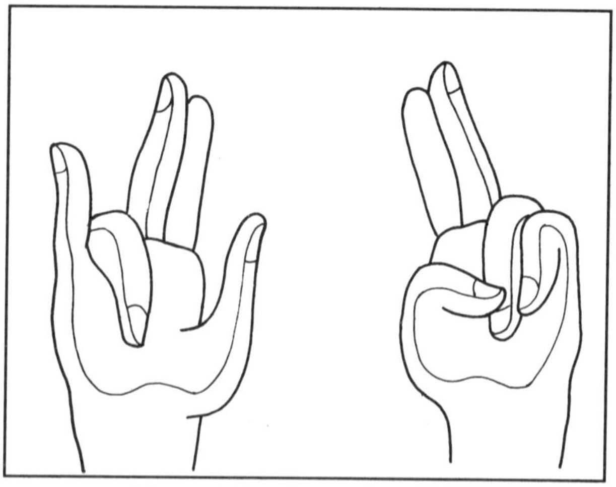

Figure 307 -- kuruvaka mudra
(as seen by another)

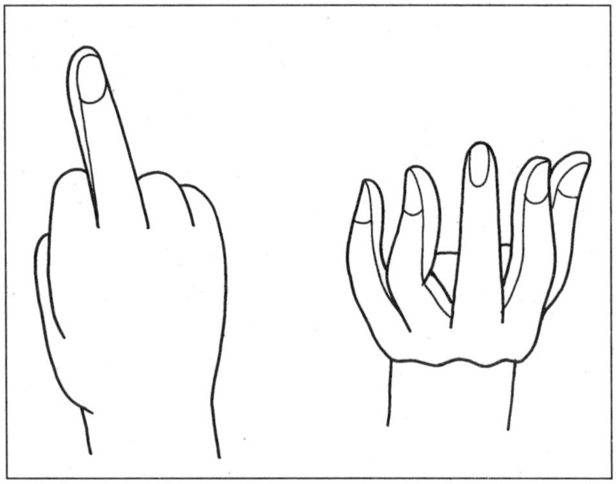

Figure 308 -- Kuvera mudra
(as seen by another)

by: right in *gada mudra*[51]; left palm faces upwards, fingers and thumb are separated and gently curl inwards, towards the hollowed palm. Thus formed the hands are held at shoulder level. (ACG 46) (See: **Figure 308**)

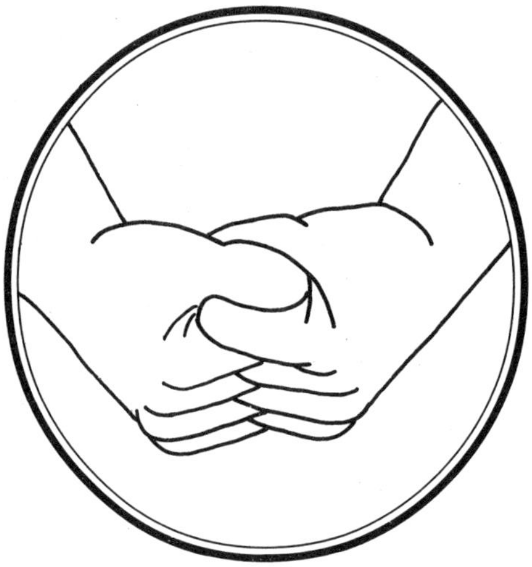

-- L --

Lakshmi mudra -- (Ind.: *Lakṣmī-mudrā*) A hand pose, a seal, a dramatic (Ind.: *nāṭya*) mudra or gesture (Ind.: *darpaṇa*) held or formed by a performer, dancer or actor which denotes a specific deity. The *Lakshmi mudra* is a combined (Ind.: *saṁyutta*) form, held by both hands. It denotes *Lakshmi*. This *mudra* is formed by: right palm faces the midline, the middle, ring and little fingers fold into the palm, the thumb lies over the first phalanges of the middle finger, index finger curls over the top of the thumb; left palm faces the midline, the middle, ring and little fingers fold into the palm, the thumb lies over the first phalanges of the middle finger, index finger curls over the top of the thumb. Thus formed the hands are held at shoulder level. (ACG 45) (See: **Figure 309**)

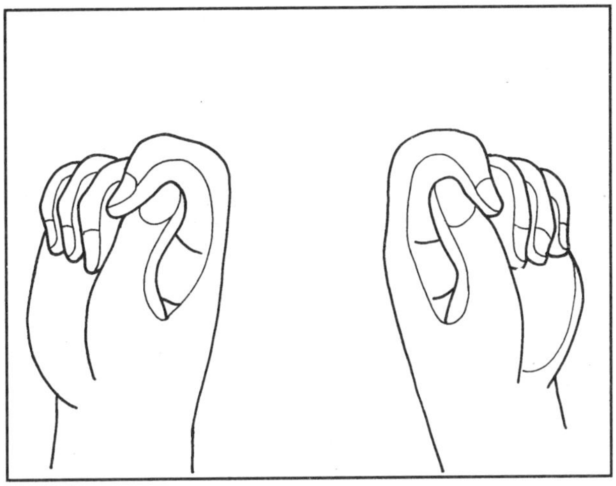

Figure 309 -- Lakshmi mudra
(as seen by another)

lakucha mudra -- (Ind.: *lakuca-mudrā*) A hand pose, a seal, a dramatic (Ind.: *nāṭya*) *mudra* or gesture (Ind.: *darpaṇa*) held or formed by a performer, dancer or actor. It denotes the *lakucha* tree. The *mudra* employed is identical in form to the *bhramara mudra*. (See: *bhramara mudra*) (ACG 48)

lalita mudra -- (Ind.: *lalita-mudrā*) A hand pose, a seal, a dramatic (Ind.: *nāṭya*) *mudra* or gesture (Ind.: *darpaṇa*) held or formed by a performer, dancer or actor. The *lalita mudra* is a combined (Ind.: *saṁyutta*) form, held by both hands. It denotes a sal-tree and a mountain. This *mudra* is formed by: the palms face upwards, the thumbs and fingers splay, stiff; so formed, the little fingers are at 90° to the palms and the ring fingers are at 45° to the palms. Thus formed, the two hands are crossed and held "near the head." (ACG 44) (See: **Figure 310**)

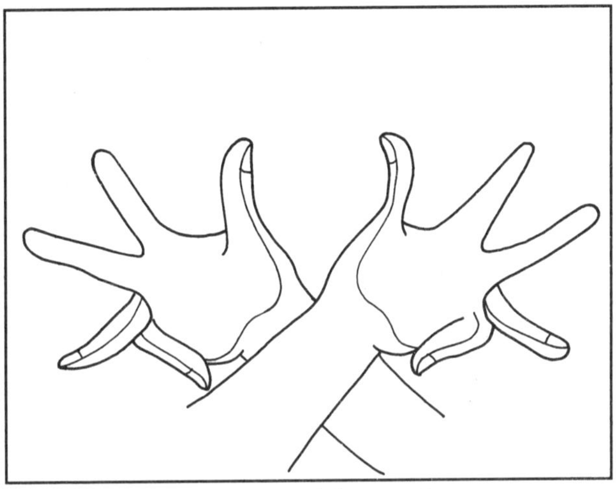

Figure 310 -- lalita mudra
(as seen by another)

langula mudra -- (Ind.: *lāṅgula-mudrā*) ("tail" or "plough") A *mudra*, a ritual hand pose, a seal, which is common to the Hindu tradition and is depicted or held by a deity. Also, a hand pose, a seal, a dramatic (Ind.: *nāṭya*) *mudra* or gesture (Ind.: *darpaṇa*) held or formed by a performer, dancer or actor. The *langula mudra*[1] is a single (Ind.: *asaṁyutta*) form, held by one hand. It rep-

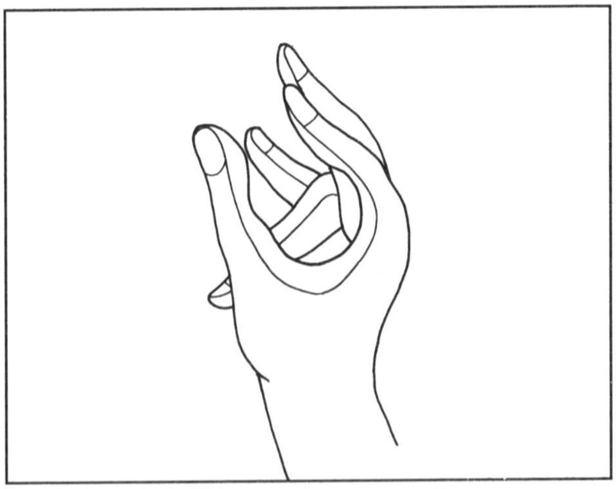

Figure 311 -- langula mudra
(as seen by the holder)

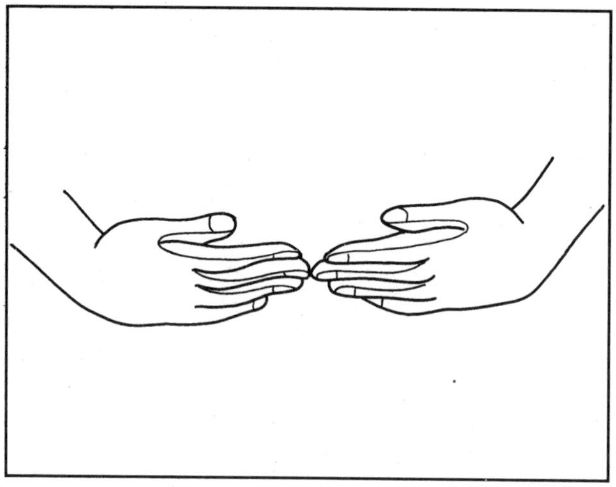

Figure 312 -- lata mudra
(as seen by another)

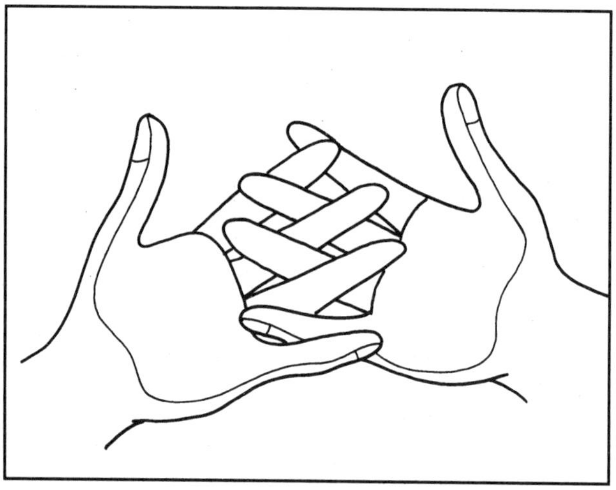

Figure 313 -- lina-karkata mudra
(as seen by the holder)

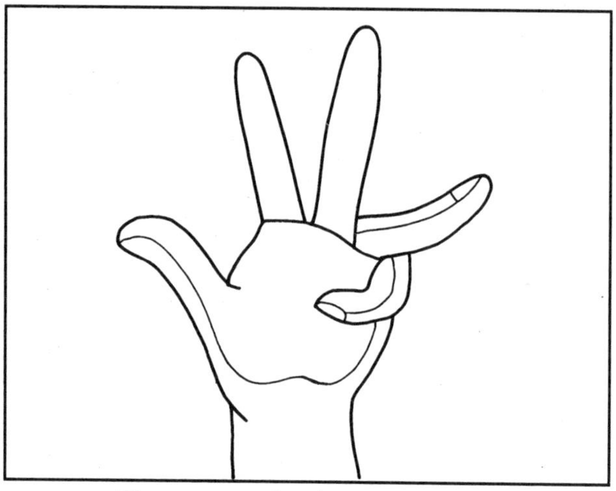

Figure 314 -- linalapadma mudra
(as seen by another)

resents an areca nut, partridge, anything that is small, etc.[2] This *mudra* is formed by: palm upwards, the thumb, index, middle and little fingers are cupped slightly as in the *padmakosha mudra*, ring finger is bent and rests in the palm, extended. (ACG 34, KVa 36 [36], GLi 151, MJS 80) (See: **Figure 311**)

lata mudra -- (Ind.: *latā-mudrā*) ("the creeper") A hand pose, a seal, a dramatic (Ind.: *nāṭya*) *mudra* or gesture (Ind.: *darpaṇa*) held or formed by a performer, dancer or actor. The *lata mudra* is a combined (Ind.: *saṁyutta*) form, held by both hands. It denotes lines, the state of union, etc.[3] This *mudra* is formed by: palms facing upwards, fingers and thumbs extended towards the midline, Thus formed the fingers touch at their tips and the hands are held in front of the groin, arms gently curved. (ACG 42) (See: **Figure 312**)

lina mudra -- (Ind.: *līna-mudrā*) A hand pose, a seal, a dramatic (Ind.: *nāṭya*) mudra or gesture (Ind.: *darpaṇa*) held or formed by a performer, dancer or actor noted in ACG but without description. (ACG 44)

lina-karkata mudra -- (Ind.: *līna-karkaṭa-mudrā*) A hand pose, a seal, a dramatic (Ind.: *nāṭya*) *mudra* or gesture (Ind.: *darpaṇa*) held or formed by a performer, dancer or actor. It denotes a crab. The *lina-karkata mudra* is a combined (Ind.: *saṁyutta*) form, held by both hands. This *mudra* is formed by: palms facing upwards, right over left, the fingers are interlocked. (ACG 51) (See: **Figure 313**)

linalapadma mudra -- (Ind.: *līnālapadma-mudrā*) A hand pose, a seal, a dramatic (Ind.: *natya*) *mudra* or gesture (Ind.: *darpaṇa*) held or formed by a performer, dancer or actor. The *linalapadma mudra* is a single (Ind.: *asaṁyutta*) form, held by one hand. This *mudra* is formed by: the palm turned upwards, the thumb and fingers are stretched far apart, stiff; so formed, the little finger folds into the palm and the ring finger is at 45° to the palm. (ACG 50) (See: **Figure 314**)

linga mudra -- (Ind.: *liṅga-mudrā*) A *mudra*, a ritual hand pose, a seal, a *mudra* which is common to yogic tradition, particularly the *Yoga Tatva Mudra Vigyan* form, and is held by a devotee or practitioner. The *linga* *mudra* is a combined (Ind.: *saṁyutta*) form, held by both hands. It is utilized for diseases of phlegm, catarrh, cough and cold. It is also one of the eight *mudras* held after the *Gayatri Jap* of the thirty-two total *Gayatri mudras*.[4] This *mudra* is formed by: the palms are brought together, the fingers are interlaced and rest on the backs of the hands, the left hand is superior and the right thumb extends upwards. Thus formed, the *mudra* is held at chest level. (KDe 60, 90 & 108) (See: **Figure 315**)

Lochana mudra -- (Ind.: *Locana-mudrā*) A *mudra*, a ritual hand pose, a seal, a *tantric mudra* which is common to the Japanese Buddhist (*Vajrayana, Mantrayana*) tradition and is held or formed by a devotee or priest during the rites of *Garbhadhatu Mandala, Vajradhatu Mandala, Homa Rites* and other rites. It may be accompanied by a *mantra*. The *Lochana mudra*[5] is a combined (Ind.: *saṁyutta*) form, held by both hands. This *mudra* is formed by: palms facing midline, thumbs extended and touching along their length, index fingers extend and curve slightly, middle and ring fingers extend and touch at their tips, little fingers extend straight upward. (GDe 130) (See: **Figure 316**)

lolahasta (mudra) -- (Ind.: *lolahasta* [*mudrā*]) A *mudra*, a ritual hand pose, a seal, which is common to both the Buddhist and Hindu traditions for deities which have few or no symbols to hold and deities of lesser rank. As such, it denotes an inferior status. It is frequently associated with female attendants, demi-deities. The form is held in one hand: palm faces midline, fingers gracefully extended, all are pointing downwards to the side. The *mudra* thus formed is held next to the thigh. The arm and hand "hangs freely 'like the tail of a cow.'"[6] (MJS 82) (See: **Figure 317**)

lolahasta-abhaya mudra I -- (Ind.: *lolahasta-abhaya mudrā*; Eng.: restraining the sandalwood image; Thai: *pang ham-phra-kaen-chan*) This is a descriptive term.[7] See: *pang ham-phra-kaen-chan*. (DRN 36, JBo 205, KIM 10, ODD 680, PSS)

lolahasta-abhaya mudra II -- (Ind.: *lolahasta-abhaya-mudrā*; Thai: *pang lila I*) This is a descriptive term.[8] See: *pang lila I*. (JBo 55, ODD 679 #35)

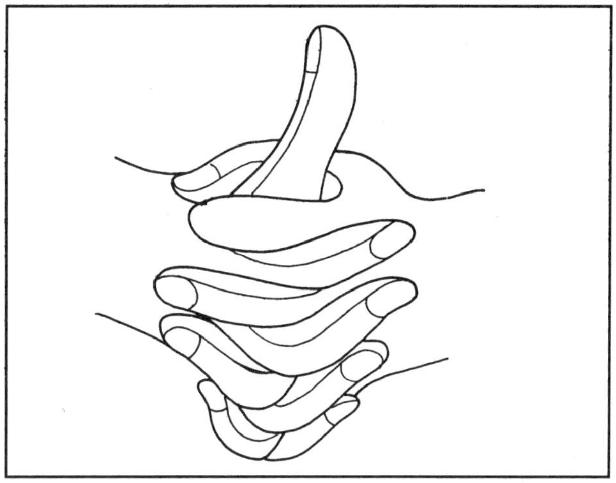

Figure 315 -- linga mudra
(as seen by another)

Figure 316 -- Lochana mudra
(as seen by the holder)

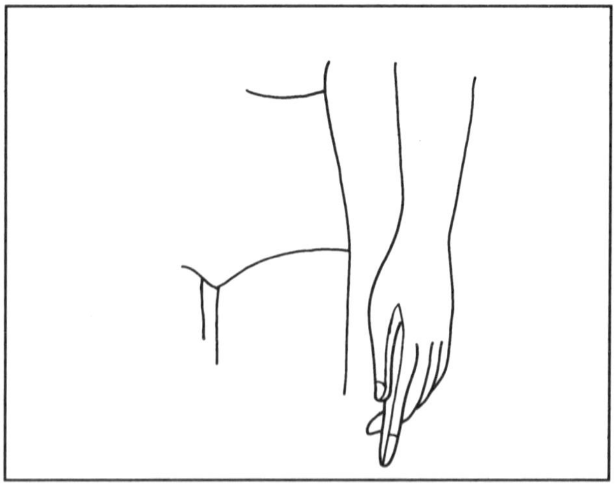

Figure 317 -- lolahasta (mudra)
(as seen by another)

lolahasta-dhyana mudra -- (Ind.: *lolahasta-dhyāna-mudrā*; Eng.: elephant glance akalooking back at *Vaisali mudra*; Thai: *pang nakawalok*) This is a descriptive term.[9] See: *pang nakawalok II*. (OFr 35)

lolahasta-lolahasta mudra II -- (Indic: *lolahasta-lolahasta-mudrā*; Eng.: standing *mudra*; Thai: *pang phratopyun*) This is a descriptive term.[10] See: *pang phratopyun*. (PSS, DRN 36, JBo 205, ODD 679)

lolahasta-vitarka mudra -- (Indic: *lolahasta-vitarka-mudrā*; Eng.: walking *mudra*; Thai: *pang lila II*) This is a descriptive term.[11] See: *pang lila II*. (JBo 132)

looking back at the city of Vaisali mudra -- (Eng.: aka elephant glance *mudra*;[12] Indic: *lolahasta-dhyana mudra*; Thai: *pang nakawalok*) The English descriptive phrase for the Thai *pang nakawalok*. See: *pang nakawalok*. (DRN 36, JBo 205, ODD 680, OFr 35, PSS)

-- M --

madhya-pataka mudra -- (Ind.: *madhya-patākā-mudrā*) A hand pose, a seal, a dramatic (Ind.: *nāṭya*) *mudra* or gesture (Ind.: *darpaṇa*) held or formed by a performer, dancer or actor. The *madhya-pataka mudra* is a combined (Ind.: *saṁyutta*) form, held by both hands. This *mudra* is formed by: the hand is raised, index, middle and ring fingers and thumb extended, together and pointing upwards, relaxed, slightly cupped, the little finger is bent, palm facing outward. (ACG 50) (See: **Figure 318**)

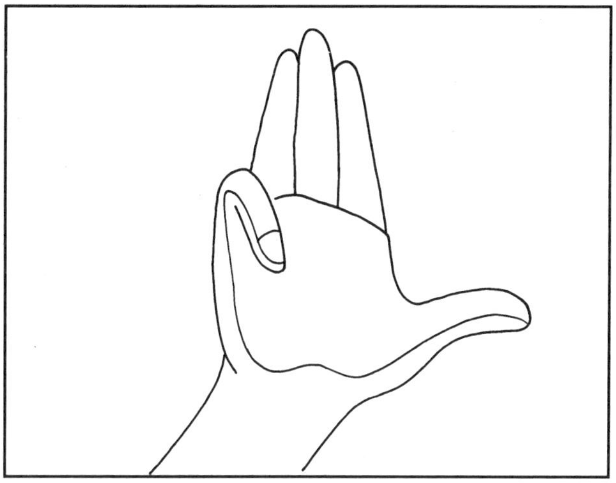

Figure 318 -- madhya-pataka mudra
(as seen by another)

Maha-Akashagarbha mudra -- (Ind.: *Mahā-Ākāśagarbha-mudrā*) A *mudra*, a ritual hand pose, a seal, a *tantric mudra* which is common to the Japanese Buddhist (*Vajrayana, Mantrayana*) tradition and is held or formed by a devotee or priest during the rites of *Garbhadhatu Mandala, Vajradhatu Mandala* and other rites. It may be accompanied by a mantra. The *Maha-Akashagarbha mudra* is a combined (Ind.: *saṁyutta*) form, held by both hands. This *mudra* is formed by: palms close, thumbs, index, middle and little fingers extend and touch at their tips, ring fingers fold to the outside. (LCS 94) (See: **Figure 319**)

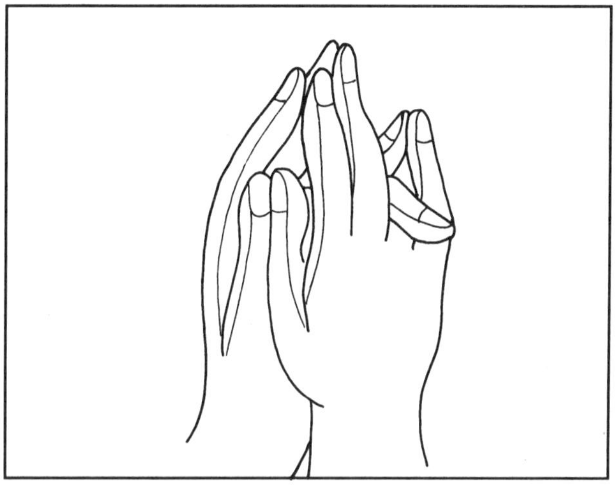

Figure 319 -- Maha-Akashagarbha mudra
(as seen by the holder)

maha-bana mudra -- (Ind.: *mahā-bāna-mudrā*]; Jap.: *ju-ni kushi ji shin-in* [*mudra*]) The Indic term for *ju-ni kushi ji shin-in* (*mudra*). See: *ju-ni kushi ji shin-in* (*mudra*). (GDe 17)

maha-jnana-khadga mudra -- (Ind.: *mahā-jñāna-khaḍga-mudrā*) A *mudra*, a ritual hand pose, a seal, a *tantric mudra* which is common to the Japanese Buddhist (*Vajrayana, Mantrayana*) tradition and is held or formed by a devotee or priest during the rites of *Garbhadhatu Mandala* and other rites. It may be accompanied by a *mantra*. The *maha-jnana-khadga mudra* is a combined (Ind.: *saṁyutta*) form, held by both hands. This *mudra* is formed by: palms close thumbs extended and touching along their length, index fingers curled, their tips touching the corresponding thumb tips, middle, ring and little fingers extend and interlace at their tips. (LCS 153) (See: **Figure 320**)

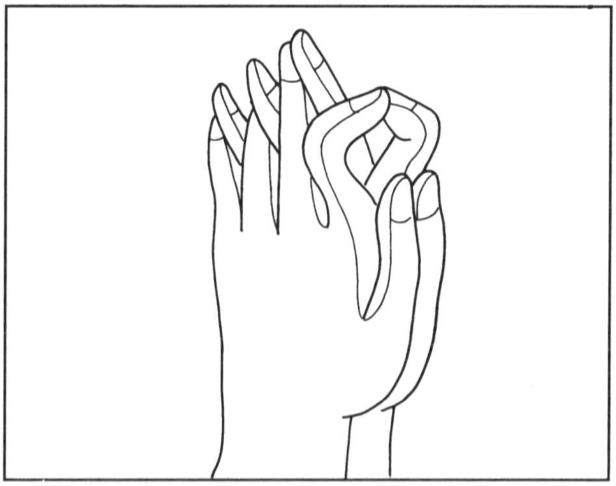

Figure 320 -- maha-jnana-khadga mudra
(as seen by the holder)

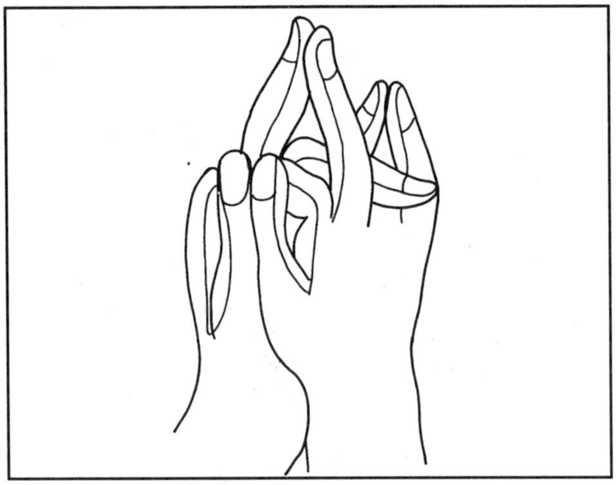

Figure 321 -- Mahakala mudra
(as seen by the holder)

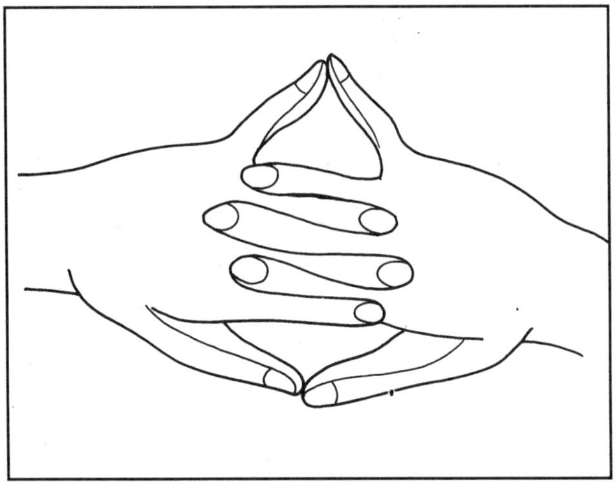

Figure 322 -- maha-karma mudra
(as seen by the holder)

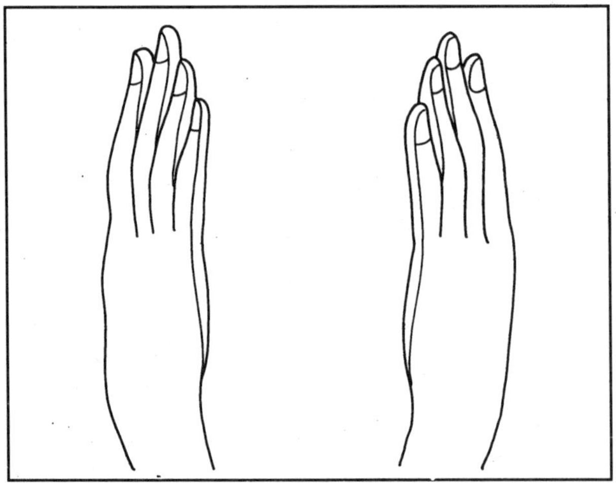

Figure 323 -- mahakrant mudra
(as seen by another)

Mahakala mudra -- (Ind.: *Mahākāla-mudrā*) A *mudra*, a ritual hand pose, a seal, a *tantric mudra* which is common to the Japanese Buddhist (*Vajrayana, Mantrayana*) tradition and is held or formed by a devotee or priest during various rites. It may be accompanied by a *mantra*. The *Mahakala mudra*[1] is a combined (Ind.: *saṁyutta*) form, held by both hands. It denotes *Mahakaḷa*. This *mudra* is formed by: palms face the midline, thumbs, index and middle fingers interlace inwards towards the palms, ring and little fingers extend upward. (LCS 302) (See: **Figure 321**)

maha-karma mudra -- (Jap.: *mahā-karma-mudrā*) A *mudra*, a ritual hand pose, a seal, a *tantric mudra* which is common to the Japanese Buddhist (*Vajrayana, Mantrayana*) tradition and is held or formed by a devotee or priest during the rites of *Vajradhatu Mandala* and other rites. It may be accompanied by a *mantra*. The *maha-karma mudra* is a combined (Ind.: *saṁyutta*) form, held by both hands. This *mudra* is formed by: palms facing downwards, thumbs and little fingers splayed and touch at their respective tips, index, middle and ring fingers interlace, their tips touching the base of their counterparts. (LCS 92) (See: **Figure 322**)

mahakrant mudra -- (Ind.: *mahākrānt-mudrā* aka *mahākrāntam mudrā*) A *mudra*, a ritual hand pose, a seal, a *mudra* which is common to yogic tradition, particularly the *Yoga Tatva Mudra Vigyan* form, and is held by a devotee or practitioner. The *mahakrant mudra* is a combined (Ind.: *saṁyutta*) form, held by both hands. It is one of the twenty-four *mudras* held before the *Gayatri Jap* of the thirty-two total *Gayatri mudras*.[2] It is utilized for all sickness, especially cancer. This *mudra* is formed by: hands are raised, fingers and thumbs extended upward and together, relaxed, palms facing the midline. Thus formed the hands are held close to the shoulders and a little to the side. (KDe 108, RLM 74) (See: **Figure 323**)

mahakrantam mudra -- (Ind.: *mahākrāntam-mudrā* aka *mahākrānt mudrā*) A variant (spelling) of *mahakrant mudra*. See: *mahakrant mudra*. (RLM 74)

maha-nabhi mudra -- (Ind.: *mahā-nābhi-mudrā*; Jap.: *nyorai hosso-in* [*mudra*]) The Indic term for *nyorai hosso-in* (*mudra*). See: *nyorai hosso-in* (*mudra*). (GDe 26)

maha-samaya mudra -- (Ind.: *mahā-samaya-mudrā*) A *mudra*, a ritual hand pose, a seal, a *tantric mudra* which is common to the Japanese Buddhist (*Vajrayana, Mantrayana*) tradition and is held or formed by a devotee or priest during the rites of *Garbhadhatu Mandala, Vajradhatu Mandala, Homa Rites* and other rites. It may be accompanied by a *mantra*. The *maha-samaya mudra* is a combined (Ind.: *saṁyutta*) form, held by both hands. It denotes the "supreme vow." This *mudra* is formed by: palms touching along their outer edge, ring and little fingers interlaced inwards (towards the palms, thumbs extend upwards, index and middle fingers extend together and curve slightly, tips of middle fingers touch. (GDe 221, LCS 64) (See: **Figure 324**)

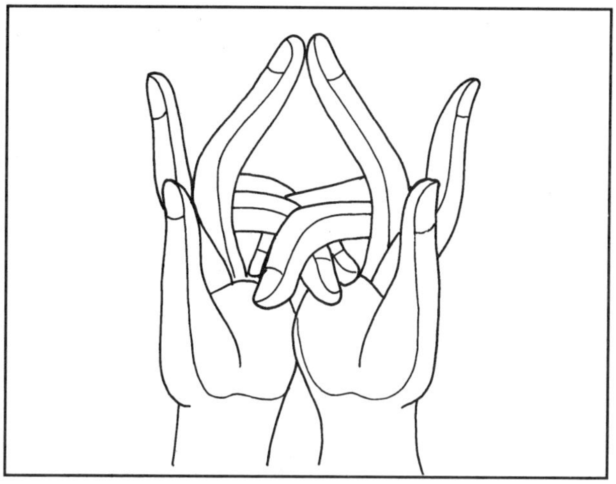

Figure 324 -- maha-samaya mudra
(as seen by the holder)

Mahasthamaprapta (mudra) -- (Ind.: *Mahāsthāmaprāpta* [*mudrā*]) A *mudra*, a ritual hand pose, a seal, a *tantric mudra* which is common to the Japanese Buddhist (*Vajrayana, Mantrayana*) tradition and is held or formed by a devotee or priest during various rites in which a deity is acknowledged. It is a *mudra* which is associated with the deity *Mahasthamaprapta*. It may be accompanied by a *mantra*. The *Mahasthamaprapta* (*mudra*)[3] is a combined (Ind.: *saṁyutta*) form, held by both hands. This *mudra* is formed by: the palms brought close together, thumbs touch along their length, index, ring and little fingers touch at their tips, and middle fingers extend straight upwards. (LCS 213) (See: **Figure 325**)

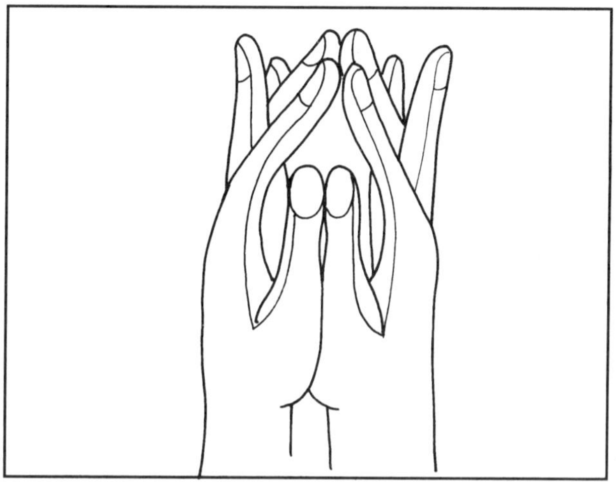

Figure 325 -- Mahasthamaprapta (mudra)
(as seen by the holder)

maha-vajra-chakra mudra -- (Ind.: *mahā-vajra-cakra-mudrā*) A *mudra*, a ritual hand pose, a seal, a *tantric mudra* which is common to the Japanese Buddhist (*Vajrayana, Mantrayana*) tradition and is held or formed by a devotee or priest during the *Eighteen Rites*. It may be accompanied by a *mantra*. The *maha-vajra-chakra*[4] is a combined (Ind.: *saṁyutta*) form, held by both hands. This *mudra* is formed by: palms face midline, ring and little fingers are interlaced towards the inside (palm-side), index fingers extend straight upwards, middle fingers curl over the back of the index fingers their tips resting on the outside edge of the respective index fingers, thumbs touch along their outside edges. (GDe 396, LCS 60) (See: **Figure 326**)

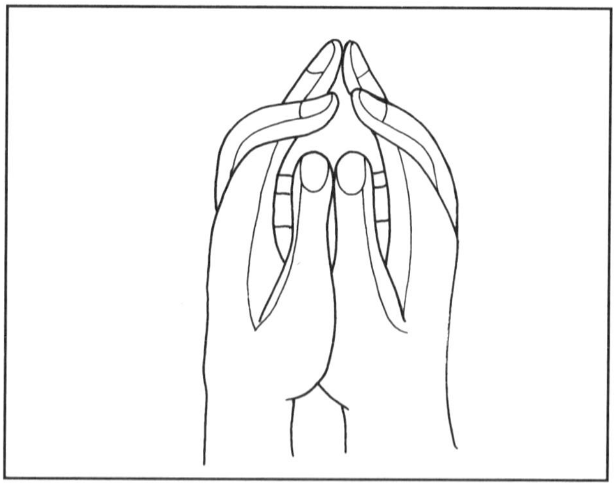

Figure 326 -- maha-vajra-chakra mudra
(as seen by the holder)

makara mudra -- (Ind.: *makara-mudrā*) A hand pose, a seal, a dramatic (Ind.: *nāṭya*) *mudra* or gesture (Ind.:

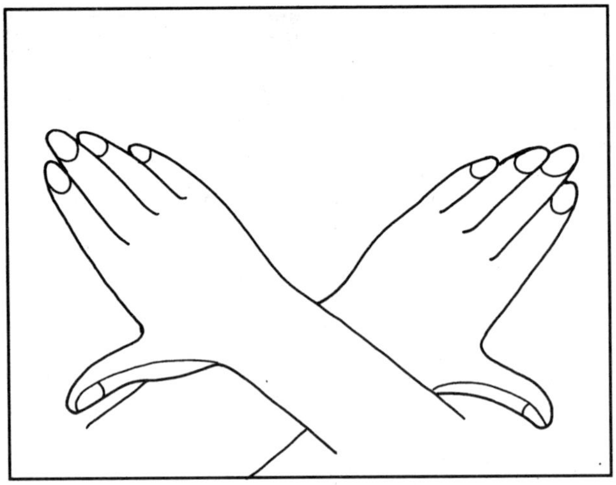

Figure 327 -- makara mudra
(as seen by the holder)

darpaṇa) held or formed by a performer, dancer or actor. The *makara mudra* is a combined (Ind.: *saṁyutta*) form, held by both hands. It denotes the sea, overflowing of a river, solidity, etc.[5] This *mudra* is formed by: palms facing downward, fingers extend straight from palm, thumbs at right angles to the fingers. Thus formed, the right palm covers the back of the left at right angles, the thumbs "move." (ACG 43) (See: **Figure 327**)

making the four alms bowls into one mudra -- (Eng.; Ind.: *buddhaśramaṇa-dhyaṇa mudrā*; Thai; *pang phrasarnbhatr*) The English descriptive phrase for the Thai: *pang phrasarnbhatr*. See: *pang phrasarnbhatr*. (DRN 36, JBo 204, ODD 680, OFr 14, PSS)

making a gift of hair mudra -- (Eng.; Ind.: *ardhāñjali-dhyāna mudrā*; Thai: *pang phra-keit-tatu*) The English descriptive phrase for the Thai: *pang phra-keit-tatu*. See: *pang phra-keit-tatu*. (DRN 36, JBo 205, ODD 680, OFr 15, PSS)

making the venerable Vakkali move away mudra -- (Eng.; Ind.: *patākā-dhyāna mudrā*; Thai: *pang khabphrawakkali*) The English descriptive phrase for the Thai *pang khabphrawakkali*. See: *pang khabphrawakkali*. (DRN 37, JBo, ODD 38, OFr 26, PSS)

ma-mo-mdos mudra(s) -- (Tibeto-Ind.: *ma-mo-mdos mudrā*) This is an assigned term.[6] A series of ritual hand pose, a seals, which are common to the Buddhist (*Vajrayana*) tradition, a *tantric mudra*. It consists of six gestures (*mudras*) which are dedicated to the *ma-mo-mdos* offering. They are associated with the white *gtor-ma* (sacrificial cake) offering and are part of the worship of the powerful *Vajrayana* goddess, *Tara*. The six *mudras* are: the *sarva-dharmah mudra, sarva-tathagatebhyo mudra, vajra-amrita-kundali mudra, sarva-tathagata-avalokite mudra, jnana-avalokite mudra,* and the *samanta-buddhanam mudra*. See each separately. (SBe 146)

mandala mudra -- (Ind.: *maṇḍala-mudrā*) This is an assigned term.[7] A *mudra*, a ritual hand pose, a seal, which is common to the Buddhist (*Vajrayana*) tradition, a *tantric mudra*. It denotes the presentation to the deity of the entire world, particularly as associated with the worship of the powerful *Vajrayana* goddess, *Tara*. The *mandala mudra* is a combined (Ind.: *saṁyutta*) form, held by both hands. This *mudra* is most complicated and formed by: palms face upwards, initially the fingers are interlocked upon the open palms, then the the thumbs extend upwards, the first two phalanges of the index fingers extend upwards, the two ring fingers extend upwards from the palm and touch along their back surface, the middle and little fingers remain interlocked. The *mudra* so formed is held at chest level. Two *mantras* are associated with this *mudra*: "*OM Vajra-bhumi AH HUM*" and "*OM Vajra-Rekhe AH HUM*.ö[8] (SBe 168) (See: **Figure 328**)

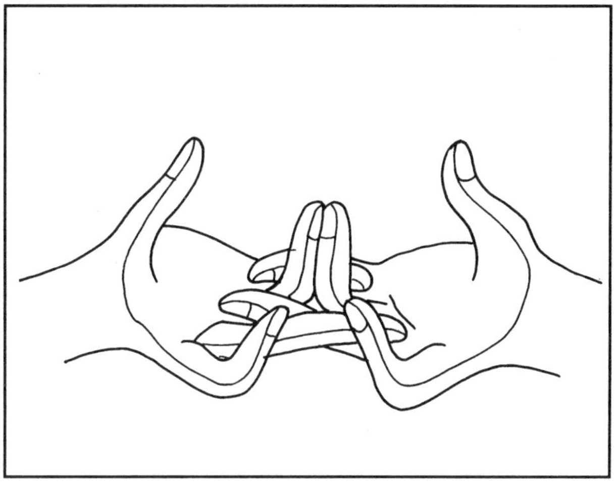

Figure 328 -- mandala mudra
(as seen by another)

mandara mudra -- (Ind.: *mandāra-mudrā*) A hand pose, a seal, a dramatic (Ind.: *nāṭya*) *mudra* or gesture (Ind.: *darpaṇa*) held or formed by a performer, dancer or actor. It denotes the *mandara* tree. The *mudra* employed is the *khanda-chatura mudra*. See: *khanda-chatura mudra*. (ACG 48)

mani-ratna mudra -- (Ind.: *maṇi-ratna-mudrā*) This is an assigned term.[9] A *mudra*, a ritual hand pose, a seal, which is common to the Buddhist (*Vajrayana*) tradition, a *tantric mudra*. It denotes the gift of the wish fulfilling jewel (Tib.: *nor-bu*) associated with the *saptaratna* (Tib.: *rgyal-srid sna-bdun*) or seven gems of sovereignty (Tib.: *nor-bu-chab-bdun*), also referred to as the 'space vast treasury,' particularly as it is associated with the worship of the powerful *Vajrayana* goddess, *Tara*. The *mani-ratna mudra* is a combined (Ind.: *saṁyutta*) form, held by both hands. This *mudra* is formed by: palms face the midline, tips of index fingers and thumb touch, middle, ring and little fingers are extended upwards. Thusly formed, the touching tips of the index fingers and thumbs are brought together, they touch and are held chest high. This *mudra* is said to resemble a flying bird. The *mantra* associated with this *mudra* is: "*OM Mani-ratna Praticcha HUM SVAHA*."[10] (SBe 152) (See: **Figure 329**)

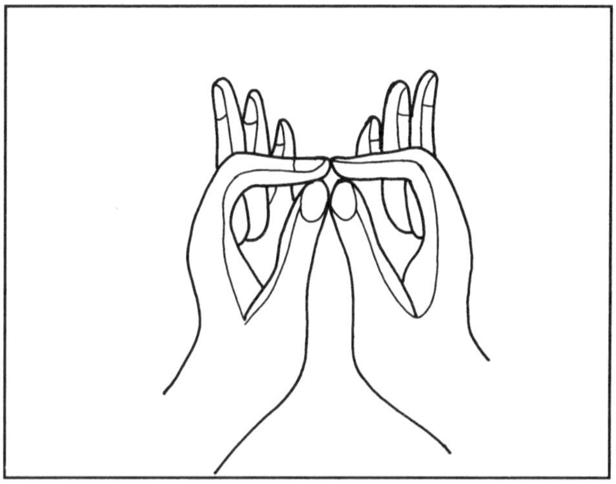

Figure 329 -- mani-ratna mudra
(as seen by the holder)

Manmatha mudra -- (Ind.: *Manmatha-mudrā*) A hand pose, a seal, a dramatic (Ind.: *nāṭya*) *mudra* or gesture (Ind.: *darpaṇa*) held or formed by a performer, dancer or actor which denotes a specific deity. The *Manmatha mudra* is a combined (Ind.: *saṁyutta*) form, held by both

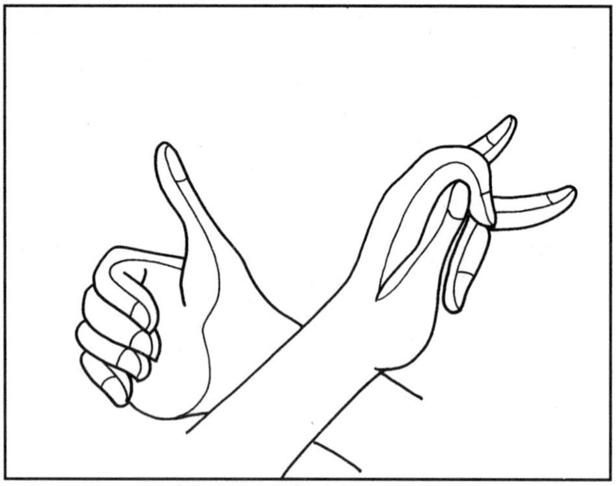

Figure 330 -- Manmatha mudra
(as seen by the holder)

hands. It denotes *Manmatha*. This *mudra* is formed by: right palm faces midline, the index and middle fingers curve and their tips touch the thumb, the ring and the little fingers also curve towards the palm; left palm faces mid-line, fingers brought into the palm forming a fist, thumb extends upwards. Thus formed the hands are held at shoulder level. (ACG 45) (See: **Figure 330**)

ma no cho jo-in[11] **(mudra)** -- (Jap.: *ma nō chō jō-in* [*mudrā*]; Ind.: *pothī mudrā*) The Japanese term for *pothi mudra*. See: *pothi mudra* (GDe 33)

manwichai (mudra) -- (Thai.: *manwichai* aka *pang maravichai*, [*pang*] *sadung-man*; Chin.: *an-shan-yin, ch'u-ti-yin*; Eng.: *adamantine posture*; Ind.: *bhasparśa mudrā, bhūmiśparśa mudrā, bhūmisparśana mudra, bhumisparśa mudrā, bhūsparśa mudrā, bhūsparśa mudrā, māravijaya mudra*; Jap.: *anzan-in* [*mudra*], *sokuchi-in* [*mudra*]) The Thai term for *bhumisparsha mudra*. See: *bhumisparsha mudra*. (KIM)

maravijaya mudra -- (Ind.: *māravijaya-mudrā* aka *bhasparśa mudrā, bhūmisparśa mudrā, bhūmisparśana mudrā, bhūmiśparśa mudrā, bhūsparś mudrā, bhūsparśa mudrā*; Chin.: *an-shan-yin, ch'u-ti-yin*; Eng.: *adamantine posture*; Jap.: *anzan-in* [*mudra*], *sokuchi-in* [*mudra*]; Thai: *manwichai* [*mudra*], *pang maravichai*, [*pang*] *sadung-man*) A variant term applied to *bhumisparsha mudra*. See: *bhumisparsha mudra*. (JBo)

marishitenhobyo-in (mudra) -- (Jap.: *marishitenhōbyō-in* [*mudrā*] aka *ongyo-in*) A variant term applied to *ongyo-in*. See: *ongyo-in*. (EDS 117)

marjara mudra -- (Ind.: *mārjarā-mudrā*) A hand pose, a seal, a dramatic (Ind.: *nāṭya*) mudra or gesture (Ind.: *darpaṇa*) held or formed by a performer, dancer or actor. It denotes an animal, in this case a cat. The *marjara mudra*[12] is a combined (Ind.: *saṁyutta*) form, held by both hands. It is identical in form to the *ardha-mukha mudra*. See: *ardha-mukha mudra*. (ACG 49)

matri mudra -- (Ind.: *mātṛ-mudrā*) A hand pose, a seal, a dramatic (Ind.: *nāṭya*) mudra or gesture (Ind.: *darpaṇa*) held or formed by a performer, dancer or actor. The matri mudra is a combined (Ind.: *saṁyutta*) form, held by both hands. One of eleven *mudras* representing "relationships" and one which denotes mother. This *mudra* is formed by: left palm faces outward, fingers extended, together and pointing upwards, relaxed, the thumb extends away from the fingers, and level with the chest; right palm faces upwards, fingers and thumb are separated and gently curl inwards, towards the hollowed palm except the middle finger which is held straight out. (ACG 44) (See: **Figure 331**)

matsya mudra -- (Ind.: *matsya-mudrā*) A *mudra*, a ritual hand pose, a seal, a *tantric mudra* which is common to the Buddhist and Hindu Buddhist (*Vajrayana, Mantrayana*) traditions and is held or formed by a devotee or priest. Also, a *mudra*, a ritual hand pose, a seal, a *mudra* which is common to yogic tradition, particularly the *Yoga Tatva Mudra Vigyan* form, and is held by a devotee or practitioner. It may be accompanied by a *mantra*. Also, a hand pose, a seal, a dramatic (Ind.: *nāṭya*) mudra or gesture (Ind.: *darpaṇa*) held or formed by a performer, dancer or actor. The matsya mudra is a combined (Ind.: *saṁyutta*) form, held by both hands. This *mudra* is formed by: right palm facing downwards, fingers together and extended outwards, thumb at right angle to the fingers, left palm facing downwards, fingers together and extended outwards, thumb at right angle to the fingers. Thus formed the right hand is placed over the left hand and touching it, and held waist high. The form of this *mudra* represents a fish and is associated with the *Matsyavatara* of the Lord *Vishnu*. (ACG 41, AMK 141, KDe 85, RLM 73) (See: **Figure 332**)

Matsyavatara mudra -- (Ind.: *Matsyāvatāra-mudrā*) A hand pose, a seal, a dramatic (Ind.: *nāṭya*) *mudra* or gesture (Ind.: *darpaṇa*) held or formed by a performer, dancer or actor. The *Matsyavatara mudra* is a combined (Ind.: *saṁyutta*) form, held by both hands. It denotes the fish *avatar*, one of the ten *avatars* (Ind.: *daśāvatāras*) of the Lord *Vishnu* The *Matsyavatara mudra* is a combined (Ind.: *saṁyutta*) form, held by both hands. This *mudra* requires movement and is formed by: right palm facing downwards, fingers together and extended outwards, thumb at right angle to the fingers, left palm facing downwards, fingers together and extended outwards, thumb at right angle to the fingers. Thus formed

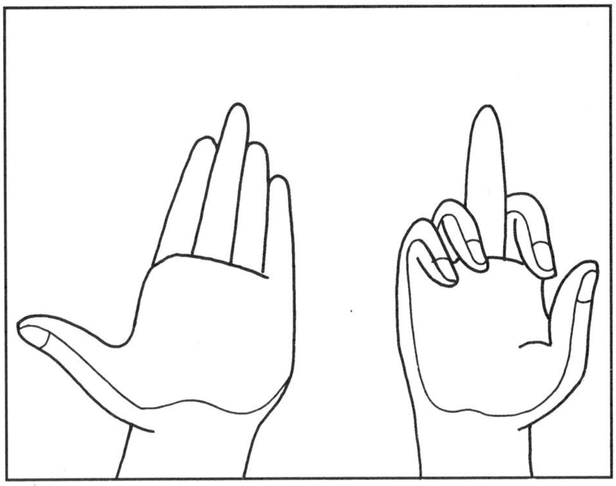

Figure 331 -- matri mudra
(as seen by the holder)

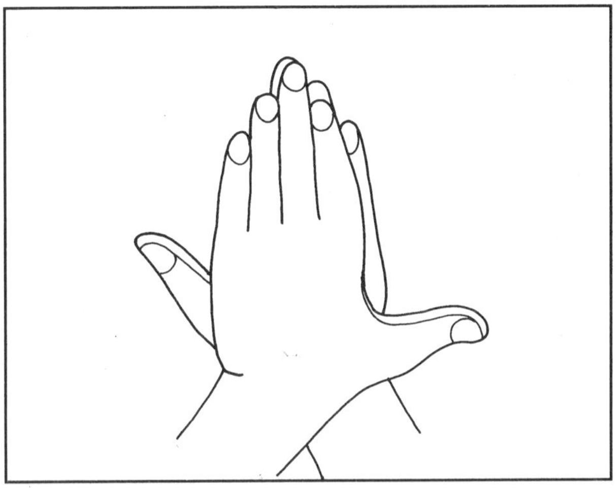

Figure 332 -- matsya mudra
(as seen by the holder)

Figure 333 -- Matsyavatara mudra
(as seen by another)

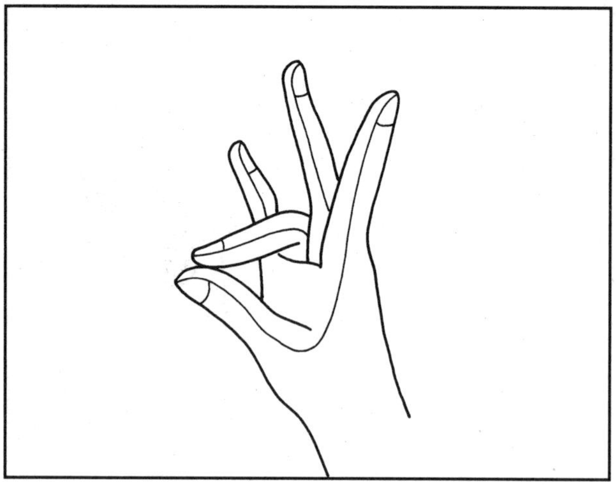

Figure 334 -- mayura mudra
(as seen by the holder)

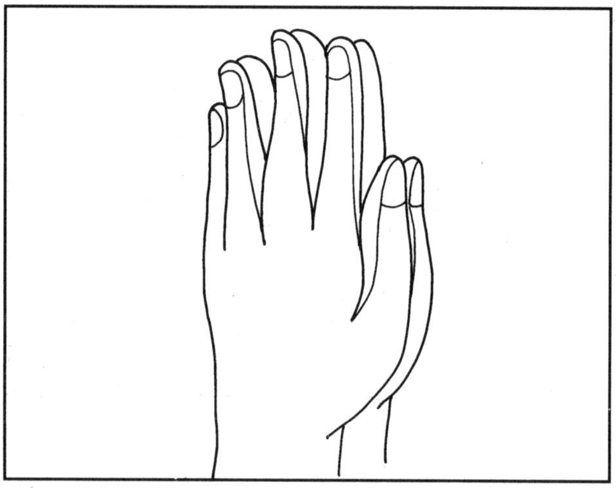

Figure 335 -- mifu renge-in (mudra) I
(as seen by the holder)

the right hand is placed over the left hand and touching it, and held level with the shoulder. It is then formed by both hands held: palms facing outward, index, middle and little fingers and thumbs extend, together and pointing upwards, ring fingers are bent towards the palms. (ACG 46) (See: **Figure 333**)

mayura mudra -- (Ind.: *mayūra-mudrā*) A *mudra*, a ritual hand pose, a seal, which is common to both the Buddhist and Hindu traditions and is depicted or held by a deity. The *mayura mudra* is a single (Ind.: *asaṁyutta*) form, held by one hand. It denotes a peacock which is an iconographic symbol of immortality and love. This *mudra* is formed by: palm facing outwards, tips of the thumb and ring finger touch and extend outwards, the index and middle fingers are straight and slightly separated, the little fingers is slightly bent. The form resembles the head of a peacock and may also represent a bird of ominous omen. It is similar to the *kartari* (*hasta*) *mudra*. (ACG 29, MJS 92) (See: **Figure 334**)

meditating mudra -- (Eng.; Chin.: *ting-yin* [*mudra*]; Ind.: *dhyāna mudrā, dhyānahasta mudrā, samādhi mudrā, yoga mudrā*; Jap.: *jo-in* [*mudra*]; Thai: *pang phra-nang*; Tib.: *bsam-gtan phyag-rgya*) The English descriptive phrase for the *dhyana mudra*. See: *dhyana mudra*. (DRN 35, JBo, KIM 5)

mi be renge gassho (mudra) -- (Jap.: *mi be renge gasshō* [*mudrā*] aka *boda gassho* [*mudra*]) A variant term applied to *boda gassho* (*mudra*). See: *boda gassho* (*mudra*). (GDe 6)

mifu renge-gassho (mudra) -- (Jap.: *mifu renge-gasshō* [*mudrā*] aka *mifu renge-in* [*mudra*] *III*) A variant term applied to *mifu renge-in* (*mudra*) *III*. See: *mifu renge-in* (*mudra*) *III*. (GDe 14)

mifu renge-in (mudra) I -- (Jap.: *mifu renge-in* [*mudrā*]) A *mudra*, a ritual hand pose, a seal, which is common to the Buddhist *Mahayana* and *Vajrayana* traditions and is depicted or held by a deity. The *mifu renge-in* (*mudra*)[13] is a combined (Ind.: *saṁyutta*) form, held by both hands. It denotes adoration. This *mudra* is related to the *kenjisshin-gassho*, and is formed by: bringing the palms, thumbs and fingers together, fingers and thumbs extending upwards, the index, middle and ring fingers are separated or splayed, the little fingers rest against the ring fingers. (EDS 79) (See: **Figure 335**)

mifu renge-in (mudra) II -- (Jap.: *mifu renge-in* [*mudrā*]) A *mudra*, a ritual hand pose, a seal, which is common to the Buddhist *Mahayana* and *Vajrayana* traditions and is depicted or held by a deity. The *mifu renge-in* (*mudra*) *II* is a combined (Ind.: *saṁyutta*) form, held by both hands. It denotes adoration. This *mudra* is related to the *kenjisshin-gassho*, and is formed by: bringing the palms, thumbs and fingers together, fingers and thumbs extending upwards, the index, middle and ring fingers are separated or slightly folded back from their counterparts, forming an opening. (EDS 79) (See: **Figure 336**)

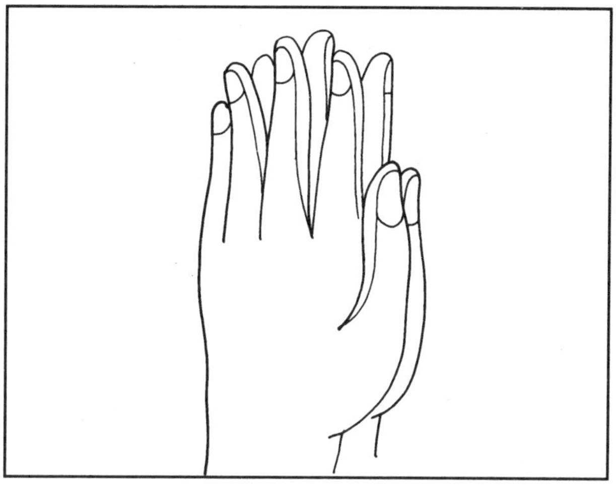

Figure 336 -- mifu renge-in (mudra) II
(as seen by the holder)

mifu renge-in (mudra) III -- (Jap.: *mifu renge-in* [*mudrā*] aka *mifu renge-gassho* [*mudra*]) A *mudra*, a ritual hand pose, a seal, which is common to the Buddhist *Mahayana* and *Vajrayana* traditions and is depicted or held by a deity. The *mifu renge-in* (*mudra*) *III* is a combined (Ind.: *saṁyutta*) form, held by both hands. It denotes adoration. This *mudra* is formed by: bringing the palms, thumbs and fingers together, fingers and thumbs extending upwards, the middle and ring fingers are separated or slightly held away from their counterparts, forming an opening. (GDe 14) (See: **Figure 337**)

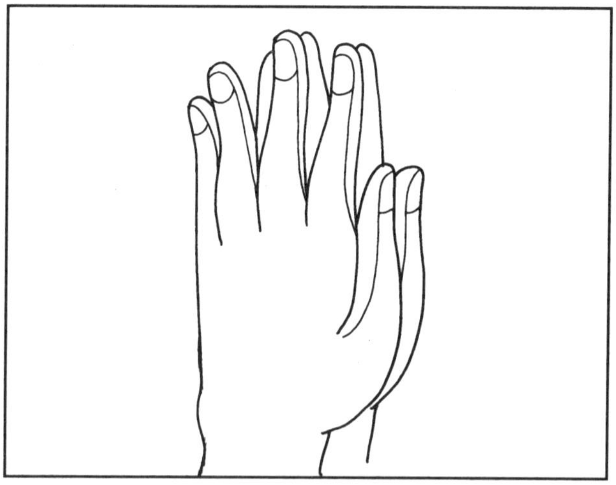

Figure 337 -- mifu renge-in (mudra) III
(as seen by the holder)

miharita gassho (mudra) -- (Jap.: *miharita gasshō* [*mudrā*]; Ind.: *viparīta mudrā*) A *mudra*, a ritual hand pose, a seal, which is common to the Japanese Buddhist tradition. Specifically one of the twelve, elemental "hand clasps" (Jap. *junigosho* or *junigassho*). The *miharita gassho* (*mudra*) is a combined (Ind.: *saṁyutta*) form, held by both hands. This *mudra* is formed by: the two hands touch, back to back and the fingers and thumbs of the right overlap (interlock) with those of the left. This is known as the "backhand clasp."[14] (EDS 40) (See: **Figure 338**)

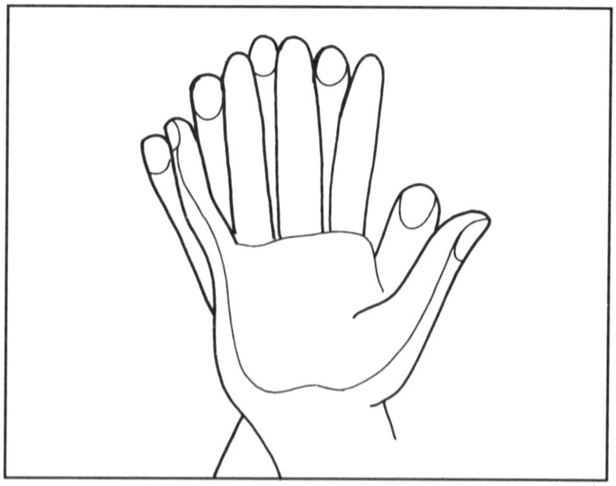

Figure 338 -- miharita gassho (mudra)
(as seen by the holder)

Milarepa's mudra -- A *mudra*, a ritual hand pose, a seal, which is common to the Buddhist (*Vajrayana*) tradition. It is associated exclusively with *Milarepa* who is said to vahe listened to the sounds of nature. The *Milarepa's mudra* is a single (Ind.: *asaṁyutta*) form, held by one hand. This *mudra* is formed by: right hand held

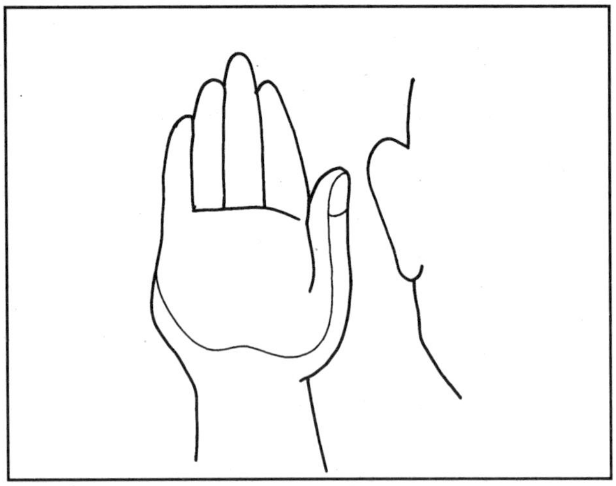

Figure 339 -- Milarepa's mudra
(as seen by another)

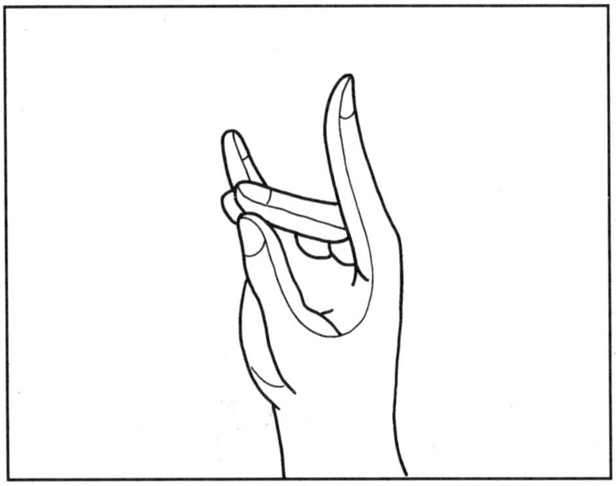

Figure 340 -- mragi mudra
(as seen by the holder)

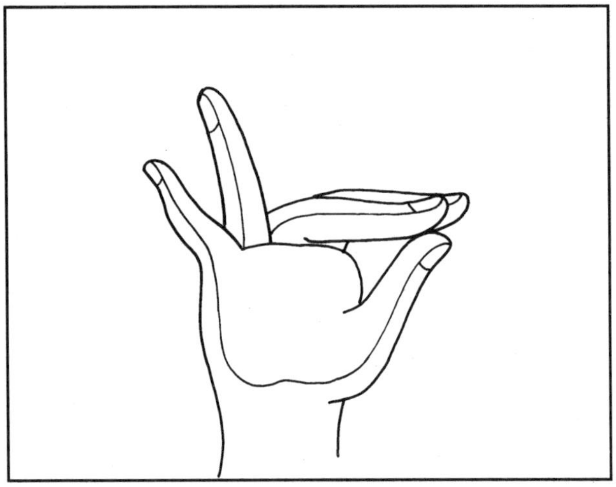

Figure 341 -- mrigashirsha mudra I
(as seen by another)

up to his right ear. It is said to refer to his listening to the sounds of nature. (MMR 240) (See: **Figure 339**)

mriagi mudra -- (Ind.: *mṛgī-mudrā*) A *mudra*, a ritual hand pose, a seal, a *mudra* which is common to yogic tradition, particularly the *Yoga Tatva Mudra Vigyan* form, and is held by a devotee or practitioner. The *mriagi mudra* is a single (Ind.: *asaṁyutta*) form, held by one hand. It is utilized for peace and restorative needs. This *mudra* is formed by: the palm facing forward, index and little fingers extend straight upwards, middle and ring fingers together and curl towards the palm, the tip of the thumb touches the first phalanges of the two fingers. It is similar to the *harina mudra*. (KDe 64) (See: **Figure 340**)

mrigashirsha mudra I -- (Ind.: *mṛga-śīrṣa-mudrā*) ("deer head") A hand pose, a seal, a dramatic (Ind.: *nāṭya*) *mudra* or gesture (Ind.: *darpaṇa*) held or formed by a performer, dancer or actor. The *mrigashirsha mudra* is a single (Ind.: *asaṁyutta*) form, held by one hand. This *mudra* is formed by: palm faces forward, index and middle fingers are straight and fold towards the palm and they are touched by the tip of the thumb, the ring and the little fingers extend upwards. (KVa 135 [24]) (See: **Figure 341**)

mrigashirsha mudra II -- (Ind.: *mṛga-śīrṣa-mudrā*) ("deer head") A hand pose, a seal, a dramatic (Ind.: *nāṭya*) *mudra* or gesture (Ind.: *darpaṇa*) held or formed by a performer, dancer or actor. The *mrigashirsha mudra* is a single (Ind.: *asaṁyutta*) form, held by one hand and a variation of the above. It denotes discussion, women, fear, etc.[15] This *mudra* is formed by: palm faces forward, index, middle and ring fingers curl at their first and second joints (towards the palm), the thumb is extended outward, and the little fingers extend upwards. (ACG 33-34) (See: **Figure 342**)

Mrit-Sanjivani mudra -- (Ind.: *Mṛt-Sañjīvanī-mudrā* aka *apāna-vāyu mudrā*) A variant term applied to *apan-vayu mudra*. See: *apan-vayu mudra*. (KDe 131)

mudgaram mudra -- (Ind.: *mudgaram-mudrā* aka *mugdharam mudrā*) A variant (spelling) of *mugdhram mudra*. See: *mugdhram mudra*. (RLM 74)

mugdhram mudra -- (Ind.: *mugdharam-mudrā* aka *mudgaram mudrā*) A *mudra*, a ritual hand pose, a seal, a *mudra* which is common to yogic tradition, particularly the *Yoga Tatva Mudra Vigyan* form, and is held by a devotee or practitioner. The *mugdhram mudra*[16] is a combined (Ind.: *saṁyutta*) form, held by both hands. It is one of the twenty-four *mudras* held before the *Gayatri Jap* of the thirty-two total *Gayatri mudras*.[17] It is utilized for all sickness, especially cancer. This *mudra* is formed by: the right forearm at right angles to the ground, hand in the *padma-mushti* (*mudra*), palm facing the midline; left palm faces upwards, fingers and thumb straight and extended to the right. Thus formed, the elbow of the right hand rests in the palm of the left. (KDe 87 & 108, RLM 74) (See: **Figure 343**)

mukha mudra -- (Ind.: *mukha-mudrā*; Jap.: *nyorai cho-in*) ("head *mudra*") A *mudra*, a ritual hand pose, a seal, a *tantric mudra* which is common to the Japanese Buddhist (*Vajrayana, Mantrayana*) tradition and is held or formed by a devotee or priest during the rites of *Garbhadhatu Mandala, Vajradhatu Mandala, Homa Rites* and other rites. It may be accompanied by a *mantra*. The *mukha mudra* is a combined (Ind.: *saṁyutta*) form, held by both hands. It symbolizes the face or head of the Buddha. This *mudra* is similar to the *kavacha mudra* and is formed by: the heels of the palms joined the thumbs extend upward an touch their counterparts, the index fingers' tips touch the second of the respective phalanges of the middle fingers, the middle fingers curve slightly and touch at their tips, the ring and little fingers interlace and fold towards the palms (being enclosed by the palms). (GDe 23, LCS 264) (See: **Figure 344**)

mukula mudra -- (Ind.: *mukula-mudrā*) ("bud") A *mudra*, a ritual hand pose, a seal, which is common to the Hindu tradition. As well as a hand pose, a seal, a dramatic (Ind.: *nāṭya*) mudra or gesture (Ind.: *darpaṇa*) held or formed by a performer, dancer or actor. It denotes the bud of a flower (lotus) and also virginity. The *mukula mudra* is a single (Ind.: *asaṁyutta*) form, held by one hand. This *mudra* is formed by: palm faces outwards, the tips of the fingers and thumb are brought together, but not necessarily touching, pointing forwards. The *mudra* may be pointing upwards as well. It is similar to the *padmakosha* except that here the fin-

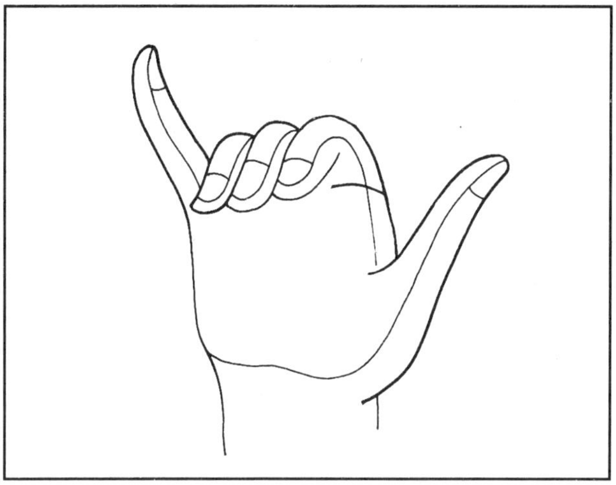

Figure 342 -- mrigashirsha mudra II
(as seen by another)

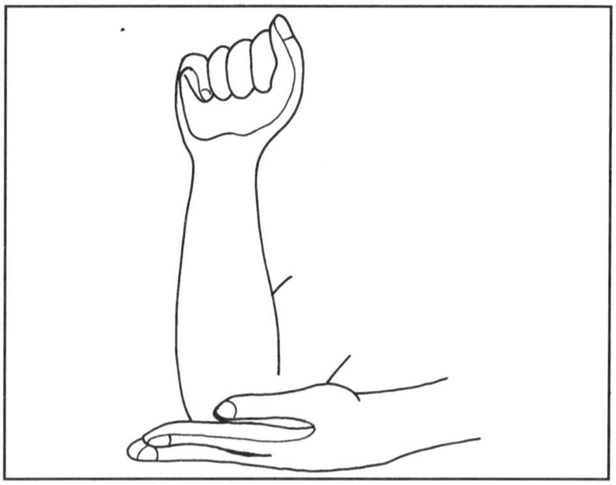

Figure 343 -- mugdhram mudra
(as seen by another)

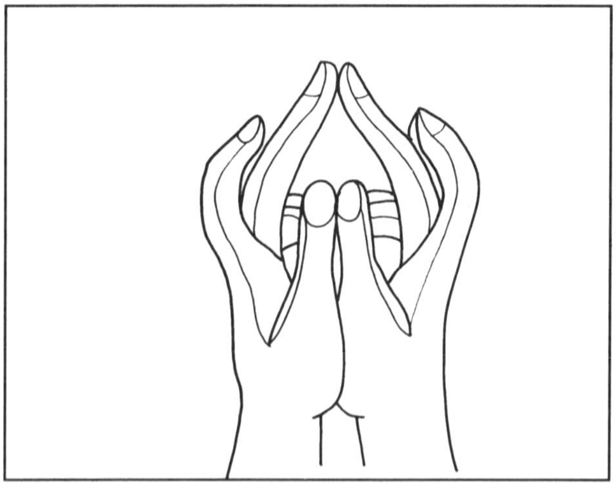

Figure 344 -- mukha mudra
(as seen by the holder)

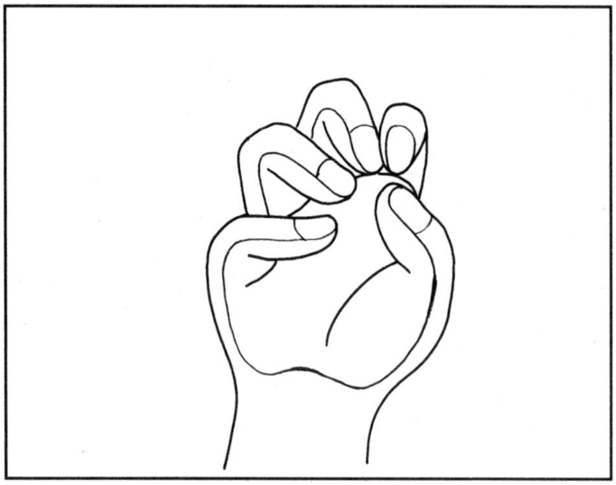

Figure 345 -- mukula mudra
(as seen by another)

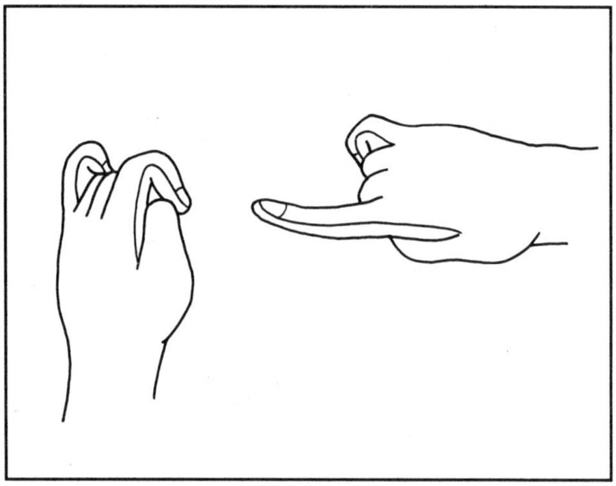

Figure 346 -- mu no sho shu-go-in (mudra)
(as seen by the holder)

gers are closer together and the palm faces outwards, and it is also similar to the *urnanabha mudra* except the latter's curved fingers are more pronounced. (ACG 26, KVa 136 [34], MJS 94) (See: **Figure 345**)

mula-guhya mudra -- (Ind.: *mūla-guhya-mudrā* aka *cakṣur mudrā*) A variant term applied to *chakshur mudra*. The first of "fourteen *mula-mudras*." See: *chakshur mudra*. (GDe 325)

mu no sho shu-go-in (mudra) -- (Jap.: *mu no shō shu-gō-in* [*mudrā*]) ("invincible guardians") A *mudra*, a ritual hand pose, a seal, a *tantric mudra* which is common to the Japanese Buddhist (*Vajrayana, Mantrayana*) tradition and is held or formed by a devotee or priest during the rites of *Garbhadhatu Mandala, Vajradhatu Mandala, Homa Rites* and other rites. It may be accompanied by a *mantra*. The *mu no sho shu-go-in* (*mudra*) is a combined (Ind.: *saṁyutta*) form, held by both hands. It denotes the destruction of demons. This *mudra* is formed by: left palm generally facing outward, thumb folded into the palm, middle and ring fingers folded over the thumb, index and little fingers curl at their first two knuckles, third phalanges remains erect (upward), the right thumb is folded into the palm, the middle, ring and little fingers fold over an enclose the thumb, the index finger extends and points towards the left hand. (GDe 46) (See: **Figure 346**)

mushaka mudra -- (Ind.: *mūṣaka-mudrā*) A hand pose, a seal, a dramatic (Ind.: *nāṭya*) mudra or gesture (Ind.: *darpaṇa*) held or formed by a performer, dancer or actor. It denotes an animal, in this case a mouse. The *mushaka mudra*[18] is a single (Ind.: *asaṁyutta*) form, held by one hand. This *mudra* is identical to the *khanda-mukula mudra*. See: *khanda-mukula mudra*. (ACG 49)

mushofushi-in (mudra) I -- (Jap.: *mushofushi-in* [*mudrā*] aka *Biroshana-in* [*mudra*], *butsubu sotoba-in* [*mudra*], *dai sotoba-in* [*mudra*], *hen hokkai mushofushi-in* [*mudra*], *mushofushi to-in* [*mudra*], *rito-in* [*mudra*]; Chin.: *wu-so-pu-chih-yin*; Ind.: *stūpa mudrā*) ("the *mudra* of ubiquity") A *mudra*, a ritual hand pose, a seal, which is common to the Japanese and Chinese Buddhist tradition. Also, a *tantric mudra* which is common to the Japanese Buddhist (*Vajrayana, Mantrayana*) tradition and is held or formed by a devotee or priest during the rites of

Garbhadhatu Mandala, Vajradhatu Mandala, Homa Rites and other rites. It may be accompanied by a *mantra.* It denotes the Supreme Principle or the Three Mysteries. The *mushofushi-in (mudra)*[19] is a combined (Ind.: *saṁyutta*) form, held by both hands. This *mudra* is formed by: the palms touch at the 'heels,' middle, ring and little fingers extend and touch at their tips, a narrow space is left between the hands, the index fingers bend at the second joint and their tips touch, the thumbs touch along their outer length and their tips rest on the tips of the joining index fingers. The mudra so formed is held at chest level. (EDS 115, GDe 32, LCS 221) (See: **Figure 347**)

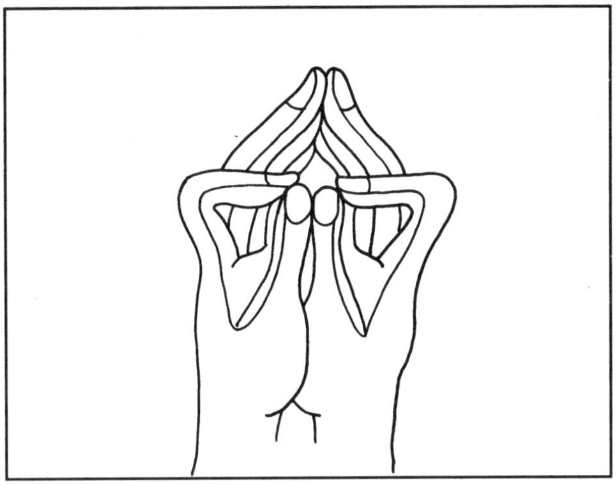

Figure 347 -- mushofushi-in (mudra) I
(as seen by the holder)

mushofushi-in (mudra) II -- (Jap.: *mushofushi-in* [*mudrā*]) A *tantric mudra* which is common to the Japanese Buddhist (*Vajrayana, Mantrayana*) tradition and is held or formed by a devotee or priest during the rites of *Garbhadhatu Mandala, Vajradhatu Mandala, Homa Rites* and other rites. It may be accompanied by a *mantra.* It denotes the Supreme Principle or the Three Mysteries. The *mushofushi-in (mudra) II,*[20] a variation on the *mushofushi-in (mudra) I,* is a combined (Ind.: *saṁyutta*) form, held by both hands. This *mudra* is formed by: the palms touch at the 'heels,' middle, ring and little fingers extend and interlace at their tips, a narrow space is left between the hands, the index fingers bend at the second joint and their tips touch, the thumbs touch along their outer length and their tips rest on the tips of the joining index fingers. The mudra so formed is held at chest level. (GDe 131) (See: **Figure 348**)

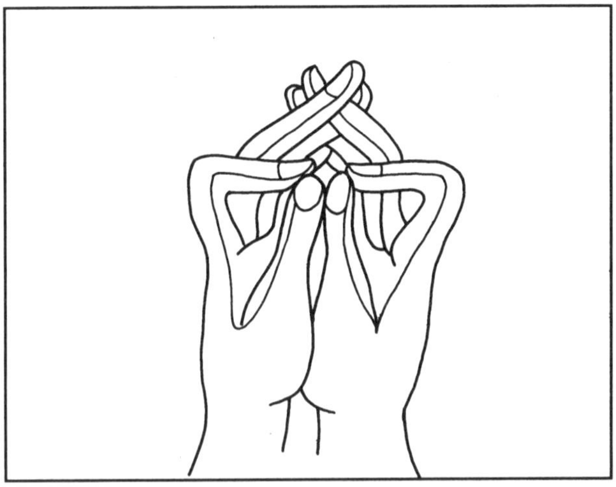

Figure 348 -- mushofushi-in (mudra) II
(as seen by the holder)

mushofushi-in (mudra) III -- (Jap.: *mushofushi-in* [*mudrā*]; Ind.: *stūpā mudrā*) ("the *mudra* of ubiquity") A *mudra,* a ritual hand pose, a seal, which is common to the Japanese and Chinese Buddhist tradition. Also, a *tantric mudra* which is common to the Japanese Buddhist (*Vajrayana, Mantrayana*) tradition and is held or formed by a devotee or priest during the rites of *Garbhadhatu Mandala, Vajradhatu Mandala, Homa Rites* and other rites. It may be accompanied by a *mantra.* The *mushofushi-in*[21] *(mudra) III* is a combined (Ind.: *saṁyutta*) form, held by both hands. This *mudra* is formed by: the palms touch at the 'heels,' middle fingers touch at their tips, ring and little fingers are folded into the palms, a narrow space is left between the

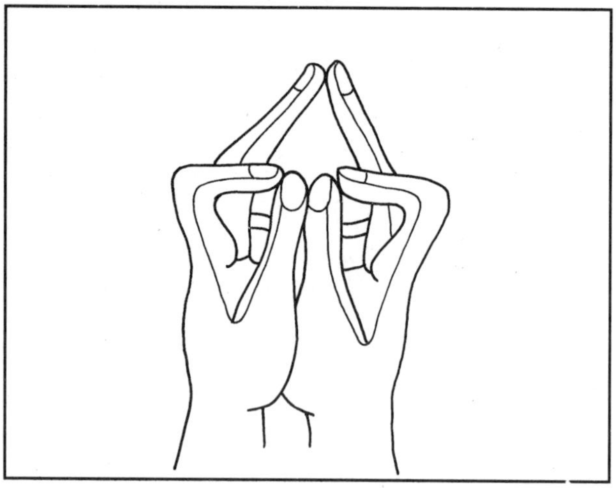

Figure 349 -- mushofushi-in (mudra) III
(as seen by the holder)

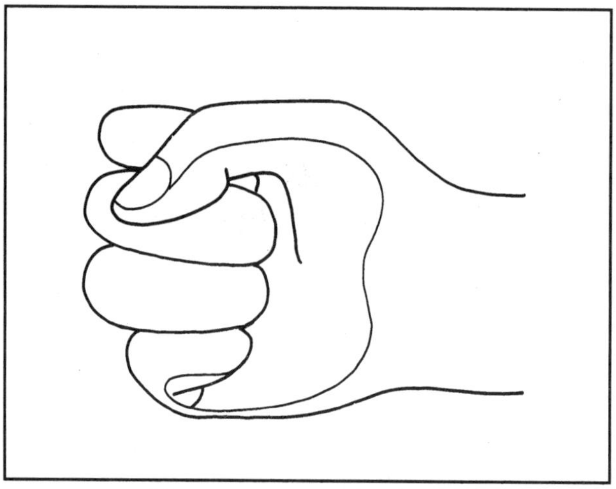

Figure 350 -- mushti mudra
(as seen by the holder)

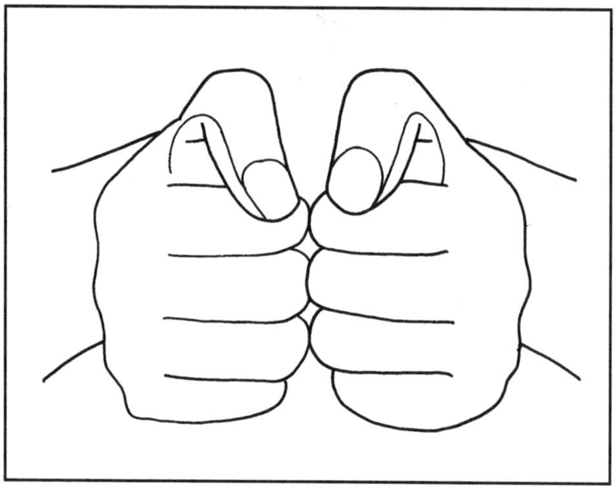

Figure 351 -- mushtikam mudra
(as seen by another)

hands, the index fingers bend at the second joint and their tips touch, the thumbs touch along their outer length and their tips rest on the tips of the joining index fingers. The *mudra* so formed is held at chest level. (EDS 144) (See: **Figure 349**)

mushofushi to-in (mudra) -- (Jap.: *mushofushi tō-in* [*mudrā*] aka *mushofushi-in* [*mudra*], *Biroshana-in* [*mudra*], *butsubu sotoba-in* [*mudra*], *dai sotoba-in* [*mudra*], *hen hokkai mushofushi-in* [*mudra*], *rito-in* [*mudra*]; Chin.: *wu-so-pu-chih-yin*; Ind.: *stūpā mudrā*) ("omnipresent *stupa mudra*") A variant term applied to *mushofushi-in* (*mudra*). See: *mushofushi-in* (*mudra*). (EDS 115)

mushti mudra -- (Ind.: *muṣṭi-mudrā*) ("the mist *mudra*") A *mudra*, a ritual hand pose, a seal, which is common to the Hindu tradition and is depicted or held by a deity. The *mushti mudra* is a single (Ind.: *asaṁyutta*) form, held by one hand. It denotes strength, power, steadiness and is used when holding a spear or lance. The form is held in one hand, frequently the left: the palm faces the midline, the fingers are fisted, the thumb lies over the first phalanges of the fingers. It is similar to the *kataka mudra*[22] and the *renge ken-in*.[23] (ACG 30, KVa 134 [10], MJS 95) (See: **Figure 350**)

mushtikam mudra -- (Ind.: *muṣṭikam-mudrā*) A *mudra*, a ritual hand pose, a seal, a *mudra* which is common to yogic tradition, particularly the *Yoga Tatva Mudra Vigyan* form, and is held by a devotee or practitioner. The *mushtikam mudra* is a combined (Ind.: *saṁyutta*) form, held by both hands. It is one of the twenty-four mudras held before the *Gayatri Jap* of the thirty-two total *Gayatri mudras*.[24] It is utilized for all sickness, especially cancer. This *mudra* is formed by: both hands forming the *padma-mushti* (*mudra*) (Jap.: *renge ken-in* [*mudra*]). Thus formed they are brought together so that the second phalanges of the fingers touch and the thumbs touch along their length. (KDe 85, RLM 73) (See: **Figure 351**)

mushti-mriga mudra -- (Ind.: *muṣṭi-mṛga-mudrā*) A hand pose, a seal, a dramatic (Ind.: *nāṭya*) *mudra* or gesture (Ind.: *darpaṇa*) held or formed by a performer, dancer or actor. The *mushti-mriga mudra* is a single (Ind.: *asaṁyutta*) form, held by one hand. This *mudra* is formed by: palm generally facing forward, index, middle and ring fingers folded into the palm, thumb and little finger extend upward and slightly outward. (ACG 49) (See: **Figure 352**)

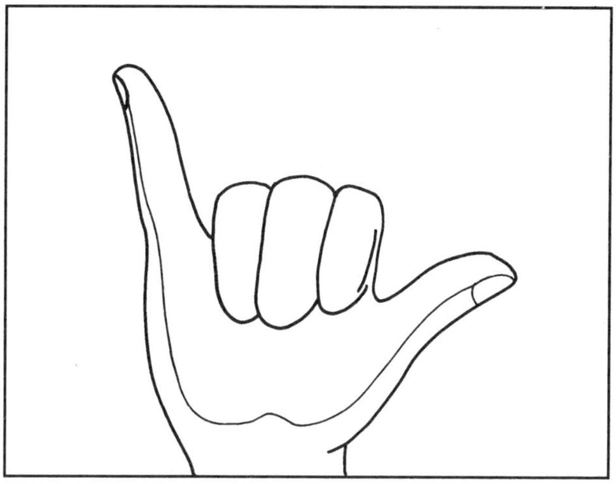

Figure 352 -- mushti-mriga mudra
(as seen by another)

mushti-svastika mudra -- (Ind.: *muṣṭi-svastika-mudrā*) A hand pose, a seal, a dramatic (Ind.: *nāṭya*) *mudra* or gesture (Ind.: *darpaṇa*) held or formed by a performer, dancer or actor. The *mushti-svastika mudra* is a combined (Ind.: *saṁyutta*) form,2 held by both hands. It denotes bashfulness, boxing, etc.[25] This *mudra* is formed by: palms facing the midline, fingers curled into the palm, thumb folded over fingers. Thus formed the hands are crossed at the wrists and held level with the abdomen. (ACG 43) (See: **Figure 353**)

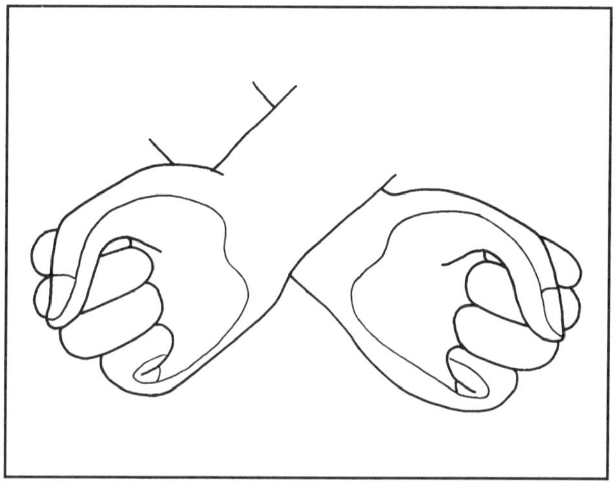

Figure 353 -- mushti-svastika mudra
(as seen by the holder)

myosenden-in[26] (mudra) -- (Jap.: *myōsenden-in* [*mudrā*] aka *ko-in* [*mudra*]; Ind.: *kavaca mudrā*) A variant term applied to *ko-in mudra*. See: *ko-in mudra*. (GDe 210)

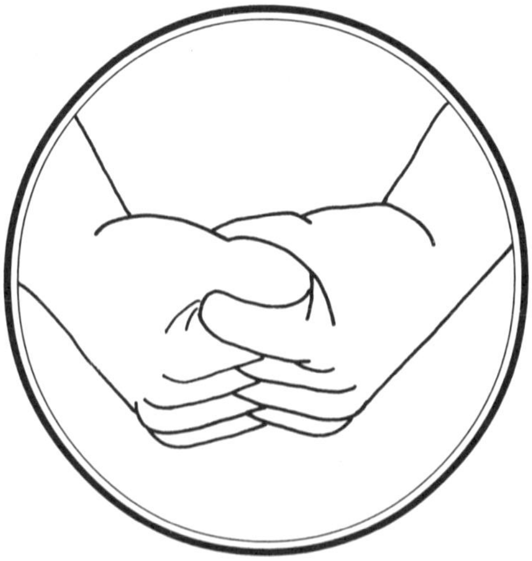

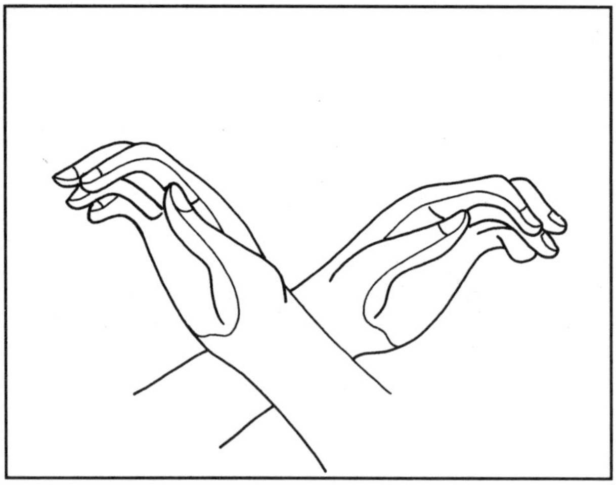

Figure 354 -- naga-bandha mudra
(as seen by the holder)

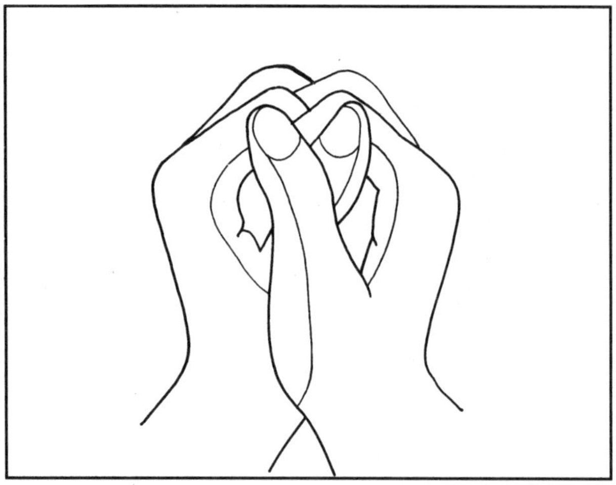

Figure 355 -- naibaku ken-in (mudra) I
(as seen by the holder)

-- N --

naga mudra -- (Ind.: *nāgamudrā* aka *sarpa mudrā, sarpaśirṣa mudrā*) A variant term applied to *sarpashirsha mudra*. See: *sarpashirsha mudra.* (MJS 97)

naga-bandha mudra -- (Ind.: *nāga-bandha-mudrā*) ("the serpent-tie") A hand pose, a seal, a dramatic (Ind.: *nāṭya*) *mudra* or gesture (Ind.: *darpaṇa*) held or formed by a performer, dancer or actor. The *naga-bandha mudra* is a combined (Ind.: *saṁyutta*) form, held by both hands. It denotes snakes and the spells of the *Atharva Veda*. This *mudra* is formed by: essentially from the *pataka mudra* for both hands--the palm facing forwards, the thumb is against the index finger's base, the index, middle, ring and little fingers curl, half-way towards the palm. Thus formed, the hands are crossed at the wrist. (ACG 41) (See: **Figure 354**)

Nahusha mudra -- (Ind.: *Nahuṣa-mudrā*) A hand pose, a seal, a dramatic (Ind.: *nāṭya*) mudra or gesture (Ind.: *darpaṇa*) held or formed by a performer, dancer or actor. The *Nahusha mudra* is a single (Ind.: *asaṁyutta*) form, held by one hand. It denotes *Nahusha*, one of a number of famous rulers or heroes. The *mudra* employed is identical withthe *shikhara mudra* moving back and forth. See: *shikhara mudra.* (ACG 47)

naibaku ken-in (mudra) I -- (Jap.: *naibaku ken-in* [*mudrā*]) A *mudra*, a ritual hand pose, a seal, which is common to the Japanese Buddhist tradition. It denotes the moon and is called the "inner bonds fist."[1] The *naibaku ken-in* (*mudra*) is a combined (Ind.: *saṁyutta*) form, held by both hands. This *mudra* is formed by: palms face each other, fingers and thumbs are interlaced with fingers and thumbs inside (palm-side) the 'fist.' (EDS 119, GDe 40) (See: **Figure 355**)

naibaku ken-in (mudra) II -- (Jap.: *naibaku ken-in* [*mudrā*]) A *mudra*, a ritual hand pose, a seal, a *tantric mudra* which is common to the Japanese Buddhist (*Vajrayana, Mantrayana*) tradition and is held or formed by a devotee or priest during the rites of *Garbhadhatu* and *Eighteen Rites*. It may be accompanied by a *mantra*.

The *naibaku ken-in* (*mudra*) *II*[2] is a combined (Ind.: *saṁyutta*) form, held by both hands. It denotes evocation. This *mudra* is formed by: palms face each other, fingers are interlaced with fingers and left thumb inside (palm-side) the 'fist,' right thumb is on the outside. (GDe 40, LCS 62) (See: **Figure 356**)

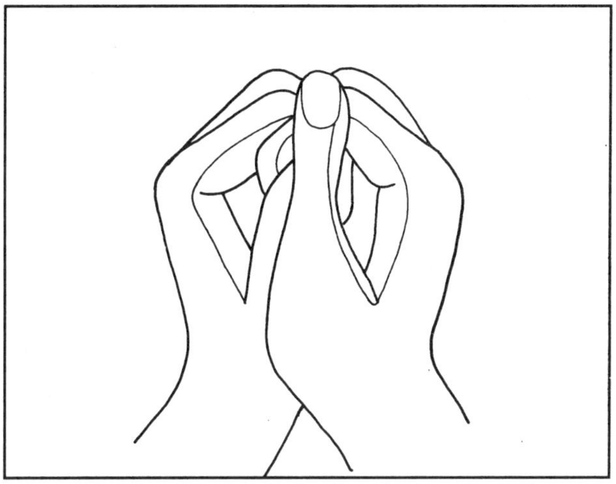

Figure 356 -- naibaku ken-in (mudra) II
(as seen by the holder)

naibaku ken-in (mudra) III -- (Jap.: *naibaku ken-in* [*mudrā*]) A *mudra*, a ritual hand pose, a seal, a *tantric mudra* which is common to the Japanese Buddhist (*Vajrayana, Mantrayana*) tradition and is held or formed by a devotee or priest during the rites of *Garbhadhatu* and *Eighteen Rites*. It may be accompanied by a *mantra*. The *naibaku ken-in* (*mudra*) *III*[3] is a combined (Ind.: *saṁyutta*) form, held by both hands. It denotes evocation. This *mudra* is formed by: palms face each other, fingers are interlaced with fingers and right thumb inside (palm-side) the 'fist,' left thumb is on the outside. (GDe 40) (See: **Figure 357**)

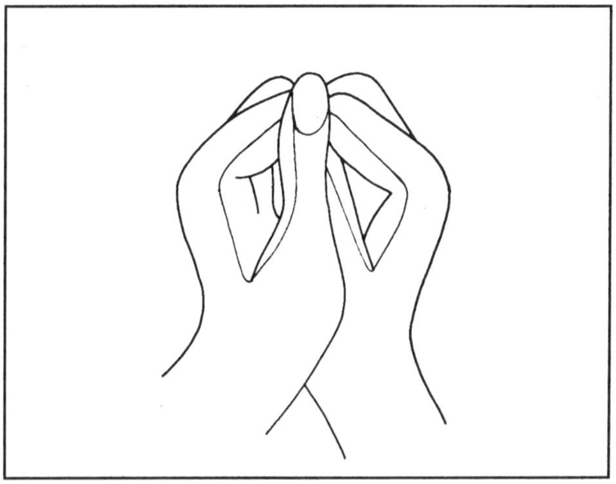

Figure 357 -- naibaku ken-in (mudra) III
(as seen by the holder)

Nairriti mudra -- (Ind.: *Nairṛti-mudrā*) A hand pose, a seal, a dramatic (Ind.: *nāṭya*) *mudra* or gesture (Ind.: *darpaṇa*) held or formed by a performer, dancer or actor which denotes a specific deity. The *Nairriti mudra* is a combined (Ind.: *saṁyutta*) form, held by both hands. It denotes *Nairriti*. This *mudra* is formed by: right palm faces forwards, index finger curls towards the palm, the middle, ring and little fingers are extended upwards, and splayed, the thumb is extended and splayed; left palm faces upwards, middle and ring fingers fold straight towards the palm, thumb touches the second knuckle of these two fingers, index and little fingers extend straight downwards. Thus formed the hands are held at shoulder level. (ACG 45) (See: **Figure 358**)

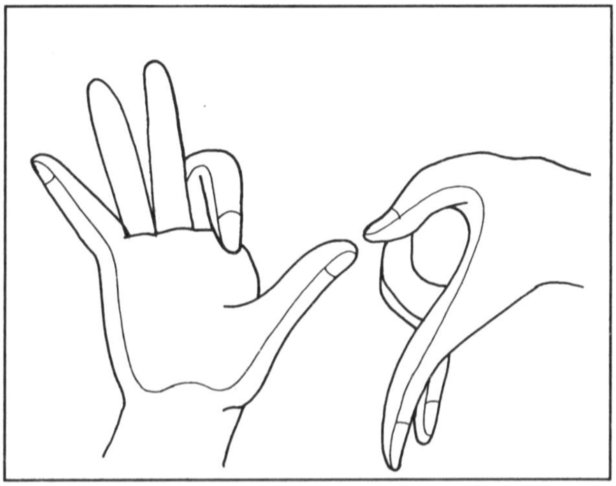

Figure 358 -- Nairriti mudra
(as seen by another)

naivedye mudra -- (Ind.: *naivedye-mudrā*) This is an assigned term.[4] A *mudra*, a ritual hand pose, a seal, which is common to the Buddhist (*Vajrayana*) tradition, a *tantric mudra*. It denotes food, which is one of the five 'gifts' or 'outer offerings' proffered to a divine guest--the other four being: flowers, lamps, perfume and incense--during the early stages worship, particularly as associated with the worship of the powerful *Vajrayana* goddess, *Tara*. The *naivedye mudra* is a combined (Ind.: *saṁyutta*) form, held by both hands. This *mudra* is formed in mirror-pose by: the palms face

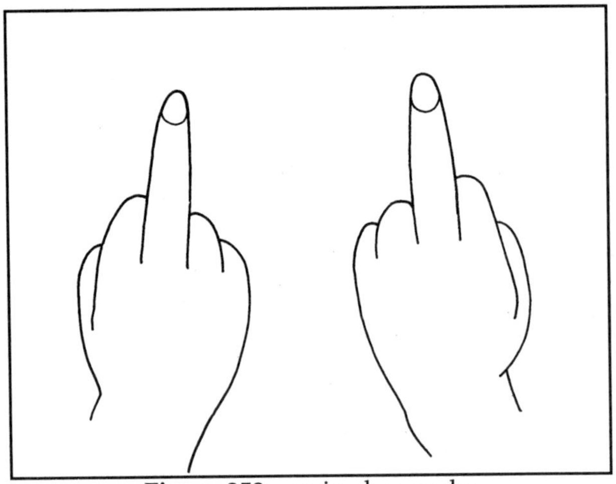

Figure 359 -- naivedye mudra
(as seen by another)

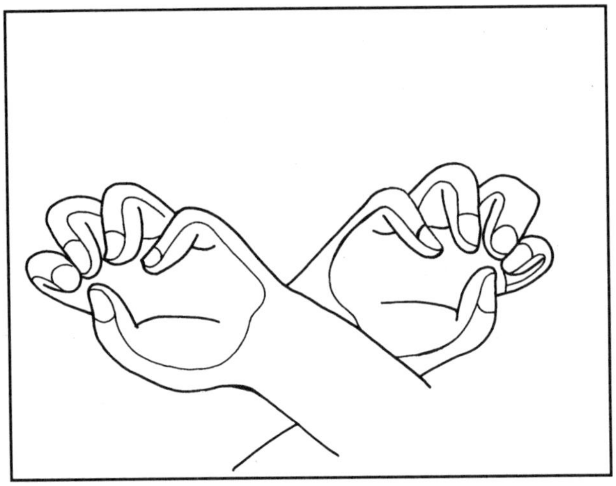

Figure 360 -- nalini-padmakosha mudra
(as seen by another)

the midline, the fingers are fisted, except the middle finger which extends upwards, the two hands are brought close together, level with each other, but not touching. The *mudra* so formed is held level with the chest. The *mantra* associated with this *mudra* is: "*OM Guru-sarva-Tathagata Naivedye Puja-megha-samudra-spharana-samaye HUM.*"[5] (SBe 147) (See: **Figure 359**)

Nakula mudra -- (Ind.: *Nakula-mudrā*) A hand pose, a seal, a dramatic (Ind.: *nāṭya*) *mudra* or gesture (Ind.: *darpaṇa*) held or formed by a performer, dancer or actor. The *Nakula mudra* is a single (Ind.: *asaṁyutta*) form, held by one hand. It denotes *Nakula*, one of a number of famous rulers or heroes. The *mudra* employed is identical in form to the *kataka mudra*. See: *kataka mudra*. (ACG 47)

Nala mudra -- (Ind.: *Nala-mudrā*) A hand pose, a seal, a dramatic (Ind.: *nāṭya*) *mudra* or gesture (Ind.: *darpaṇa*) held or formed by a performer, dancer or actor. The *Nala mudra* is a single (Ind.: *asaṁyutta*) form, held by one hand. It denotes *Nala*, one of a number of famous rulers or heroes. The *mudra* employed is identical in form to the *mayura mudra*. See: *mayura mudra*. (ACG 47)

nalini-padmakosha mudra -- (Ind.: *nalinī-padmakośa-mudrā*) A hand pose, a seal, a dramatic (Ind.: *nāṭya*) *mudra* or gesture (Ind.: *darpaṇa*) held or formed by a performer, dancer or actor. The *nalini-padmakosha mudra* is a combined (Ind.: *saṁyutta*) form, held by both hands. It denotes buds, cluster of flowers, etc.[6] This *mudra* is formed by: palms faces outwards, fingers and thumbs are separated and gently curl inwards, towards the hollowed palms. Thus formed the hands are crossed at the wrists. (ACG 44) (See: **Figure 360**)

namaskara mudra I -- (Ind.: *namaskāra-mudrā*; Tib.: *phyag-htshal phyag-rgya*) A *mudra*, a ritual hand pose, a seal, which is common to both the Buddhist and Hindu traditions, although this form is more frequently seen amongst Hindu practices. It denotes adoration and greetings. The *namaskara mudra I* is a combined (Ind.: *saṁyutta*) form, held by both hands. This *mudra* is formed by: palms face the midline and are brought together, fingers extended upwards, slightly cupped and held with the tips of the fingers touching. Thus formed, the *mudra* is held against the forehead.[7] (MJS 98) (See: **Figure 361**)

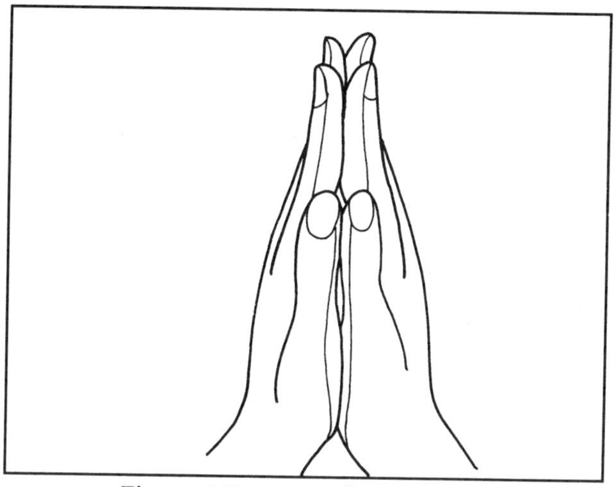

Figure 361 -- namaskara mudra I
(as seen by the holder)

namaskara mudra II -- (Ind.: *namaskāra-mudrā;* Tib.: *phyag-htshal phyag-rgya*) A *mudra*, a ritual hand pose, a seal, which is common to both the Buddhist and Hindu traditions, although this form is more frequently seen amongst Buddhist practices.[8] It denotes adoration through the bearing of a gift and greetings. Also, a *tantric mudra* which is common to the Japanese and Chinese Buddhist (*Vajrayana, Mantrayana*) tradition and is held or formed by a devotee or priest. It may be accompanied by a *mantra*. The *namaskara mudra II* is a combined (Ind.: *saṁyutta*) form, held by both hands. This *mudra* is formed by: palms face the midline and are close, fingers extended upwards, slightly cupped and held with the tips of the fingers touching. Thus formed, the *mudra* is held against the chest and often with an object is enfolded between the cupped hands. The *chatur-bhuja* form of *Avalokiteshvara* (Tib.: *spyan-ras-gzigs phyag-bzhi-pa*) is shown with this *mudra*, frequently holding the wish-fulfilling jewel (Ind.: *cintāmaṇi*; Tib.: *yod-bzhin-nor-bu*) in the hollow space of the two hands. (AKG 22, BCO 214, BBh 194, ERJ 7, ERJ II 23, GDe 393, RSG 3) (See: **Figure 362**)

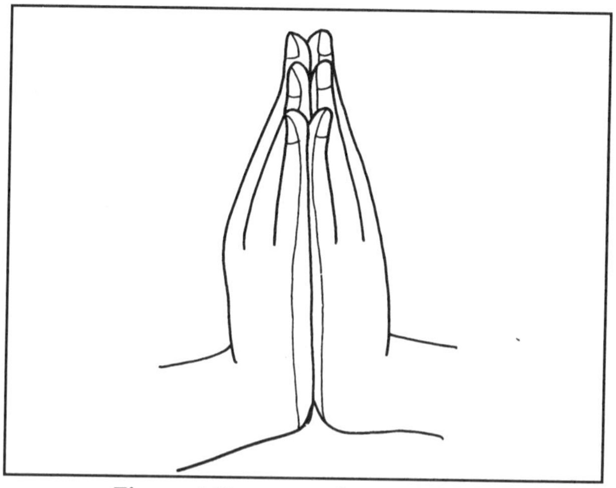

Figure 362 -- namaskara mudra II
(as seen by another)

nananda mudra -- (Ind.: *nananda-mudrā*) A hand pose, a seal, a dramatic (Ind.: *nāṭya*) *mudra* or gesture (Ind.: *darpaṇa*) held or formed by a performer, dancer or actor. The *nananda mudra* is a combined (Ind.: *saṁyutta*) form, held by both hands. One of eleven *mudras* representing "relationships" and one which denotes sister-in-law. This *mudra* is formed by: right palm faces outward, index, middle fingers and thumb extended, pointing upwards, the index and middle fingers are slightly separated, ring and little fingers bent towards the palm; left palm faces midline, fingers and thumb extended together towards the midline, and placed on the lower abdomen. (ACG 45) (See: **Figure 363**)

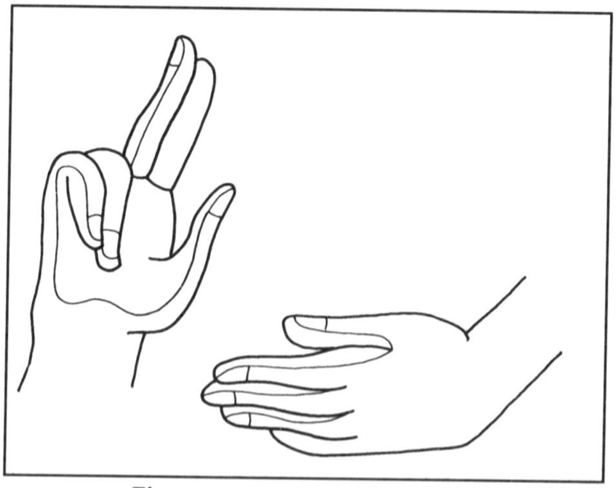

Figure 363 -- nananda mudra
(as seen by another)

nan kan-nin-in (mudra) -- (Jap.: *nan kan-nin-in* [*mudrā*]) A *mudra*, a ritual hand pose, a seal, a *tantric mudra* which is common to the Japanese Buddhist (*Vajrayana, Mantrayana*) tradition and is held or formed by a devotee or priest during the rites of *Garbhadhatu Mandala, Vajradhatu Mandala, Homa Rites* and other

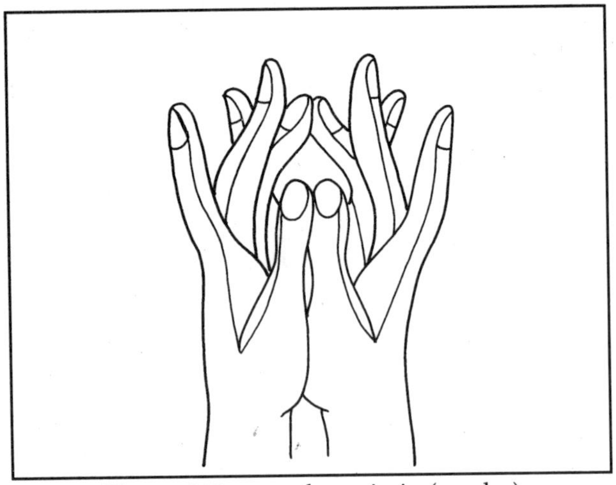

Figure 364 -- nan kan-nin-in (mudra)
(as seen by the holder)

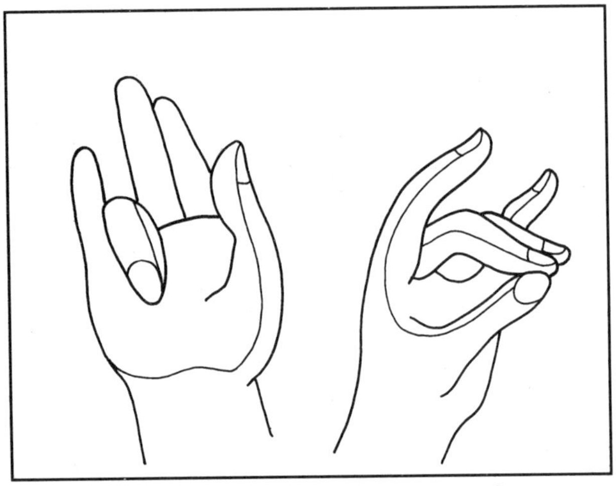

Figure 365 -- Narasimhavatara mudra
(as seen by another)

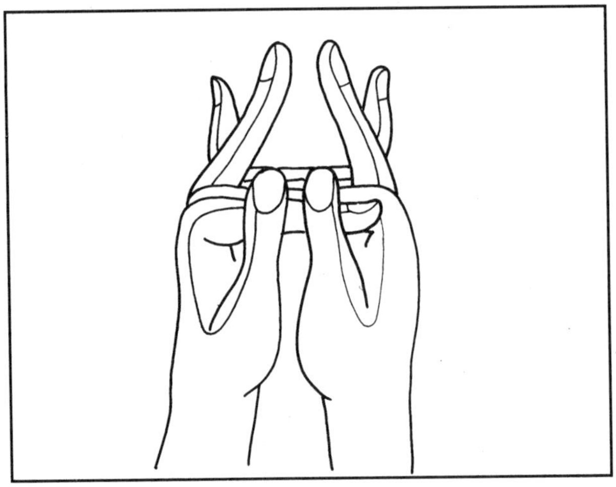

Figure 366 -- Naya-sutra mudra I
(as seen by the holder)

rites. It may be accompanied by a *mantra*. The *nan kan-nin-in (mudra)*[9] is a combined (Ind.: *saṁyutta*) form, held by both hands. It denotes difficult patience. This *mudra* is formed by: bringing the palms, thumbs extend upwards together, index fingers curl at first and second knuckles and tips rest behind thumbs' first phalanges, middle and little fingers extend and touch at their tips, ring fingers extend straight upward and apart, forming an opening. (GDe 44) (See: **Figure 364**)

narangi mudra -- (Ind.: *nāraṅgī-mudrā*) A hand pose, a seal, a dramatic (Ind.: *nāṭya*) mudra or gesture (Ind.: *darpaṇa*) held or formed by a performer, dancer or actor. It denotes the *narangi* or orange tree. The *mudra* employed is identical in form to the *padmakosha mudra*. See: *padmakosha mudra*. (ACG 48)

Narasimhavatara mudra -- (Ind.: *Narasiṁhāvatāra-mudrā*) A hand pose, a seal, a dramatic (Ind.: *nāṭya*) *mudra* or gesture (Ind.: *darpaṇa*) held or formed by a performer, dancer or actor. The *Narasimhavatara mudra* is a combined (Ind.: *saṁyutta*) form, held by both hands. It denotes lion-man *avatar*, one of the ten *avatars* (Ind.: *daśāvatāras*) of the Lord *Vishnu* This *mudra* is formed by: right palm facing outward, index, middle and little fingers and thumb extended, together and pointing upwards, ring finger is bent towards the palm; left palm facing forward, the index and little fingers extended upwards and straight, the middle and ring fingers are curl into the palm, the first phalanges of the thumb lays across the first phalanges of the middle and ring fingers. (ACG 46) (See: **Figure 365**)

Narmada mudra -- (Ind.: *narmadā-mudrā*) A hand pose, a seal, a dramatic (Ind.: *nāṭya*) *mudra* or gesture (Ind.: *darpaṇa*) held or formed by a performer, dancer or actor. It denotes the *Narmada*, one of the famous rivers of India. The *mudra* employed is identical in form to the *ardha-pataka mudra*. See: *ardha-pataka mudra*. (ACG 48)

Naya-sutra mudra I -- (Ind.: *Naya-sūtra-mudrā*]) A *mudra*, a ritual hand pose, a seal, a *tantric mudra* which is common to the Japanese Buddhist (*Vajrayana, Mantrayana*) tradition and is held or formed by a devotee or priest during various rites in which a deity is acknowledged. It is a *mudra* which is associated with the deity Naya-sutra. It may be accompanied by a *mantra*. The *Naya-sutra mudra*[10] is a combined (Ind.: *saṁyutta*) form, held by both hands. This *mudra* is formed by: palms facing the midline and close, thumbs extend upward and touch at their tips, index and middle fingers interlace on top, ring fingers are folded into the palm, little fingers extend upwards and touch at their tips. (LCS 229) (See: **Figure 366**)

Naya-sutra mudra II -- (Jap.: *Naya-sūtra-mudrā*) A *mudra*, a ritual hand pose, a seal, a *tantric mudra* which is common to the Japanese Buddhist (*Vajrayana, Mantrayana*) tradition and is held or formed by a devotee or priest during various rites. It may be accompanied by a *mantra*. The *Naya-sutra mudra*[11] is a combined (Ind.: *saṁyutta*) form, held by both hands. This *mudra* is formed by: palms facing midline, thumbs extended and touch along their length, index and ring fingers interlaced and fold over top, middle fingers fold into the palms, little fingers extend upward and touch at their tips. (GDe 187) (See: **Figure 367**)

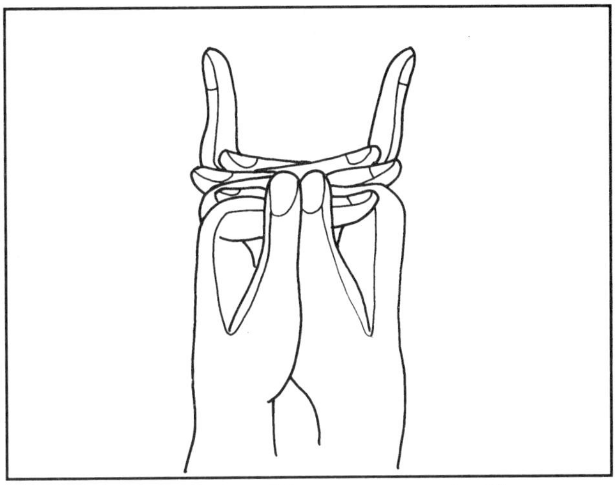

Figure 367 -- Naya-sutra mudra II
(as seen by the holder)

nebina gassho (mudra) -- (Jap.: *nebina gasshō* [*mudrā*] aka *kenjisshin-gassho* [*mudra*]) A *mudra*, a ritual hand pose, a seal, which is common to the Japanese Buddhist tradition. Specifically one of the twelve, elemental "hand clasps" (Jap. *junigosho* or *junigassho*). The *nebina gassho* (*mudra*) is a combined (Ind.: *saṁyutta*) form, held by both hands. This *mudra* is formed by: the hands are brought together, palm to palm, fingers extended upwards, there is no cupping of the hands. This *mudra* is referred to as the "clasp of the firm and sincere heart."[12] (EDS 40) (See: **Figure 368**)

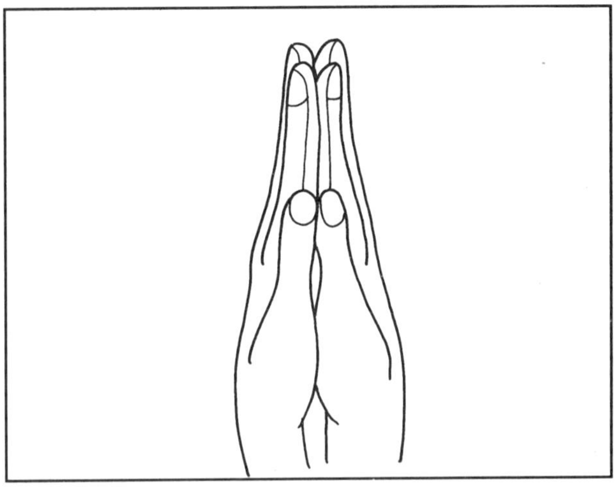

Figure 368 -- nebina gassho (mudra)
(as seen by the holder)

netra mudra I -- (Ind.: *netra-mudrā*) A *mudra*, a ritual hand pose, a seal, which is common to both the Buddhist and Hindu traditions. It denotes the eye(s). The *netra mudra I* is a single (Ind.: *asaṁyutta*) form, held by one hand. This *mudra* is formed by: palm faces the midline, tips of the thumb and little finger are touching forming a circular opening, index, middle and ring fingers extend upwards. The *mudra* thus formed is held "in front of the eyes."[13] (MJS 102) (See: **Figure 369**)

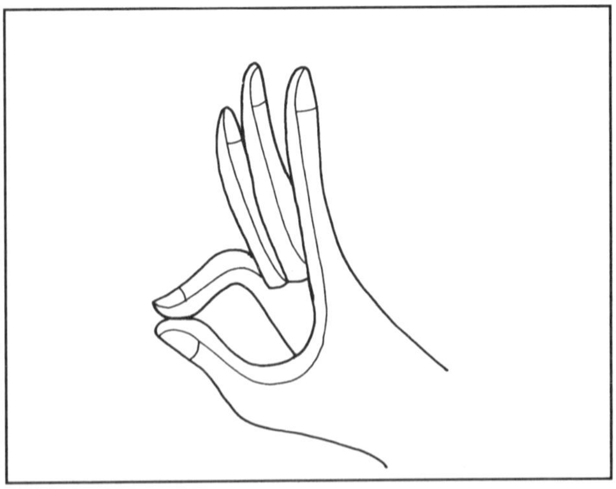

Figure 369 -- netra mudra I
(as seen by the holder)

netra mudra II -- (Ind.: *netra-mudrā*) A *mudra*, a ritual hand pose, a seal, which is common to both the Buddhist and Hindu traditions. It denotes the eye(s). The *netra mudra II* is a combined (Ind.: *saṁyutta*) form,

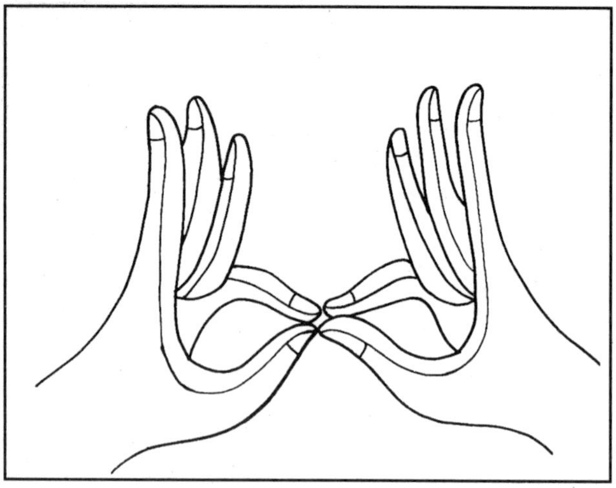

Figure 370 -- netra mudra II
(as seen by the holder)

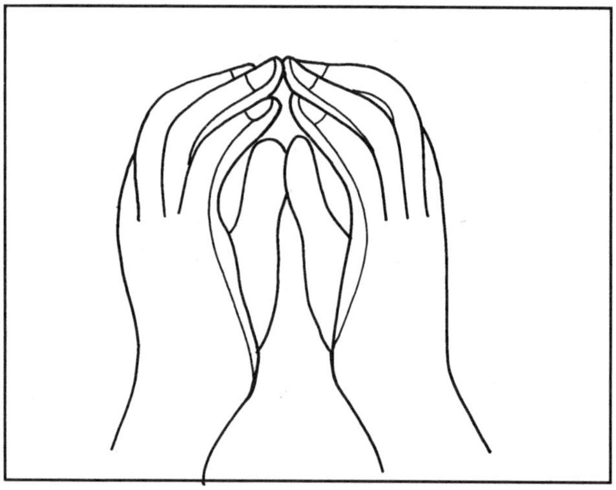

Figure 371 -- nidhi-ghata mudra
(as seen by another)

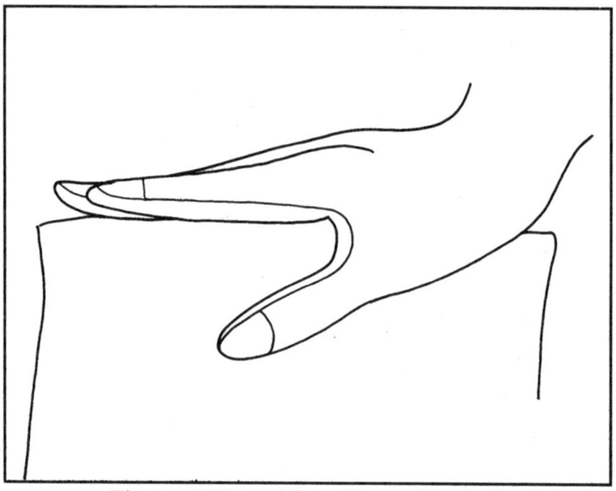

Figure 372 -- nidratahasta (mudra)
(as seen by another)

held by both hands. This *mudra* is formed by: palms face the midline, tips of the thumbs and little fingers are touching forming a circular opening, index, middle and ring fingers extend upwards. The *mudra* thus formed is held "in front of the eyes." (MJS 102) (See: **Figure 370**)

nidhi-ghata mudra -- (Ind.: *nidhi-ghaṭa-mudrā*) This is an assigned term.[14] A *mudra*, a ritual hand pose, a seal, which is common to the Buddhist (*Vajrayana*) tradition, a *tantric mudra*. It denotes the treasure vase or flask (Tib.: *gter-chen-pohi bum-pa*), one of eight signs of good fortune (Indi.: *aṣṭa-maṅgala*, Tib.: *bkra-shis rtags-brgyad*), an 'outer offering'--the other seven being: the knot, wheel, lotus, golden fish, umbrella, victory banner and conch shell--which is proffered to a divine guest during worship, particularly as associated with the ceremonies of the powerful *Vajrayana* goddess, *Tara*. The form is held by two hands in mirror-pose: palms face each other and touch at the 'heel,' tips of the fingers and thumbs touch, forming a hollow space between the two hands. The *mudra* thus formed is held at chest level. The *mantra* associated with this *mudra* is: "*OM Nidhi-ghata Praticcha SVAHA*."[15] (SBe 155) (See: **Figure 371**)

nidratahasta (mudra) -- (Ind.: *nidrātahasta* [*mudrā*]) A *mudra*, a ritual hand pose, a seal, which is common to the Hindu tradition. It indicates the supporting of the relaxed body and is called "the sleeping hand."[16] The *nidratahasta* (*mudra*) is a single (Ind.: *asaṁyutta*) form, held by one hand. This *mudra* is formed by: palm down, fingers extended, the hand rests on a plinth or other flat surface. Thus formed the *mudra* supports the body. (MJS 102) (See: **Figure 372**)

nidratahasta-vitarka mudra -- (Ind.: *nidrātahasta-vitarka-mudrā*; Eng.: expounding the constituent elements *mudra*; Thai: **pang ODD #53**) This is a descriptive term.[17] (See: pang **ODD #53**) (PSS, DRN 37, JBo 205, ODD 680)

nidratahasta-nidratahasta mudra -- (Ind.: *nidrātahasta-nidrātahasta-mudrā*; Thai: pang song-picharanacharatham) This is a descriptive term.[18] See: *pang song-picharanacharatham*. (DRN 37, JBo 205, PSS)

nimbasala mudra -- (Ind.: *nimbasala-mudrā*) A hand pose, a seal, a dramatic (Ind.: *nāṭya*) *mudra* or gesture (Ind.: *darpaṇa*) held or formed by a performer, dancer or actor. It denotes the *nimbasala* tree. The *nimbasala mudra* is a combined (Ind.: *saṁyutta*) form, held by both hands. This *mudra* is formed by: palms face outwards, thumbs, middle and little fingers extend upwards, index and ring fingers curve towards the palm. Thus formed the hands are crossed at the wrist. (ACG 49) (See: **Figure 373**)

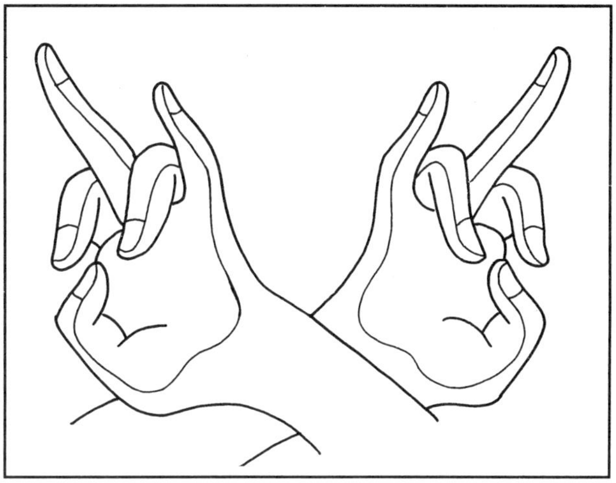

Figure 373 -- nimbasala mudra
(as seen by another)

nirvan(a) mudra -- (Ind.: *nirvāṇa-mudrā*) A *mudra*, a ritual hand pose, a seal, a *mudra* which is common to yogic tradition, particularly the *Yoga Tatva Mudra Vigyan* form, and is held by a devotee or practitioner. The *nirvan(a) mudra* is a combined (Ind.: *saṁyutta*) form, held by both hands. It is one of the eight mudras held after the *Gayatri Jap* of the thirty-two total *Gayatri mudras*.[19] It is utilized for all sickness, especially cancer. The *nirvan(a) mudra* is a combined (Ind.: *saṁyutta*) form, held by both hands. This *mudra* is formed by: left palm faces left, right palm faces right (in both cases the hand is approximately at 30° to the forearm) fingers and thumb together, all extended upwards and cupped. Thus formed, the hands cross at the wrist, left in front of the right and the cupped hands and fingers are brought together. It appears similar to the *namaskara mudra*, except in this *mudra* the thumbs are at the front. (KDe 90 & 108, RLM 77) (See: **Figure 374**)

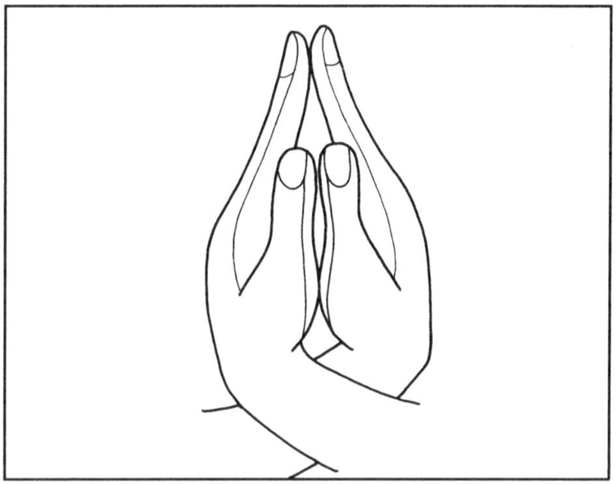

Figure 374 -- nirvan(a) mudra
(as seen by another)

nishedha mudra -- (Ind.: *niṣedha-mudrā*) ("defense") A hand pose, a seal, a dramatic (Ind.: *nāṭya*) *mudra* or gesture (Ind.: *darpaṇa*) held or formed by a performer, dancer or actor. The *nishedha mudra* is a combined (Ind.: *saṁyutta*) form, held by both hands. It denotes truth, "verily," holding the nipples, etc.[20] This *mudra* is formed by: left palm faces midline, fingers and thumb, slightly extended, tips together and touching the palm of the right hand; right hand palm faces the midline, thumb up, index finger curls over the top of the thumb, middle, ring and little fingers fold towards the palm covering the tips of the fingers and thumb of the left hand. (ACG 43) (See: **Figure 375**)

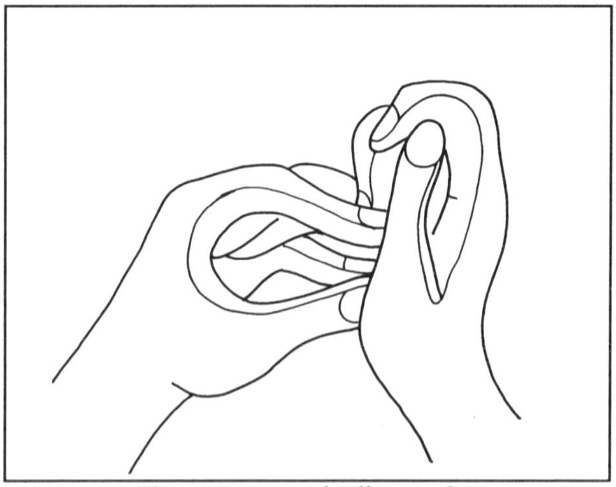

Figure 375 -- nishedha mudra
(as seen by the holder)

nitamba mudra -- (Ind.: *nitamba-mudrā*) ("buttocks") A hand pose, a seal, a dramatic (Ind.: *nāṭya*) *mudra* or gesture (Ind.: *darpaṇa*) held or formed by a performer,

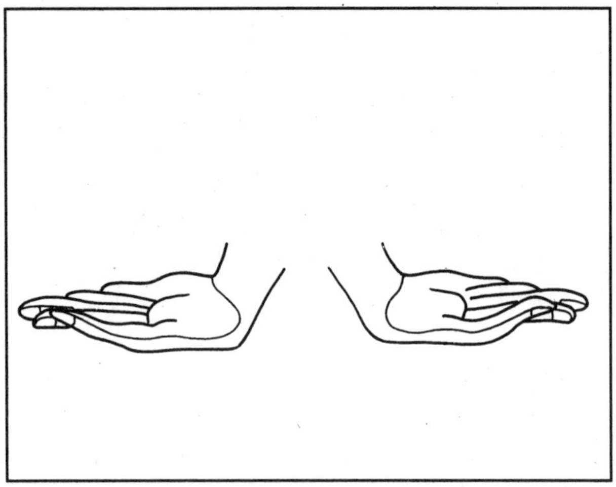

Figure 376 -- nitamba mudra
(as seen by another)

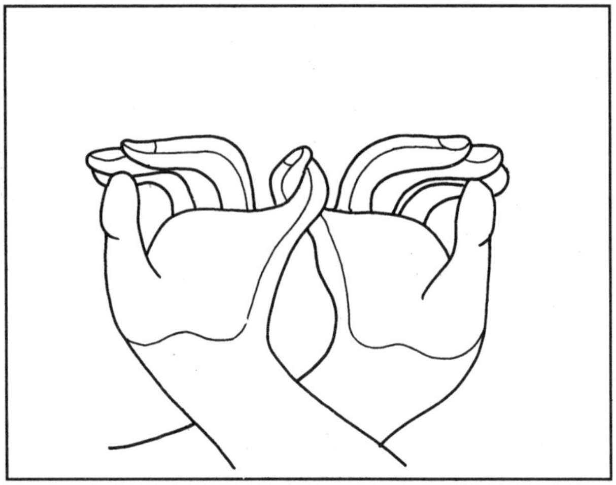

Figure 377 -- niwa-in (mudra)
(as seen by another)

dancer or actor. The *nitamba mudra* is a combined (Ind.: *saṁyutta*) form, held by both hands. It denotes weariness, descent, ecstasy, etc.[21] This *mudra* is formed by: palms face upwards, fingers and thumbs together extend outwards. Thus formed, the arms are at the sides and the hands extend outward or away from the body.22 (ACG 42) (See: **Figure 376**)

niwa-in (mudra) -- (Jap.: *niwa-in* [*mudrā*] aka *an-i-in*) A *mudra*, a ritual hand pose, a seal, which is common to the Buddhist tradition, particularly in Japan and China and is a variant of the *an-i-in* (*mudra*). It denotes appeasement. The *niwa-in* (*mudra*) is a combined (Ind.: *saṁyutta*) form, held by both hands. This *mudra* is formed by: the palms face outward, the thumb is turned in towards the palm, the first phalanges of the middle finger rests on the first phalanges of the thumb, the index and ring fingers curl in towards the palm, the left hand crosses at the wrist in front of the right hand and the little fingers interlock. The *mudra* thus formed is held in front of the chest. (EDS 75) (See: **Figure 377**)

nometsumumyokokuan-in mudra -- (Jap.: *nōmetsu-mumyōkokuan-in* [*mudrā*] aka *bodaiindo-daiichichi-in* [*mudra*], *chi ken-in* [*mudra*], *biroshananyoraidaimyochi-in* [*mudra*]; Chin.: *Chih-ch'ṃan-yin* (*mudra*); Ind.: *vajra mudrā, jñāna mudrā, bodhaśrī mudrā*) A variant term applied to *chi ken-in* (*mudra*). It means "*mudra* which is capable of suppressing darkness and spiritual shadows."[23] See: *chi ken-in* (*mudra*). (EDS 102)

nritya mudra[24] -- (Ind.: *nṛtya mudrā*; Jap.: *bu bosatsu-in* [*mudra*]) The Indic term for *bu bosatsu-in* (*mudra*). See: *bu bosatsu-in* (*mudra*). (GDe 79)

nyo-i-shu-in (mudra) -- (Jap.: *nyo-i-shu-in* [*mudrā*]; Ind.: *cintāmaṇi mudrā*) The Japanese term for *chintamani mudra*. See: *chintamani mudra*. (GDe 32)

nyorai cho-in (mudra) -- (Jap.: *nyorai cho-in* [*mudra*]; Ind.: *mukha mudrā*) The Japanese term for *mukha mudra* See: *mukha mudra*. (GDe 55)

nyorai getsu-in (mudra) -- (Jap.: *nyorai getsu-in* [*mudrā*]) ("the tongue of the Buddha") A *mudra*, a ritual hand pose, a seal, a tantric mudra which is common to the

Japanese Buddhist (*Vajrayana, Mantrayana*) tradition and is held or formed by a devotee or priest during the rites of *Garbhadhatu Mandala*. It may be accompanied by a *mantra*. The *nyorai getsu-in* (*mudra*)[25] is a combined (Ind.: *saṁyutta*) form, held by both hands. This *mudra* is formed by: the palms brought together, fingers extended upwards and together, the thumbs are folded into the palms. (GDe 28) (See: **Figure 378**)

nyorai hosso-in (mudra) -- (Jap.: *nyorai hossō-in* [*mudrā*]; Ind.: *mahā-nābhi mudrā*) A *mudra*, a ritual hand pose, a seal, a *tantric mudra* which is common to the Japanese Buddhist (*Vajrayana, Mantrayana*) tradition and is held or formed by a devotee or priest during the rites of *Garbhadhatu Mandala*. It may be accompanied by a *mantra*. The *nyorai hosso-in* (*mudra*)[26] is a combined (Ind.: *saṁyutta*) form, held by both hands. It denotes the attainment of happiness and peace. This *mudra* is formed by: he palms brought close, thumbs, index, middle and little fingers interlace inwards--between the palms--ring fingers extend upwards and touch at their tips. (GDe 26) (See: **Figure 379**)

nyorai ken-in (mudra) -- (Jap.: *nyorai ken-in* [*mudrā*]; Ind.: *jñāna-muṣṭi mudrā, tathāgata-muṣṭi mudrā*) A *mudra*, a ritual hand pose, a seal, which is common to the Japanese Buddhist tradition. It is one of the six, elemental fist positions. The *nyorai ken-in* (*mudra*) is a combined (Ind.: *saṁyutta*) form, held by both hands. This *mudra* is formed by: the right hand is fisted, palm towards the midline and grasps the left index finger; the left palm faces the midline, index finger extends straight upward, middle, ring and little finger are folded into the palm, first phalanges of the thumb touches the second phalanges of the index finger. (EDS 40) (See: **Figure 380**)

nyorai saku-in (mudra) -- (Jap.: *nyorai saku-in* [*mudrā*]) ("the cord of *Tathagata*") A *mudra*, a ritual hand pose, a seal, a *tantric mudra* which is common to the Japanese Buddhist (*Vajrayana, Mantrayana*) tradition and is held or formed by a devotee or priest during the rites of *Garbhadhatu Mandala*. It may be accompanied by a *mantra*. The *nyorai saku-in* (*mudra*)[27] is a combined (Ind.: *saṁyutta*) form, held by both hands. It denotes great compassion.[28] This *mudra* is formed by: the palms

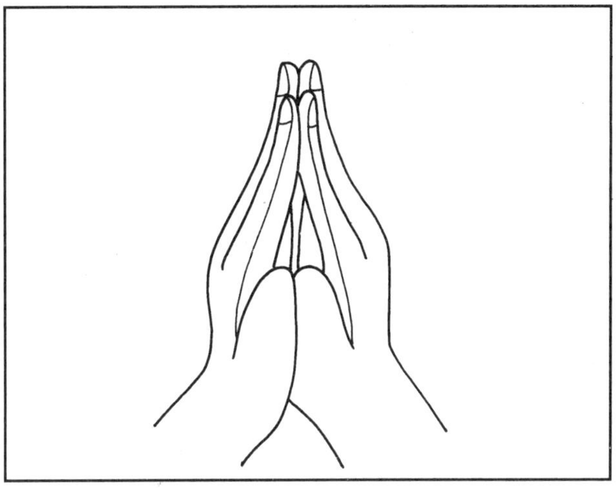

Figure 378 -- nyorai getsu-in (mudra)
(as seen by the holder)

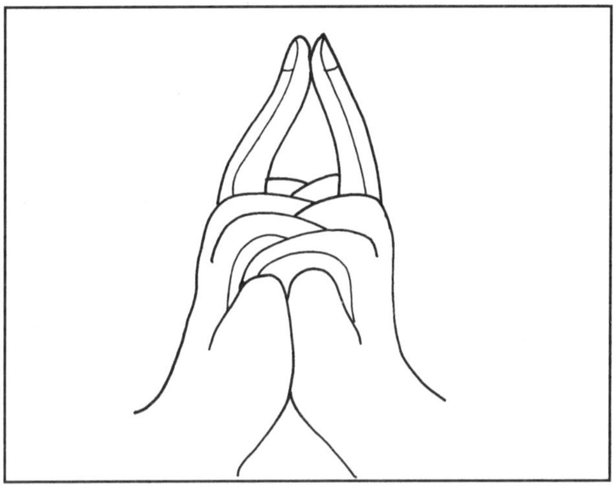

Figure 379 -- nyorai hosso-in (mudra)
(as seen by the holder)

Figure 380 -- nyorai ken-in (mudra)
(as seen by another)

Figure 381 -- nyorai saku-in (mudra)
(as seen by the holder)

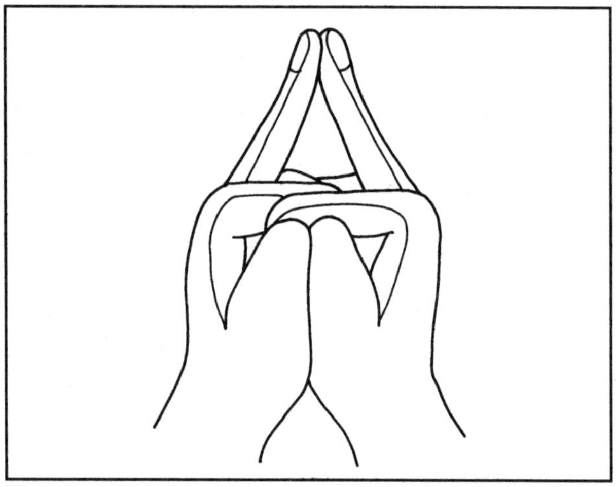

Figure 382 -- nyorai shin-in (mudra)
(as seen by the holder)

Figure 383 -- nyorai zo-in (mudra)
(as seen by the holder)

brought close, thumbs, middle, ring and little fingers interlace inwards--between the palms--index fingers gently arch over and touch the tips. (GDe 26) (See: **Figure 381**)

nyorai shin-in (mudra) -- (Jap.: *nyorai shin-in* [*mudrā*]) A *mudra*, a ritual hand pose, a seal, a *tantric mudra* which is common to the Japanese Buddhist (*Vajrayana, Mantrayana*) tradition and is held or formed by a devotee or priest during the rites of *Garbhadhatu Mandala*. It may be accompanied by a *mantra*. The *nyorai shin-in* (*mudra*)[29] is a combined (Ind.: *saṁyutta*) form, held by both hands. It denotes the acquisition of great knowledge of Buddha. This *mudra* is formed by: the the palms brought close, thumbs, index, ring and little fingers interlace inwards--between the palms--middle fingers extend upwards and touch the tips. (GDe 26) (See: **Figure 382**)

nyorai zo-in (mudra) -- (Jap.: *nyorai zō-in* [*mudra*]) A *mudra*, a ritual hand pose, a seal, a *tantric mudra* which is common to the Japanese Buddhist (*Vajrayana, Mantrayana*) tradition and is held or formed by a devotee or priest during the rites of *Garbhadhatu Mandala*. It may be accompanied by a *mantra*. The *nyorai zo-in* (*mudra*)[30] is a combined (Ind.: *saṁyutta*) form, held by both hands. It denotes the container for the Buddha. This *mudra* is formed by: the palms facing the midline and close, thumbs erect and together, index fingers curled and their tips behind their respective thumbs, the middle and the little fingers erect and their tips touch their counterparts, the ring fingers cross and are interlaced. (GDe 27) (See: **Figure 383**)

-- O --

ongyo-in (mudra) I -- (Jap.: *ongyō-in* [*mudrā*] aka *marishitenhobyo-in*; Chin.: *yin-hsing-yin*) A *mudra*, a ritual hand pose, a seal, which is common to the Japanese Buddhist tradition. It denotes the hiding from others or to remove oneself from others. The *ongyo-in* (*mudra*) *I* is a combined (Ind.: *saṁyutta*) form, held by both hands. This *mudra* is formed by: right palm faces downwards, fingers and thumb extend to the left (horizontal with the ground), the left hand's palm faces downwards, the fingers and thumb are fisted into the *kuken* fist. thus formed, the right hand hovers over the left and the *mudra* is held at chest level or slightly lower. (EDS 117) (See: **Figure 384**)

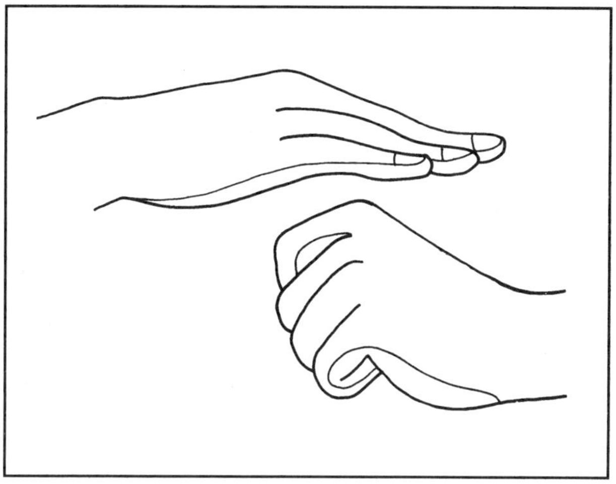

Figure 384 -- ongyo-in (mudra) I
(as seen by another)

ongyo-in (mudra) II -- (Jap.: *ongyō-in* [*mudrā*]) ("hiding *mudra*") A *mudra*, a ritual hand pose, a seal, a *tantric mudra* which is common to the Japanese Buddhist (*Vajrayana, Mantrayana*) tradition and is held or formed by a devotee or priest during various rites. It may be accompanied by a *mantra*. The *on gyo-in* (*mudra*) is a combined (Ind.: *saṁyutta*) form, held by both hands. This *mudra* is formed by: right palm faces downwards, thumb and fingers extend towards midline, left palm faces the midline, middle, ring and little fingers folded into palm, thumb folds over fingers, index finger extends towards midline. Thus formed the right hand is held over the left hand as if hiding it. (GDe 397) (See: **Figure 385**)

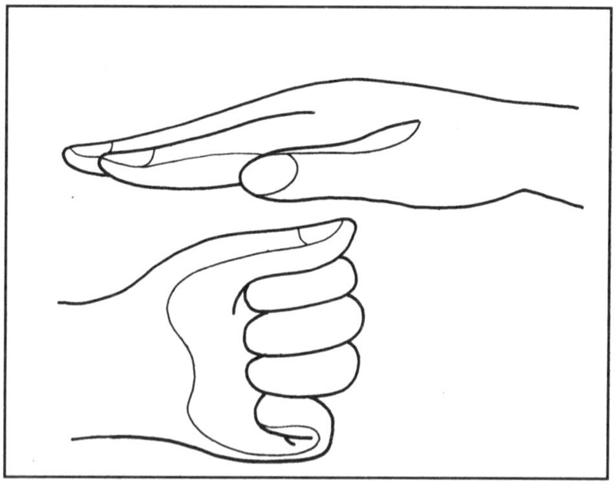

Figure 385 -- ongyo-in (mudra) II
(as seen by the holder)

on the jeweled walkway mudra -- (Eng.; Indic: *hastasvastika mudra*; Thai: *pang chong-krom-keaw*) The English descriptive phrase for the Thai *pang chong-krom-keaw*. See: *pang chong-krom-keaw*. (DRN 35, JBo)

ottanasha gassho (mudra) -- (Jap.: *ottanasha gasshō* [*mudrā*]; Ind.: *uttanaja mudrā*) A *mudra*, a ritual hand pose, a seal, which is common to the Japanese Buddhist tradition. Specifically one of the twelve, elemental "hand clasps" (Jap. *junigosho* or *junigassho*). The *ottanasha gassho* (*mudra*) is a combined (Ind.: *saṁyutta*) form, held by both hands. This *mudra* is formed by: palms face the midline, fingers and thumbs pointing

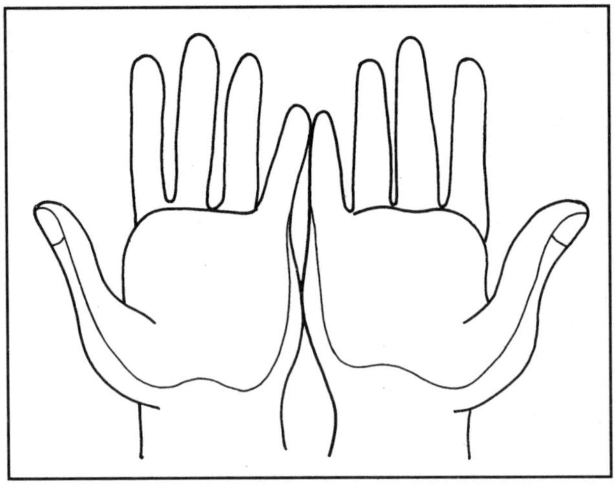

Figure 386 -- ottanasha gassho (mudra)
(as seen by the holder)

upwards, outside edges of palms and little fingers touching their whole length. This is known as the "clasp of clear exposition."[1] (EDS 41) (See: **Figure 386**)

-- P --

padma mudra I -- (Ind.: *padma-mudrā*) A *mudra*, a ritual hand pose, a seal, which is common to the Hindu Tantric tradition. The *padma mudra I* is a combined (Ind.: *saṁyutta*) form, held by both hands. This *mudra* is formed by: The hands are raised to chest level, palms facing the midline and the heels of the hands touch, all the fingers curl somewhat inward, towards the palm, their tips drawn close together, but not touching. (AMK 141) (See: **Figure 387**)

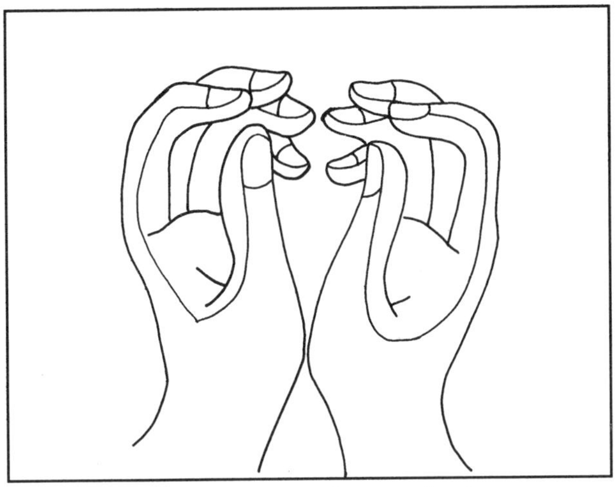

Figure 387 -- padma mudra I
(as seen by the holder)

padma mudra II -- (Ind.: *padma-mudrā* aka *padmakośa* [*mudrā*]) A variant term applied to *padmakosha* (*mudra*). See: *padmakosha* (*mudra*). (MJS 105)

padmahasta (mudra) -- (Ind.: *padmahasta* [*mudrā*]) A *mudra*, a ritual hand pose, a seal, which is common to the Hindu tradition, although it is certainly applicable to the Buddhist tradition as well. The *padmahasta* (*mudra*) is a combined (Ind.: *saṁyutta*) form, held by both hands. This *mudra* is formed by: palms face outward, fingers curl inwards as does the thumb, and the clasp a lotus (*padma*) stem. (MJS 105) (See: **Figure 388**)

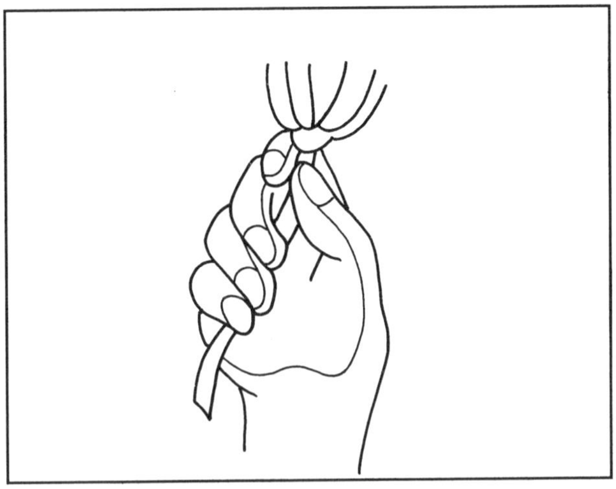

Figure 388 -- padmahasta (mudra)
(as seen by another)

padmakosha mudra -- (Ind.: *padma-kośa-mudrā* aka *padma mudrā*) ("lotus bud") A *mudra*, a ritual hand pose, a seal, which is common to the Hindu tradition and is depicted or held by a deity. The *padmakosha mudra* is a single (Ind.: *asaṁyutta*) form, held by one hand. It represents a lotus bud or blossom, brilliance, etc.[1] This *mudra* is formed by: palm faces upwards, fingers and thumb are separated and gently curl inwards, towards the hollowed palm. (ACG 32-33, KVa 135 [22-23], MJS 105) (See: **Figure 389**)

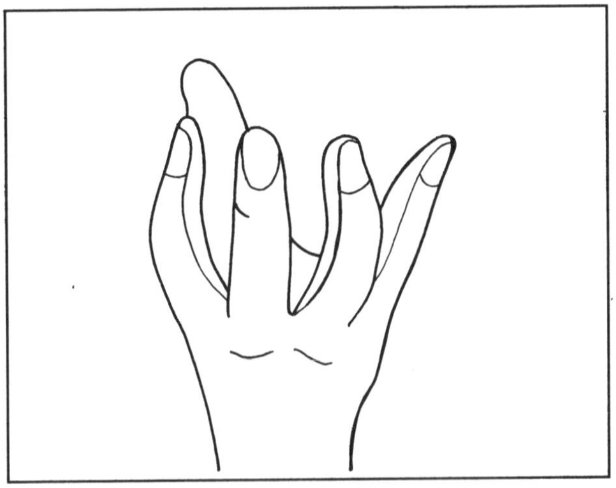

Figure 389 -- padmakosha mudra
(as seen by another)

padma-kunjara mudra -- (Ind.: *padma-kuñjara-mudrā*) This is an assigned term.[2] A *mudra*, a ritual hand pose, a seal, which is common to the Buddhist (*Vajrayana*) tradition, a *tantric mudra*. It denotes the excellent lotus (Tib.: *pad-ma bzang-po*), one of eight signs of good fortune (Ind.: *aṣṭa-maṅgala*, Tib.: *bkra-shis rtags-brgyad*), an 'outer offering'--the other seven being: the knot, wheel, victory banner, golden fish, umbrella, treasure vase and

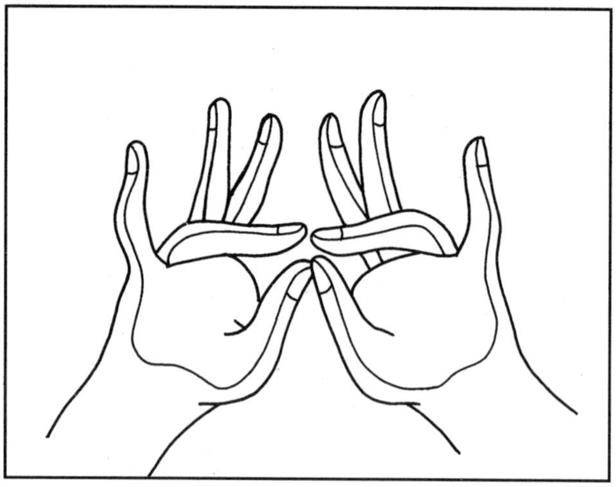

Figure 390 -- padma-kunjara mudra
(as seen by another)

Figure 391 -- padyam mudra
(as seen by the holder)

conch shell--which is proffered to a divine guest during worship, particularly as associated with the ceremonies of the powerful *Vajrayana* goddess, *Tara*. The *padma-kunjara mudra* is a combined (Ind.: *saṁyutta*) form, held by both hands. This *mudra* is formed by: palms face the midline, index, middle and little fingers are extended upwards the tips of the thumbs touches the tips of the ring fingers. Both hand hold the same pose and the tips of the thumbs and ring fingers touch. Thus held, the mudra is held level with the chest The *mantra* associated with this *mudra* is: "*OM Padma-kunjara Praticcha SVAHA*."[3] (SBe 155) (See: **Figure 390**)

padma-mushti (mudra) -- (Ind.: *padma-muṣṭi* [*mudrā*]; Eng.: lotus fist; Jap.: *renge ken-in* [*mudra*]) The Indic term for *renge ken-in* (*mudra*) See: *renge ken-in* (*mudra*). (EDS 39)

padmanjali mudra -- (Ind.: *padmāñjali-mudrā* aka *añjali mudrā, añjalikarma mudrā, samputāñjali mudrā, sarvarājendra mudrā, vajra-añjalikarma mudrā*; Chin.: *chin-kang ho-chang*; Jap.: *kongo-gassho, nebina-gassho*) A variant term applied to *anjali mudra*. See: *anjali mudra*. (GDe 57, LCS)

padyam mudra -- (Ind.: *pādyam-mudrā*) This is an assigned term.[4] A *mudra*, a ritual hand pose, a seal, which is common to the Buddhist (*Vajrayana*) tradition, a *tantric mudra*. It denotes 'water for the feet,' which is one of the two 'waters' or 'outer offerings' proffered to a divine guest--the other one being: water for the face--during the early stages worship, particularly as associated with the worship of the powerful *Vajrayana* goddess, *Tara*. The *padyam mudra* is a combined (Ind.: *saṁyutta*) form, held by both hands. This *mudra* is formed by: the palms face towards each other, thumb, index, ring and little fingers are fisted, middle finger extends outward (away from the body, the hands thus formed are brought together, the tips of the middle finger touch as well as the first two phalanges of thumb, index, ring and little fingers. The *mudra* thus formed is held level with the chest. The *mantra* associated with this mudra is: "*OM Guru-sarva-Tathagata Maha-padyam Praticcha HUM SVAHA*."[5] (SBe 147) (See: **Figure 391**)

paksha-pradyota mudra -- (Ind.: *pakṣa-pradyota-mudrā*) ("the shining wing") A hand pose, a seal, a dramatic (Ind.: *nāṭya*) *mudra* or gesture (Ind.: *darpaṇa*) held or formed by a performer, dancer or actor. The *paksha-pradyota mudra* is a combined (Ind.: *saṁyutta*) form, held by both hands. It denotes despondence, strangeness, etc.[6] This *mudra* is formed by: palms upwards, thumbs, index, middle and little fingers extend outward (straight from the palms), ring fingers are folded into the palm, Thus formed the hands are held against the hips. (ACG 42) (See: **Figure 392**)

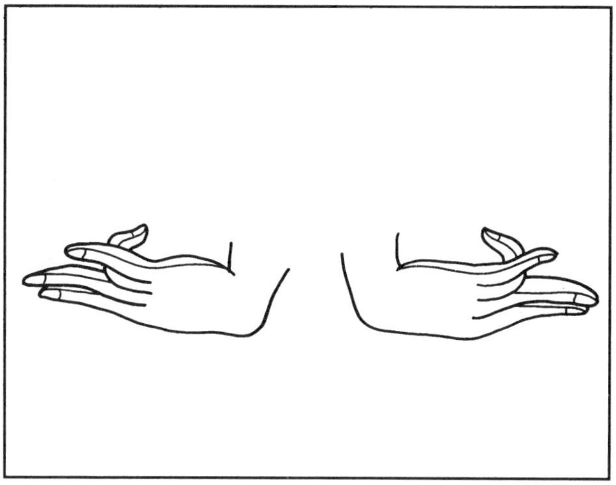

Figure 392 -- paksha-pradyota mudra
(as seen by another)

paksha-vanchita mudra -- (Ind.: *pakṣa-vañcita-mudrā*) ("the bent wing") A hand pose, a seal, a dramatic (Ind.: *nāṭya*) mudra or gesture (Ind.: *darpaṇa*) held or formed by a performer, dancer or actor. The *paksha-vanchita mudra* is a combined (Ind.: *saṁyutta*) form, held by both hands. It denotes indifference and the movement of the thighs. This *mudra* is formed by: palms face mid-line or forward, thumbs, index, middle and little fingers extend downward (straight from the palms), ring fingers are folded into the palm, Thus formed the hands are held on the hips. (ACG 42) (See: **Figure 393**)

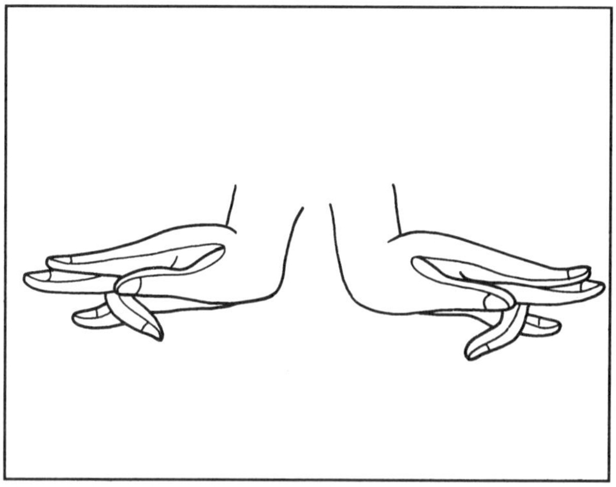

Figure 393 -- paksha-vanchita mudra
(as seen by another)

palasa mudra -- (Ind.: *palāśa-mudrā*) A hand pose, a seal, a dramatic (Ind.: *nāṭya*) *mudra* or gesture (Ind.: *darpaṇa*) held or formed by a performer, dancer or actor. It denotes the *palasa* tree. The *mudra* employed is identical in form to the *ardha-chandra mudra*. See: *ardha-chandra mudra*. (ACG 49)

pallava mudra -- (Ind.: *pallava-mudrā*) A hand pose, a seal, a dramatic (Ind.: *nāṭya*) *mudra* or gesture (Ind.: *darpaṇa*) held or formed by a performer, dancer or actor noted in ACG but without description. (ACG 44)

pallavam mudra -- (Ind.: *pallavam-mudrā*) A *mudra*, a ritual hand pose, a seal, a *mudra* which is common to yogic tradition, particularly the *Yoga Tatva Mudra Vigyan* form, and is held by a devotee or practitioner. The *palavam mudra* is a single (Ind.: *asaṁyutta*) form, held by one hand. It is one of the twenty-four *mudras* held before the *Gayatri Jap* of the thirty-two total *Gayatri mudras*.[7] It is utilized for all sickness, especially cancer. The *pallavam mudra* is a single (Ind.: *asaṁyutta*) form, held by one hand. This *mudra* is formed by: the

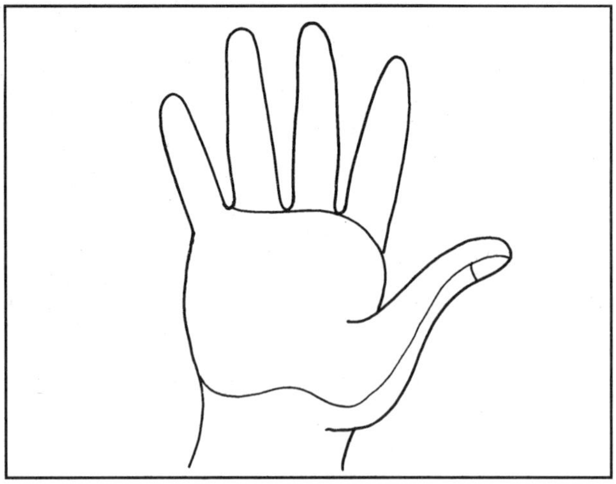

Figure 394 -- pallavam mudra
(as seen by another)

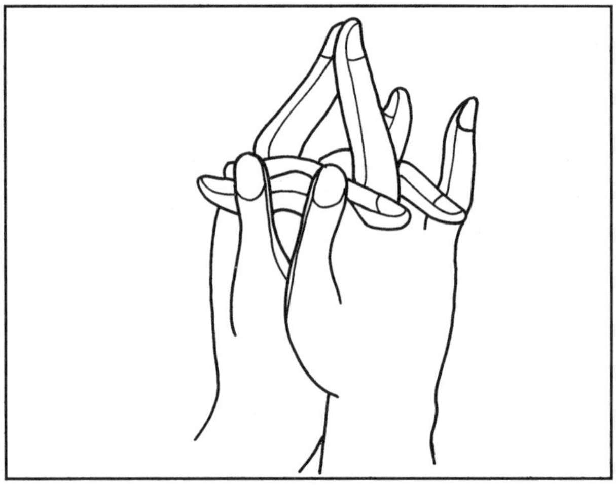

Figure 395 -- pancha-guhya mudra
(as seen by the holder)

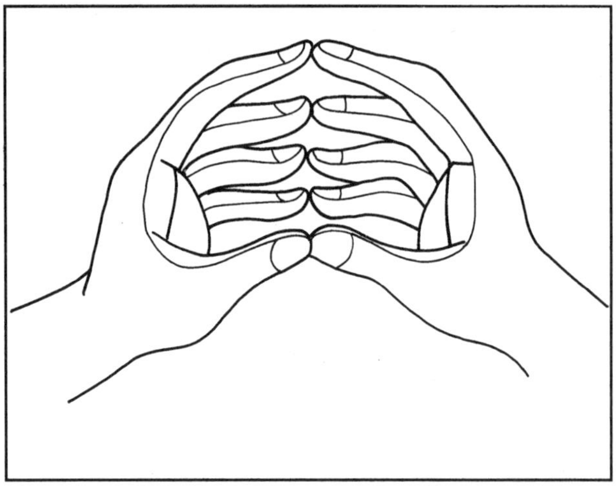

Figure 396 -- pancha-mukham mudra
(as seen by the holder)

right palm facing forwards, fingers and thumb extended upwards, slightly separated, in a relaxed manner and held shoulder high. This *mudra* is similar to *abhaya mudra I.* (KDe 108, RLM 74) (See: **Figure 394**)

panasa mudra -- (Ind.: *panāsa-mudrā*) A hand pose, a seal, a dramatic (Ind.: *nāṭya*) *mudra* or gesture (Ind.: *darpaṇa*) held or formed by a performer, dancer or actor. It denotes the *panasa* or bread-fruit tree. The *mudra* employed is identical in form to the *chatura mudra*. See: *chatura mudra*. (ACG 48)

Pancha-guhya mudra -- (Ind.: *pañca-guhya-mudrā*) A *mudra*, a ritual hand pose, a seal, a *tantric mudra* which is common to the Japanese Buddhist (*Vajrayana, Mantrayana*) tradition and is held or formed by a devotee or priest during the rites of *Garbhadhatu Mandala, Vajradhatu Mandala, Homa Rites* and other rites. It may be accompanied by a *mantra*. The *Pancha-guhya mudra*[8] is a combined (Ind.: *saṁyutta*) form, held by both hands. This *mudra* is formed by: palms facing midline, thumbs extend straight upward and are separated except for meeting at their base, index and ring fingers interlace and are straight, middle fingers touch at their tips, little fingers extend straight upward. (GDe 256, LCS 246) (See: **Figure 395**)

pancha-mukham mudra -- (Ind.: *pañca-mukham-mudrā*) A *mudra*, a ritual hand pose, a seal, a *mudra* which is common to yogic tradition, particularly the *Yoga Tatva Mudra Vigyan* form, and is held by a devotee or practitioner. The *pancha-mukham mudra* is a combined (Ind.: *saṁyutta*) form, held by both hands. It is one of the twenty-four mudras held before the *Gayatri Jap* of the thirty-two total *Gayatri mudras*.[9] It is utilized for all sickness, especially cancer. This *mudra* is formed by: palms facing midline, fingers splayed and parallel to the ground, tips of the thumb, index, middle, ring and little fingers touch, thumbs extends upwards. Thus formed, the *mudra* is held waist high. (KDe 82, RLM 72) (See: **Figure 396**)

pancha-nayana mudra -- (Ind.: *pañca-nayana-mudrā*; Chin.: *pu mu-yin* [*mudra*]; Jap.: *bu mo-in* [*mudra*]) The Indic term for *bu mo-in* (*mudra*). See: *bu mo-in* (*mudra*). (GDe 51)

Panchoshnisha mudra -- (Ind.: *Pañcoṣṇīṣa-mudrā*) A *mudra*, a ritual hand pose, a seal, a *tantric mudra* which is common to the Japanese Buddhist (*Vajrayana, Mantrayana*) tradition and is held or formed by a devotee or priest during the rites of *Garbhadhatu Mandala, Vajradhatu Mandala, Homa Rites* and other rites. It may be accompanied by a *mantra*. The *Panchoshnisha mudra* is a combined (Ind.: *saṁyutta*) form, held by both hands. It denotes the five *Ushnishas*. This *mudra* is formed by: palms facing midline and apart, tips of thumbs touch, index, middle and little fingers arch and touch at their tips, ring fingers cross at their tips. (GDe 286, LCS 253) (See: **Figure 397**)

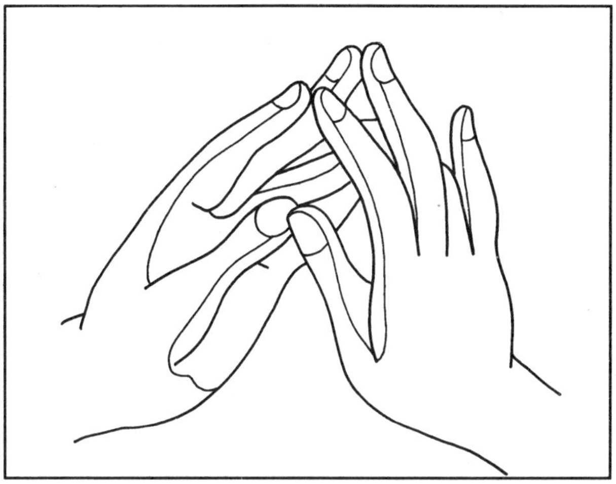

Figure 397 -- Panchoshnisha mudra
(as seen by the holder)

pang chan-samor -- (Thai: *pang chan-samor*; Eng.: eating the myrobalan fruit *mudra*; Ind.: *añcita-dhyāna mudrā*) A *mudra*, a ritual hand pose, a seal, which is common to the Thai Buddhist tradition. One of forty *mudras* and *asanas* compiled by the Prince Patriarch Paramanujita Jinorasa and established during the reign of Rama III as being acceptable for the depiction of images of The Lord Buddha--i.e., "eating the *myrobalan* fruit *mudra*" the tenth of the forty attitudes noted.[10] The *pang chan-samor* (*anchita-dhyana mudra*) is a combined (Ind.: *saṁyutta*) form, held by both hands. The form is: right palm upwards, fingers cupped somewhat, the thumb slightly bent towards the fingertips, fingers pointing outward and holding the fruit; left hand is relaxed, palm upward, the right hand rests in the lap. The figure is sitting in the *virasana* or *vajrasana* position. (DRN 36, OFr 13, JBo 204, PSS) (See: **Figure 398**)

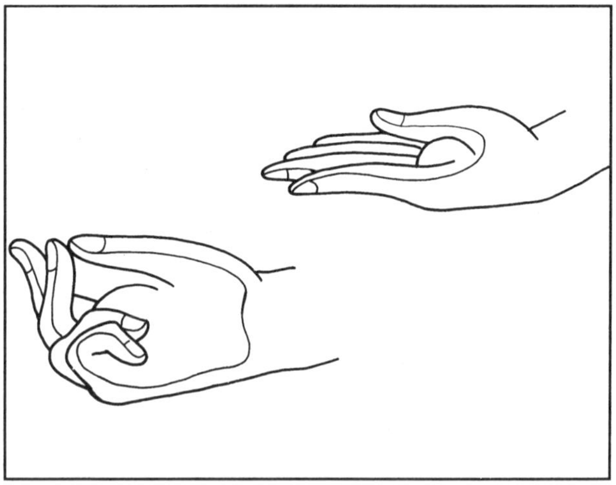

Figure 398 -- pang chan-samor
(as seen by another)

pang chong-krom-keaw -- (Thai: *pang chong-krom-keaw*; Eng.: on the jewelled walkway *mudra*; Ind.: *hastavastika mudrā III*) A *mudra*, a ritual hand pose, a seal, which is common to the Thai Buddhist tradition. One of forty *mudras* and *asanas* compiled by the Prince Patriarch Paramanujita Jinorasa and established during the reign of Rama III as being acceptable for the depiction of images of The Lord Buddha--i.e., "on the jewelled walkway" the eighth of the forty attitudes noted.[11] The *pang chong-krom-keaw* is a combined (Ind.: *saṁyutta*) form, held by both hands. This *mudra* is formed by: the right hand crosses over the left at the wrist, both palms face backwards, fingers and thumbs extended downwards. The *mudra* is thus held in front of the groin and the figure is standing on right foot with the left raised as if

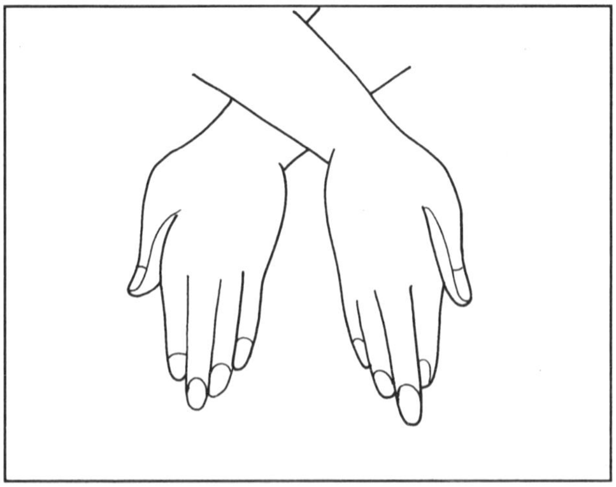

Figure 399 -- pang chong-krom-keaw
(as seen by another)

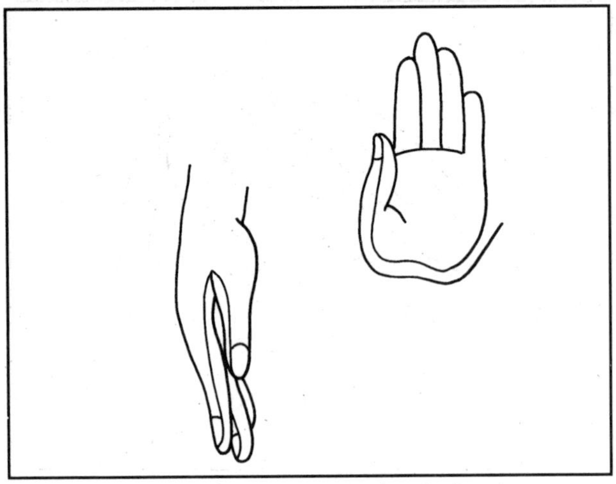

Figure 400 -- pang ham-phra-kaen-chan
(as seen by another)

stepping. (PSS, DRN 35, JBo, ODD 680) (See: **Figure 399**)

pang ham-phra-kaen-chan -- (Thai: *pang ham-phra-kaen-chan*; Ind.: *lolahasta-abhaya mudrā*) A *mudra*, a ritual hand pose, a seal, which is common to the *Theravada* Buddhist tradition in Thailand. It denotes the time when the Lord Buddha returning from the *Tavatimsa* heaven was met by a sandalwood image, commissioned by King Udyana, which miraculously sprang to life. The gesture known as "restraining the sandalwood image" halted the image and he requested that it be used as a model after his death. It is one of forty Thai Buddhist *mudras* and *asanas* compiled by the Prince Patriarch Paramanujita Jinorasa and established during the reign of Rama III as being acceptable for the depiction of images of The Lord Buddha--i.e., "restraining the sandalwood image" the twenty-first of the forty attitudes noted.[12] The *pang ham-phra-kaen-chan* is a combined (Ind.: *saṁyutta*) form, held by both hands. This *mudra* is formed by; right hand hangs in a relaxed manner to the side (*lolahasta*); the left palm faces outwards, fingers and thumb extended upwards (*abhaya*), slightly cupped. The figure is standing. (DRN 36, JBo 205, KIM 10, ODD 680, PSS) (See: **Figure 400**)

pang ham-samut -- (Thai: *pang ham-samut*; Ind.: *abhaya mudrā*) The Thai for restraining the waters.[13] See: *abhaya mudra III*. (KIM 40, DRN 36, JBo, ODD 680)

pang hamyat -- (Thai: *pang hamyat*; Eng.: restraining the kinsmen *mudra*; Ind: *abhaya-lolahasta mudrā*[14]) A *mudra*, a ritual hand pose, a seal, which is common to the Theravada Buddhist tradition in Thailand. One of forty *mudras* and *asanas* compiled by the Prince Patriarch Paramanujita Jinorasa and established during the reign of Rama III as being acceptable for the depiction of images of The Lord Buddha--i.e., "restraining the kinsmen"[15] the nineteenth of the forty attitudes noted.[16] It denotes calming the family. The *pang hamyat* (*abhaya-lolahasta mudra*) is a combined (Ind.: *saṁyutta*) form, held by both hands. The form is: the right hand is raised, fingers and thumb extended and together, relaxed, slightly cupped, palm facing outward; left palm faces the midline, fingers gracefully extended and all are pointing downwards at the side. The figure is standing. (DRN 36, JBo 205, ODD 680) (See: **Figure 401**)

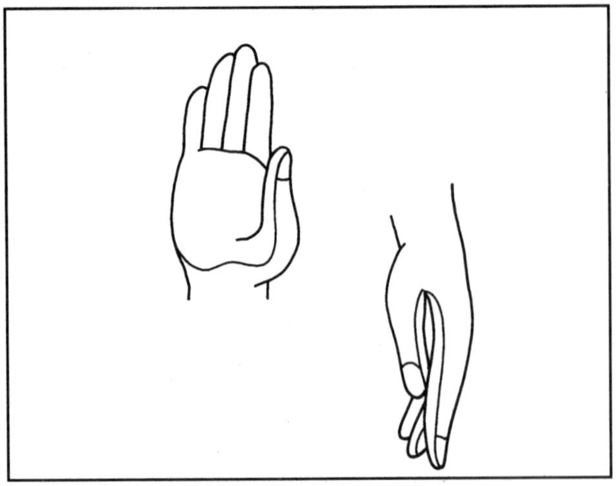

Figure 401 -- pang hamyat
(as seen by another)

pang harm-marn -- (Thai: *pang harm-marn*; Ind.: *abhaya-dhyāna mudrā*; Eng.: restraining *Mara mudra*[17]) A *mudra*, a ritual hand pose, a seal, which is common to the Thai Buddhist tradition. One of forty *mudras* and *asanas* compiled by the Prince Patriarch Paramanujita Jinorasa and established during the reign of Rama III as being acceptable for the depiction of images of The Lord Buddha--i.e., "restraining *Mara*" the thirty-seventh of the forty attitudes noted.[18] It is different from the *bhumisparsha mudra*. The *pang harm-marn* is a combined (Ind.: *saṁyutta*) form, held by both hands. The form is: the right hand is raised, fingers and thumb extend upwards and together, relaxed, slightly cupped, palm facing outward and generally on a line level with the chest; the left hand relaxed, palm upward and rests in the lap. The figure is seated upon a throne or plinth in the *virasana*. (PSS, DRN 37, JBo 205, ODD 680, OFr 8) (See: **Figure 402**)

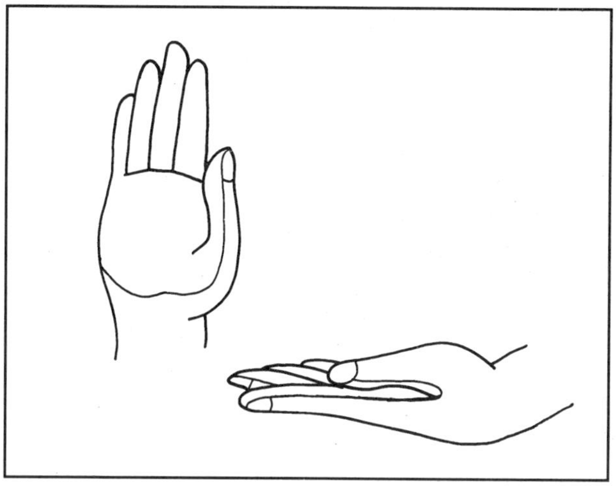

Figure 402 -- pang harm-marn
(as seen by another)

pang khabphrawakkali -- (Thai: *pang khabphrawakkali*; Eng.: making the venerable *Vakkali* move away *mudra*; Ind.: *patākā-dhyāna mudrā*) A *mudra*, a ritual hand pose, a seal, which is common to the Thai Buddhist tradition. One of forty *mudras* and *asanas* compiled by the Prince Patriarch Paramanujita Jinorasa and established during the reign of Rama III as being acceptable for the depiction of images of The Lord Buddha--i.e., "making the venerable *Vakkali* move away" the thirty-fourth of the forty attitudes noted.[19] The *pang khabphrawakkali* is a combined (Ind.: *saṁyutta*) form, held by both hands. This *mudra* is formed by: right palm facing backward, fingers and thumb extended to the left and held close to the chest;[20] the left hand relaxed, palm upward and the hand rests in the lap. The figure is in the *virasana* or *vajrasana* pose.[21] (DRN 37, JBo, ODD 38, OFr 26, PSS) (See: **Figure 403**)

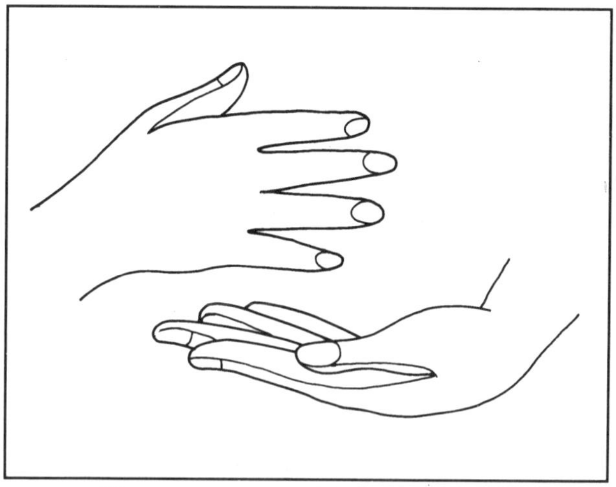

Figure 403 -- pang khabphrawakkali
(as s(as seen by another)en by 0000)

pang khor-phon -- (Thai: *pang khor-phon*; Eng.: calling down the rain *mudra*; Ind.: *añcita-ahāyavarada mudrā, gandhararaṭṭha mudrā*) A *mudra*, a ritual hand pose, a seal, which is common to the Thai Buddhist tradition. One of forty *mudras* and *asanas* compiled by the Prince Patriarch Paramanujita Jinorasa and established during the reign of Rama III as being acceptable for the depiction of images of The Lord Buddha--i.e., "*gandhararattha mudra*" or "calling down the rain" the

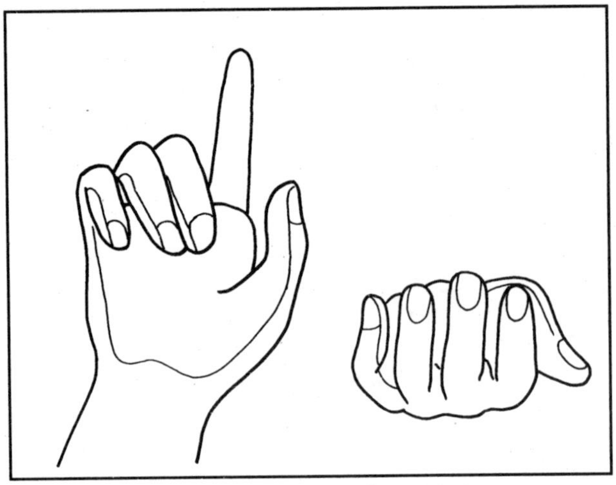

Figure 404 -- pang khor-phon
(as seen by another)

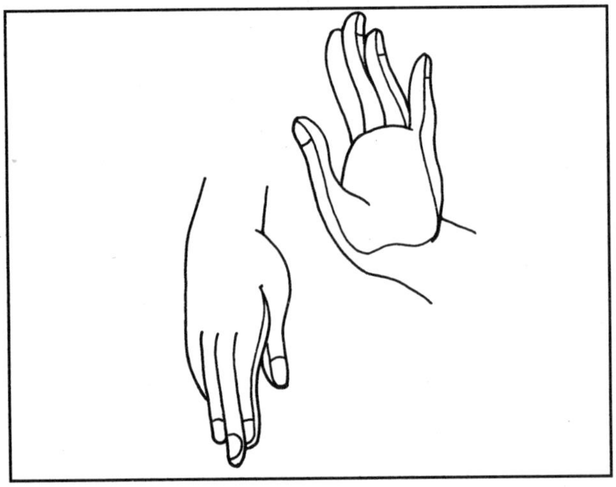

Figure 405 -- pang lila I
(as seen by another)

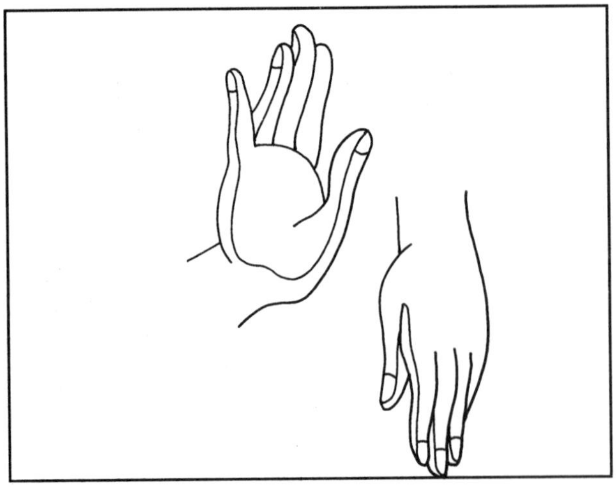

Figure 406 -- pang lila II
(as seen by another)

twenty-seventh of the forty attitudes noted.[22] The *gandhararattha mudra* is a combined (Ind.: *saṁyutta*) form, held by both hands. The *pang khor-phon* is a combined (Ind.: *saṁyutta*) form, held by both hands. This *mudra* is formed by: the right palm upwards, fingers cupped somewhat, the thumb slightly bent towards the fingertips, fingers pointing outward resting on the corresponding thigh or knee; the left is similar to the *abhaya mudra* in that the fingers and thumb are extended and together, relaxed, slightly cupped, palm facing outward and downward at approximately 45°, away from the body and generally at the level of the chest. (DRN 37, JBo 205, MSD, ODD 680, SVB) (See: **Figure 404**)

pang lila I -- (Thai: *pang lila*; Eng.: walking *mudra*; Ind.: *lolahasta-abhaya mudrā*) The Thai for walking.[23] A mudra, a ritual hand pose, a seal, which is common to the Thai Buddhist tradition. One of forty *mudras* and *asanas* compiled by the Prince Patriarch Paramanujita Jinorasa and established during the reign of Rama III as being acceptable for the depiction of images of The Lord Buddha ("walking *mudra*"). The *pang lila I* is a combined (Ind.: *saṁyutta*) form, held by both hands. The form is: left hand is raised, fingers and thumb extended and together, relaxed, slightly cupped, palm facing outward and generally on a line level with the chest; right palrds, fingers gracefully extended and all are poi nting downwards to the side. Specifically, the left foot is raised as if taking a step while the right rests flat on the ground. (PSS, DRN 36, JBo 165, ODD 680) (See: **Figure 405**)

pang lila II -- (Thai: *pang lila*; Eng.: walking *mudra*; Ind.: *lolahasta-vitarka mudrā*[24]) A *mudra*, a ritual hand pose, a seal, which is common to the Thai Buddhist tradition. One of forty *mudras* and *asanas* compiled by the Prince Patriarch Paramanujita Jinorasa and established during the reign of Rama III as being acceptable for the depiction of The Lord Buddha--i.e., "walking *mudra*" the eleventh of the forty attitudes noted.[25] The form is held in both hands: right hand is raised, fingers and thumb extended and together, relaxed, slightly cupped, palm facing outward and generally on a line level with the chest; left palm faces the midline, fingers gracefully extended and all are pointing downwards to the side. Specifically, the left foot is raised as if taking a step while the right rests flat on the ground. (JBo 132) (See: **Figure 406**)

pang loy-tard -- (Thai: *pang loy-tard;* Eng.: setting the dish afloat *mudra;* Ind.: *anchita-katyavalambita mudra*) A *mudra,* a ritual hand pose, a seal, which is common to the Thai Buddhist tradition. One of forty *mudras* and *asanas* compiled by the Prince Patriarch Paramanujita Jinorasa and established during the reign of Rama III as being acceptable for the depiction of images of The Lord Buddha--i.e., "setting the dish afloat" the third of the forty attitudes noted.[26] The *pang loy-tard* is a combined (Ind.: *saṁyutta*) form, held by both hands. The form is: the right palm upwards, fingers cupped somewhat, the thumb slightly bent towards the fingertips, fingers pointing outward and holding a dish; the left hand rests on the thigh (upper), fingers to the front, thumb to the back, the thumb may also rest along side the fingers. The figure is kneeling. (DRN 35, OFr 6, JBo 204, PSS, ODD 680) (See: **Figure 407**)

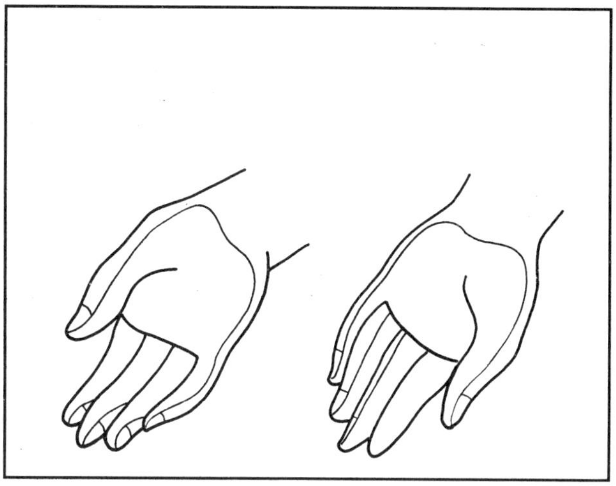

Figure 407 -- pang loy-tard
(as seen by another)

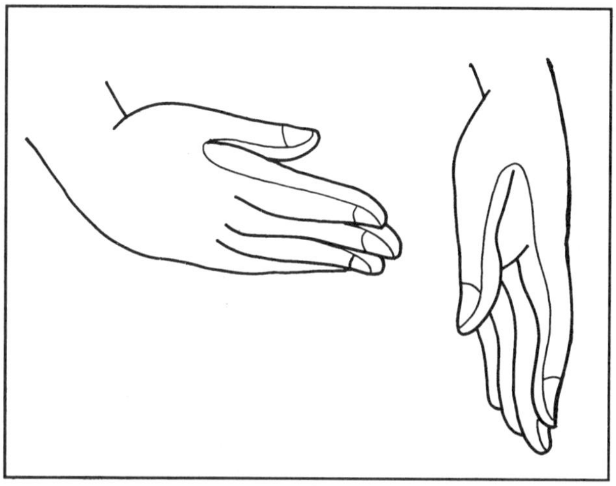

Figure 408 -- pang nakawalok I
(as seen by another)

pang maravichai -- (Thai: *pang maravichai* aka *manwichai* [*mudra*], [*pang*] *sadung-man;* Chin.: *an-shan-yin, ch'u-ti-yin;* Eng.: adamantine posture; Ind.: *bhasparśa-mudrā, bhūmiśparśa mudra, bhūmisparśana mudrā, bhūmisparśa mudrā, bhūsparś mudrā, bhūsparśa mudrā, māravijaya mudra;* Jap.: *anzan-in* [*mudra*], *sokuchi-in* [*mudra*]) The Thai for subduing *Mara.*[27] See: *bhumisparsha mudra.* (PSS, DRN 35, JBo, ODD 680)

pang nakawalok I -- (Thai: *pang nakawalok;* Eng.: elephant glance *mudra;* Ind.: *jñāna-lolahasta mudrā*) A *mudra,* a ritual hand pose, a seal, which is common to the Thai Buddhist tradition and refers to the Lord Buddha subduing the wild elephant. One of forty *mudras* and *asanas* compiled by the Prince Patriarch Paramanujita Jinorasa and established during the reign of Rama III as being acceptable for the depiction of images of The Lord Buddha.[28] The *pang nakawalok* is a combined (Ind.: *saṁyutta*) form, held by both hands. This *mudra* is formed by: the right palm turns towards the midline, the tips of the thumb and the index finger touch, the other fingers are relaxed and extend to the left; the left palm towards midline, fingers gracefully extended and all are pointing downwards. The head

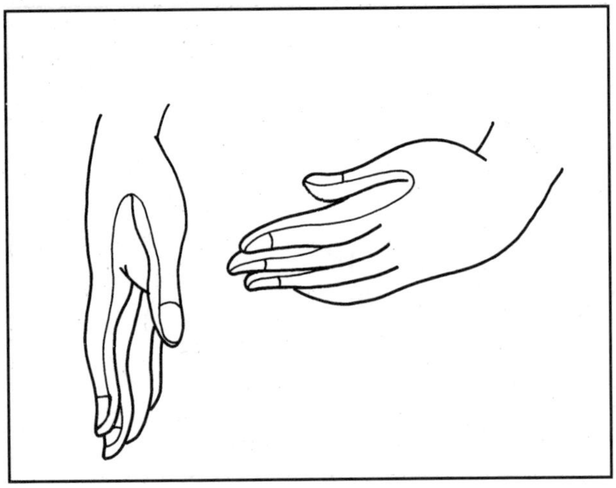

Figure 409 -- pang nakawalok II
(as seen by another)

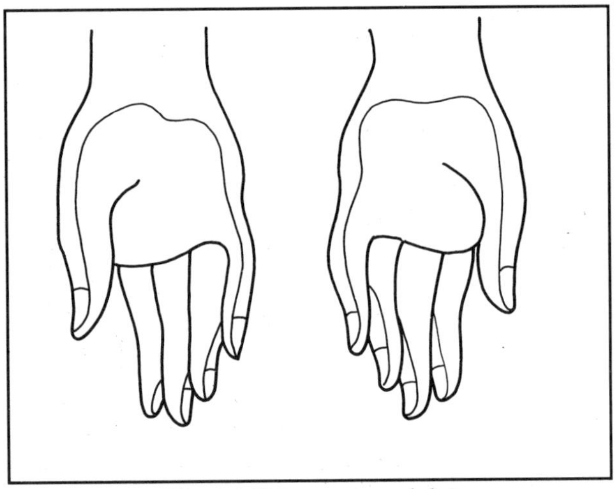

Figure 410 -- pang palelai
(as seen by another)

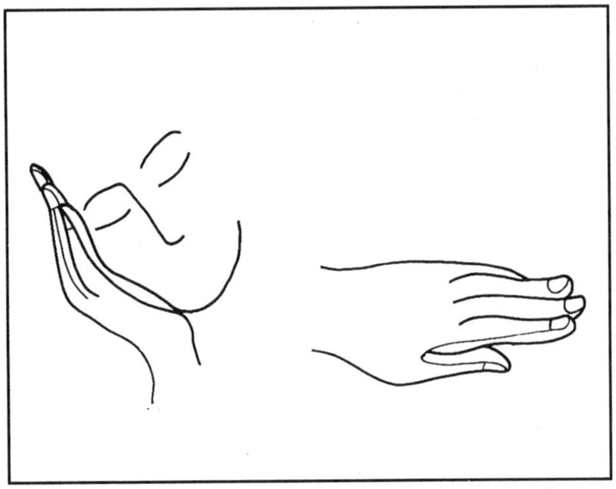

Figure 411 -- pang parinippharn
(as seen by another)

is turned to the left and the figure is standing. (DRN 36, JBo 205, ODD 680, OFr 35, PSS) (See: **Figure 408**)

pang nakawalok II -- (Thai: *pang nakawalok*; Eng.: elephant glance *mudra*; Ind.: *jñāna-lolahasta mudrā*) A *mudra*, a ritual hand pose, a seal, which is common to the Thai Buddhist tradition. One of forty *mudras* and *asanas* compiled by the Prince Patriarch Paramanujita Jinorasa and established during the reign of Rama III as being acceptable for the depiction of images of The Lord Buddha--i.e., "looking back at *Vaisali mudra*" the twenty-second of the forty attitudes noted.[29] The form is held in both hands: the right palm faces the midline, the tips of the thumb and the index finger touch, the other fingers are relaxed and extend to the left; the left palm inwards, fingers gracefully extended and all are pointing downwards. The head is turned to the left and the figure is standing.[30] (OFr 35) (See: **Figure 409**)

pang palelai -- (Thai: *pang palelai*; Eng.: in the *Palelayaka* forest *mudra*; Ind.: *añcita-nidrātahasta mudrā*) A *mudra*, a ritual hand pose, a seal, which is common to the Thai Buddhist tradition. One of forty *mudras* and *asanas* compiled by the Prince Patriarch Paramanujita Jinorasa and established during the reign of Rama III as being acceptable for the depiction of images of The Lord Buddha--i.e., "in the *Palelayaka* forest" the twentieth of the forty attitudes noted.[31] The *pang palelai* is a combined (Ind.: *saṁyutta*) form, held by both hands. The form is: right palm upwards, fingers cupped somewhat, the thumb slightly bent towards the fingertips, fingers pointing outward and resting on right knee; left rests palm down, fingers extended (generally, the hand rests on a plinth or other flat surface) and is known as the "sleeping hand" in the lap. The figure is in a *pralambapadasana* pose. (DRN 36, JBo 205, ODD 680, OFr [#25], PSS) (See: **Figure 410**)

pang parinippharn -- (Thai: *pang parinippharn* aka *pang s[h]aiyas*; Eng.: reclining *mudra*; Ind.: *śayana mudrā*) A *mudra*, a ritual hand pose, a seal, which is common to the Thai Buddhist tradition. One of forty *mudras* and *asanas* compiled by the Prince Patriarch Paramanujita Jinorasa and established during the reign of Rama III as being acceptable for the depiction of images of The Lord Buddha--i.e., "reclining" the thirty-fifth of the forty attitudes noted.[32] It denotes imminent death and the contemplation of *Nirvana*. The *pang parinippharn* is a combined (Ind.: *saṁyutta*) form, held by both hands. This *mudra* is formed by: right hand supports the head; left hand rests along the body on left thigh in a relaxed manner. The figure is reclining on the right side. (DRN 37, JBo 205, ODD 680, OFr [#33],PSS) (See: **Figure 411**)

pang pattakit-- (Thai: *pang pattakit*; Eng.: partaking of food; Ind.: *varada-dhyāna mudrā*) A *mudra*, a ritual hand pose, a seal, which is common to the Thai Buddhist tradition. One of forty *mudras* and *asanas* compiled by the Prince Patriarch Paramanujita Jinorasa and established during the reign of Rama III as being acceptable for the depiction of images of The Lord Buddha--i.e., "partaking of food *mudra*" the sixteenth of the forty attitudes noted.[33] The *pang pattakit* is a combined (Ind.: *saṁyutta*) form, held by both hands. This *mudra* is formed by: right palm facing forward, fingers and thumb extended and pointing downwards as if reaching towards the bowl; the left hand is relaxed, palm upward, rests in the lap and holds a bowl. The figure is seated in either the *virasana* or *vajrasana* position. (DRN 36, JBo 205, ODD 680, PSS) (See: **Figure 412**)

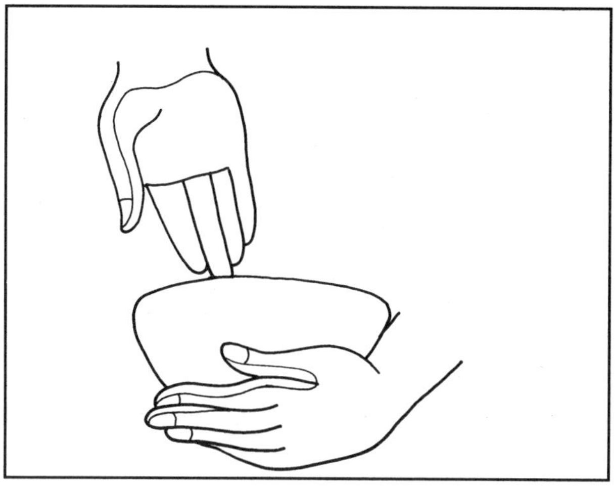

Figure 412 -- pang pattakit
(as seen by another)

pang perdlok -- (Thai: *pang perdlok*; Eng.: revealing the three worlds *mudra*; Ind.: *siṁhakarna-siṁhakarṇa mudrā*) A *mudra*, a ritual hand pose, a seal, which is common to the Thai Buddhist tradition. One of forty *mudras* and *asanas* compiled by the Prince Patriarch Paramanujita Jinorasa and established during the reign of Rama III as being acceptable for the depiction of images of The Lord Buddha--i.e., "revealing the three worlds" the last of the forty attitudes noted.[34] The pang *pang perdlok* is a combined (Ind.: *saṁyutta*) form, held by both hands. This *mudra* is formed by: the right and left hands hang down, bent at wrist, palm downward, fingers and thumbs point outwards. The figure is standing. (DRN 36, JBo 205, ODD 680, PSS) (See: **Figure 413**)

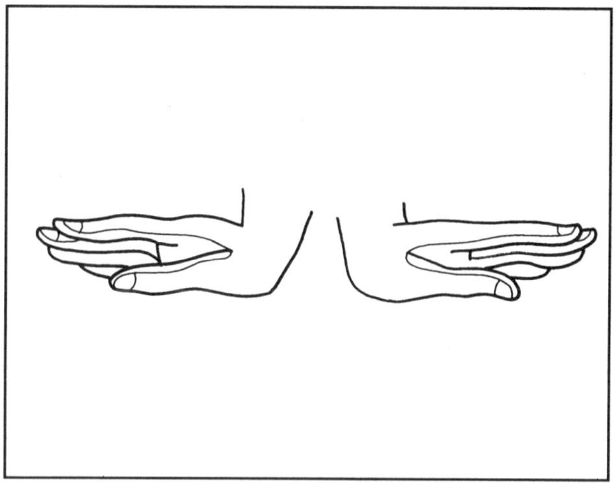

Figure 413 -- pang perdlok
(as seen by another)

pang phraditthanroy-phrabuddhabatr -- (Thai: *pang phraditthanroy-phrabuddhabatr*; Eng.: making his footprint *mudra*; Ind.: *hastavastika mudrā*[35]) A mudra, a ritual hand pose, a seal, which is common to the Thai Buddhist tradition. One of forty *mudras* and *asanas* compiled by the Prince Patriarch Paramanujita Jinorasa and

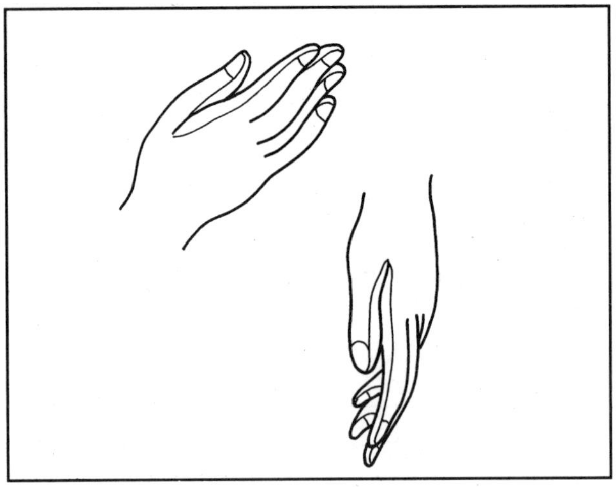

Figure 414 -- pang phraditthanroy-phrabuddhabatr
(as seen by another)

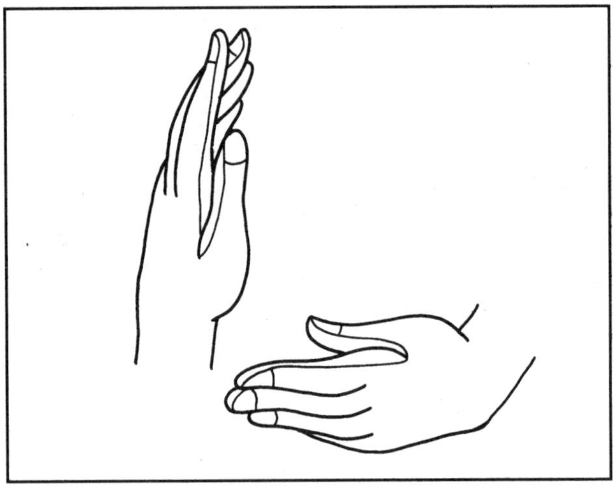

Figure 415 -- pang phra-keit-tatu
(as seen by another)

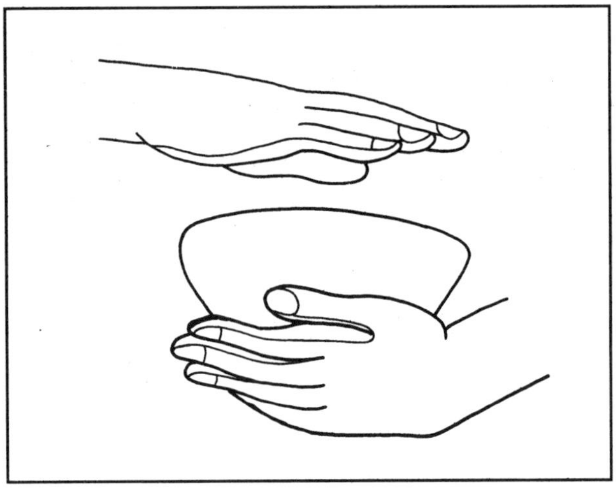

Figure 416 -- pang phrasarnbhatr
(as seen by another)

established during the reign of Rama III as being acceptable for the depiction of images of The Lord Buddha--i.e., "stamping his footprint in the ground" the thirty-first of the forty attitudes noted.[36] The *pang phraditthanroy-phrabud-dhabatr* is a combined (Ind.: *saṁyutta*) form, held by both hands. This *mudra* is formed by: the right hand, palm backward, rests in the middle of the chest. The left hand hangs, loosely at the side, palm towards the midline, fingers and thumb pointing downwards. The figure is standing on right foot with the left raised as if stepping.[37] (PSS, DRN 37, JBo, ODD 780) (See: **Figure 414**)

pang phra-keit-tatu -- (Thai: *pang phra-keit-tatu*; Eng.: making a gift of hair *mudra*; Ind.: *ardhāñjali-dhyāna mudrā*[38]) A *mudra*, a ritual hand pose, a seal, which is common to the Thai Buddhist tradition. One of forty *mudras* and *asanas* compiled by the Prince Patriarch Paramanujita Jinorasa and established during the reign of Rama III as being acceptable for the depiction of images of The Lord Buddha--i.e., "making a gift of hair" the seventeenth of the forty attitudes noted.[39] The *pang phra-keit-tatu* (*ardhanjali-dhyana mudra*) is a combined (Ind.: *saṁyutta*) form, held by both hands. The form is: the right fingers extended upwards, slightly cupped and palm facing the midline and touching the hair; left hand is relaxed, palm upward, and rests in the lap. The figure sits in the *virasana* or *vajrasana* position. (DRN 36, JBo 205, ODD 680, OFr 15, PSS) (See: **Figure 415**)

pang phra-nang -- (Thai: *pang phra-nang*; Chin.: *ting-yin* [*mudra*]; Ind.: *dhyāna mudrā, dhyānahasta mudrā, samādhi mudrā, yoga mudrā*; Jap.: *jo-in* [*mudra*]; Tib.: *bsam-gtan phyag-rgya*) The Thai for meditating.[40] See: *dhyana mudra*. (KIM 5, DRN 35, JBo, ODD 680)

pang phrasarnbhatr -- (Thai: *pang phrasarnbhatr*; Eng.: making the four alms bowls into one *mudra*; Ind.: *buddhaśramaṇa-dhyāna mudrā*) A *mudra*, a ritual hand pose, a seal, which is common to the Thai Buddhist tradition. One of forty *mudras* and *asanas* compiled by the Prince Patriarch Paramanujita Jinorasa and established during the reign of Rama III as being acceptable for the depiction of images of The Lord Buddha--i.e., "making the four alms bowls into one *mudra*" the ninth of the forty attitudes noted.[41] The *pang* *phrasarnbhatr* is a combined (Ind.: *saṁyutta*) form, held by both hands. This *mudra* is formed by: the right palm facing downward, the fingers extended turned slightly outward or away from the body as if touching the bowl; the left hand is relaxed, palm upward and rests in the lap, holding a bowl. The figure sits in the *virasana* or *vajrasana* pose. (DRN 36, JBo 204, ODD 680, OFr 14, PSS) (See: **Figure 416**)

pang phratabreakhanan I -- (Thai: *pang phratabreakhanan;* Eng.: traveling by boat *mudra*[42]; Ind.: *abhaya-kaṭyāvalambita mudrā*) A *mudra,* a ritual hand pose, a seal, which is common to the Thai Buddhist tradition. One of forty *mudras* and *asanas* compiled by the Prince Patriarch Paramanujita Jinorasa and established during the reign of Rama III as being acceptable for the depiction of images of The Lord Buddha--i.e., "traveling by boat" the eighteenth of the forty attitudes noted.[43] The *pang phratabreakhanan I* (*abhaya-katyavalambita mudra*) is a combined (Ind.: *saṁyutta*) form, held by both hands. The form is: the right hand is raised, fingers and thumb extended and together, relaxed, slightly cupped, palm facing outward and generally on a line level with the chest; the left hand relaxed, rests in the lap, palm down. The figure is seated upon a throne or plinth in the *pralambapadasana* position. (PSS, DRN 36, JBo 205, ODD 680) (See: **Figure 417**)

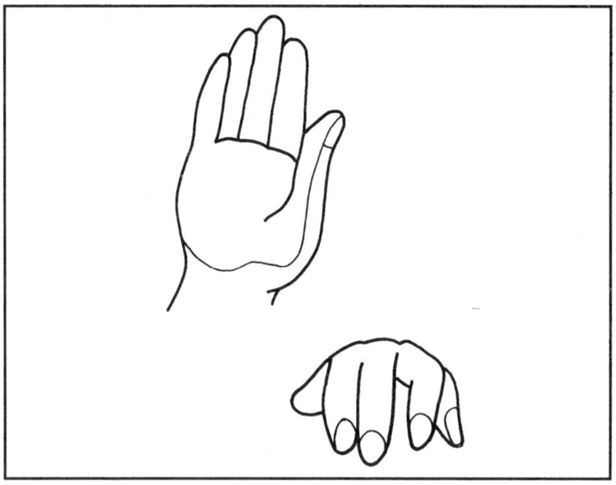

Figure 417 -- pang phratabreakhanan I
(as seen by another)

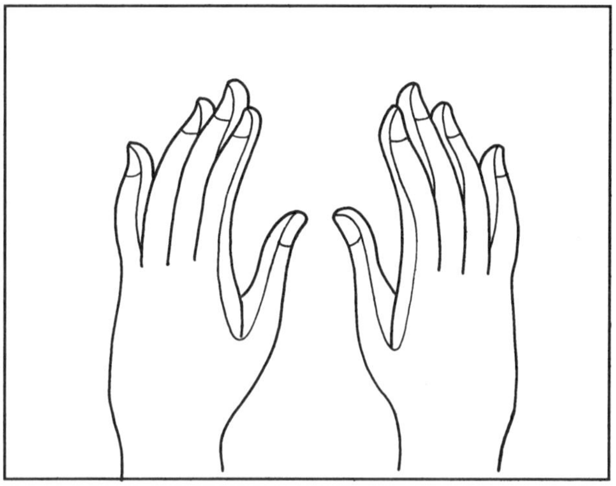

Figure 418 -- pang phratabreakhanan II
(as seen by another)

pang phratabreakhanan II -- (Thai: *pang phratabreakhanan;* Eng.: traveling by boat[44]; Ind.: *kūrpara-kūrpara mudrā*) A *mudra,* a ritual hand pose, a seal, which is common to the Thai Buddhist tradition. One of forty *mudras* and *asanas* compiled by the Prince Patriarch Paramanujita Jinorasa and established during the reign of Rama III as being acceptable for the depiction of images of The Lord Buddha--i.e., "traveling by boat" the eighteenth of the forty attitudes noted.[45] The *pang phratabreakhanan II* (*kurpara-kurpara mudra*) is a combined (Ind.: *saṁyutta*) form, held by both hands. It is formed by: palms downward resting in a relaxed manner upon the knees. The figure sits in the "European manner" upon a plinth. (DRN 36, ODD 679, OFr 27, #24, PSS) (See: **Figure 418**)

pang phratarn-ehibhikkhu -- (Thai: *pang phratarn-ehibhikkhu;* Eng.: bestowing ordination *mudra;* Ind.:

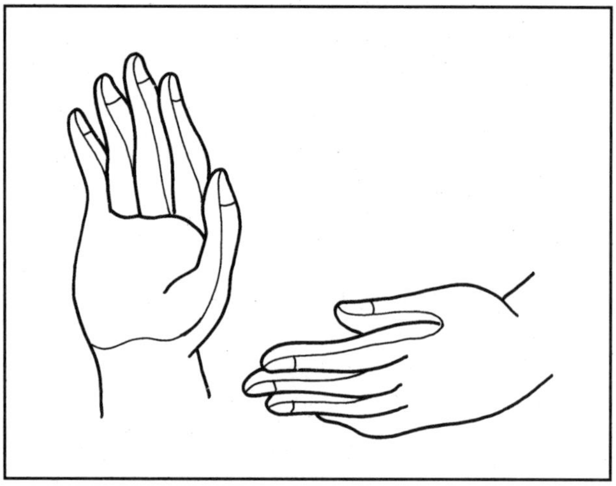

Figure 419-- pang phratarn-ehibhikkhu
(as seen by another)

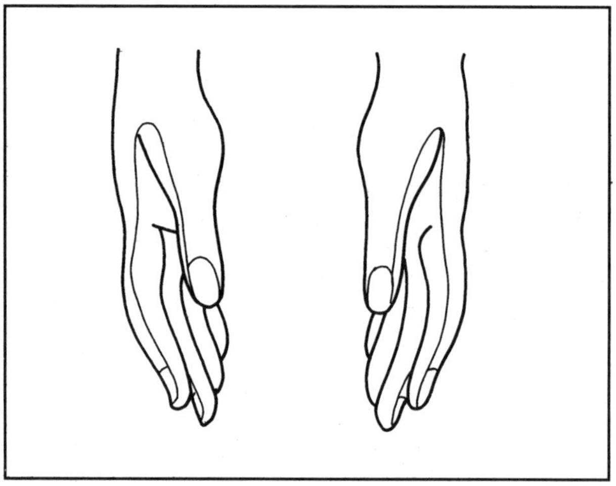

Figure 420-- pang phratopyun
(as seen by another)

ahāyavarada-dhyāna mudrā) A *mudra*, a ritual hand pose, a seal, which is common to the Thai Buddhist tradition. One of forty *mudras* and *asanas* compiled by the Prince Patriarch Paramanujita Jinorasa and established during the reign of Rama III as being acceptable for the depiction of images of The Lord Buddha--i.e., "bestowing ordination *mudra*" the twelfth of the forty attitudes noted.[46] The *pang phratarn-ehibhikkhu* is a combined (Ind.: *saṁyutta*) form, held by both hands. The *mudra* is formed: right hand: fingers and thumb are extended and together, relaxed, slightly cupped, palm facing outward and downward at approximately 45°, away from the body and generally at the level of the chest; the left hand is relaxed, palm upward, and thusly formed rest in the lap or the folded legs. The figure is sitting in the *dhyanasana* or *virasana* position. (PSS, DRN 36, JBo, ODD 680) (See: **Figure 419**)

pang phratopyun -- (Thai: *pang phratopyun*; Eng.: standing *mudra*; Ind.: *lolahasta-lolahasta-mudrā*) A *mudra*, a ritual hand pose, a seal, which is common to the Thai Buddhist tradition. One of forty *mudras* and *asanas* compiled by the Prince Patriarch Paramanujita Jinorasa and established during the reign of Rama III as being acceptable for the depiction of images of The Lord Buddha--i.e., "standing " the twenty-sixth of the forty attitudes noted.[47] The form is held in both hands: right palm inwards, fingers gracefully extended and all are pointing downwards to the side; left palm inwards, fingers gracefully extended and all are pointing downwards to the side. The figure is standing. (PSS, DRN 36, JBo 205, ODD 679) (See: **Figure 420**)

pang plong-aryusangkharn -- (Thai: *pang plong-aryusangkharn*; Eng.: contemplating the corpse or reflecting on worldly impermanence; Ind.: *jñāna-nidrātahasta mudrā*) A *mudra*, a ritual hand pose, a seal, which is common to the Thai Buddhist tradition. One of forty *mudras* and *asanas* compiled by the Prince Patriarch Paramanujita Jinorasa and established during the reign of Rama III as being acceptable for the depiction of images of The Lord Buddha--i.e., "contemplating the corpse" or "reflecting on worldly transience" the thirteenth of the forty attitudes n.[48] The *pang plong-aryusangkharn* is a combined (Ind.: *saṁyutta*) form, held by both hands. The form is: the right palm upwards, fingers cupped somewhat, the thumb slightly bent towards the fingertips, fingers pointing outward a slight distance from the torso; the left palm faces the midline, the fingers curve in towards the palm and the tip of the thumb touches the tip of the index finger. The figure is in a standing position. (DRN 36, JBo 204, ODD 279, OFr 34, PSS) (See: **Figure 421**)

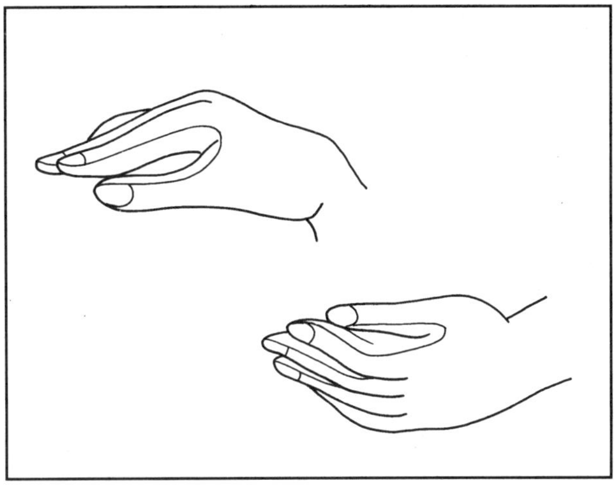

Figure 421 -- pang plong-aryusangkharn
(as seen by another)

pang plong-kammathan -- (Thai: *pang plong-kammathan*; Eng.: contemplating the corpse or reflecting on worldly impermanence[49]; Ind.: *ahayavarada-jñāna mudrā, ahāyavarada-kaṭaka mudrā*) A *mudra*, a ritual hand pose, a seal, which is common to the Thai Buddhist tradition. One of forty *mudras* and *asanas* compiled by the Prince Patriarch Paramanujita Jinorasa and established during the reign of Rama III as being acceptable for the depiction of images of The Lord Buddha--i.e., "contemplating the corpse" or "reflecting on worldly impermanence" the thirteenth of the forty attitudes noted.[50] The *pang plong-kammathan* is a combined (Ind.: *saṁyutta*) form, held by both hands. The form is: the right palm upwards, fingers cupped somewhat, the thumb slightly bent towards the fingertips, fingers pointing outward a slight distance from the torso; the left palm faces the midline, the fingers curve in towards the palm and the tip of the thumb touches the tip of the index finger. The figure is in a standing position. (See: *ahayavarada-jnana mudra* or *ahayavarada-kataka mudra*) (PSS, DRN 36, JBo 204, ODD 680) (See: **Figure 422**)

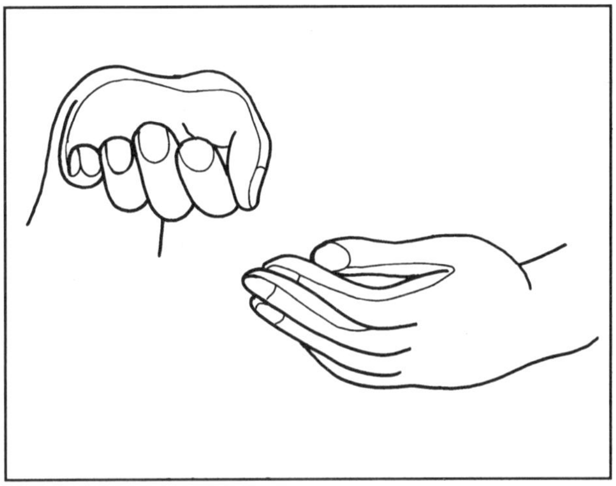

Figure 422-- pang plong-kammathan
(as seen by another)

pang prongahyuksankhan -- (Thai: *pang prongahyuksankhan*; Eng.: expounding the constituent elements *mudra*; Ind.: *nidrātahasta-vitarka mudrā*) A *mudra*, a ritual hand pose, a seal, which is common to the Thai Buddhist tradition. One of forty *mudras* and *asanas* compiled by the Prince Patriarch Paramanujita Jinorasa and established during the reign of Rama III as being acceptable for the depiction of images of The Lord Buddha--i.e., "expounding the constituent elements" the thirty-second of the forty attitudes noted.[51] The form is held in both hands: the right palm down, fingers extended (generally, the hand rests on a plinth or other flat surface) and is known as the "sleeping hand" rests on right knee; the left palm facing outwards, tips of the thumb and index finger touch, middle, ring and little fingers are relaxed and point upwards. It is held against the middle of the chest. The figure is in the

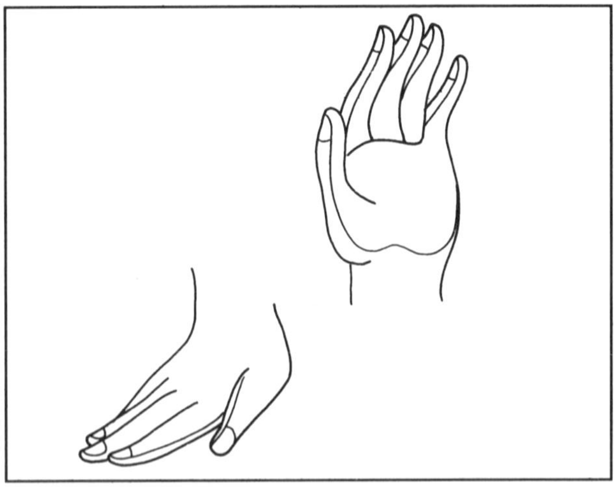

Figure 423-- pang prongahyuksankhan
(as seen by another)

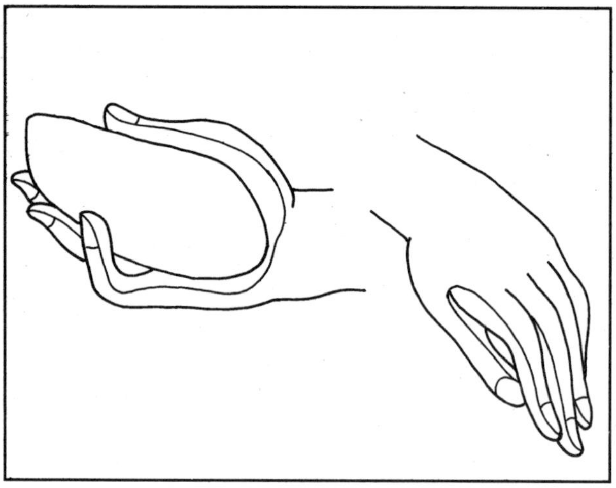

Figure 424 -- pang rab-pholmamuang
(as seen by another)

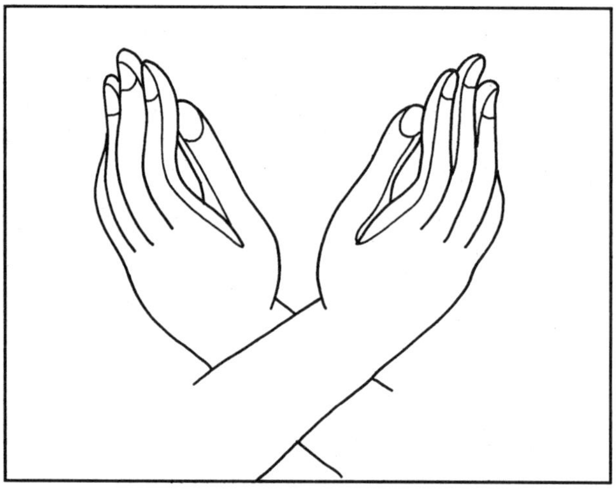

Figure 425 -- pang ram-pueng
(as seen by another)

virasana or *vajrasana* position. (PSS, DRN 37, JBo 205, ODD 680) (See: **Figure 423**)

pang rab-pholmamuang -- (Thai: *pang rab-pholmamuang*; Eng.: receiving the mango *mudra*; Ind.: *añcita-nidrātahasta mudrā*) A *mudra*, a ritual hand pose, a seal, which is common to the Thai Buddhist tradition. One of forty *mudras* and *asanas* compiled by the Prince Patriarch Paramanujita Jinorasa and established during the reign of Rama III as being acceptable for the depiction of images of The Lord Buddha--i.e., "receiving the mango" the thirty-third of the forty attitudes noted.[52] The *pang rab-pholmamuang* (*anchita-nidratahasta mudra I*) is a combined (Ind.: *saṁyutta*) form, held by both hands. The form is: right hand, palm upwards, fingers extended outward and slightly curved hold a mango; left hand, palm down, fingers extended (generally, the hand rests on a plinth or other flat surface) and is known as the "sleeping hand" rest on corresponding knee. The figure is seated in either the *virasana* or *vajrasana* position. (DRN 37, JBo 205, ODD 680, OFr 22, PSS) (See: **Figure 424**)

pang ram-pueng -- (Thai: *pang ram-pueng*; Eng.: reflecting; Ind.: *jñāna-jñāna-mudrā*) A *mudra*, a ritual hand pose, a seal, which is common to the Thai Buddhist tradition. One of forty *mudras* and *asanas* compiled by the Prince Patriarch Paramanujita Jinorasa and established during the reign of Rama III as being acceptable for the depiction of images of The Lord Buddha--i.e., "reflecting *mudra*" the twenty-eighth of the forty attitudes noted.[53] The *pang ram-pueng* is a combined (Ind.: *saṁyutta*) form, held by both hands. This *mudra* is formed by: right hand crosses over left,right palm is turns towards midline, the tips of the thumb and the index finger touch, the other fingers are relaxed and extend to the left; left palm is turned inwards, the tips of the thumb and the index finger touch, the other fingers are relaxed and extend to the right. The figure is standing. (DRN 37, JBo 205, ODD 279, OFr [#13], PSS) (See: **Figure 425**)

pang sanghlupnammamuangduaibaht -- (Thai: *pang sanghlupnammamuangduaibaht*; Eng.: receiving the offering of water *mudra*; Ind.: *dhyāna-nidrātahasta mudrā*) A *mudra*, a ritual hand pose, a seal, which is common to the Thai Buddhist tradition. One of forty *mudras* and *asanas* compiled by the Prince Patriarch Paramanujita Jinorasa and established during the reign of Rama III as being acceptable for the depiction of images of The Lord Buddha--i.e., "receiving the offering of water" the twenty-fourth of the forty attitudes noted.[54] The *pang sanghlupnammamuangduaibaht* is a combined (Ind.: *saṁyutta*) form, held by both hands.[55] This *mudra* is formed by: both hands clasping the bowl at its base and holding it over the right knee. The figure is seated in either the *virasana* position. (OFr 23, DRN 36, JBo 205, ODD 678, PSS) (See: **Figure 426**)

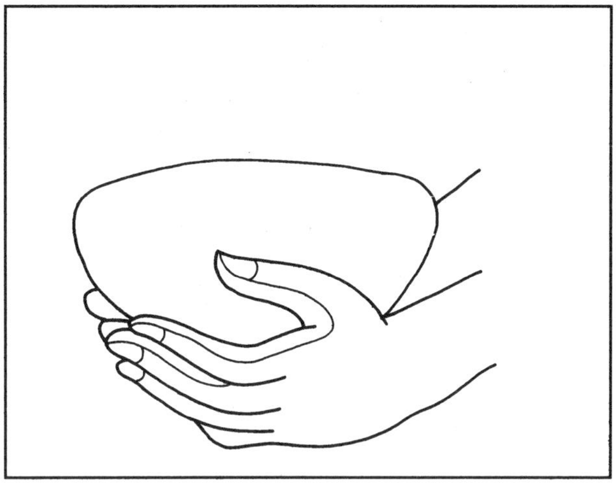

Figure 426 -- pang sanghlupnammamuangduaibaht
(as seen by another)

pang sawoimathupayas -- (Thai: *pang sawoimathupayas*; Eng.: eating the rice gruel *mudra*; Ind.: *varada-dhyāna mudrā*) A *mudra*, a ritual hand pose, a seal, which is common to the Thai Buddhist tradition. One of forty *mudras* and *asanas* compiled by the Prince Patriarch Paramanujita Jinorasa and established during the reign of Rama III as being acceptable for the depiction of images of The Lord Buddha--i.e., "eating the rice gruel" the thirty-sixth of the forty attitudes noted.[56] The *pang sawoimathupayas* is a combined (Ind.: *saṁyutta*) form, held by both hands. This *mudra* is formed by: right palm facing forward, fingers and thumb extended and pointing downwards as if reaching towards the dish; left hand is relaxed, palm upward, rests in the lap and holds a bowl. The figure is in the *virasana* or *vajrasana* pose. (DRN 37, JBo 205, ODD 680, PSS) (See: **Figure 427**)

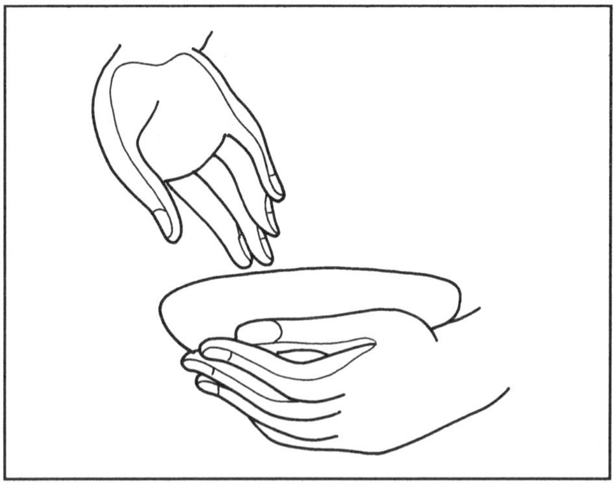

Figure 427 -- pang sawoimathupayas
(as seen by another)

pang sedetphutthadannernpai -- (Thai: *pang sedetphutthadannernpai*; Eng.: walking *mudra*; Ind.: *abhaya-lolahasta mudrā*) The Thai for walking.[57] A *mudra*, a ritual hand pose, a seal, which is common to the Thai Buddhist tradition. One of forty *mudras* and *asanas* compiled by the Prince Patriarch Paramanujita Jinorasa and established during the reign of Rama III as being acceptable for the depiction of images of The Lord Buddha--i.e., "walking *mudra*" the thirty-seventh of the forty attitudes noted.[58] The *pang sedetphutthadannernpai* (*abhaya-lolahasta mudra*) is a combined (Ind.: *saṁyutta*) form, held by both hands. The form is: right hand is raised, fingers and thumb extended and together, relaxed, slightly cupped, palm facing outward and generally on a line level with the chest; left palm faces midline, fingers gracefully extended and all are pointing downwards to the side. Specifically, the left foot is

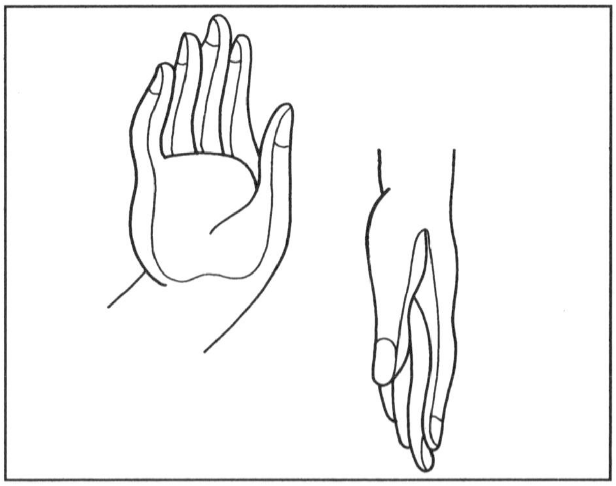

Figure 428 -- pang sedetphutthadannernpai
(as seen by another)

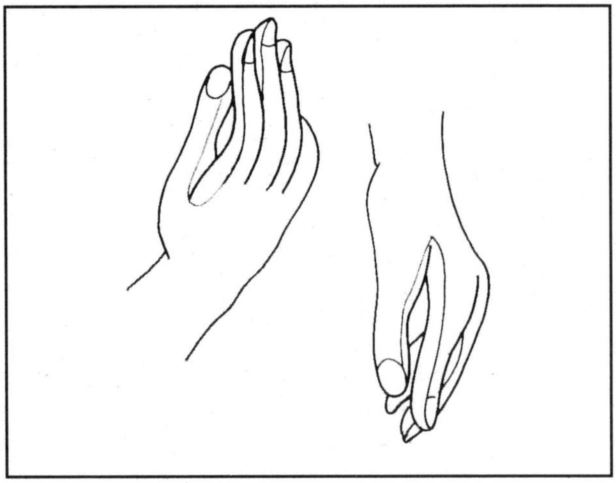

Figure 429 -- pang song-nam-phon
(as seen by another)

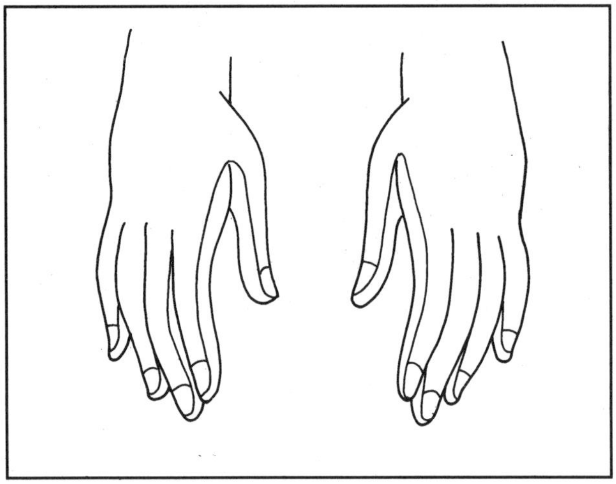

Figure 430 -- pang song-picharanacharatham
(as seen by another)

raised as if taking a step while the right rests flat on the ground. (PSS, DRN 36, JBo 165, OFr #17) (See: **Figure 428**)

pang s(h)aiyas -- (Thai: *pang s[h]aiyas* aka *pang parinippharn;* Eng.: reclining *mudra;* Ind.: *śayana mudrā*) The Thai for reclining.[59] See: *pang parinippharn.* (DRN 37, JBo 205, ODD 680, OFr [#33],PSS)

pang song-nam-phon -- (Thai: *pang song-nam-phon;* Eng.: bathing *mudra;* Ind.: *jñāna-lolahasta mudrā*) A *mudra,* a ritual hand pose, a seal, which is common to the Thai Buddhist tradition. One of forty *mudras* and *asanas* compiled by the Prince Patriarch Paramanujita Jinorasa and established during the reign of Rama III as being acceptable for the depiction of images of The Lord Buddha--i.e., "bathing" the twenty-fifth of the forty attitudes noted.[60] The *pang song-nam-phon* is a combined (Ind.: *saṁyutta*) form, held by both hands. This *mudra* is formed by: right palm faces the midline, the tips of the thumb and the index finger touch, the other fingers are relaxed and extend to the left and held against the middle of the chest; the left hand hangs in a relaxed manner to the side of the figure. The figure is standing with a bathing cloth over left shoulder. (DRN 36, JBo 205, OFr 30, PSS) (See: **Figure 429**)

pang song-picharanacharatham -- (Thai: *pang song-picharanacharatham;* Eng.: discoursing on the decrepitude of old age *mudra;* Ind.: *nidrātahasta-nidrātahasta mudrā*[61]) A *mudra,* a ritual hand pose, a seal, which is common to the Thai Buddhist tradition. One of forty *mudras* and *asanas* compiled by the Prince Patriarch Paramanujita Jinorasa and established during the reign of Rama III as being acceptable for the depiction of images of The Lord Buddha--i.e., "discoursing on the decrepitude of old age" the thirtieth of the forty attitudes noted.[62] The form is held in both hands: each hand rests palm down, fingers extended (generally, the hand rests on a plinth or other flat surface) and is known as the "sleeping hand" on their respective knees. The figure is seated in either the *virasana* or *vajrasana* position. (DRN 37, JBo 205, PSS) (See: **Figure 430**)

pang songruputkang -- (Thai: *pang songruputkang;* Eng.: receiving the offering of water *mudra;* Ind.: *dhyāna-nidrātahasta mudrā*) A *mudra,* a ritual hand pose, a seal, which is common to the Thai Buddhist tradition. One of forty *mudras* and *asanas* compiled by the Prince Patriarch Paramanujita Jinorasa and established during the reign of Rama III as being acceptable for the depiction of images of The Lord Buddha--i.e., "receiving the offering of water" the twenty-fourth of the forty attitudes noted.[63] The *pang songruputkang* is a combined (Ind.: *saṁyutta*) form, held by both hands. This *mudra* is formed by: right hand is relaxed, palm upward, rests in the lap; left hand palm down, fingers extended (generally, the hand rests on a plinth or other flat surface) and is known as the "sleeping hand" rests on the knee. The figure is seated in either the *virasana* or *vajrasana* position. (DRN 36, JBo 205, ODD 678, OFr 23, PSS) (See: **Figure 431**)

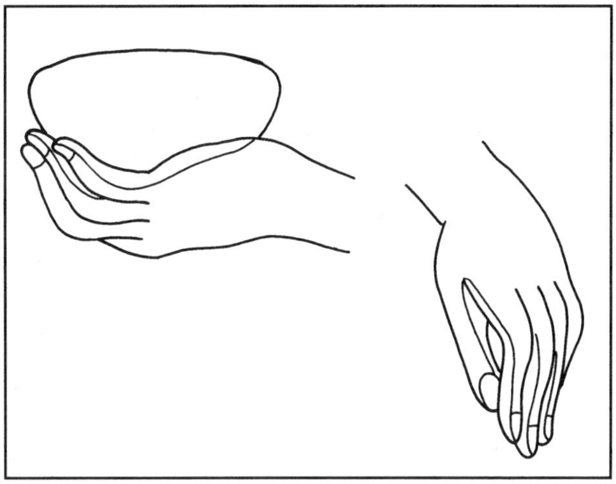

Figure 431 -- pang songruputkang
(as seen by another)

pang sonkhem -- (Thai: *pang sonkhem*; Eng.: threading the needle *mudra*; Jap: *temborin-in mudra*) A *mudra*, a ritual hand pose, a seal, which is common to the Thai Buddhist tradition. One of forty *mudras* and *asanas* compiled by the Prince Patriarch Paramanujita Jinorasa and established during the reign of Rama III as being acceptable for the depiction of images of The Lord Buddha--i.e., "threading the needle" the thirty-eighth of the forty attitudes noted.[64] The *pang sonkhem* is a combined (Ind.: *saṁyutta*) form, held by both hands. This *mudra* is formed by: the tip of the thumb and the index finger touch, the middle, ring and little fingers are extended, the palm of the right faces outward while the palm of the left faces upwards and the tips of the index fingers and thumbs are brought together and touch as if threading a needle. The figure is seated in either the *virasana* or *vajrasana* position. (DRN 37, JBo 205, ODD 680, OFr 26, PSS) (See: **Figure 432**)

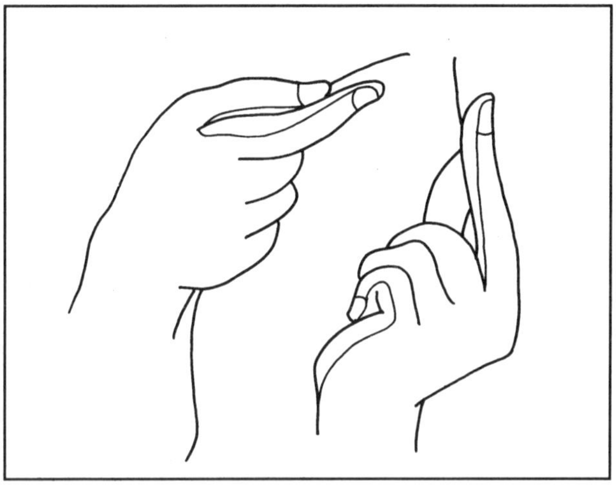

Figure 432 -- pang sonkhem
(as seen by another)

pang sung-rabmathupayas -- (Thai: *pang sung-rabmathupayas*; Eng.: accepting the rice-gruel offering; Ind.: *añcita-añcita mudrā*) A *mudra*, a ritual hand pose, a seal, which is common to the *Theravada* Buddhist tradition in Thailand. It denotes the time when the Lord Buddha accepted the simple offering after performing long and difficult austerities. It is one of forty Thai Buddhist *mudras* and *asanas* compiled by the Prince Patriarch Paramanujita Jinorasa and established during the reign of Rama III as being acceptable for the depiction of images of The Lord Buddha--i.e., "accepting the rice-gruel offering" the second of the forty atti-

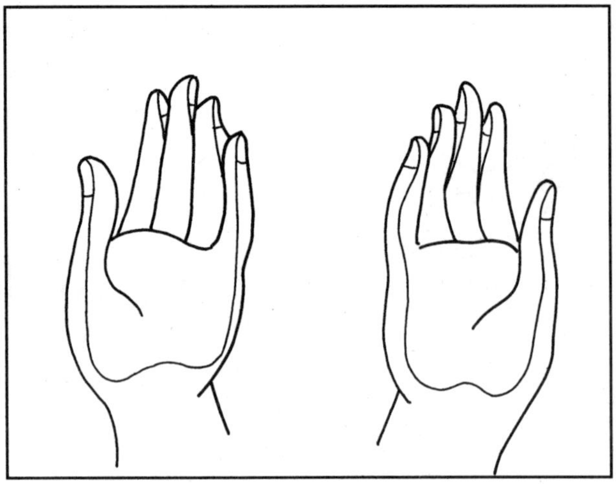

Figure 433 -- pang sung-rabmathupayas
(as seen by the holder)

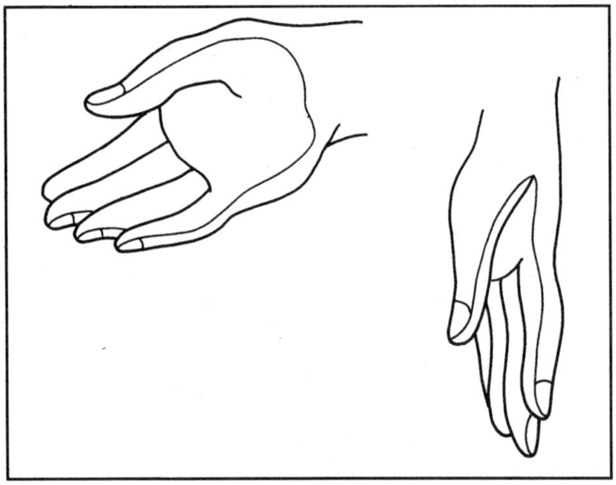

Figure 434 -- pang sung-rabyaka
(as seen by another)

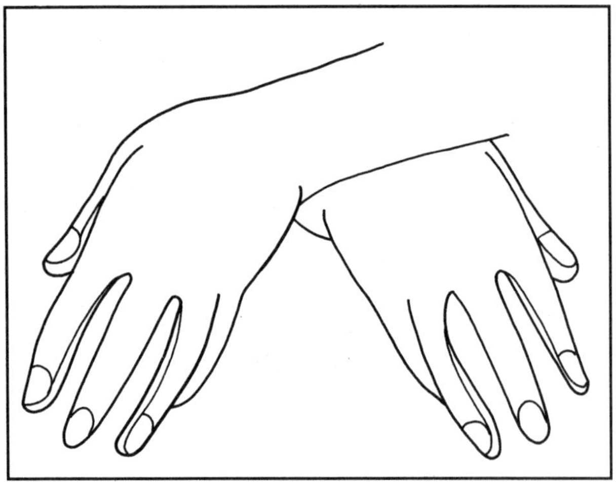

Figure 435 -- pang tavainetr
(as seen by another)

tudes noted.[65] The *pang sung-rabmathupayas* (*anchita-anchita mudra*) is a combined (Ind.: *saṁyutta*) form, held by both hands. The *mudra* is: hands resting on corresponding knee, palm facing upwards, fingers and thumb extended, slightly cupped. The figure is seated in the *pralambapadasana*. (DRN 35, JBo 204, ODD 680, PSS) (See: **Figure 433**)

pang sung-rabyaka -- (Thai: *pang sung-rabyaka*; Eng.: accepting the bundle of grass *mudra*; Ind.: *añcita-lolahasta mudrā*) A *mudra*, a ritual hand pose, a seal, which is common to the Thai Buddhist tradition. One of forty *mudras* and *asanas* compiled by the Prince Patriarch Paramanujita Jinorasa and established during the reign of Rama III as being acceptable for the depiction of images of The Lord Buddha--i.e., "accepting the bundle of grass" the fourth of the forty attitudes noted.[66] The *pang sung-rabyaka* (*anchita-lolahasta mudra*) is a combined (Ind.: *saṁyutta*) form, held by both hands. The form is: right hand extended, palm facing upwards, fingers and thumb extended outwards and held at waist level; left hand is hanging in a relaxed manner at the Buddha's side. The figure is in a standing pose. (DRN 35, JBo 204, ODD 680, OFr 7, PSS) (See: **Figure 434**)

pang tavainetr -- (Thai: *pang tavainetr*; Eng.: gazing at the bodhi tree *mudra*) A *mudra*, a ritual hand pose, a seal, which is common to the Thai Buddhist tradition. One of forty *mudras* and *asanas* compiled by the Prince Patriarch Paramanujita Jinorasa and established during the reign of Rama III as being acceptable for the depiction of images of The Lord Buddha--i.e., "gazing at the bodhi tree *mudra*" the seventh of the forty attitudes noted.[67] The *pang tavainetr* is a combined (Ind.: *saṁyutta*) form, held by both hands. This *mudra* is formed by: the right hand crosses over the left at the wrist, both palms face the midline, fingers and thumbs extended downwards. The *mudra* is thus held in front of the groin and the figure is standing.[68] (PSS, DRN 35, JBo, ODD 680) (See: **Figure 435**)

pang thong-tang-etatakkasatarn -- (Thai: *pang thong-tang-etatakkasatarn*; Eng.: choosing the chief disciples *mudra*; Ind.: *tarjanī-dhyāna mudrā*) A *mudra*, a ritual hand pose, a seal, which is common to the Thai Buddhist tradition. One of forty *mudras* and *asanas* compiled by the Prince Patriarch Paramanujita Jinorasa and established during the reign of Rama III as being acceptable for the depiction of images of The Lord Buddha--i.e., "choosing the chief disciples" the thirty-ninth of the forty attitudes noted.[69] The *pang thong-tang-etatakkasatarn* is a combined (Ind.: *saṁyutta*) form, held by both hands. This *mudra* is formed by: the right palm faces forward or downwards, index finger extends straight outward, parallel to the ground or slightly upward, middle, ring and little finger are folded into the palm, first phalanges of the thumb touches the second phalanges of the index finger; the left hand is relaxed, palm upward, and rest in the lap. The figure is in the *virasana* or *vajrasana* position.[70] (DRN 37, JBo 205, ODD 680, OFr 18, PSS) (See: **Figure 436**)

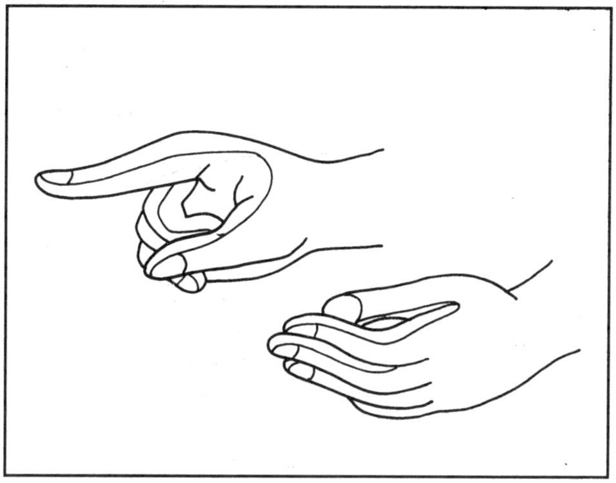

Figure 436 -- pang thong-tang-etatakkasatarn
(as seen by another)

pang tukkarakiriya -- (Thai: *pang tukkarakiriya;* Eng.: performing austerities *mudra;* Ind.: *jñāna-jñāna mudrā*) A *mudra*, a ritual hand pose, a seal, which is common to the Thai Buddhist tradition. One of forty *mudras* and *asanas* compiled by the Prince Patriarch Paramanujita Jinorasa and established during the reign of Rama III as being acceptable for the depiction of images of The Lord Buddha--i.e., "performing austerities" the first of the forty attitudes noted.[71] The *pang tukkarakiriya* is a combined (Ind.: *saṁyutta*) form, held by both hands. This *mudra* is formed by: the right palm is turned towards midline, the tips of the thumb and the index finger touch, the other fingers are relaxed and extend to the left; the left, crossing over the right, the palm faces the midline, the tips of the thumb and the index finger touch, the other fingers are relaxed and extend to the right. The figure is in the *virasana* or *vajrasana* pose. (DRN 35, JBo 204, PSS) (See: **Figure 437**)

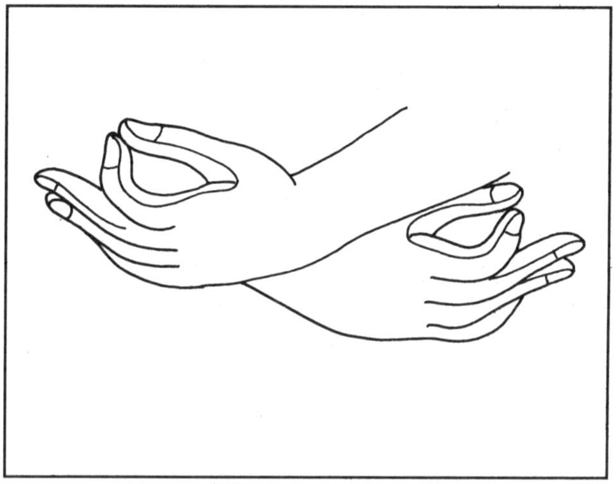

Figure 437 -- pang tukkarakiriya
(as seen by another)

pang uhm-bhatr -- (Thai: *pang uhm-bhatr;* Eng.: carrying the alms bowl *mudra;* Ind.: *añcita-añcita mudrā*) A *mudra*, a ritual hand pose, a seal, which is common to the Thai Buddhist tradition. It denotes the simplicity of the Lord Buddha when he went abroad seeking food and sustenance. It is one of forty Thai Buddhist *mudras* and *asanas* compiled by the Prince Patriarch Paramanujita Jinorasa and established during the reign of Rama III as being acceptable for the depiction of images of The Lord Buddha-- "carrying the alms bowl *mudra*" the fifteenth of the forty attitudes noted.[72] The *pang uhm-bhatr* is a combined (Ind.: *saṁyutta*) form,

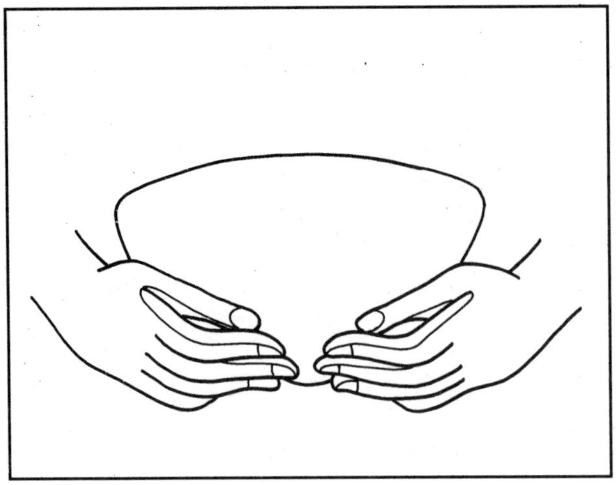

Figure 438 -- pang uhm-bhatr
(as seen by another)

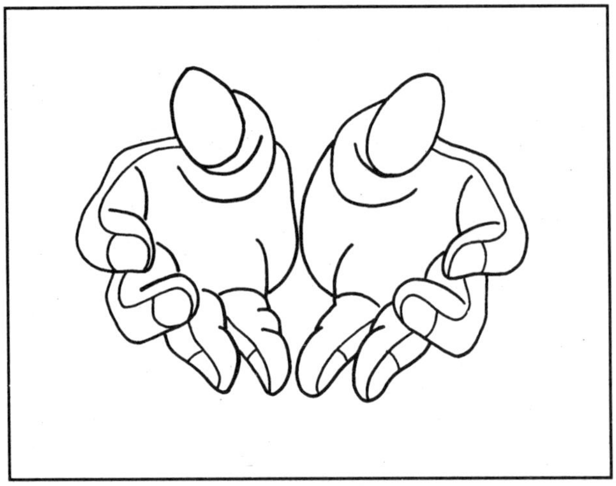

Figure 439 -- pankaj mudra
(as seen by another)

held by both hands. The *mudra* is formed by: hands holding an alms bowl at waist level, palms facing upwards, fingers and thumbs extended, slightly cupped. The figure is standing. (DRN 36, JBo 205, ODD 680, PSS) (See: **Figure 438**)

pankajam mudra -- (Ind.: *pañkajam-mudrā* aka *pankaj mudrā*) A variant (spelling) of *pankaj mudra*. See: *pankaj mudra*. (RLM 77)

pankaj mudra -- (Ind.: *pañkaj-mudrā* aka *pañkajam mudrā*) A *mudra*, a ritual hand pose, a seal, a *mudra* which is common to yogic tradition, particularly the *Yoga Tatva Mudra Vigyan* form, and is held by a devotee or practitioner. The *pankaj mudra* is a combined (Ind.: *saṁyutta*) form, held by both hands. It is one of the eight *mudras* held after the *Gayatri Jap* of the thirty-two total *Gayatri mudras*.[73] It is utilized for all sickness, especially cancer. The *pankaj mudra* is a combined (Ind.: *saṁyutta*) form, held by both hands. This *mudra* is formed by: the heels of the two palms touch and a hollow space is formed, the thumbs touch along their outer edges, the little fingers touch along the first phalanges, the index, middle and ring fingers are separated and all face outward. Thus formed, the *mudra* is held at waist level. This *mudra* is similar to the *ashtadala mudra* except that the latter is oriented upwards. (KDe 89 & 108, RLM 77) (See: **Figure 439**)

Papanasini mudra -- (Ind.: *Pāpanāśinī-mudrā*) A hand pose, a seal, a dramatic (Ind.: *nāṭya*) *mudra* or gesture (Ind.: *darpaṇa*) held or formed by a performer, dancer or actor. It denotes the *Papanasini*, one of the famous rivers of India. The *mudra* employed is identical in form to the *shukatunda mudra*. See: *shukatunda mudra*. (ACG 48)

Parashuramavatara mudra -- (Ind.: *Paraśurāmāvatāra-mudrā*) A hand pose, a seal, a dramatic (Ind.: *nāṭya*) mudra or gesture (Ind.: *darpaṇa*) held or formed by a performer, dancer or actor. The *Parashuramavatara mudra* is a combined (Ind.: *saṁyutta*) form, held by both hands. It denotes *Rama* with a battle-axe *avatar*, one of the ten *avaturs* (Ind.: *daśāvatāras*) of the Lord Vishnu This *mudra* is formed by: right palm facing outward, index, middle fingers and thumb extended, together and pointing upwards, ring and little fingers bent towards the palm; left arm is relaxed, hangs loosely at the side, the hand rests on the hip (just below the waist), fingers to the front, thumb to the back, the thumb may also rest along side of the fingers. (ACG 46) (See: **Figure 440**)

pardisha-mukula mudra -- (Ind.: *pardiṣa-mukula-mudrā*) A hand pose, a seal, a dramatic (Ind.: *nāṭya*) *mudra* or gesture (Ind.: *darpaṇa*) held or formed by a performer, dancer or actor. The *pardisha-mukula mudra* is a single (Ind.: *asaṁyutta*) form, held by one hand. This *mudra* is formed by: palm faces outwards, the tips of the index, middle and ring fingers and thumb are brought together, but not necessarily touching, pointing forwards, the little finger is gently curled and separate. (ACG 50) (See: **Figure 441**)

parijata mudra -- (Ind.: *pārījāta-mudrā*) A hand pose, a seal, a dramatic (Ind.: *nāṭya*) *mudra* or gesture (Ind.: *darpaṇa*) held or formed by a performer, dancer or actor. It denotes the *parijata* tree. The *mudra* employed is identical in form to the *trijnana mudra*. See: *trijnana mudra*. (ACG 49)

partaking of food mudra -- (Eng.; Ind.: *varada-dhyāna mudrā*; Thai: *pang pattakit*) The English descriptive phrase for the Thai: *pang pattakit*. **See:** *pang pattakit*. (DRN 36, JBo)

Parvati mudra -- (Ind.: *Pārvatī-mudrā*) A hand pose, a seal, a dramatic (Ind.: *nāṭya*) *mudra* or gesture (Ind.: *darpaṇa*) held or formed by a performer, dancer or actor which denotes a specific deity. The *Parvati mudra* is a combined (Ind.: *saṁyutta*) form, held by both hands. It denotes *Parvati*. This *mudra* is formed by: right palm facing outward, fingers extended, together and pointing downwards, relaxed, the thumb extends away from the fingers; left palm facing outward, fingers extended, together and pointing upwards, relaxed, the thumb extends away from the fingers. Thus formed the hands are held at shoulder level. (ACG 45) (See: **Figure 442**)

pasha mudra I -- (Ind.: *pāśa-mudrā*) ("the noose") A hand pose, a seal, a dramatic (Ind.: *nāṭya*) *mudra* or gesture (Ind.: *darpaṇa*) held or formed by a performer, dancer or actor. The *pasha mudra* is a combined (Ind.: *saṁyutta*) form, held by both hands. It denotes enmity.

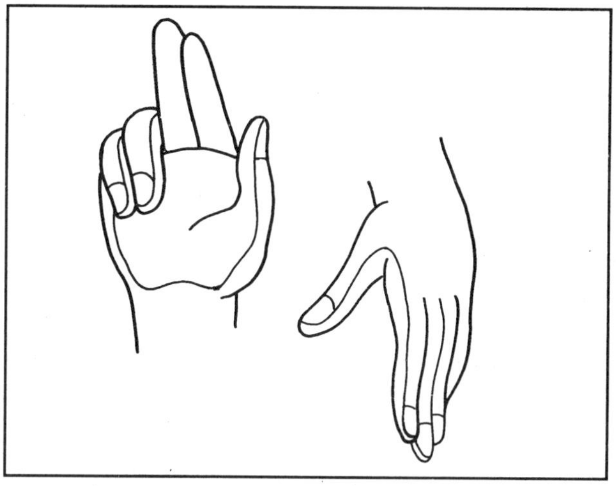

Figure 440 -- Parashuramavatara mudra
(as seen by another)

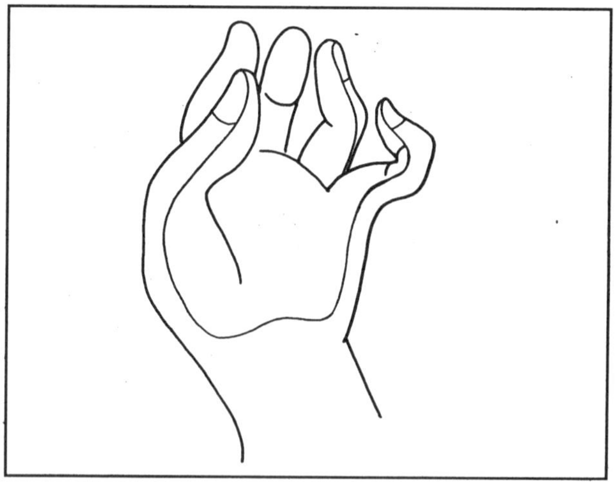

Figure 441 -- pardisha-mukula mudra
(as seen by another)

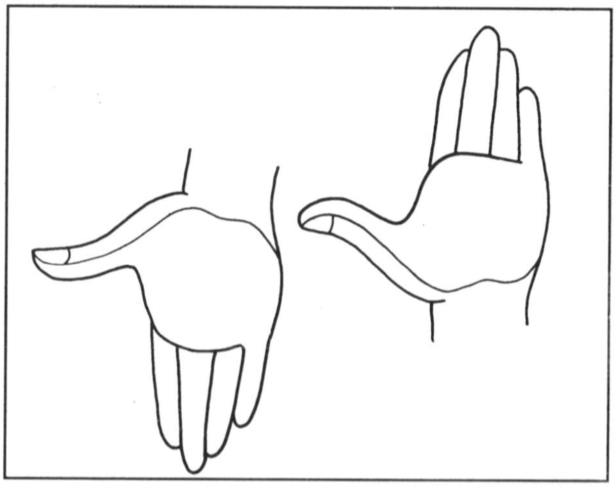

Figure 442 -- Parvati mudra
(as seen by another)

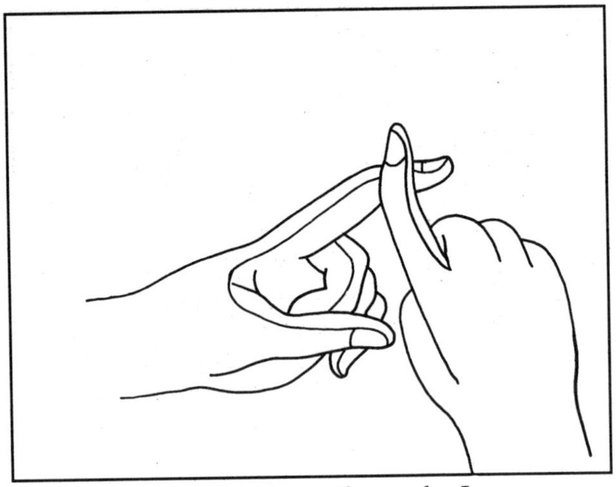

Figure 443 -- pasha mudra I
(as seen by the holder)

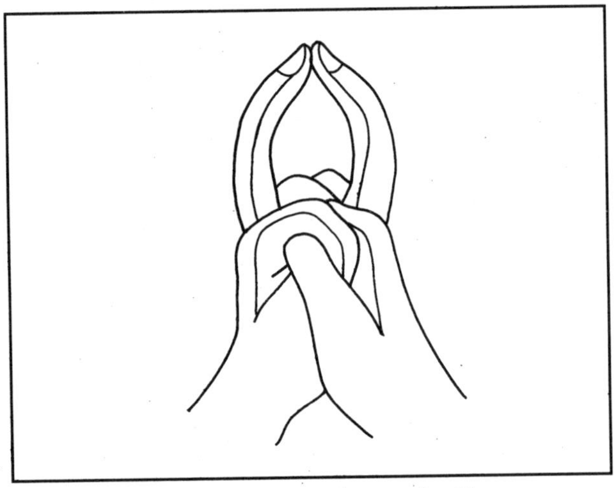

Figure 444 -- pasha mudra II
(as seen by the holder)

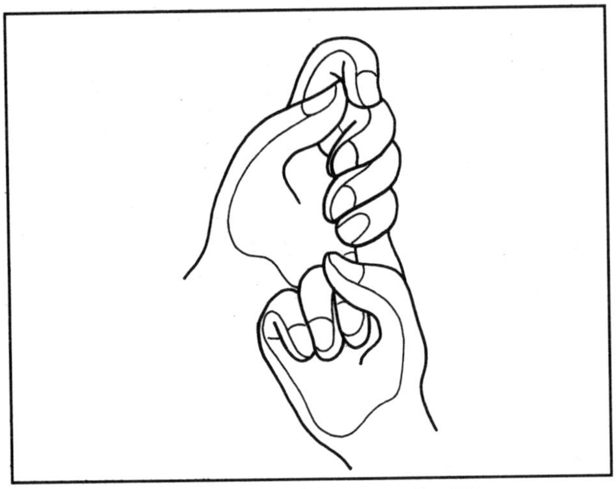

Figure 445 -- pasha mudra III
(as seen by the holder)

This *mudra* is formed by: the right palm faces outwards, the index finger and the thumb point upwards, together, the middle, ring and little fingers are folded into the palm, the left is similar, the palm faces the midline. Thus formed, the two are joined by hooking the index fingers together. (ACG 41) (See: **Figure 443**)

pasha mudra II -- (Ind.: *pāśa-mudrā*) ("the noose *mudra*") A *mudra*, a ritual hand pose, a seal, a *tantric mudra* which is common to the Japanese Buddhist (*Vajrayana, Mantrayana*) tradition and is held or formed by a devotee or priest during the rites of *Garbhadhatu Mandala, Vajradhatu Mandala, Homa Rites* and other rites. It may be accompanied by a mantra. The *pasha mudra II* is a combined (Ind.: *saṁyutta*) form, held by both hands. It denotes the subduing of evil forces. This *mudra* is formed by: palms face each other, index, ring and little fingers and thumbs are interlaced with fingers and thumbs inside (palm-side) the 'fist,' middle gingers arch upwards and touch at their tips. (GDe 289, LCS 256) (See: **Figure 444**)

pasha mudra III -- (Ind.: *pāśa-mudrā*) ("the noose *mudra*") A *mudra*, a ritual hand pose, a seal, a *tantric mudra* which is common to the Japanese Buddhist (*Vajrayana, Mantrayana*) tradition and is held or formed by a devotee or priest during various rites. It may be accompanied by a *mantra*. The *pasha mudra III* is a combined (Ind.: *saṁyutta*) form, held by both hands. This *mudra* is formed by: right palm faces midline, middle, ring and little fingers folded into palm, thumb folded over fingers, index extended upwards, left palm faces midline, middle, ring and little fingers folded into palm and over extended right index finger, left index flexed at first two knuckles, thumb tip touched tip of index finger. (GDe 337) (See: **Figure 445**)

pashatarjani mudra -- (Ind.: *pāśatarjanī-mudrā* aka *tarjanī mudrā, tarjanīpaśa mudrā*) A *mudra*, a ritual hand pose, a seal, which is common to the Buddhist tradition. It denotes warning. The form is the *tarjani mudra* with a noose or snare (*pasha*), the loop of which is held in the extended index finger. (BCO 216)

pataka mudra I -- (Ind.: *patākā-mudrā*) ("the flag hand") A hand pose, a seal, a dramatic (Ind.: *nāṭya*) *mudra* or gesture (Ind.: *darpaṇa*) held or formed by a performer, dancer or actor. The *pataka-mudra* is a single (Ind.: *asaṁyutta*) form, held by one hand, frequently the right. It denotes: a flag, victory, forbidding,, removal of hindrance, closing a dispute, etc.[74] It is identical to the deity-centered *abhaya-mudra*. The form of this *mudra* is generally held by the right hand: the hand is raised, fingers and thumb extended, together and pointing upwards, relaxed, slightly cupped, palm facing outward and generally on a line level with the chest.[75] (ACG 26, KVa 134 [1]) (See: **Figure 446**)

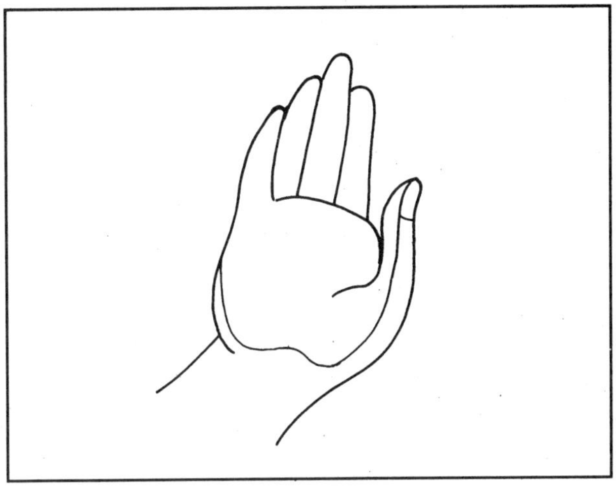

Figure 446 -- pataka mudra I
(as seen by another)

pataka mudra II -- (Ind.: *patākā-mudrā*) A *mudra*, a ritual hand pose, a seal, which is common to the Hindu tradition. It denotes a flag and symbolizes strength and power. The form is held in one hand (right): arm is extended (right) level with the shoulder, palm facing downwards, fingers and thumb extended away from the body.[76] (ERJ II 24, MJS 110) (See: **Figure 447**)

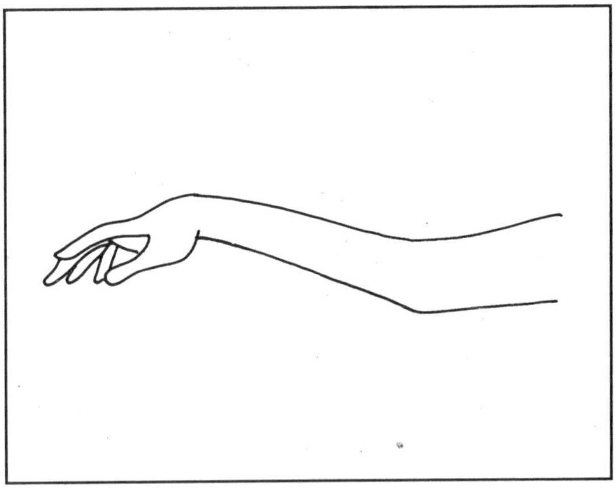

Figure 447 -- pataka mudra II
(as seen by another)

pataka-dhyana mudra -- (Ind.: *patākā-dhyāna-mudrā; Thai: pang khabphrawakkali*) This is a descriptive term.[77] See: *pang khabphrawakkali*. (DRN 37, JBo, ODD 38, OFr 26, PSS)

patali mudra -- (Ind.: *pāṭalī-mudrā*) A hand pose, a seal, a dramatic (Ind.: *nāṭya*) *mudra* or gesture (Ind.: *darpaṇa*) held or formed by a performer, dancer or actor. It denotes the *patali* tree. The *mudra* employed is identical in form to the *shukatunda mudra*. See: *shukatunda mudra*. (ACG 48)

patra mudra -- (Ind.: *pātra-mudrā* aka *akṣata mudrā*) ("the bowl *mudra*") A *mudra*, a ritual hand pose, a seal, a *tantric mudra* which is common to the Japanese Buddhist (*Vajrayana, Mantrayana*) tradition and is held or formed by a devotee or priest during the *Eighteen Rites* and the rites of *Garbhadhatu Mandala*. It denotes either the offering of rice (*akshata*) or an alms bowl (*patra*). It may be accompanied by a *mantra* and denotes protection against evil. The *patra mudra*[78] is a combined (Ind.: *saṁyutta*) form, held by both hands. This *mudra* is formed by: palms of both hands facing nearly upwards, fingers and thumbs of both hands extended outwards and parallel to the ground and are slightly cupped. Thus formed, the hands touch along the outer edge of the palms and little fingers. (GDe 15, LCS 155) (See: **Figure 448**)

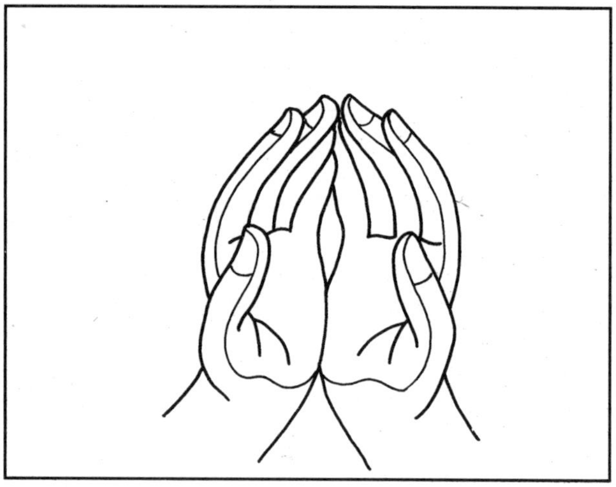

Figure 448 -- patra mudra
(as seen by the holder)

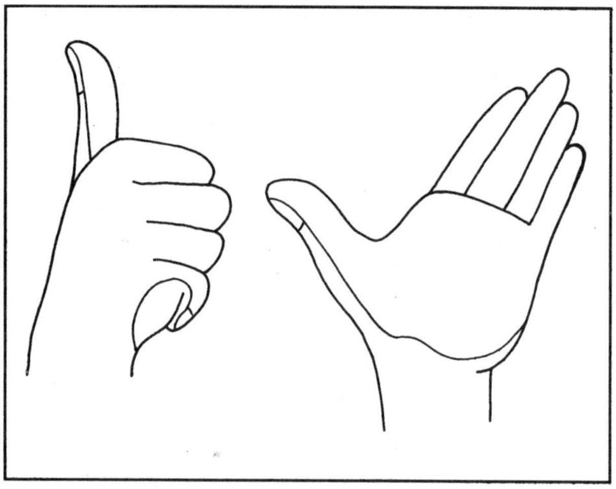

Figure 449 -- pitri mudra
(as seen by another)

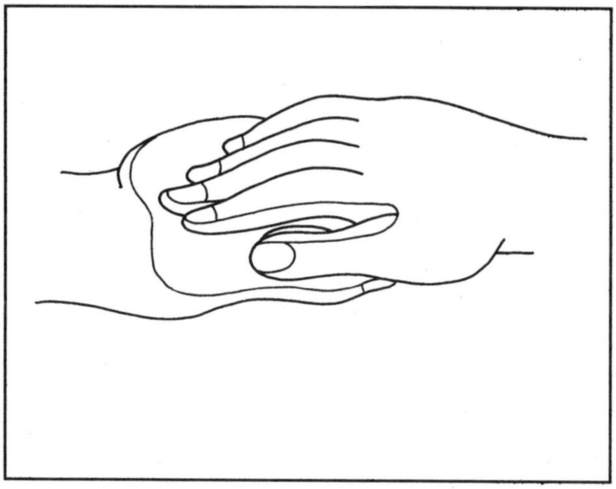

Figure 450 -- pothi mudra
(as seen by the holder)

performing austerities mudra -- (Eng.; Ind.: *jñāna-jñāna mudrā*; Thai: *pang tukkarakiriya*) The English descriptive phrase for the Thai: *pang tukkarakiriya*. See: *pang tukkarakiriya*. (DRN 35, JBo, PSS)

pitri mudra -- (Ind.: *pitṛ-mudrā*) A hand pose, a seal, a dramatic (Ind.: *nāṭya*) *mudra* or gesture (Ind.: *darpaṇa*) held or formed by a performer, dancer or actor. The *pitri mudra* is a combined (Ind.: *saṁyutta*) form, held by both hands. One of eleven mudras representing "relationships" and one which denotes father. This *mudra* is formed by: left palm faces outward, fingers extended, together and pointing upwards, relaxed, the thumb extends away from the fingers, and level with the chest; right palm faces mid-line, fingers brought into the palm forming a fist, thumb extends upwards. (ACG 44) (See: **Figure 449**)

porcupine deer mudra -- (Eng.; Ind.: *candra-mṛga mudra*) The English term for *chandra-mriga mudra*. See: *chandra-mriga mudra*. (ACG 49)

pothi mudra -- (Ind.: *pothī-mudrā* aka *tripiṭaka mudrā*; Jap.: *ma no cho jo-in* [*mudra*]) A *mudra*, a ritual hand pose, a seal, a *tantric mudra* which is common to the Japanese Buddhist (*Vajrayana, Mantrayana*) tradition and is held or formed by a devotee or priest during the rites of *Garbhadhatu Mandala, Vajradhatu Mandala, Homa Rites* and other rites. It may be accompanied by a *mantra*. The *pothi mudra* is a combined (Ind.: *saṁyutta*) form, held by both hands. It denotes invulnerability to malevolent spirits. This *mudra* is formed by: left palm facing upwards, fingers and thumb extended towards the midline, right palm facing downwards, fingers and thumb extended towards the midline and resting upon the left hand. Thus formed the *mudra* is held in the lap. (GDe 172, LCS 156) (See: **Figure 450**)

pralambam mudra -- (Ind.: *pralambam-mudrā*) A mudra, a ritual hand pose, a seal, a mudra which is common to yogic tradition, particularly the *Yoga Tatva Mudra Vigyan* form, and is held by a devotee or practitioner. The *pralambam*[79] *mudra* is a combined (Ind.: *saṁyutta*) form, held by both hands. It is one of the twenty-four *mudras* held before the *Gayatri Jap* of the thirty-two total *Gayatri mudras*.[80] It is utilized for all sickness, especially cancer. This *mudra* is formed by: palms face midline, fingers and thumbs are together and point downwards. Thus formed the two hands are held side by side, but not touching and the *mudra* is held at and below the waist. (KDe) (See: **Figure 451**)

pranama mudra -- (Ind.: *praṇāma mudrā*; Jap.: *haranama gassho* [*mudra*]) The Indic term for *haranama gassho* (*mudra*). See: *haranama gassho* (*mudra*). (EDS 41)

pran mudra -- (Ind.: *prāṇa-mudrā*) A *mudra*, a ritual hand pose, a seal, a *mudra* which is common to yogic tradition, particularly the *Yoga Tatva Mudra Vigyan* form, and is held by a devotee or practitioner. The *pran mudra* is a single (Ind.: *asaṁyutta*) form, held by one hand. It is utilized for lack of energy and recuperation. This *mudra* is formed by: the palm forward, the index and middle fingers extended upwards, the ring and little fingers curl together towards the palm and the tip of the thumb touches the tips of those two fingers. (KDe 39) (See: **Figure 452**)

prasada mudra -- (Ind.: *prasāda-mudrā* aka *varada mudrā*) A variant term applied to *varada mudra*. See: *varada mudra*. (MJS 113)

pravartita mudra -- (Ind.: *pravartita-mudrā* aka *pravartitahasta*) A variant term applied to *pravartitahasta*. See: *pravartitahasta*. (RSG 63)

pravartitahasta (mudra) -- (Ind.: *pravartitahasta* [*mudrā*] aka *pravartita mudrā*) A *mudra*, a ritual hand pose, a seal, which is common to the Hindu tradition. It is generally used in the dance and denotes turning or a resolve. The form is held in one hand: upper arm parallel with the shoulders, forearm bent at the elbow, palm faces backwards), fingers and thumb are extended upwards. (MJS 113, RSG 63) (See: **Figure 453**)

prithvi mudra -- (Ind.: *pṛthvī-mudrā*) A *mudra*, a ritual hand pose, a seal, a *mudra* which is common to yogic tradition, particularly the *Yoga Tatva Mudra Vigyan* form, and is held by a devotee or practitioner. The *prithvi mudra* is a single (Ind.: *asaṁyutta*) form, held by one hand. It is utilized for vitamin deficiency, foster broad mindedness and patience. This *mudra* is formed

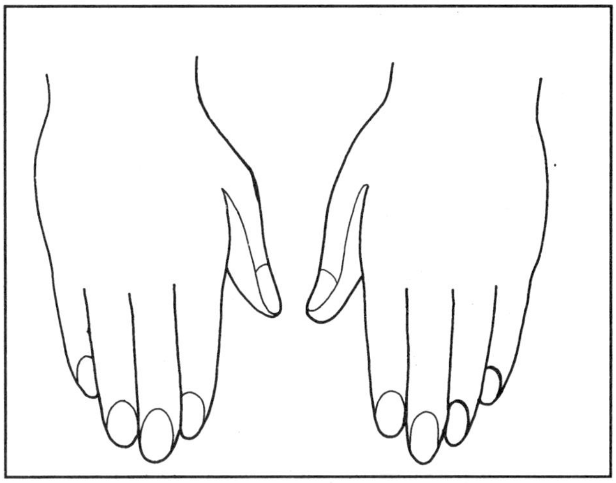

Figure 451 -- pralambam mudra
(as seen by another)

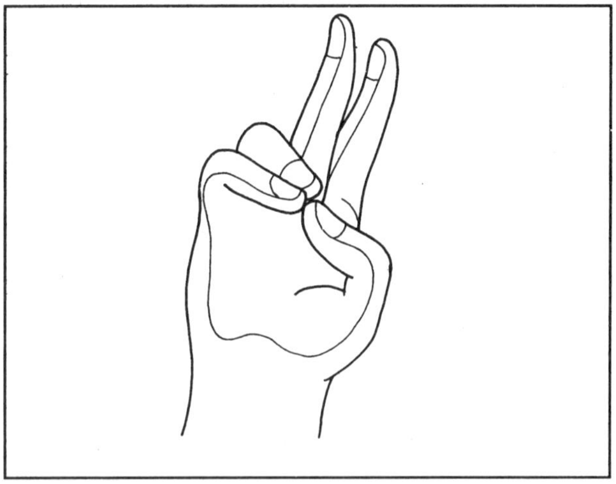

Figure 452 -- pran mudra
(as seen by another)

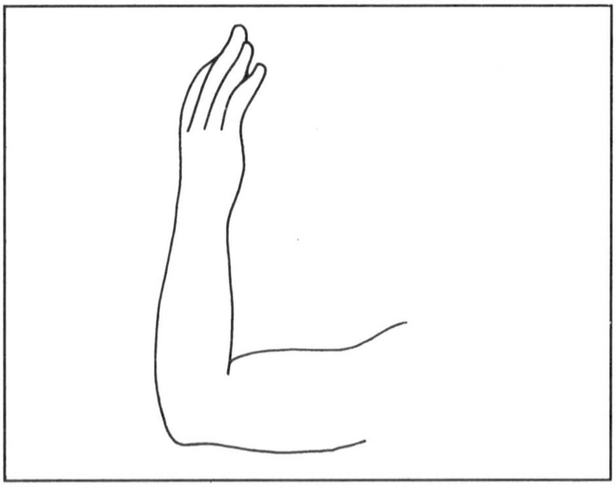

Figure 453 -- pravartitahasta (mudra)
(as seen by another)

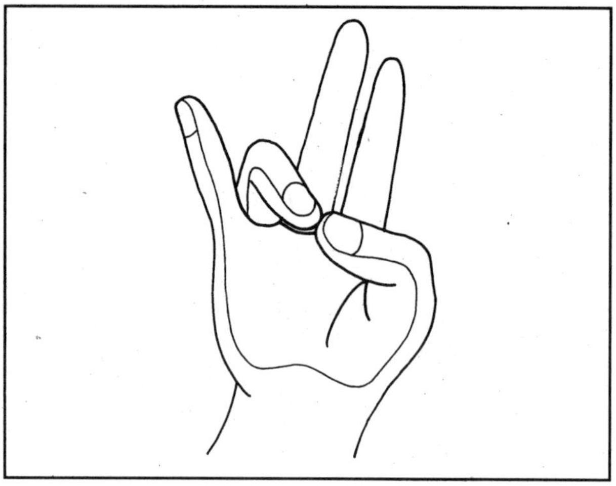

Figure 454 -- prithvi mudra
(as seen by another)

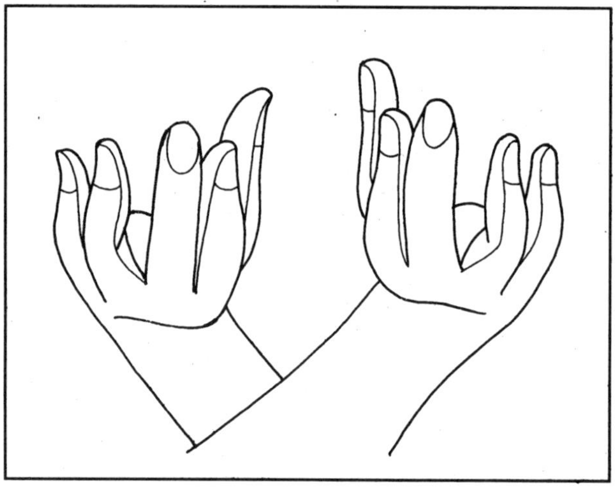

Figure 455 -- puga mudra
(as seen by another)

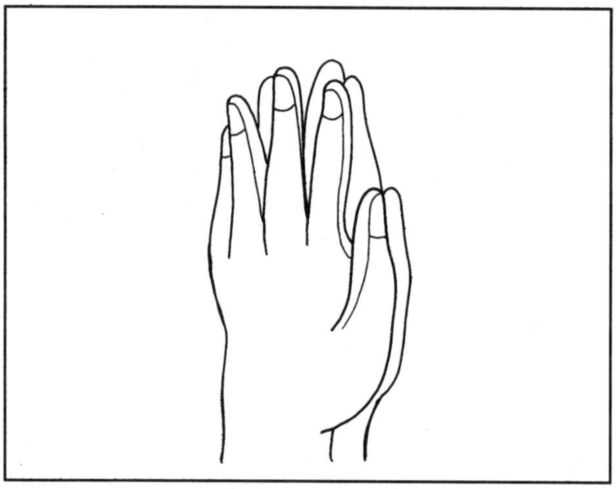

Figure 456 -- puna mudra
(as seen by the holder)

by: palm facing forwards, index, middle and little fingers extend upwards, ring finger folds towards the palm and its tip is touched by the tip of the thumb. It resembles the *kartari mudra*. (KDe 41) (See: **Figure 454**)

puga mudra -- (Ind.: *pūga-mudrā*) A hand pose, a seal, a dramatic (Ind.: *nāṭya*) *mudra* or gesture (Ind.: *darpaṇa*) held or formed by a performer, dancer or actor. It denotes the *puga* or *areca*-nut tree. The *puga mudra* is a combined (Ind.: *saṁyutta*) form, held by both hands. This *mudra* is formed by; palms faces upwards, fingers and thumbs are separated and gently curl inwards, towards the hollowed palms. Thus formed the hands are crossed at the wrist. It is based upon the *padmakosha mudra*. (ACG 49) (See: **Figure 455**)

pu mu-yin (mudra) -- (Chin.: *pu mu-yin* [*mudrā*]; Ind.: *pañca-nayana mudrā*; Jap.: *bu mo-in* [*mudra*]) The Chinese term for *bu mo-in* (*mudra*). See: *bu mo-in* (*mudra*). (GDe 51)

puna mudra -- (Ind.: *pūṇa-mudrā*; Jap.: *boda gassho* [*mudra*], *mi be renge gassho* [*mudra*]) A *mudra*, a ritual hand pose, a seal, a *tantric mudra* which is common to the Japanese Buddhist (*Vajrayana, Mantrayana*) tradition and is held or formed by a devotee or priest during the rites of *Garbhadhatu Mandala, Vajradhatu Mandala, Homa Rites* and other rites. It may be accompanied by a *mantra*. The *puna mudra* is a combined (Ind.: *saṁyutta*) form, held by both hands. It denotes purification. This *mudra* is similar to the *anjali mudra* and is formed by: bring the hands together, palm to palm, fingers and thumbs extended upwards and together--i.e., touching their counterparts--except the middle and ring fingers which are separated slightly. (GDe 6, LCS 73) (See: **Figure 456**)

purn-gyan mudra -- (Ind.: *pūrṇa-gyān-mudrā* aka *pūrṇa-jñāna-mudrā*) A *mudra*, a ritual hand pose, a seal, a *mudra* which is common to yogic tradition, particularly the *Yoga Tatva Mudra Vigyan* form, and is held by a devotee or practitioner. The *purn-gyan mudra* is a combined (Ind.: *saṁyutta*) form, held by both hands. It is utilized for controlling addiction as well as controlling excess passion. This *mudra* is formed in both hands by: the tips of the thumb and index finger touch, middle, ring and little fingers are relaxed, slightly separated and point upwards. Thus formed the right hand is held in front of the right side of the chest, while the left rests, palm upwards on the left knee. (KDe 24) (See: **Figure 457**)

punnaga mudra -- (Ind.: *punnāga-mudrā*) A hand pose, a seal, a dramatic (Ind.: *nāṭya*) *mudra* or gesture (Ind.: *darpaṇa*) held or formed by a performer, dancer or actor. It denotes the *punnaga* tree. The *punnaga mudra* is a combined (Ind.: *saṁyutta*) form, held by both hands. This mudra is formed by: right palm facing outward, fingers and thumb extended, together and pointing upwards, relaxed, slightly cupped and generally on a line level with the chest; left palm facing forwards, the fingers, together and extended upwards, the little finger is separated slightly, the tip of the thumb crosses the palm and touches the base of the ring finger. This *mudra* is derived from the *pataka mudra* and *chatura mudra*. (ACG 48) (See: **Figure 458**)

Purukutsa mudra -- (Ind.: *Purukutsa-mudrā*) A hand pose, a seal, a dramatic (Ind.: *nāṭya*) *mudra* or gesture (Ind.: *darpaṇa*) held or formed by a performer, dancer or actor. The *Purukutsa mudra* is a single (Ind.: *asaṁyutta*) form, held by one hand. It denotes *Purukutsa*, one of a number of famous rulers or heroes. The *mudra* employed is identical in form to the *alapadma mudra*. See: *alapadma mudra*. (ACG 47)

Pururavas mudra -- (Ind.: *Purūravas-mudrā*) A hand pose, a seal, a dramatic (Ind.: *nāṭya*) *mudra* or gesture (Ind.: *darpaṇa*) held or formed by a performer, dancer or actor. The *Pururavas mudra* is a single (Ind.: *asaṁyutta*) form, held by one hand. It denotes *Pururavas*, one of a number of famous rulers or heroes. The *mudra* employed is identical in form to the *mushti mudra*. See: *mushti mudra*. (ACG 47)

purusha-ratna mudra -- (Ind.: *puruṣa-ratna-mudrā*) This is an assigned term.[81] A *mudra*, a ritual hand pose, a seal, which is common to the Buddhist (*Vajrayana*) tradition, a *tantric mudra*. It denotes the gift of a precious minister (Tib.: *blon-po*) associated with the *saptaratna* (Tib.: *rgyal-srid sna-bdun*) or seven gems of sovereignty (Tib.: *nor-bu-chab-bdun*), also referred to as the 'space vast treasury,' particularly as it is associated with the worship of the powerful *Vajrayana* goddess, *Tara*. The *purusha-ratna mudra* is a combined (Ind.: *saṁyutta*)

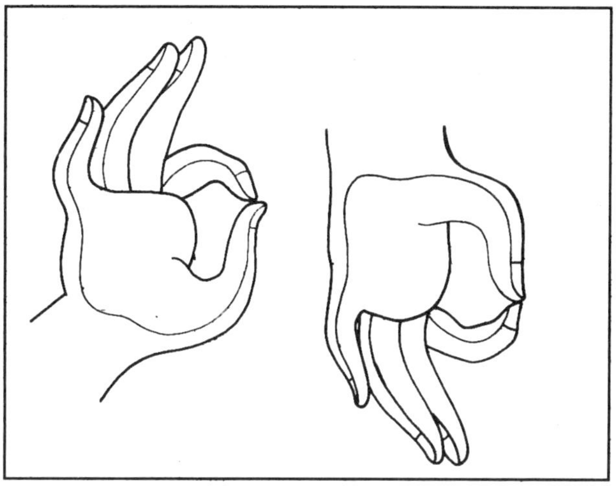

Figure 457 -- purn-gyan mudra
(as seen by another)

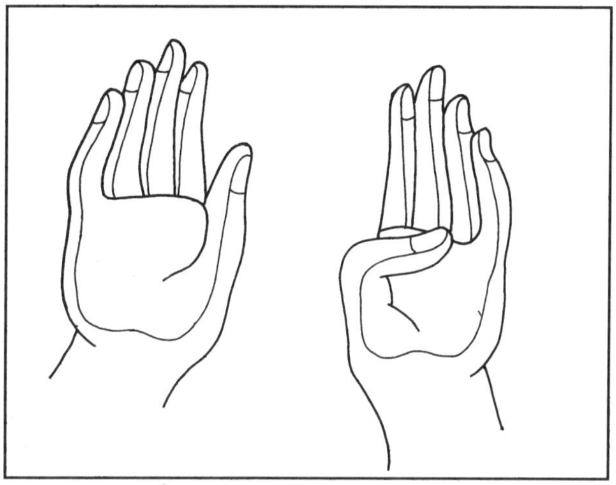

Figure 458 -- punnaga mudra
(as seen by another)

Figure 459 -- purusha-ratna mudra
(as seen by another)

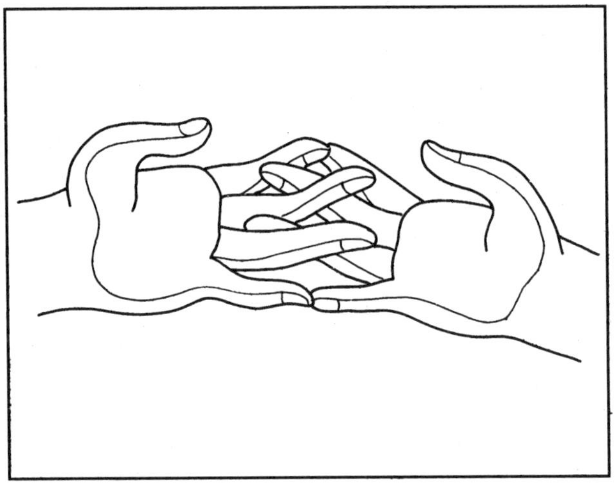

Figure 460 -- pushpa-mala mudra I
(as seen by the holder)

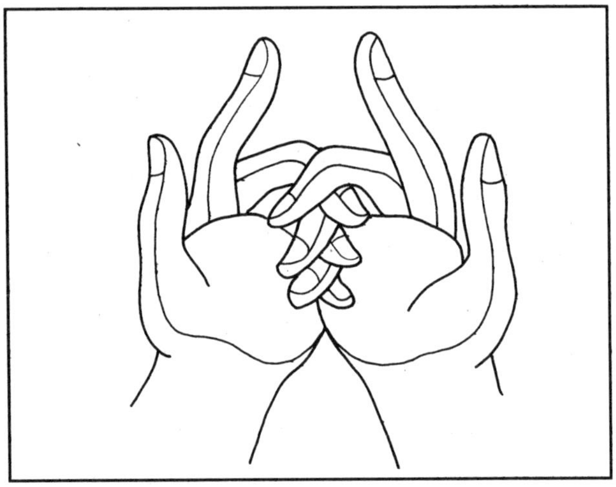

Figure 461 -- pushpa-mala mudra II
(as seen by the holder)

form, held by both hands. This *mudra* is identical in both hands and formed by: palms face downwards, tip of the thumb touches index finger's tip, middle finger extends upwards, ring and little fingers curl towards the palm, thus formed the tips of the middle fingers touch as do the whole of the second phalanges of the index, ring and little fingers. The *mantra* associated with this *mudra* is: "*OM Stri-ratna Praticcha HUM SVAHA.*"[82] (SBe 152) (See: **Figure 459**)

pushpa-mala mudra I -- (Ind.: *puṣpa-mālā-mudrā*); Jap.: *ke man-in* [*mudra*]) A *mudra*, a ritual hand pose, a seal, a *tantric mudra* which is common to the Japanese Buddhist (*Vajrayana, Mantrayana*) tradition and is held or formed by a devotee or priest during various rites. It may be accompanied by a *mantra*. The *pushpa-mala mudra* is a combined (Ind.: *saṁyutta*) form, held by both hands. It denotes a garland of flowers. This *mudra* is formed by: palms face upwards, fingers and thumbs extend towards the midline, slightly curled, first phalanges of the fingers interlace. (GDe 47) (See: **Figure 460**)

pushpa-mala mudra II -- (Ind.: *puṣpa-mālā-mudrā*) A *mudra*, a ritual hand pose, a seal, a *tantric mudra* which is common to the Japanese Buddhist (*Vajrayana, Mantrayana*) tradition and is held or formed by a devotee or priest during the *Eighteen Rites*. It may be accompanied by a *mantra*. The *pushpa-mala mudra* is a combined (Ind.: *saṁyutta*) form, held by both hands. It denotes a garland of flowers. This *mudra* is formed by: outside edges of the hand are brought together, middle, ring and little fingers interlace towards the palms, index fingers extend upward and curl slightly but do not touch, thumbs extend upwards. (LCS 61) (See: **Figure 461**)

pushpanjali (mudra) -- (Ind.: *puṣpāñjali* [*mudrā*]) ("a salutation of flowers") A *mudra*, a ritual hand pose, a seal, which is common to the Hindu tradition. It denotes the offering of flowers or worship. The *pushpanjali* (*mudra*) is a combined (Ind.: *saṁyutta*) form, held by both hands. This *mudra* is formed by: both hands are cupped, touching along the outside edge and the depression may hold flowers. (MJS 114) (See: **Figure 462**)

pushpa mudra[83] -- (Ind.: *puṣpa* [*mudrā*]; Jap.: *ke bosatsu* [*mudra*]) The Indic term for *ke bosatsu* (*mudra*). See: *ke bosatsu* (*mudra*). (GDe 79)

pushpaputa mudra -- (Ind.: *puṣpapuṭa-mudrā*) ("flower casket") A *mudra*, a ritual hand pose, a seal, which is common to the Hindu tradition. Also, a hand pose, a seal, a dramatic (Ind.: *nāṭya*) *mudra* or gesture (Ind.: *darpaṇa*) held or formed by a performer, dancer or actor. The *pushpaputa mudra* is a combined (Ind.: *saṁyutta*) form, held by both hands. It denotes the offering of water, flowers (Ind.: *puṣpa*), etc.[84] This *mudra* is formed by: palms face upwards, fingers and thumbs extended and are slightly cupped, thus formed the hands are brought together and touch along the outer edge of the palms and little fingers. Thus posed, the *mudra* is held at chest level. (ACG 40, MJS 114) (See: **Figure 463**)

pushpe mudra -- (Ind.: *puṣpe-mudrā*) This is an assigned term.[85] A *mudra*, a ritual hand pose, a seal, which is common to the Buddhist (*Vajrayana*) tradition, a *tantric mudra*. It denotes flowers, which is one of the five 'gifts' or 'outer offerings' proffered to a divine guest--the other four being: incense, lamps, perfume and food--during the early stages worship, particularly as associated with the worship of the powerful *Vajrayana* goddess, *Tara*. The *pushpe mudra* is a combined (Ind.: *saṁyutta*) form, held by both hands. This *mudra* is formed by hands in mirror-pose: palms face upwards, middle, ring and little fingers are brought into the palm, the thumb holds the three fingers in place by touching the first phalanges, the index finger extends outwards, so formed the two hands are brought together, touching along the third phalanges of the little fingers. Thus posed, the *mudra* is held at chest level. The *mantra* associated with this mudra is: "*OM Guru-sarva-Tathagata Dhupe Puja-megha-samudra-spharana-samaye HUM*."[86] (SBe 147) (See: **Figure 464**)

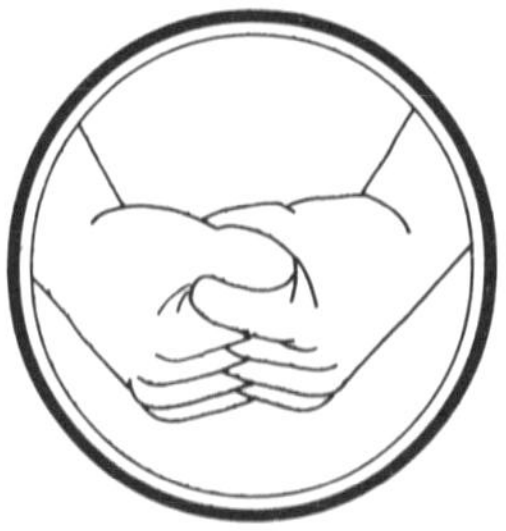

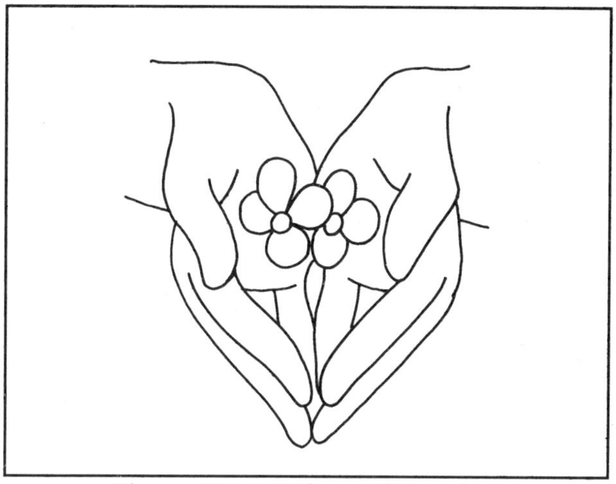

Figure 462 -- pushpanjali (mudra)
(as seen by another)

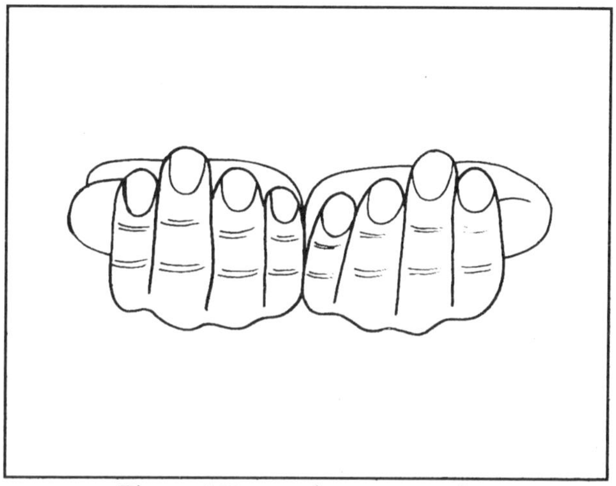

Figure 463 -- pushpaputa mudra
(as seen by another)

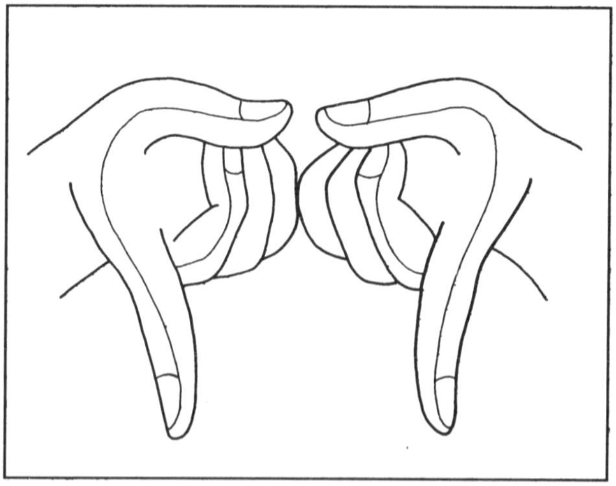

Figure 464 -- pushpe mudra
(as seen by another)

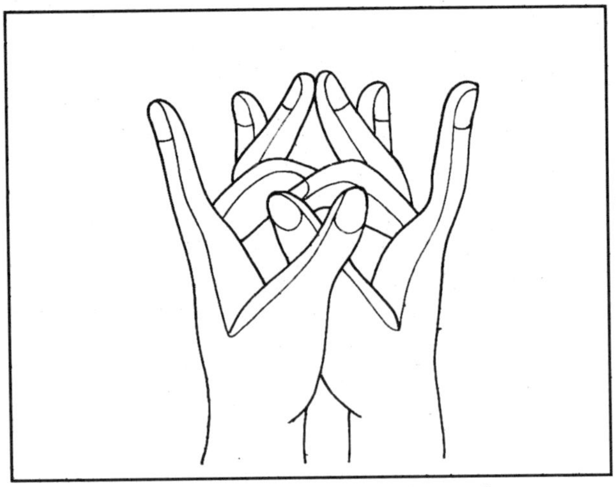

Figure 465 -- Ragaraja Mula-mudra
(as seen by the holder)

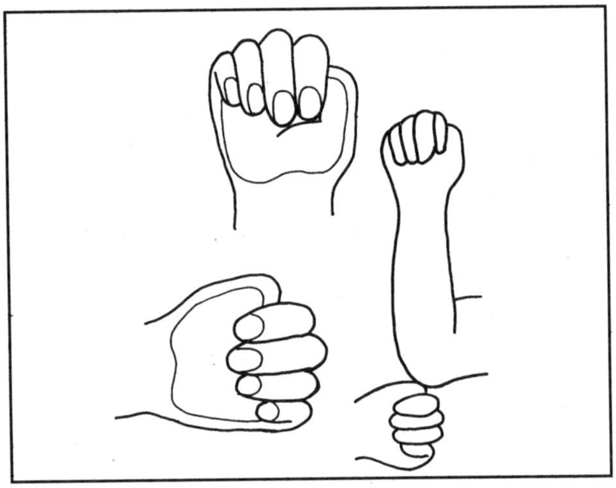

Figure 466 -- Ragavajra mudra
(as seen by the holder)

-- R --

Ragaraja Mula-mudra -- (Ind.: *Rāgarāja Mūla-mudrā*) A *mudra*, a ritual hand pose, a seal, a *tantric mudra* which is common to the Japanese Buddhist (*Vajrayana, Mantrayana*) tradition and is held or formed by a devotee or priest during various rites in which a deity is acknowledged. It is a *mudra* which is associated with the deity *Ragaraja*. It may be accompanied by a *mantra*. The *Ragaraja Mula-mudra* is a combined (Ind.: *saṁyutta*) form, held by both hands. This *mudra* is formed by: palms facing midline and close thumbs and ring fingers touch at their tips forming a circle, index and little fingers extend upwards, middle fingers touch at their tips. Thus formed the 'circled' thumbs and ring fingers inter-link.[1] (LCS 261) (See: **Figure 465**)

Ragavajra mudra -- (Ind.: *Rāgavajra-mudrā*) A *mudra*, a ritual hand pose, a seal, a *tantric mudra* which is common to the Japanese Buddhist (*Vajrayana, Mantrayana*) tradition and is held or formed by a devotee or priest during the rites of *Garbhadhatu Mandala, Vajradhatu Mandala, Homa Rites* and other rites. It may be accompanied by a *mantra*. The *Ragavajra mudra* is a combined (Ind.: *saṁyutta*) form, held by both hands. It This *mudra* is formed by: thumbs folded into the palms, index, middle ring and little fingers folded into the palms and over the thumbs. Thus formed, the right palm faces midline and held level with the chin, the left hand faces the midline and the "fist" touches the right elbow. (GDe 245, LCS 103) (See: **Figure 466**)

Raghuramavatara mudra -- (Ind.: *Raghurāmāvatāra-mudrā*) ("the descent of *Raghu*") A hand pose, a seal, a dramatic (Ind.: *nāṭya*) *mudra* or gesture (Ind.: *darpaṇa*) held or formed by a performer, dancer or actor. The *Raghuramavatara mudra* is a combined (Ind.: *saṁyutta*) form, held by both hands. It denotes *Ramavatara*, one of the ten *avatars* (Ind.: *daśāvatāras*) of the Lord *Vishnu* This *mudra* is formed by: right palm faces the midline, the middle, ring and little fingers fold into the palm, the thumb lies over the first phalanges of the fingers, index finger curls over the top of the thumb; left palm faces mid-line, fingers brought into the palm forming a fist, thumb extends upwards. (ACG 46) (See: **Figure 467**)

Rahu mudra -- (Ind.: *Rāhu-mudrā*) A hand pose, a seal, a dramatic (Ind.: *nāṭya*) *mudra* or gesture (Ind.: *darpaṇa*) held or formed by a performer, dancer or actor. The *Rahu mudra* is a combined (Ind.: *saṁyutta*) form, held by both hands. It denotes the ascending node of the moon, one of the nine planets (Ind.: *navagraha*). This *mudra* is formed by: right palm faces outwards, the index finger and the thumb point upwards, together, the middle, ring and little fingers are folded into the palm; left palm facing forwards, the thumb is against the index finger's base, the index, middle, ring and little fingers curl, half-way towards the palm. (ACG 46) (See: **Figure 468**)

rasala mudra -- (Ind.: *rasāla-mudrā*) A hand pose, a seal, a dramatic (Ind.: *nāṭya*) *mudra* or gesture (Ind.: *darpaṇa*) held or formed by a performer, dancer or actor. It denotes the *rasala* or mango tree. The *mudra* employed is identical in form to the *tripitaka mudra*. See: *tripitaka mudra*. (ACG 49)

ratna-ghata mudra -- (Ind.: *ratna-ghaṭa-mudrā* aka *citta mudrā*) ("*mudra* of the jewel jar") A *mudra*, a ritual hand pose, a seal, a *tantric mudra* which is common to the Japanese Buddhist (*Vajrayana, Mantrayana*) tradition and is held or formed by a devotee or priest during various rites. It may be accompanied by a *mantra*. The *ratna-ghata mudra* is a combined (Ind.: *saṁyutta*) form, held by both hands. This *mudra* is formed by: the palms touch at the 'heels,' middle, ring and little fingers extend and touch at their tips, a narrow space is left between the hands, the thumbs touch along their outer length and extend upward, the index fingers bend at the first and second joints and their tips rest behind the tips of the thumbs. The *mudra* so formed is held at chest level. (GDe 141) (See: **Figure 469**)

ratna mudra I -- (Ind.: *ratna-mudrā*) ("the *mudra* of the jewel") A *mudra*, a ritual hand pose, a seal, a *tantric mudra* which is common to the Japanese Buddhist (*Vajrayana, Mantrayana*) tradition and is held or formed by a devotee or priest during the rites of *Garbhadhatu Mandala, Vajradhatu Mandala, Homa Rites* and other rites. It may be accompanied by a *mantra*. The *ratna*

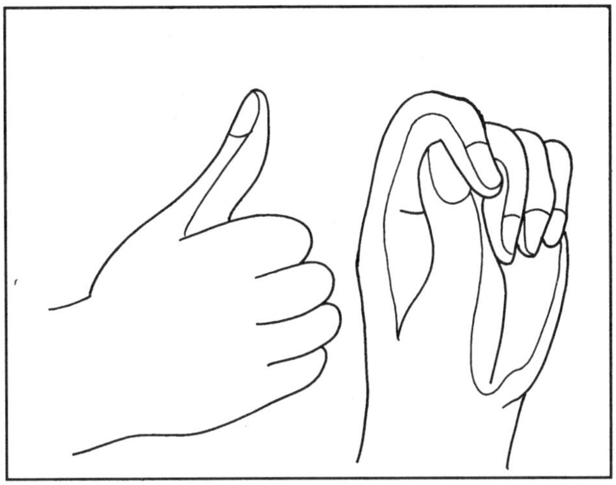

Figure 467 -- Raghuramavatara mudra
(as seen by another)

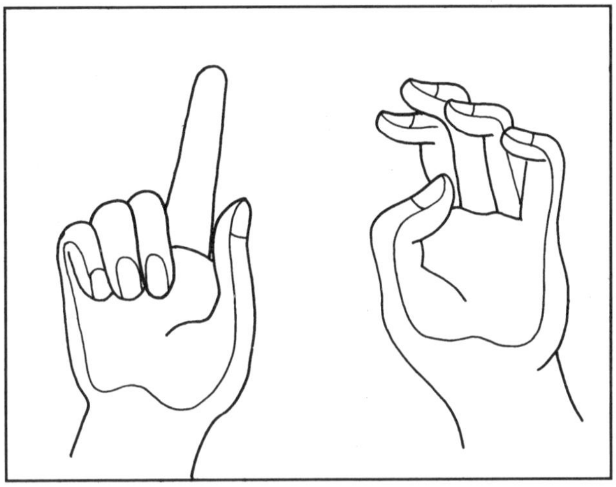

Figure 468 -- Rahu mudra
(as seen by another)

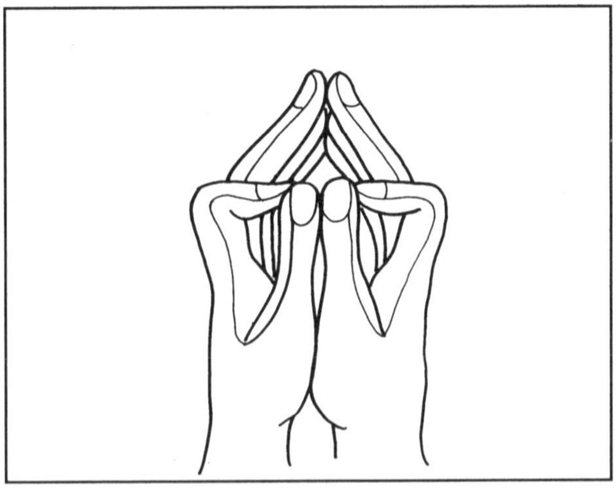

Figure 469 -- ratna-ghata mudra
(as seen by the holder)

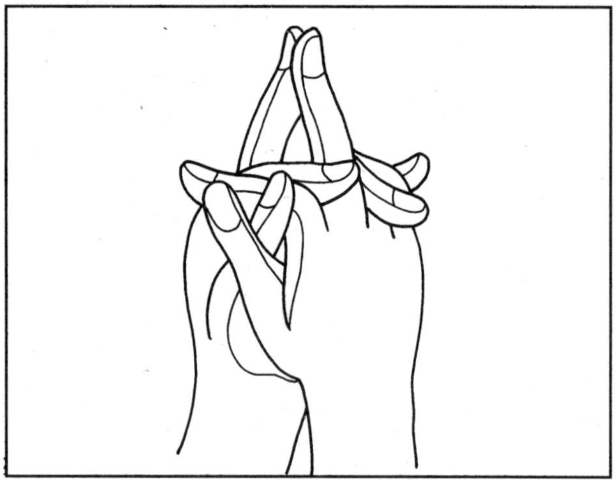

Figure 470 -- ratna mudra I
(as seen by the holder)

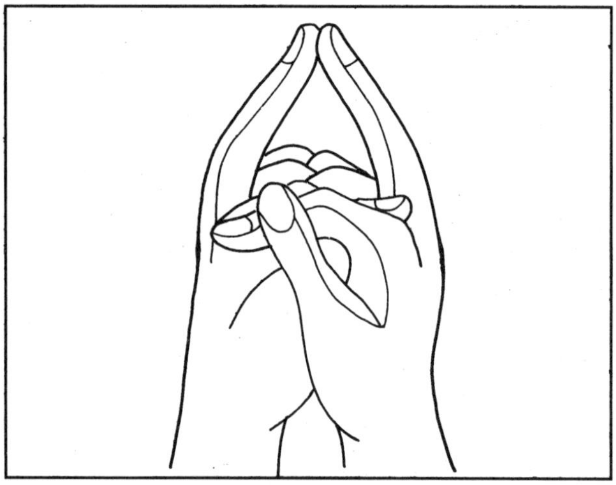

Figure 471 -- ratna mudra II
(as seen by the holder)

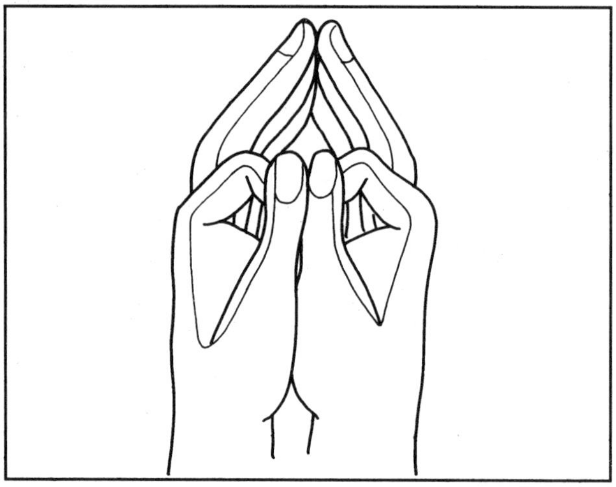

Figure 472 -- ratna-kalasha mudra
(as seen by the holder)

mudra is a combined (Ind.: *saṁyutta*) form, held by both hands. It denotes the jewel which is often associated with *Ratnasambhava*. This *mudra* is formed by: palms brought close together, thumbs cross, index, ring and little fingers interlace and rest on the backs of the opposite hand, middle fingers extend upwards and touch at the tip. (GDe 259, LCS 87) (See: **Figure 470**)

ratna mudra II -- (Ind.: *ratna-mudrā*) ("the *mudra* of the jewel") A *mudra*, a ritual hand pose, a seal, a *tantric mudra* which is common to the Japanese Buddhist (*Vajrayana, Mantrayana*) tradition and is held or formed by a devotee or priest. It may be accompanied by a *mantra*. The *ratna mudra* is a combined (Ind.: *saṁyutta*) form, held by both hands. It denotes the jewel which is often associated with *Ratnasambhava*. This *mudra* is formed by: palms brought close together, thumbs cross, left tucked inward, index, ring and little fingers interlace and rest on the backs of the opposite hand, middle fingers curls slightly and touch at the tip. (LCS 223) (See: **Figure 471**)

ratna-kalasha mudra -- (Ind.: *ratna-kalaśa-mudrā*) A *mudra*, a ritual hand pose, a seal, a *tantric mudra* which is common to the Japanese Buddhist (*Vajrayana, Mantrayana*) tradition and is held or formed by a devotee or priest during the rites of *Garbhadhatu Mandala* and other rites. It may be accompanied by a mantra. The *ratna-kalasha mudra*[2] is a combined (Ind.: *saṁyutta*) form, held by both hands. This *mudra* is formed by: palms face midline and touch, thumbs extend upward and touch along their length, index fingers curl , their tips behind the tips of the thumbs, middle, ring and little fingers extend and touch at their tips. (LCS 254) (See: **Figure 472**)

Ratnaprabha-Akashagarbha mudra -- (Ind.: *Ratnaprabhā-Ākāśagarbha-mudrā*) A *mudra*, a ritual hand pose, a seal, a *tantric mudra* which is common to the Japanese Buddhist (*Vajrayana, Mantrayana*) tradition and is held or formed by a devotee or priest during various rites in which a deity is acknowledged. It is a mudra which is associated with the deity *Ratnaprabha-Akashagarbha*. It may be accompanied by a *mantra*. The *Ratnaprabha-Akashagarbha mudra*[3] is a combined (Ind.: *saṁyutta*) form, held by both hands. This *mudra* is formed by: palms facing the midline and close, thumbs crossed, right over left, index and middle fingers arch over and touch at tips, ring and little fingers interlace on top of the hands. (LCS 247) (See: **Figure 473**)

ratna-vahana mudra -- (Ind.: *ratna-vāhana-mudrā*) A *mudra*, a ritual hand pose, a seal, a *tantric mudra* which is common to the Japanese Buddhist (*Vajrayana, Mantrayana*) tradition and is held or formed by a devotee or priest during the *Eighteen Rites*. It may be accompanied by a *mantra*. The *ratna-vahana mudra*[4] is a combined (Ind.: *saṁyutta*) form, held by both hands. It denotes the reception of a deity. This *mudra* is formed by: palms face midline and are brought together, touching along the outside edges of the palms and thumbs. index, ring and little fingers curl slightly touching at their tips, middle finger folds at the third knuckle and interlaces with its opposite. See also: *ratna-ghata-mudra*. (LCS 62) (See: **Figure 474**)

Ravana mudra -- (Ind.: *Rāvaṇa-mudrā*) A hand pose, a seal, a dramatic (Ind.: *nāṭya*) mudra or gesture (Ind.: *darpaṇa*) held or formed by a performer, dancer or actor. The *Ravana mudra* is a combined (Ind.: *saṁyutta*) form, held by both hands. It denotes the *rakshasa Ravana*, one of a number of famous rulers or heroes. The *Ravana mudra* is a combined (Ind.: *saṁyutta*) form, held by both hands. This *mudra* is formed by: palms facing outward, fingers and thumbs extended, pointing upwards, splayed and generally on a line level with the chest. Thus formed the *mudra* is held chest high, hands to the side of the shoulders. (ACG 47) (See: **Figure 475**)

receiving the mango mudra -- (Eng.; Ind.: *añcita-nidrātahasta mudrā*; Thai: *pang rab-pholmamuang*) The English descriptive phrase for the Thai *pang rab-pholmamuang*. See: *pang rab-pholmamuang*. (DRN 37, JBo 205, ODD 680, OFr 22, PSS)

receiving the offering of water mudra -- (Eng.; Ind.: *dhyāna-nidrātahasta mudrā*; Thai: **pang ODD #55**) The English descriptive phrase for the Thai: **pang ODD #55**. See: **pang ODD #55**. (DRN 36, JBo 205, ODD 678, OFr 23, PSS)

rechita mudra -- (Ind.: *recita-mudrā*) A hand pose, a seal, a dramatic (Ind.: *nāṭya*) *mudra* or gesture (Ind.:

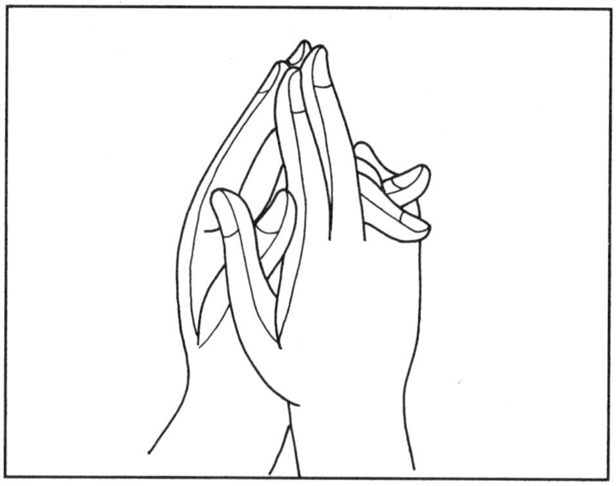

Figure 473 -- Ratnaprabha-Akashagarbha mudra
(as seen by the holder)

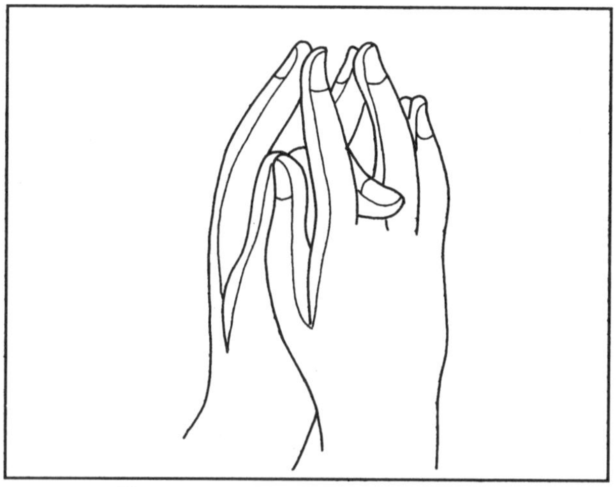

Figure 474 -- ratna-vahana mudra
(as seen by the holder)

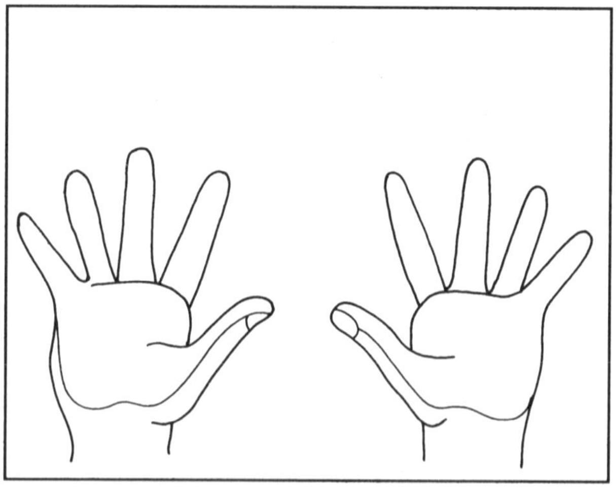

Figure 475 -- Ravana mudra
(as seen by the holder)

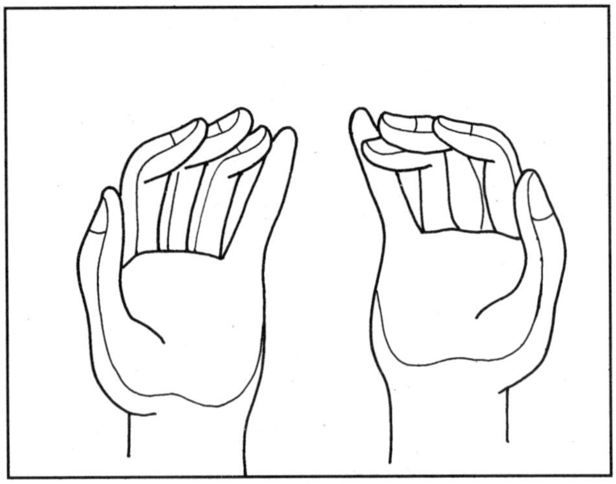

Figure 476 -- rechita mudra
(as seen by the holder)

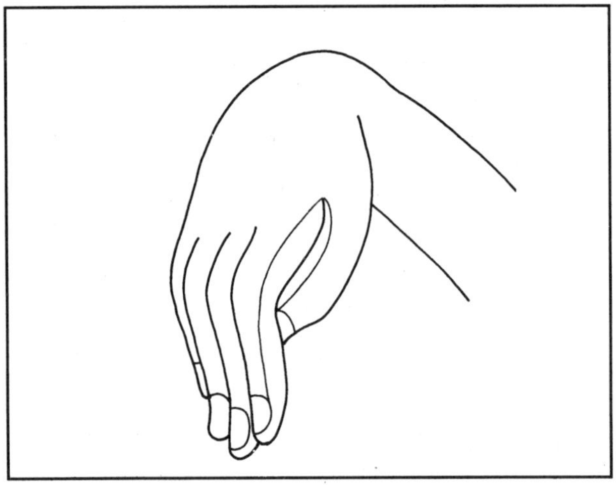

Figure 477 -- rei-in (mudra)
(as seen by another)

darpaṇa) held or formed by a performer, dancer or actor. The *rechita mudra* is a combined (Ind.: *saṁyutta*) form, held by both hands. It denotes holding children and holding a painted panel. This *mudra* is formed by: palms face upwards, the index, middle and ring fingers curl towards the palms, the thumbs rests along the curled index fingers, the little fingers are straight and pointing outwards, Thus formed the hands are held in front of the trunk, close, but not touching. (ACG 42) (See: **Figure 476**)

reclining mudra -- (Eng.; Ind.: *śayana mudrā*; Thai: *pang parinippharn, pang s[h]aiyas*; Indic: *shayana mudra*) The English descriptive phrase for the Thai pang *parinippharn* or *pang s(h)aiyas*. See: *shayana mudra*. (DRN 37, JBo 205, ODD 680, OFr [#33],PSS)

reflecting mudra -- (Eng.; Ind.: *jñāna-jñāna mudrā*; Thai: *pang ram-pueng*) The English descriptive phrase for the Thai *pang ram-pueng*. See: *pang ram-pueng II*. (DRN 37, JBo 205, ODD 279, OFr 16, PSS)

reflecting on worldly impermanence mudra -- (Eng. aka *contemplating the corpse mudra*; Ind.: *ahāyavarada-jñāna mudrā, ahayavarada-kaṭaka mudrā*; Thai: *pang plong-kammathan*) An English descriptive phrase for the Thai *pang plong-kammathan*. See: *pang plong-kammathan*. (ODD 680, OFr 25, DRN, JBo)

rei-in (mudra) -- (Jap.: *rei-in [mudrā]*; Ind.: *ghaṇṭā mudrā*) ("the bell") A *mudra*, a ritual hand pose, a seal, a *tantric mudra* which is common to the Japanese Buddhist (*Vajrayana, Mantrayana*) tradition and is held or formed by a devotee or priest during the rites of *Garbhadhatu Mandala, Vajradhatu Mandala, Homa Rites* and other rites. It may be accompanied by a *mantra*. The *rei-in* (*mudra*) is a single (Ind.: *asaṁyutta*) form, held by one hand. It denotes joy, contentment and the arrival of deities in the temple. This *mudra* is formed by: the right hand, fingers together, thumb rests on the inside touching the middle finger. Thus formed, the hand bends downward at the wrist and is rotated towards the midline. (GDe 41) (See: **Figure 477**)

rekha mudra -- (Ind.: *rekhā-mudrā*) A hand pose, a seal, a dramatic (Ind.: *nāṭya*) mudra or gesture (Ind.: *darpaṇa*) held or formed by a performer, dancer or actor noted in ACG but without description. (ACG 44)

renge-bu shu-in (mudra) -- (Jap.: *renge-bu shu-in* [*mudrā*]) A *mudra*, a ritual hand pose, a seal, a *tantric mudra* which is common to the Japanese Buddhist (*Vajrayana, Mantrayana*) tradition and is held or formed by a devotee or priest during the rites of *Garbhadhatu Mandala, Vajradhatu Mandala, Homa Rites* and other rites. It may be accompanied by a *mantra*. The *renge-bu shu-in*[5] (*mudra*) is a combined (Ind.: *saṁyutta*) form, held by both hands. This *mudra* is formed by: the palms brought together, index, middle and ring fingers interlaced and resting on the back of the hand, thumb and little fingers extend straight up and touch their counterparts. (GDe 64, LCS 83) (See: **Figure 478**)

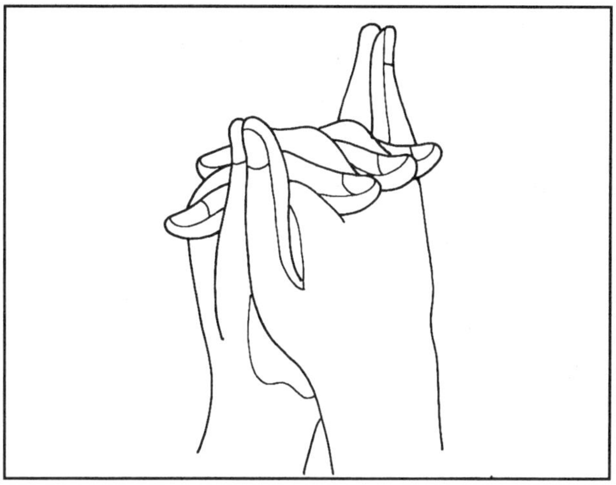

Figure 478 -- renge-bu shu-in (mudra)
(as seen by the holder)

renge ken-in (mudra) -- (Jap.: *renge ken-in* [*mudrā*]; Ind.: *padma-muṣṭi*) A *mudra*, a ritual hand pose, a seal, which is common to the Japanese Buddhist tradition. It is one of the six, elemental fist positions, is considered to be a mother sign and may represent an lotus bud. The *renge ken-in* (*mudra*) is a single (Ind.: *asaṁyutta*) form, held by one hand. This *mudra* is formed by the right hand: the hand is fisted, thumb outside, resting against the index finger. Thus formed, the *mudra* is usually held chest-high. (EDS 39) (See: **Figure 479**)

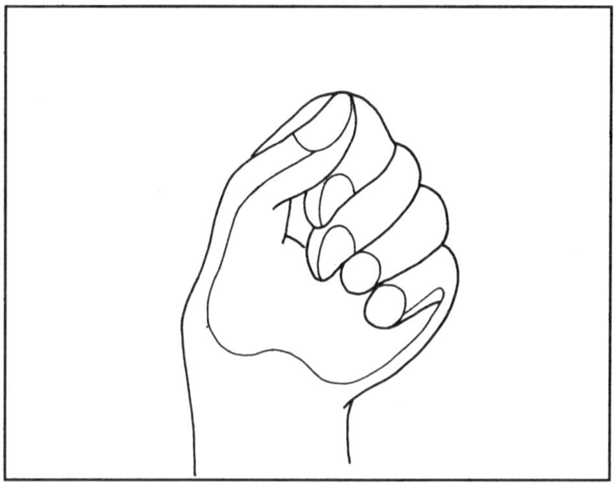

Figure 479 -- renge ken-in (mudra)
(as seen by the holder)

renge-no-in (mudra) -- (Jap.; Ind.: *uttarabodhi mudrā*) The Japanese term for *uttarabodhi mudra*. See: *uttarabodhi mudra*. (AGe)

ren renge-in (mudra) -- (Jap.: *ren renge-in* [*mudrā*]) A *mudra*, a ritual hand pose, a seal, a *tantric mudra* which is common to the Japanese Buddhist (*Vajrayana, Mantrayana*) tradition and is held or formed by a devotee or priest during the rites of *Garbhadhatu Mandala, Vajradhatu Mandala, Homa Rites* and other rites. It may be accompanied by a *mantra*. The *ren renge-in* (*mudra*)[6] is a combined (Ind.: *saṁyutta*) form, held by both hands. It denotes the pressing of lotus. This *mudra* is formed by two '*san-ko*' hand: palms face the midline, thumbs and little fingers folded into the palms and touch at their tips, index, middle and ring fingers extend straight upwards. Thus formed the hands are brought together, the tips of the index, middle and ring fingers touch. (GDe 68) (See: **Figure 480**)

Figure 480 -- ren renge-in (mudra)
(as seen by the holder)

restraining Mara mudra -- (Eng.; Ind: *abhaya-dhyāna mudrā* ; Thai: *pang harm-marn*) The English descriptive phrase for the Thai *pang harm-marn*. See: *pang harm-marn*. (DRN 37, JBo, PSS, ODD 680)

restraining the kinsmen mudra -- (Eng.; Ind.: *abhaya-lolahasta mudrā*; Thai: **pang ODD #33**) The English descriptive phrase for the Thai **pang ODD #33**. See: **pang ODD #33.** (DRN 36, JBo, ODD 680)

restraining the sandalwood image mudra -- (Eng.; Ind.: *lolahasta-abhaya mudrā*; Thai: *pang ham-phra-kaen-chan*) The English descriptive phrase for the Thai *pang ham-phra-kaen-chan*. See: *pang ham-phra-kaen-chan*. (DRN 36, JBo 205, KIM 10, ODD 680, PSS)

restraining the waters mudra -- (Eng.; Ind.: *abhaya-abhaya mudrā*; Thai: *pang ham-samut*) The English descriptive phrase for the Thai *pang ham-samut*. See: *pang ham-samut*. (KIM 40, DRN 36, JBo)

revealing the three worlds mudra -- (Eng.; Thai: **pang ODD #32**; Ind.: *siṁhakarṇa-siṁhakarṇa mudrā*) The English descriptive phrase for the Thai **pang ODD #32**. See: **ODD #32 mudra**. (DRN 36, JBo 205, ODD 680, PSS)

rgya-chen shugs-ldan phyag-rgya (mudra) -- (Tib.; Ind.: *sarva-tathāgata-avalokite mudrā*) The Tibetan transliteral term for *sarva-tathagata-avalokite mudra*. See: *sarva-tathagata-avalokite mudra*. (SBe 347)

rin-chen sgrom-bu'i phyag-rgya (mudra) -- (Tib.; Ind.: *sarva-tathāgatebhyo mudrā*) The Tibetan transliteral term for *sarva-tathagatebhyo mudra*. See: *sarva-tathagatebhyo mudra*. (SBe 347)

rishabha mudra -- (Ind.: *r̥ṣabha-mudrā*) A hand pose, a seal, a dramatic (Ind.: *nāṭya*) *mudra* or gesture (Ind.: *darpaṇa*) held or formed by a performer, dancer or actor. It denotes an animal, in this case a bull. The *rishabha mudra*[7] is a combined (Ind.: *saṁyutta*) form, held by both hands. This *mudra* is identical to the *tala-simha mudra*. See: *tala-simha mudra*. (ACG 50)

rito-in (mudra) -- (Jap.: *ritō-in* [*mudrā*] aka *mushofushi-in* [*mudra*], *Biroshana-in* [*mudra*], *butsubu sotoba-in* [*mudra*], *dai sotoba-in* [*mudra*], *hen hokkai mushofushi-in* [*mudra*]; Chin.: *wu-so-pu-chih-yin*; Ind.: *stūpa mudrā*) A variant term applied to *mushofushi-in* (*mudra*). ("*mudra* of the primary *stupa*") See: *mushofushi-in* (*mudra*). (EDS 115)

rupa mudra -- (Ind.: *rūpa-mudrā*) A *mudra*, a ritual hand pose, a seal, a *tantric mudra* which is common to the Japanese Buddhist (*Vajrayana, Mantrayana*) tradition and is held or formed by a devotee or priest during various rites. It may be accompanied by a *mantra*. The *rupa mudra* is a combined (Ind.: *saṁyutta*) form, held by both hands. It denotes "form." This *mudra* is formed by: palms facing outward, thumbs folded into the palms, middle and ring fingers folded over the thumbs, index and little fingers extend straight upwards. Thus formed, the right hand is crossed over the left at the wrists and the little fingers "hook." (GDe 449) (See: **Figure 481**)

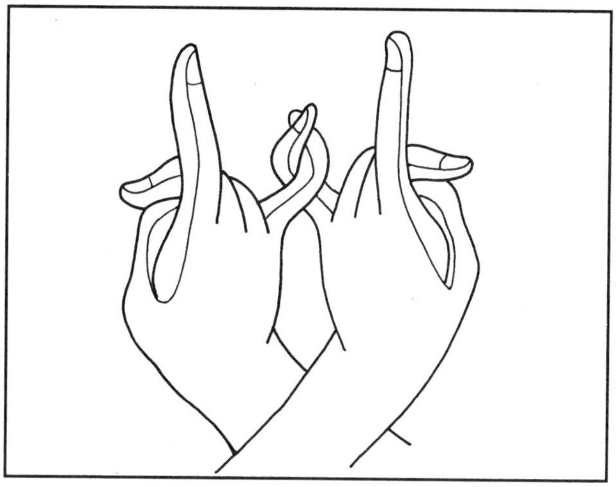

Figure 481 -- rupa mudra
(as seen by the holder)

Figure 482 -- Sahasra-bhuja Avalokiteshvara mudra
(as seen by the holder)

-- S --

Sachittotpada-Bodhisattva mudra -- (Ind.: *Sacittotpāda-Bodhisattva-mudrā* aka *dharma-cakra-pravartana-bodhisattva-varga-mudrā*) A variant term applied to *dharmachakra-pravartana-bodhisattva-varga-mudra*. See: *dharmachakra-pravartana-bodhisattva-varga-mudra*. (LCS 231)

sadung-man (mudra) -- (Thai.: [*pang*] *sadung-man* aka *manwichai* [*mudra*], *pang maravichai*, [*pang*]; Chin.: *an-shan-yin, ch'u-ti-yin*; Eng.: *adamantine posture*; Ind.: *bhasparśa mudrā, bhūmisparśa mudrā, bhūmisparśana mudrā, bhūmiśparśa mudrā, bhūsparś mudrā, bhūsparśa mudrā, māravijaya mudra*; Jap.: *anzan-in* [*mudra*], *sokuchi-in* [*mudra*]) A variant Thai term applied to *bhumisparsha mudra*. See: *bhumisparsha mudra*. (KIM 8)

Sagara mudra -- (Ind.: *Sagara-mudrā*) A hand pose, a seal, a dramatic (Ind.: *nāṭya*) mudra or gesture (Ind.: *darpaṇa*) held or formed by a performer, dancer or actor. The *Sagara mudra* is a single (Ind.: *asaṁyutta*) form, held by one hand. It denotes *Sagara*, one of a number of famous rulers or heroes. The *mudra* employed is identical in form to the *ala-padma mudra*. See: *ala-padma mudra*. (ACG 47)

Sahadeva mudra -- (Ind.: *Sahadeva-mudrā*) A hand pose, a seal, a dramatic (Ind.: *nāṭya*) *mudra* or gesture (Ind.: *darpaṇa*) held or formed by a performer, dancer or actor. The *Sahadeva mudra* is a single (Ind.: *asaṁyutta*) form, held by one hand. It denotes *Sahadeva*, one of a number of famous rulers or heroes. The *mudra* employed is identical in form to the *shikhara mudra*. See: *shikhara mudra*. (ACG 47)

Sahasra-bhuja Avalokiteshvara mudra -- (Ind.: *Sahasra-bhuja Avalokiteśvara-mudrā*) A *mudra*, a ritual hand pose, a seal, a *tantric mudra* which is common to the Japanese Buddhist (*Vajrayana, Mantrayana*) tradition and is held or formed by a devotee or priest during various rites. It may be accompanied by a *mantra*. The *Sahasra-bhuja Avalokiteshvara mudra*[1] is a combined

(Ind.: *saṁyutta*) form, held by both hands. This *mudra* is formed by: Palms face midline, thumbs extend upward, index and ring fingers cross their counterparts at their tips, middle fingers touch at their tips, little fingers extend straight upward. (GDe 215) (See: **Figure 482**)

sai butsu-in (mudra) -- (Jap.: *sai butsu-in* [*mudrā*]) ("the Buddha of the west") A *mudra*, a ritual hand pose, a seal, a *tantric mudra* which is common to the Japanese Buddhist (*Vajrayana, Mantrayana*) tradition and is held or formed by a devotee or priest during the rites of *Vajradhatu Mandala* and other rites. It may be accompanied by a *mantra*. The *sai butsu-in* (*mudra*) is a combined (Ind.: *saṁyutta*) form, held by both hands. It denotes *Amitabha* (Jap.: *Amida*). This *mudra* is formed by: palms facing midline and are close, thumbs crossed, index, ring and little fingers interlace touching the back of the opposite hands, middle fingers extend and touch at their tips. (GDe 69) (See: **Figure 483**)

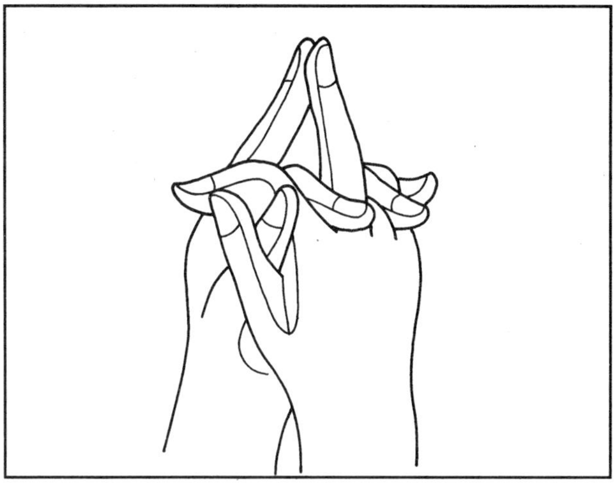

Figure 483 -- sai butsu-in (mudra)
(as seen by the holder)

sai fuku sho ma-in (mudra) -- (Jap.: *sai fuku shoā ma-in* [*mudrā*]; Ind.: *tarjanī mudrā*) ("victory over demons")[2] The Japanese term for *tarjani mudra* See: *tarjani mudra*. (GDe 44)

sa-in (mudra) -- (Jap.: *sa-in* [*mudrā*]; Ind.: *vajra-śṛṅkhalā mudrā*) A *mudra*, a ritual hand pose, a seal, a *tantric mudra* which is common to the Japanese Buddhist (*Vajrayana, Mantrayana*) tradition and is held or formed by a devotee or priest during the rites of *Garbhadhatu Mandala, Vajradhatu Mandala, Homa Rites* and other rites. It may be accompanied by a *mantra*. The *sa-in* (*mudra*) is a combined (Ind.: *saṁyutta*) form, held by both hands. It denotes keeping of the deities within the precincts of the temple. This *mudra* is formed by: both hands forming a fist with the thumbs on the outside, the left palm faces left and the right palm faces right. Thus formed the two fists are crossed at the wrist, left in front of the right and the thumbs of the two fists touch and held chest high. (GDe 41, LCS 156) (See: **Figure 484**)

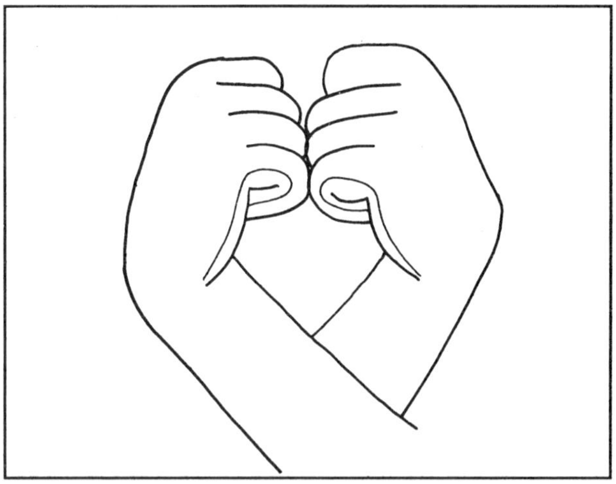

Figure 484 -- sa-in (mudra)
(as seen by the holder)

sai zai-in (mudra) -- (Jap.: *sai zai-in* [*mudrā*]) A *mudra*, a ritual hand pose, a seal, a *tantric mudra* which is common to the Japanese Buddhist (*Vajrayana, Mantrayana*)

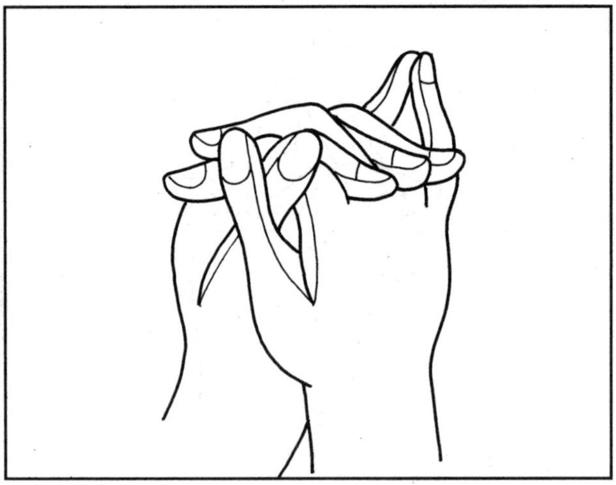

Figure 485 -- sai zai-in (mudra)
(as seen by the holder)

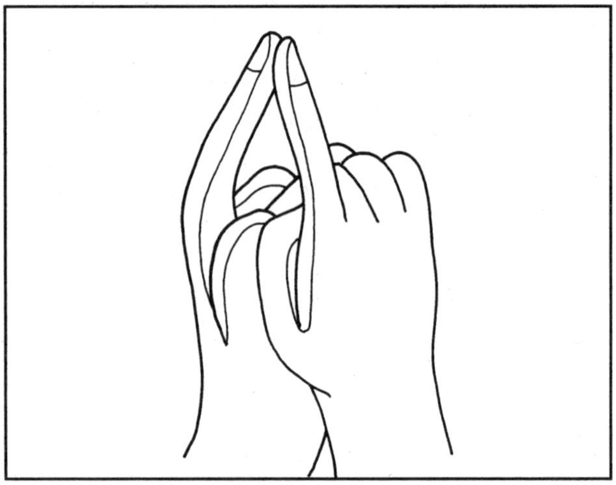

Figure 486 -- saku-in (mudra)
(as seen by the holder)

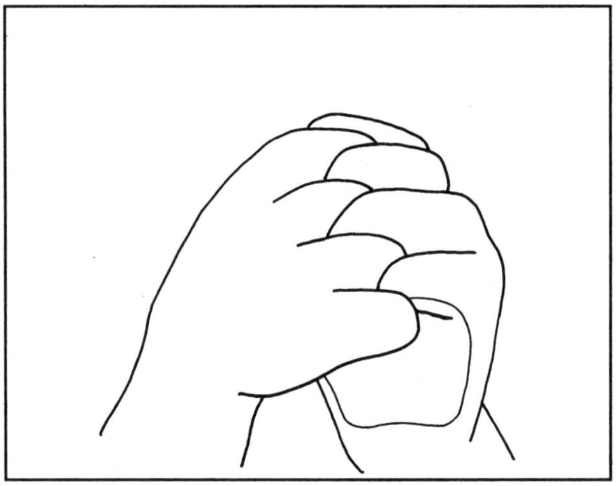

Figure 487 -- samanta-buddhanam mudra
(as seen by another)

tradition and is held or formed by a devotee or priest during the rites of *Vajradhatu Mandala* and other rites. It may be accompanied by a *mantra*. The *sai zai-in*[3] (*mudra*) is a combined (Ind.: *saṁyutta*) form, held by both hands. It denotes the destruction of crimes. This *mudra* is formed by: the palms facing the midline and close, thumbs cross, index, ring and middle fingers interlace and are folded touching with their tips the third knuckle of their opposites, the middle fingers extend and touch at their tips. (GDe 66) (See: **Figure 485**)

saku-in (mudra) -- (Jap.: *saku-in* [*mudrā*]) ("the cord") A *mudra*, a ritual hand pose, a seal, a *tantric mudra* which is common to the Japanese Buddhist (*Vajrayana, Mantrayana*) tradition and is held or formed by a devotee or priest during the rites of *Garbhadhatu Mandala, Vajradhatu Mandala, Homa Rites* and other rites. It may be accompanied by a *mantra*. The *saku-in* (*mudra*) is a combined (Ind.: *saṁyutta*) form, held by both hands. It denotes the retention of the deities within the sacred precincts. This *mudra* is formed by: the palms brought close, thumbs, middle, ring and little fingers interlace inwards--between the palms--index fingers touch at the tips. It is a variation of the *nyorai saku-in* (*mudra*). (GDe 40) (See: **Figure 486**)

samadhi mudra -- (Ind.: *samādhi-mudrā* aka *dhyāna mudrā, dhyānahasta mudrā, yoga mudrā*; Chin.: *ting-yin* [*mudra*]; Jap.: *jo-in* [*mudra*]; Thai: *pang phra-nang*; Tib.: *bsam-gtan phyag-rgya*) A variant term applied to *dhyana mudra*. See: *dhyana mudra*. (AKG 20, BBh 196, RSG 3)

samanta-buddhanam mudra -- (Ind.: *samanta-buddhanām-mudrā*; Tib.: *dbang-sgyur 'khor-lo'i phyag-rgya*) This is an assigned term.[4] A *mudra*, a ritual hand pose, a seal, which is common sixth the Buddhist (*Vajrayana*) tradition, a *tantric mudra*. It is the sixth gesture of six of the *ma-mo-mdos mudras*. It denotes the universal sovereignty, particularly as associated with the white *gtor-ma* (sacrificial cake) offering and the presentation of the thread cross (Tib.: *ma-mo-mdos* or *ma-mdos*) as part of the worship of the powerful *Vajrayana* goddess, *Tara*. The *samanta-buddhanam mudra* is a combined (Ind.: *saṁyutta*) form, held by both hands. This *mudra* is formed by: palms face the midline, the fingers and thumbs of both hands are interlaced (inward) and held between the palms. The *mantra* associated with this *mudra* is: "*Namah samanta-buddhanam Graheshvara-prabha-jyotena Maha-samaye SVAHA.*"[5] (SBe 347) (See: **Figure 487**)

samdamsa mudra I -- (Ind.: *saṁdaṁśa-mudrā*) ("grasping") A hand pose, a seal, a dramatic (Ind.: *nāṭya*) *mudra* or gesture (Ind.: *darpaṇa*) held or formed by a performer, dancer or actor. The *samdamsa mudra* is a single (Ind.: *asaṁyutta*) form, held by one hand. It denotes generosity, apprehension, etc.[6] This *mudra* requires motion and is formed by: palm faces upwards, fingers and thumb are separated and gently curl inwards, towards the hollowed palm. Thus formed the fingers are opened and closed repeatedly. (ACG 37) (See: **Figure 488**)

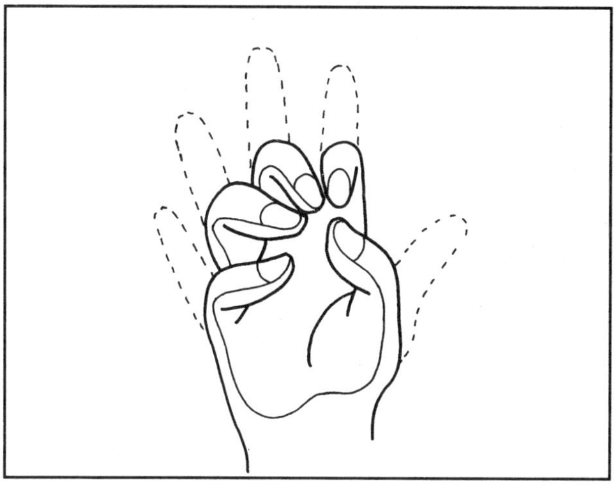

Figure 488 -- samdamsa mudra I
(as seen by the holder)

samdamsa mudra II -- (Ind.: *saṁdaṁśa-mudrā*) ("grasping") A hand pose, a seal, a dramatic (Ind.: *nāṭya*) *mudra* or gesture (Ind.: *darpaṇa*) held or formed by a performer, dancer or actor. The *samdamsa mudra* is a single (Ind.: *asaṁyutta*) form, held by one hand. It denotes truth, singing, solitude, etc.[7] This *mudra* is formed by: palm faces upwards, fingers and thumb are separated and gently curl inwards, towards the hollowed palm except the middle finger which is held straight out. (ACG 37) (See: **Figure 489**)

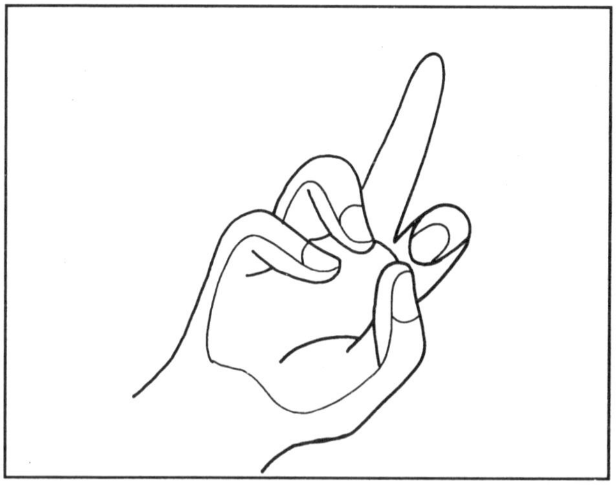

Figure 489 -- samdamsa mudra II
(as seen by the holder)

samdamsa-mukula mudra -- (Ind.: *saṁdaṁśa-mukula-mudrā*) A hand pose, a seal, a dramatic (Ind.: *nāṭya*) *mudra* or gesture (Ind.: *darpaṇa*) held or formed by a performer, dancer or actor. The *samdamsa-mukula mudra* is a single (Ind.: *asaṁyutta*) form, held by one hand. It denotes a crow. This *mudra* is formed by: the tips of the index and middle fingers touch the joint between the first and middle phalanges of the thumb, the ring and little fingers are extended upwards, and splayed. (ACG 50) (See: **Figure 490**)

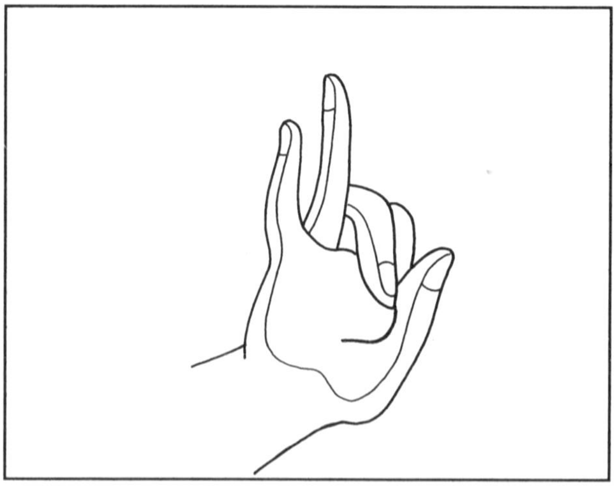

Figure 490 -- samdamsa-mukula mudra
(as seen by another)

samputa mudra I -- (Ind.: *sampuṭa-mudrā*; Jap.: *sanfuta gassho* [*mudra*]) ("the casket" or "box") A hand pose, a seal, a dramatic (Ind.: *nāṭya*) *mudra* or gesture (Ind.: *darpaṇa*) held or formed by a performer, dancer or actor. The *samputa mudra*[8] is a combined (Ind.: *saṁyutta*) form, held by both hands. It denotes concealment. This *mudra* is formed by: right palm facing downwards and rotated 45° to the left, fingers curled towards the palm, the thumb extends away from the fingers; left palm facing upwards and rotated 45° to the right, fingers curled towards the palm, the thumb extends away from the fingers. Thus formed, the palms are somewhat apart, forming a hollow. (ACG 41) (See: **Figure 491**)

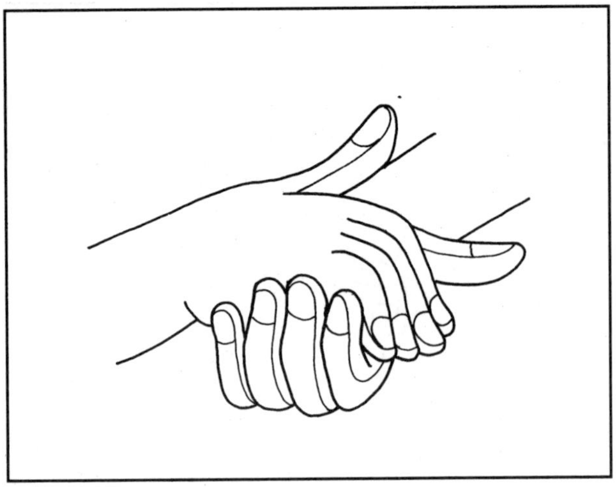

Figure 491 -- samputa mudra I
(as seen by another)

samputa mudra II -- (Ind.: *saṁputa mudrā*; Jap.: *sanfuta gassho* [*mudra*]) The Indic term for *sanfuta gassho* (*mudra*). See: *sanfuta gassho* (*mudra*); see also: *samputam mudra*. (EDS 40)

samputam mudra -- (Ind.: *saṁpuṭam-mudrā* aka *sampuṭa mudrā*; Jap.: *sanfuta gasshoµ* [*mudraµ*]) A *mudra*, a ritual hand pose, a seal, a *mudra* which is common to yogic tradition, particularly the *Yoga Tatva Mudra Vigyan* form, and is held by a devotee or practitioner. The *samputam mudra* is a combined (Ind.: *saṁyutta*) form, held by both hands. It is one of the twenty-four mudras held before the *Gayatri Jap* of the thirty-two total *Gayatri mudras*.[9] It is utilized for all sickness, especially cancer. This *mudra* is formed by: palms facing the midline, fingers extended outwards,[10] cupped and held with the tips of the fingers and heels of the palms touching. This *mudra* is similar to the *namaskara mudra*, except for the direction in which the fingers point. (KDe 80, RLM 70) (See: **Figure 492**)

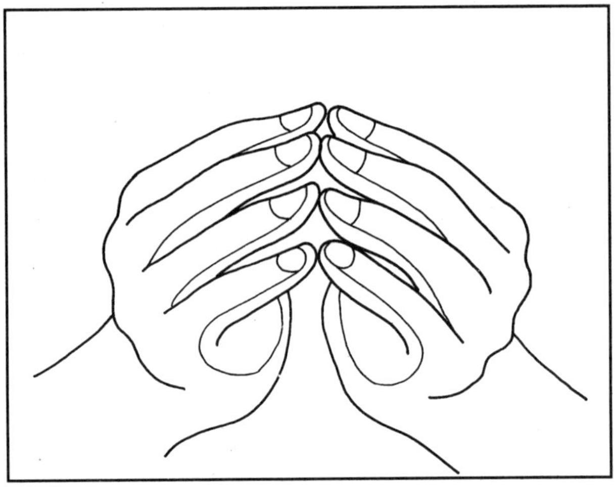

Figure 492 -- samputam mudra
(as seen by another)

samputanjali mudra -- (Ind.: *saṁpuṭāñjali-mudrā* aka *añjali mudrā*) A variant term applied to *anjali mudra*. See: *anjali mudra*. (BBh 189)

samyama mudra -- (Ind.: *saṁyama-mudrā*) A hand pose, a seal, a dramatic (Ind.: *nāṭya*) mudra or gesture (Ind.: *darpaṇa*) held or formed by a performer, dancer or actor noted in ACG but without description. See: *samyama-nayaka mudra*. (ACG 44)

samyama-nayaka mudra -- (Ind.: *saṁyama-nāyaka-mudrā*) A hand pose, a seal, a dramatic (Ind.: *nāṭya*) *mudra* or gesture (Ind.: *darpaṇa*) held or formed by a performer, dancer or actor. The *samyama-nayaka mudra* is a single (Ind.: *asaṁyutta*) form, held by one hand. It denotes an Amalaka tree. This *mudra* is formed by: palm facing outward, index and middle finger folded into the palm, thumb, ring and little fingers extended upwards. (ACG 49) (See: **Figure 493**)

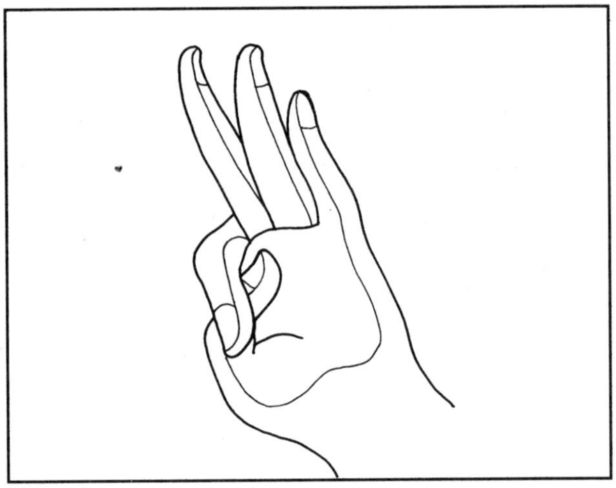

Figure 493 -- samyama-nayaka mudra
(as seen by another)

sandarshana mudra -- (Ind.: *sandarśana-mudrā* aka *cin mudrā*) A variant term applied to *chin mudra*. See: *chin mudra*. (MJS 123, RSG 3)

sanfuta gassho (mudra) -- (Jap.: *sanfuta gasshō* [*mudrā*]; Ind.: *saṁpuṭa mudrā*) A *mudra*, a ritual hand pose, a seal, which is common to the Japanese Buddhist tradition. Specifically one of the twelve, elemental "hand clasps" (Jap. *junigosho* or *junigassho*). The *sanfuta gassho* (*mudra*) is a combined (Ind.: *saṁyutta*) form, held by both hands. This *mudra* is formed by: the hands are brought together, palm to palm, fingers extended upwards, there is slight cupping of the hands. This mudra is referred to as the clasp of the "empty heart."[11] (EDS 40) (See: **Figure 494**)

sanjali mudra -- (Ind.: *sañjali-mudrā* aka *namaskāra mudrā*) A *mudra*, a ritual hand pose, a seal, which is common to both the Buddhist and Hindu traditions, although it is applied to Hindu practice. The *sanjali mudra* is a combined (Ind.: *saṁyutta*) form, held by both hands. This *mudra* is formed in mirror-pose: palm to palm, fingers extended upwards, slightly cupped and held with the tips of the fingers at the level of the chin. A gift or object is held in the hollow of the hands. It is related to the *anjali mudra* and the *namaskara mudra*. (MJS 123) (See: **Figure 495**)

sankaisaisho-in (mudra) -- (Jap.: *sankaisaishō-in* [*mudrā*]) A *mudra*, a ritual hand pose, a seal, which is common to the Japanese Buddhist tradition and a variation of the *basara-un-kongo-in* (*mudra*). It denotes the victory over the three worlds and is related to the *trailokyavijaya mudra*. The *sankaisaisho-in* (*mudra*) is a combined (Ind.: *saṁyutta*) form, held by both hands. This *mudra* is formed by hands in mirror-pose: palm faces the midline, fingers and thumb fisted, thumb inside, right hand crosses in front of left at wrist. This posed, the *mudra* he held at chest level. (EDS 114) (See: **Figure 496**)

sankirna mudra -- (Ind.: *saṅkīrṇa-mudrā*) A hand pose, a seal, a dramatic (Ind.: *nāṭya*) *mudra* or gesture (Ind.: *darpaṇa*) held or formed by a performer, dancer or actor. It denotes an animal, in this case a cow. The *sankirna mudra*[12] is a combined (Ind.: *saṁyutta*) form, held by

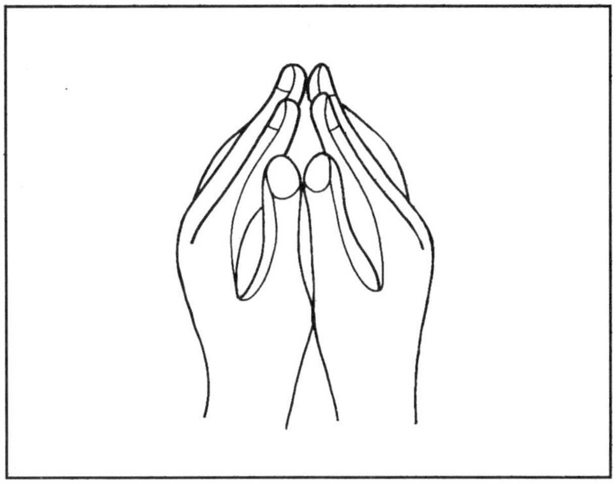

Figure 494 -- sanfuta gassho (mudra)
(as seen by the holder)

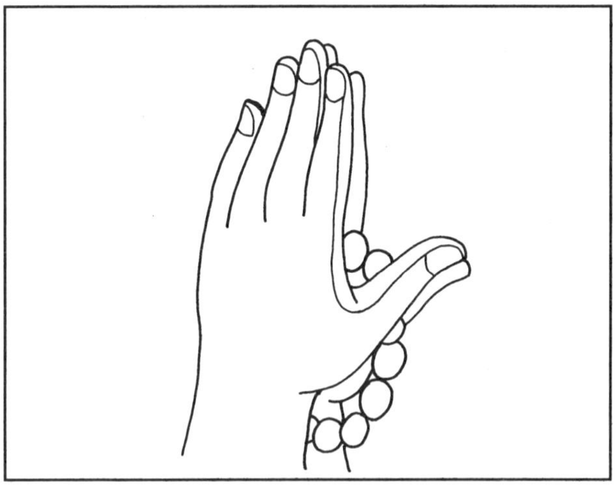

Figure 495 -- sanjali mudra
(as seen by the holder)

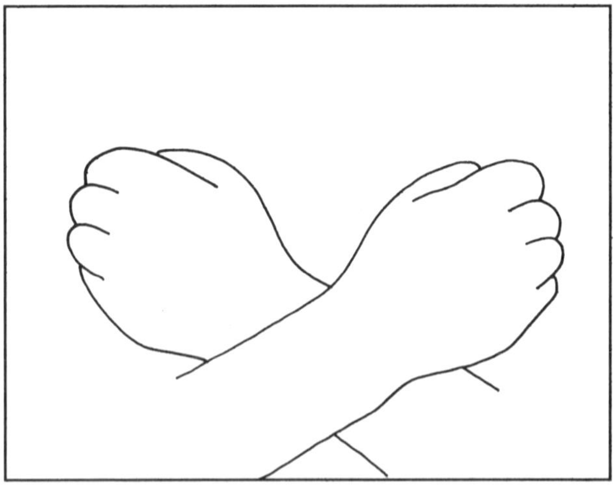

Figure 496 -- sankaisaisho-in (mudra)
(as seen by another)

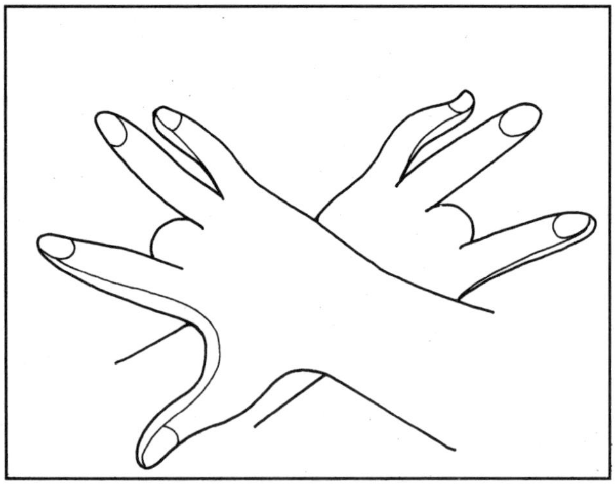

Figure 497 -- sankirna mudra
(as seen by the holder)

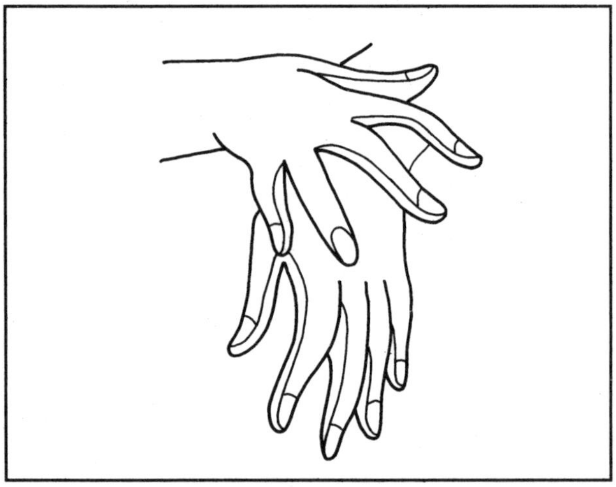

Figure 498 -- sankirna-makara mudra
(as seen by another)

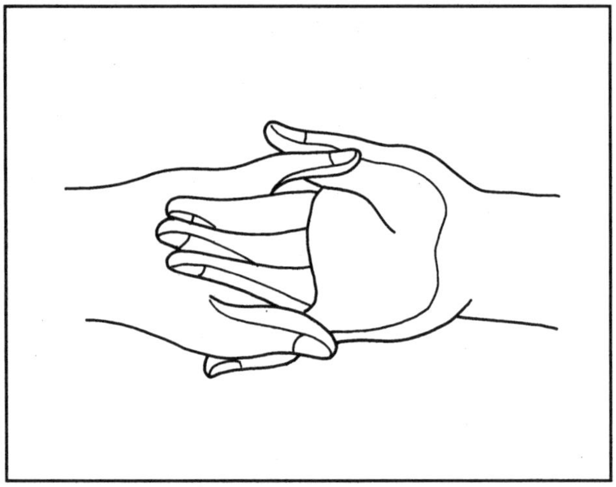

Figure 499 -- san-ko-cho-in (mudra)
(as seen by the holder)

both hands. This *mudra* is formed by: right palm facing downwards, fingers slightly separated, extended outwards, thumb at right angle to the fingers; left palm facing downwards, fingers together and extended outwards except the middle finger which is bent palmward, thumb at right angle to the fingers. Thus formed the right hand is placed over the left hand and touching it, and held waist high. (ACG 50) (See: **Figure 497**)

sankirna-makara mudra -- (Ind.: *saṅkīrṇa-makara-mudrā*) A hand pose, a seal, a dramatic (Ind.: *nāṭya*) *mudra* or gesture (Ind.: *darpaṇa*) held or formed by a performer, dancer or actor. It denotes a boar. The *sankirna-makara mudra* is a combined (Ind.: *saṁyutta*) form, held by both hands. This *mudra* is formed by: right palm facing downwards, fingers slightly separated, extended outwards, thumb at right angle to the fingers; left palm facing downwards, fingers together and extended outwards, thumb at right angle to the fingers. Thus formed the right hand is placed over the left hand and touching it, and held waist high. (ACG 49) (See: **Figure 498**)

san-ko-cho-in (mudra) -- (Jap.: *san-kō-chō-in* [*mudrā*]) A *mudra*, a ritual hand pose, a seal, a *tantric mudra* which is common to the Japanese Buddhist (*Vajrayana, Mantrayana*) tradition and is held or formed by a devotee or priest during the rites of *Garbhadhatu*. It may be accompanied by a *mantra*. The *san-ko-cho-in*[13] (*mudra*) is a combined (Ind.: *saṁyutta*) form, held by both hands. It denotes a salutation to the Buddhas and is also related to the *dhyana mudra*. This *mudra* is formed by: right palm face upwards, fingers and thumb extended towards the midline; left palm face downwards, fingers and thumb extended towards the midline. Thus formed the upturned right hand is placed upon the down turned left hand; the right thumb is placed under the little finger of the left and the thumb of the left is placed over the little finger of the right. Thus formed the *mudra* is generally held in the lap. (GDe 15, LCS 58) (See: **Figure 499**)

san-ko-in (mudra) I -- (Jap.: *san-kō-in* [*mudrā*]) ("three-pronged *vajra*") A *mudra*, a ritual hand pose, a seal, a *tantric mudra* which is common to the Japanese Buddhist (*Vajrayana, Mantrayana*) tradition and is held or formed by a devotee or priest during the rites of *Garbhadhatu Mandala, Vajradhatu Mandala, Homa Rites* and other rites. It may be accompanied by a *mantra*. The *san-ko-in*[14] (*mudra*) is a single (Ind.: *asaṁyutta*) form, held by one hand. It denotes a three-pronged scepter. This *mudra* is formed by: thumb and little fingers folded into the palm and touching at their tips, index, middle and ring fingers extend straight upwards. (GDe 68) (See: **Figure 500**)

san-ko-in (mudra) II -- (Jap.: *san-kō-in* [*mudrā*]) ("three-pronged *vajra*") A *mudra*, a ritual hand pose, a seal, a *tantric mudra* which is common to the Japanese Buddhist (*Vajrayana, Mantrayana*) tradition and is held or formed by a devotee or priest during the rites of *Garbhadhatu Mandala, Vajradhatu Mandala, Homa Rites* and other rites. It may be accompanied by a *mantra*. The *san-ko-in*[15] (*mudra*) is a combined (Ind.: *saṁyutta*) form, held by both hands. It denotes a three-pronged scepter. This *mudra* is formed by: thumbs together and extended, index fingers extended and bent slightly "backwards." middle fingers tips touch, ring and little fingers interlace, inwards towards the palms. (GDe 151, LCS 220) (See: **Figure 501**)

santi mudra -- (Ind.: *śānti-mudrā* aka *abhaya mudrā*) A *mudra*, a ritual hand pose, a seal, which is common to both the Buddhist and Hindu traditions. The *mudra* is noted by RSG as: "similar to *Abhaya*."[16] (RSG 3)

sapatni mudra -- (Ind.: *sapatnī-mudrā*) A hand pose, a seal, a dramatic (Ind.: *nāṭya*) *mudra* or gesture (Ind.: *darpaṇa*) held or formed by a performer, dancer or actor. The *sapatni mudra* is a combined (Ind.: *saṁyutta*) form, held by both hands. One of eleven *mudras* representing "relationships" and one which denotes co-wife. This *mudra* requires movement from one *mudra* to another and is formed by first both hands hold: right palm faces outwards, the index finger and the thumb point upwards, together, the middle, ring and little fingers are folded into the palm, the left is similar but the palm faces the midline. Thus formed, the two are joined by hooking the index fingers together; then they both hold: palms face inwards, fingers and thumbs extended together towards the midline, and placed on the lower abdomen. (ACG 45) (See: **Figure 502**)

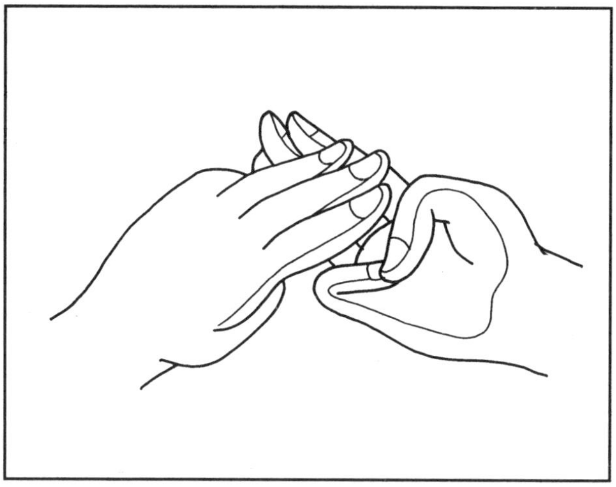

Figure 500 -- san-ko-in (mudra) I
(as seen by the holder)

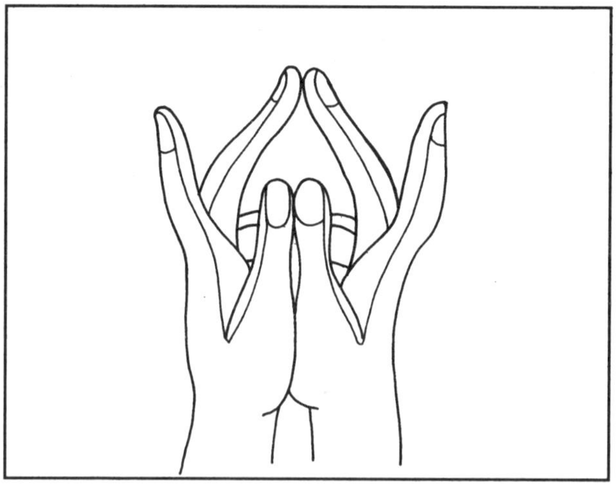

Figure 501 -- san-ko-in (mudra) II
(as seen by the holder)

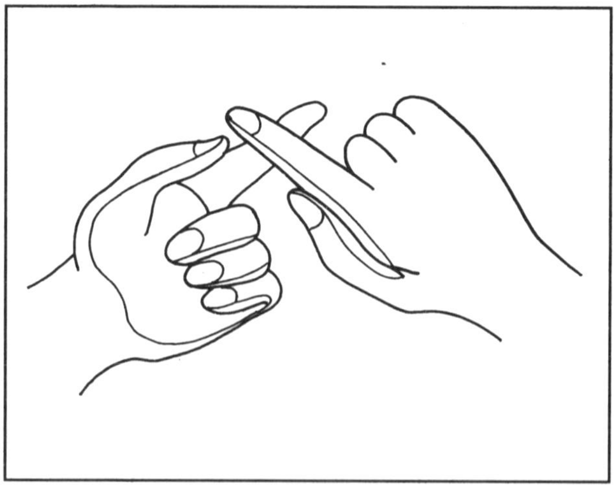

Figure 502 -- sapatni mudra
(as seen by the holder)

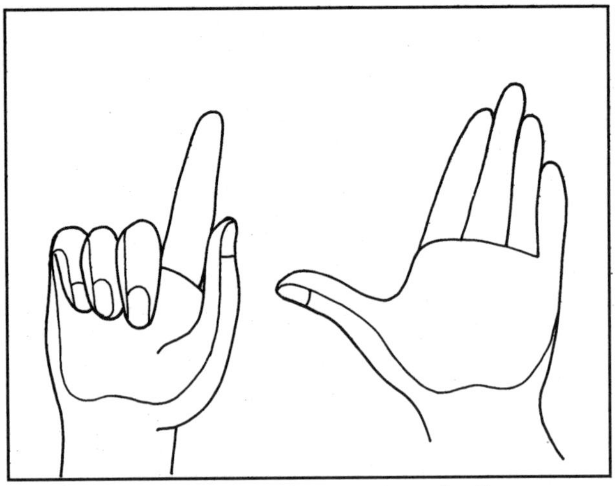

Figure 503 -- Sarasvati mudra I
(as seen by another)

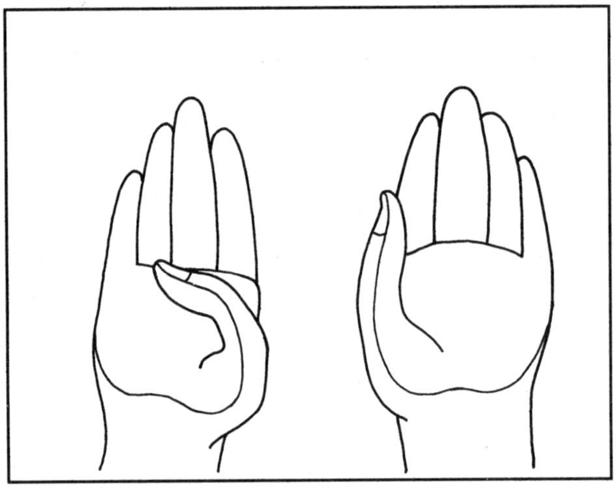

Figure 504 -- Sarasvati mudra II
(as seen by another)

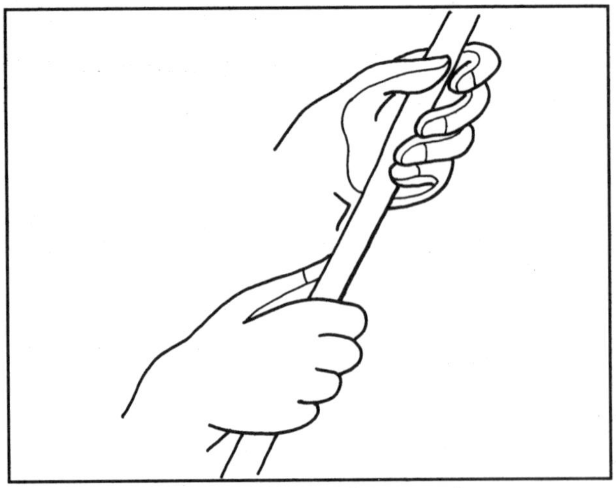

Figure 505 -- sarpakara mudra
(as seen by another)

sarasa mudra -- (Ind.: *sārasa-mudrā*) A hand pose, a seal, a dramatic (Ind.: *nāṭya*) *mudra* or gesture (Ind.: *darpaṇa*) held or formed by a performer, dancer or actor. It denotes a bird, in this case a crane. The *sarasa mudra*[17] is a combined (Ind.: *saṁyutta*) form, held by both hands. This *mudra* is identical to the *pardisha-mukula mudra*. (See: *pardisha-mukula mudra*) (ACG 50)

Sarasvati mudra I -- (Ind.: *Sarasvatī-mudrā*) A hand pose, a seal, a dramatic (Ind.: *nāṭya*) *mudra* or gesture (Ind.: *darpaṇa*) held or formed by a performer, dancer or actor which denotes a specific deity. The *Sarasvati mudra* is a combined (Ind.: *saṁyutta*) form, held by both hands. It denotes the deity *Sarasvati*. This *mudra* is formed by: right palm faces outwards, the index finger and the thumb point upwards, together, the middle, ring and little fingers are folded into the palm; left palm facing outward, fingers extended, together and pointing upwards, relaxed, the thumb extends away from the fingers. Thus formed the hands are held at shoulder level. (ACG 45) (See: **Figure 503**)

Sarasvati mudra II -- (Ind.: *Sarasvatī-mudrā*) A hand pose, a seal, a dramatic (Ind.: *nāṭya*) *mudra* or gesture (Ind.: *darpaṇa*) held or formed by a performer, dancer or actor. It denotes the *Sarasvati*, one of the famous rivers of India. The *Sarasvati mudra II* is a combined (Ind.: *saṁyutta*) form, held by both hands. This *mudra* is made up of the *pataka mudra* and *chatura mudra* being formed by: right palm facing outward, fingers and thumb extended, together, pointing upwards, relaxed, slightly cupped and generally on a line level with the chest; left palm facing forwards, the fingers, together and extended upwards, the little finger is separated slightly, the tip of the thumb crosses the palm and touches the base of the ring finger. (ACG 48) (See: **Figure 504**)

sarpakara mudra -- (Ind.: *sarpakāra-mudrā*) A *mudra*, a ritual hand pose, a seal, which is common to the Hindu tradition. It denotes the handling of a serpent and is used in holding an object such as Indian lute (Indi: *vīṇa*). The *sarpakara mudra* is a combined (Ind.: *saṁyutta*) form, held by both hands. This *mudra* is formed by: the left hand is raised to shoulder level, left palm faces upwards fingers and thumb curled (similar to *kataka mudra*), the right hand is held at waist level, right palm faces downwards fingers and thumb curled. Thus formed the two hands grasp a long narrow object.18 (TGR 290) (See: **Figure 505**)

sarpa mudra -- (Ind.: *sarpa-mudrā* aka *nāga mudrā, sarpaśīrṣa mudrā*) A variant term applied to *sarpashirsha mudra*. See: *sarpashirsha mudra*. (TGR 282)

sarpashirsha mudra -- (Ind.: *sarpa-śīrṣa-mudrā* aka *nāga mudrā, sarpa mudrā*) ("snake head") A hand pose, a seal, a dramatic (Ind.: *nāṭya*) *mudra* or gesture (Ind.: *darpaṇa*) held or formed by a performer, dancer or actor. The *sarpashirsha mudra* is a single (Ind.: *asaṁyutta*) form, held by one hand. It denotes a snake, slowness, cherishing, etc.[19] This *mudra* is formed by: essentially from the *pataka mudra*--the palm facing forwards, the thumb is against the index finger's base, the index, middle, ring and little fingers curl, half-way towards the palm resembling the hood of a cobra. (ACG 33, KVa 136 [29]) (See: **Figure 506**)

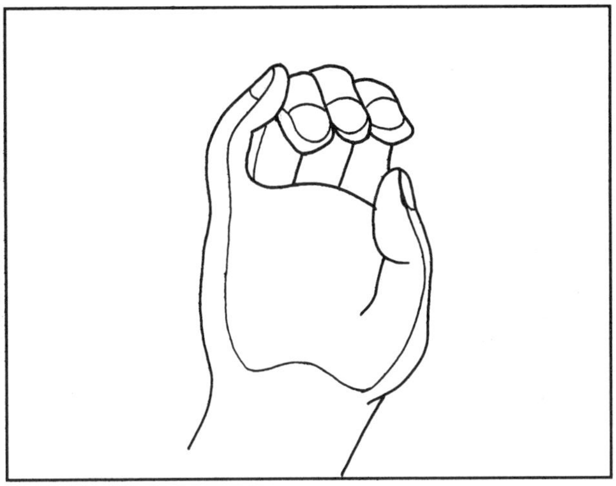

Figure 506 -- sarpashirsha mudra
(as seen by another)

sarva-buddha-bodhisattvanam mudra -- (Ind.: *sarva-buddha-bodhisattvānām-mudrā;* Tib: *Bya-lding phyag-rgya* [*mudra*]) This is an assigned term.[20] A *mudra*, a ritual hand pose, a seal, which is common to the Buddhist (*Vajrayana*) tradition, a *tantric mudra*. It signifies the "empowering flying-bird"[21] which is invoked during the first presentations of the *torma*, particularly as associated with the worship of the powerful *Vajrayana* goddess, *Tara*. The *sarva-buddha-bodhisattvanam mudra* is a combined (Ind.: *saṁyutta*) form, held by both hands. This *mudra* is formed in mirror-pose: palms face the mid-line, tips of the index finger touches the tips of the thumb, middle, ring and little fingers extend upwards. The hands so posed are brought together and the tips of the index fingers and the tips of the thumbs touch. Thus formed, the *mudra* is held at chest level. The *mantra* associated with this *mudra* is: "*Namah Sarva-buddha-bodhisattvanam aparatihata-shasananam He He Bhagavate Mahasattva-sarva-buddha-avalokite Mavilamba Mavilamba Idam Balim Grihnapaya Grihnapaya Hum Hum Ja Ja Sarva-visan-chare Svaha.*"[22] (SBe 218) (See: **Figure 507**)

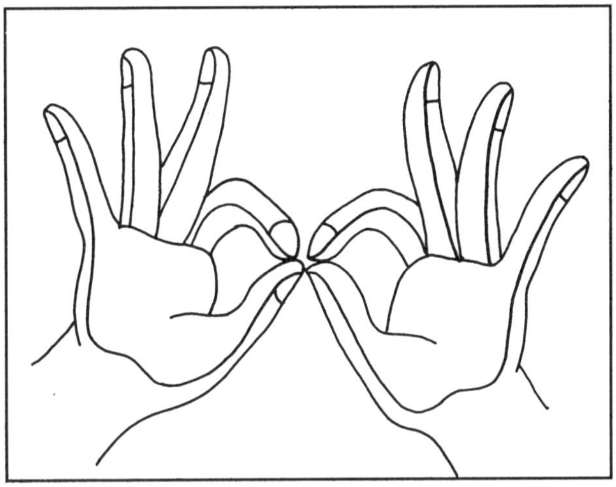

Figure 507 -- sarva-buddha-bodhisattvanam mudra
(as seen by another)

sarva-dharmah mudra -- (Ind.: *sarva-dharmāḥ-mudrā;* Tib: *Chos-dbying rnam-dag phyag-rgya*) This is an assigned term.[23] A *mudra*, a ritual hand pose, a seal,

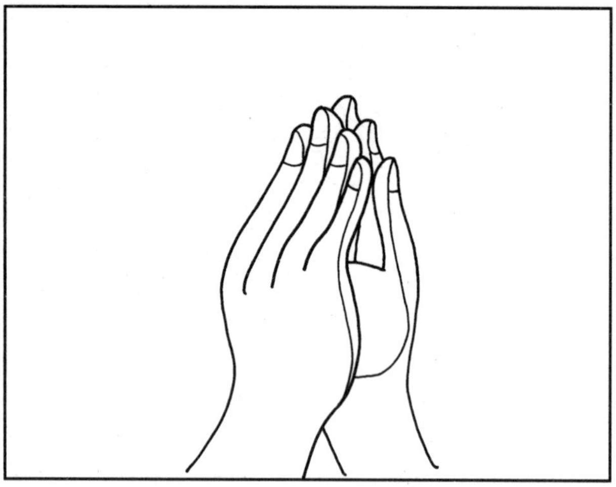

Figure 508 -- sarva-dharmah mudra
(as seen by another)

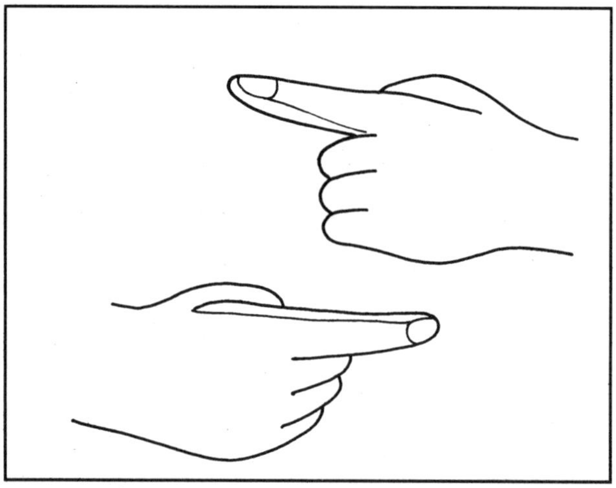

Figure 509 -- sarva-tathagata-avalokite mudra
(as seen by another)

which is common to the Buddhist (*Vajrayana*) tradition. It is the first gesture of six of the *ma-mo-mdos mudras*. It denotes the purity of the *dharma* realm, particularly as associated with the white *gtor-ma* (sacrificial cake) offering and the presentation of the thread cross (Tib.: *ma-mo-mdos* or *ma-mdos*) as part of the worship of the powerful *Vajrayana* goddess, *Tara*. The *sarva-dharmah mudra* is a combined (Ind.: *saṁyutta*) form, held by both hands. This *mudra* is formed by: fingers, thumbs and palms are together as in *anjali mudra I* including the snapping of fingers. Thus held, the *mudra* is held level with the nose. The *mantra* associated with this *mudra* is: "*Om Svabhava-shuddham Sarva-dharmah Sva-bhava-shuddho Ham.*"[24] (SBe 347) (See: **Figure 508**)

sarvarajendra mudra -- (Ind.: *sarvarājendra-mudrā* aka *añjali mudrā*) A variant term applied to *anjali mudra*. See: *anjali mudra*. (BBh 189)

sarva-tathagata-avalokite mudra -- (Ind.: *sarva-tathāgata-avalokite-mudrā*; Tib.: *rgya-chen shugs-ldan phyag-rgya*) This is an assigned term.[25] A *mudra*, a ritual hand pose, a seal, which is common to the Buddhist (*Vajrayana*) tradition, a *tantric mudra*. It is the fourth gesture of six of the *ma-mo-mdos mudras*. It denotes the vast potency, particularly as associated with the white *gtor-ma* (sacrificial cake) offering and the presentation of the thread cross (Tib.: *ma-mo-mdos* or *ma-mdos*) as part of the worship of the powerful *Vajrayana* goddess, *Tara*. The *sarva-tathagata-avalokite mudra* is a combined (Ind.: *saṁyutta*) form, held by both hands. This *mudra* is formed in mirror image by: the right palm faces the midline, thumb, middle, ring and little fingers are fisted, index finger extends to the left; the left palm faces inwards, thumb, middle, ring and little fingers are fisted, index finger extends to the right. So posed, the left hand is held slightly above the right hand, and the *mudra* is held at chest level. The *mantra* associated with this *mudra* is: "*Namah Sarva-tathagata-avalokite OM Sambhara Sambhara HUM.*"[26] (SBe 347) (See: **Figure 509**)

sarva-tathagatebhyo mudra -- (Ind.: *sarva-tathāgatebhyo-mudrā*; Tib.: *rin-chen sgrom-bu'i phyag-rgya*) This is an assigned term.[27] A *mudra*, a ritual hand pose, a seal, which is common to the Buddhist (*Vajrayana*) tradition, a *tantric mudra*. It is the second gesture of six of the *ma-mo-mdos mudras*. It denotes the jeweled casket, particularly as associated with the white *gtor-ma* (sacrificial cake) offering and the presentation of the thread cross (Tib.: *ma-mo-mdos* or *ma-mdos*) as part of the worship of the powerful *Vajrayana* goddess, *Tara*. The *sarva-tathagatebhyo mudra* is a combined (Ind.: *saṁyutta*) form, held by both hands. This *mudra* is formed in mirror-pose: right palm faces the mid-line, fingers and thumb extending upwards are slightly cupped; left palm faces the mid-line, fingers and thumb extending upwards are slightly cupped. Thus posed, the tips of the fingers and thumbs of both hand touch, and the *mudra* moves in a small circle between the eyebrows. The *mantra* associated with this *mudra* is: "*Namah Sarva-tathagatebhyo Vishva-mukhebhyh Sarvatha-kham Udgate Spharana Imam Gagana-kham SVAHA*."[28] (SBe 347) (See: **Figure 510**)

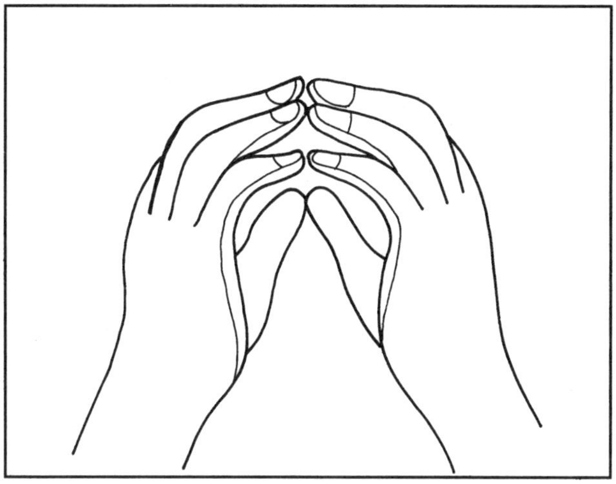

Figure 510 -- sarva-tathagatebhyo mudra
(as seen by another)

sashu-gassho (mudra) -- (Jap.: *sashu-gasshō* [*mudrā*]; Ind.: *añjalikarma mudrā*) A Japanese term for *anjalikarma mudra*. See: *anjalikarma mudra*. (EDS 76)

segan-in (mudra) -- (Jap.: *segan-in* [*mudrā*]; Chin.: *shih-yṃan-yin*; Ind.: *vara mudrā, varada mudrā*) The Japanese term for *varada mudra*. See: *varada mudra*. (EDS 51)

segan-semui-in (mudra) -- (Jap.: *segan-semui-in* [*mudrā*]) A *mudra*, a ritual hand pose, a seal, which is common to the Japanese Buddhist tradition. It is a compound mudra being composed of the *semui-in* and the *segan-in* (*mudras*). The *segan-semui-in* (*mudra*) is a combined (Ind.: *saṁyutta*) form, held by both hands. This *mudra* is formed by: right palm faces outwards, fingers and thumb extended upwards (*semui-in*), left palm faces outwards, fingers and thumb extended downwards (*segan-in*). Frequently this *mudra* is held by a standing figure, right hand at chest level, left hand at waist level. (EDS 58) (See: **Figure 511**)

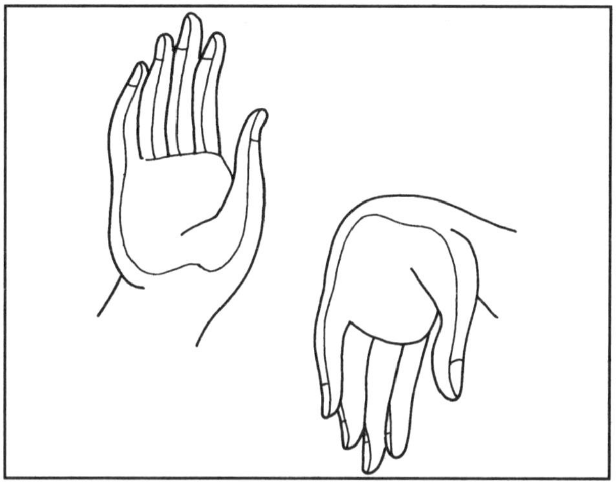

Figure 511 -- segan-semui-in (mudra)
(as seen by another)

sems-ma rdo-rje-ma'i phyag-rgya (mudra) -- (Tib.; Ind.: *vajra-manas mudrā*) The Tibetan transliteral term for *vajra-manas mudra*. See: *vajra-manas mudra*. (SBe 179)

semui-in (mudra) -- (Jap.: *semui-in* [*mudrā*]; Chin.: *shih-wu-wei-yin*; Ind.: *abhaya mudrā, abhayamdada mudrā*) A mudra, a ritual hand pose, a seal, which is common to the Japanese Buddhist tradition. It denotes the granting of a boon of fearlessness. The *semui-in* (*mudra*) is a

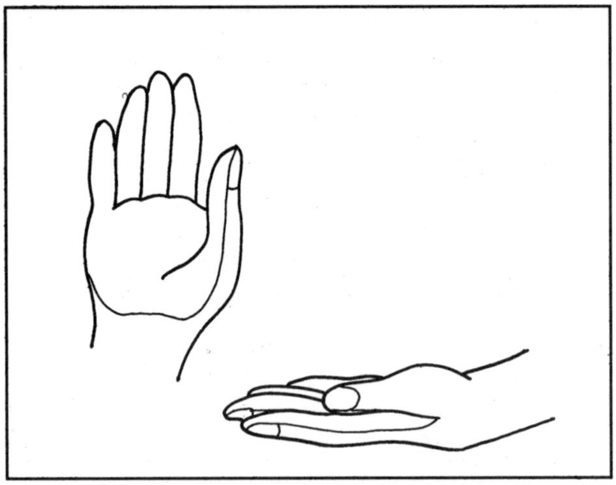

Figure 512 -- semui-in (mudra)
(as seen by another)

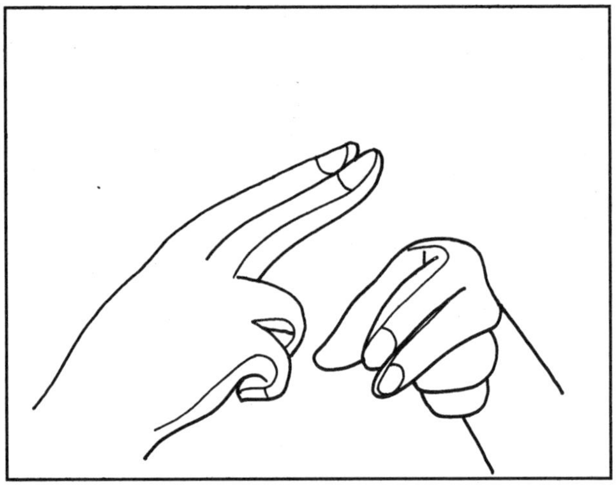

Figure 513 -- shabda mudra I
(as seen by another)

combined (Ind.: *saṁyutta*) form, held by both hands. This *mudra* is formed by: right palm facing outward and generally at the level of the chest (identical to the *abhaya mudra*), fingers and thumb extended upwards and together, relaxed, slightly cupped; left palm facing upwards and generally held at the level of the waist or, if the figure is seated, in the lap (identical to the left hand's pose in the *dhyana mudra*), fingers and thumb extended and together, relaxed, slightly cupped. The position of the left hand may be seen as holding or supporting the gift. (EDS 55) (See: **Figure 512**)

se-ten cho sho no-in (mudra) -- (Jap.: *se-ten chō shō no-in* [*mudrā*] aka *cho butsu fu-in* [*mudra*]) A variant term applied to *cho butsu fu-in* (*mudra*). See: *cho butsu fu-in* (*mudra*). (GDe 94)

setting the dish afloat mudra -- (Eng.; Ind.: *añcita-kaṭyāvalambita mudrā*; Thai: *pang loy tard*) The English descriptive phrase for the Thai: *pang loy tard*. See: *pang loy tard*. (DRN 35, JBo 204, OFr 6, PSS, ODD 680)

shabda mudra I -- (Ind.: *śabda-mudrā*) This is an assigned term.[29] A *mudra*, a ritual hand pose, a seal, which is common to the Buddhist (*Vajrayana*) tradition, a *tantric mudra*. It denotes 'music,' which is one of the 'outer offerings' proffered to a divine guest during the early stages worship, particularly as associated with the worship of the powerful *Vajrayana* goddess, *Tara*. The *shabda mudra I* is a combined (Ind.: *saṁyutta*) form, held by both hands. This *mudra* is formed in mirror-pose: right palm faces downwards, index and middle fingers point to the midline and slightly upwards, ring and little fingers are folded into the palm, the thumb touches the first phalanges of the ring and little fingers; left palm faces the midline, index and middle fingers point to the midline, ring and little fingers are folded into the palm, the thumb touches the first phalanges of the ring and little fingers, the right hand is slightly above the left. The hands so formed, hold the *mudra* at chest level. The *mantra* associated with this *mudra* is: "*OM Guru-sarva-Tathagata Shabda Puja-megha-samudra-spharana-samaye HUM*."[30] (SBe 147) (See: **Figure 513**)

shabda mudra II -- (Ind.: *śabda-mudrā*) A *mudra*, a ritual hand pose, a seal, a *tantric mudra* which is common to the Japanese Buddhist (*Vajrayana, Mantrayana*) tradition and is held or formed by a devotee or priest during various rites. It may be accompanied by a *mantra*. The *shabda mudra* is a combined (Ind.: *saṁyutta*) form, held by both hands. It denotes "sound." This *mudra* is formed by: palms facing outward, thumbs folded into the palms, middle and ring fingers folded over the thumbs, index and little fingers extend straight upwards. Thus formed, the back of the right hand is crossed over rests against the back of the left hand, index fingers touch along their length, and the little fingers "hook." (GDe 450) (See: **Figure 514**)

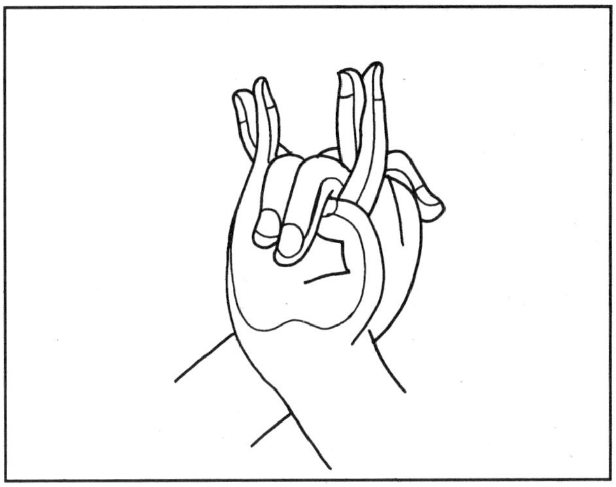

Figure 514 -- shabda mudra II
(as seen by the holder)

Shaibya mudra -- (Ind.: *Śaibya-mudrā*) A hand pose, a seal, a dramatic (Ind.: *nāṭya*) *mudra* or gesture (Ind.: *darpaṇa*) held or formed by a performer, dancer or actor. The *Shaibya mudra* is a combined (Ind.: *saṁyutta*) form, held by both hands. It denotes *Shaibya*, one of a number of famous rulers or heroes. This *mudra* is formed by hands in mirror pose, being: palm facing upwards,. index finger extends downwards, middle and ring fingers fold into the palm, little finger bends towards the palm, thumb touches middle finger. Thus formed the hands are held at shoulder level. The form of the individual hands is related to the *suchi mudra*. (ACG 47) (See: **Figure 515**)

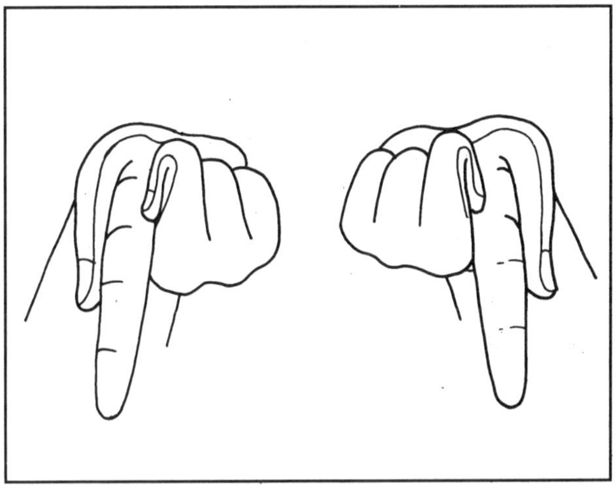

Figure 515 -- Shaibya mudra
(as seen by the holder)

shakata mudra I -- (Ind.: *śakaṭa-mudrā*) A *mudra*, a ritual hand pose, a seal, a *mudra* which is common to yogic tradition, particularly the *Yoga Tatva Mudra Vigyan* form, and is held by a devotee or practitioner. The *shaktam mudra* is a combined (Ind.: *saṁyutta*) form, held by both hands. It is one of the twenty-four mudras held before the *Gayatri Jap* of the thirty-two total *Gayatri mudras*.[31] It is utilized for all sickness, especially cancer. This *mudra* is formed by: palms facing downwards, index finger extended outwards and parallel to the ground, middle, ring and little fingers are folded into the palm, thumb held at 90° to the hand. Thus formed the tips of the thumbs of each hand touch and the mudra is held waist high. (KDe 83) (See: **Figure 516**)

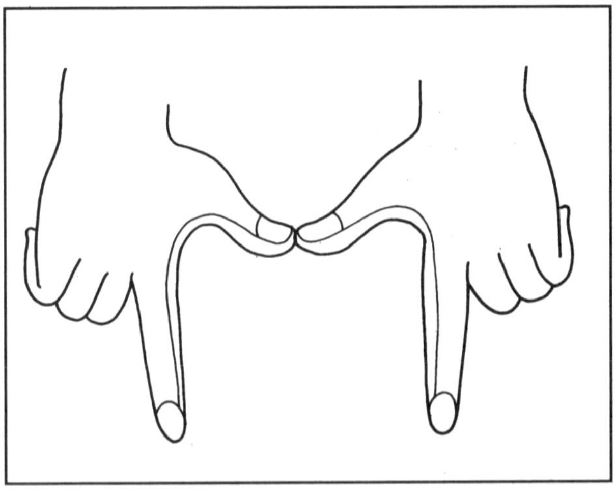

Figure 516 -- shakata mudra I
(as seen by another)

shakata mudra II-- (Ind.: *śakaṭa-mudrā*) ("the car" or "vehicle") A hand pose, a seal, a dramatic (Ind.: *nāṭya*) *mudra* or gesture (Ind.: *darpaṇa*) held or formed by a performer, dancer or actor. The *shakata mudra* is a combined (Ind.: *saṁyutta*) form, held by both hands. It de-

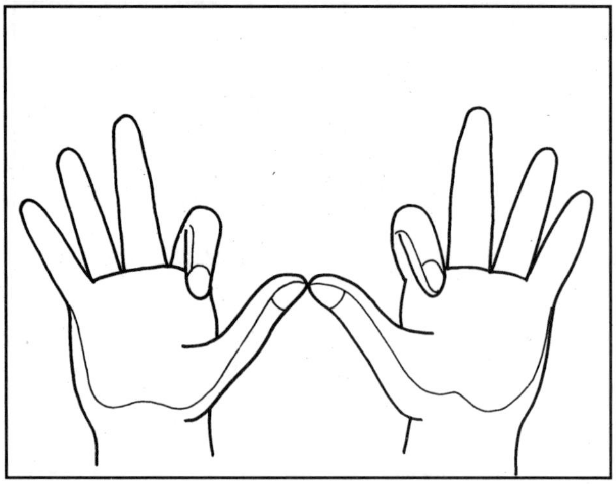

Figure 517 -- shakata mudra II
(as seen by another)

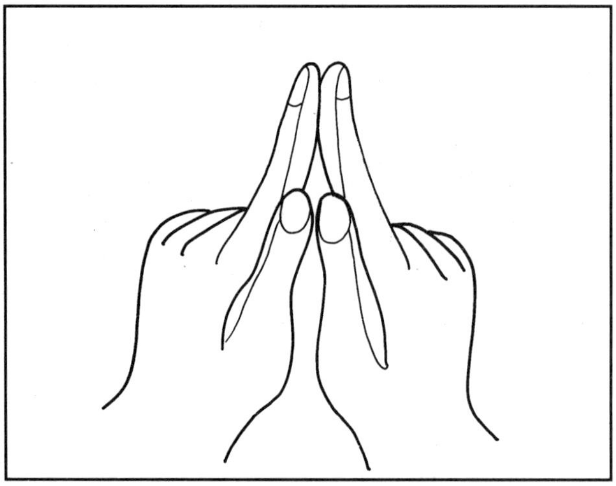

Figure 518 -- Shakra mudra
(as seen by the holder)

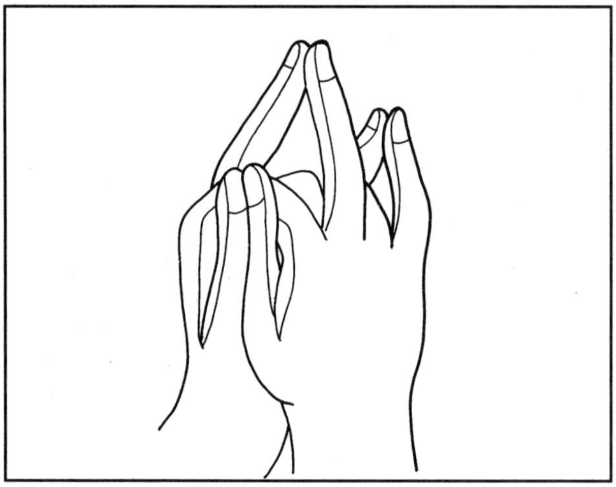

Figure 519 -- Shakyamuni (mudra)
(as seen by the holder)

notes a gesture of a *rakshasas*. This *mudra* is formed by: the index finger curls towards the palm, the middle, ring and little fingers are extended upwards, and splayed, the thumb is extended and splayed. Thus formed the hands are joined by touching the thumbs.[32] (ACG 40) (See: **Figure 517**)

Shakra mudra -- (Ind.: *Śakra-mudrā*) A *mudra*, a ritual hand pose, a seal, a *tantric mudra* which is common to the Japanese Buddhist (*Vajrayana, Mantrayana*) tradition and is held or formed by a devotee or priest during various rites in which a deity is acknowledged. It is a *mudra* which is associated with the deity *Shakra*. It may be accompanied by a *mantra*. The *Shakra mudra*[33] is a combined (Ind.: *saṁyutta*) form, held by both hands. This *mudra* is formed by: thumbs and index fingers extended upwards, middle, ring and little fingers fold into the palm. Thus formed the hands are brought together touching along the extended thumbs and index fingers. (LCS 275) (See: **Figure 518**)

Shakyamuni (mudra) -- (Ind.: *Śākyamuni* [*mudrā*]) A *mudra*, a ritual hand pose, a seal, a *tantric mudra* which is common to the Japanese Buddhist (*Vajrayana, Mantrayana*) tradition and is held or formed by a devotee or priest during various rites in which a deity is acknowledged. It is a *mudra* which is associated with the deity *Shakyamuni* (Buddha). It may be accompanied by a *mantra*. The *Shakyamuni* (*mudra*)[34] is a combined (Ind.: *saṁyutta*) form, held by both hands. It denotes the *Buddha Shakyamuni*. This *mudra* is formed by: the palms brought together, thumbs extend upwards and touch along their length, index and ring fingers are folded inward (between the palms), middle and little fingers extend straight upwards and touch at their tips. (LCS 213) (See: **Figure 519**)

Shambhu mudra -- (Ind.: *Śambhu-mudrā*) A hand pose, a seal, a dramatic (Ind.: *nāṭya*) *mudra* or gesture (Ind.: *darpaṇa*) held or formed by a performer, dancer or actor which denotes a specific deity. The *Shambhu mudra* is a combined (Ind.: *saṁyutta*) form, held by both hands. It denotes *Shambhu*. This *mudra* is formed by: right palm facing outward, index, middle and little fingers and thumb extended, together and pointing upwards, ring finger is bent towards the palm; left palm faces forward, index, middle and ring fingers curl at their first and second joints (towards the palm), the thumb is extended outward, and the little fingers extend upwards. Thus formed the hands are held at shoulder level. (ACG 45) (See: **Figure 520**)

Shanaischara mudra -- (Ind.: *Śanaiścara-mudrā*) A hand pose, a seal, a dramatic (Ind.: *nāṭya*) *mudra* or gesture (Ind.: *darpaṇa*) held or formed by a performer, dancer or actor. The *Shanaischara mudra* is a combined (Ind.: *saṁyutta*) form, held by both hands. It denotes Saturn, one of the nine planets (Ind.: *navagraha*). This *mudra* is formed by: right palm faces forward, the index, middle and ring fingers extend upward and are slightly separated, the thumb and the little finger curl towards the palm; left palm facing forwards, the thumb is against the index finger's base, the index, middle, ring and little fingers curl, half-way towards the palm resembling the hood of a cobra. (ACG 46) (See: **Figure 521**)

shami mudra -- (Ind.: *śamī-mudrā*) A hand pose, a seal, a dramatic (Ind.: *nāṭya*) *mudra* or gesture (Ind.: *darpaṇa*) held or formed by a performer, dancer or actor. It denotes the *shami* tree. The *shami mudra* is a combined (Ind.: *saṁyutta*) form, held by both hands. This *mudra* is formed by: the hands raised, index, middle fingers and thumbs extended, pointing upwards, the index and middle fingers are crossed, ring and little fingers bent towards the palms, palms facing outward. Thus formed the hands are level with the chest and interlocked. The separate hands are related to the *kartari-mukha mudra*. (ACG 49) (See: **Figure 522**)

shankha mudra I -- (Ind.: *śaṅkha-mudrā*) A *mudra*, a ritual hand pose, a seal, a *mudra* which is common to yogic tradition, particularly the *Yoga Tatva Mudra Vigyan* form, and is held by a devotee or practitioner. The *shankha mudra* is a combined (Ind.: *saṁyutta*) form, held by both hands. It is one of the eight *mudras* held after the *Gayatri Jap* of the thirty-two total *Gayatri mudras*.[35] It is utilized for all sickness, especially cancer. This *mudra* is formed by: left palm faces upwards, the tips of the fingers are brought together, pointing upwards, the thumb extends upwards; right hand is fisted, thumb outside, resting against the index finger (*padma-mushti* [*mudra*]). Thus formed the thumb of the left hand is grasped within the folded fingers of the

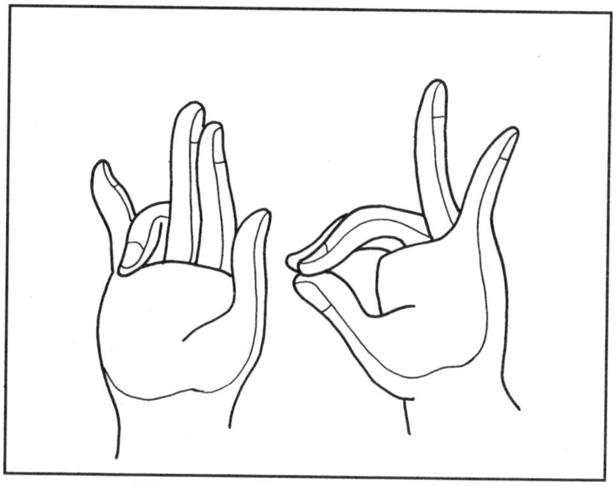

Figure 520 -- Shambhu mudra
(as seen by another)

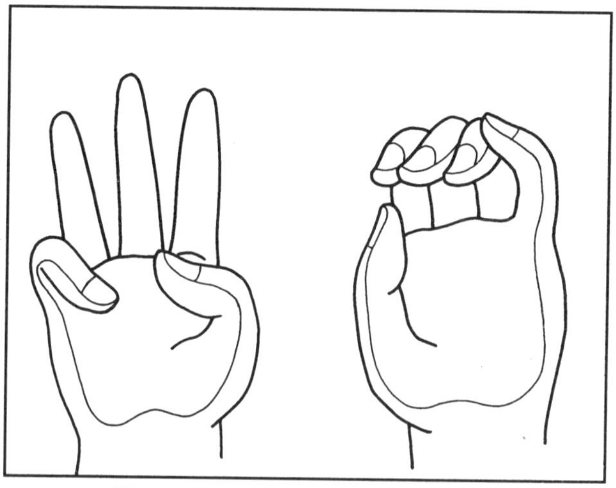

Figure 521 -- Shanaischara mudra
(as seen by another)

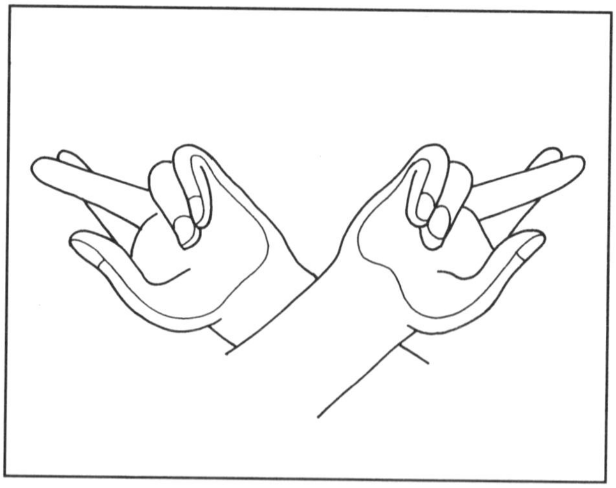

Figure 522 -- shami mudra
(as seen by another)

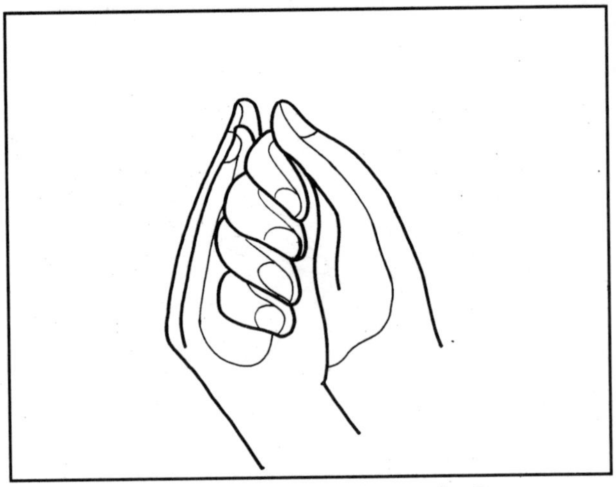

Figure 523 -- shankha mudra I
(as seen by the holder)

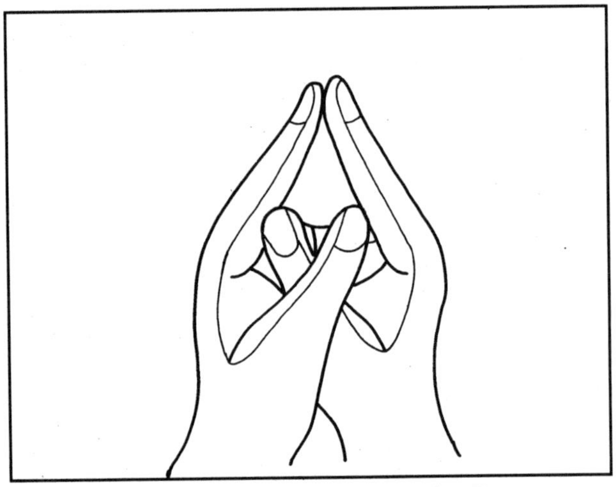

Figure 524 -- shankha mudra II
(as seen by the holder)

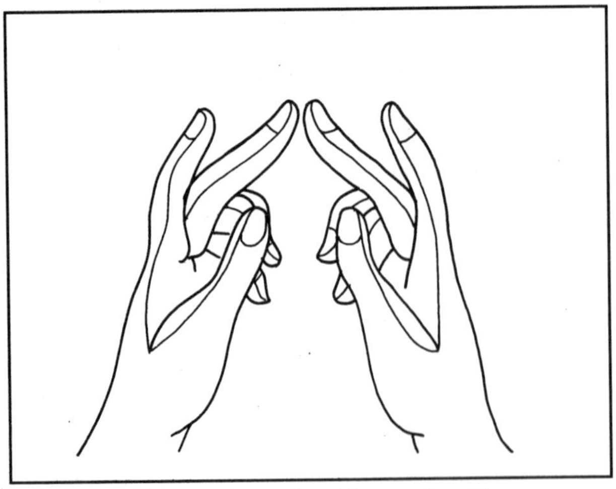

Figure 525 -- shankha mudra III
(as seen by the holder)

right fist. This *mudra* clearly resembles the *shankha* (conch shell). (KDe 89 & 108, RLM 77) (See: **Figure 523**)

shankha mudra II -- (Ind.: *śaṁkha-mudrā*) A hand pose, a seal, a dramatic (Ind.: *nāṭya*) *mudra* or gesture (Ind.: *darpaṇa*) held or formed by a performer, dancer or actor. The *shankha mudra* is a combined (Ind.: *saṁyutta*) form, held by both hands. This *mudra* is formed by: palms facing midline, middle, ring and little fingers folded into the palm, index and thumb extended. Thus formed the hands are brought together so that the folded fingers touch along their second phalanges, thumbs cross (usually right over left), tips of the index fingers touch. (ACG 41) (See: **Figure 524**)

shankha mudra III -- (Ind.: *śaṁkha-mudrā*) A *mudra*, a ritual hand pose, a seal, a *tantric mudra* which is common to the Japanese Buddhist (*Vajrayana, Mantrayana*) tradition and is held or formed by a devotee or priest during the rites of *Garbhadhatu Mandala, Vajradhatu Mandala, Homa Rites* and other rites. It may be accompanied by a *mantra*. The *shankha mudra III* is a combined (Ind.: *saṁyutta*) form, held by both hands. It denotes a conch shell. This *mudra* is formed by: middle fingers touching at their tips, index fingers extended and gently arched, ring and little fingers folded into the palms, thumbs folded towards the palms and touching the tips of the ring fingers. (GDe 335) (See: **Figure 525**)

shankha mudra IV -- (Ind.: *śaṁkha-mudrā*) A *mudra*, a ritual hand pose, a seal, a *tantric mudra* which is common to the Japanese Buddhist (*Vajrayana, Mantrayana*) tradition and is held or formed by a devotee or priest during the rites of *Garbhadhatu Mandala, Vajradhatu Mandala, Homa Rites* and other rites. It may be accompanied by a *mantra*. The *shankha mudra IV is* a combined (Ind.: *saṁyutta*) form, held by both hands. It denotes a conch shell. This *mudra* is formed by: palms facing the midline, ring and little fingers folded into the palms, thumbs folded towards the palms and touching the tips of the ring fingers, the hands touch along the curled little fingers, middle fingers touch at their tips, index fingers extended and gently arched. (LCS 210) (See: **Figure 526**)

shankha mudra V -- (Ind.: *śaṅkha-mudrā*; Jap.: *hora no-in* [*mudra*]) The Indic term for *hora no-in* (*mudra*). See: *hora no-in* (*mudra*). (GDe 22)

shankha-varta mudra -- (Ind.: *śaṅkha-varta mudrā*) This is an assigned term.[36] A mudra, a ritual hand pose, a seal, which is common to the Buddhist (*Vajrayana*) tradition, a *tantric mudra*. It denotes the conch (Tib.: *dung-kat gyas-ḥkhil*), one of eight signs of good fortune (Indic: *aṣṭa-maṅgala*, Tib.: *bkra-shis rtags-brgyad*), an 'outer offering'--the other seven being: the knot, wheel, lotus, victory banner, umbrella, treasure vase and golden fish--which is proffered to a divine guest during worship, particularly as associated with the ceremonies of the powerful *Vajrayana* goddess, *Tara*. The *shankha-varta mudra* is a combined (Ind.: *saṁyutta*) form, held by both hands. This *mudra* is formed by: the right palm faces the mid-line, fingers extended and point downwards, thumb upwards, the left palm faces the mid-line, middle, ring and little fingers extended and point downwards, index finger curls towards the palm, thumb upwards, thus formed the tips of the thumb, middle, ring and little fingers touch. The *mudra* is held at chest level. The *mantra* associated with this *mudra* is: "*OM Shankha-varta Praticcha SVAHA*."[37] (SBe 155) (See: **Figure 527**)

Shanmukha mudra -- (Ind.: *Ṣanmukha-mudrā*) A hand pose, a seal, a dramatic (Ind.: *nāṭya*) *mudra* or gesture (Ind.: *darpaṇa*) held or formed by a performer, dancer or actor which denotes a specific deity. The *Shanmukha mudra* is a combined (Ind.: *saṁyutta*) form, held by both hands. It denotes *Shanmukha*. This *mudra* is formed by: right palm faces mid-line, fingers brought into the palm forming a fist, thumb extends upwards; left palm faces forward, the index, middle and ring fingers extend upward and are slightly separated, the thumb and the little finger curl towards the palm. Thus formed the hands are held at shoulder level. (ACG 45) (See: **Figure 528**)

shan-mukham mudra -- (Ind.: *ṣaṇ-mukham-mudrā*) A *mudra*, a ritual hand pose, a seal, a *mudra* which is common to yogic tradition, particularly the *Yoga Tatva Mudra Vigyan* form, and is held by a devotee or practitioner. The *shan-mukham mudra* is a combined (Ind.: *saṁyutta*) form, held by both hands. It is one of the

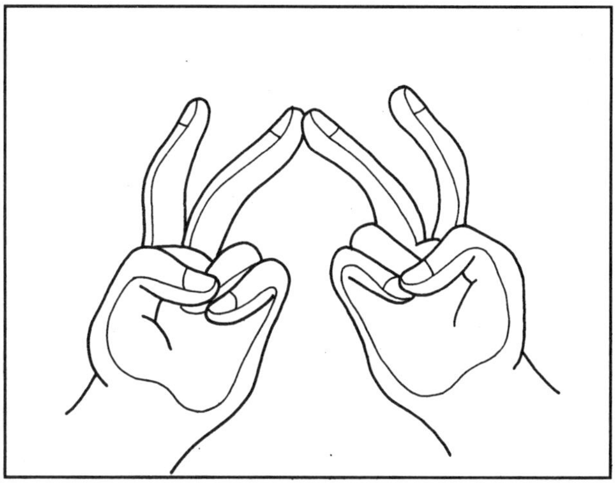

Figure 526 -- shankha mudra IV
(as seen by the holder)

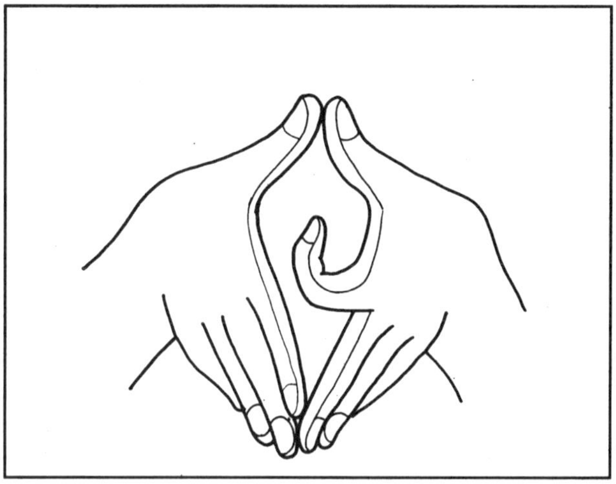

Figure 527 -- shankha-varta mudra
(as seen by another)

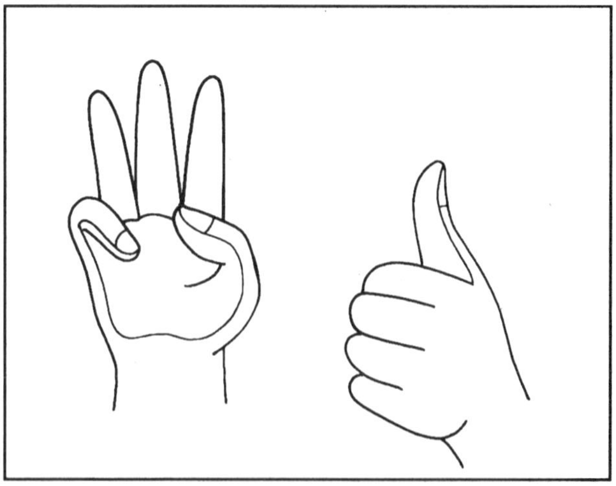

Figure 528 -- Shanmukha mudra
(as seen by another)

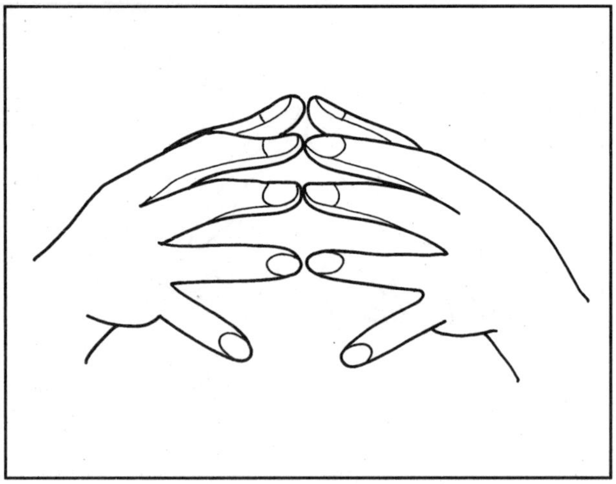

Figure 529 -- shan-mukham mudra
(as seen by another)

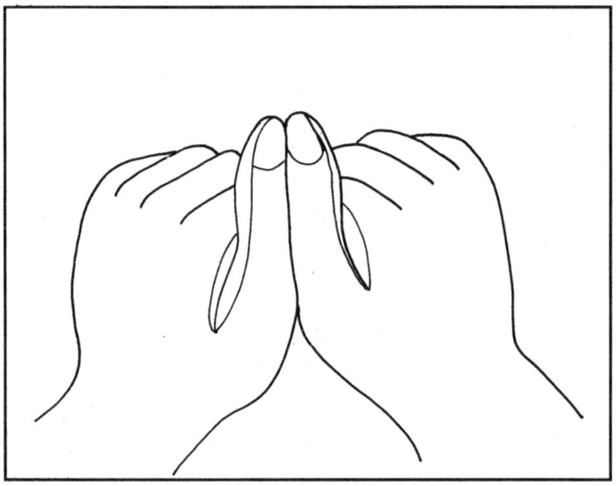

Figure 530 -- sharad mudra
(as seen by the holder)

twenty-four mudras held before the *Gayatri Jap* of the thirty-two total *Gayatri mudras*.[38] It is utilized for all sickness, especially cancer. This *mudra* is formed by: palms facing midline, fingers splayed and parallel to the ground, tips of the thumb, index, middle and ring fingers touch, thumbs extends upwards, little fingers are separated and extend. Thus formed, the mudra is held waist high. (KDe 82, RLM 72) (See: **Figure 529**)

shantida mudra -- (Ind.: *śāntida-mudrā* aka *abhaya mudrā*) A *mudra*, a ritual hand pose, a seal, which is common to both the Buddhist and Hindu traditions (although this term implies a specifically Hindu usage) and which denotes the "causing of tranquility." A variant term applied to *abhaya mudra*. It is a name that is applied to the Lord *Vishnu*[39] being one of the thousand names of the Lord *Vishnu* (*Vishnu-sahasranama*). See: *abhaya mudra*. (MJS 124)

sharad mudra -- (Ind.: *śarad-mudrā*) ("autumn mudra") A *mudra*, a ritual hand pose, a seal, a *tantric mudra* which is common to the Japanese Buddhist (*Vajraÿana, Mantrayana*) tradition and is held or formed by a devotee or priest during various rites. It may be accompanied by a *mantra*. The *sharad mudra* is a combined (Ind.: *saṁyutta*) form, held by both hands. It denotes autumn. This *mudra* is formed by: palms face outwards, fingers fold into the palms, thumbs extend upwards and touch along their length. (GDe 447) (See: **Figure 530**)

Sharasvati mudra -- (Ind.: *Sarasvatī-mudrā*) A hand pose, a seal, a dramatic (Ind.: *nāṭya*) *mudra* or gesture (Ind.: *darpaṇa*) held or formed by a performer, dancer or actor. It denotes the *Sharasvati*, one of the famous rivers of India. The *mudra* employed is identical in form to the *bana mudra*. See: *bana mudra*. (ACG 48)

Sharayu mudra -- (Ind.: *Sarayu-mudrā*) A hand pose, a seal, a dramatic (Ind.: *nāṭya*) *mudra* or gesture (Ind.: *darpaṇa*) held or formed by a performer, dancer or actor. It denotes the *Sharayu*, one of the famous rivers of India. The *mudra* employed is identical in form to the *padma mudra*. See: *padma mudra*. (ACG 48)

shashanka mudra -- (Ind.: *śaśāṅka-mudrā*) A hand pose, a seal, a dramatic (Ind.: *nāṭya*) *mudra* or gesture (Ind.: *darpaṇa*) held or formed by a performer, dancer or actor. It denotes an animal, in this case a hare. The *shashanka mudra*[40] is a single (Ind.: *asaṁyutta*) form, held by one hand. It is identical in form to the *tala-pataka mudra* moved horizontally (Ind.: *tiryak*). See: *tala-pataka mudra*) (ACG 50.

shayana mudra -- (Indic: *śayana-mudrā*; Eng.: reclining *mudra*; Thai: *pang parinippharn, pang s[h]aiyas*) This is a descriptive term.[41] See: *pang parinippharn*. (DRN 37, JBo 205, ODD 680, OFr [#33],PSS)

Shibi mudra -- (Ind.: *Śibi-mudrā*) A hand pose, a seal, a dramatic (Ind.: *nāṭya*) *mudra* or gesture (Ind.: *darpaṇa*) held or formed by a performer, dancer or actor. The *Shibi mudra* is a single (Ind.: *asaṁyutta*) form, held by one hand. It denotes *Shibi*, one of a number of famous rulers or heroes. The *mudra* employed is identical in form to the *kapittha mudra*. See: *kapittha mudra*. (ACG 47)

shih-wu-wei-yin -- (Chin.; Ind.: *abhaya mudrā, abhayamdada mudrā*) The Chinese term for *abhaya mudra* or *abhayamdada mudra*. See: *abhaya mudra*. (EDS 55)

shih-yṃan-yin (mudra) -- (Chin.; Ind.: *varada mudrā*) The Chinese term for *varada mudra*. See: *varada mudra*. (EDS 51)

shikhara mudra -- (Ind.: *śikhara-mudrā*) ("the spire") A *mudra*, a ritual hand pose, a seal, which is common to both the Buddhist and Hindu traditions and is depicted or held by a deity. The *shikhara mudra* is a single (Ind.: *asaṁyutta*) form, held by one hand. It denotes silence, steadiness, etc.[42] This *mudra* is formed by: palm faces mid-line, fingers brought into the palm forming a fist, thumb extends upwards. It is the masculine counterpart of the *kapittha mudra*. (ACG 30-31, KVa 134 [11 & 12], MJS 129) (See: **Figure 531**)

Figure 531 -- shikhara mudra
(as seen by the holder)

shimshapa mudra -- (Ind.: *śiṁśapa-mudrā*) A hand pose, a seal, a dramatic (Ind.: *nāṭya*) *mudra* or gesture (Ind.: *darpaṇa*) held or formed by a performer, dancer or actor. It denotes the *shimshapa* tree. The *mudra* employed is identical in form to the *ardha-chandra mudra*. See: *ardha-chandra mudra*. (ACG 49)

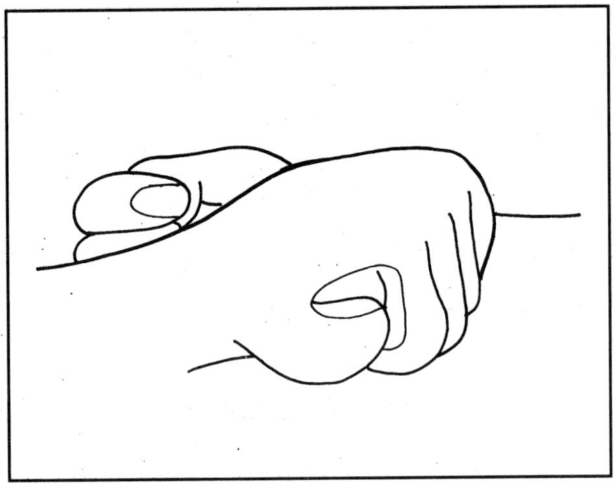

Figure 532 -- shirsha mudra
(as seen by the holder)

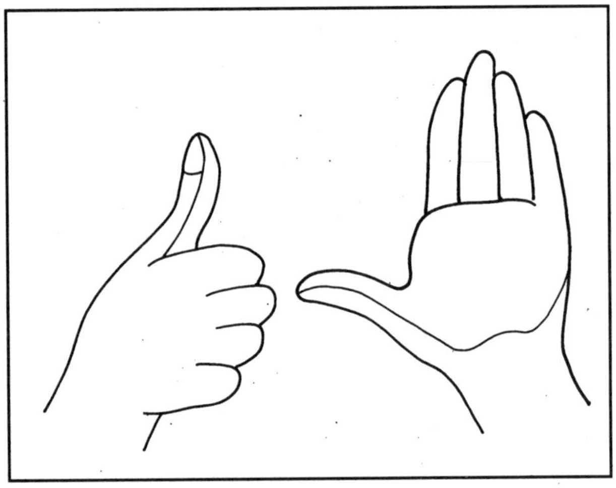

Figure 533 -- Shiva-linga mudra
(as seen by another)

shirsha mudra -- (Ind.: *śirṣa-mudrā*) ("*mudra* of the head") A *mudra*, a ritual hand pose, a seal, a *tantric mudra* which is common to the Japanese Buddhist (*Vajrayana, Mantrayana*) tradition and is held or formed by a devotee or priest during the rites of *Garbhadhatu Mandala* and other rites. It may be accompanied by a *mantra*. The *shirsha mudra* is a combined (Ind.: *saṁyutta*) form, held by both hands. This *mudra* is formed by: right palm faces inwards, thumb folded into the palm, fingers folded into the palm and over the thumb; left palm faces outwards, thumb folded into the palm, fingers folded into the palm and over the thumb. Thus formed, the folded fingers of the right hand touch the folded fingers of the left. (LCS 208) (See: **Figure 532**)

Shiva-linga mudra -- (Ind.: *Śiva-liṅga-mudrā*) A hand pose, a seal, a dramatic (Ind.: *nāṭya*) *mudra* or gesture (Ind.: *darpaṇa*) held or formed by a performer, dancer or actor. The *Shiva-linga mudra* is a combined (Ind.: *saṁyutta*) form, held by both hands. It denotes the *linga*. This *mudra* is formed by: right palm faces mid-line, fingers brought into the palm forming a fist, thumb extends upwards (*shikhara mudra*); left palm faces mid-line, thumb and fingers clasp or hold the right. This *mudra* is a variation of the *linga mudra*. (ACG 40) (See: **Figure 533**)

shizaige ken-in (mudra) -- (Jap.: *shizaige ken-in* [*mudra*] aka *gebaku ken-in* [*mudra*]; Chin.: *wai-fu ch'ṃan-yin*; Ind.: *granthitam mudrā*) A variant term applied to *gebaku ken-in* (*mudra*). See: *gebaku ken-in* (*mudra*). (EDS 119)

sho cha ro-in (mudra) -- (Jap.: *shō cha rō-in* [*mudrā*]) ("the receiving of the carts") A *mudra*, a ritual hand pose, a seal, a *tantric mudra* which is common to the Japanese Buddhist (*Vajrayana, Mantrayana*) tradition and is held or formed by a devotee or priest during the *Eighteen Rites* and other rites. It may be accompanied by a *mantra*. The *sho cha ro-in*[43] (*mudra*) is a combined (Ind.: *saṁyutta*) form, held by both hands. It denotes the reception of the Buddhas who arrive in carts. This *mudra* is formed by: palms face upwards, middle, ring and little fingers extend towards the midline, slightly curled and the first phalanges interlace, index fingers extend straight and their tips touch, tips of the thumbs touch the tips of the middle fingers. (GDe 105) (See: **Figure 534**)

sho ko-in (mudra) -- (Jap.: *shō kō-in* [*mudrā*]; Ind.: *dhūpa mudrā*) ("burning incense") A *mudra*, a ritual hand pose, a seal, a *tantric mudra* which is common to the Japanese Buddhist (*Vajrayana, Mantrayana*) tradition and is held or formed by a devotee or priest during the rites of *Garbhadhatu Mandala, Vajradhatu Mandala, Homa Rites* and other rites. It may be accompanied by a *mantra*. The *sho ko-in* (*mudra*) is a combined (Ind.: *saṁyutta*) form, held by both hands. It denotes an offering to the deities. This *mudra* is formed by: palms facing generally upward index fingers extend straight, thumbs rest along the index fingers, middle, ring and little fingers curl halfway towards the palms. Thus formed the hands are brought together so that the tips of the index fingers touch as well as the second knuckles of the middle, ring and little fingers. (GDe 47) (See: **Figure 535**)

shri-vatsya mudra -- (Ind.: *śrī-vatsya-mudrā*) This is an assigned term.[44] A *mudra*, a ritual hand pose, a seal, which is common to the Buddhist (*Vajrayana*) tradition, a *tantric mudra*. It denotes the the endless knot (Tib.: *dpal-gyi behu*), one of eight signs of good fortune (Indic: *ashta-mangala*, Tib.: *bkra-shis rtags-brgyad*), an 'outer offering'--the other seven being: the victory banner, wheel, lotus, golden fish, umbrella, treasure vase and conch shell--which is proffered to a divine guest during worship, particularly as associated with the ceremonies of the powerful *Vajrayana* goddess, *Tara*. The *shri-vatsya mudra* is a combined (Ind.: *saṁyutta*) form, held by both hands. This *mudra* is formed by: right hand palm faces upwards, index and middle finger extends outward, ring and little finger folds into the palm, first phalanges of the thumb covers the first phalanges of the ring and little finger, the left hand is formed in the same manner, except the palm faces downwards. Thus posed the first two phalanges of the index hand middle fingers of the left hand rest on the first two phalanges of the index hand middle fingers of the right hand. Thus formed, the *mudra* is held at chest level. The mantra associated with this mudra is: "*OM Shrivatsya Praticcha SVAHA*."[45] (SBe 155) (See: **Figure 536**)

Shudra mudra -- (Ind.: *Śūdra-mudrā*) A hand pose, a seal, a dramatic (Ind.: *nāṭya*) *mudra* or gesture (Ind.: *darpaṇa*) held or formed by a performer, dancer or ac-

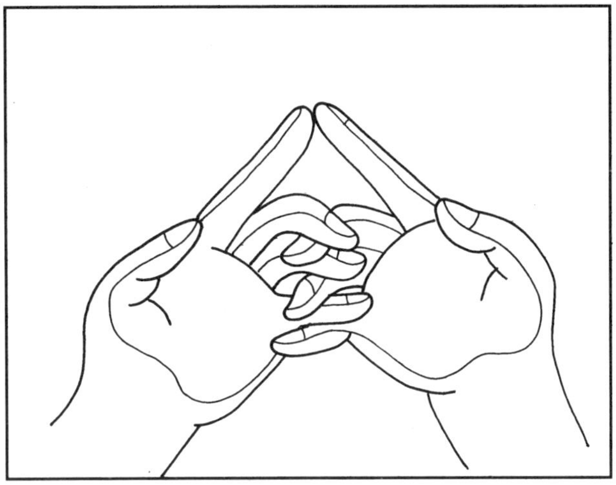

Figure 534 -- sho cha ro-in (mudra)
(as seen by the holder)

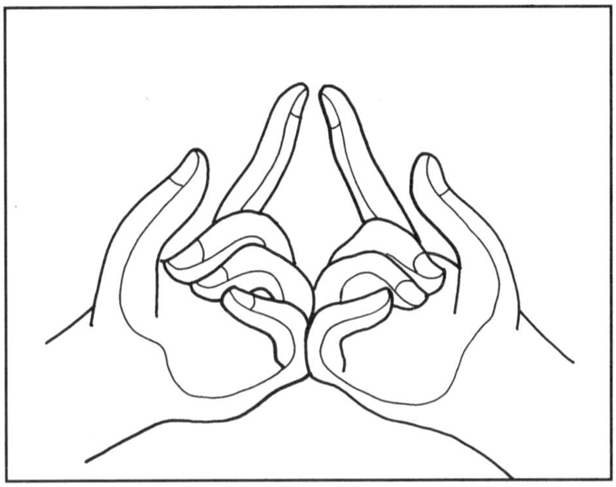

Figure 535 -- sho ko-in (mudra)
(as seen by the holder)

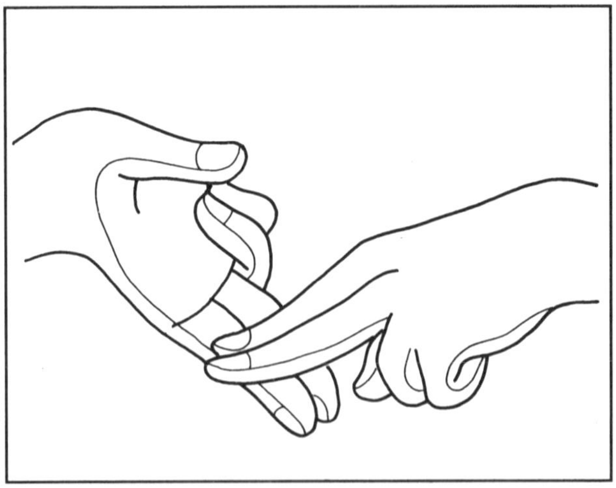

Figure 536 -- shri-vatsya mudra
(as seen by another)

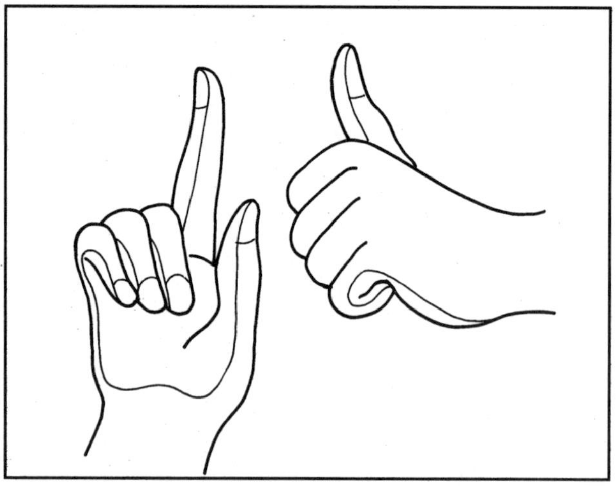

Figure 537 -- Shudra mudra
(as seen by another)

Figure 538 -- shukatunda mudra
(as seen by another)

tor. The *Shudra mudra* is a combined (Ind.: *saṁyutta*) form, held by both hands. It denotes *Shudra*, one of the four castes. This *mudra* is formed by: right palm faces outwards, the index finger and the thumb point upwards, together, the middle, ring and little fingers are folded into the palm; left palm faces mid-line, fingers brought into the palm forming a fist, thumb extends upwards. (ACG 47) (See: **Figure 537**)

shuka mudra -- (Ind.: *śuka-mudrā*) A hand pose, a seal, a dramatic (Ind.: *nāṭya*) *mudra* or gesture (Ind.: *darpaṇa*) held or formed by a performer, dancer or actor. It denotes a bird, in this case a parrot. The *shuka mudra*[46] is a combined (Ind.: *saṁyutta*) form, held by both hands. This *mudra* is identical in form to the *shukatunda mudra*. See: *shukatunda mudra*. (ACG 50)

shukatunda mudra -- (Ind.: *śukatuṇḍa-mudrā* aka *śukatuṇḍaka-mudrā*) ("the parrot beak") A *mudra*, a ritual hand pose, a seal, which is common to the Hindu tradition and is depicted or held by a deity. Also, a hand pose, a seal, a dramatic (Ind.: *nāṭya*) *mudra* or gesture (Ind.: *darpaṇa*) held or formed by a performer, dancer or actor. The *shukatunda mudra* is a single (Ind.: *asaṁyutta*) form, held by one hand. It denotes shooting an arrow or fierceness.[47] This *mudra* is formed by: palm faces outwards, thumb, middle and little fingers extend upwards, index and ring fingers curve towards the palm. (ACG 30, GLi 285, KVa 134 [9], MJS 136) (See: **Figure 538**)

shukatundaka mudra -- (Ind.: *śukatuṇḍaka-mudrā* aka *śukatuṇḍa mudrā*) A variant (spelling) of *shukatunda mudra*. See: *shukatunda mudra*. (ACG 30)

Shukra mudra -- (Ind.: *Śukra-mudrā*) A hand pose, a seal, a dramatic (Ind.: *nāṭya*) *mudra* or gesture (Ind.: *darpaṇa*) held or formed by a performer, dancer or actor. The *Shukra mudra* is a combined (Ind.: *saṁyutta*) form, held by both hands. It denotes Venus, one of the nine planets (Ind.: *navagraha*). This *mudra* is formed by: right palm faces the midline, the fingers are fisted, the thumb lies over the first phalanges of the fingers and held so that fingers are down; left palm faces the midline, the fingers are fisted, the thumb lies over the first phalanges of the fingers, and held so that fingers are upwards. (ACG 46) (See: **Figure 539**)

shumi sen ho-in (mudra) -- (Jap.: *shumi sen hō-in* [*mudrā*]; Ind.: *Sumeru mudrā*) ("*mudra* of Mt. Sumeru") A *mudra*, a ritual hand pose, a seal, a *tantric mudra* which is common to the Japanese Buddhist (*Vajrayana, Mantrayana*) tradition and is held or formed by a devotee or priest during the rites of *Homa* and other rites. It may be accompanied by a *mantra*. The *shumi sen ho-in* (*mudra*) is a combined (Ind.: *saṁyutta*) form, held by both hands. This *mudra* is formed by: the left palm facing the midline, thumb folded into the palm, index, middle, ring and little fingers folded over the thumb; right palm faces outwards, thumb, index, middle, ring and little fingers extend upwards. Thus formed, the left hand rests upon the left thigh, the left is held chest high. (GDe 95) (See: **Figure 540**)

shunya mudra -- (Ind.: *śūnya-mudrā*) A *mudra*, a ritual hand pose, a seal, a *mudra* which is common to yogic tradition, particularly the *Yoga Tatva Mudra Vigyan* form, and is held by a devotee or practitioner. The *shunya mudra*[48] is a single (Ind.: *asaṁyutta*) form, held by one hand. It is utilized for the heart and hearing. This *mudra* is formed by: palm facing forwards, index, ring and little fingers extend straight upwards, the middle finger folds into the palm, the thumb cross over that finger at the second phalanges. It resembles the *karana mudra*. (KDe 52) (See: **Figure 541**)

shvan mudra -- (Ind.: *śvān-mudrā*) A hand pose, a seal, a dramatic (Ind.: *nāṭya*) *mudra* or gesture (Ind.: *darpaṇa*) held or formed by a performer, dancer or actor. It denotes an animal, in this case a dog. The *shvan mudra*[49] is a combined (Ind.: *saṁyutta*) form, held by both hands. This *mudra* is identical in form to the *madhya-pataka mudra*. See: *madhya-pataka mudra*. (ACG 50)

shvashri mudra -- (Ind.: *śvaśrī-mudrā*) A hand pose, a seal, a dramatic (Ind.: *nāṭya*) *mudra* or gesture (Ind.: *darpaṇa*) held or formed by a performer, dancer or actor. The *shvashri mudra* is a combined (Ind.: *saṁyutta*) form, held by both hands. One of eleven mudras representing "relationships" and one which denotes mother-in-law. This *mudra* is formed by: right palm faces upwards, fingers and thumb are separated and gently curl inwards, towards the hollowed palm except the middle finger which is held straight out and

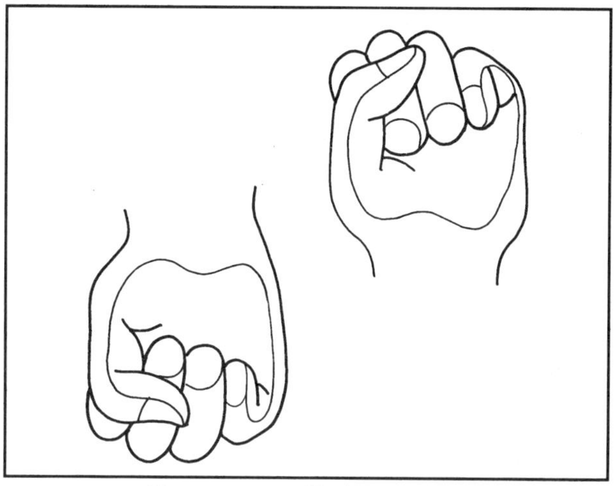

Figure 539 -- Shukra mudra
(as seen by another)

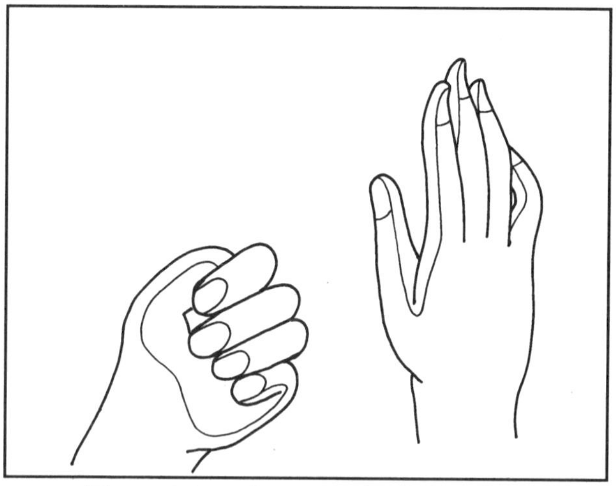

Figure 540 -- shumi sen ho-in (mudra)
(as seen by the holder)

Figure 541 -- shunya mudra
(as seen by another)

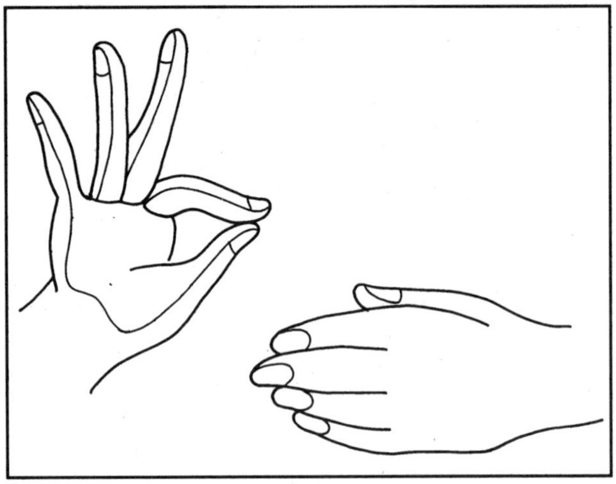

Figure 542 -- shvashri mudra
(as seen by another)

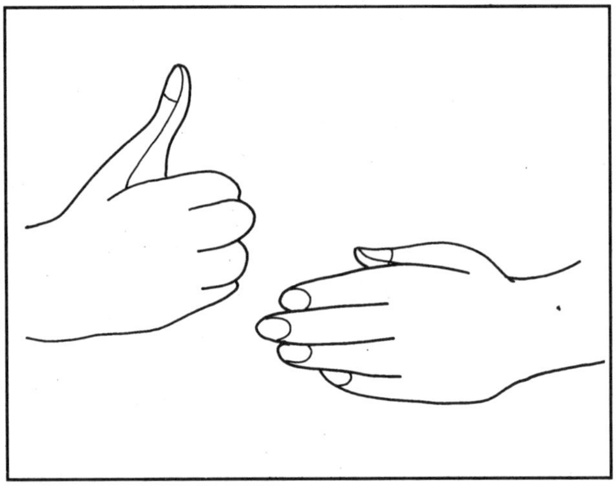

Figure 543 -- shvashura mudra
(as seen by another)

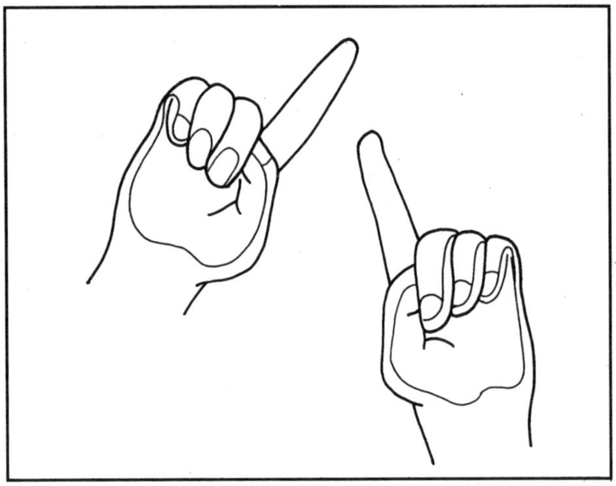

Figure 544 -- sima-bandha mudra I
(as seen by another)

held at the throat; left palm face the midline, fingers and thumb extended together towards the midline, and on the lower abdomen. (ACG 44) (See: **Figure 542**)

shvashura mudra -- (Ind.: *śvaśura-mudrā*) A hand pose, a seal, a dramatic (Ind.: *nāṭya*) *mudra* or gesture (Ind.: *darpaṇa*) held or formed by a performer, dancer or actor. The *shvashura mudra* is a combined (Ind.: *saṁyutta*) form, held by both hands. One of eleven *mudras* representing "relationships" and one which denotes father-in-law. This *mudra* is formed by: right palm faces midline, fingers brought into the palm forming a fist, thumb extends upwards; left palm face the midline, fingers and thumb extended together towards the midline, and placed on the lower abdomen. (ACG 45) (See: **Figure 543**)

sima-bandha mudra I -- (Ind.: *sīmā-bandha-mudrā*) A mudra, a ritual hand pose, a seal, a *tantric mudra* which is common to the Japanese Buddhist (*Vajrayana, Mantrayana*) tradition and is held or formed by a devotee or priest during the rites of the *Vajradhatu Mandala* rites. It may be accompanied by a *mantra*. The *sima-bandha mudra*[50] is a combined (Ind.: *saṁyutta*) form, held by both hands. This *mudra* is similar to the *zen-in* (*mudra*) and is identical for both hands and is formed by: palm facing outward, the middle, ring and little fingers folded into the palm, the thumb touches the second phalange of the middle finger, the index finger extends straight. Thus formed the two hands are rotated slightly so that the index fingers point towards the mid-line--i.e. approximately 30°--and the left hand is slightly lower than the right. (LCS 74) (See: **Figure 544**)

sima-bandha mudra II -- (Ind.: *sīmā-bandha-mudrā* aka *vajra-bandha mudrā*) A variant term applied to *vajra-bandha mudra*.[51] See: *vajra-bandha mudra*. (LCS 61)

simha mudra -- (Ind.: *siṃha-mudrā*) A hand pose, a seal, a dramatic (Ind.: *nāṭya*) *mudra* or gesture (Ind.: *darpaṇa*) held or formed by a performer, dancer or actor. It denotes an animal, in this case a lion. The *simha mudra*[52] is a combined (Ind.: *saṁyutta*) form, held by both hands. The *simha mudra* is a combined (Ind.: *saṁyutta*) form, held by both hands. This *mudra* is formed by: right palm facing forward, the index and little fingers extended upwards and straight, the middle and ring fingers are curl into the palm, the first phalanges of the thumb lays across the first phalanges of the middle and ring fingers; left hand is raised, fingers and thumb extended, together and pointing upwards, relaxed, slightly cupped, palm facing outward and touching the back of the right hand. (ACG 49) (See: **Figure 545**)

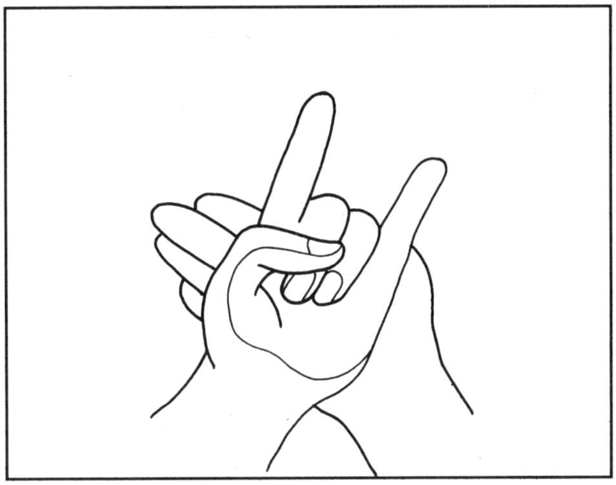

Figure 545 -- simha mudra
(as seen by another)

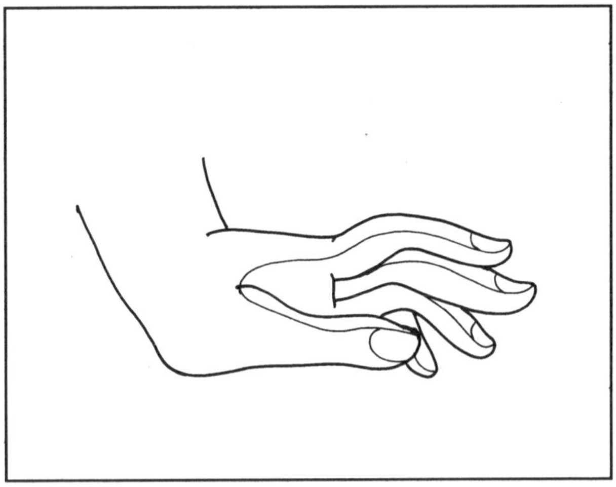

Figure 546 -- simhakarna mudra I
(as seen by another)

simhakarna mudra I -- (Ind.: *siṁhakarṇa-mudrā*) A *mudra*, a ritual hand pose, a seal, which is common to the Hindu tradition. It is viewed as a purely aesthetic pose.[53] The *simhakarna mudra I* is a single (Ind.: *asaṁyutta*) form, held by one hand. This *mudra* is formed by: arm held down, slightly and gracefully away from the body, the hand, palm down, fingers and thumbs extended in a relaxed manner, fingertips point outward (away from the body). (HKS 267) (See: **Figure 546**)

simhakarna mudra II -- (Ind.: *siṁhakarṇa-mudrā* aka *kaṭaka mudrā*) The *simhakarna mudra II*[54] is a variant term applied to *kataka mudra*. See: *kataka mudra*. (MJS 129, RSG 3, TGR 15)

simhakarna-simhakarna mudra -- (Ind.: *siṁhakarṇa-siṁhakarṇa-mudrā*; Eng.: revealing the three worlds mudra; Thai: **pang ODD #32**) This is a descriptive term.[55] See: **pang ODD #32**. (DRN 36, JBo 205, ODD 680, PSS)

simhakrantam mudra -- (Ind.: *siṁhakrāntam-mudrā* aka *singhakrānt mudrā*) A variant (spelling) of *singhakrant mudra*. See: *singhakrant mudra*. (RLM 74)

simha-mukha mudra -- (Ind.: *siṁha-mukha-mudrā*) ("lion head") A hand pose, a seal, a dramatic (Ind.: *nāṭya*) *mudra* or gesture (Ind.: *darpaṇa*) held or formed by a performer, dancer or actor. The *simha-mukha mudra* is a single (Ind.: *asaṁyutta*) form, held by one hand. It denotes a lion's head, fragrance, salvation, etc.[56] This *mudra* is formed by: palm facing forward, the index and little fingers extended upwards and straight, the middle and ring fingers are curl into the palm, the first phalanges of the thumb lays across the first phalanges of the middle and ring fingers. It is similar to the *karana mudra*. (ACG, 34) (See: **Figure 547**)

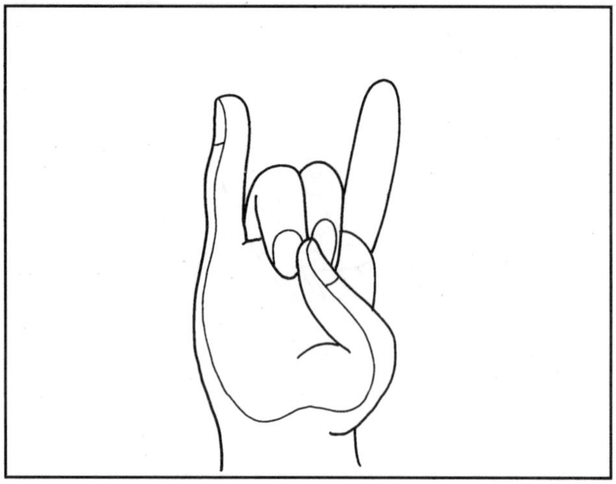

Figure 547 -- simha-mukha mudra
(as seen by another)

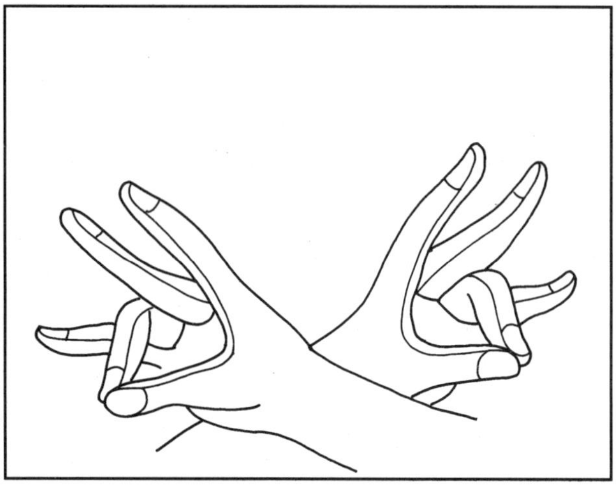

Figure 548 -- sindhuvara mudra
(as seen by another)

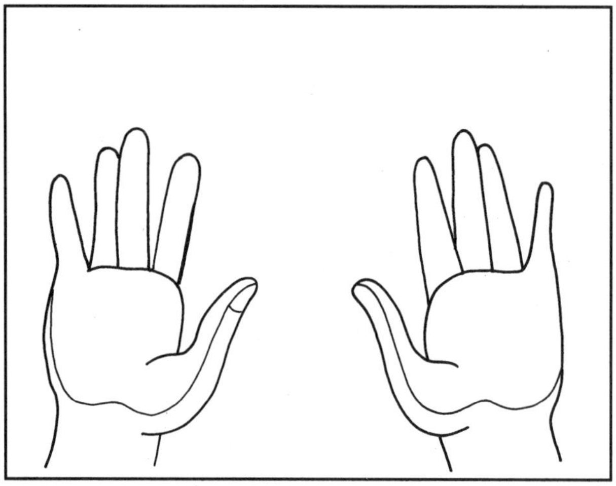

Figure 549 -- singhakrant mudra
(as seen by another)

sindhuvara mudra -- (Ind.: *sindhuvara-mudrā*) A hand pose, a seal, a dramatic (Ind.: *nāṭya*) *mudra* or gesture (Ind.: *darpaṇa*) held or formed by a performer, dancer or actor. It denotes the *sindkuvara tree.* The *sindhuvara mudra* is a combined (Ind.: *saṁyutta*) form, held by both hands. This *mudra* is formed in mirror pose by: palms facing outwards, tips of the thumbs and ring finger touch and extend outwards, the index and middle fingers are straight and slightly separated, the little fingers are slightly bent. Thus formed the hands are hands "interlocked" or crossed at the wrists. The individual hands form the *mayura mudra.* (ACG 49) (See: **Figure 548**)

singhakrant mudra -- (Ind.: *singhakrānt-mudrā* aka *siṁhakrāntam mudrā*) A mudra, a ritual hand pose, a seal, a *mudra* which is common to yogic tradition, particularly the *Yoga Tatva Mudra Vigyan* form, and is held by a devotee or practitioner. The *singhakrant mudra*[57] is a combined (Ind.: *saṁyutta*) form, held by both hands. It is one of the twenty-four *mudras* held before the *Gayatri Jap* of the thirty-two total *Gayatri mudras*.58 It is utilized for all sickness, especially cancer. This *mudra* is formed by: hands are raised, fingers and thumbs extended upwards and together, relaxed, slightly cupped, palm facing outward and on a line level with the chest or shoulders. Thus formed, the hands are held at either side of the shoulders. It is one of the four *Gayatri mudras* which make reference to the Lord *Vishnu*'s first five (animal) *avatars*. (KDe 86 & 108, RLM 74) (See: **Figure 549**)

sitatapatra mudra -- (Ind.: *sitātapatra-mudrā*) This is an assigned term.[59] A *mudra*, a ritual hand pose, a seal, which is common to the Buddhist (*Vajrayana*) tradition, a *tantric mudra*. It denotes the white parasol (Tib.: *rinchen gdugs*), one of eight signs of good fortune (Ind.: *aṣṭa-maṅgala*, Tib.: *bkra-shis rtags-brgyad*), an 'outer offering'--the other seven being: the knot, wheel, lotus, golden fish, victory banner, treasure vase and conch shell--which is proffered to a divine guest during worship, particularly as associated with the ceremonies of the powerful *Vajrayana* goddess, *Tara*. The *sitatapatra mudra* is a combined (Ind.: *saṁyutta*) form, held by both hands. This *mudra* is formed by: the right palm faces downwards, fingers and thumb extend towards the mid-line, left palm faces the mid-line, middle, ring and little fingers fold into the palm, thumb touches the first phalanges of the middle finger, index finger points upward. Thus posed the left index finger touches the palm of the right hand and the *mudra* is held at chest level. The *mantra* associated with this *mudra* is: "*OM Sitatapatra Praticcha SVAHA.*"[60] (SBe 155) (See: **Figure 550**)

snusha mudra -- (Ind.: *snuṣa-mudrā*) A hand pose, a seal, a dramatic (Ind.: *nāṭya*) *mudra* or gesture (Ind.: *darpaṇa*) held or formed by a performer, dancer or actor. The *snusha mudra* is a combined (Ind.: *saṁyutta*) form, held by both hands. One of eleven *mudras* representing "relationships" and one which denotes daughter-in-law. This *mudra* is formed by: right palm face the midline, fingers and thumb extended together towards the midline, and placed on the lower abdomen; left palm facing the midline, tips of the thumb and ring finger touch and extend inwards, the index and middle fingers are straight and slightly separated, the little fingers is slightly bent. (ACG 45) (See: **Figure 551**)

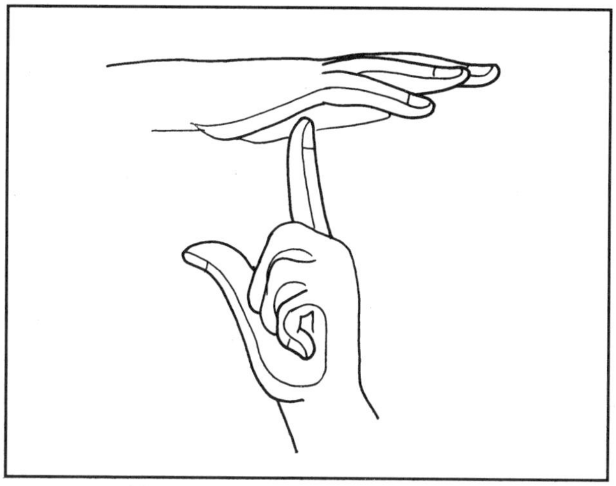

Figure 550 -- sitatapatra mudra
(as seen by another)

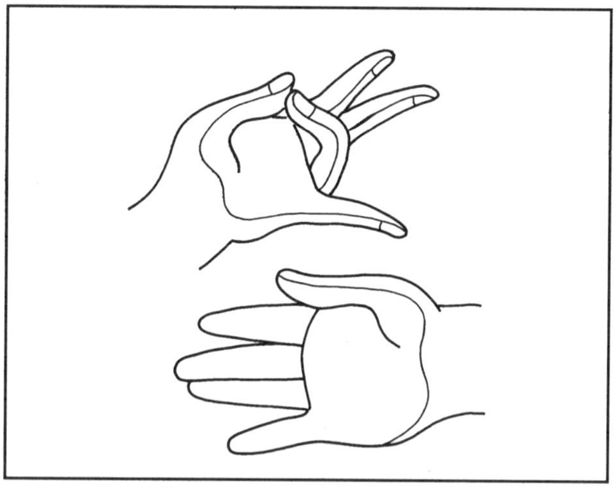

Figure 551 -- snusha mudra
(as seen by the holder)

so cha ro-in mudra -- (Jap.: *sō cha rō-in* [*mudrā*] aka *ke man-in* [*mudra*]) ("sending the cart") A variant term applied to ke man-in (*mudra*). See: *ke man-in* (*mudra*); see: *pushpa-mala mudra*. (GDe 104)

so ko shu-go-in (mudra) -- (Jap.: *sō kō shu-gō-in* [*mudrā*]) ("guardian of the face") A *mudra*, a ritual hand pose, a seal, a *tantric mudra* which is common to the Japanese Buddhist (*Vajrayana, Mantrayana*) tradition and is held or formed by a devotee or priest during the rites of *Garbhadhatu Mandala, Vajradhatu Mandala, Homa Rites* and other rites. It may be accompanied by a *mantra*. The *so ko shu-go-in* (*mudra*) is a combined (Ind.: *saṁyutta*) form, held by both hands. It denotes the destruction of demons. This *mudra* is formed by: left palm generally facing outward, thumb folded into the palm, middle and ring fingers folded over the thumb, index and little fingers curl at their first two knuckles, third phalanges remains erect (upward), the right thumb is folded into the palm, the middle, ring and little fingers fold over an enclose the thumb, the index finger extends and points towards the left hand. (GDe 46) (See: **Figure 552**)

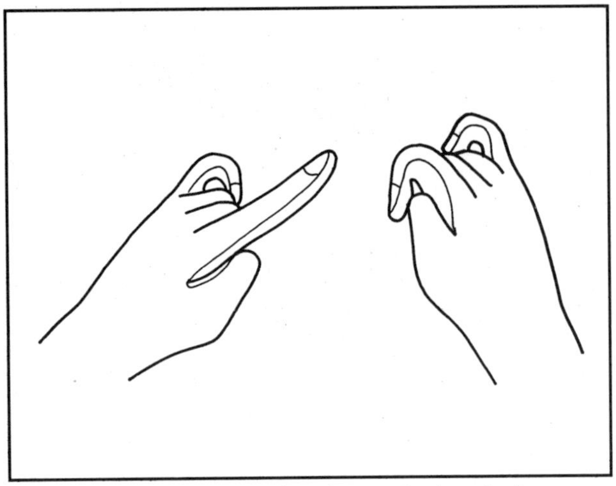

Figure 552 -- so ko shu-go-in (mudra)
(as seen by the holder)

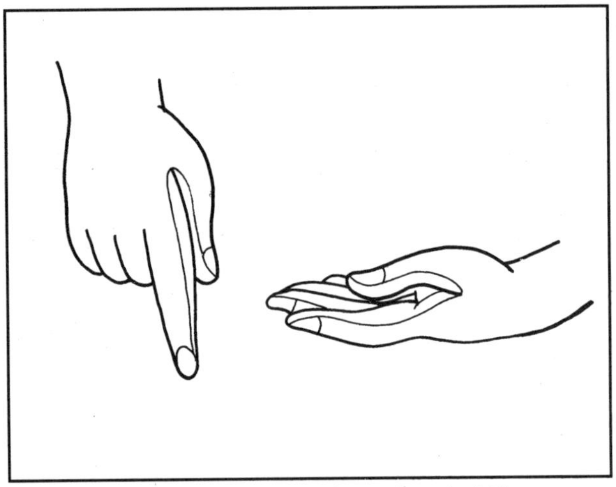

Figure 553 -- sokuchi-in (mudra) II
(as seen by another)

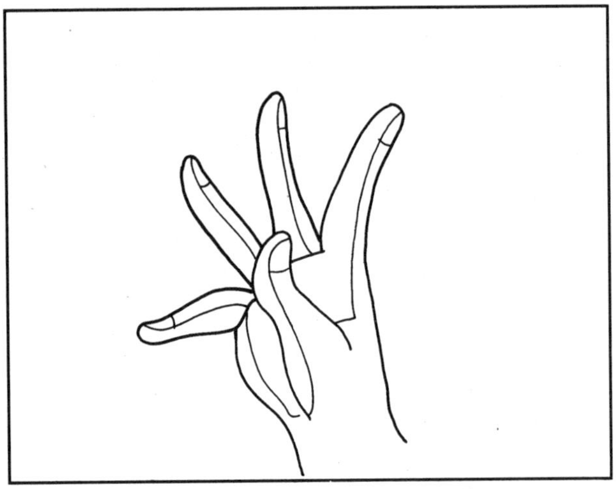

Figure 554 -- sola-padma mudra
(as seen by another)

sokuchi-in (mudra) I -- (Jap.: *sokuchi-in* [*mudrā*] aka *anzan-in* [*mudra*]; Chin.: *an-shan-yin, ch'u-ti-yin;* Eng.: adamantine posture; Ind.: *bhasparsha mudrā, bhūmisparśa mudrā, bhūmisparśana mudrā, bhūmiśparśa mudrā, bhūsparś mudrā, bhūsparśa mudrā, māravijaya mudrā;* Thai: *manwichai* [*mudra*], *pang maravichai,* [*pang*] *sadung-man*) The Japanese term for *bhumisparsha mudra*. See: *bhumisparsha mudra*. (EDS 80)

sokuchi-in (mudra) II -- (Jap.: *sokuchi-in* [*mudrā*] aka *anzan-in* [*mudra*]; Chin.: *an-shan-yin, ch'u-ti-yin;* Eng.: adamantine posture; Ind.: *bhasparśa mudrā, bhūmiśparśa mudrā, bhūmisparśana mudrā, bhūmisparśa mudrā, bhūsparś mudrā, bhūsparśa mudrā, māravijaya mudrā;* Thai: *manwichai* [*mudra*], *pang maravichai,* [*pang*] *sadung-man*) A *mudra*, a ritual hand pose, a seal, which is common to the Japanese Buddhist tradition and a variation of *sokuchi-in (mudra) I*. The *sokuchi-in (mudra) II* is a combined (Ind.: *saṁyutta*) form, held by both hands. This *mudra* is formed by: right forearm rest upon the right thigh, the hand is relaxed and bends at the wrist, palm faces the midline, the index finger points downward (frequently touching the ground), the thumb rests along the index finger, the middle, ring and little fingers are curled into the palm (similar to the *tarjani mudra*); the relaxed left hand rests in the lap, palm facing upwards (*dhyana mudra*). (EDS 80) (See: **Figure 553**)

sola-padma mudra -- (Ind.: *sola-padma-mudrā* aka *ala-padma mudrā*) ("full-blown lotus") A hand pose, a seal, a dramatic (Ind.: *nāṭya*) *mudra* or gesture (Ind.: *darpaṇa*) held or formed by a performer, dancer or actor. The *sola-padma mudra* is a single (Ind.: *asaṁyutta*) form, held by one hand. It denotes turning, yearning, crown, etc.[61] This *mudra* is formed by: the palm turned upwards, the thumb and fingers are stretched far apart, stiff; so formed, the little finger is at 90° to the palm and the ring finger is at 45° to the palm. (ACG 34-35 & Plate 12-C, KVa 135 [18-19]) (See: **Figure 554**)

stamping his footprint in the ground mudra -- (Eng.; Ind.: *hastasvastika mudrā IV;* Thai: *pang phraditthanroy-phrabuddhabatr*) The English descriptive phrase for the Thai *pang phraditthanroy-phrabuddhabatr*. See: *pang phraditthanroy-phrabuddhabatr*. (DRN 37, JBo, PSS, ODD 780)

standing mudra -- (Eng.; Indic: *lolahasta-lolahasta mudra*; Thai: **pang ODD #34**) The English descriptive phrase for the Thai **pang ODD #34**. See: **pang ODD #34**. (DRN 37, JBo, ODD 679)

sthirabodhi mudra -- (Ind.: *sthirabodhi-mudrā*) A *mudra*, a ritual hand pose, a seal, a *tantric mudra* which is common to the Japanese Buddhist (*Vajrayana, Mantrayana*) tradition and is held or formed by a devotee or priest during the rites of *Garbhadhatu Mandala* and other rites. It may be accompanied by a *mantra*. The *sthirabodhi mudra* is a combined (Ind.: *saṁyutta*) form, held by both hands. This *mudra* is formed by: thumbs extend upwards and touch along their length, index fingers extend straight upwards, middle, ring and little fingers interlace and fold inwards (into the palms). (LCS 169) (See: **Figure 555**)

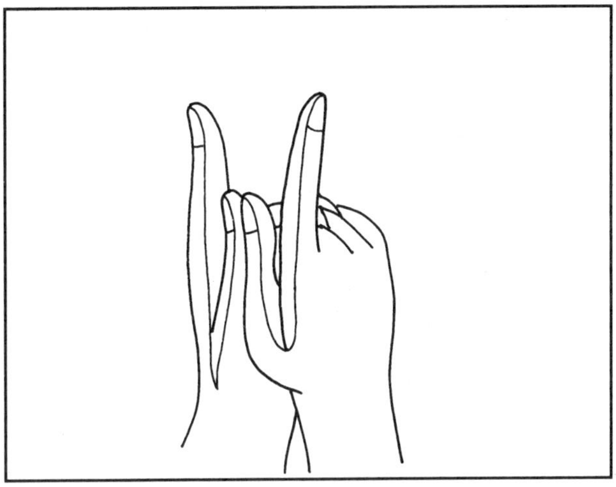

Figure 555 -- sthirabodhi mudra
(as seen by the holder)

stri mudra -- (Ind.: *strī-mudrā*) A hand pose, a seal, a dramatic (Ind.: *nāṭya*) *mudra* or gesture (Ind.: *darpaṇa*) held or formed by a performer, dancer or actor. The *stri mudra* is a single (Ind.: *asaṁyutta*) form, held by one hand. It denotes the womb. This *mudra* is formed by: either hand, palm face the midline, fingers and thumb extended towards the midline, and placed on the lower abdomen. (ACG 44) (See: **Figure 556**)

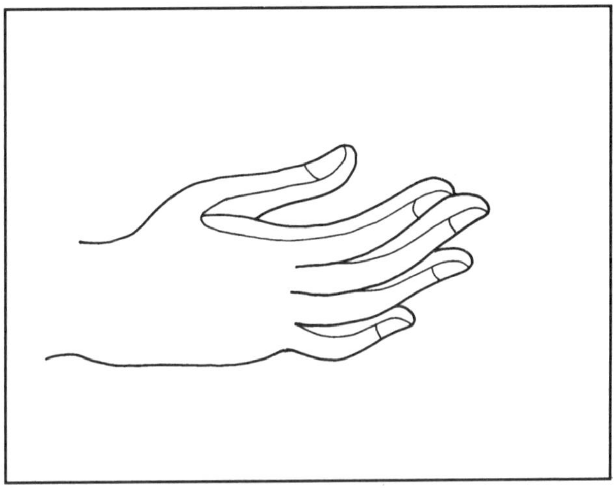

Figure 556 -- stri mudra
(as seen by another)

stri-ratna mudra -- (Ind.: *strī-ratna-mudrā*) This is an assigned term.[62] A *mudra*, a ritual hand pose, a seal, which is common to the Buddhist (*Vajrayana*) tradition, a *tantric mudra*. It denotes the gift of a precious queen (Tib.: *btsun-mo*) associated with the *saptaratna* (Tib.: *rgyal-srid sna-bdun*) or seven gems of sovereignty (Tib.: *nor-bu-chab-bdun*), also referred to as the 'space vast treasury,' particularly as it is associated with the worship of the powerful *Vajrayana* goddess, *Tara*. The *stri-ratna mudra* is a combined (Ind.: *saṁyutta*) form, held by both hands. This *mudra* is formed in mirror-pose: palm faces the midline, index, middle and little fingers are folded into the palm, thumb lays across the first phalanges of the folded fingers, ring finger extends upwards. Thus posed the two hands are close, but not touching and the *mudra* is held at chest level. The *mantra* associated with this *mudra* is: "*OM Stri-ratna Praticcha HUM SVAHA*."[63] (SBe 152) (See: **Figure 557**)

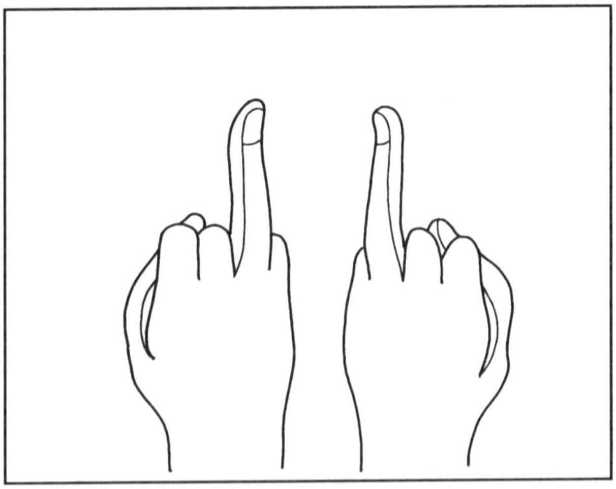

Figure 557 -- stri-ratna mudra
(as seen by another)

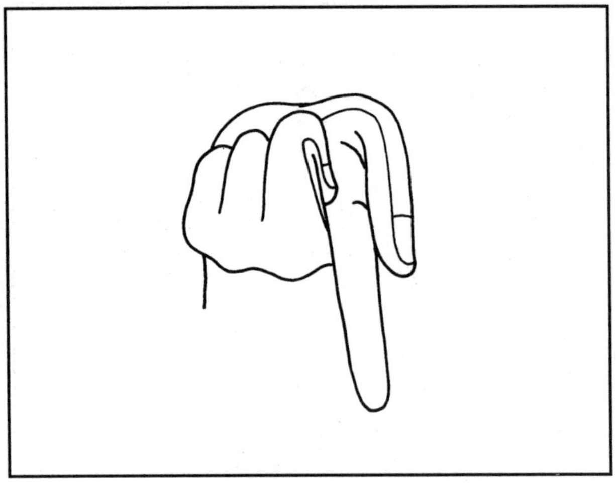

Figure 558 -- suchi mudra I
(as seen by another)

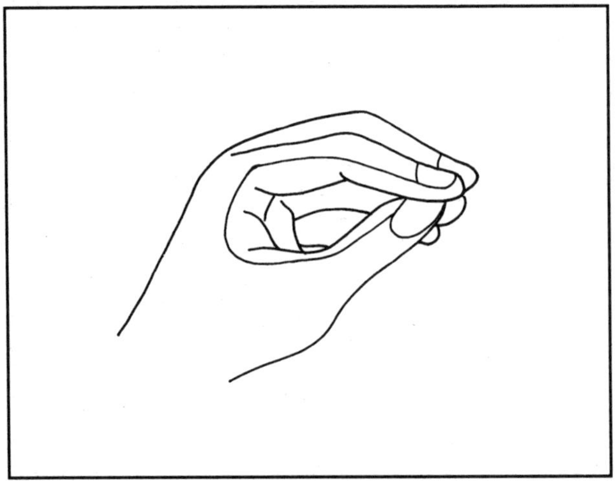

Figure 559 -- suchi mudra II
(as seen by the holder)

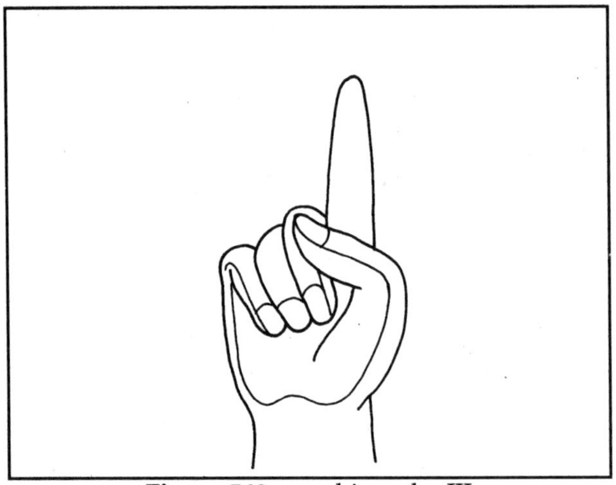

Figure 560 -- suchi mudra III
(as seen by another)

stupa mudra -- (Ind.: *stūpa mudrā;* Chin.: *wu-so-pu-chih-yin;* Jap.: *Biroshana-in* [*mudra*], *butsubu sotoba-in* [*mudra*], *dai sotoba-in* [*mudra*], *hen hokkai mushofushi-in* [*mudra*], *mushofushi-in* [*mudra*], *mushofushi to-in* [*mudra*], *rito-in* [*mudra*]) The Chinese term for *mushofushi-in* (*mudra*). See: *mushofushi-in* (*mudra*). (EDS 115, GDe 32, LCS 221)

suchi mudra I -- (Ind.: *sūcī-mudra*) ("the needle") A *mudra*, a ritual hand pose, a seal, which is common to both the Buddhist and Hindu traditions and is depicted or held by a deity. It is more frequently found within Hindu practice. The *suchi mudra* is a single (Ind.: *asaṁyutta*) form, held by one hand. It denotes an elephant tusk, transgression or the universe. This *mudra* is formed by: palm facing upwards, index finger extends downwards, middle and ring fingers fold into the palm, little finger bends towards the palm, thumb touches middle finger. It is similar to the *tarjani mudra* except that it points downward rather than upward. (ACG Plate XIII-A, BBh 197, HKS 271, MJS 135, RSG 3, TGR 14) (See: **Figure 558**)

suchi mudra II -- (Ind.: *sūcī-mudrā*) ("the needle") A *mudra*, a ritual hand pose, a seal, which is common to both the Buddhist and Hindu traditions and is depicted or held by a deity. It is more frequently found within Hindu practice. The *suchi mudra* is a single (Ind.: *asaṁyutta*) form, held by one hand. This *mudra* a variation, is formed by: "all fingers are stretched with the tips joining at the end, so as to resemble a needle (*suchi*)."[64] (BBh 197) (See: **Figure 559**)

suchi mudra III -- (Ind.: *sūcī-mudrā*) ("the needle") A hand pose, a seal, a dramatic (Ind.: *nāṭya*) *mudra* or gesture (Ind.: *darpaṇa*) held or formed by a performer, dancer or actor. The *suchi mudra* is a single (Ind.: *asaṁyutta*) form, held by one hand. It denotes threatening, astonishment, turning the potters wheel, etc.[65] This *mudra* a variation, is formed by: the palm faces outwards, the index finger and the thumb point upwards, together, the middle, ring and little fingers are folded into the palm. It is similar to the *tarjani mudra*. (ACG 32, KVa 135 ([17]) (See: **Figure 560**)

suchi mudra IV -- (Ind.: *sūcī-mudra*) ("the needle") A *mudra*, a ritual hand pose, a seal, a *tantric mudra* which is common to the Japanese Buddhist (*Vajrayana*,

Mantrayana) tradition and is held or formed by a devotee or priest during the rites of *Garbhadhatu Mandala, Vajradhatu Mandala, Homa Rites* and other rites. It may be accompanied by a *mantra*. The *suchi mudra*[66] is a combined (Ind.: *saṁyutta*) form, held by both hands. This *mudra* is formed by: the two hands are brought together, palm to palm, the index, ring and little fingers and thumbs are interlaced, the left thumb over the right and so forth, the fingers resting on the back of the hand, the middle fingers extend upward and are pressed together. (GDe 69, LCS 86) (See: **Figure 561**)

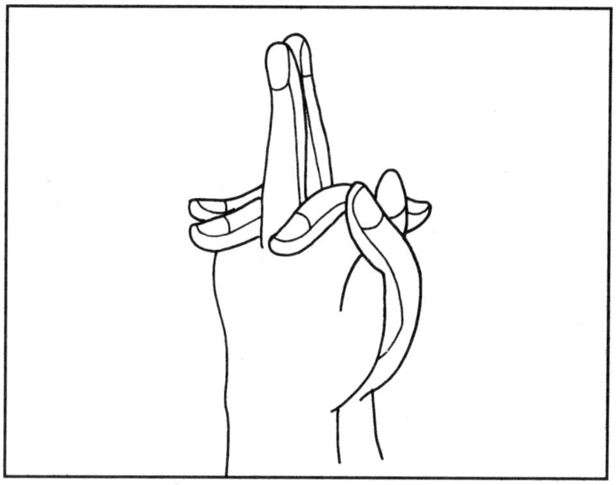

Figure 561 -- suchi mudra IV
(as seen by the holder)

suchi-viddha mudra -- (Ind.: *sūcī-viddha-mudrā*) A hand pose, a seal, a dramatic (Ind.: *nāṭya*) *mudra* or gesture (Ind.: *darpaṇa*) held or formed by a performer, dancer or actor noted in ACG but without description. (ACG 44)

suchyasya mudra -- (Ind.: *sucyāsya-mudrā*) ("needle face") A hand pose, a seal, a dramatic (Ind.: *nāṭya*) *mudra* or gesture (Ind.: *darpaṇa*) held or formed by a performer, dancer or actor. The *suchyasya mudra* is a combined (Ind.: *saṁyutta*) form, held by both hands. It denotes yearning for the beloved one, "look here," etc.[67] This *mudra* requires movement and is formed by: palms face outwards, the index finger and the thumbs point upwards, together, the middle, ring and little fingers are folded into the palms, and held in front of the chest. Thus formed the hands are moved to the respective sides simultaneously. (ACG 43) (See: **Figure 562**)

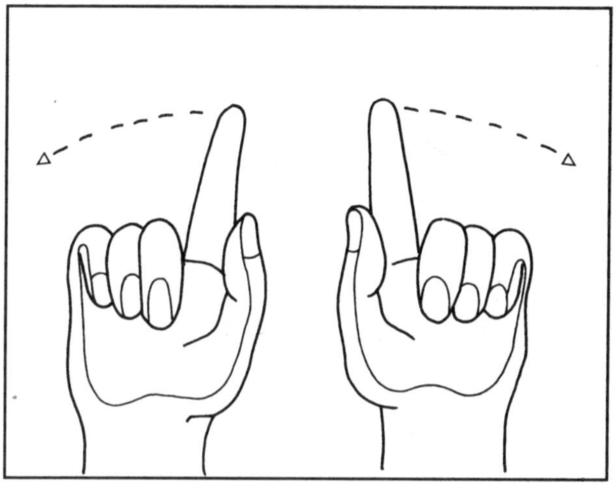

Figure 562 -- suchyasya mudra
(as seen by another)

sukri mudra -- (Ind.: *sukri-mudrā*) A *mudrā*, a ritual hand pose, a seal, a *mudra* which is common to yogic tradition, particularly the *Yoga Tatva Mudra Vigyan* form, and is held by a devotee or practitioner. The *sukri mudra* is a single (Ind.: *asaṁyutta*) form, held by one hand. It is utilized for peace and restorative needs. This *mudra* is formed by: palm facing forwards, the tips of the index, middle, ring and little finger touch the tip of the thumb. (KDe 64) (See: **Figure 563**)

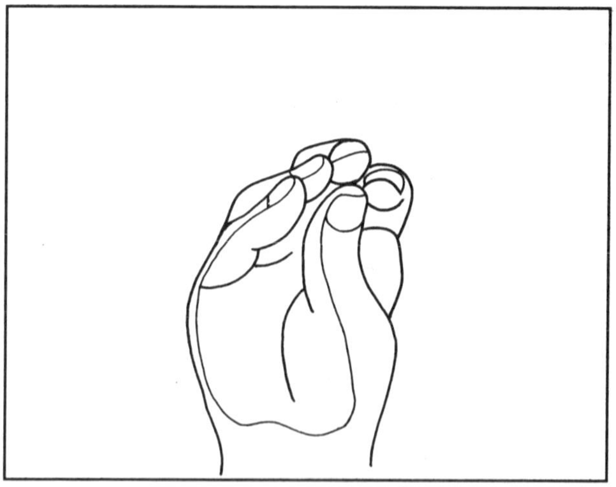

Figure 563 -- sukri mudra
(as seen by another)

Sumeru mudra -- (Ind.: *Sumeru* [*mudrā*]; Jap.: *shumi sen ho-in* [*mudra*]) The Indic term for *shumi sen ho-in* (*mudra*). See: *shumi sen ho-in* (*mudra*). (GDe 95)

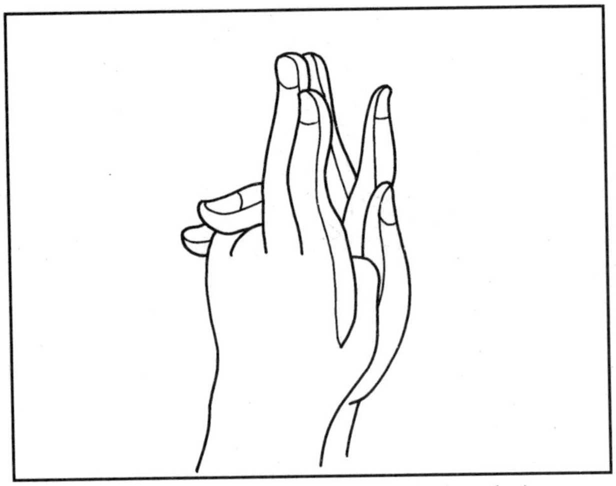

Figure 564 -- summoning sins (mudra)
(as seen by the holder)

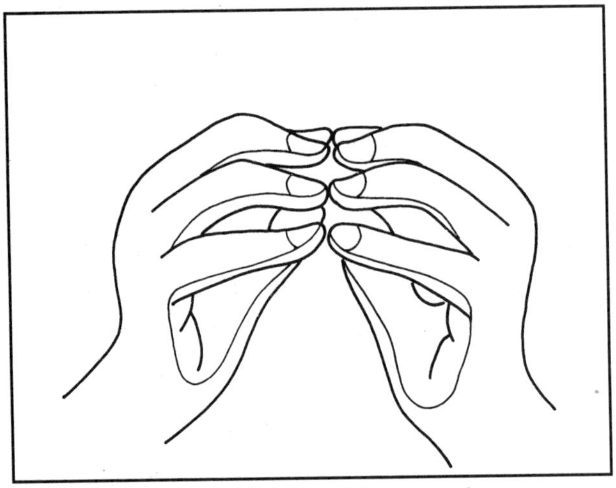

Figure 565 -- sumukham mudra
(as seen by another)

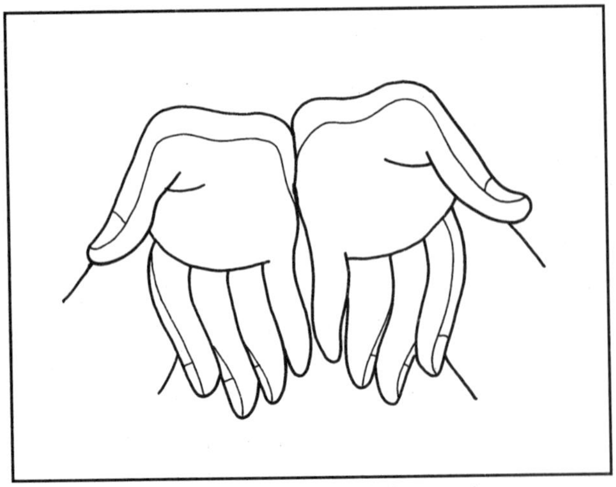

Figure 566 -- supratishtha mudra
(as seen by another)

summoning sins (mudra) -- (Eng.) A *mudra*, a ritual hand pose, a seal, a *tantric mudra* which is common to the Japanese Buddhist (*Vajrayana, Mantrayana*) tradition and is held or formed by a devotee or priest during the rites of *Vajradhatu Mandala* and other rites. It may be accompanied by a *mantra*. The "summoning sins"[68] (*mudra*) is a combined (Ind.: *saṁyutta*) form, held by both hands. This *mudra* is formed by: palms touching, right thumb extended upwards, left is folded towards the palm, index fingers extend upwards and curl slightly, middle fingers touch at their tips, ring and little fingers interlace across the back of the palms. (LCS 84) (See: **Figure 564**)

sumukham mudra -- (Ind.: *sumukham-mudrā*) A *mudra*, a ritual hand pose, a seal, a *mudra* which is common to yogic tradition, particularly the *Yoga Tatva Mudra Vigyan* form, and is held by a devotee or practitioner. The *sumukham mudra* is a combined (Ind.: *saṁyutta*) form, held by both hands. It is one of the twenty-four mudras held before the *Gayatri Jap* of the thirty-two total *Gayatri mudras*.[69] It is utilized for all sickness, especially cancer. This *mudra* is formed by: palm faces the midline, the index, middle, ring and little fingers curl together towards the palm, the thumb touches the side of the first phalanges of the index finger. Thus formed, the two hands are brought together so that the tips of the thumbs and fingers touch their opposite counterpart. This *mudra* is held in front of the chest. (KDe 79, RLM 70) (See: **Figure 565**)

supratishtha mudra -- (Ind.: *supratiṣṭha-mudrā*; Tib.: *gshegs-gsol phyag-rgya* [*mudra*]) This is an assigned term.[70] A *mudra*, a ritual hand pose, a seal, which is common to the Buddhist (*Vajrayana*) tradition, a *tantric mudra*. It denotes the gathering in or praying to depart, particularly as associated with the worship of the powerful *Vajrayana* goddess, *Tara*. The *supratishtha mudra* is a combined (Ind.: *saṁyutta*) form, held by both hands. This *mudra* is formed by: palm faces upwards, fingers and thumb extended outwards. Thus formed the hands are brought together along the edge of the palms and little fingers. The mudra thus formed is held chest high. (SBe 224) (See: **Figure 566**)

surabhi mudra I -- (Ind.: *surabhi-mudrā*) A *mudra*, a ritual hand pose, a seal, which is common to the Hindu tradition. It denotes the udder of the sacred cow, *Surabhi*. The *surabhi mudra I* is a single (Ind.: *asaṁyutta*) form, held by one hand. This *mudra* is formed by: thumb brought into the palm, fingers extend downward as to form the four udders of a cow. (MJS 137) (See: **Figure 567**)

surabhi mudra II -- (Ind.: *surabhi-mudrā*) A *mudra*, a ritual hand pose, a seal, a *mudra* which is common to yogic tradition, particularly the *Yoga Tatva Mudra Vigyan* form, and is held by a devotee or practitioner. The *surabhi mudra* is a combined (Ind.: *saṁyutta*) form, held by both hands. It is utilized for bile, cough and internal balance. It is also one of the eight *mudras* held after the *Gayatri Jap* of the thirty-two total *Gayatri mudras*.[71] This *mudra* is formed by: palms facing the midline and separated, the tips of both ring fingers touch the tips of both little fingers of the opposite hand, the tips of both index fingers touch the tips of both middle fingers of the opposite hand, the fingers are parallel to the ground, the thumbs stretch upwards and are separated from each other. (KDe 43) (See: **Figure 568**)

surya mudra I -- (Ind.: *Sūrya-mudrā*) A *mudra*, a ritual hand pose, a seal, a *mudra* which is common to yogic tradition, particularly the *Yoga Tatva Mudra Vigyan* form, and is held by a devotee or practitioner. The *surya mudra I* is a single (Ind.: *asaṁyutta*) form, held by one hand. It is utilized for mental depression and weight reduction. This *mudra* is formed by: palm forward, index, middle and little fingers extend straight upwards, the ring finger is folded into the palm its tip resting on the pad of the thumb, the thumb crosses this finger at the second phalanges. It is similar to the *kartari-hasta*. (KDe 46) (See: **Figure 569**)

Surya mudra II -- (Ind.: *Sūrya-mudrā*) A hand pose, a seal, a dramatic (Ind.: *nāṭya*) *mudra* or gesture (Ind.: *darpaṇa*) held or formed by a performer, dancer or actor. The *Surya mudra II* is a combined (Ind.: *saṁyutta*) form, held by both hands. It denotes the sun, one of the nine planets (Ind.: *navagraha*). This *mudra* is formed by: right palm faces the midline, middle, ring and little fingers are folded into the palm, the thumb lies next to the first phalanges of the middle finger, the index finger curls over the top of the thumb; left palm turned

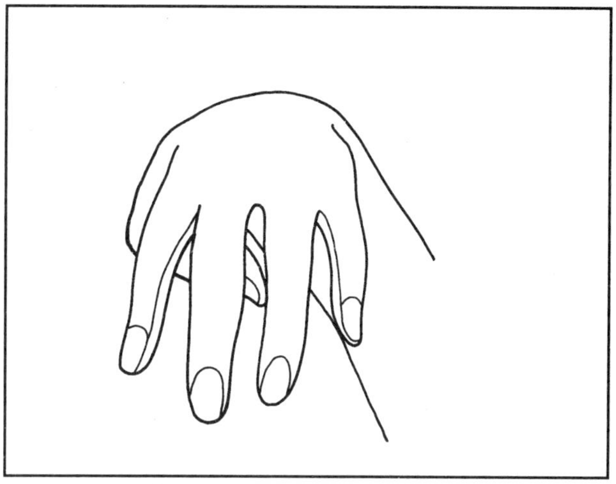

Figure 567 -- surabhi mudra I
(as seen by another)

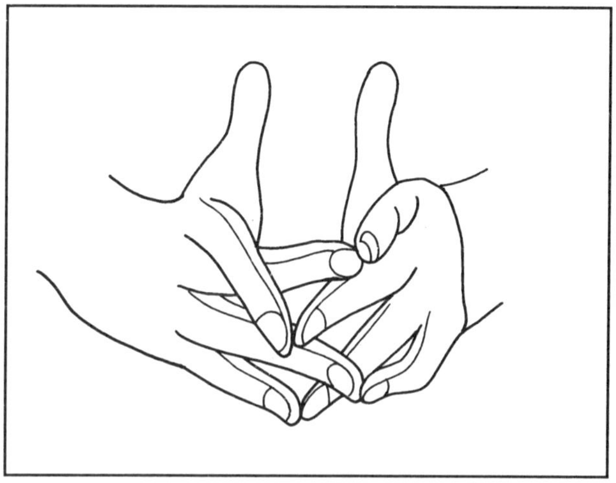

Figure 568 -- surabhi mudra II
(as seen by another)

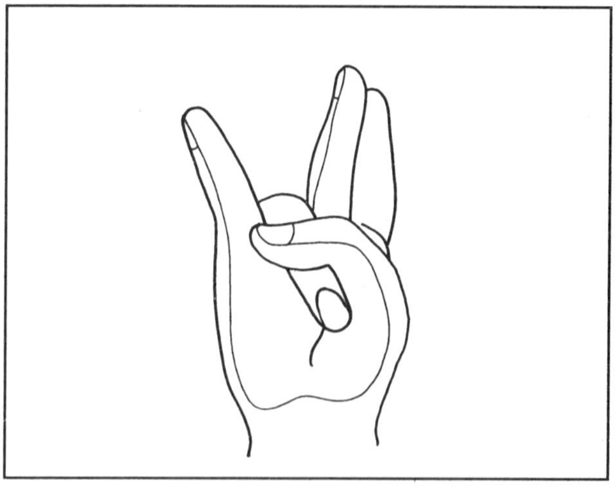

Figure 569 -- Surya mudra I
(as seen by another)

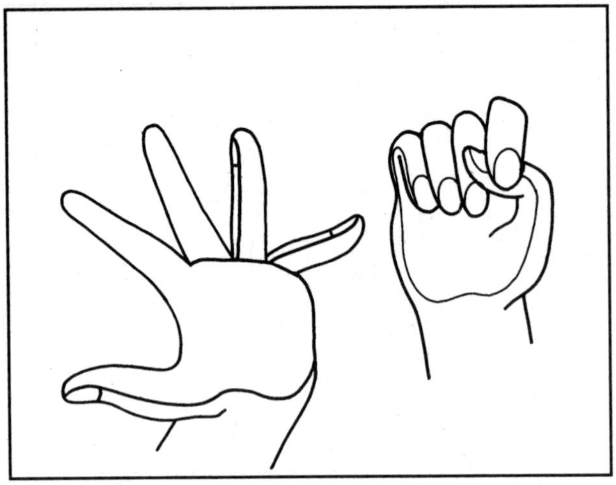

Figure 570 -- Surya mudra II
(as seen by the holder)

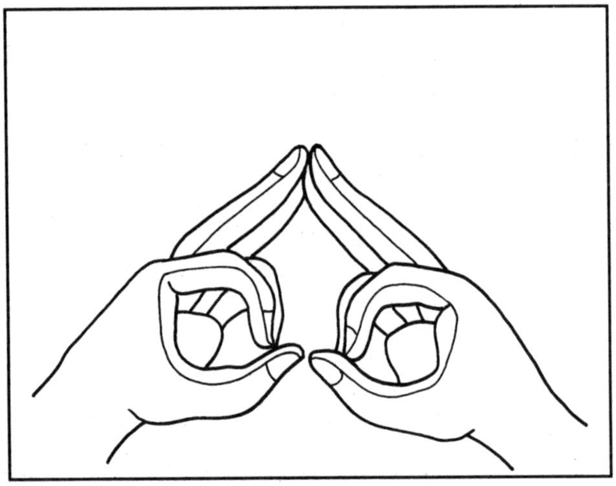

Figure 571 -- sutra mudra
(as seen by the holder)

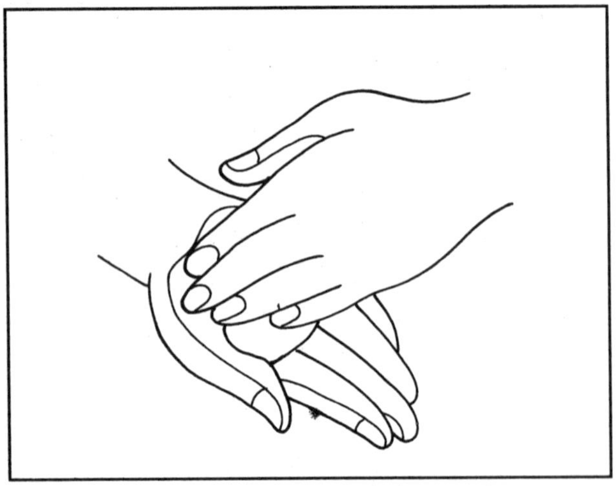

Figure 572 -- suvarna-chakra mudra
(as seen by another)

upwards, the thumb and fingers are stretched far apart, stiff; so formed, the little finger is at 90° to the palm and the ring finger is at 45° to the palm. (ACG 46) (See: **Figure 570**)

sutra mudra -- (Ind.: *sūtra-mudrā*]) A *mudra*, a ritual hand pose, a seal, a *tantric mudra* which is common to the Japanese Buddhist (*Vajrayana, Mantrayana*) tradition and is held or formed by a devotee or priest during various rites in which a deity is acknowledged. It may be accompanied by a *mantra*. The *sutra mudra* is a combined (Ind.: *saṁyutta*) form, held by both hands. This *mudra* is formed by: palms face inwards, index and little fingers folded into the palm, thumbs folded over first phalanges of index and little fingers, middle and ring fingers extended. Thus formed the hands are brought together so that the tips of the middle and ring fingers touch, as well as the first phalanges of the thumb. (LCS 225) (See: **Figure 571**)

suvarna-chakra mudra -- (Ind.: *suvarṇa-cakra-mudrā*) This is an assigned term.[72] A *mudra*, a ritual hand pose, a seal, which is common to the Buddhist (*Vajrayana*) tradition, a *tantric mudra*. It denotes the the golden wheel (Tib.: *gser-gyi hkhor-lo*), one of eight signs of good fortune (Ind.: *aṣṭa-maṅgala*, Tib.: *bkra-shis rtags-brgyad*), an 'outer offering'--the other seven being: the victory banner, endless knot, lotus, golden fish, umbrella, treasure vase and conch shell--which is proffered to a divine guest during worship, particularly as associated with the ceremonies of the powerful *Vajrayana* goddess, *Tara*. The *suvarna-chakra mudra* is a combined (Ind.: *saṁyutta*) form, held by both hands. This *mudra* is formed by: palm upwards, fingers extended, pointed outward; the left hand: palm downward, fingers extended, touching the right palm or slightly above it, and at a 90° angle to the right hand. The *mantra* associated with this *mudra* is: "*OM Suvarna-chakra Praticcha SVAHA*."[73] (SBe 155) (See: **Figure 572**)

Suvarnamukhi mudra -- (Ind.: *Suvarṇamukhī-mudrā*) A hand pose, a seal, a dramatic (Ind.: *nāṭya*) *mudra* or gesture (Ind.: *darpaṇa*) held or formed by a performer, dancer or actor. It denotes the *Suvarnamukhi*, one of the famous rivers of India. The *mudra* employed is identical in form to the *ardha-chatura mudra*. See: *ardha-chatura mudra*. (ACG 48)

svakuchagraha mudra -- (Ind.: *svakucagraha-mudrā*) A *mudra*, a ritual hand pose, a seal, which is common to both the Buddhist and Hindu traditions. It denotes resignation or recognition. The *svakuchagraha mudra* is a single (Ind.: *asaṁyutta*) form, held by one hand. This *mudra* is formed by: the right hand, palm faces the midline, is placed on the chest covering the heart. It is a *mudra* that is generally applied to *Hayagriva*. (MJS 139) (See: **Figure 573**)

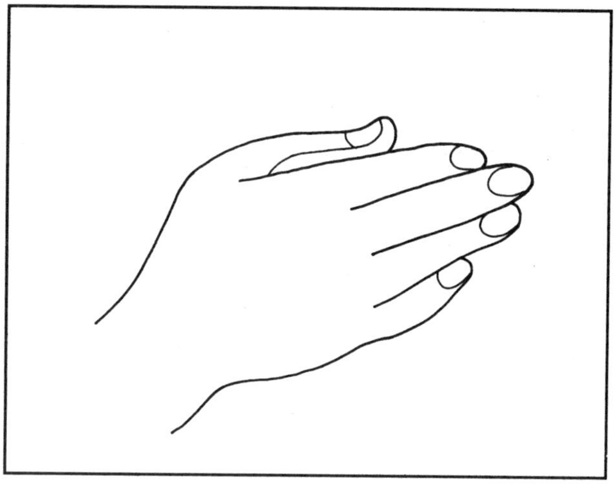

Figure 573 -- svakuchagraha mudra
(as seen by another)

svastika mudra I[74] -- (Ind.: *svastika-mudrā* aka *swastika mudrā*) A *mudra*, a ritual hand pose, a seal, which is common to both the Buddhist and Hindu traditions and is depicted or held by a deity. The *svastika mudra I* is a combined (Ind.: *saṁyutta*) form, held by both hands. It denotes the sun or *nagas*. This *mudra* is formed by: hands are brought together, palm towards palm, the fingers overlap approximately at a 30°, but are kept straight. (MJS 139) (See: **Figure 574**)

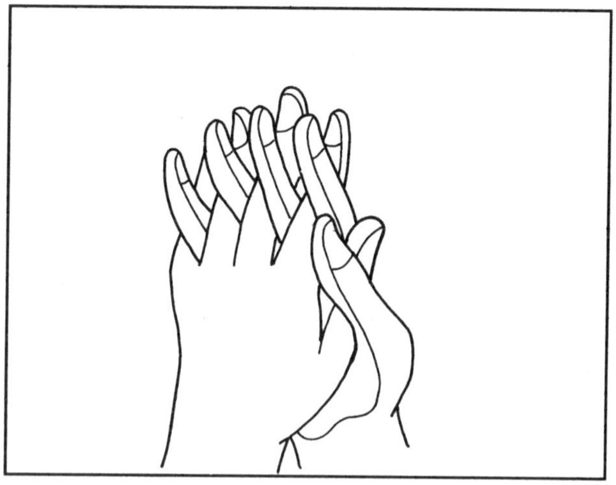

Figure 574 -- svastika mudra I
(as seen by the holder)

svastika mudra II -- (Ind.: *svastika-mudrā* aka *swastika mudrā*) A *mudra*, a ritual hand pose, a seal, which is common to both the Buddhist and Hindu traditions and is depicted or held by a deity. The *svastika mudra II* is a combined (Ind.: *saṁyutta*) form, held by both hands. A variation of *svastika I*. This *mudra* is formed by: palms face the midline, fingers and thumb extended towards mid-line (*pataka mudra*). Thus formed the hands cross at the wrist. (MJS 139) (See: **Figure 575**)

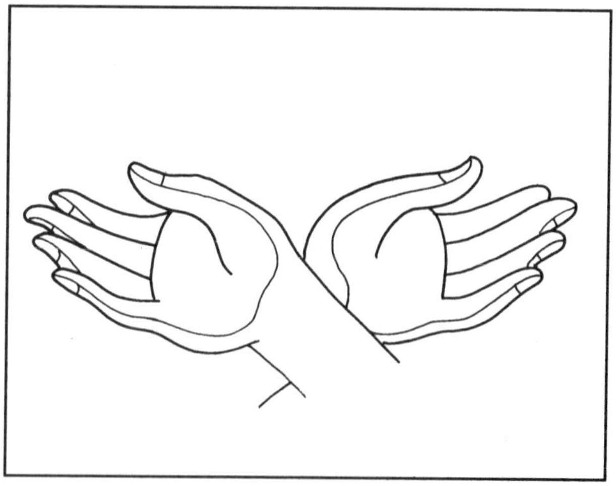

Figure 575 -- svastika mudra II
(as seen by the holder)

svastika mudra III -- (Ind.: *svastika-mudrā* aka *swastika mudrā*) A mudra, a ritual hand pose, a seal, which is common to both the Buddhist and Hindu traditions and is depicted or held by a deity. The *svastika mudra III* is a combined (Ind.: *saṁyutta*) form, held by both hands. It denotes the sun or *nagas*. This *mudra* is formed by: right hand palm faces the midline, fingers and thumb extended towards mid-line (*pataka mudra*); left palm upwards and fingers slightly cupped resembling a crescent or half moon, the thumb is at right angle to the fingers, and similarly bent (*ardhachandra mudra*).[75] (TGR 260) (See: **Figure 576**)

svastika mudra IV -- (Ind.: *svastika-mudrā* aka *swastika mudrā*) A hand pose, a seal, a dramatic (Ind.: *nāṭya*) *mudra* or gesture (Ind.: *darpaṇa*) held or formed by a

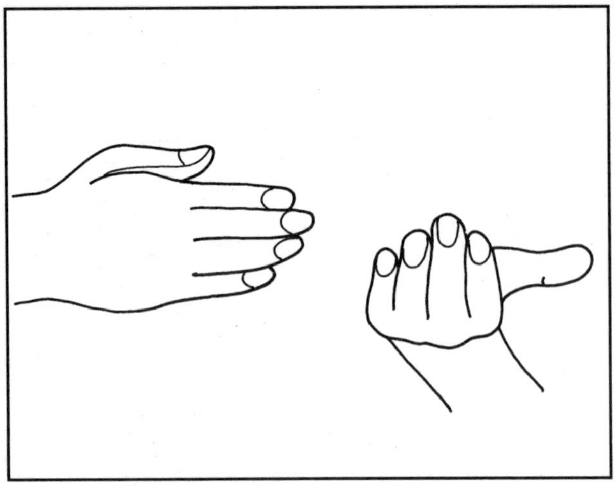

Figure 576 -- svastika mudra III
(as seen by another)

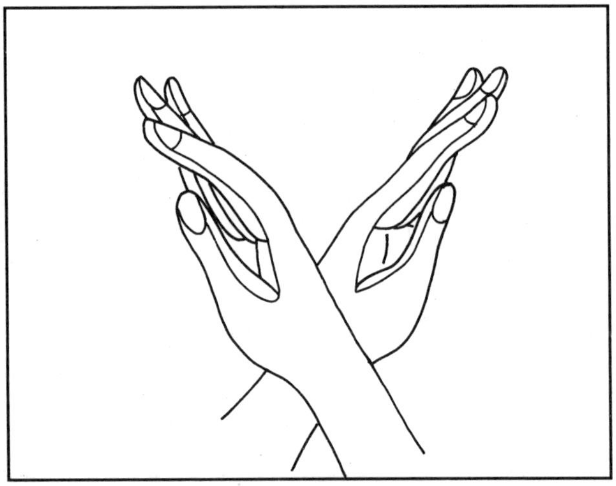

Figure 577 -- svastika mudra IV
(as seen by the holder)

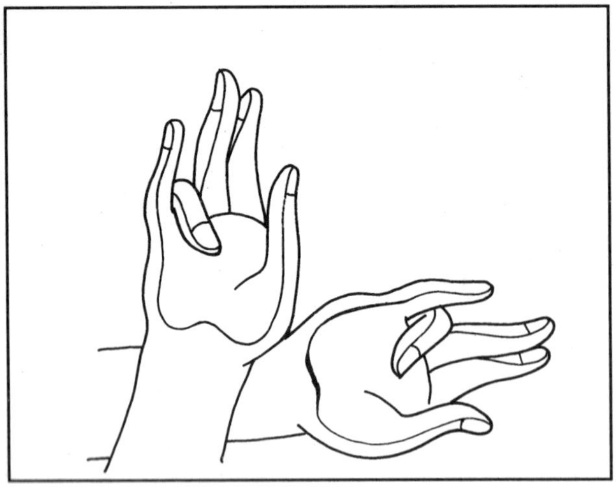

Figure 578 -- svastika mudra V
(as seen by another)

performer, dancer or actor. The *svastika mudra IV* is a combined (Ind.: *saṁyutta*) form, held by both hands. It denotes timid speech, dispute, etc.[76] This *mudra* is formed by: hand is raised, fingers and thumb extended, together and pointing upwards, relaxed, slightly cupped, palm facing the midline. Thus formed the hands are "held together at the wrist."[77] (ACG) (See: **Figure 577**)

svastika mudra V -- (Ind.: *svastika-mudrā*) ("crossed") A hand pose, a seal, a dramatic (Ind.: *nāṭya*) *mudra* or gesture (Ind.: *darpaṇa*) held or formed by a performer, dancer or actor. The *svastika mudra V* is a combined (Ind.: *saṁyutta*) form, held by both hands. It denotes a wishing tree and mountains. This *mudra* is a second *svastika mudra* noted by ACG, and is formed by: palms facing outward, index, middle and little fingers, and thumbs extend, together and point upwards, ring fingers are bent towards the palms. Thus formed the hands are crossed at the wrist, and held to the left of chest. (ACG 42) (See: **Figure 578**)

swastika mudra -- (Ind.: *swastika-mudrā* aka *svastika mudra*) A variant (spelling) of *svastika mudra*. See: *svastika mudra*. (MJS 139 TGR 260)

-- T --

tai-ken-in (mudra) -- (Jap.: *tai-ken-in* [*mudrā*] aka *renge ken-in* [*mudra*]; Ind.: *padma-muṣṭi*) A variant term applied to to *renge ken-in* (*mudra*). See: *renge ken-in* (*mudra*). (EDS 39)

tala-mukha mudra -- (Ind.: *tāla-mukha-mudrā*) A hand pose, a seal, a dramatic (Ind.: *nāṭya*) *mudra* or gesture (Ind.: *darpaṇa*) held or formed by a performer, dancer or actor. The *tala-mukha mudra* is a combined (Ind.: *saṁyutta*) form, held by both hands. It denotes embrace, wide objects, a thick pillar, etc.[1] This *mudra* is formed by: palms facing the midline, fingers and thumbs extended, together and upwards, relaxed and slightly cupped. Thus formed, the hands are in front of the chest and are apart. (ACG 42) (See: **Figure 579**)

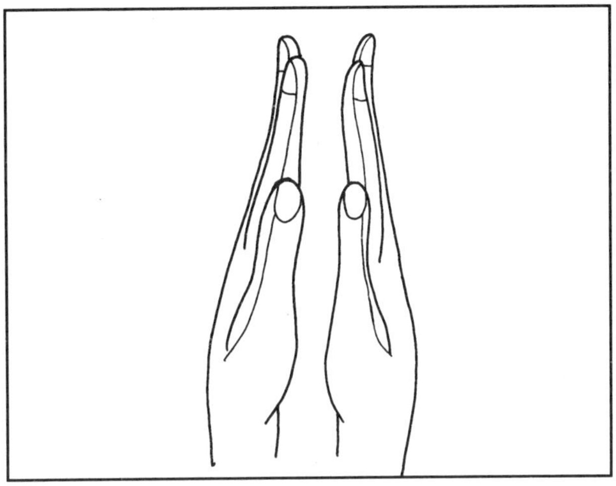

Figure 579 -- tala-mukha mudra
(as seen by the holder)

tala-pataka mudra -- (Ind.: *tāla-patākā-mudrā*) A hand pose, a seal, a dramatic (Ind.: *nāṭya*) *mudra* or gesture (Ind.: *darpaṇa*) held or formed by a performer, dancer or actor. The *tala-pataka mudra* is a single (Ind.: *asaṁyutta*) form, held by one hand. This *mudra* is formed by: palm facing outward, hand is raised, fingers and thumb extended, together and pointing upwards, relaxed, slightly cupped, except the thumb and little finger which are extended straight. (ACG 49) (See: **Figure 580**)

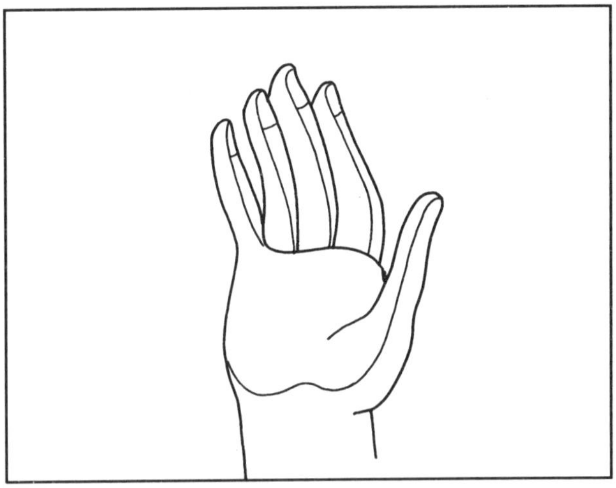

Figure 580 -- tala-pataka mudra
(as seen by another)

tala-simha mudra -- (Ind.: *tāla-siṁha-mudrā*) A hand pose, a seal, a dramatic (Ind.: *nāṭya*) *mudra* or gesture (Ind.: *darpaṇa*) held or formed by a performer, dancer or actor. The *tala-simha mudra* is a single (Ind.: *asaṁyutta*) form, held by one hand. This *mudra* is formed by: palm facing downward, the index and little fingers extended upwards and straight, the middle and ring fingers are curl into the palm, the first phalanges of the thumb lays across the first phalanges of the middle and ring fingers. (ACG 50) (See: **Figure 581**)

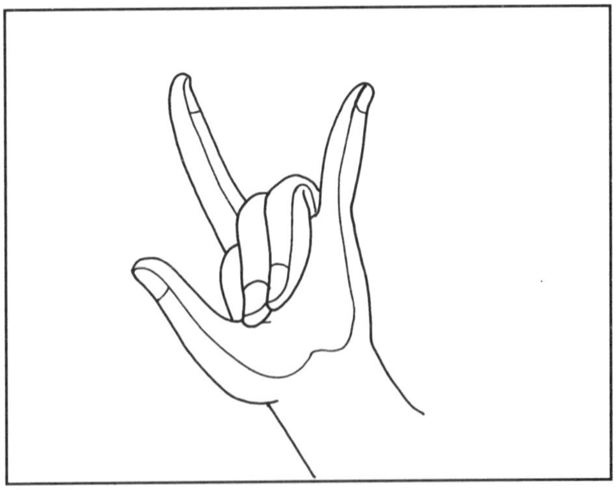

Figure 581 -- tala-simha mudra
(as seen by another)

tamrachuda mudra I -- (Ind.: *tāmracūḍa-mudrā*) ("red crest") A *mudra*, a ritual hand pose, a seal, which is common to the Hindu tradition and is depicted or held

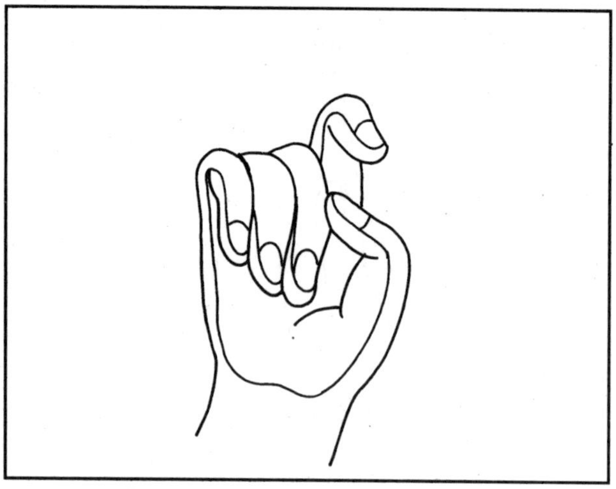

Figure 582 -- tamrachuda mudra I
(as seen by another)

Figure 583 -- tamrachuda mudra II
(as seen by another)

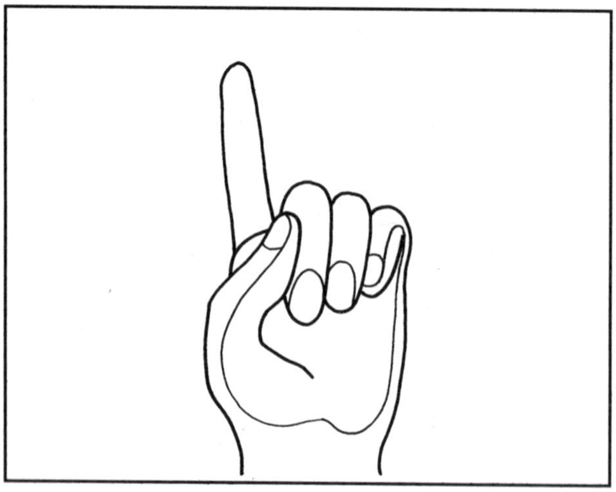

Figure 584 -- tarjani mudra I
(as seen by another)

by a deity. Also, a hand pose, a seal, a dramatic (Ind.: *nāṭya*) *mudra* or gesture (Ind.: *darpaṇa*) held or formed by a performer, dancer or actor. The *tamrachuda mudra* is a single (Ind.: *asaṁyutta*) form, held by one hand. It denotes a rooster, crane, writing, etc.[2] This *mudra* is formed by: palm faces forwards, index finger bends slightly towards palm, middle, ring and little fingers bend into the palm, tip of thumb touches the tips of the middle finger. (ACG 38, KVa 136 [35], MJS 141) (See: **Figure 582**)

tamrachuda mudra II -- (Ind.: *tāmracūḍa-mudrā*) ("red crest") A hand pose, a seal, a dramatic (Ind.: *nāṭya*) *mudra* or gesture (Ind.: *darpaṇa*) held or formed by a performer, dancer or actor. The *tamrachuda mudra* is a single (Ind.: *asaṁyutta*) form, held by one hand. It denotes a trident, the three worlds, the *Vedas*, etc.[3] This *mudra* is a variation formed by: palm faces forwards, index, middle and ring fingers are straight upwards, the tip of the thumb crosses the palm and touches the tip of the bent little finger. (ACG 38) (See: **Figure 583**)

tarjani mudra I -- (Ind.: *tarjanī-mudrā* aka *pāśatarjanī mudrā, tarjanīpāśa mudrā*; Jap.: *sai fuku sho ma-in* [*mudra*]; Tib.: *khro-bohi sdigs-mdzub phyag-rgya*) A *mudra*, a ritual hand pose, a seal, which is common to both the Buddhist and Hindu traditions, although the form appears to differ slightly between the two faiths.[4] It denotes warning, threatening or warding off evil. The *tarjani mudra I* is a single (Ind.: *asaṁyutta*) form, held by one hand in the Hindu tradition. This *mudra* is formed by: palm faces forward or rotated slightly towards the mid-line, index finger extends straight upward, middle, ring and little finger are folded into the palm, first phalanges of the thumb touches the second phalanges of the index finger. Thus formed the *mudra* is held at shoulder level. (AKG 22, ERJ II 22, HKS 271, MJS 142, RSG 3, TGR 15) (See: **Figure 584**)

tarjani mudra II -- (Ind.: *tarjanī-mudrā* aka *pāśatarjanī mudrā, tarjanīpāśa mudrā*; Tib.: *khro-bohi sdigs-mdzub phyag-rgya*) A *mudra*, a ritual hand pose, a seal, which is common to both the Buddhist and Hindu traditions, although the form appears to differ slightly between the two faiths. It denotes warning, threatening or warding off evil. In the Buddhist tradition, the *tarjani mudra II* is a single (Ind.: *asaṁyutta*) form, held by one hand.

This *mudra* is formed by: palm faces forward, index finger extends straight outward, parallel to the ground or slightly upward, middle, ring and little finger are folded into the palm, first phalanges of the thumb touches the second phalanges of the index finger. Thus formed the *mudra* is held below shoulder level. (BCO 218) (See: **Figure 585**)

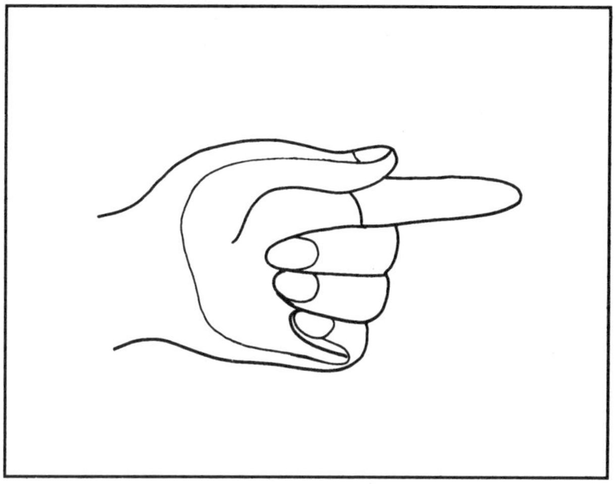

Figure 585 -- tarjani mudra II
(as seen by another)

tarjani (II)-dhyana mudra -- (Indic: *tarjanī-dhyāna-mudrā;* Eng.: choosing the chief disciples *mudra;* Thai: *pang thong-tang-etatakkasatarn*) This is a descriptive term.[5] See: *pang thong-tang-etatakkasatarn*. (DRN 37, JBo 205, ODD 680, OFr 18, PSS)

tarjanipasha mudra -- (Ind.: *tarjanīpāśa-mudrā* aka *tarjanī mudrā, paśatarjanī mudrā*) A variant term applied to *pashatarjani mudra*. See: *pashatarjani mudra*. (BBh 197)

tarpana mudra -- (Ind.: *tarpaṇa-mudrā*) A *mudra*, a ritual hand pose, a seal, which is common to the Buddhist tradition. It denotes paying homage, particularly to the departed 'Fathers.' The *tarpana mudra* is a single (Ind.: *asaṁyutta*) form, held by one hand. This *mudra* is formed by: forearm bent at the elbow, palm faces downwards, fingers and thumb extend towards the mid-line, tips of fingers point to or touch the shoulder. (AKG 22, BBh 197, RSG 4) (See: **Figure 586**)

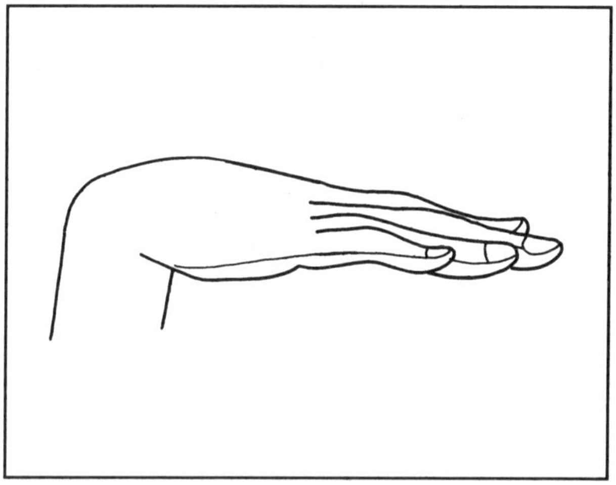

Figure 586 -- tarpana mudra
(as seen by another)

Tathagata-damshtra mudra -- (Jap.: *Tathāgata-daṁṣṭra-mudrā*) A *mudra*, a ritual hand pose, a seal, a *tantric mudra* which is common to the Japanese Buddhist (*Vajrayana, Mantrayana*) tradition and is held or formed by a devotee or priest during the rites of *Garbhadhatu Mandala* and other rites. It may be accompanied by a *mantra*. The *Tathagata-damshtra mudra* is a combined (Ind.: *saṁyutta*) form, held by both hands. This *mudra* is formed by: palms facing midline, thumbs extend straight up, index fingers folded into the palms, middle, ring and little fingers extend upward and touch at their tips. (LCS 200) (See: **Figure 587**)

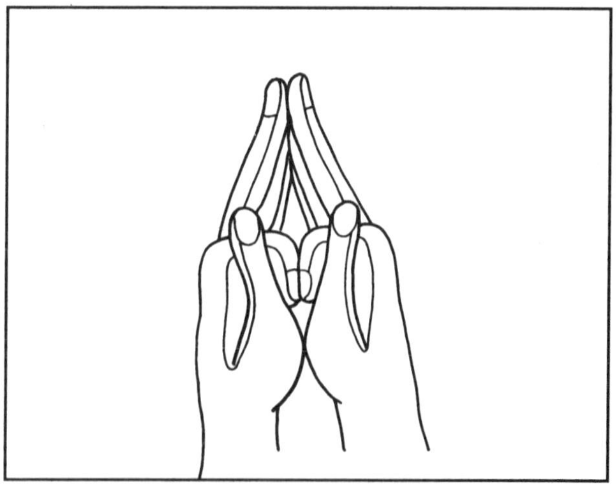

Figure 587 -- Tathagata-damshtra mudra
(as seen by the holder)

tathagata-kukshi mudra -- (Jap.: *tathāgata-kukṣī-mudrā*) A *mudra*, a ritual hand pose, a seal, a *tantric mudra* which is common to the Japanese Buddhist (*Vajrayana, Mantrayana*) tradition and is held or formed by a devotee or priest during the rites of *Garbhadhatu Mandala, Vajradhatu Mandala, Homa Rites* and other rites. It may

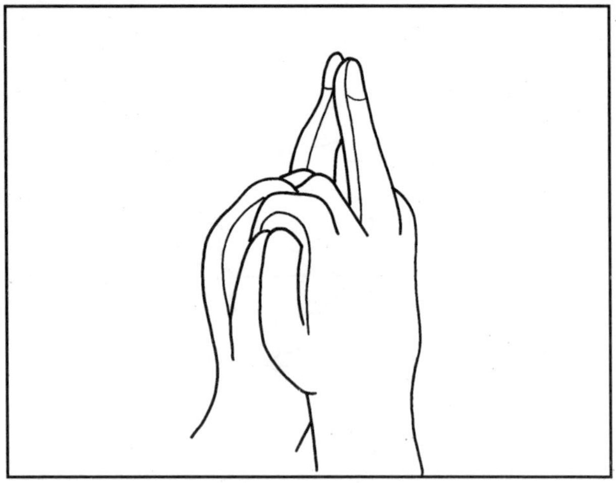

Figure 588 -- tathagata-kukshi mudra
(as seen by the holder)

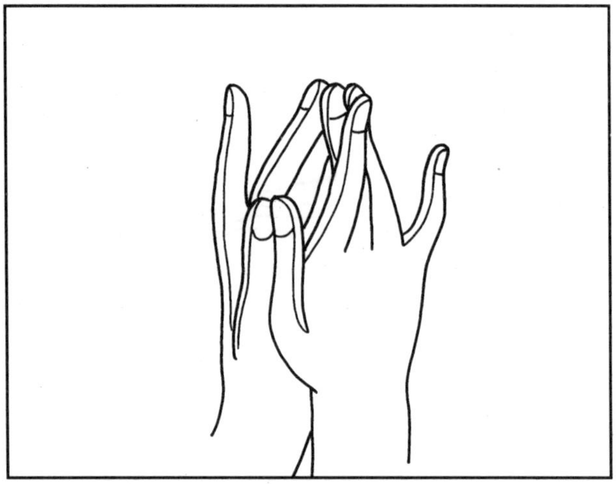

Figure 589 -- tathagata-vachana mudra
(as seen by the holder)

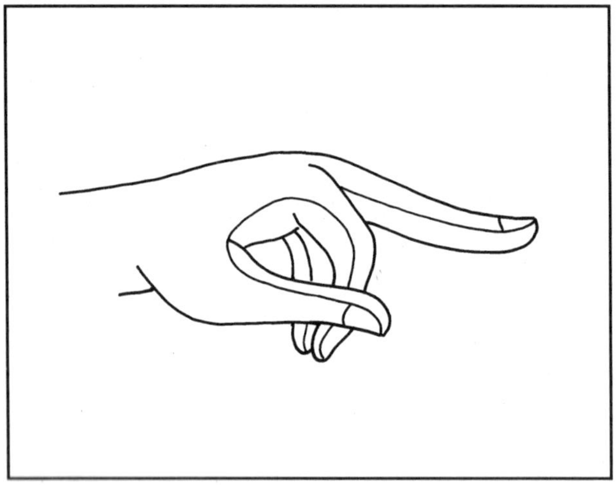

Figure 590 -- tattva mudra
(as seen by the holder)

be accompanied by a *mantra*. The *tathagata-kukshi*[6] *mudra* is a combined (Ind.: *saṁyutta*) form, held by both hands. This *mudra* is formed by: palms close, thumbs, index, middle and little fingers interlace inwards towards the palms, ring fingers extend and touch at their tips. (LCS 198) (See: **Figure 588**)

tathagata-mushti (mudra) -- (Ind.: *tathāgata-muṣṭi* [*mudrā*]aka *jñāna-muṣṭi mudra*) A variant term applied to *jnana-mushti mudra* See: *jnana-mushti mudra*. (EDS 40)

tathagata-vachana mudra -- (Ind.: *tathāgata-vacana-mudrā*) A *mudra*, a ritual hand pose, a seal, a *tantric mudra* which is common to the Japanese Buddhist (*Vajrayana, Mantrayana*) tradition and is held or formed by a devotee or priest during the rites of *Garbhadhatu Mandala* and other rites. It may be accompanied by a *mantra*. The *tathagata-vachana mudra* is a combined (Ind.: *saṁyutta*) form, held by both hands. This *mudra* is formed by: palms facing midline, thumbs, index and little fingers extend upwards, thumbs touch along their length, middle and ring fingers touch at their tips. (LCS 200) (See: **Figure 589**)

tattva mudra -- (Ind.: *tattva-mudrā*) A *mudra*, a ritual hand pose, a seal, which is common to the Hindu tradition. It denotes truth. The *tattva mudra* is a single (Ind.: *asaṁyutta*) form, held by one hand. This *mudra* is formed by either hand: hand extended in front of the body, palm facing downwards, the index, ring and little fingers curl inwards towards the palm, the first phalanges of the thumb touches the first phalanges of the index finger while the middle finger extends straight, outward. (AMK 141) (See: **Figure 590**)

teiriei gassho (mudra) -- (Jap.: *teiriei gasshō* [*mudrā*]) A *mudra*, a ritual hand pose, a seal, which is common to the Japanese Buddhist tradition. Specifically one of the twelve, elemental "hand clasps" (Jap. *junigosho* or *junigassho*). The *teiriei gassho* (*mudra*) is a combined (Ind.: *saṁyutta*) form, held by both hands. This *mudra* is formed by: palms inwards, outside edges of palms touching their whole length, the tips of the little and middle fingers touch, the ring and index fingers flare outwards, and the thumbs are turned outward. This *mudra* represents the "clasp of the construction-support-fingers."[7] (EDS 40) (See: **Figure 591**)

tejas-bodhisattva mudra -- (Jap.: *tejas-bodhisattva-mudrā*]) A *mudra*, a ritual hand pose, a seal, a *tantric mudra* which is common to the Japanese Buddhist (*Vajrayana, Mantrayana*) tradition and is held or formed by a devotee or priest during the rites of *Garbhadhatu Mandala, Vajradhatu Mandala, Homa Rites* and other rites. It may be accompanied by a *mantra*. The *tejas-bodhisattva mudra*[8] is a combined (Ind.: *saṁyutta*) form, held by both hands. This *mudra* is formed by: palms facing outward, fingers slightly splayed, thumbs erect and together along their length, tips of index fingers touch. (GDe 127, LCS 112) (See: **Figure 592**)

temborin-in (mudra) -- (Jap.: *tembōrin-in* [*mudrā*] aka *gandharan temborin-in, horyuji temborin-in*; Chin.: *chuan-fa-lun-yin*; Ind.: *dharmacakra mudrā, dharmacakra-pravartana mudrā*) ("turning the wheel of the law") A *mudra*, a ritual hand pose, a seal, which is common to the Japanese and Chinese Buddhist traditions. It denotes setting the wheel of the Law into motion as well as preaching. The *temborin-in* (*mudra*) is similar to the *dharmachakra mudra*, but there are subtle variations. The *temborin-in* (*mudra*) is a combined (Ind.: *saṁyutta*) form, held by both hands. This *mudra* is formed by: the tip of the thumb and the index finger touch, the middle, ring and little fingers are extended, the palm of the right faces outward while the palm of the left faces upwards and the tips of the index fingers and thumbs are brought together and touch. It is the touching of the tips of the index fingers and thumbs and the orientation of the palms which are the significant differences from the *dharmachakra mudra* that is described above. (EDS 95) (See: **Figure 593**)

temborin-in mudra II -- (Jap: *tembōrin-in-mudrā*; Eng.: threading the needle *mudra*; Thai: *pang sonkhem*) This is a descriptive term.[9] See: *pang sonkhem*. (DRN 37, JBo 205, ODD 680, OFr 26, PSS)

threading the needle mudra -- (Eng.; Jap: *temborin-in mudra*; Thai: *pang sonkhem*) The English descriptive phrase for the Thai *pang sonkhem*. See: *pang sonkhem*. (DRN 37, JBo 205, ODD 680, OFr 26, PSS)

Tibetan temborin-in (mudra) -- (Jap.; Indic.: *dharmachakra mudra*) The English/Japanese term for

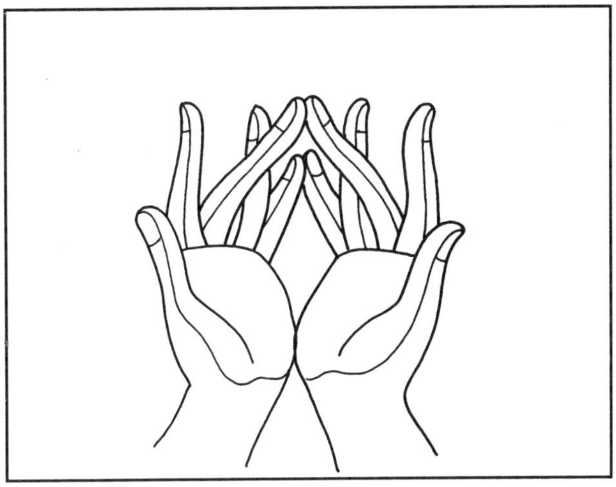

Figure 591 -- teiriei gassho (mudra)
(as seen by the holder)

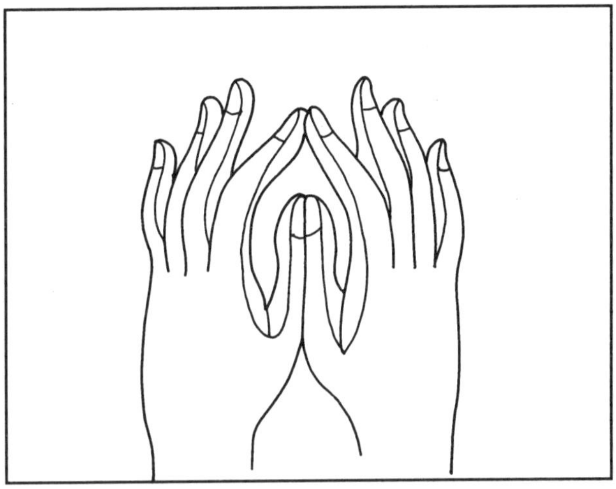

Figure 592 -- tejas-bodhisattva mudra
(as seen by the holder)

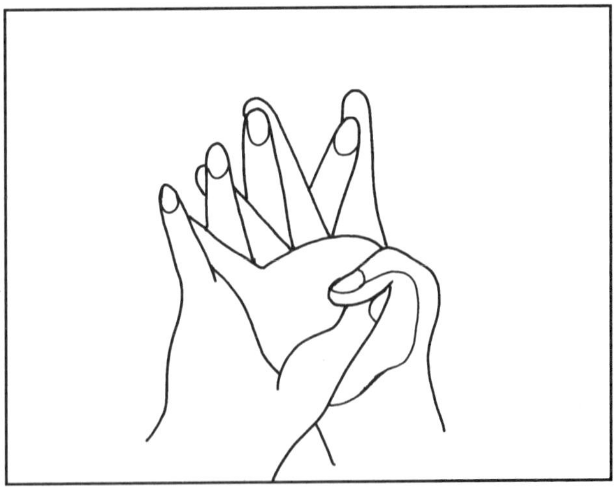

Figure 593 -- temborin-in (mudra)
(as seen by the holder)

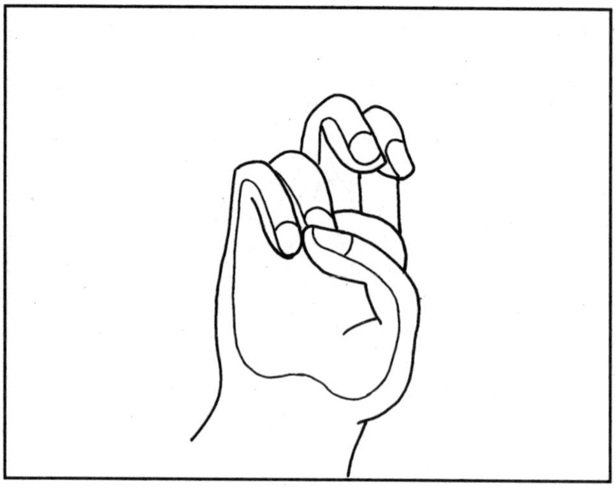

Figure 594 -- to myo-in (mudra)
(as seen by another)

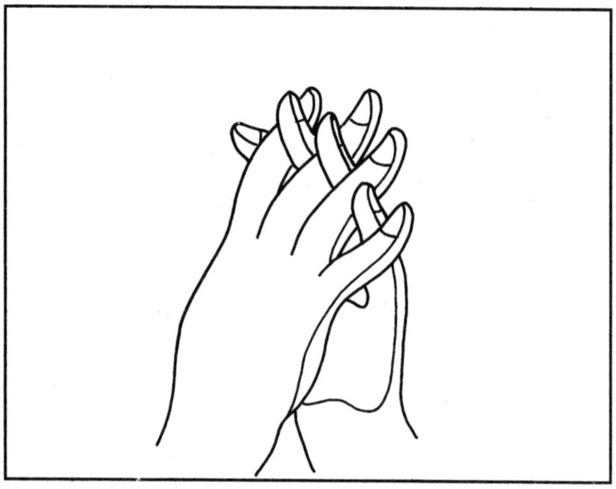

Figure 595 -- torma mudra
(as seen by another)

dharmachakra mudra. The form is closely parallel with the *dharmachakra mudra*. See: *dharmachakra mudra*. (EDS 94)

tilaka mudra -- (Ind.: *tilaka-mudrā*) A hand pose, a seal, a dramatic (Ind.: *nāṭya*) *mudra* or gesture (Ind.: *darpaṇa*) held or formed by a performer, dancer or actor noted in ACG but without description. (ACG 44)

ting-yin (mudra) -- (Chinese.; Ind.: *dhyāna mudrā*; Ind.: *dhyāna mudrā, dhyānahasta mudrā, samādhi mudrā, yoga mudrā*; Jap.: *jo-in* [*mudra*]; Thai: *pang phra-nang*; Tib.: *bsam-gtan phyag-rgya*) The Chinese term for *dhyana mudra* (Jap.: *jo-in* [*mudra*]). See: *dhyana mudra*. (EDS 85)

to myo-in (mudra) -- (Jap.: *tō myo-in* [*mudra*]; Ind.: *dipa mudra*) ("the lamp") A *mudra*, a ritual hand pose, a seal, a *tantric mudra* which is common to the Japanese Buddhist (*Vajrayana, Mantrayana*) tradition and is held or formed by a devotee or priest during the rites of *Garbhadhatu Mandala, Vajradhatu Mandala, Homa Rites* and other rites. It may be accompanied by a *mantra*. The *to myo-in* (*mudra*) is a combined (Ind.: *saṁyutta*) form, held by both hands. It denotes the dissolving of the darkness of ignorance. This *mudra* is formed by: palm facing outwards, ring and little fingers fold into the palm, thumb folds into the palm, its tip touching the first knuckle of the ring finger, index and middle fingers are separated and flex at their first and second knuckles, hook-like. (GDe 47) (See: **Figure 594**)

torma mudra -- (Ind.: *torma-mudrā*) This is an assigned term.[10] A *mudra*, a ritual hand pose, a seal, which is common to the Buddhist (*Vajrayana*) tradition, a *tantric mudra*. It is a gesture that is offered after the *sarva-buddha-bodhisattvanam mudra* (the 'empowering flying-bird' gesture), and before the offering of the second *torma*, as associated with the worship of the powerful *Vajrayana* goddess, *Tara*. The *torma mudra* is a combined (Ind.: *saṁyutta*) form, held by both hands. This *mudra* is formed by: palms face mid-line, fingers and thumbs extend upwards and interlace at the second phalanges, the *mudra* so formesd is held in front of the face. The *mantra* associated with this *mudra* is: "*Om A-Karo Mukham, Sarva-dharmanam Ady-anutpanatnvat Om Ah Hum Phat Svaha.*" (SBe 220) (See: **Figure 595**)

Trailokyavijaya mudra I -- (Ind.: *Trailokyavijaya-mudra*) A *mudra*, a ritual hand pose, a seal, a *tantric mudra* which is common to the Japanese Buddhist (*Vajrayana, Mantrayana*) tradition and is held or formed by a devotee or priest during the rites of *Garbhadhatu Mandala, Vajradhatu Mandala, Homa Rites* and other rites. It may be accompanied by a *mantra*. The *Trailokyavijaya mudra* is a combined (Ind.: *saṁyutta*) form, held by both hands. This *mudra* is formed by: palms facing outwards, thumbs folded into the palm, middle and ring fingers folded over the thumbs, index and little fingers extend straight upwards. Thus formed, the right hand crosses over (behind) the left and the little fingers of both hook (entwine). (GDe 156, LCS 83) (See: **Figure 596**)

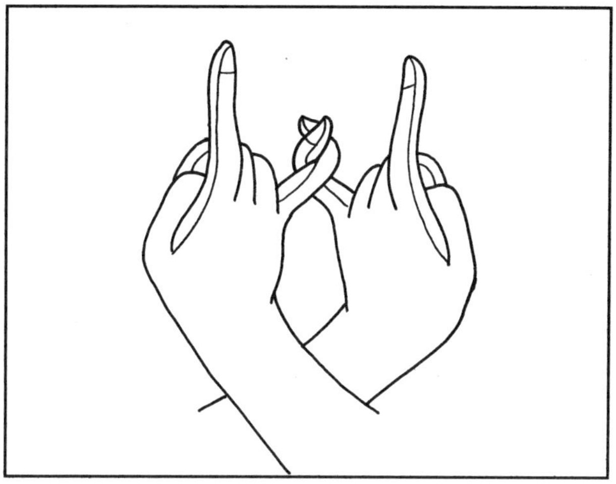

Figure 596 -- Trailokyavijaya mudra I
(as seen by the holder)

Trailokyavijaya mudra II -- (Ind.: *Trailokyavijaya-mudrā* aka *bhutadamara mudra, vajrahumkara mudra*) A variant term applied to both *bhutadamara mudra*[11] and *vajrahumkara mudra*.[12] See: *bhutadamara mudra* or *vajrahumkara mudra*. (AKG 20, BCO 217, BBh 198)

traveling by boat mudra -- (Eng.; Ind.: *abhaya-kaṭyāvalambita mudrā*; Thai: *pang phratabreakhanan*) The English descriptive phrase for the Thai *pang phratabreakhanan*. See: *pang phratabreakhanan*. (DRN 36, JBo, PSS)

trijnana mudra -- (Ind.: *trijñāna-mudrā*) A hand pose, a seal, a dramatic (Ind.: *nāṭya*) *mudra* or gesture (Ind.: *darpaṇa*) held or formed by a performer, dancer or actor. The *trijnana mudra* is a combined (Ind.: *saṁyutta*) form, held by both hands. This *mudra* is formed by: the palms face upwards, fingers and thumb extended, together and pointing outwards, relaxed, slightly cupped, and generally on a line level with the chest or higher. (ACG 49) (See: **Figure 597**)

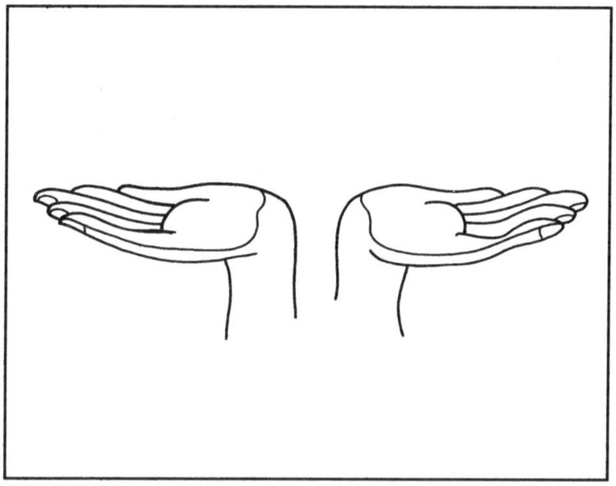

Figure 597 -- trijnana mudra
(as seen by another)

tri-mukham mudra -- (Ind.: *tri-mukham-mudrā*) A *mudra*, a ritual hand pose, a seal, a *mudra* which is common to yogic tradition, particularly the *Yoga Tatva Mudra Vigyan* form, and is held by a devotee or practitioner. The *tri-mukham mudra* is a combined (Ind.: *saṁyutta*) form, held by both hands. It is one of the twenty-four mudras held before the *Gayatri Jap* of the thirty-two total *Gayatri mudras*.[13] It is utilized for all sickness, especially cancer. This *mudra* is formed by:

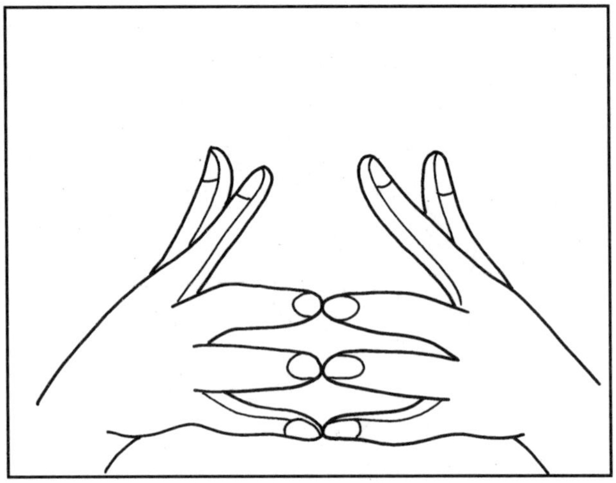

Figure 598 -- tri-mukham mudra
(as seen by another)

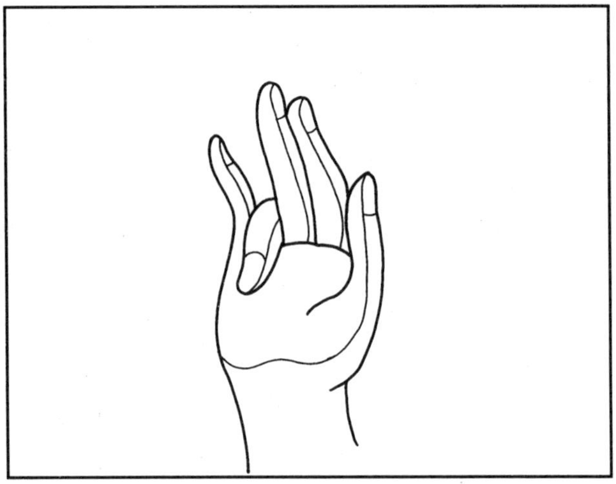

Figure 599 -- tripitaka mudra I
(as seen by another)

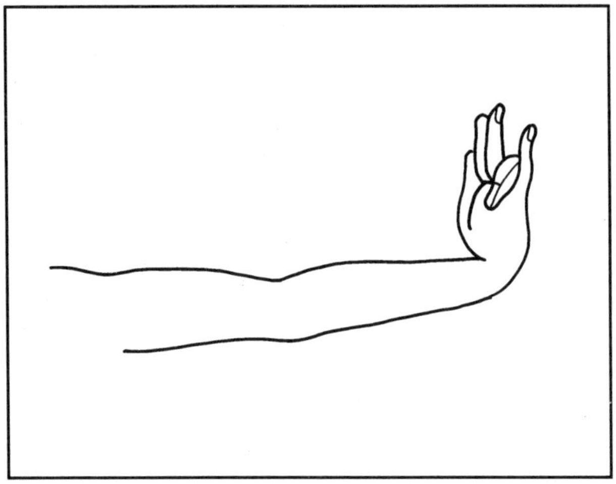

Figure 600 -- tripitaka mudra II
(as seen by another)

palms facing midline, fingers splayed and parallel to the ground, tips of middle, ring and little fingers touch, thumb extends upwards. Thus formed, the *mudra* is held waist high. (KDe 81, RLM 70) (See: **Figure 598**)

trintrini mudra -- (Ind.: *trintrīṇī-mudrā*) A hand pose, a seal, a dramatic (Ind.: *nāṭya*) *mudra* or gesture (Ind.: *darpaṇa*) held or formed by a performer, dancer or actor. It denotes the *trintrini* tree. The *mudra* employed is identical in form to the *langula mudra*. See: *langula mudra*. (ACG 49)

tripitaka mudra I -- (Ind.: *tripiṭaka-mudrā* or *tripitākā-mudrā*) ("three parts of the flag") A hand pose, a seal, a dramatic (Ind.: *nāṭya*) *mudra* or gesture (Ind.: *darpaṇa*) held or formed by a performer, dancer or actor. The *tripataka-mudra* is a single (Ind.: *asaṁyutta*) form, held by one hand. It denotes: a crown, a *vajra*, light, etc.[14] The *mudra* is formed by: the hand raised, index, middle and little fingers and thumb extended, together and pointing upwards, ring finger is bent towards the palm, palm facing outward and generally on a line level with the chest. This *mudra* is held by *Shiva-Nataraja* in the *Katisama* dance.[15] (ACG 27-28, KVa 134 [2], RSG 63) (See: **Figure 599**)

tripitaka mudra II -- (Ind.: *tripiṭaka-mudrā* or *tripitākā-mudrā*) A *mudra*, a ritual hand pose, a seal, which is common to both the Buddhist and Hindu traditions. This is a variation on *tripitaka mudra I*. The *tripitaka mudra II* is a single (Ind.: *asaṁyutta*) form, held by one hand. This *mudra* is formed by: palm faces upwards, thumb, index, middle and little fingers extend outwards, ring finger folds into palm. This *mudra* is held by the Lords *Vishnu* and *Shiva* when they hold certain weapons.[16] (MJS 145) (See: **Figure 600**)

tripitaka mudra III -- (Ind.: *tripiṭaka-mudrā* or *tripitākā-mudrā*) A *mudra*, a ritual hand pose, a seal, which is common to both the Buddhist and Hindu traditions. The *tripitaka mudra III* is a single (Ind.: *asaṁyutta*) form, held by one hand. This *mudra* is formed by: palm faces outwards, index, middle and ring fingers extend upwards, little finger folds into palm, the tips of the little finger and the thumb touch. This *mudra* is held by *Katisama* dance and by *Paramashva*.[17] (BBh 147) (See: **Figure 601**)

tripitaka mudra IV -- (Ind.: *tripiṭaka-mudrā* aka *pothī mudrā*) A variant term applied to *pothi mudra*. See: *pothi mudra*. (GDe 33)

trisharana mudra -- (Ind.: *triśaranā-mudrā*) A *mudra*, a ritual hand pose, a seal, which is common to the Buddhist tradition. It is called the Three Refuges Gesture and denotes the *Buddha, Dharma* and *Sangha*. The *trisharana mudra* is a single (Ind.: *asaṁyutta*) form, held by one hand. This *mudra* is formed by: palm facing outwards, tips of the thumb and index finger touch, middle, ring and little fingers are extended, separated and point upwards. (MMR 391) (See: **Figure 602**)

trishula mudra I -- (Ind.: *triśūla-mudrā*) ("the trident") A hand pose, a seal, a dramatic (Ind.: *nāṭya*) *mudra* or gesture (Ind.: *darpaṇa*) held or formed by a performer, dancer or actor. The *trishula mudra I* is a single (Ind.: *asaṁyutta*) form, held by one hand. It denotes a wood-apple leaf and groups of three. This *mudra* is formed by: the palm faces forward, the index, middle and ring fingers extend upward and are slightly separated, the thumb and the little finger curl towards the palm. (ACG 38) (See: **Figure 603**)

trishula mudra II -- (Ind.: *triśūla-mudrā*) ("the trident") A *mudra*, a ritual hand pose, a seal, a *tantric mudra* which is common to the Japanese Buddhist (*Vajrayana, Mantrayana*) tradition and is held or formed by a devotee or priest during the rites of the *Garbhadhatu Mandala* and *Vajradhatu Mandala*. It may be accompanied by a *mantra*. The *trishula mudra*[18] is a single (Ind.: *asaṁyutta*) form, held by one hand. It denotes a trident and the extinguishing of impediments. The *trishula mudra II* is a single (Ind.: *asaṁyutta*) form, held by one hand. This *mudra* is formed by either hand: palm facing out, little finger folded into the palm, thumb folded into the palm and pressing down the little finger, the index, middle and ring fingers are erect and together. (GDe 8) (See: **Figure 604**)

trishula mudra III -- (Ind.: *triśūla-mudrā*) ("the trident") A *mudra*, a ritual hand pose, a seal, a *tantric mudra* which is common to the Japanese Buddhist (*Vajrayana, Mantrayana*) tradition and is held or formed by a devo-

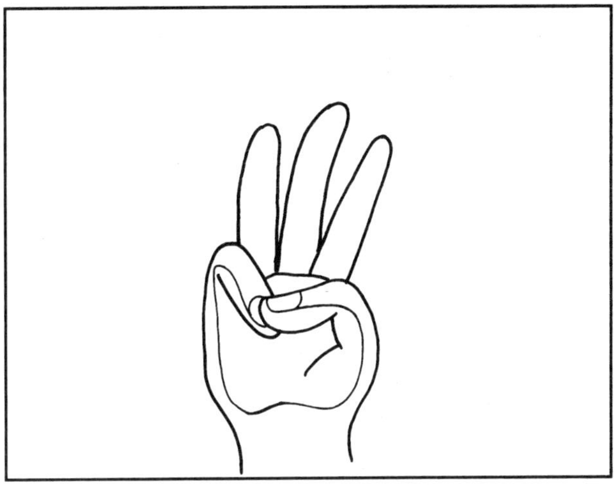

Figure 601 -- tripitaka mudra III
(as seen by another)

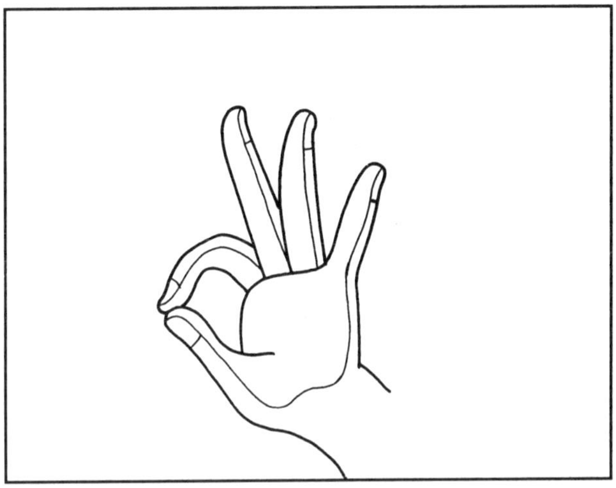

Figure 602 -- trisharana mudra
(as seen by another)

Figure 603 -- trishula mudra I
(as seen by another)

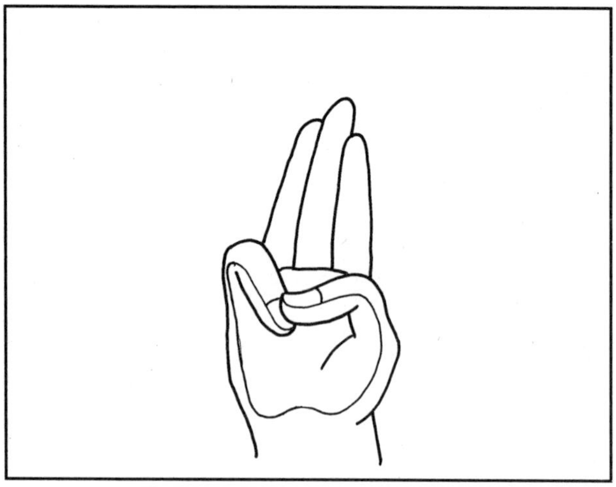

Figure 604 -- trishula mudra II
(as seen by another)

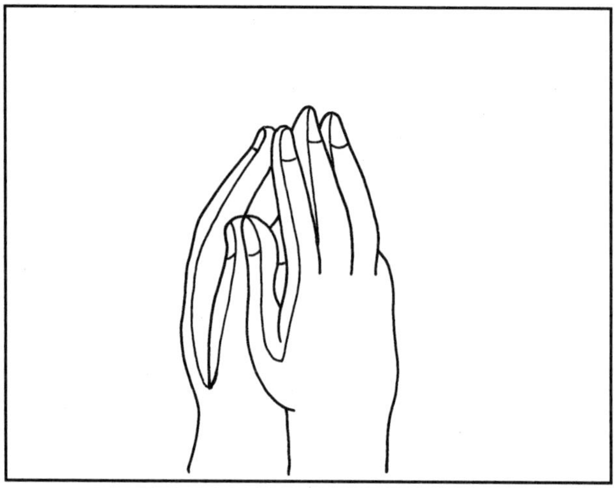

Figure 605 -- trishula mudra III
(as seen by the holder)

tee or priest during the rites of *Garbhadhatu Mandala, Vajradhatu Mandala, Homa Rites* and other rites. It may be accompanied by a *mantra*. The *trishula mudra III* is a combined (Ind.: *saṁyutta*) form, held by both hands. It denotes a trident, an offensive weapon used to destroy or subdue the enemies of religion. This *mudra* is formed by: palms facing midline and close, thumbs extend upwards and touch along their length, index, middle and ring fingers extend upward, touch at their tips and are slightly splayed, little fingers are folded into the palms. (GDe 299, LCS 257) (See: **Figure 605**)

Tungabhadra mudra -- (Ind.: *Tuṅgabhadrā-mudrā*) A hand pose, a seal, a dramatic (Ind.: *nāṭya*) *mudra* or gesture (Ind.: *darpaṇa*) held or formed by a performer, dancer or actor. It denotes the *Tungabhadra*, one of the famous rivers of India. The *mudra* employed is identical in form to the *hamsasya mudra*. See: *hamsasya mudra*. (ACG 48)

-- U --

uddhrita mudra -- (Ind.: *uddhṛta-mudrā*) A hand pose, a seal, a dramatic (Ind.: *nāṭya*) *mudra* or gesture (Ind.: *darpaṇa*) held or formed by a performer, dancer or actor noted in ACG but without description. (ACG 44)

udveshtitalapadma mudra -- (Ind.: *udveṣṭitāla-padma-mudrā*) ("dissimulation") A hand pose, a seal, a dramatic (Ind.: *nāṭya*) *mudra* or gesture (Ind.: *darpaṇa*) held or formed by a performer, dancer or actor. It denotes the breast, holding a ball and is often used in an erotic dance. The *udveshtitalapadma mudra*[1] is a combined (Ind.: *saṁyutta*) form, held by both hands. This *mudra* is formed by: the palms face upwards, the thumbs and fingers splay, stiff; so formed, the little fingers are at 90° to the palms and the ring fingers are at 45° to the palms. Thus formed, the two hands are held in front of and close to the chest. (ACG 44) (See: **Figure 606**)

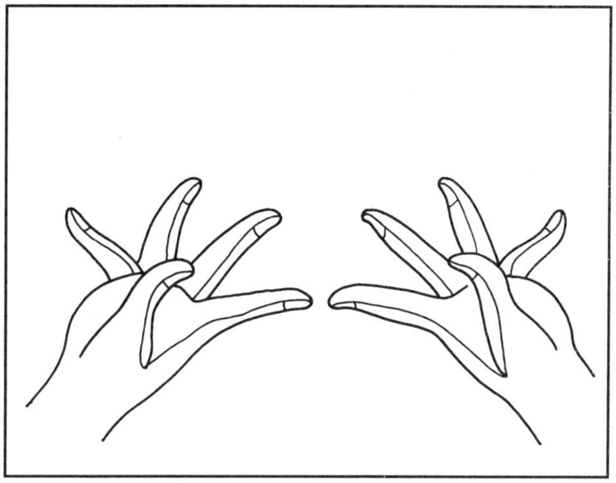

Figure 606 -- udveshtitalapadma mudra
(as seen by another)

udvritta mudra -- (Ind.: *udvṛtta-mudrā*) ("asunder") A hand pose, a seal, a dramatic (Ind.: *nāṭya*) *mudra* or gesture (Ind.: *darpaṇa*) held or formed by a performer, dancer or actor. The *udvritta mudra* is a combined (Ind.: *saṁyutta*) form, held by both hands. It denotes modesty, simile, torment, etc.[2] This *mudra* requires movement and is first formed by: left palm faces downwards, the index, middle and ring fingers curl towards the palm, the thumb rests along the curled index finger, the little finger is extending straight; right palm faces upwards, the index, middle and ring fingers curl towards the palm, the thumb rests along the curled index finger, the little finger is extending straight. The two hands are close. (ACG 43) (See: **Figure 607**)

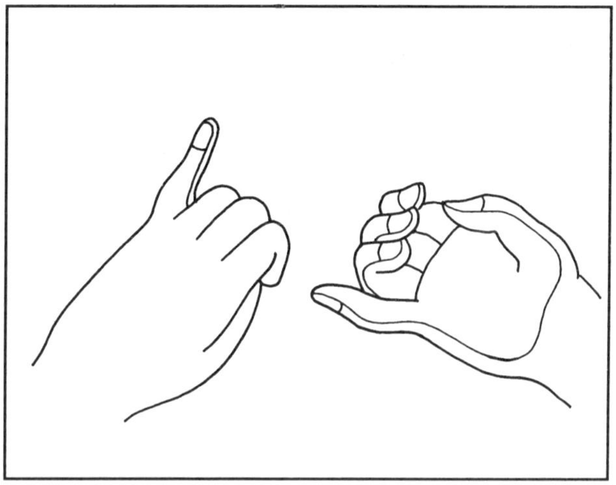

Figure 607 -- udvritta mudra
(as seen by the holder)

ulbana mudra -- (Ind.: *ulbaṇa-mudrā*) A hand pose, a seal, a dramatic (Ind.: *nāṭya*) *mudra* or gesture (Ind.: *darpaṇa*) held or formed by a performer, dancer or actor. The *ulbana mudra* is a combined (Ind.: *saṁyutta*) form, held by both hands. It denotes clusters of flowers and eyes. This *mudra* is formed by: the palms face upwards, the thumbs and fingers splay, stiff; so formed, the little fingers are at 90° to the palms and the ring

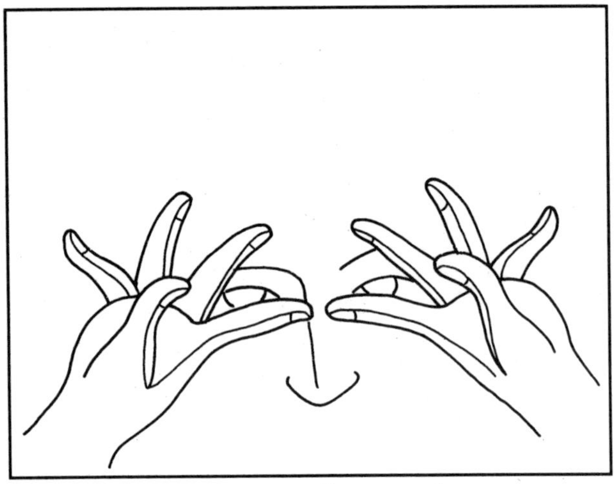

Figure 608 -- ulbana mudra
(as seen by another)

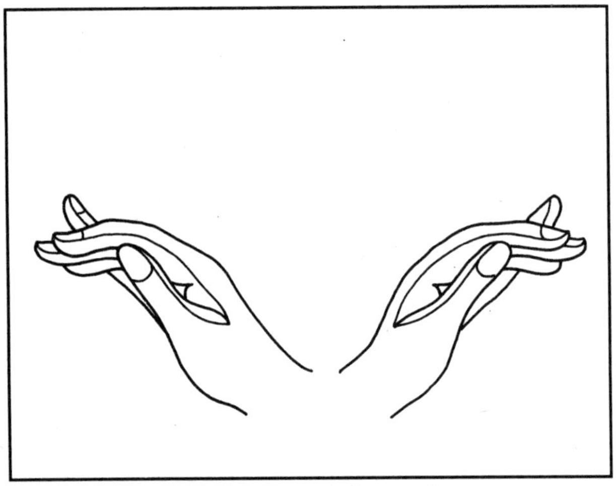

Figure 609 -- uluka mudra
(as seen by the holder)

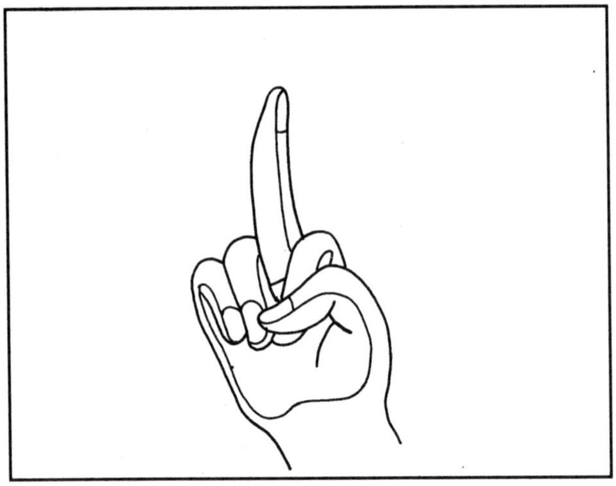

Figure 610 -- Upakeshini mudra
(as seen by another)

fingers are at 45° to the palms. Thus formed, the two hands are held in front of and close to the eyes. (ACG 44) (See: **Figure 608**)

uluka mudra -- (Ind.: *ulūka-mudrā*) A hand pose, a seal, a dramatic (Ind.: *nāṭya*) *mudra* or gesture (Ind.: *darpaṇa*) held or formed by a performer, dancer or actor. It denotes a bird, in this case an owl. The *uluka mudra*[3] is a combined (Ind.: *saṁyutta*) form, held by both hands. This *mudra* is formed by: palms facing each other, the thumbs are against the index fingers' base, the index, middle, ring and little fingers curl, half-way towards the palms. Thus formed the forearms are crossed close to the elbows. (ACG 50) (See: **Figure 609**)

unmukhonmukham mudra -- (Ind.: *unmukhon-mukham-mudrā* aka *conmukhmukham mudrā*) A variant (spelling) of *chonmukhmukham mudra*. See: *chonmukhmukham mudra*. (RLM 73)

Upakeshini mudra -- (Ind.: *Upakeśinī-mudrā*) A *mudra*, a ritual hand pose, a seal, a *tantric mudra* which is common to the Japanese Buddhist (*Vajrayana, Mantrayana*) tradition and is held or formed by a devotee or priest during the rites of *Garbhadhatu Mandala, Vajradhatu Mandala, Homa Rites* and other rites. It may be accompanied by a *mantra*. It denotes the deity *Upakeshini*. The *Upakeshini mudra* is a single (Ind.: *asaṁyutta*) form, held by one hand. This *mudra* is formed by: the index, ring and little fingers folded into the palm, thumb folded over the three fingers, middle finger extends straight upwards. (GDe 279, LCS 252) (See: **Figure 610**)

uparatna mudra -- (Ind.: *uparatna-mudrā*) This is an assigned term.[4] A *mudra*, a ritual hand pose, a seal, which is common to the Buddhist (*Vajrayana*) tradition, a *tantric mudra*. It denotes the gift of a subsidiary precious offerings associated with the *saptaratna* (Tib.: *rgyal-srid sna-bdun*) or seven gems of sovereignty (Tib.: *nor-bu-chab-bdun*), also referred to as the 'space vast treasury,' particularly as it is associated with the worship of the powerful *Vajrayana* goddess, *Tara*. The *uparatna mudra* is a combined (Ind.: *saṁyutta*) form, held by both hands. This *mudra* is formed by both hands in mirror-pose: palms face the mid-line, fingers and thumb are cupped, so formed the tips of the fingers and thumbs touch. Thus formed, the *mudra* is held at chest level. The *mantra* associated with this *mudra* is: "*OM Uparatna Praticcha HUM SVAHA*."[5] (SBe 152) (See: **Figure 611**)

Upaya-paramita mudra -- (Ind.: *Upāya-pāramitā-mudrā*) A *mudra*, a ritual hand pose, a seal, a *tantric mudra* which is common to the Japanese Buddhist (*Vajrayana, Mantrayana*) tradition and is held or formed by a devotee or priest during the rites of *Garbhadhatu Mandala* and other rites. It may be accompanied by a mantra. The *Upaya-paramita mudra*[6] is a combined (Ind.: *saṁyutta*) form, held by both hands. This *mudra* is formed by: palms facing inwards, thumbs folded into palms, middle and ring fingers fold over thumbs, index and little fingers extend straight and touch (across the folded middle and ring fingers) at their tips. Thus formed the hands touch along the outside edges of the little fingers and palms. (LCS 171) (See: **Figure 612**)

urnanabha mudra -- (Ind.: *ūrṇa-nābha-mudrā*) ("the spider") A hand pose, a seal, a dramatic (Ind.: *nāṭya*) *mudra* or gesture (Ind.: *darpaṇa*) held or formed by a performer, dancer or actor. Also, a *tantric mudra* which is common to the Japanese and Chinese Buddhist (*Vajrayana, Mantrayana*) tradition and is held or formed by a devotee or priest. It may be accompanied by a *mantra*. The *urnanabha mudra* is a single (Ind.: *asaṁyutta*) form, held by one hand. It denotes ferocity, thievery,fear, etc.[7] This *mudra* is formed by: the fingers and thumb separated and curled inward, towards the palm. The curve of the fingers are more exaggerated than the *padmakosha mudra*. (ACG 32, GDe 474, KVa 136 [30-32]) (See: **Figure 613**)

urusamsthita mudra -- (Ind.: *urusaṁsthita-mudrā*) A *mudra*, a ritual hand pose, a seal, which is common to both the Buddhist and Hindu traditions, although it is more frequently seen in Hindu practice. It denotes relaxation. The *urusamsthita mudra* is a single (Ind.: *asaṁyutta*) form, held by one hand. This *mudra* is formed by: the hand, usually the left, rests casually, palm down on the thigh of a seated figure. (MJS 149) (See: **Figure 614**)

ushnisha mudra -- (Ind.: *uṣṇīṣa-mudrā*) A *mudra*, a ritual hand pose, a seal, a *tantric mudra* which is com-

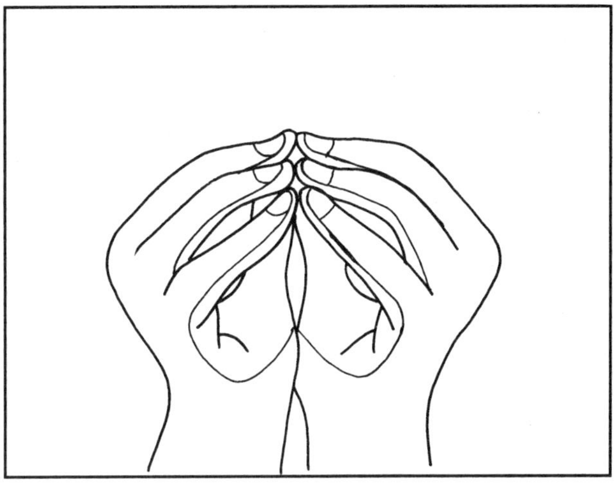

Figure 611 -- uparatna mudra
(as seen by another)

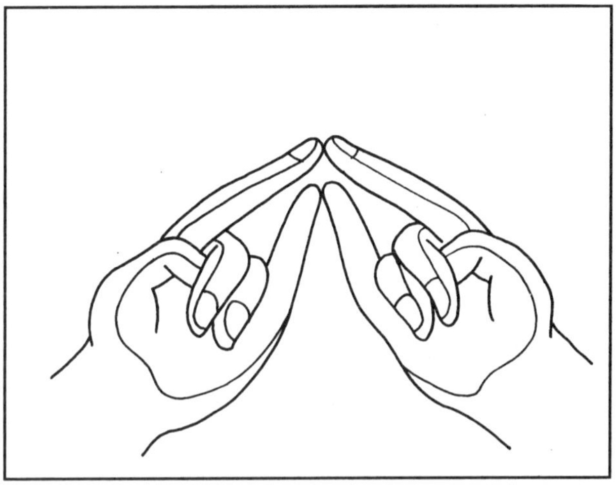

Figure 612 -- Upaya-paramita mudra
(as seen by the holder)

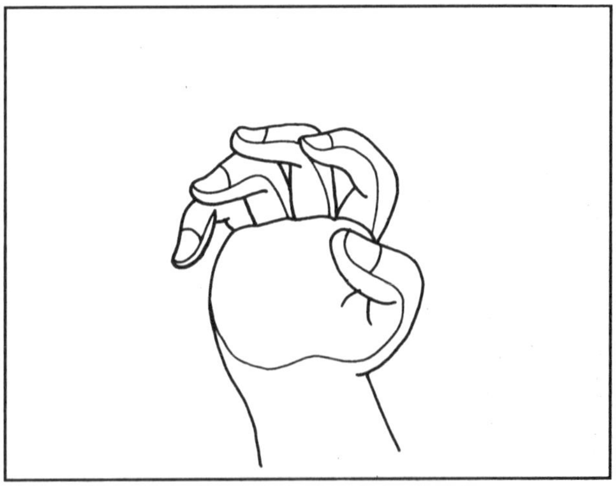

Figure 613 -- urnanabha mudra
(as seen by another)

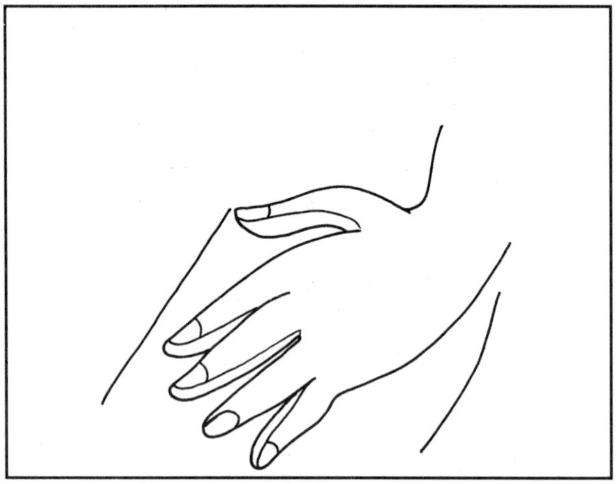

Figure 614 -- urusamsthita mudra
(as seen by another)

Figure 615 -- ushnisha mudra
(as seen by the holder)

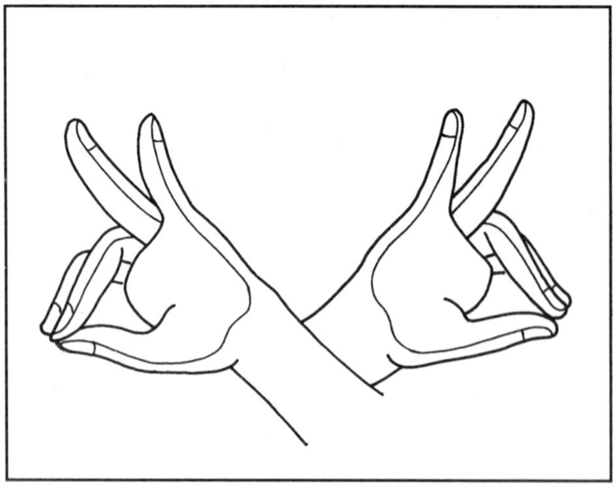

Figure 616 -- utsanga mudra
(as seen by another)

mon to the Japanese Buddhist (*Vajrayana, Mantrayana*) tradition and is held or formed by a devotee or priest during the rites of *Garbhadhatu Mandala, Vajradhatu Mandala, Homa Rites* and other rites. It may be accompanied by a mantra. The *ushnisha mudra* is a combined (Ind.: *saṁyutta*) form, held by both hands. This *mudra* is formed by: palms facing the midline, thumbs folded into the palms, middle, ring and little fingers interlaced and folded inwards (into the palms), index fingers curl palm-ward and touch along the outside surface of the first phalanges. (GDe 312, LCS 164) (See: **Figure 615**)

ushtra mudra -- (Ind.: *uṣṭra-mudrā*) A hand pose, a seal, a dramatic (Ind.: *nāṭya*) *mudra* or gesture (Ind.: *darpaṇa*) held or formed by a performer, dancer or actor. It denotes an animal, in this case a camel. The *ushtra mudra*[8] is a combined (Ind.: *saṁyutta*) form, held by both hands. This *mudra* is identical in form to the *kandanjali mudra*. See: *kandanjali mudra*. (ACG 50)

ut-pal kha-bye-ba'i phyag-rgya (mudra) -- (Tib.; Ind.: *vikasitapadma mudrā*) The Tibetan transliteral term for *vikasitapadma mudra*. See: *vikasitapadma mudra*. (SBe 338)

utsanga mudra -- (Ind.: *utsaṅga-mudrā*) ("the embrace") A hand pose, a seal, a dramatic (Ind.: *nāṭya*) *mudra* or gesture (Ind.: *darpaṇa*) held or formed by a performer, dancer or actor. It denotes modesty, cold, etc.[9] The *utsanga mudra* is a combined (Ind.: *saṁyutta*) form, held by both hands. This *mudra* is formed by: palm faces forward, index and middle fingers curl towards the palm and they are touched by the tip of the thumb, the ring and the little fingers extend upwards. Thus formed, the hands cross and the *mudra* is held in front of and against the opposite armpit. (ACG 40) (See: **Figure 616**)

uttanaja mudra -- (Ind.: *uttānaja mudrā*; Jap.: *ottanasha gassho* [*mudra*]) The Indic term for *ottanasha gassho* [*mudra*]. See: *ottanasha gassho* [*mudra*]. (EDS 41)

uttarabodhi mudra -- (Ind.: *uttarabodhi-mudrā*) A *mudra*, a ritual hand pose, a seal, which is common to both the Buddhist and Hindu traditions and is depicted or held by a deity. Also, a *mudra*, a ritual hand pose, a seal, a *tantric mudra* which is common to the Japanese Buddhist (*Vajrayana, Mantrayana*) tradition and is held or formed by a devotee or priest. It may be accompanied by a *mantra*. It denotes perfection or supreme enlightenment. The *uttarabodhi mudra* is a combined (Ind.: *saṁyutta*) form, held by both hands. This *mudra* is formed by: palm to palm, all fingers and thumbs interlace except the index fingers which point upwards. Thus formed the mudra is held at chest level, or above the head.10 (AKG 22, ERJ 9, GDe 310, RSG 4) (See: **Figure 617**)

utthana-vanchita mudra -- (Ind.: *utthāna-vañcita-mudrā*) A hand pose, a seal, a dramatic (Ind.: *nāṭya*) *mudra* or gesture (Ind.: *darpaṇa*) held or formed by a performer, dancer or actor noted in ACG but without description. (ACG 44)

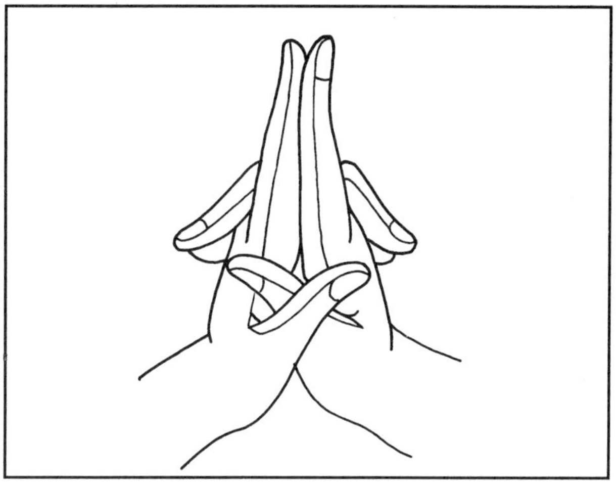

Figure 617 -- uttarabodhi mudra
(as seen by the holder)

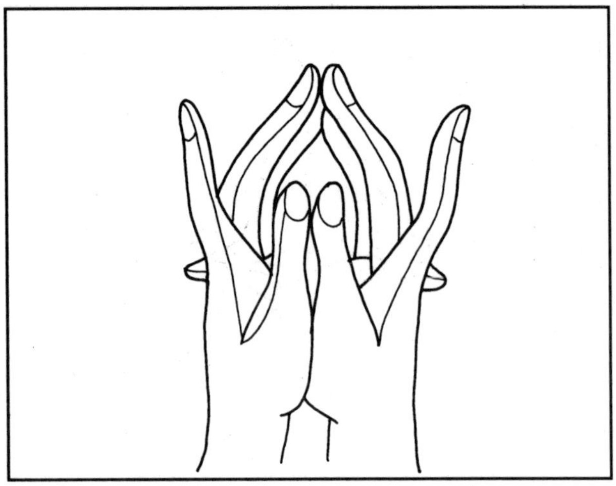

Figure 618 -- Vaishravana mudra
(as seen by the holder)

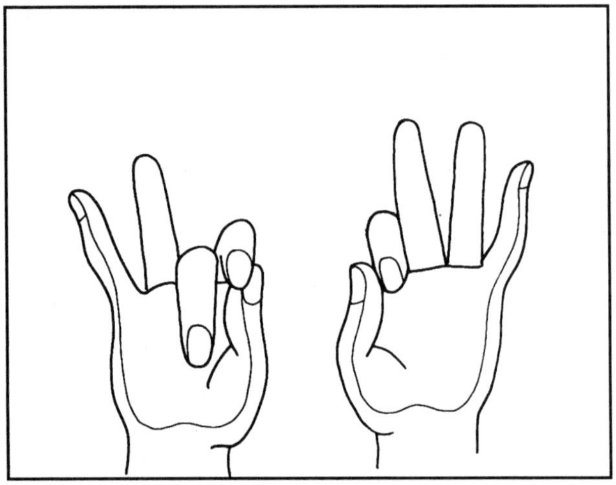

Figure 619 -- Vaishya mudra
(as seen by another)

-- V --

vairagyam mudra -- (Ind.: *vairāgyam-mudrā* aka *verāgya mudrā*) A variant (spelling) of *veragya mudra*. See: *veragya mudra*. (RLM 77)

vaishnava mudra -- (Ind.: *vaiṣṇava-mudrā*) A hand pose, a seal, a dramatic (Ind.: *nāṭya*) *mudra* or gesture (Ind.: *darpaṇa*) held or formed by a performer, dancer or actor noted in ACG but without description. (ACG 44)

Vaishravana mudra -- (Ind.: *Vaiśravaṇa-mudrā*) A *mudra*, a ritual hand pose, a seal, a *tantric mudra* which is common to the Japanese Buddhist (*Vajrayana, Mantrayana*) tradition and is held or formed by a devotee or priest during the rites of *Garbhadhatu Mandala* and other rites. It may be accompanied by a mantra. The *Vaishravana mudra* is a combined (Ind.: *saṁyutta*) form, held by both hands. This *mudra* is formed by: palms facing midline and touching, thumbs and index fingers extend upwards, thumbs touch along their length, middle and ring fingers touch at tips, little fingers fold into the palms. (GDe 239, LCS 184) (See: **Figure 618**)

Vaishya mudra -- (Ind.: *Vaiśya-mudrā*) A hand pose, a seal, a dramatic (Ind.: *nāṭya*) *mudra* or gesture (Ind.: *darpaṇa*) held or formed by a performer, dancer or actor. The *Vaishya mudra* is a combined (Ind.: *saṁyutta*) form, held by both hands. It denotes *Vaishya*, one of the four castes. This *mudra* is formed by: right palm faces inward, the index and middle fingers curve and their tips touch the thumb, the ring and the little fingers also curve towards the palm; left palm faces forwards, the first phalanges of the thumb and index finger are touching and extended, the middle, ring and little fingers are separated, straight and pointing upwards. (ACG 47) (See: **Figure 619**)

vajra mudra I -- (Ind.: *vajra-mudrā* aka *jñāna mudrā*[?], *bodhaśrī mudrā*[?]) A *mudra*, a ritual hand pose, a seal, a *tantric mudra* which is common to the Japanese Buddhist (*Vajrayana, Mantrayana*) tradition and is held or formed by a devotee or priest. It may be accompanied by a *mantra*. The *vajra mudra*[1] is a combined (Ind.: *saṁyutta*) form, held by both hands. This *mudra* is formed by: hands brought together and touching along the outer edges of the thumbs and little fingers, the palms form a hollow space, the digits (generally) extend upwards or outwards, except the ring fingers which curl towards the palms and touch along the second phalanges, and the middle fingers which touch at their tips. (GDe 294) (See: **Figure 620**)

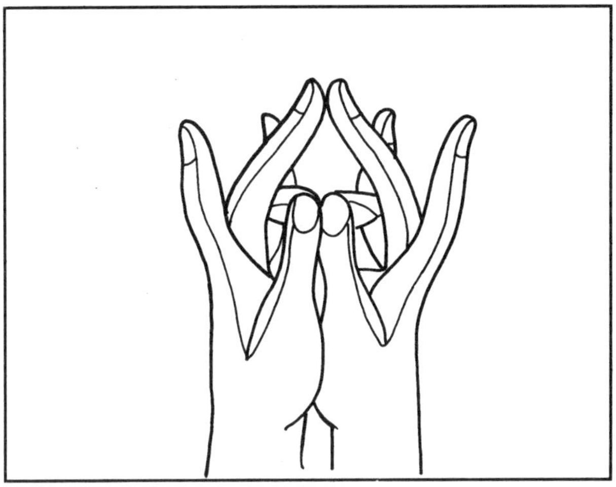

Figure 620 -- vajra mudra I
(as seen by the holder)

vajra mudra II -- (Ind.: *vajra-mudrā*) (called "small *sanko*"[2]) A *mudra*, a ritual hand pose, a seal, a *tantric mudra* which is common to the Japanese Buddhist (*Vajrayana, Mantrayana*) tradition and is held or formed by a devotee or priest during various rites. It may be accompanied by a *mantra*. The *vajra* (small *sanko*) *mudra* is a single (Ind.: *asaṁyutta*) form, held by one hand. It denotes the diamond scepter. This *mudra* is formed by: right palm forward, index, middle, ring fingers extend upwards, tip of the thumb touches the tip of the curled little finger. (GDe 67, LCS 58) (See: **Figure 621**)

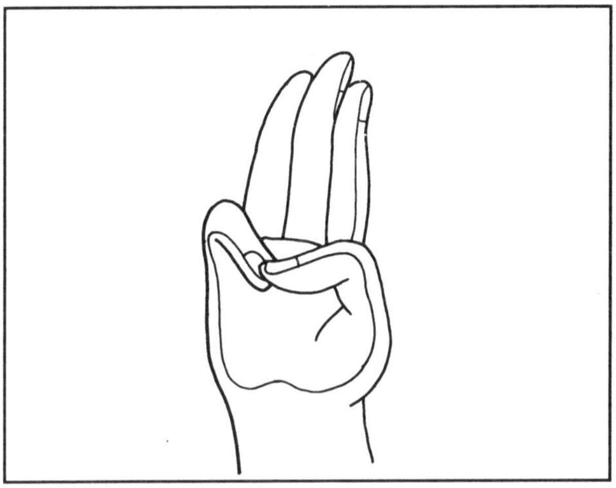

Figure 621 -- vajra mudra II
(as seen by another)

vajra mudra III -- (Ind.: *vajra-mudrā* aka *jñāna mudrā, bodhaśrī mudra*; Chin.: *chih-ch'ṃan-yin* [*mudra*]; Jap.: *biroshananyoraidaimyochi-in* [*mudra*]; *bodaiindodaiichichi-in* [*mudra*], *chi ken-in* [*mudra*], *nometsumumyokokuan-in* [*mudra*]) A variant term applied to *chi ken-in* (*mudra*). See: *chi ken-in* (*mudra*); see also: *jnana mudra*. (EDS 102, MMR 348)

vajra mudra IV -- (Ind.: *vajra-mudrā*; Jap.: *kongo ken-in* [*mudra*];) ("*vajra* fist [*mudra*])" The Indic transliteral term applied to *kongo ken-in* (*mudra*) *I*. See: *kongo ken-in* (*mudra*) *I*. (EDS 39)

Vajra-Akashagarbha mudra -- (Ind.: *Vajra-Ākāśa-garbha-mudrā*) A *mudra*, a ritual hand pose, a seal, a *tantric mudra* which is common to the Japanese Buddhist (*Vajrayana, Mantrayana*) tradition and is held or formed by a devotee or priest during various rites in which a deity is acknowledged. It is a *mudra* which is associated with the deity *Vajra-Akashagarbha*. It may be accompanied by a *mantra*. The *Vajra-Akashagarbha mudra*[3] is a combined (Ind.: *saṁyutta*) form, held by both hands. This *mudra* is formed by: palms facing inwards and close, thumbs crossed, right over left, in-

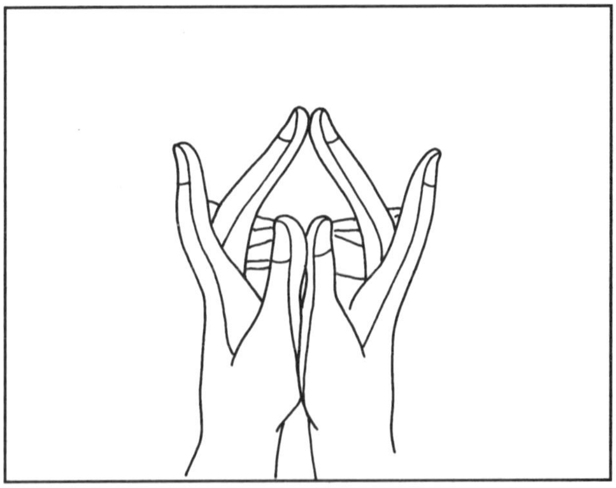

Figure 622 -- Vajra-Akashagarbha mudra
(as seen by the holder)

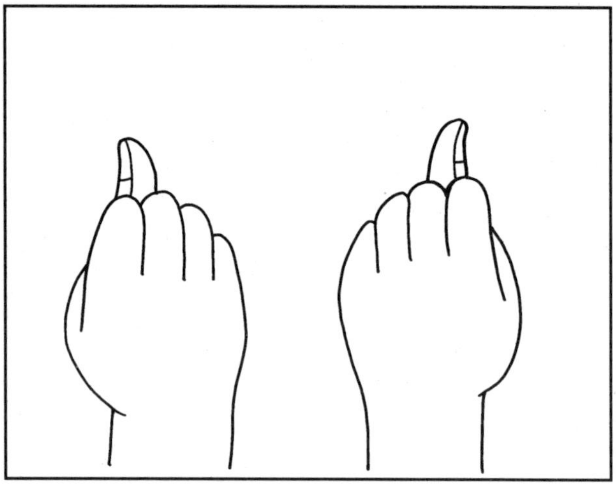

Figure 623 -- vajra-aloke mudra
(as seen by another)

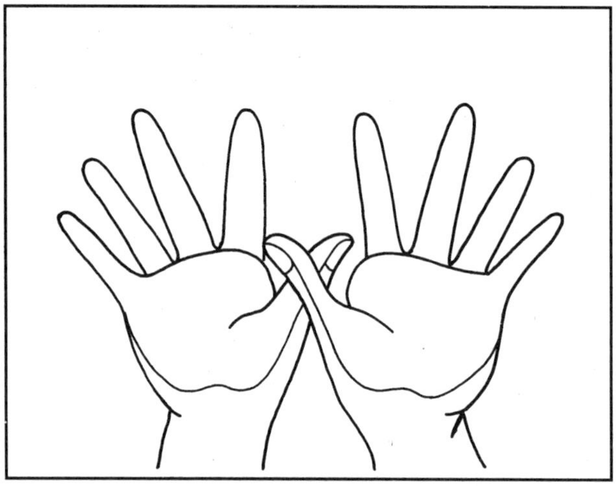

Figure 624 -- vajra-amrita-kundali mudra
(as seen by another)

dex fingers extend and are slightly curved, middle fingers touch at tips, ring and little fingers interlace on top of the hands. (LCS 247) (See: **Figure 622**)

vajra-aloke mudra -- (Ind.: *vajra-āloke-mudrā*) This is an assigned term.[4] A *mudra*, a ritual hand pose, a seal, which is common to the Buddhist (*Vajrayana*) tradition, a *tantric mudra*. It denotes one of the sixteen inner offerings which follow the presentation of the eight signs of good fortune (Indic: *aṣṭa-maṅgala*, Tib.: *bkra-shis rtags-brgyad*). These secret offerings are presented to one of the sixteen goddesses of sensual enjoyment, particularly as associated with the worship of the powerful *Vajrayana* goddess, *Tara*. The *vajra-aloke mudra* is a combined (Ind.: *saṁyutta*) form, held by both hands. This *mudra* is formed by hands in mirror-pose: the palm faces inwards, the fingers are folded into the palm, the thumb extends upwards, so formed the hands are brought close together but not touching. The *mudra* is held in front of the chest. The *mantra* associated with this *mudra* is: "*OM AH Vajra-aloke HUM.*"[5] (SBe 160) (See: Figure 623)

vajra-amrita-kundali mudra -- (Ind.: *vajra-amṛta-kuṇḍalī-mudrā*; Tib.: *bdud-rtsi thabs-sbyor phyag-rgya*) This is an assigned term.[6] A *mudra*, a ritual hand pose, a seal, which is common to the Buddhist (*Vajrayana*) tradition, a *tantric mudra*. It is the third gesture of six of the *ma-mo-mdos mudras*. It denotes the swirling nectar, particularly as associated with the white *gtor-ma* (sacrificial cake) offering and the presentation of the thread cross (Tib.: *ma-mo-mdos* or *ma-mdos*) as part of the worship of the powerful *Vajrayana* goddess, *Tara*. The *vajra-amrita-kundali mudra* is a combined (Ind.: *saṁyutta*) form, held by both hands. This *mudra* is formed by both hands in mirror pose: palm faces outwards, fingers extend upwards (*abhaya mudra*), thumb held at 45°, so posed the thumbs overlap at the joint of the first phalanges. The *mudra* is held in front of the chest. The *mantra* associated with this mudra is: "*Vajra-amrita-kundali Hana Hana HUM Phat.*"[7] (SBe 347) (See: **Figure 624**)

vajra-anjalikarma mudra -- (Ind.: *vajra-añjalikarma-mudrā* aka *añjali mudrā, añjalikarma-mudrā*) A variant term applied to *anjali mudra*. See: *anjali mudra*. (EDS 76)

vajra-bandha mudra -- (Ind.: *vajra-bandha-mudrā* aka *bhūmi-bandha mudrā, sīma-bandha mudrā*; Jap.: *ji ketsu-in* [*mudra*]) A *mudra*, a ritual hand pose, a seal, a *tantric mudra* which is common to the Japanese Buddhist (*Vajrayana, Mantrayana*) tradition and is held or formed by a devotee or priest during the *Eighteen Rites*. It may be accompanied by a *mantra*. The *vajra-bandha mudra*[8] is a combined (Ind.: *saṁyutta*) form, held by both hands. It denotes delineation of the sacred precinct. This *mudra* is formed by: palms facing downwards, middle and ring fingers interlace on top (the back of the hand), index and little fingers are straight and point slightly upwards, their tips touch, tips of the thumbs also touch. (GDe 103, LCS 61) (See: **Figure 625**)

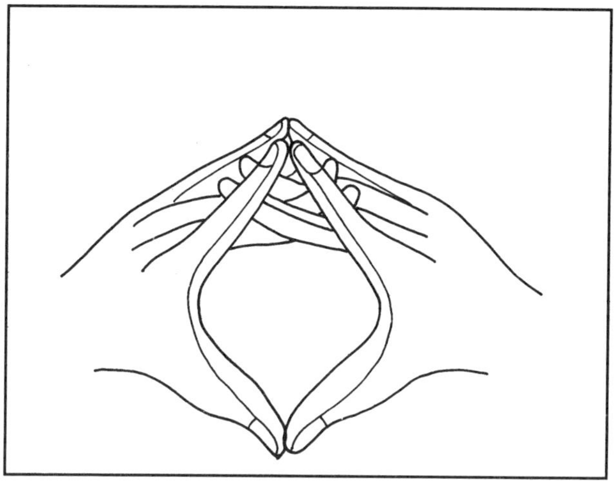

Figure 625 -- vajra-bandha mudra
(as seen by the holder)

vajranjali mudra -- (Ind.: *vajrāñjali-mudrā* aka *vajra-añjalikarma-mudrā*; Chin.: *chin-kang ho-chang*; Jap.: *kongo-gassho*) ("*vajra* or adamantine clasped-hands") A popular and frequently employed *mudra*, a ritual hand pose, a seal, a *tantric mudra* which is common to the Japanese Buddhist (*Vajrayana, Mantrayana*) tradition and is held or formed by a devotee or priest during numerous tantric rites. It may be accompanied by a *mantra*. The *vajranjali mudra*[9] is a combined (Ind.: *saṁyutta*) form, held by both hands. It denotes prayerful salutation and spiritual subjugation. This *mudra* is formed by: right palm touching the left palm, fingers extended upwards, slightly cupped, the first phalanges of the fingers and thumbs are interlaced with their opposites and held at the level of the chin.. (EDS 76, GDe 6, LCS 57) (See: **Figure 626**)

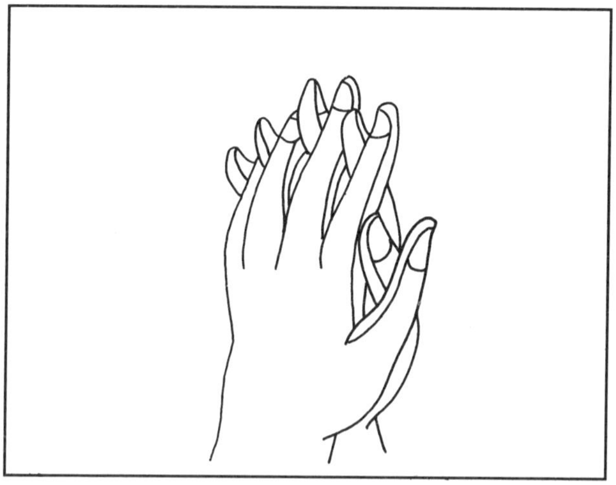

Figure 626 -- vajranjali mudra
(as seen by the holder)

vajra-darshe mudra -- (Ind.: *vajra-darśe-mudrā*) This is an assigned term.[10] A *mudra*, a ritual hand pose, a seal, which is common to the Buddhist (*Vajrayana*) tradition, a *tantric mudra*. It denotes one of the sixteen inner offerings which follow the presentation of the eight signs of good fortune (Indi: *aṣṭa-maṅgala*, Tib.: *bkra-shis rtags-brgyad*). These secret offerings are presented to one of the sixteen goddesses of sensual enjoyment, particularly as associated with the worship of the powerful *Vajrayana* goddess, *Tara*. The *vajra-darshe mudra* is a combined (Ind.: *saṁyutta*) form, held by both hands. This *mudra* is formed by: right hand's palm faces downwards, index finger extends towards the mid-line, thumb, middle, ring and little fingers fold into the palm

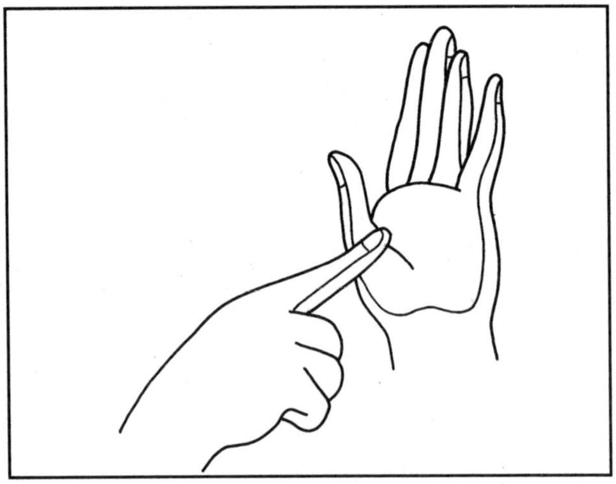

Figure 627 -- vajra-darshe mudra
(as seen by another)

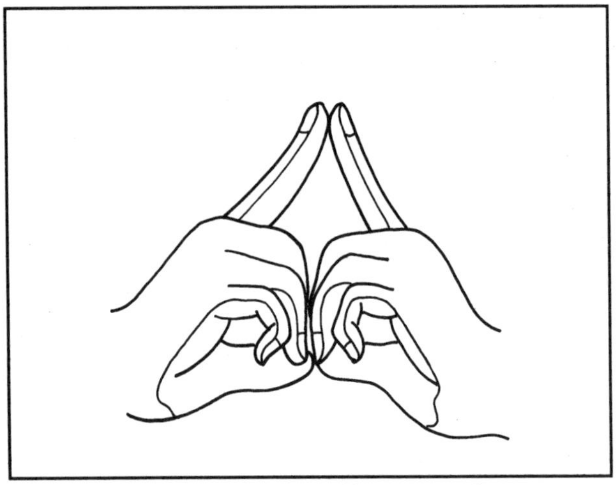

Figure 628 -- vajra-dharme mudra
(as seen by another)

(*tarjani mudra*); left hand's palm faces the mid-line, thumb and fingers extended upwards, the index finger of the right hand touches the palm of the left hand. The *mudra* so posed is held level with the chest. The *mudra* is held in front of the chest. The *mantra* associated with this *mudra* is: "*OM AH Vajra-darshe HUM*."[11] (SBe 161) (See: **Figure 627**)

vajra-dharme mudra -- (Ind.: *vajra-dharme-mudrā*) This is an assigned term.[12] A *mudra*, a ritual hand pose, a seal, which is common to the Buddhist (*Vajrayana*) tradition, a *tantric mudra*. It denotes one of the sixteen inner offerings which follow the presentation of the eight signs of good fortune (Indi: *aṣṭa-maṅgala*, Tib.: *bkra-shis rtags-brgyad*). These secret offerings are presented to one of the sixteen goddesses of sensual enjoyment, particularly as associated with the worship of the powerful *Vajrayana* goddess, *Tara*. The *vajra-dharme mudra* is a combined (Ind.: *saṁyutta*) form, held by both hands. This *mudra* is formed in mirror-pose: palm faces mid-line and slightly downwards, index finger extended slightly upwards, middle, ring and little fingers curl towards the palm, tip of thumb touches tip of middle finger, so formed the first phalanges of the index fingers touch, and the second phalanges of the middle, ring and little fingers come together. Thus formed the *mudra* is held level with the chest. The *mudra* is held in front of the chest. The *mantra* associated with this mudra is: "*OM AH Vajra-dharme HUM*."[13] (SBe 161) (See: **Figure 628**)

vajra-dhupe mudra -- (Ind.: *vajra-dhūpe-mudrā*) This is an assigned term.[14] A *mudra*, a ritual hand pose, a seal, which is common to the Buddhist (*Vajrayana*) tradition, a *tantric mudra*. It denotes one of the sixteen inner offerings which follow the presentation of the eight signs of good fortune (Ind.: *aṣṭa-maṅgala*, Tib.: *bkra-shis rtags-brgyad*). These secret offerings are presented to one of the sixteen goddesses of sensual enjoyment, particularly as associated with the worship of the powerful *Vajrayana* goddess, *Tara*. The *vajra-dhupe mudra* is a combined (Ind.: *saṁyutta*) form, held by both hands. This *mudra* is formed in mirror-pose: palms face inward, thumb and fingers are fisted,thumb inside the fingers, so posed the 'fists' are brought close to each other. The *mudra* is held in front of the chest. The *mantra* associated with this *mudra* is: "*OM AH Vajra-dhupe HUM*."[15] (SBe 161) (See: **Figure 629**)

vajra-gandhe mudra -- (Ind.: *vajra-gandhe-mudrā*) This is an assigned term.[16] A *mudra,* a ritual hand pose, a seal, which is common to the Buddhist (*Vajrayana*) tradition, a *tantric mudra*. It denotes one of the sixteen inner offerings which follow the presentation of the eight signs of good fortune (Ind.: *aṣṭa-maṅgala*, Tib.: *bkra-shis rtags-brgyad*). These secret offerings are presented to one of the sixteen goddesses of sensual enjoyment, particularly as associated with the worship of the powerful *Vajrayana* goddess, *Tara*. The *vajra-gandhe mudra* is a combined (Ind.: *saṁyutta*) form, held by both hands. This *mudra* is formed in mirror-pose: palms face the mid-line, tips of the middle finger touches the tips of the thumb, index, ring and little fingers extend upwards. The hands so posed are brought together and the tips of the index fingers and the tips of the thumbs touch. The *mudra* is held in front of the chest. The *mantra* associated with this mudra is: "*OM AH Vajra-gandhe HUM*."[17] (SBe 161) (See: **Figure 630**)

vajra-gita mudra -- (Ind.: *vajra-gītā-mudrā*) ("song *mudra*") A *mudra,* a ritual hand pose, a seal, a *tantric mudra* which is common to the Japanese Buddhist (*Vajrayana, Mantrayana*) tradition and is held or formed by a devotee or priest during the rites of *Garbhadhatu Mandala, Vajradhatu Mandala, Homa Rites* and other rites. It may be accompanied by a *mantra*. The *vajra-gita mudra*[18] is a combined (Ind.: *saṁyutta*) form, held by both hands. In this *mudra* both hands holds the same position. This *mudra* is formed by: palms facing upwards, fingers and thumbs interlaced and resting on the back of the hands. The *vajra-gita mudra's* orientation is opposite to the *vajra-mala mudra*. (GDe 83, LCS 115) (See: **Figure 631**)

vajra-gite mudra -- (Ind.: *vajra-gīte-mudrā*) This is an assigned term.[19] A *mudra,* a ritual hand pose, a seal, which is common to the Buddhist (*Vajrayana*) tradition, a *tantric mudra*. It denotes one of the sixteen inner offerings which follow the presentation of the eight signs of good fortune (Ind.: *aṣṭa-maṅgala*, Tib.: *bkra-shis rtags-brgyad*). These secret offerings are presented to one of the sixteen goddesses of sensual enjoyment, particularly as associated with the worship of the powerful *Vajrayana* goddess, *Tara*. The *vajra-gite mudra* is a combined (Ind.: *saṁyutta*) form, held by both hands.

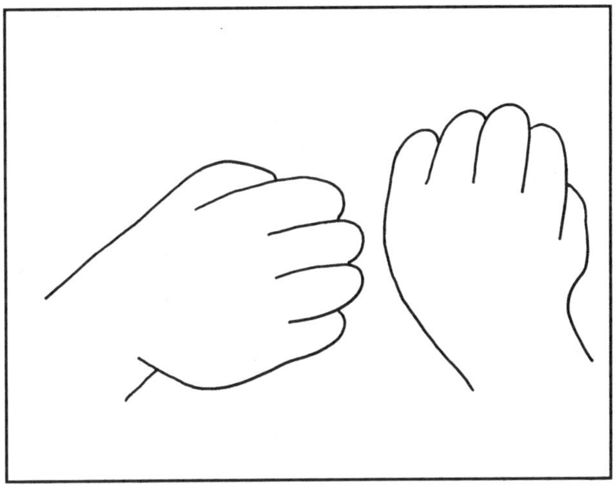

Figure 629 -- vajra-dhupe mudra
(as seen by another)

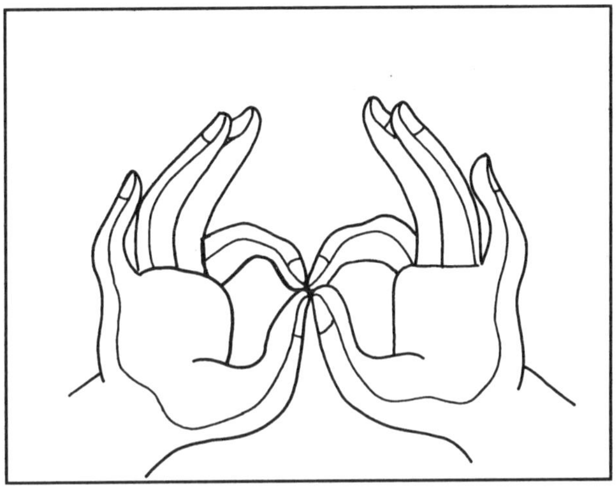

Figure 630 -- vajra-gandhe mudra
(as seen by another)

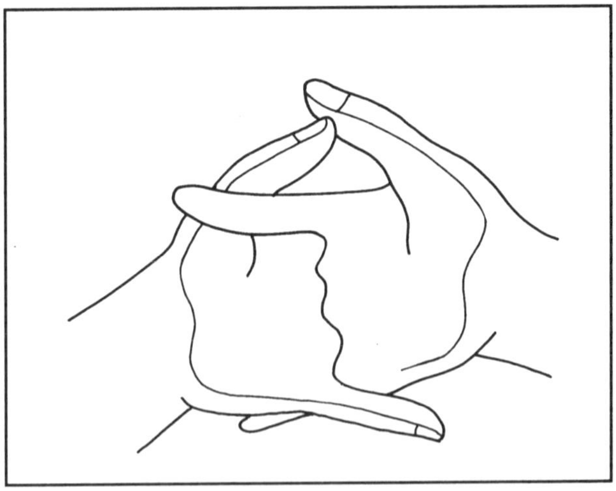

Figure 631 -- vajra-gita mudra
(as seen by the holder)

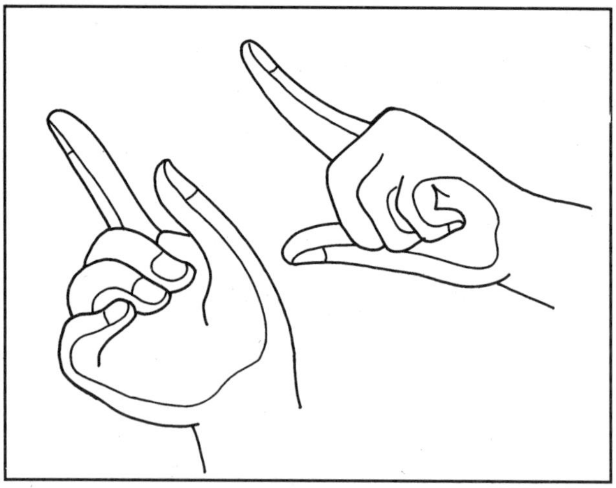

Figure 632 -- vajra-gite mudra
(as seen by another)

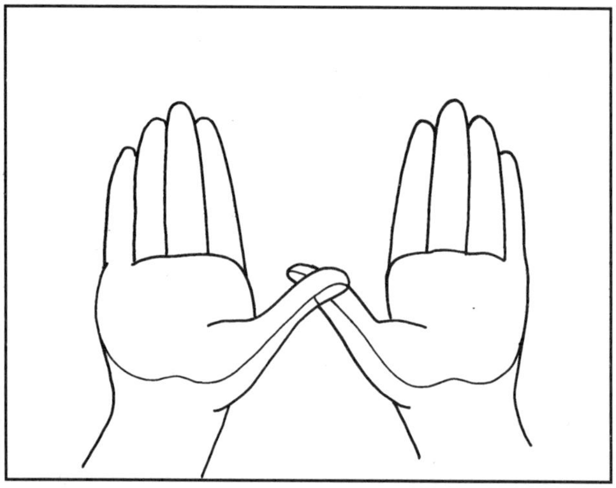

Figure 633 -- vajra-hasye mudra
(as seen by another)

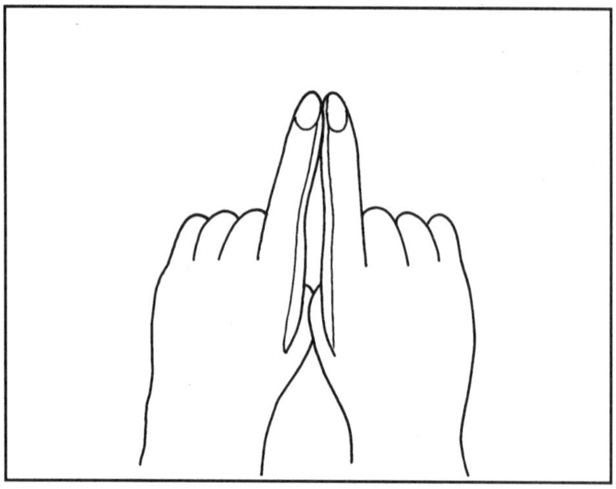

Figure 634 -- Vajrahetu mudra
(as seen by the holder)

This *mudra* is formed in mirror-pose: palm faces the mid-line, index finger extends upwards as does the thumb, middle, ring and little fingers fold into the palm (similar to the *tarjani mudra*), so posed the hands are brought close together but do not touch. The *mantra* associated with this mudra is: "*OM AH Vajra-gite HUM*."[20] (SBe 160) (See: **Figure 632**)

vajra-hasye mudra -- (Ind.: *vajra-hāsye-mudrā*) This is an assigned term.[21] A *mudra*, a ritual hand pose, a seal, which is common to the Buddhist (*Vajrayana*) tradition, a *tantric mudra*. It denotes one of the sixteen inner offerings which follow the presentation of the eight signs of good fortune (Ind.: *aṣṭa-maṅgala*, Tib.: *bkra-shis rtags-brgyad*). These secret offerings are presented to one of the sixteen goddesses of sensual enjoyment, particularly as associated with the worship of the powerful *Vajrayana* goddess, *Tara*. The *vajra-hasye mudra* is a combined (Ind.: *saṁyutta*) form, held by both hands. This *mudra* is formed in mirror pose: palm faces outwards, fingers and thumb extend upwards (*abhaya mudra*), so posed the tips of the thumbs touch. The *mudra* is held in front of the chest. The *mantra* associated with this *mudra* is: "*OM AH Vajra-hasye HUM*."[22] (SBe 160) (See: **Figure 633**)

Vajrahetu mudra -- (Ind.: *Vajrahetu-mudrā*) A *mudra*, a ritual hand pose, a seal, a *tantric mudra* which is common to the Japanese Buddhist (*Vajrayana, Mantrayana*) tradition and is held or formed by a devotee or priest during the rites of *Vajradhatu Mandala* and other rites. It may be accompanied by a *mantra*. The *Vajrahetu mudra*[23] is a combined (Ind.: *saṁyutta*) form, held by both hands. This *mudra* is formed by: palms facing outward, thumbs folded into the palm, middle, ring and little fingers fold into the palm over the thumbs, index fingers extend straight upwards. Thus formed the hands are brought together so that the index fingers touch along their length. (LCS 104) (See: **Figure 634**)

vajrahumkara mudra I -- (Ind.: *vajrahuṁkāra-mudrā* aka *vajrahuṅkāra mudra, vajrakarma mudrā*; Chin.: *chuan-yṃeh-lo-hung chin-kang-yin*; Jap.: *basara-un-kongo-in, kongo-karuma bosatsu-in*) A *mudra*, a ritual hand pose, a seal, which is common to both the Buddhist and

Hindu traditions. It denotes that path and purpose are one, or the Buddha Supreme. The *vajrahumkara mudra I* is a combined (Ind.: *saṁyutta*) form, held by both hands. This *mudra* is formed by: right palm faces inward, thumb, middle and ring fingers grasp *vajra*, index and little fingers extend; left palm faces inward, thumb, middle and ring fingers grasp ghanta, index and little fingers extend. So formed the two hands cross at the wrist, right over (on the outside of) left. Thus formed the *mudra* is held at chest level. (AKG 22, BBh 198, BCO 151, ERJ 8, RSG 4) (See: **Figure 635**)

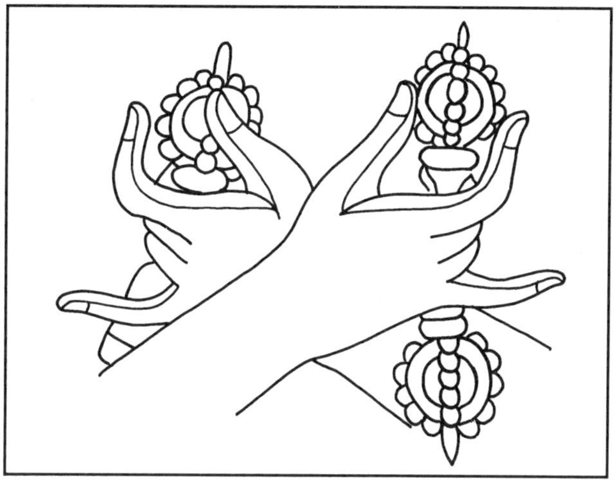

Figure 635 -- vajrahumkara mudra I
(as seen by another)

vajrahumkara mudra II -- (Ind.: *vajrahuṁkāra-mudrā* aka *vajrahuṅkāra mudrā, vajrakarma mudrā*; Chin.: *chuan-yṃeh-lo-hung chin-kang-yin*; Jap.: *basara-un-kongo-in, kongo-karuma bosatsu-in*) A *mudra*, a ritual hand pose, a seal, a *tantric mudra* which is common to the Japanese Buddhist (*Vajrayana, Mantrayana*) tradition and is held or formed by a devotee or priest during the rites of *Homa* and other rites. It may be accompanied by a *mantra*. The *vajrahumkara*[24] *mudra II* (Jap.: *kongo-karuma bosatsu-in*) is a combined (Ind.: *saṁyutta*) form, held by both hands. This *mudra* is formed by: right palm faces upwards, thumb and ring fingers touch at their tips forming a circle, index, middle and little fingers extend; left palm faces upwards, thumb and ring fingers touch at their tips forming a circle, index, middle and little fingers extend. So formed the two hands cross at the wrist, right over the left. (GDe 91) (See: **Figure 636**)

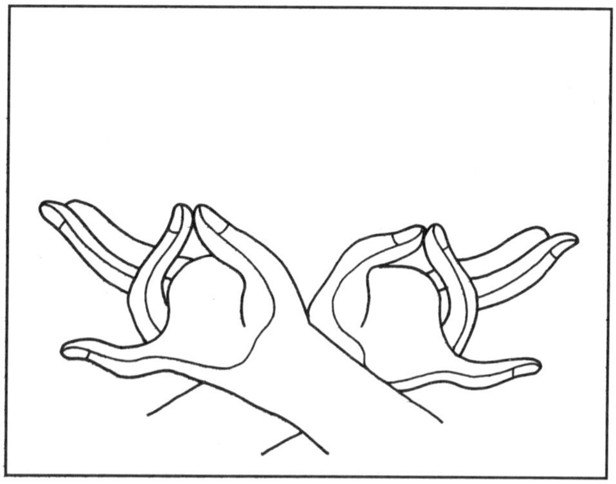

Figure 636 -- vajrahumkara mudra II
(as seen by the holder)

vajrahunkara mudra -- (Ind.: *vajrahuṅkāra-mudrā* aka *vajrahuṁkāra mudrā*) A variant (spelling) of *vajrahumkara mudra*. See: *vajrahumkara mudra*. (BBh 198)

vajra-jala mudra -- (Ind.: *vajra-jāla-mudrā*] aka *ākāśa-jāla mudrā*; Jap.: *kongo mo-in* [*mudra*]) The Indic term for *kongo mo-in* (*mudra*). See: *kongo mo-in* (*mudra*). (GDe 106. LCS 63)

vajra-jvala mudra -- (Ind.: *vajra-jvālā-mudrā* aka *agni-śāla mudrā*) A variant term applied to *agni-shala mudra*. See: *agni-shala mudra*. (LCS 64)

vajrakarma mudra -- (Ind.: *vajrakarma mudrā* aka *vajrahuṁkāra mudrā, vajrahuṅkāra mudrā*) A variant term

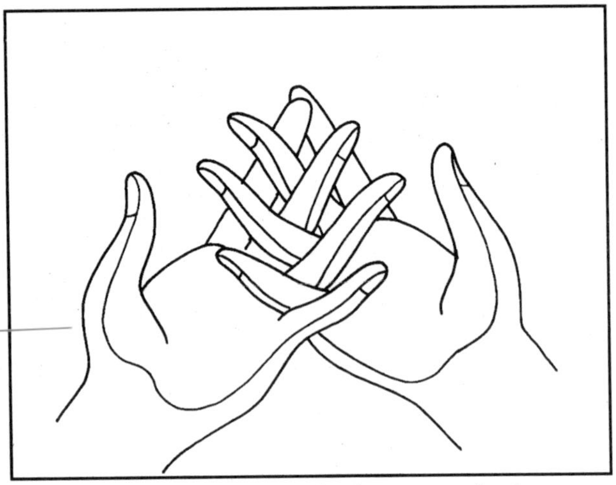

Figure 637 -- vajra-kashyapa mudra I
(as seen by the holder)

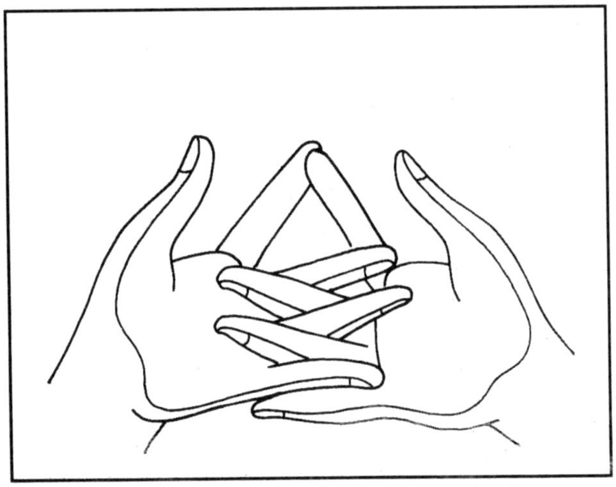

Figure 638 -- vajra-kashyapa mudra II
(as seen by the holder)

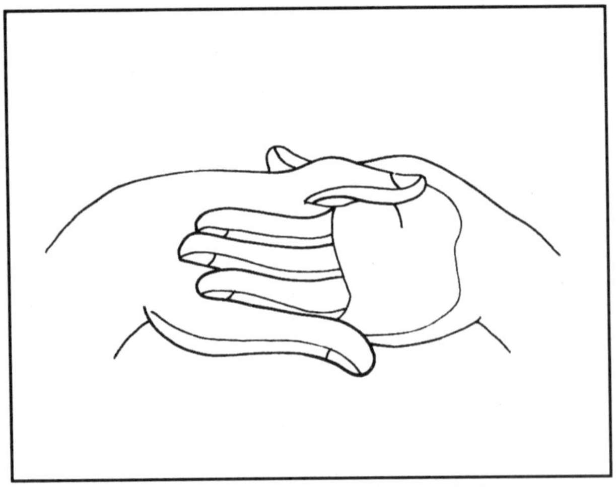

Figure 639 -- Vajrakula (mudra)
(as seen by the holder)

applied to *vajrahumkara mudra*. See: *vajrahumkara mudra*. (GDe 91)

vajra-kashyapa mudra I -- (Ind.: *vajra-kaśyapa-mudrā*) A *mudra*, a ritual hand pose, a seal, a *tantric mudra* which is common to the Japanese Buddhist (*Vajrayana, Mantrayana*) tradition and is held or formed by a devotee or priest during the rites of the *Vajradhatu Mandala*. It may be accompanied by a *mantra*. The *vajra-kashyapa mudra* is a combined (Ind.: *saṁyutta*) form, held by both hands. This *mudra* is formed by: palms facing away from each other (back to back, but not touching), middle, ring and little fingers extended and interlace at approximately 30°, index fingers extend and tips touch, thumbs extend upwards. (LCS 93) (See: **Figure 637**)

vajra-kashyapa mudra II -- (Ind.: *vajra-kaśyapa-mudrā*) A *mudra*, a ritual hand pose, a seal, a *tantric mudra* which is common to the Japanese Buddhist (*Vajrayana, Mantrayana*) tradition and is held or formed by a devotee or priest during the rites of the *Vajradhatu Mandala*. It may be accompanied by a *mantra*. The vajra-*kashyapa mudra II* is a combined (Ind.: *saṁyutta*) form, held by both hands. This *mudra* is a variation on the former and is formed by: palms facing upwards, middle, ring and little fingers extend towards midline and interlace, index fingers extend outward and tips touch, thumbs extend outwards. (LCS 93) (See: **Figure 638**)

Vajrakula (mudra) -- (Ind.: *Vajrakula* [*mudrā*]) A *mudra*, a ritual hand pose, a seal, a *tantric mudra* which is common to the Japanese Buddhist (*Vajrayana, Mantrayana*) tradition and is held or formed by a devotee or priest during various rites in which a deity is acknowledged. It is a *mudra* which is associated with the deity *Vajrakula*. It may be accompanied by a *mantra*. The *Vajrakula* (*mudra*) is a combined (Ind.: *saṁyutta*) form, held by both hands. It denotes *Vajrakula*. This *mudra* is formed by: right palm faces upwards, fingers and thumb extended towards midline, left palm faces downwards, fingers and thumb extended towards midline. Thus formed the back of the right hand rests on the back of the left, the right thumb lies under the left little finger and the right little finger lies under the left thumb. (LCS 301) (See: **Figure 639**)

vajra-lasye mudra -- (Ind.: *vajra-lāsye-mudrā*) This is an assigned term.[25] A *mudra*, a ritual hand pose, a seal, which is common to the Buddhist (*Vajrayana*) tradition, a *tantric mudra*. It denotes one of the sixteen inner offerings which follow the presentation of the eight signs of good fortune (Ind.: *aṣṭa-maṅgala*, Tib.: *bkra-shis rtags-brgyad*). These secret offerings are presented to one of the sixteen goddesses of sensual enjoyment, particularly as associated with the worship of the powerful *Vajrayana* goddess, *Tara*. Also, a *mudra* which is common to the Japanese Buddhist (*Vajrayana, Mantrayana*) tradition and is held or formed by a devotee or priest during the rites of *Garbhadhatu Mandala, Vajradhatu Mandala, Homa Rites* and other rites. It may be accompanied by a *mantra*. The *vajra-lasye mudra* is a combined (Ind.: *saṁyutta*) form, held by both hands. This *mudra* is formed in mirror pose: palm faces inwards, fingers and thumb extend upwards (*abhaya mudra*), so posed the hands are brought close together, but do not touch.[26] The *mudra* is held in front of the chest. The *mantra* associated with this mudra is: "*OM AH Vajra-lasye HUM*."[27] (GDe 60. LCS 88, SBe 160) (See: **Figure 640**)

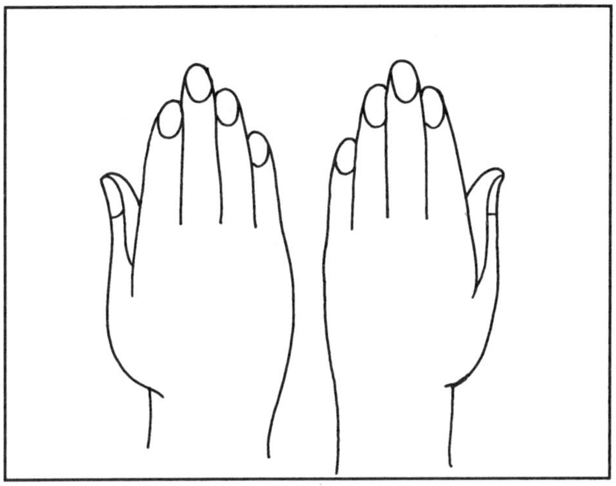

Figure 640 -- vajra-lasye mudra
(as seen by another)

vajra-mala mudra -- (Ind.: *vajra-mālā-mudrā*) ("garland *mudra*") A *mudra*, a ritual hand pose, a seal, a *tantric mudra* which is common to the Japanese Buddhist (*Vajrayana, Mantrayana*) tradition and is held or formed by a devotee or priest during the rites of *Garbhadhatu Mandala, Vajradhatu Mandala, Homa Rites* and other rites. It may be accompanied by a *mantra*. The *vajramala mudra* is a combined (Ind.: *saṁyutta*) form, held by both hands. This *mudra* is formed by: palms facing downwards, fingers and thumbs interlaced and resting on the back of the hands. This *mudra* resembles the *granthitam mudra* in which the palms are separated and parallel to the ground. (GDe 83) (See: **Figure 641**)

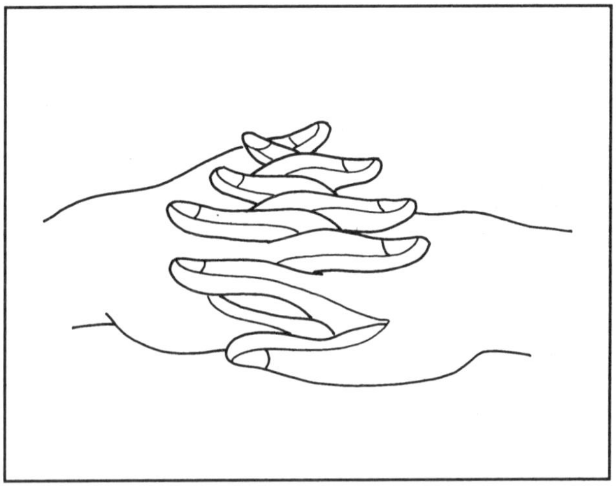

Figure 641 -- vajra-mala mudra
(as seen by the holder)

vajra-manas mudra -- (Ind.: *vajra-manas-mudrā*; Tib: *sems-ma rdo-rje-ma'i phyag-rgya* [*mudra*]) This is an assigned term.[28] A *mudra*, a ritual hand pose, a seal, which is common to the Buddhist (*Vajrayana*) tradition, a *tantric mudra*. It denotes the 'diamond lady of the mind' and is used making the cleansing water powerful;, particularly as associated with the worship of the powerful *Vajrayana* goddess, *Tara*. The *vajra-manas mudra* is

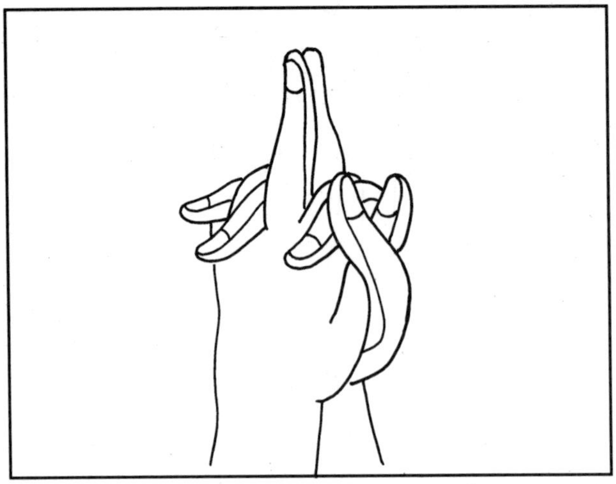

Figure 642 -- vajra-manas mudra
(as seen by the holder)

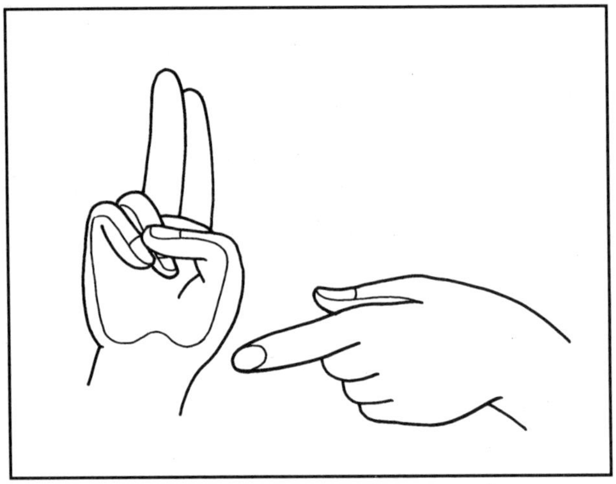

Figure 643 -- vajra-mridamge mudra
(as seen by another)

a combined (Ind.: *saṁyutta*) form, held by both hands. This *mudra* is formed by: palm to palm, thumbs and fingers are interlaced, except the middle fingers which extend upwards, touching along their inner length. Thus formed, the *mudra* is held level with the chest. The *mantra* associated with this *mudra* is: "*OM Amrita HUM PHAT*." (SBe 179) (See: **Figure 642**)

vajra-mridamge mudra -- (Ind.: *vajra-mṛdaṁge-mudrā*) This is an assigned term.[29] A *mudra*, a ritual hand pose, a seal, which is common to the Buddhist (*Vajrayana*) tradition, a *tantric mudra*. It denotes one of the sixteen inner offerings which follow the presentation of the eight signs of good fortune (Ind.: *aṣṭa-maṅgala*, Tib.: *bkra-shis rtags-brgyad*). These secret offerings are presented to one of the sixteen goddesses of sensual enjoyment, particularly as associated with the worship of the powerful *Vajrayana* goddess, *Tara*. The *vajra-mridamge mudra* is a combined (Ind.: *saṁyutta*) form, held by both hands. This *mudra* is formed by: right palm faces outwards, index and middle fingers extend upwards, ring and little fingers fold into the palm, first phalanges of the thumb touches first phalanges of ring finger; left palm faces inwards, index finger extends towards the mid-line, middle, ring and little fingers fold into the palm, the first phalanges of the thumb touches the first phalanges of the middle and ring fingers (*tarjani mudra*), so formed, the left index finger points close to and towards the right palm. The *mudra* is held in front of the chest. The *mantra* associated with this *mudra* is: "*OM AH Vajra-mridamge HUM*."[30] (SBe 160) (See: **Figure 643**)

vajra-muraje mudra -- (Ind.: *vajra-muraje-mudrā*) This is an assigned term.[31] A *mudra*, a ritual hand pose, a seal, which is common to the Buddhist (*Vajrayana*) tradition, a *tantric mudra*. It denotes one of the sixteen inner offerings which follow the presentation of the eight signs of good fortune (Ind.: *aṣṭa-maṅgala*, Tib.: *bkra-shis rtags-brgyad*). These secret offerings are presented to one of the sixteen goddesses of sensual enjoyment, particularly as associated with the worship of the powerful *Vajrayana* goddess, *Tara*. The *vajra-muraje mudra* is a combined (Ind.: *saṁyutta*) form, held by both hands. This mudra is formed in mirror-pose: palm faces outwards, index, middle and little fingers extend downwards, ring finger folds into the palm, first phalanges of the thumb touches first phalanges of the ring finger, so formed the hands are held close to each other, but not touching. The *mudra* is held in front of the chest. The *mantra* associated with this *mudra* is: "*OM AH Vajra-muraje HUM.*"[32] (SBe 160) (See: **Figure 644**)

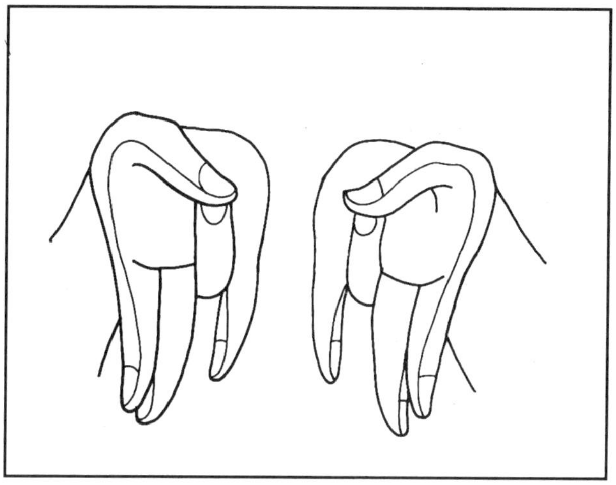

Figure 644 -- vajra-muraje mudra
(as seen by another)

vajra-mushti I -- (Ind.: *vajra-muṣṭi;* Jap.: *kongo ken-in, kenro kongo ken-in*) ("diamond fist") A *mudra,* a ritual hand pose, a seal, a *tantric mudra* which is common to the Japanese Buddhist (*Vajrayana, Mantrayana*) tradition and is held or formed by a devotee or priest during the rites of *Garbhadhatu Mandala, Vajradhatu Mandala, Homa Rites* and other rites. It may be accompanied by a *mantra.* The *vajra-mushti* (*mudra*) is a single (Ind.: *asaṁyutta*) form, held by one hand. It denotes strength and is considered as a "mother" symbol. This *mudra* is generally formed by the right hand: the thumb is folded into the palm, the middle, ring and little fingers fold over an enclose the thumb, the index finger curls and touches the knuckle of the thumb. (EDS 38) (See: **Figure 645**)

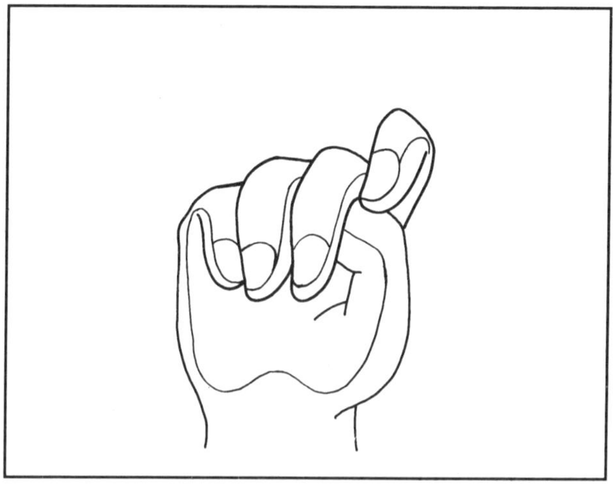

Figure 645 -- vajra-mushti I
(as seen by another)

vajra-mushti II -- (Ind.: *vajra-muṣṭi;* Jap.: *kongo ken-in, kenro kongo ken-in*) ("diamond fist") A variation on the above *mudra.* The *vajra-mushti II* is a single (Ind.: *asaṁyutta*) form, held by one hand. This *mudra* is formed by the right hand: the thumb is folded into the palm, the index, middle, ring and little fingers fold over and enclose the thumb.[33] (GDe 8) (See: **Figure 646**)

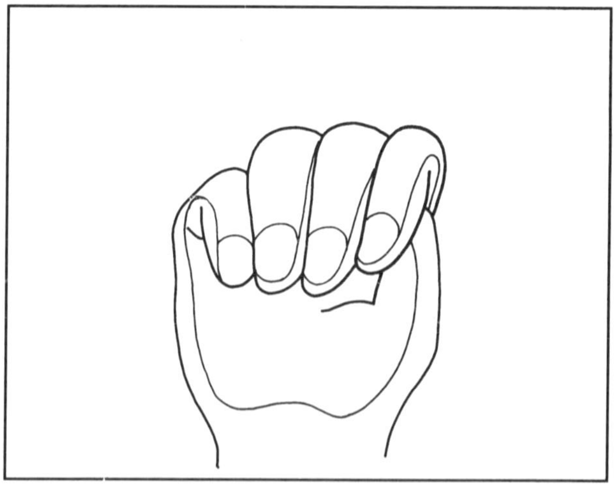

Figure 646 -- vajra-mushti II
(as seen by another)

vajra-mushti III -- (Ind.: *vajra-muṣṭi;* Jap.: *kongo ken-in, kenro kongo ken-in*) ("diamond fist") A variation on the above *mudra.* The *vajra-mushti III* is a single (Ind.: *asaṁyutta*) form, held by one hand. This *mudra* is formed by the right hand: the thumb is folded into the palm, the middle, ring and little fingers fold over an enclose the thumb, the index finger extends. (GDe 45) (See: **Figure 647**)

vajra-mushti (kai mon) mudra -- (Ind.: *vajra-muṣṭi-mudrā;* Jap.: *kongo ken-in*) A *mudra,* a ritual hand pose, a seal, a *tantric mudra* which is common to the Japanese Buddhist (*Vajrayana, Mantrayana*) tradition and is held or formed by a devotee or priest during the rites of *Vajradhatu.* It may be accompanied by a *mantra.* The *vajra-mushti* (*kai mon*[34]) is a combined (Ind.: *saṁyutta*)

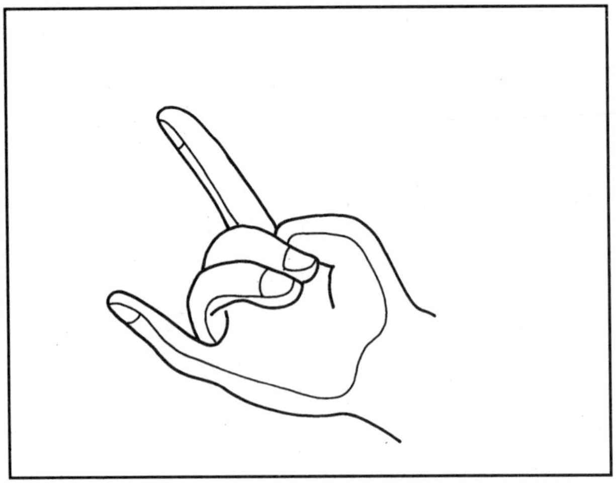

Figure 647 -- vajra-mushti III
(as seen by the holder)

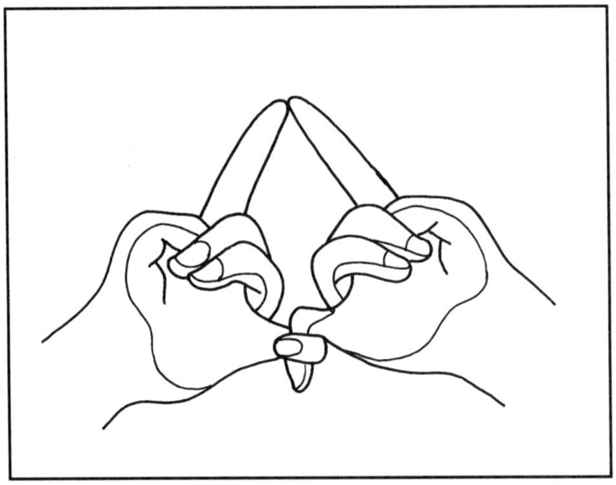

Figure 648 -- vajra-mushti (kai mon) mudra
(as seen by the holder)

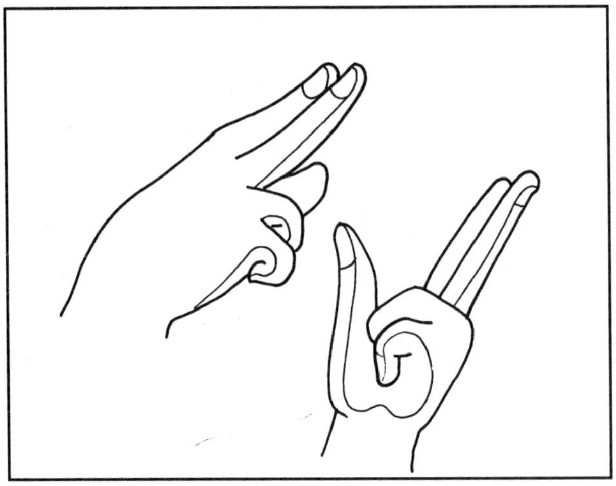

Figure 649 -- vajra-nritye mudra
(as seen by another)

form, held by both hands. It denotes opening the gates. This *mudra* is formed by: palms face inwards, middle and ring fingers fold into the palm, the thumb folds into the palm and is covered by the two fingers, index and little fingers extend. Thus formed the index fingers touch at their tips and the little fingers hook at the first knuckle. (GDe 75, LCS 59) (See: **Figure 648**)

vajra-nritye mudra -- (Ind.: *vajra-nṛtye-mudrā*) This is an assigned term.[35] A *mudra*, a ritual hand pose, a seal, which is common to the Buddhist (*Vajrayana*) tradition, a *tantric mudra*. It denotes one of the sixteen inner offerings which follow the presentation of the eight signs of good fortune (Ind.: *aṣṭa-maṅgala*, Tib.: *bkra-shis rtags-brgyad*). These secret offerings are presented to one of the sixteen goddesses of sensual enjoyment, particularly as associated with the worship of the powerful *Vajrayana* goddess, *Tara*. The *vajra-nritye mudra* is a combined (Ind.: *saṁyutta*) form, held by both hands. This *mudra* is formed by: right palm faces downwards, index and middle fingers extend outwards and slightly upwards, ring and little fingers fold into the palm, the thumb touches the ring and little fingers, the left hand is so formed, except the palm faces upwards, the right hand is over the left hand, close, but not touching. The *mudra* is held in front of the chest. The *mantra* associated with this *mudra* is: "*OM AH Vajra-nritye HUM*."[36] (SBe 160) (See: **Figure 649**)

vajrapataka mudra -- (Ind.: *vajrapatākā-mudrā*) A *mudra*, a ritual hand pose, a seal, which is common to the Hindu tradition. It denotes the *vajra*. The *vajrapataka mudra* is a single (Ind.: *asaṁyutta*) form, held by one hand. This *mudra* is formed by: palm facing forward, index, middle and little fingers extend outwards, ring finger curls towards palm, tip of thumb touches tip of ring finger. Thus formed, the *mudra* is held below the shoulder, but above the waist. (MJS 151) (See: **Figure 650**)

vajra-pushpe mudra -- (Ind.: *vajra-puṣpe-mudrā*) This is an assigned term.[37] A *mudra*, a ritual hand pose, a seal, which is common to the Buddhist (*Vajrayana*) tradition, a *tantric mudra*. It denotes one of the sixteen inner offerings which follow the presentation of the eight signs of good fortune (Ind.: *aṣṭa-maṅgala*, Tib.: *bkra-shis* *rtags-brgyad*). These secret offerings are presented to one of the sixteen goddesses of sensual enjoyment, particularly as associated with the worship of the powerful *Vajrayana* goddess, *Tara*. The *vajra-pushpe mudra* is a combined (Ind.: *saṁyutta*) form, held by both hands. This *mudra* is formed in mirror-pose: palm faces the mid-line and slightly upwards, index finger extends downwards as does the thumb, the middle, ring and little fingers fold into the palm (similar to the *tarjani mudra*), so posed the the tips of the index fingers and thumbs touch, as well as the joints between the second and third phalanges of the middle fingers. The *mudra* is held in front of the chest. The *mantra* associated with this *mudra* is: "*OM AH Vajra-pushpe HUM*."[38] (SBe 161) (See: **Figure 651**)

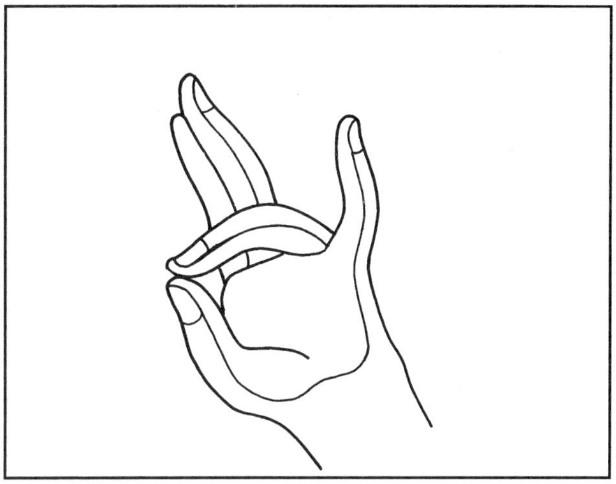

Figure 650 -- vajrapataka mudra
(as seen by another)

vajra-rasye mudra -- (Ind.: *vajra-rāsye-mudrā*) This is an assigned term.[39] A *mudra*, a ritual hand pose, a seal, which is common to the Buddhist (*Vajrayana*) tradition, a *tantric mudra*. It denotes one of the sixteen inner offerings which follow the presentation of the eight signs of good fortune (Ind.: *aṣṭa-maṅgala*, Tib.: *bkra-shis rtags-brgyad*). These secret offerings are presented to one of the sixteen goddesses of sensual enjoyment, particularly as associated with the worship of the powerful *Vajrayana* goddess, *Tara*. The *vajra-rasye mudra* is a combined (Ind.: *saṁyutta*) form, held by both hands. This *mudra* is formed in mirror-pose: palm faces inwards, fingers slightly splayed, extend towards the mid-line, thumb extends upwards, so posed the extended, splayed fingers interlace, left index over right index, etc. The *mudra* is held in front of the chest. The *mantra* associated with this *mudra* is: "*OM AH Vajra-rasye HUM*."[40] (SBe 161) (See: **Figure 652**)

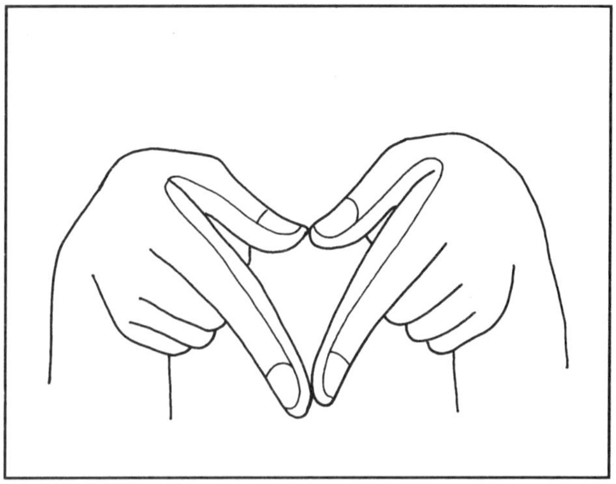

Figure 651 -- vajra-pushpe mudra
(as seen by another)

Vajrasattva mudra -- (Ind.: *Vajrasattva-mudrā*) A *mudra*, a ritual hand pose, a seal, a *tantric mudra* which is common to the Japanese Buddhist (*Vajrayana, Mantrayana*) tradition and is held or formed by a devotee or priest during the rites of *Garbhadhatu Mandala, Vajradhatu Mandala, Homa Rites* and other rites. It may be accompanied by a *mantra*. The *Vajrasattva mudra*[41] is a combined (Ind.: *saṁyutta*) form, held by both hands. It denotes *Vajrasattva bodhisattva*. This *mudra* is formed by: palms facing midline, thumbs extended upward, index fingers interlaced on top of the hands, middle fingers extend straight upward and touch along their

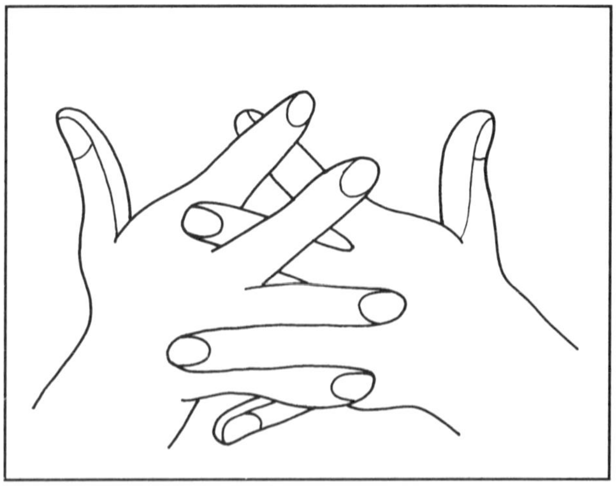

Figure 652 -- vajra-rasye mudra
(as seen by another)

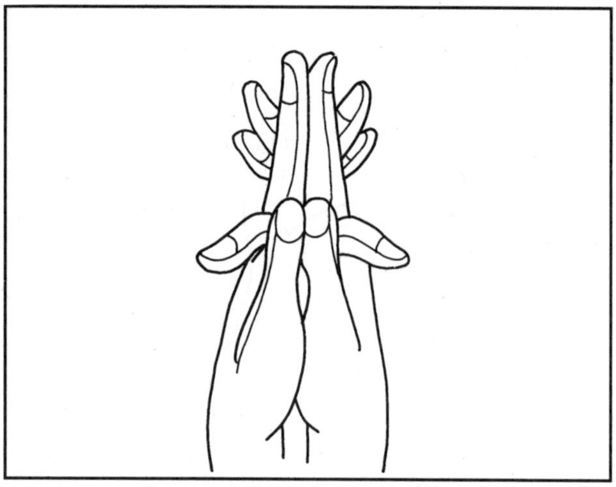

Figure 653 -- Vajrasattva mudra
(as seen by the holder)

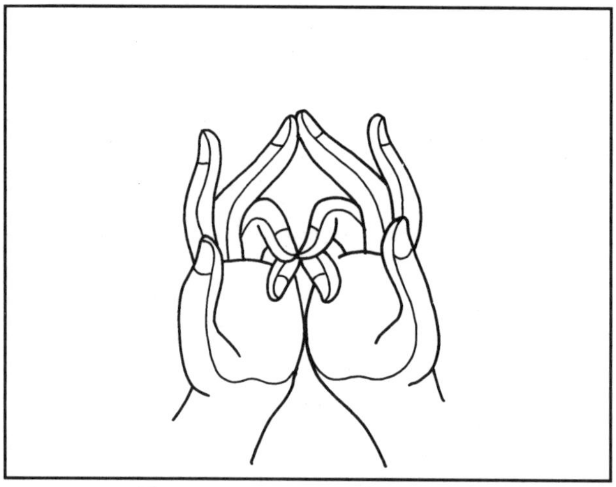

Figure 654 -- vajra-shri mudra
(as seen by the holder)

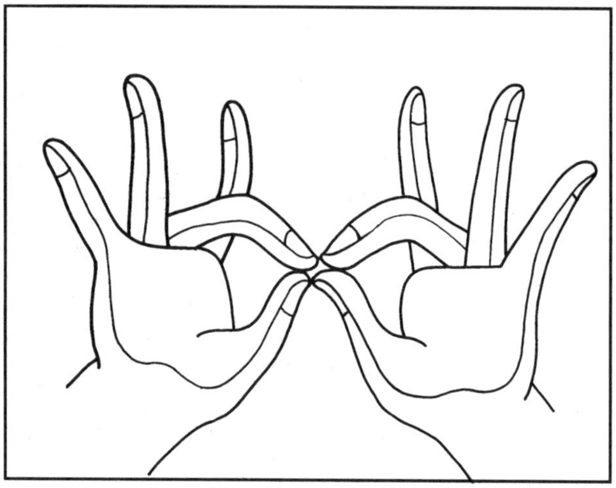

Figure 655 -- vajra-sparshe mudra
(as seen by another)

length, ring and little fingers interlace at their tips. (LCS 111) (See: **Figure 653**)

vajra-shri mudra -- (Ind.: *vajra-śrī-mudrā*) A *mudra*, a ritual hand pose, a seal, a *tantric mudra* which is common to the Japanese Buddhist (*Vajrayana, Mantrayana*) tradition and is held or formed by a devotee or priest during the rites of *Garbhadhatu Mandala* and other rites. It may be accompanied by a *mantra*. The *vajra-shri mudra*[42] is a combined (Ind.: *saṁyutta*) form, held by both hands. This *mudra* is formed by: palms facing midline and close, thumb extends upwards, index fingers extends and curves slightly, middle fingers touch at tip, ring and little fingers fold into palm and touch their counterparts along their second phalanges. (GDe 136, LCS 249) (See: **Figure 654**)

vajra-shrinkhala mudra -- (Ind.: *vajra-śṛṅkhalā-mudrā*; Jap.: *sa-in* [*mudra*]) The Indic term for *sa-in* (*mudra*). See: *sa-in* (*mudra*). (LCS 156)

vajra-sparshe mudra -- (Ind.: *vajra-sparśe-mudrā*) This is an assigned term.[43] A *mudra*, a ritual hand pose, a seal, which is common to the Buddhist (*Vajrayana*) tradition, a *tantric mudra*. It denotes one of the sixteen inner offerings which follow the presentation of the eight signs of good fortune (Ind.: *aṣṭa-maṅgala*, Tib.: *bkra-shis rtags-brgyad*). These secret offerings are presented to one of the sixteen goddesses of sensual enjoyment, particularly as associated with the worship of the powerful *Vajrayana* goddess, *Tara*. The *vajra-sparshe mudra* is a combined (Ind.: *saṁyutta*) form, held by both hands. This *mudra* is formed in mirror-pose: palms face the mid-line, tips of the middle finger touches the tips of the thumb, index, ring and little fingers extend upwards (similar to the *vitarka mudra*). The hands so posed are brought together and the tips of the index fingers and the tips of the thumbs touch. The *mudra* is held in front of the chest. The *mantra* associated with this *mudra* is: "*OM AH Vajra-sparshe HUM*."[44] (SBe 161) (See: **Figure 655**)

vajra-suchi mudra -- (Ind.: *vajra-sūci-mudrā*) A *mudrā*, a ritual hand pose, a seal, a *tantric mudra* which is common to the Japanese Buddhist (*Vajrayana, Mantrayana*) tradition and is held or formed by a devotee or priest during the rites of *Garbhadhatu Mandala* and other rites. It may be accompanied by a *mantra*. The *vajra-suchi mudra* is a combined (Ind.: *saṁyutta*) form, held by both hands. This *mudra* is formed by: palms facing thumbs, middle, right and little fingers interlace inwards (between the palms), index fingers extend upwards and touch at their tips. (LCS 156) (See: **Figure 656**)

vajravali mudra -- (Ind.: *vajrāvalī-mudrā* aka *catur-dig-bandha mudrā*; Jap.: *kongo cho-in* [*mudra*]) A variant term applied to *chatur-dig-bandha mudra*. See: *chatur-dig-bandha mudra*. (GDe 508)

vajra-vamshe mudra -- (Ind.: *vajra-vaṁśe-mudrā*) This is an assigned term.[45] A *mudra*, a ritual hand pose, a seal, which is common to the Buddhist (*Vajrayana*) tradition, a *tantric mudra*. It denotes one of the sixteen inner offerings which follow the presentation of the eight signs of good fortune (Ind.: *aṣṭa-maṅgala*, Tib.: *bkra-shis rtags-brgyad*). These secret offerings are presented to one of the sixteen goddesses of sensual enjoyment, particularly as associated with the worship of the powerful *Vajrayana* goddess, *Tara*. The *vajra-vamshe mudra* is a combined (Ind.: *saṁyutta*) form, held by both hands. This *mudra* is formed by: right palm faces inwards, thumb and fingers extend towards midline, below the left hand's palm faces inwards, thumb and fingers extend towards midline. The *mudra* is held in front of the chest. The *mantra* associated with this *mudra* is: "*OM AH Vajra-vamshe HUM*."[46] (SBe 160) (See: **Figure 657**)

vajra-vine mudra -- (Ind.: *vajra-vīne-mudrā*) This is an assigned term.[47] A *mudra*, a ritual hand pose, a seal, which is common to the Buddhist (*Vajrayana*) tradition, a *tantric mudra*. It denotes one of the sixteen inner offerings which follow the presentation of the eight signs of good fortune (Ind.: *aṣṭa-maṅgala*, Tib.: *bkra-shis rtags-brgyad*). These secret offerings are presented to one of the sixteen goddesses of sensual enjoyment, particularly as associated with the worship of the powerful *Vajrayana* goddess, *Tara*. The *vajra-vine mudra* is a combined (Ind.: *saṁyutta*) form, held by both hands. This *mudra* is formed by: right palm faces downwards, fingers fold into the palm, thumb extends towards midline, the left hand's palm faces upwards, fingers fold into the palm, thumb extends towards the left, so

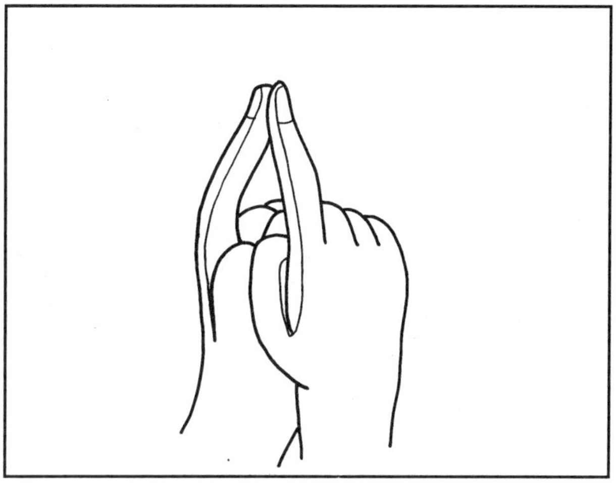

Figure 656 -- vajra-suchi mudra
(as seen by the holder)

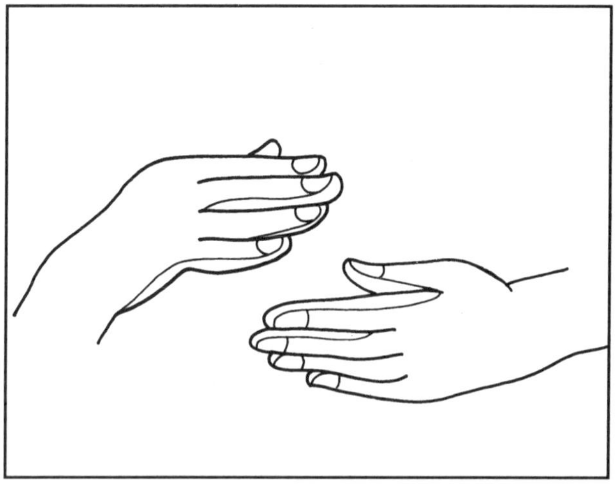

Figure 657 -- vajra-vamshe mudra
(as seen by another)

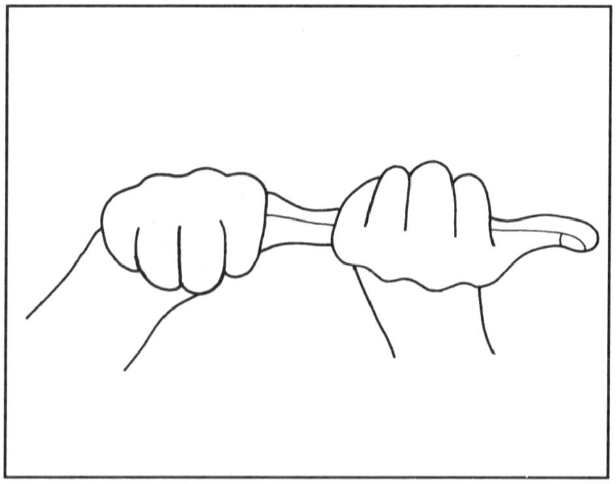

Figure 658 -- vajra-vine mudra
(as seen by another)

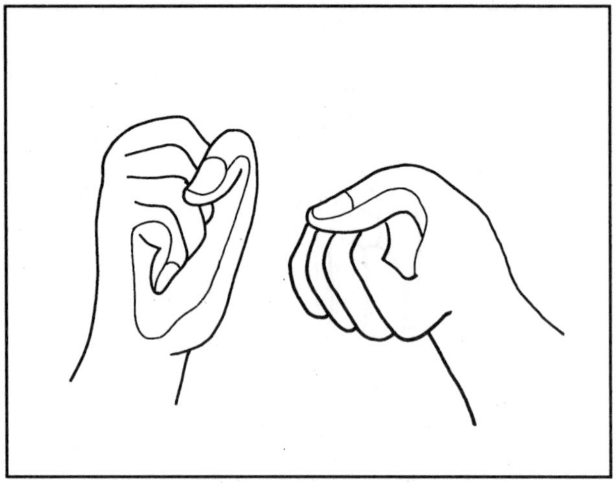

Figure 659 -- Vamanavatara mudra
(as seen by another)

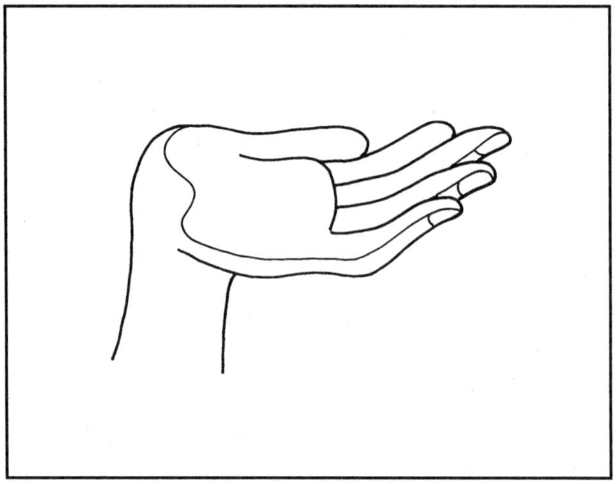

Figure 660 -- vandana mudra I
(as seen by another)

formed the first phalanges of the right thumb in inserted into the fisted fingers of the left hand. The *mudra* is held in front of the chest. The *mantra* associated with this *mudra* is: "*OM AH Vajra-vine HUM*."[48] (SBe 160) (See: **Figure 658**)

vakula mudra -- (Ind.: *vakula-mudrā*) A hand pose, a seal, a dramatic (Ind.: *nāṭya*) *mudra* or gesture (Ind.: *darpaṇa*) held or formed by a performer, dancer or actor. It denotes the *vakula* tree. The *mudra* employed is identical in form to the *samdamsa mudra*. See: *samdamsa mudra*. (ACG 48)

Vamanavatara mudra -- (Ind.: *Vāmanāvatāra-mudrā*) A hand pose, a seal, a dramatic (Ind.: *nāṭya*) *mudra* or gesture (Ind.: *darpaṇa*) held or formed by a performer, dancer or actor. The *Vamanavatara mudra* is a combined (Ind.: *saṁyutta*) form, held by both hands. It denotes the dwarf *avatar*, one of the ten *avatars* (Ind.: *daśāvatāras*) of the Lord *Vishnu* This *mudra* is formed by: right palm faces the midline, the fingers are fisted, the thumb lies over the first phalanges of the fingers, fingers face downwards; left palm faces the midline, the fingers are fisted, the thumb lies over the first phalanges of the fingers, fingers face upwards. Thus formed the hands are held towards the right side. (ACG 46) (See: **Figure 659**)

vanara mudra -- (Ind.: *vānara-mudrā*) A hand pose, a seal, a dramatic (Ind.: *nāṭya*) *mudra* or gesture (Ind.: *darpaṇa*) held or formed by a performer, dancer or actor. It denotes an animal, in this case a monkey. The *vanara mudra*[49] is a combined (Ind.: *saṁyutta*) form, held by both hands. This *mudra* is identical in form to the *adho-mushti-mukula mudra*. *See: adho-mushti-mukula mudra*. (ACG 49)

vandana mudra I -- (Ind.: *vandanā-mudrā*) A *mudra*, a ritual hand pose, a seal, which is common to both the Buddhist and Hindu traditions. It denotes the containment of precious object or thought. The *vandana mudra I* is a single (Ind.: *asaṁyutta*) form, held by one hand. This *mudra* is formed by: palm faces upwards, fingers and thumb extended and slightly cupped, facing away from the mid-line. The form of the *mudra* is such that it could hold an object. (PBa) (See: **Figure 660**)

vandana mudra II -- (Ind.: *vandanā-mudrā* aka *vandanī-mudrā*) A *mudra*, a ritual hand pose, a seal, which is common to the Hindu tradition. It denotes the greeting or salutation. The *vandana mudra II* is a single (Ind.: *asaṁyutta*) form, held by one hand. This *mudra* is formed by the right hand: hand held chest high, palm facing midline, fingers and thumb extended upwards in a relaxed manner.[50] (MJS 153) (See: **Figure 661**)

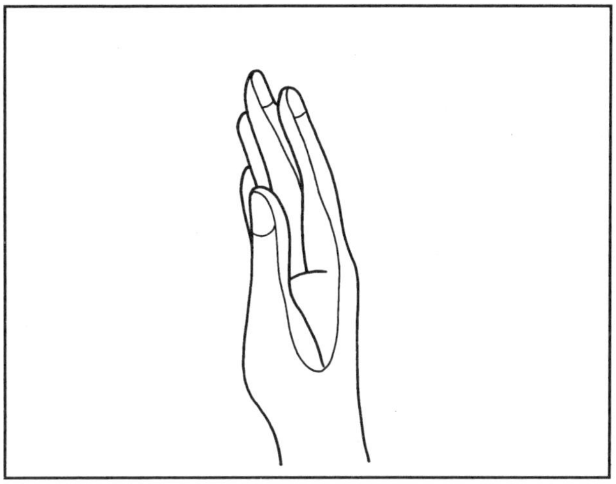

Figure 661 -- vandana mudra II
(as seen by the holder)

vandani mudra -- (Ind.: *vandanī-mudrā* aka *vandanā-mudrā*) A variant (spelling) of *vandana-mudra*. See: *vandana-mudra*. (MJS 153)

vara mudra -- (Ind.: *vara-mudrā* aka *dāna mudrā, prasāda mudrā, varada mudrā*; Chin.: *shih-yṃan-yin*; Jap.: *segan-in*) A variant (spelling) of *varada mudra*. See: *varada mudra*. (RSG 4)

varada mudra -- (Ind.: *varada-mudrā* aka *dāna mudrā, prasāda mudrā, vara mudrā*; Chin.: *shih-yṃan-yin*; Jap.: *segan-in*) A *mudra*, a ritual hand pose, a seal, which is common to both the Buddhist and Hindu traditions. It denotes the granting of a boon or the fulfillment of a vow. It is one of the more frequently encountered *mudras* and often seen in the hands of fierce deities where the sign is offered to the believers. The *varada mudra* is a single (Ind.: *asaṁyutta*) form, held by one hand. This *mudra* is formed in one hand, frequently the left hand: palm facing forward, fingers and thumb extended and pointing downwards.[51] Along with the *abhaya mudra*, the *varada mudra* is the most popular. (AKG 22, BCO 218, BBH 198, ERJ 6, ERJ II 22, HKS 271, RSG 4, TGR 14) (See: **Figure 662**)

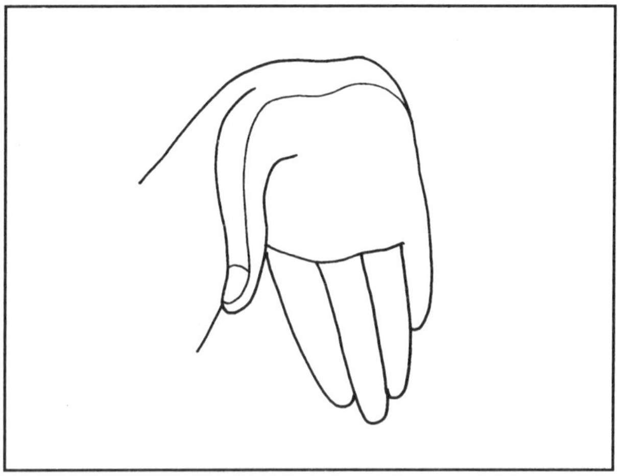

Figure 662 -- varada mudra
(as seen by another)

varada-dhyana mudra I -- (Ind.: *varada-dhyāna-mudrā*; Eng.: eating the rice gruel *mudra*; Thai: **pang ODD #6**) This is a descriptive term.[52] See: **pang ODD #6**. (DRN 37, JBo 205, ODD 680, PSS)

varada-dhyana mudra II -- (Ind.: *varada-dhyāna-mudrā*; Eng.: partaking of food *mudra*; Thai: **pang ODD #23**) This is a descriptive term.[53] See: **pang ODD #23**. (DRN 36, JBo 205, ODD 680, PSS)

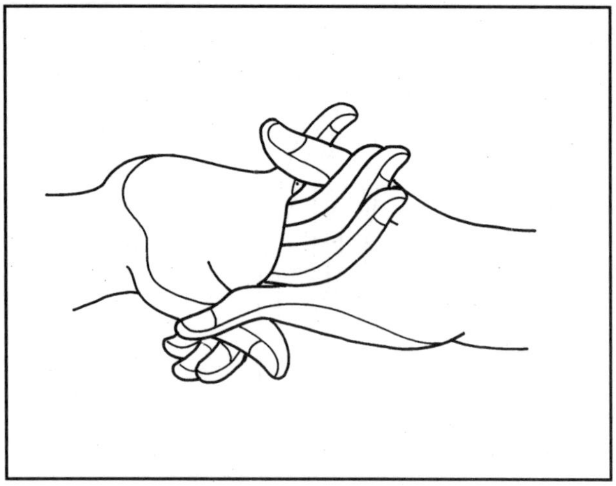

Figure 663 -- varaha mudra I
(as seen by another)

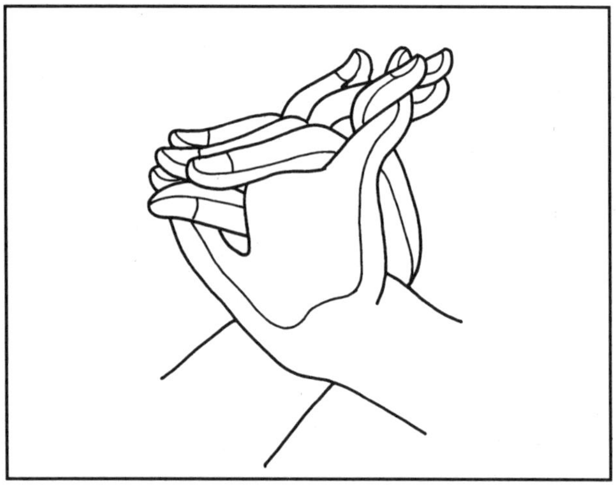

Figure 664 -- varaha mudra II
(as seen by another)

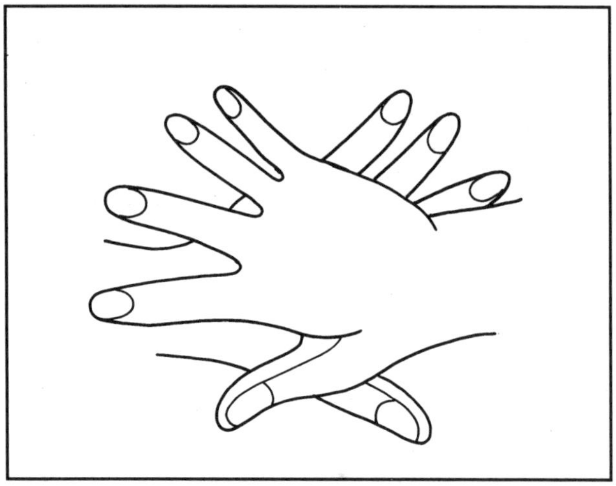

Figure 665 -- varaha mudra III
(as seen by the holder)

varaha mudra I -- (Ind.: *varāha-mudrā*) A hand pose, a seal, a dramatic (Ind.: *nāṭya*) *mudra* or gesture (Ind.: *darpaṇa*) held or formed by a performer, dancer or actor. The *varaha mudra* is a combined (Ind.: *saṁyutta*) form, held by both hands. It denotes a boar and is related to the *Varahavatara* of the Lord *Vishnu*. This *mudra* is formed by: index, middle and ring fingers curl at their first and second joints (towards the palm), the thumb is extended outward, and the little fingers extend upwards. Thus formed, the left palm faces downwards, the right faces upwards the right thumb "hooks" with the left little finger and the right little finger "hooks" with the left thumb.[54] (ACG 41) (See: **Figure 663**)

varaha mudra II -- (Ind.: *varāha-mudrā*) A hand pose, a seal, a dramatic (Ind.: *nāṭya*) *mudra* or gesture (Ind.: *darpaṇa*) held or formed by a performer, dancer or actor. This *mudra*, a variation on the above. The *varaha mudra II* is a combined (Ind.: *saṁyutta*) form, held by both hands. This *mudra* is formed by: the left palm faces right and the right palm faces left, index, middle and ring fingers curl at their first and second joints (towards the palm), thumbs are extended outward, and the little fingers extend upwards. Thus formed, the right hand is brought around the left so that the two hands are back-to-back, the thumbs and little fingers "hook" with their counterparts.[55] (ACG 41) (See: **Figure 664**)

varaha mudra III -- (Ind.: *varāha-mudrā*) A hand pose, a seal, a dramatic (Ind.: *nāṭya*) *mudra* or gesture (Ind.: *darpaṇa*) held or formed by a performer, dancer or actor. It denotes an animal, in this case a boar. The *varaha mudra*[56] is a combined (Ind.: *saṁyutta*) form, held by both hands. This *mudra* is formed by: right palm facing downwards, fingers slightly separated, extended outwards, thumb at right angle to the fingers, the fingers and thumb move slightly (as bristles); left palm facing downwards, fingers together and extended outwards, thumb at right angle to the fingers. Thus formed the right hand is placed over the left hand and touching it, and held waist high. (ACG 49) (See: **Figure 665**)

varahakam mudra -- (Ind.: *varāhakam-mudrā* aka *varahkam mudrā*) A variant (spelling) of *varahkam mudra*. See: *varahkam mudra*. (RLM 74)

varahkam mudra I -- (Ind.: *varāhkam-mudrā*) ("the boar") A *mudra*, a ritual hand pose, a seal, a *mudra* which is common to yogic tradition, particularly the *Yoga Tatva Mudra Vigyan* form, and is held by a devotee or practitioner. The *varahkam mudra*[57] is a combined (Ind.: *saṁyutta*) form, held by both hands. It is one of the twenty-four *mudras* held before the *Gayatri Jap* of the thirty-two total *Gayatri mudras*.[58] It is utilized for all sickness, especially cancer. The *varahkam mudra I* is a combined (Ind.: *saṁyutta*) form, held by both hands. This *mudra* is formed by: right palm facing midline, fingers downward and curled towards the palm, thumb extends upwards; left palm faces midline, fingers outwards and curled towards the palm, thumb extends towards the midline. Thus formed the curled fingers of the left hand enclose the the curled fingers of the right hand and the thumbs touch at their tips. It is one of the four *Gayatri mudras* which make reference to the Lord *Vishnu's* first five (animal) *avatars*. (KDe 86, RLM 74) (See: **Figure 666**)

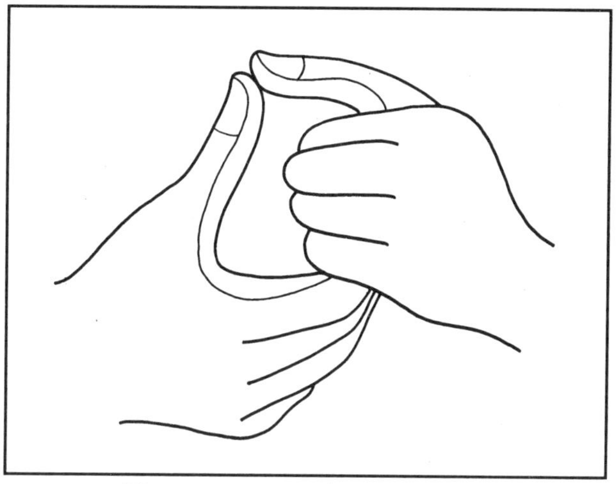

Figure 666 -- varahkam mudra I
(as seen by another)

varahkam mudra II -- (Ind.: *varāhkam-mudrā* aka *varāhakam mudrā*) A *mudra*, a ritual hand pose, a seal, a mudra which is common to yogic tradition, particularly the *Yoga Tatva Mudra Vigyan* form, and is held by a devotee or practitioner. The *varahkam mudra II* is a combined (Ind.: *saṁyutta*) form, held by both hands. It is one of the twenty-four mudras held before the *Gayatri Jap* of the thirty-two total *Gayatri mudras*.[59] It is utilized for all sickness, especially cancer. The *varahkam mudra II* is a combined (Ind.: *saṁyutta*) form, held by both hands. This *mudra* is formed by: right palm faces midline, fingers outwards and curled towards the palm, thumb extends towards the midline; left palm facing midline, fingers downward and curled towards the palm, thumb extends upwards. Thus formed the curled fingers of the right hand enclose the the curled fingers of the left hand and the thumbs touch at their tips. It is one of the four *Gayatri mudras* which make reference to the Lord *Vishnu's* first five (animal) *avatars*. (KDe 108) (See: **Figure 667**)

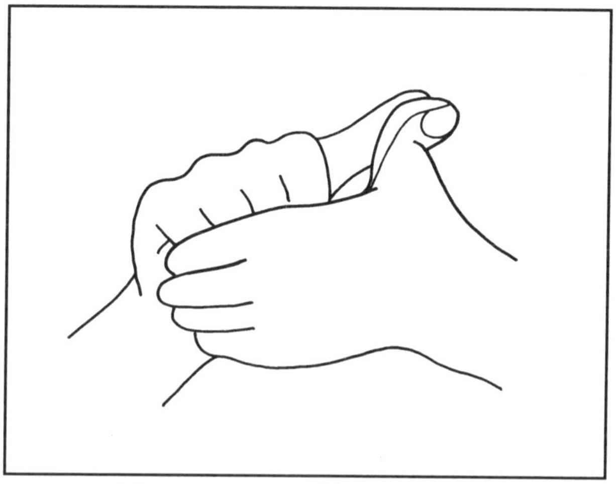

Figure 667 -- varahkam mudra II
(as seen by another)

Vara-kaya-samaya-mudra -- (Ind.: *Vara-kāya-samaya-mudrā*) A *mudra*, a ritual hand pose, a seal, a *tantric mudra* which is common to the Japanese Buddhist (*Vajrayana, Mantrayana*) tradition and is held or formed

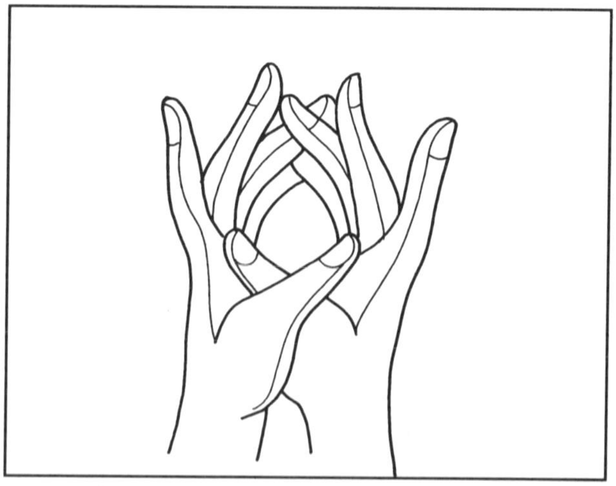

Figure 668 -- Vara-kaya-samaya-mudra
(as seen by the holder)

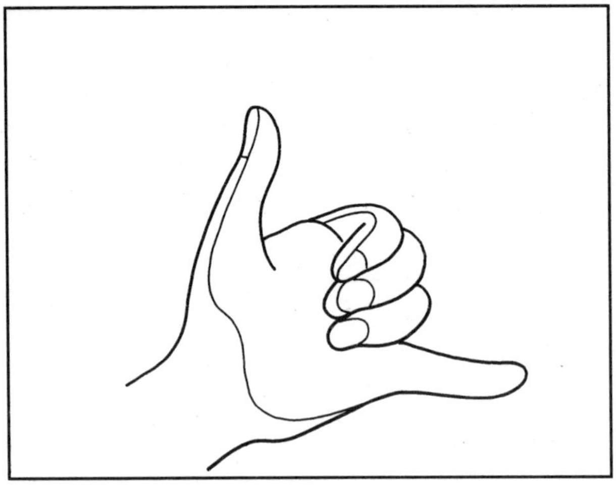

Figure 669 -- vardhamanaka mudra
(as seen by the holder)

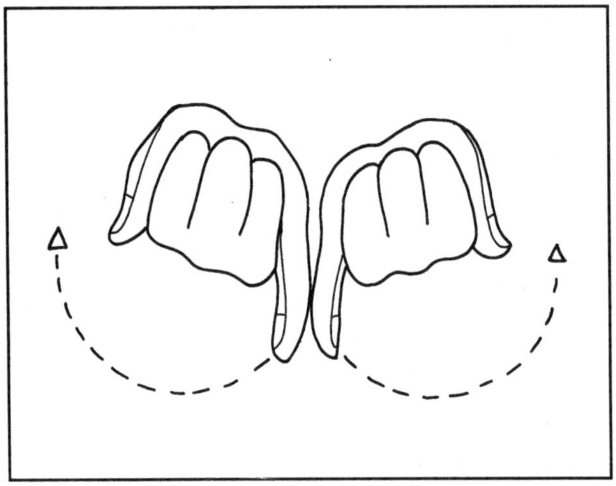

Figure 670 -- vardhamana mudra
(as seen by another)

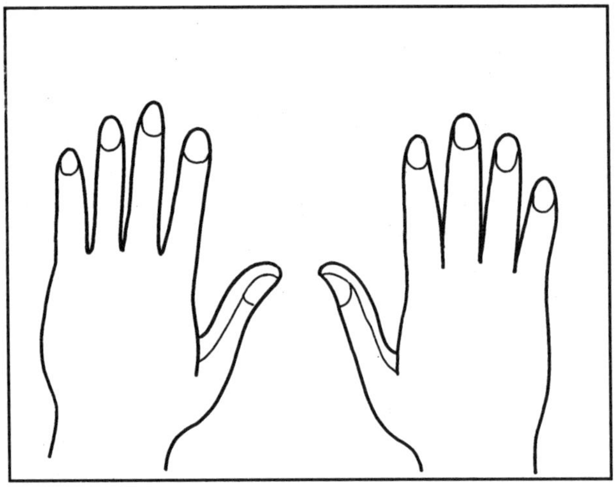

Figure 671 -- varsha mudra
(as seen by the holder)

by a devotee or priest during various rites. It may be accompanied by a *mantra*. The *Vara-kaya-samaya-mudra* is a combined (Ind.: *saṁyutta*) form, held by both hands. This *mudra* is formed by: palms facing midline, thumbs crossed, tight over left, index fingers extend upward and curve slightly, middle fingers touch at their tips, ring and little fingers interlace at their tips. (GDe 143, LCS 218) (See: **Figure 668**)

vardhamana mudra -- (Ind.: *vardhamāna-mudrā*) A hand pose, a seal, a dramatic (Ind.: *nāṭya*) *mudra* or gesture (Ind.: *darpaṇa*) held or formed by a performer, dancer or actor noted in ACG but without description. (ACG 44)

vardhamanaka mudra -- (Ind.: *vardhamānaka-mudrā*) A hand pose, a seal, a dramatic (Ind.: *nāṭya*) *mudra* or gesture (Ind.: *darpaṇa*) held or formed by a performer, dancer or actor. The *vardhamanaka mudra* is a single (Ind.: *asaṁyutta*) form, held by one hand. This *mudra* is formed by: palm (left) facing the mid-line, the thumb extends upwards, the index, middle and ring fingers are curled into the palm the little finger is slightly curled and separated slightly.[60] (KVa 136 [33]) (See: **Figure 669**)

vardhamana mudra -- (Ind.: *vardhamāna-mudrā*) A hand pose, a seal, a dramatic (Ind.: *nāṭya*) *mudra* or gesture (Ind.: *darpaṇa*) held or formed by a performer, dancer or actor. The *vardhamana mudra* is a combined (Ind.: *saṁyutta*) form, held by both hands. It denotes *Narasimha*, his glory, and the defeating of the *rakshasa*. This *mudra* requires movement and is first formed by: palms face downwards, the index, middle and ring fingers curl towards the palms, the thumbs rests along the curled index fingers, the little fingers are extending straight. The two hands are close, then rotate until the palms face upwards. (ACG 43) (See: **Figure 670**)

varsha mudra -- (Ind.: *varṣā-mudrā*) ("*mudra* of rains") A *mudra*, a ritual hand pose, a seal, a *tantric mudra* which is common to the Japanese Buddhist (*Vajrayana, Mantrayana*) tradition and is held or formed by a devotee or priest during various rites. It may be accompanied by a *mantra*. The *varsha mudra*[61] is a combined (Ind.: *saṁyutta*) form, held by both hands. In this form the hands are raised, fingers and thumbs extended upwards and together, relaxed, slightly cupped, palm facing outward. Thus formed, the hands are held close, in front of the chest. (GDe 446) (See: **Figure 671**)

Varuna mudra -- (Ind.: *Varuṇa-mudrā*) A hand pose, a seal, a dramatic (Ind.: *nāṭya*) *mudra* or gesture (Ind.: *darpaṇa*) held or formed by a performer, dancer or actor which denotes a specific deity. The *Varuna mudra* is a combined (Ind.: *saṁyutta*) form, held by both hands. It denotes *Varuna*. This *mudra* is formed by: right palm faces outward, fingers and thumb extended, together and pointing upwards, relaxed, slightly cupped; left palm faces mid-line, fingers brought into the palm forming a fist, thumb extends upwards. Thus formed the hands are held at shoulder level. (ACG 46) (See: **Figure 672**)

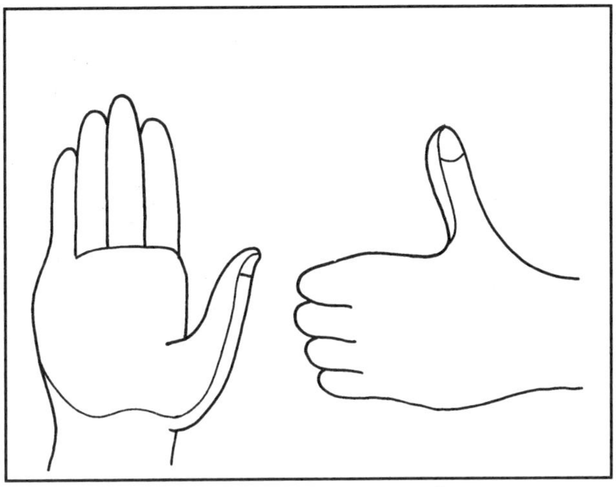

Figure 672 -- Varuna mudra
(as seen by another)

varun(a) mudra -- (Ind.: *varuṇ[a]-mudrā*) A *mudra*, a ritual hand pose, a seal, a mudra which is common to yogic tradition, particularly the *Yoga Tatva Mudra Vigyan* form, and is held by a devotee or practitioner. The *varun(a) mudra* is a single (Ind.: *asaṁyutta*) form, held by one hand. It is utilized for bodily waters and blood. This *mudra* is formed by: palm forwards, index, middle and ring fingers extend straight upwards, little finger curls towards the palm and touches the tip of the thumb which is folded towards it. (KDe 47) (See: **Figure 673**)

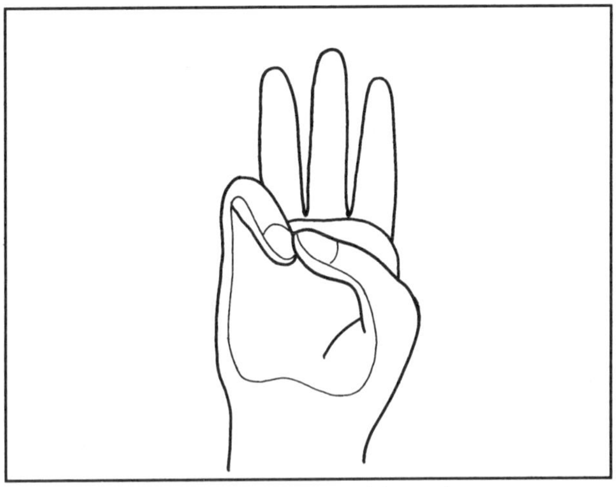

Figure 673 -- varun(a) mudra
(as seen by another)

vasanta mudra -- (Ind.: *vasanta-mudrā*) ("spring *mudra*") A *mudra*, a ritual hand pose, a seal, a *tantric mudra* which is common to the Japanese Buddhist (*Vajrayana, Mantrayana*) tradition and is held or formed by a devotee or priest during various rites. It may be accompanied by a *mantra*. The *vasanta mudra* is a combined (Ind.: *saṁyutta*) form, held by both hands. It denotes spring. This *mudra* is formed by: palms face inwards, fingers thumbs and fingers extend upwards. Thus formed the hands are close, each are slightly rotated inwards and held chest level. (GDe 445) (See: **Figure 674**)

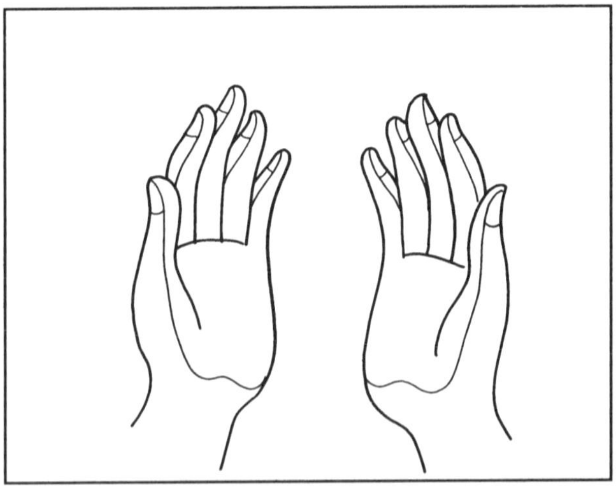

Figure 674 -- vasanta mudra
(as seen by the holder)

vata mudra -- (Ind.: *vaṭa-mudrā*) A hand pose, a seal, a dramatic (Ind.: *nāṭya*) *mudra* or gesture (Ind.: *darpaṇa*) held or formed by a performer, dancer or actor. It denotes the *vata* or banyan tree. The *mudra* employed is

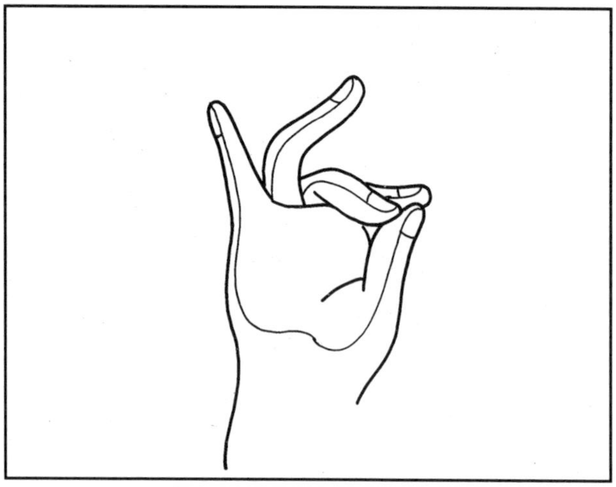

Figure 675 -- vayan mudra
(as seen by another)

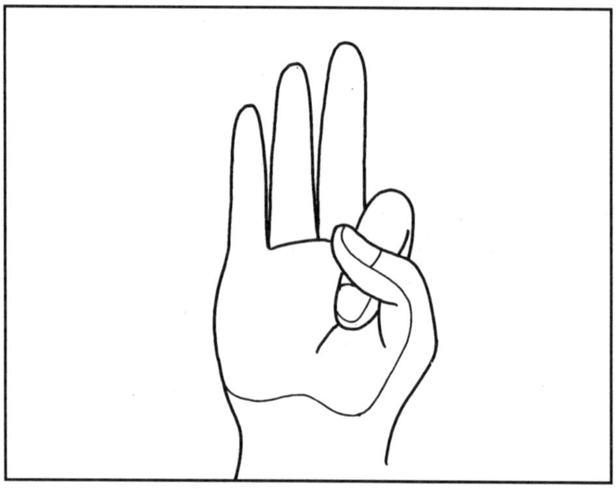

Figure 676 -- vayu mudra I
(as seen by another)

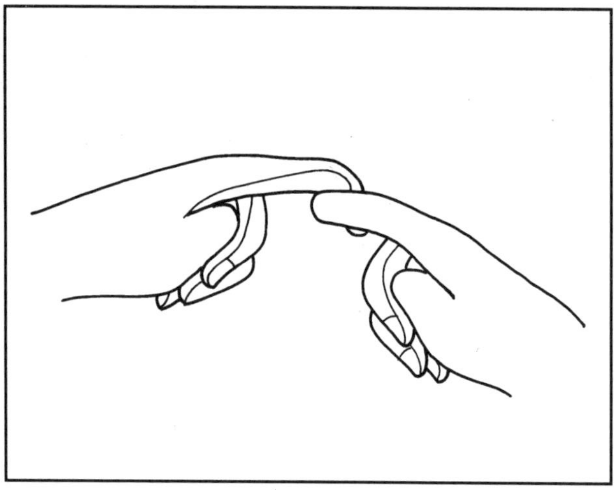

Figure 677 -- vayu mudra II
(as seen by the holder)

identical in form to the *pataka mudra*. See: *pataka mudra*. (ACG 48)

vayan mudra -- (Ind.: *vayan-mudrā*) A *mudra*, a ritual hand pose, a seal, a *mudra* which is common to yogic tradition, particularly the *Yoga Tatva Mudra Vigyan* form, and is held by a devotee or practitioner. The *vayan mudra* is a combined (Ind.: *saṁyutta*) form, held by both hands. It is utilized for problems with the blood. This *mudra* is formed by: palm forward, index and middle fingers together and curled towards the palm, the tip of the thumb touches the tips of these two fingers, the ring and little fingers are separated, upward and slightly curled. It is similar to the *mrigashirsha mudra*. (KDe 100) (See: **Figure 675**)

vayu mudra I -- (Ind.: *vāyu-mudrā*) A *mudra*, a ritual hand pose, a seal, a *mudra* which is common to yogic tradition, particularly the *Yoga Tatva Mudra Vigyan* form, and is held by a devotee or practitioner. The *vayu mudra* is a single (Ind.: *asaṁyutta*) form, held by one hand. It is utilized for Parkinson's disease, gout and polio. This *mudra* is formed by: palm forward, folding the index finger into the palm and curling the thumb over the first knuckle of the finger, the middle, ring and little fingers are straight up. (KDe 37) (See: **Figure 676**)

vayu mudra II -- (Ind.: *vāyu-mudrā*) ("the wind *mudra*") A *mudra*, a ritual hand pose, a seal, a *tantric mudra* which is common to the Japanese Buddhist (*Vajrayana, Mantrayana*) tradition and is held or formed by a devotee or priest during the rites of *Garbhadhatu Mandala, Vajradhatu Mandala*, and other rites. It may be accompanied by a *mantra*. The *vayu mudra*[62] *II* is a combined (Ind.: *saṁyutta*) form, held by both hands. It denotes the wind which blows away all impediments. This *mudra* is formed by: the thumbs folded into the palms of their respective hands, the middle, ring and little fingers folded over the thumbs into the palms, the index fingers are extended and "hooked"--i.e., flexed at the first two joints, the palm of the left hand faces inwards as does the right, except the latter is slightly rotated downwards. Thus formed the index finger of the right hand "hooks" the index finger of the left. (GDe 4, LCS 241) (See: **Figure 677**)

Vayu mudra III -- (Ind.: *Vāyu-mudrā*) A hand pose, a seal, a dramatic (Ind.: *nāṭya*) *mudra* or gesture (Ind.: *darpaṇa*) held or formed by a performer, dancer or actor which denotes a specific deity. The *Vayu mudra*[63] *III* is a combined (Ind.: *saṁyutta*) form, held by both hands. It denotes the deity *Vayu*. This *mudra* is formed by: right palm faces outwards, thumb, middle, ring and little fingers extend upwards and together, index finger curls towards the palm; left palm faces outward, index, middle fingers and thumb extend together and pointing upwards, ring and little fingers bent towards the palm. Thus formed the hands are held at shoulder level. (ACG 46) (See: **Figure 678**)

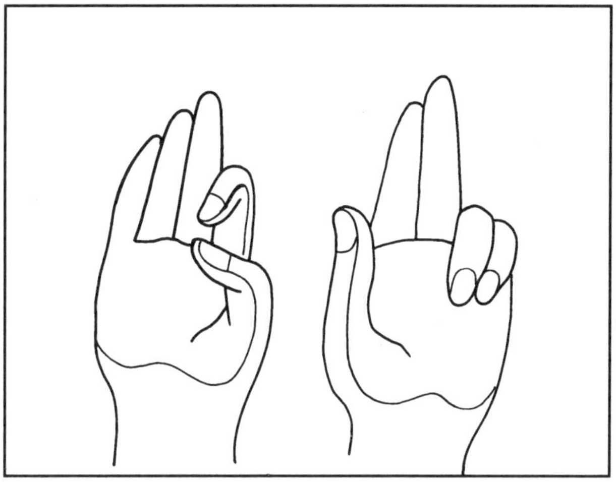

Figure 678 -- Vayu mudra III
(as seen by another)

veragya mudra -- (Ind.: *verāgya-mudrā* aka *vairāgyam mudrā*) A *mudra*, a ritual hand pose, a seal, a *mudra* which is common to yogic tradition, particularly the *Yoga Tatva Mudra Vigyan* form, and is held by a devotee or practitioner. The *veragya mudra* is a combined (Ind.: *saṁyutta*) form, held by both hands. It is utilized for depression and indecision. It is also one of the eight *mudras* held after the *Gayatri Jap* of the thirty-two total *Gayatri mudras*.[64] This *mudra* is formed in both hands by: the tips of the thumb and index finger touch, middle, ring and little fingers are relaxed, slightly separated and point upwards (outwards). Thus formed both hands rest, palm facing upwards on the corresponding knees. (KDe 27 & 108) (See: **Figure 679**)

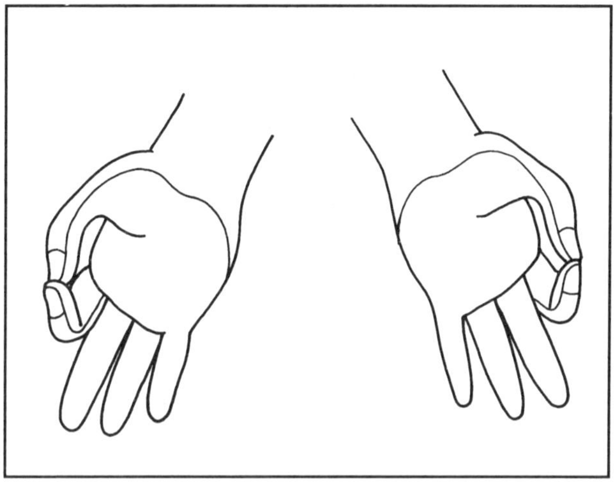

Figure 679 -- veragya mudra
(as seen by another)

Vetravati mudra -- (Ind.: *vetrāvatī-mudrā*) A hand pose, a seal, a dramatic (Ind.: *nāṭya*) *mudra* or gesture (Ind.: *darpaṇa*) held or formed by a performer, dancer or actor. It denotes the *Vetravati*, one of the famous rivers of India. The *mudra* employed is identical in form to the *suchi mudra*. See: *suchi mudra*. (ACG 48)

vhalo mudra -- (Ind.: *vhalo-mudrā*) A hand pose, a seal, a dramatic (Ind.: *nāṭya*) *mudra* or gesture (Ind.: *darpaṇa*) held or formed by a performer, dancer or actor. It denotes an animal, in this case a bear. The *vhalo mudra*[65] is a combined (Ind.: *saṁyutta*) form, held by both hands. This *mudra* is formed by: right palm facing outward, fingers and thumb extended, together and pointing upwards, relaxed, slightly cupped; left palm faces downwards, fingers and thumb are separated and gently curl inwards, towards the hollowed palm. Thus formed the heel of the right hand rests on the back of

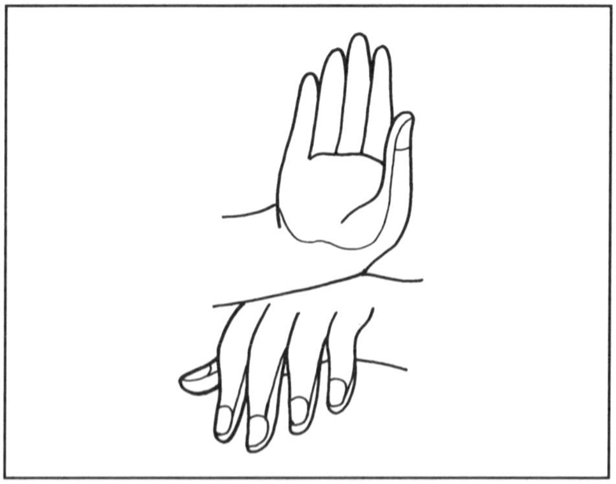

Figure 680 -- vhalo mudra
(as seen by another)

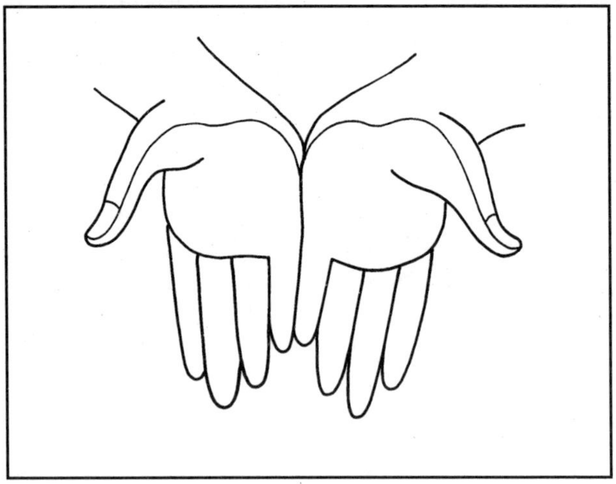

Figure 681 -- viapkanjali mudra
(as seen by another)

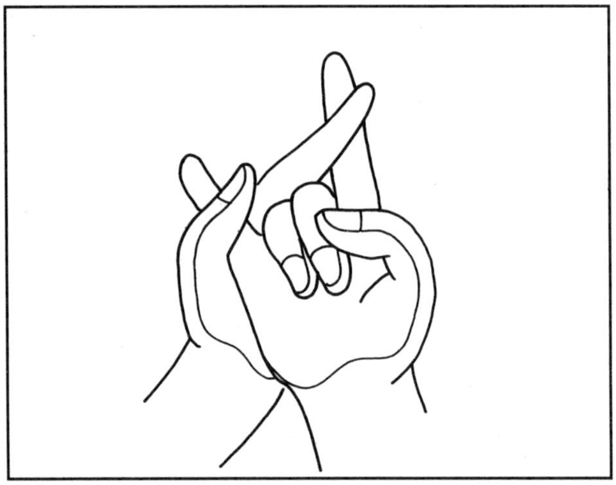

Figure 682 -- vidya mudra
(as seen by the holder)

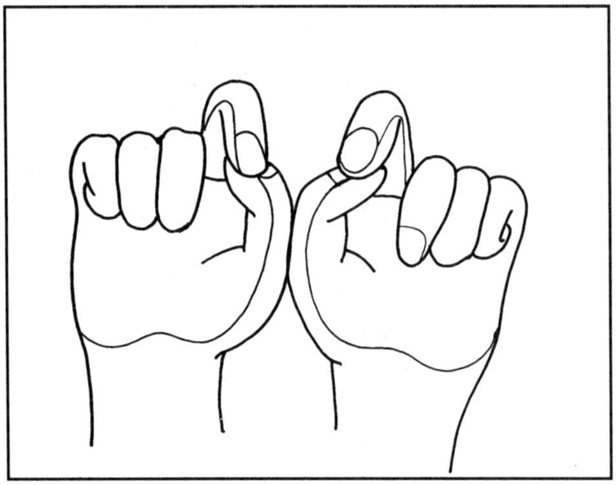

Figure 683 -- Vijneshvara mudra
(as seen by another)

the left (ACG 49) (See: **Figure 680**)

viapkanjali mudra -- (Ind.: *viāpkāñjali-mudrā* aka *vyāpkāñjali mudrā*) A *mudra*, a ritual hand pose, a seal, a *mudra* which is common to yogic tradition, particularly the *Yoga Tatva Mudra Vigyan* form, and is held by a devotee or practitioner. The *viapkanjali mudra* is a combined (Ind.: *saṁyutta*) form, held by both hands. It is one of the twenty-four *mudras* held before the *Gayatri Jap* of the thirty-two total *Gayatri mudras*.[66] It is utilized for all sickness, especially cancer. This *mudra* is formed by: palms facing upwards, fingers extend outward, thumbs extend outwards and are slightly separated from the palm. Thus formed the hands are brought together, touching along the outer edge of the palms and little fingers, and held level with the waist. (KDe 83, RLM 72) (See: **Figure 681**)

vidya mudra -- (Ind.: *vidyā-mudrā*) A *mudra*, a ritual hand pose, a seal, a *tantric mudra* which is common to the Japanese Buddhist (*Vajrayana, Mantrayana*) tradition and is held or formed by a devotee or priest during the rites of *Vajradhatu Mandala*, and other rites. It may be accompanied by a *mantra*. The *vidya mudra*[67] is a combined (Ind.: *saṁyutta*) form, held by both hands. This *mudra* is formed by: right palm faces midline, index and little fingers extend upwards, middle and ring fingers fold into the palm, thumb folds into the palm its tip touching the first knuckle of the middle finger; left thumb grasps right extended little finger, index finger is extended and rests against the inner surface of the extended right index, middle, ring and little fingers fold into the palm(?). (LCS 91) (See: **Figure 682**)

Vijneshvara mudra -- (Ind.: *Vijñeśvara-mudrā*) A hand pose, a seal, a dramatic (Ind.: *nāṭya*) *mudra* or gesture (Ind.: *darpaṇa*) held or formed by a performer, dancer or actor which denotes a specific deity. The *Vijneshvara mudra* is a combined (Ind.: *saṁyutta*) form, held by both hands. It denotes the deity *Vijneshvara*. This *mudra* is formed by: right palm faces outward, the middle, ring and little fingers fold into the palm, the thumb lies over the first phalanges of the middle finger, the index finger curls over the top of the thumb; left palm faces outward, the middle, ring and little fingers fold into the palm, the thumb lies over the first phalanges of the middle finger, the index finger curls over the top of the thumb. Thus formed the hands are held at shoulder level. (ACG 45) (See: **Figure 683**)

vikasitapadma mudra -- (Ind.: *vikasitapadma-mudrā;* Tib.: *ut-pal kha-bye-ba'i phyag-rgya*) This is an assigned term.[68] A *mudra*, a ritual hand pose, a seal, which is common to the Buddhist (*Vajrayana*) tradition, a *tantric mudra*, and called the 'full-blown-lotus-flower.'[69] It is the gesture formed after the generation of the twenty-one *Taras*, particularly as associated with the worship of the powerful *Vajrayana* goddess, *Tara*. The *vikasitapadma mudra* is a combined (Ind.: *saṁyutta*) form, held by both hands. This *mudra* is formed in mirror-pose: palm faces the midline thumb, index, middle and little fingers extend upwards, ring finger folds into the palm, so posed the hands are brought together so that the second phalanges of the ring fingers touch. Thus formed, the *mudra* is held at chest level. The *mantra* associated with this mudra is: "*JAH HUM BAM HOH.*" (SBe 338) (See: **Figure 684**)

vilva mudra -- (Ind.: *vilva-mudrā*) A hand pose, a seal, a dramatic (Ind.: *nāṭya*) *mudra* or gesture (Ind.: *darpaṇa*) held or formed by a performer, dancer or actor. It denotes the *vilva* or wood-apple tree. The *mudra* employed is identical in form to the *chatura mudra*. See: *chatura mudra*. (ACG 48)

Vinayaka mudra -- (Ind.: *Vināyaka-mudrā*) A *mudra*, a ritual hand pose, a seal, a *tantric mudra* which is common to the Japanese Buddhist (*Vajrayana, Mantrayana*) tradition and is held or formed by a devotee or priest during various rites in which a deity is acknowledged. It is a *mudra* which is associated with the deity *Vinayaka*. It may be accompanied by a *mantra*. The *Vinayaka mudra*[70] is a combined (Ind.: *saṁyutta*) form, held by both hands. This *mudra* is formed by: thumbs extend upwards, index fingers cross over the back of the middle fingers, ring and little fingers fold into palms. Thus formed the hands are brought together, touching along the outer edge of the palms, the folded little fingers and the tips of the middle fingers. (LCS 273) (See: **Figure 685**)

viparita mudra -- (Ind.: *viparīta mudrā;* Jap.: *miharita gassho* [*mudra*]) The Indic term for *miharita gassho* (*mudra*). See: *miharita gassho* (*mudra*). (EDS)

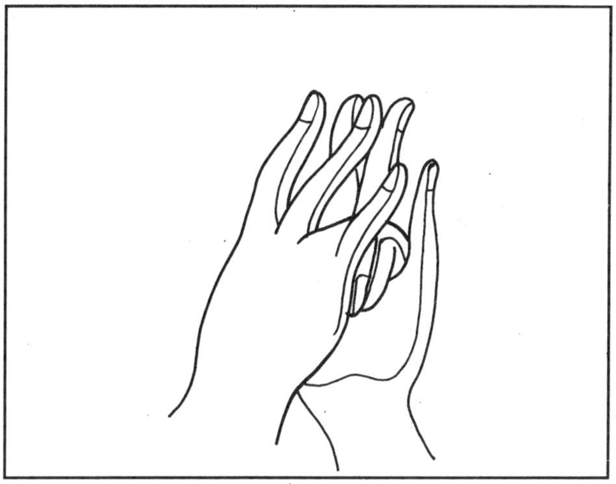

Figure 684 -- vikasitapadma mudra
(as seen by another)

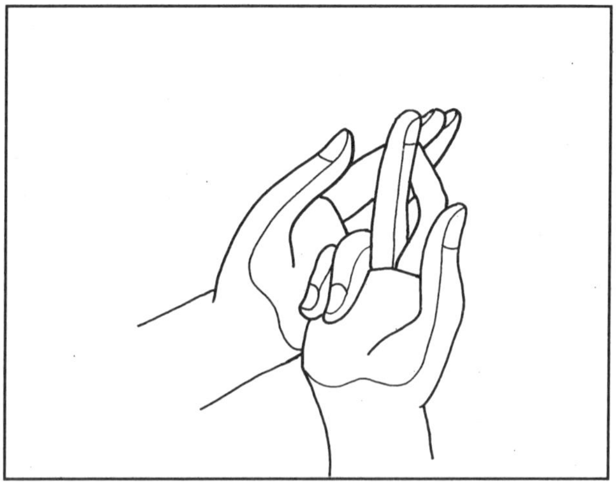

Figure 685 -- Vinayaka mudra
(as seen by the holder)

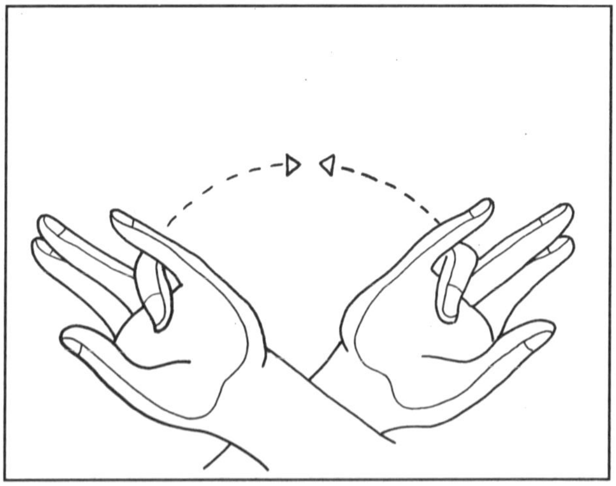

Figure 686 -- viprakirna mudra
(as seen by another)

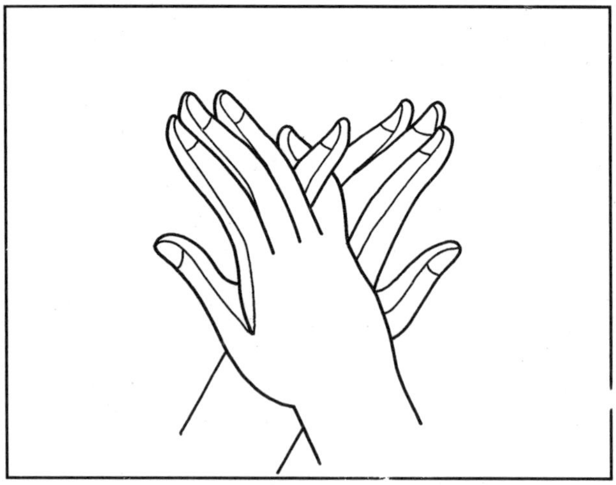

Figure 687 -- Virudhaka mudra I
(as seen by the holder)

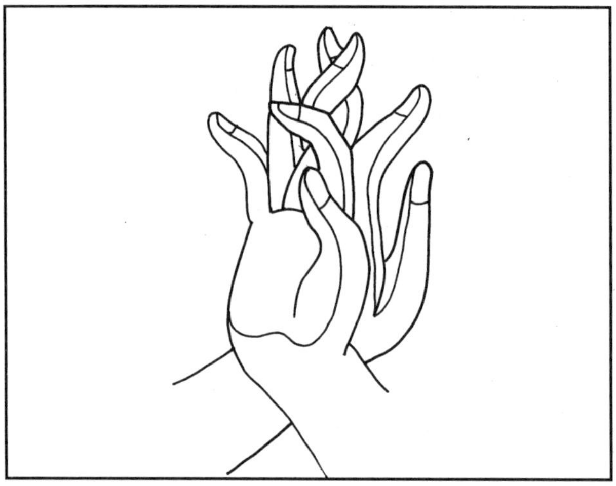

Figure 688 -- Virudhaka mudra II
(as seen by the holder)

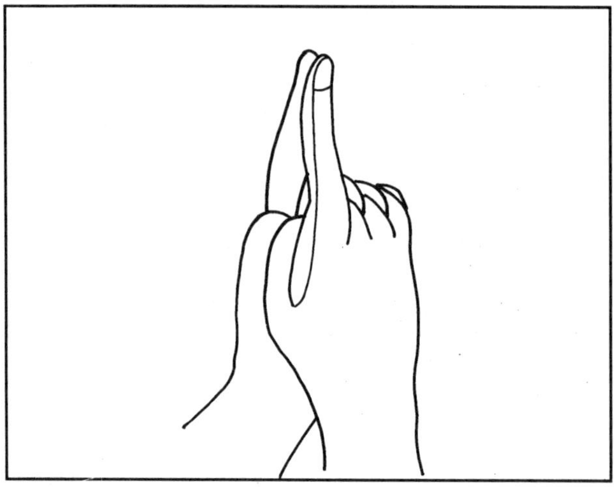

Figure 689 -- Virya-paramita mudra
(as seen by the holder)

viparyasta mudra -- (Ind.: *viparyasta mudrā*; Jap.: *bihararieisata gassho* [*mudra*]) The Indic term for *bihararieisata gassho* (*mudra*). See: *bihararieisata gassho* (*mudra*). (EDS 42)

viprakirna mudra -- (Ind.: *viprakīrṇa-mudrā*) ("loosed") A hand pose, a seal, a dramatic (Ind.: *nāṭya*) *muḍra* or gesture (Ind.: *darpaṇa*) held or formed by a performer, dancer or actor. The *viprakirna mudra* is a combined (Ind.: *saṁyutta*) form, held by both hands. It denotes releasing and opening a robe. This *mudra* requires movement and is formed by: palms facing outward, index, middle and little fingers, and thumbs extend, together and point upwards, ring fingers are bent towards the palms. Thus formed the hands are crossed at the wrist, and held to the left of chest and then quickly separated. (ACG 43) (See: **Figure 686**)

Virudhaka mudra I -- (Ind.: *Virūḍhaka-mudrā*) A *mudra*, a ritual hand pose, a seal, a *tantric mudra* which is common to the Japanese Buddhist (*Vajrayana, Mantrayana*) tradition and is held or formed by a devotee or priest during the rites of *Garbhadhatu Mandala* and other rites. It may be accompanied by a mantra. The *Virudhaka mudra* is a combined (Ind.: *saṁyutta*) form, held by both hands. This *mudra* is formed by: palms face outwards, thumbs and fingers extend upwards, Thus formed, the right hand crosses behind the left and the little fingers interlace. (LCS 178) (See: **Figure 687**)

Virudhaka mudra II -- (Ind.: *Virūḍhaka-mudrā*) A *mudra*, a ritual hand pose, a seal, a *tantric mudra* which is common to the Japanese Buddhist (*Vajrayana, Mantrayana*) tradition and is held or formed by a devotee or priest during the rites of *Garbhadhatu Mandala* and other rites. It may be accompanied by a *mantra*. The *Virudhaka mudra II* is a combined (Ind.: *saṁyutta*) form, held by both hands. This *mudra* is formed by: right palm faces left, left palm faces right, thumbs, index and little fingers curl slightly, middle and ring fingers extend upwards. Thus formed the right hand crosses behind the left, backs touching and middle fingers interlock. (GDe 237, LCS 241) (See: **Figure 688**)

Virya-paramita mudra -- (Ind.: *Vīrya-pāramitā-mudrā*) A *mudra*, a ritual hand pose, a seal, a *tantric mudra* which is common to the Japanese Buddhist (*Vajrayana, Mantrayana*) tradition and is held or formed by a devotee or priest during the rites of *Garbhadhatu Mandala* and other rites. It may be accompanied by a *mantra*. The *Virya-paramita mudra* is a combined (Ind.: *saṁyutta*) form, held by both hands. This *mudra* is formed by: thumbs, middle, ring and little fingers interlace and fold inwards (into the palms), index fingers extend straight upwards. (LCS 170) (See: **Figure 689**)

Vishnu mudra -- (Ind.: *Viṣṇu-mudra*) A hand pose, a seal, a dramatic (Ind.: *nāṭya*) *mudra* or gesture (Ind.: *darpaṇa*) held or formed by a performer, dancer or actor which denotes a specific deity. The *Vishnu mudra* is a combined (Ind.: *saṁyutta*) form, held by both hands. It denotes the Lord *Vishnu*. This *mudra* is formed by: palms facing outward, index, middle and little fingers and thumbs extend together and pointing upwards, ring fingers are bent towards the palms. Thus formed the hands are held at shoulder level. (ACG 45) (See: **Figure 690**)

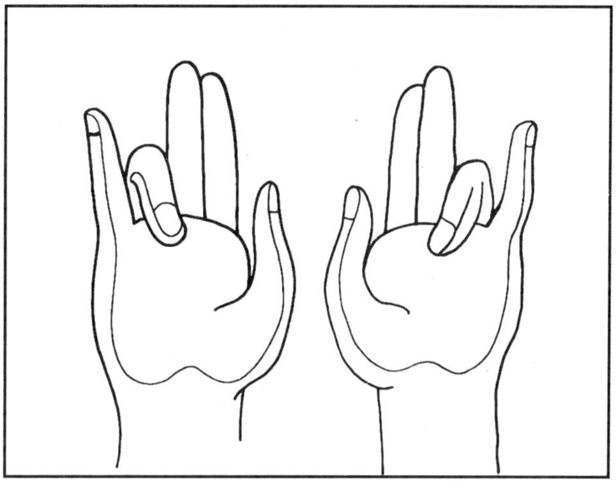

Figure 690 -- Vishnu mudra
(as seen by another)

vismaya mudra I -- (Ind.: *vismaya-mudrā* aka *āścarya mudrā*) A *mudra*, a ritual hand pose, a seal, which is common to the Hindu tradition. It denotes a state of amazement or awe. The *vismaya mudra I* is a single (Ind.: *asaṁyutta*) form, held by one hand. This *mudra* is formed by: (right) palm facing upwards, heel of the palm held close to the shoulder, index, middle and little fingers and thumb extended to the right, ring finger curls towards the palm. (HKS 271, MJS 160, RSG 4) (See: **Figure 691**)

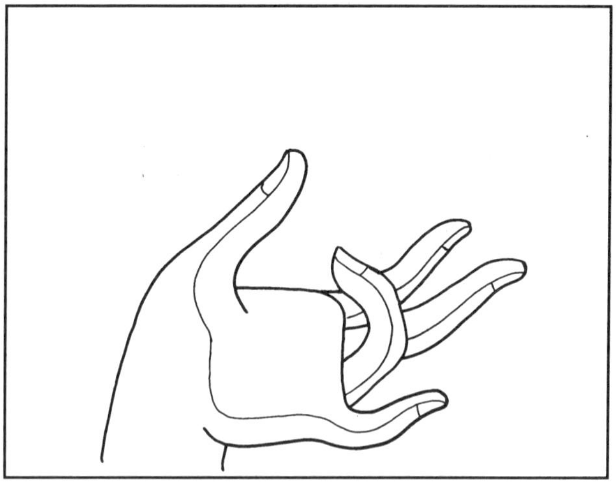

Figure 691 -- vismaya mudra I
(as seen by another)

vismaya mudra II -- (Ind.: *vismaya-mudrā* aka *āścarya mudrā*) A *mudra*, a ritual hand pose, a seal, which is common to the Hindu tradition. It denotes a state of amazement or awe. The *vismaya mudra II* is a single (Ind.: *asaṁyutta*) form, held by one hand. This *mudra* is formed by: (right) palm facing upwards, heel of the palm held close to the shoulder, fingers and thumb extended to the right. (RSG 4) (See: **Figure 692**)

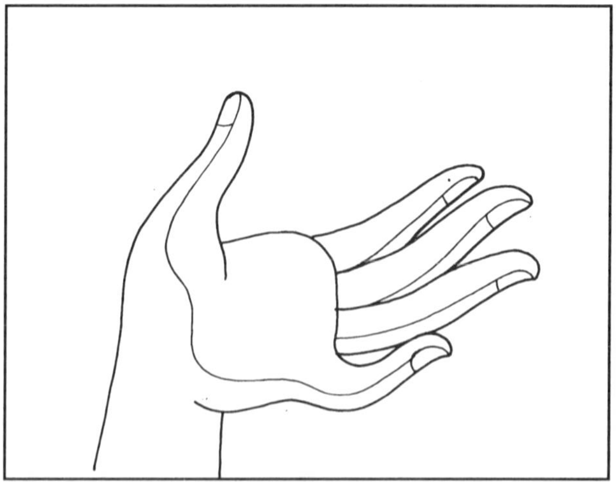

Figure 692 -- vismaya mudra II
(as seen by another)

vismaya-vitarka mudra -- (Ind.: *vismaya-vitarka-mudrā*) A *mudra*, a ritual hand pose, a seal, which is common to

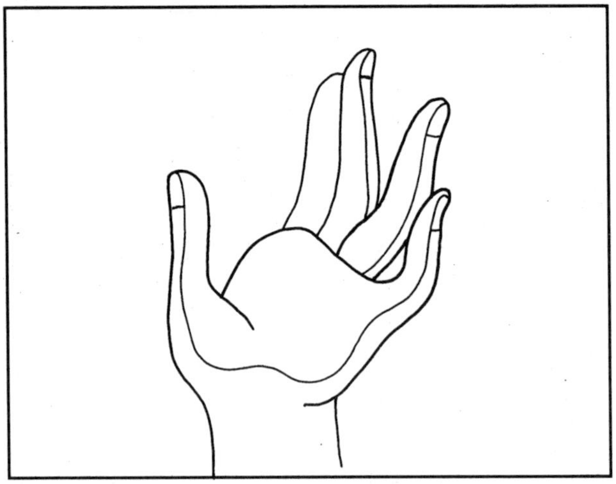

Figure 693 -- vismaya-vitarka mudra
(as seen by another)

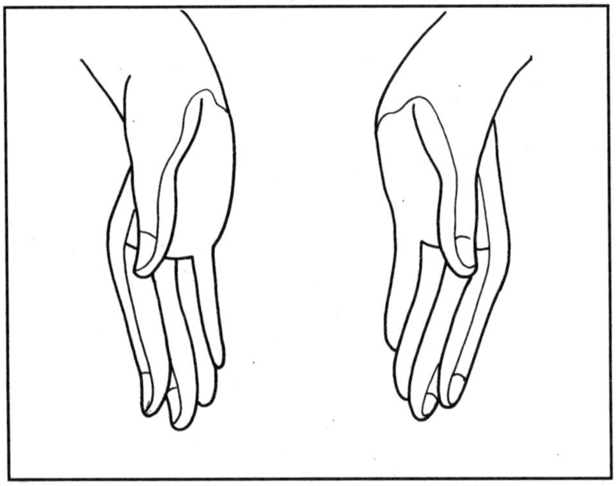

Figure 694 -- visttam mudra
(as seen by another)

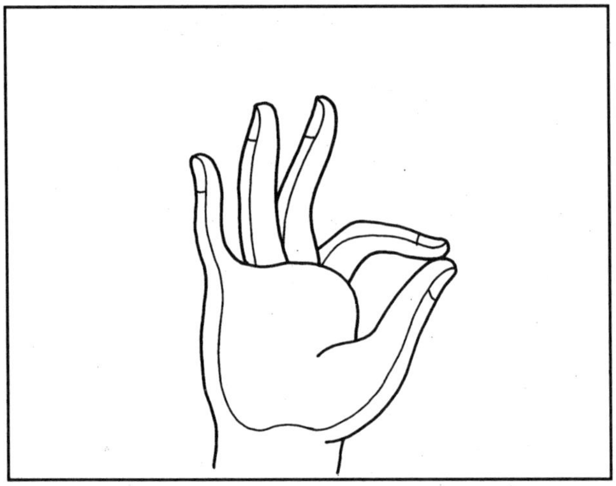

Figure 695 -- vitarka mudra
(as seen by another)

the Hindu tradition. It denotes a state of amazement or awe. The *vismaya-vitarka mudra* is a single (Ind.: *asaṁyutta*) form, held by one hand. This *mudra* is formed by: palm facing inwards, index and middle fingers touch the chin, ring and little fingers curled towards the palm. (MJS 160) (See: **Figure 693**)

vistritam mudra -- (Ind.: *vistrītam-mudrā* aka *visttam mudrā*) A variant (spelling) of *visttam mudra*. See: visttam mudra. (RLM 70)

visttam mudra -- (Ind.: *visttam-mudrā* aka *vistrītam mudrā*) A *mudra*, a ritual hand pose, a seal, a *mudra* which is common to yogic tradition, particularly the *Yoga Tatva Mudra Vigyan* form, and is held by a devotee or practitioner. The *visttam mudra* is a combined (Ind.: *saṁyutta*) form, held by both hands. It is one of the twenty-four *mudras* held before the *Gayatri Jap* of the thirty-two total *Gayatri mudras*.[71] It is utilized for all sickness, especially cancer. This *mudra* is formed by: palms facing the midline and separated by approximately a foot, fingers and thumb extended and together, relaxed, slightly cupped and pointing outwards. Thus formed, the *mudra* is held at waist level. It is similar to the *vittam mudra* except for the distance between the hands. (KDe 80) (See: **Figure 694**)

vitarka mudra -- (Ind.: *vitarka-mudrā*; Chin.: *an-wei-yin*; Jap.: *an-i-in*; Tib.: *chos-sbyin phyag-rgya*) A mudra, a ritual hand pose, a seal, which is common to the Buddhist tradition. Also, a *tantric mudra* which is common to the Japanese and Chinese Buddhist (*Vajrayana, Mantrayana*) tradition and is held or formed by a devotee or priest. It may be accompanied by a *mantra*. It denotes preaching or theological disputation or discussion. The *vitarka mudra* is a single (Ind.: *asaṁyutta*) form, held by one hand. This *mudra* is formed by: palm facing outwards, tips of the thumb and index finger touch, middle, ring and little fingers are relaxed and point upwards. It is to be noted that apparently the term *vitarka mudra* is applied exclusively to Buddhist iconography, whereas it seems that *chin mudra*, which is identical in form and meaning, but differs in orientation, is applied to the Hindu tradition. (AKG 22, BBh 199, BCO 214, GDe 128, LCS 211; RSG 4) (See: **Figure 695**)

vitatam mudra -- (Ind.: *vitatam-mudrā* aka *vittam mudrā*) A variant (spelling) of *vittam mudra*. See: *vittam mudra*. (RLM 70)

vittam mudra -- (Ind.: *vittam-mudrā* aka *vitatam mudrā*) A *mudra*, a ritual hand pose, a seal, a *mudra* which is common to yogic tradition, particularly the *Yoga Tatva Mudra Vigyan* form, and is held by a devotee or practitioner. The *vittam mudra* is a combined (Ind.: *saṁyutta*) form, held by both hands. It is one of the twenty-four mudras held before the *Gayatri Jap* of the thirty-two total *Gayatri mudras*.[72] It is utilized for all sickness, especially cancer. This *mudra* is formed by: palms facing the midline and separated by a few centimeters, fingers and thumb extended and together, relaxed, slightly cupped but not touching the opposite member and pointing outwards. Thus formed, the *mudra* is held at waist level. (KDe 80. RLM 70) (See: **Figure 696**)

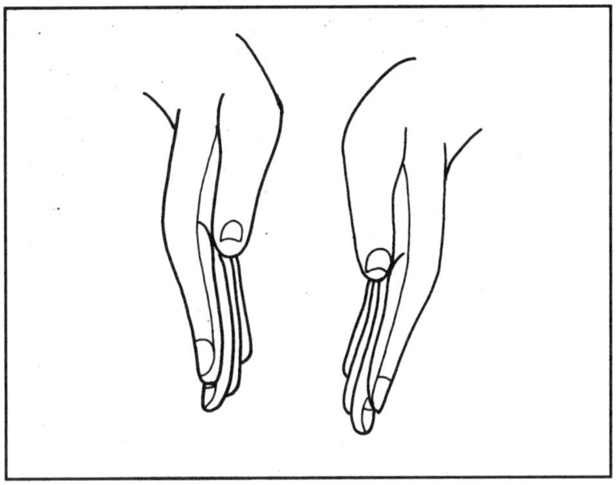

Figure 696 -- vittam mudra
(as seen by another)

vyaghra mudra I -- (Ind.: *vyāghra-mudrā*) ("tiger") A hand pose, a seal, a dramatic (Ind.: *nāṭya*) *mudra* or gesture (Ind.: *darpaṇa*) held or formed by a performer, dancer or actor. The *vyaghra mudra* is a single (Ind.: *asaṁyutta*) form, held by one hand. It denotes fierceness and aggression. This *mudra* is formed by: the palm facing forwards, the thumb is folded across the base of the fingers in the palm, the fingers are stiff (not curled) and point forwards, at 90° to the palm. (KVa 136 [26]) (See: **Figure 697**)

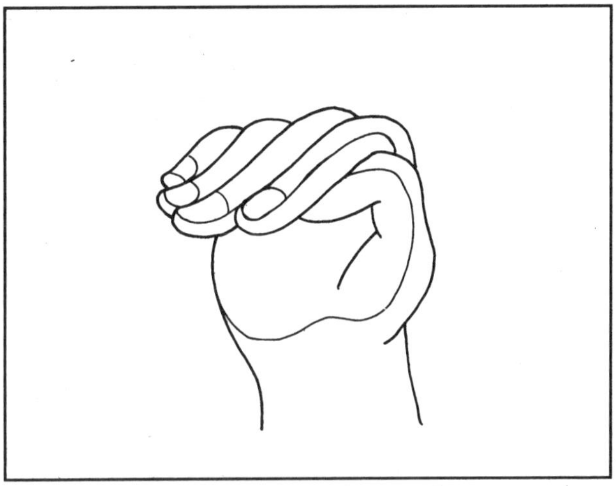

Figure 697 -- vyaghra mudra I
(as seen by another)

vyaghra mudra II -- (Ind.: *vyāghra-mudrā*) A hand pose, a seal, a dramatic (Ind.: *nāṭya*) *mudra* or gesture (Ind.: *darpaṇa*) held or formed by a performer, dancer or actor. It denotes an animal, in this case a tiger. The *vyaghra mudra*[73] is a single (Ind.: *asaṁyutta*) form, held by one hand. This *mudra* is formed by: palm faces downward, fingers extended, together and pointing outwards, relaxed, the thumb extends away from the fingers and generally held on a line level with the chest. (ACG 49) (See: **Figure 698**)

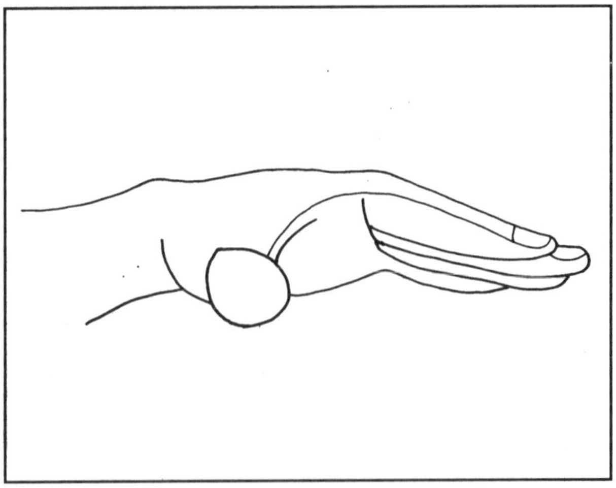

Figure 698 -- vyaghra mudra II
(as seen by the holder)

vyakhyana mudra I -- (Ind.: *vyākhyāna-mudrā* aka *dharmacakra mudrā*) A variant term applied to *dharmachakra mudra*. See: *dharmachakra mudra*.[74] (BBh 192, BCO 217)

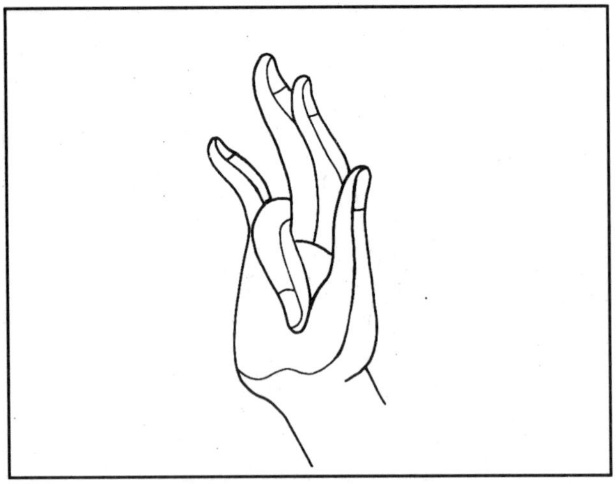

Figure 699 -- vyali mudra
(as seen by another)

vyakhyana mudra II -- (Ind.: *vyākhyāna-mudrā* aka *cin mudrā*) A variant term applied to *chin mudra*. See: *chin mudra*. (EDS 66, TGR 14)

vyakhyana mudra III -- (Ind.: *vyākhyāna-mudrā* aka *vitarka mudrā*) A variant term applied to *vitarka mudra*. See:*vitarka mudra*. (MJS 163)

vyala mudra -- (Ind.: *vyāla-mudrā*) A *mudra*, a ritual hand pose, a seal, which is common to the Hindu tradition. It denotes indication, or pointing out. The form is noted as: "the right hand of the demon pointing towards it (*vyala-mudra*?)."[75] This may be a form of *tarjani mudra* which refers to a specific object or concrete thing, rather than situations, such as, warning, threatening or warding off evil, and therefore, related to the *suchi mudra*. (HKS 79)

vyali mudra -- (Ind.: *vyāli-mudrā*) A hand pose, a seal, a dramatic (Ind.: *nāṭya*) *mudra* or gesture (Ind.: *darpaṇa*) held or formed by a performer, dancer or actor. It denotes the bird known as *vyali*. The *vyali mudra* is a combined (Ind.: *saṁyutta*) form, held by both hands. This *mudra* is formed by: palm generally faces outwards, index and middle fingers curve slightly towards the palm, tip of the ring finger touches the base of the thumb, little finger is curved slightly. (ACG 50) (See: **Figure 699**)

vyapkanjali mudra -- (Ind.: *vyāpkāñjali-mudrā* aka *viapkāñjali mudrā*) A variant (spelling) of *viapkanjali mudra*. See: *viapkanjali mudra*. (RLM 72)

-- W --

wai-fu ch'ṃan-yin (mudra) -- (Chin.; Jap.: *gebaku ken-in* [*mudra*]) The Chinese term for *gebaku ken-in* [*mudra*]. See: *gebaku ken-in* [*mudra*]. (EDS 119)

walking mudra -- (Eng.; Indic: *abhaya-lolahasta mudrā,*[1] *lolahasta-vitarka mudrā;*[2] Thai **ODD 35, F 17**) The English descriptive phrase for the Thai **ODD 35, F 17**. See: *abhaya-lolahasta mudra* or *lolahasta-vitarka mudra*. (DRN 36, JBo, ODD 680)

womb (fist mudra) -- (Ind.: *padma* [fist *mudrā*]; Jap.: *tai-ken-in*) A variant term applied to *renge ken-in* (*mudra*). See: *renge ken-in* (*mudra*). (EDS 39)

wu-so-pu-chih-yin (mudra) -- (Chin.; Ind.: *stūpa mudrā;* Jap.: *Biroshana-in* [*mudra*], *butsubu sotoba-in* [*mudra*], *dai sotoba-in* [*mudra*], *hen hokkai mushofushi-in* [*mudra*], *mushofushi-in* [*mudra*], *mushofushi to-in* [*mudra*], *rito-in* [*mudra*]) The Chinese term for *mushofushi-in* [*mudra*]. See: *mushofushi-in* [*mudra*]. (EDS 115)

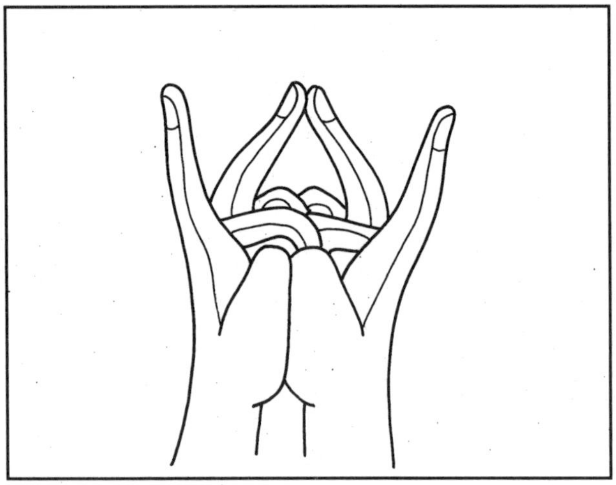

Figure 700 -- Yaksha mudra
(as seen by the holder)

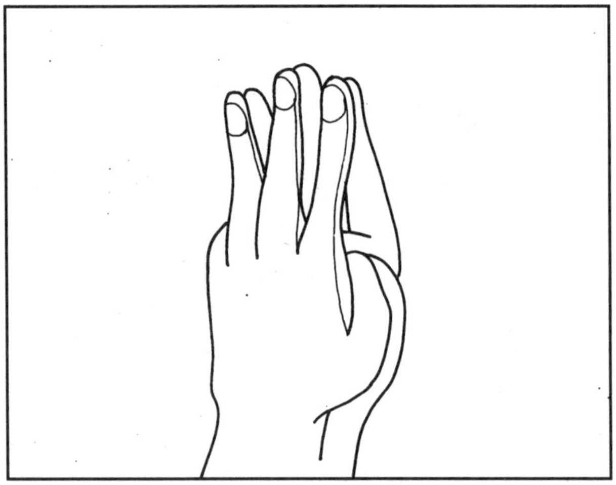

Figure 701 -- Yakshini mudra
(as seen by the holder)

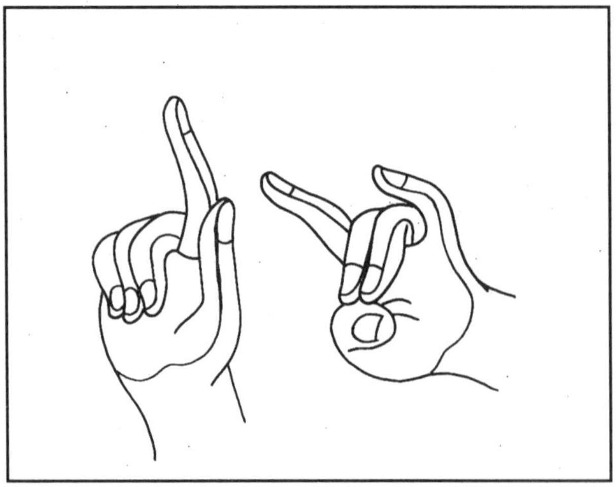

Figure 702 -- Yama mudra I
(as seen by another)

-- Y --

Yaksha mudra -- (Ind.: *Yakṣa-mudrā*) A *mudra*, a ritual hand pose, a seal, a *tantric mudra* which is common to the Japanese Buddhist (*Vajrayana, Mantrayana*) tradition and is held or formed by a devotee or priest during the rites of *Garbhadhatu Mandala* and other rites. It may be accompanied by a *mantra*. The *Yaksha mudra* is a combined (Ind.: *saṁyutta*) form, held by both hands. It denotes *Yakshas* in general. This *mudra* is formed by: palms facing midline, thumbs, middle and little fingers fold into the palms, index and ring fingers extend upward and touch at their tips. (LCS 185) (See: **Figure 700**)

Yakshini mudra -- (Ind.: *Yakṣiṇī-mudrā*) A *mudra*, a ritual hand pose, a seal, a *tantric mudra* which is common to the Japanese Buddhist (*Vajrayana, Mantrayana*) tradition and is held or formed by a devotee or priest during the rites of *Garbhadhatu Mandala* and other rites. It may be accompanied by a *mantra*. The *Yakshini mudra* is a combined (Ind.: *saṁyutta*) form, held by both hands. It denotes *Yakshinis* in general. This *mudra* is formed by: palms facing midline, thumbs and little fingers fold into the palms, index, middle and ring fingers extend upward and touch at their tips. In this mudra the touching index fingers splay from the touching middle fingers forming a "V." (LCS 185) (See: **Figure 701**)

Yama mudra I -- (Ind.: *Yama-mudrā*) A hand pose, a seal, a dramatic (Ind.: *nāṭya*) *mudra* or gesture (Ind.: *darpaṇa*) held or formed by a performer, dancer or actor which denotes a specific deity. The *Yama mudra* is a combined (Ind.: *saṁyutta*) form, held by both hands. It denotes *Yama*. This *mudra* is formed by: right palm faces outwards, the index finger and the thumb point upwards, together, the middle, ring and little fingers are folded into the palm; left palm faces inwards, the index finger and the thumb point upwards, together, the middle, ring and little fingers are folded into the palm. Thus formed the hands are held at shoulder level. (ACG 45) (See: **Figure 702**)

Yama mudra II -- (Ind.: *Yama-mudrā*) A *mudra*, a ritual hand pose, a seal, a *tantric mudra* which is common to the Japanese Buddhist (*Vajrayana, Mantrayana*) tradition and is held or formed by a devotee or priest during various rites in which a deity is acknowledged. It is a *mudra* which is associated with the deity *Yama*. It may be accompanied by a *mantra*. The *Yama mudra II*[1] is a combined (Ind.: *saṁyutta*) form, held by both hands. This *mudra* is formed by: palms face inwards and are close, thumbs extend upward and touch along their edge, index fingers flex at their first and second knuckles and are placed behind the first phalanges of the thumbs, middle and ring fingers extend upward and touch at their tips, little fingers fold inward.[2] (LCS 271) (See: **Figure 703**)

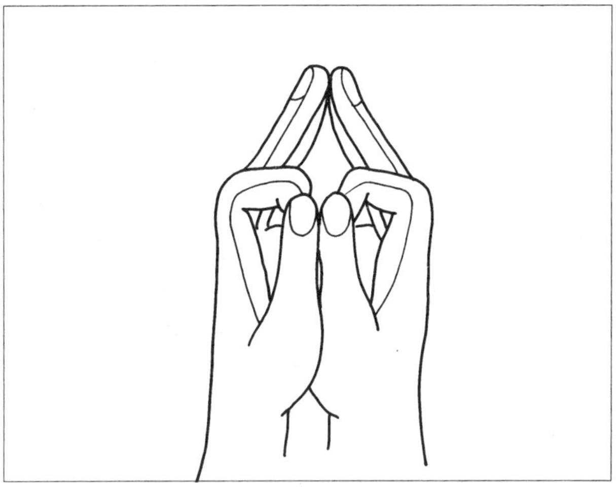

Figure 703 -- Yama mudra II
(as seen by 0000)

yampasham mudra -- (Ind.: *yampāśam-mudrā*) A *mudra*, a ritual hand pose, a seal, a *mudra* which is common to yogic tradition, particularly the *Yoga Tatva Mudra Vigyan* form, and is held by a devotee or practitioner. The *yampasham mudra* is a combined (Ind.: *saṁyutta*) form, held by both hands. It is one of the twenty-four *mudras* held before the *Gayatri Jap* of the thirty-two total *Gayatri mudras*.[3] It is utilized for all sickness, especially cancer. This *mudra* is formed by: right palm turned inwards, thumb extended upwards, middle, ring and little fingers folded into the palm, index finger curled at the first and second phalanges; left hand palm facing midline, middle, ring and little fingers folded into the palm, index finger curled at the first and second phalanges hooking the index finger of the right hand, thumb folded over "palmed" fingers. This *mudra* is held chest high. (KDe, RLM 73) (See: **Figure 704**)

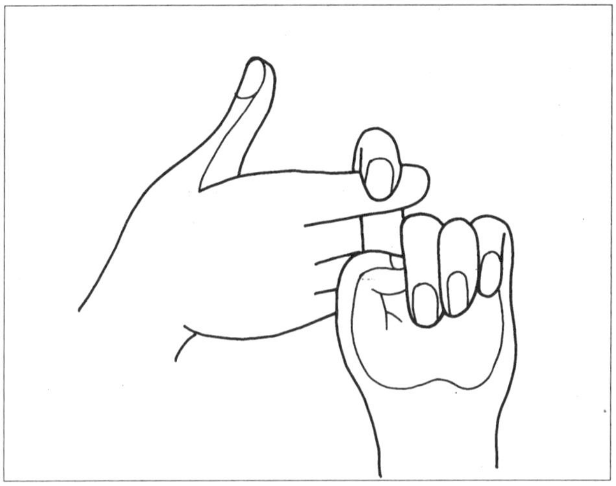

Figure 704 -- yampasham mudra
(as seen by 0000)

Yamuna mudra -- (Ind.: *Yamunā-mudrā* aka *rekhā mudrā*) A hand pose, a seal, a dramatic (Ind.: *nāṭya*) *mudra* or gesture (Ind.: *darpaṇa*) held or formed by a performer, dancer or actor. It denotes the river *Yamuna*, one of the famous rivers of India. The *mudra* employed is identical in form to the *rekha mudra*. See: *rekha mudra*. (ACG 48)

Yayati mudra -- (Ind.: *Yayāti-mudrā*) A hand pose, a seal, a dramatic (Ind.: *nāṭya*) mudra or gesture (Ind.: *darpaṇa*) held or formed by a performer, dancer or actor. The *Yayati mudra* is a single (Ind.: *asaṁyutta*) form,

Figure 705 -- yoni mudra I
(as seen by 0000)

Figure 706 -- yoni mudra II
(as seen by 0000)

held by one hand. It denotes Yayati, one of a number of famous rulers or heroes. The *mudra* employed is identical in form to the *tamrachuda mudra*. See: *tamrachuda mudra*. (ACG 47)

ye-shes skar-mda'i phyag-rgya (mudra) -- (Tib.; Ind.: *jñāna-avalokite mudrā*) The Tibetan transliteral term for *jnana-avalokite mudra*. See: *jnana-avalokite mudra*. (SBe 347)

yin-hsing-yin mudra -- (Chin.; Jap.: *ongyo-in*) The Chinese transliteral term for *ongyo-in*. See: *ongyo-in*. (EDS 117)

yo-cho jo-in (mudra) -- (Jap.: *yō-chō jō-in* [*mudrā*]; Ind.: *ratna-ghaṭa mudrā*) ("*mudra* of invitation to the astral bodies") The Japanese transliteral term applied to *ratna-ghata mudra*.[4] See: *ratna-ghata mudra*. (GDe 92)

yoni mudra I -- (Ind.: *yoni-mudrā*) A *mudra*, a ritual hand pose, a seal, a *tantric mudra* which is common to the Buddhist and Hindu Buddhist (*Vajrayana*, *Mantrayana*) traditions and is held or formed by a devotee or priest. It may be accompanied by a *mantra*. It denotes the female generative organ. The *yoni mudra* is a combined (Ind.: *saṁyutta*) form, held by both hands. The form is noted as: "The fingers are places to form a triangle (*trikona*)."[5] It is assumed that the fingers are together, pointing downwards, palms facing the midline, tips of the fingers touch, thumbs perpendicular to the fingers touch at their tips. Thus held, a downward pointed triangle is formed. (MJS 170) (See: **Figure 705**)

yoni mudra II -- (Ind.: *yoni-mudrā*) A *mudra*, a ritual hand pose, a seal, a *tantric mudra* which is common to the Buddhist and Hindu Buddhist (*Vajrayana*, *Mantrayana*) traditions and is held or formed by a devotee or priest. It may be accompanied by a *mantra*. The *yoni mudra* is a combined (Ind.: *saṁyutta*) form, held by both hands. It denotes the female generative organ. This *mudra* is formed by: the palms facing the midline, index, ring and little fingers and thumbs are interlaced, inwards towards the palm, the middle fingers extend downwards and touch at their tips. Thus formed the *mudra* is held at waist level. (AMK 141) (See: **Figure 706**)

yoni mudra III -- (Ind.: *yoni-mudrā*) A *mudra*, a ritual hand pose, a seal, a *mudra* which is common to yogic tradition, particularly the *Yoga Tatva Mudra Vigyan* form, and is held by a devotee or practitioner. The *yoni mudra* is a combined (Ind.: *saṁyutta*) form, held by both hands. It is one of the eight *mudras* held after the *Gayatri Jap* of the thirty-two total *Gayatri mudras*.[6] It is utilized for all sickness, especially cancer. This *mudra* is formed by: the palms facing upward, the hands are brought together along the outside edge of the palms and little fingers, the thumbs curl over and touch the base of the little fingers, first, middle and ring fingers extend forward, the ring finger of the right hand is placed under the middle finger of the left and its nail rests on the inner surface of the left hand's index finger's first phalanges, the ring finger of the left hand is placed under the middle finger of the right and its nail rests on the inner surface of the right hand's index finger's first phalanges. Thus formed, the *mudra* is held waist high. (KDe 89 & 108) (See: **Figure 707**)

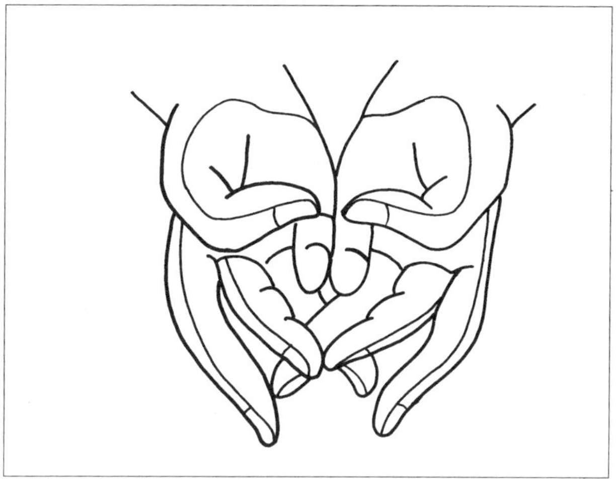

Figure 707 -- yoni mudra III
(as seen by 0000)

yoga mudra -- (Ind.: *yoga-mudrā* aka *dhyāna mudrā, dhyānahasta mudrā, samādhi mudrā*; Chin.: *ting-yin* [*mudra*]; Jap.: *jo-in* [*mudra*]; Thai: *pang phra-nang*; Tib.: *bsam-gtan phyag-rgya*) A variant term applied to *dhyana mudra*. See: *dhyana mudra*. (RSG 4)

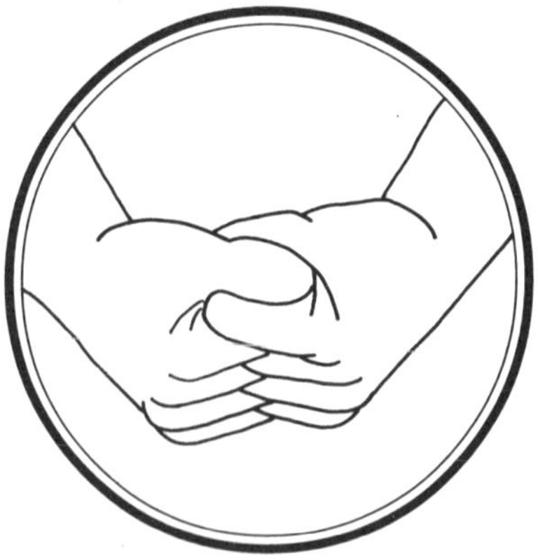

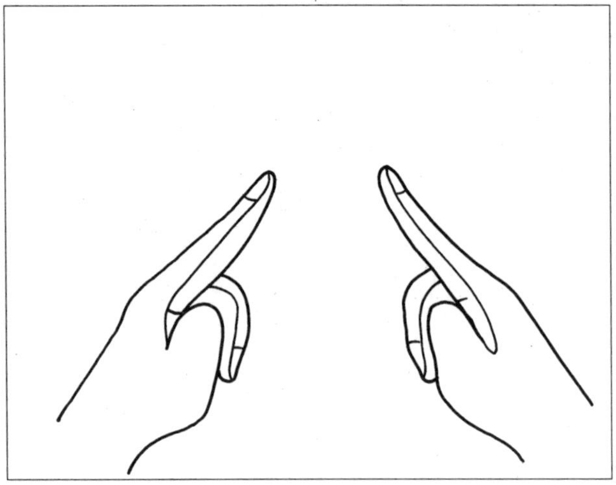

Figure 708 -- zen-in (mudra)
(as seen by 0000)

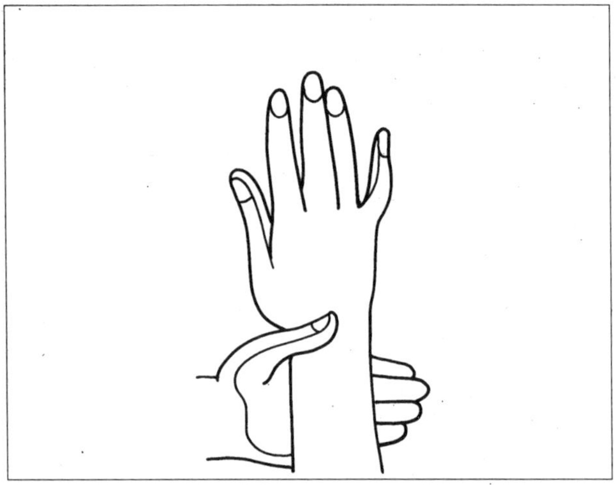

Figure 709 -- zu ko-in (mudra)
(as seen by 0000)

-- Z --

zen-in (mudra) -- (Jap.: *zen-in* [*mudrā*];) A *mudra*, a ritual hand pose, a seal, a *tantric mudra* which is common to the Japanese Buddhist (*Vajrayana, Mantrayana*) tradition and is held or formed by a devotee or priest during the rites of *Garbhadhatu Mandala* and *Vajradhatu Mandala* rites. It may be accompanied by a *mantra*. The *zen-in* (*mudra*) is a combined (Ind.: *saṁyutta*) form, held by both hands. It denotes the fastening of armor and therefore related to the *kavacha mudra*. This *mudra* is identical for both hands and is formed by: palm facing outward, the middle, ring and little fingers folded into the palm, the thumb touches the second phalange of the middle finger, the index finger extends straight. Thus formed the tips of the index fingers a brought close together, but not touching. This *mudra* involves motion1 in that the hands, specifically the index fingers make a circular motion in opposition. (GDe 5, LCS 89) (See: **Figure 708**)

zu ko-in (mudra) -- (Jap.: *zu kō-in* [*mudrā*] ; Ind.: *gandha mudrā II*) ("anointing with perfume") A *mudra*, a ritual hand pose, a seal, a *tantric mudra* which is common to the Japanese Buddhist (*Vajrayana, Mantrayana*) tradition and is held or formed by a devotee or priest during the rites of *Garbhadhatu Mandala, Vajradhatu Mandala, Homa Rites* and other rites. It may be accompanied by a *mantra*. The *zu ko-in* (*mudra*) is a combined (Ind.: *saṁyutta*) form, held by both hands. It denotes the anointing of deities, a form of worship. This *mudra* is formed by: right palm facing outwards, fingers and thumb extending upwards, left hand grasps the right forearm below the wrist, fingers extended straight on the outward side, thumb extended straight on the inward side. (GDe 46) (See: **Figure 709**)

A *Tantric* ritual known as *nyasa* (Ind.: *nyāsa*) is performed to sensitize the *chakras* (Ind.: *cakra*) of the body. This is normally accomplished with the right hand and its fingers or palm which touches the various parts of the body accompanied by a *mantra* to sensitize these *chakras*. The *sadanga-nyasa* (Ind.: *ṣaḍaṅga-nyāsa*) is the most popular form and includes the six *mudra* listed below.

hridayaya (mudra) -- (Ind.: *hṛdayāya* [*mudrā*]) A *mudra*, a ritual hand pose, a seal, a *tantric mudra* which is common to the Buddhist and Hindu Buddhist (Vajrayana, Mantrayana) traditions and is held or formed by a devotee or priest during the *sadanga-nyasa*. The *hridayaya* (*mudra*) is a single (Ind.: *asaṁyutta*) form, held by the right hand. The 'heart center' is touched with the palm and the *mantra*: *aim hridayaya namah* is recited. (AMo 141) (See: **Figure 710**)

kavachaya (mudra) -- (Ind.: *kavacāya* [*mudrā*]) A *mudra*, a ritual hand pose, a seal, a *tantric mudra* which is common to the Buddhist and Hindu Buddhist (Vajrayana, Mantrayana) traditions and is held or formed by a devotee or priest during the *sadanga-nyasa*. The *kavacaya* (*mudra*) is a combined (Ind.: *saṁyutta*) form, held by both hands. the arms are crossed and the biceps are touched with the palms while the *mantra*: *om sahuh kavacaya hum* is recited. (AMo 141) (See: **Figure 711**)

netratroyaiya (mudra) -- (Ind.: *netratroyaiya* [*mudrā*]) A mudra, a ritual hand pose, a seal, a *tantric mudra* which is common to the Buddhist and Hindu Buddhist (Vajrayana, Mantrayana) traditions and is held or formed by a devotee or priest during the *sadanga-nyasa*. The *netratroyaiya* (*mudra*) is a single (Ind.: *asaṁyutta*) form, held by the right hand. The index and middle fingers touch the closed eyes while the *mantra*: *om bhuvah netratroyaiya vausat* is recited. (AMo 141) (See: **Figure 712**)

phat (mudra) -- (Ind.: *phaṭ* [*mudrā*]) A mudra, a ritual hand pose, a seal, a *tantric mudra* which is common to the Buddhist and Hindu Buddhist (Vajrayana, Mantrayana) traditions and is held or formed by a devotee or priest during the *sadanga-nyasa*. The *phat*

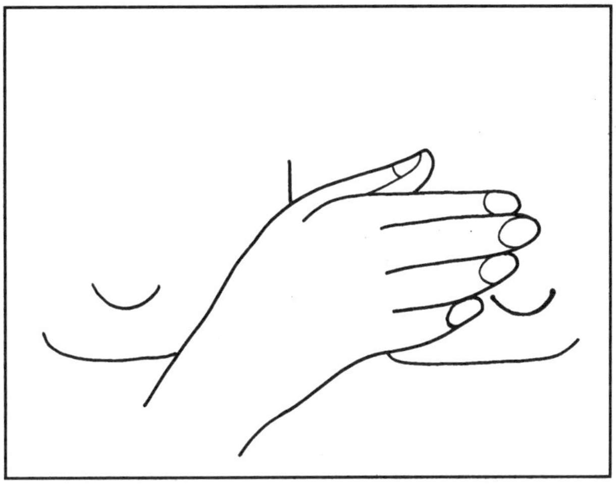

Figure 710 -- hridayaya (mudra)
(as seen by another)

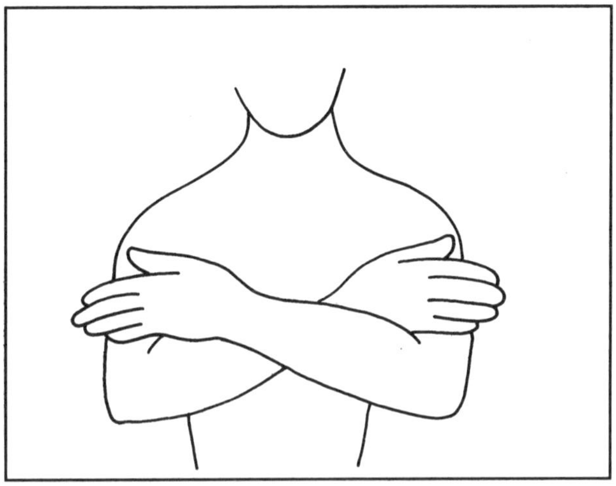

Figure 711 -- kavachaya (mudra)
(as seen by another)

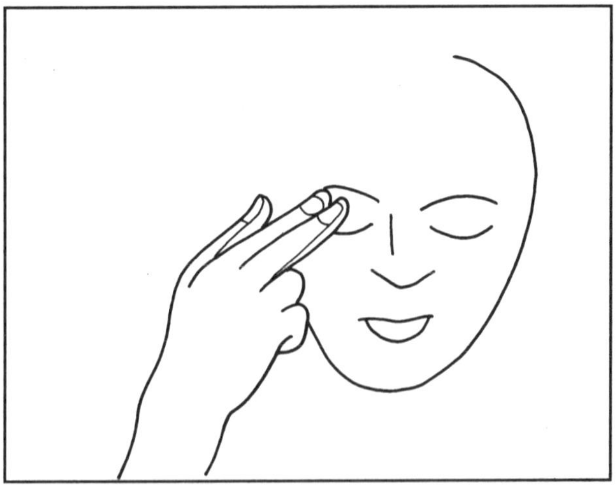

Figure 712 -- netratroyaiya (mudra)
(as seen by another)

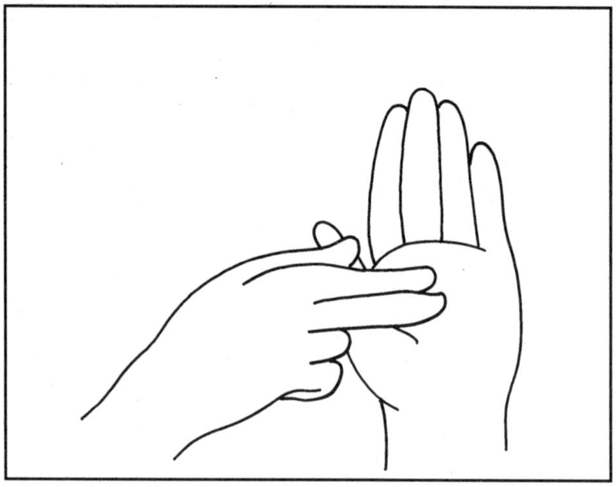

Figure 713 -- phat (mudra)
(as seen by another)

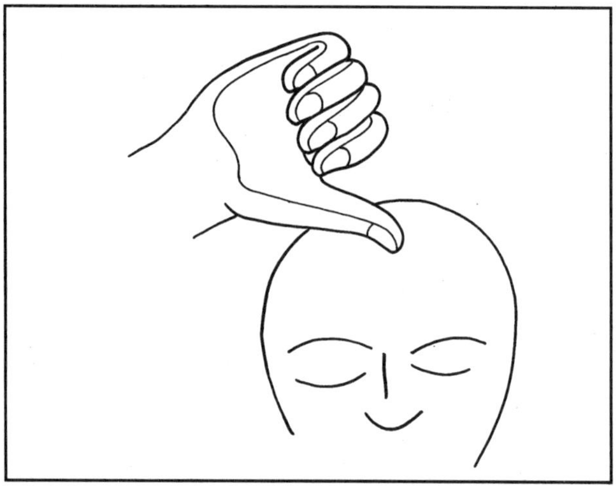

Figure 714 -- shikhayai (mudra)
(as seen by another)

Figure 715 -- shirasi (mudra)
(as seen by another)

(*mudra*) is a combined (Ind.: *saṁyutta*) form, held by both hands. index and middle fingers of the right hand touch the palm of the left while the *mantra*: *om bhur bhuvah phat* is recited. (AMo 141) (See: **Figure 713**)

shikhayai (mudra) -- (Ind.: *śikhāyai* [*mudrā*]) A *mudra*, a ritual hand pose, a seal, a *tantric mudra* which is common to the Buddhist and Hindu Buddhist (Vajrayana, Mantrayana) traditions and is held or formed by a devotee or priest during the *sadanga-nyasa*. The *sikhayai* (*mudra*) is a single (Ind.: *asaṁyutta*) form, held by the right hand. The top of the head is touched with the the tip of the thumb and the *mantra*: *om sahuh sikhayai hum* is recited. (AMo 141) (See: **Figure 714**)

shirasi (mudra) -- (Ind.: *śirasī* [*mudrā*]) A *mudra*, a ritual hand pose, a seal, a *tantric mudra* which is common to the Buddhist and Hindu Buddhist (Vajrayana, Mantrayana) traditions and is held or formed by a devotee or priest during the *sadanga-nyasa*. The *shirasi* (*mudra*) is a single (Ind.: *asaṁyutta*) form, held by the right hand. The forehead is touched with the the tips of the four fingers and the *mantra*: *om klim shirasi savah* is recited. (AMo 141) (See: **Figure 715**)

Notes to the Text

Notes to the Text

Notes for: Introduction, pages xiv-xvi

1 The notation "Indic" or "Ind." is used to denote those numerous languages whose geographic source is the Indian sub-continent. The focus, therefore, is not the etymology of the term, but its iconography. There are numerous comparative dictionaries dealing with etymology.

2 The other term that applies to ritual hand poses is: hasta. MJS, pp. 94 (*mudra*) & 54-55 (*hasta*), defines them at length and separately, but makes no distinction between them; HKS, pp. 266-267 and, likewise RSG, pp. 1-4, make no distinction; AKG, pp. 20-23, BBh, p. 194, BCO, p. 216, and MMR, p. 391, define or note the term *mudra*, but not *hasta*; and, finally TGR, pp. 14-17 clearly separates them but makes no distinction: "Each pose has its own designation, and the most common *hastas* or hand poses are . . . ." (p. 14) where he discusses briefly eight "*hastas*" and starting a paragraph with "Among the *mudras*, . . ." (p. 16) where he briefly notes three. There is, however, an implied distinction--i.e., the term *mudra* appears to be utilized exclusively by Buddhist scholars when referring to ritual hand poses that are to be found within either Theravada or Mahayana and Vajrayana Buddhism. The term "*hasta*" is not utilized by these scholars, while scholars of Hindu art and iconography are seen to uses them without distinction, generally.

3 KVa, p. 135 & 137.

4 For example: *anjali-mudra, bhutadamara-mudra, dharmachakra-mudra, dhyana-mudra, namaskara-mudra, kshepana-mudra, uttarabodhi-mudra* and *vajrahumkara-mudra* to name the most frequently seen.

5 MiS, p. 69.

6 This system was in a sense arbitrarily "set-up" for the ease of the author's identification and in no way was conceived of as being a "standard" for identification.

7 E. Dale Saunders, *Mudra: A Study of Symbolic Gestures in Japanese Buddhist Sculpture*. is an excellent and thorough example as are: N.K. Bhattasali, *Iconography of Buddhist and Brahmanical Sculptures in the Dacca Museum*; Ananda Kentish Coomaraswamy, *The Mirror of Gesture*; G. Liebert, *Iconographic Dictionary of the Indian Religions*; R. K. Poduval, *Administrative Report of the Archeological Department*; R. V. Poduval, *Kathakala and Diagram of Hand Poses*; and S.P. Tewari, *Hindu Iconography*.

8 The *abhaya-mudra* is generally held in the right hand. However, the Thai Theravada tradition recognizes two additional variations: held in the left hand and held by both hands at the same time.

9 RSG, p. 9; AKG, p. 23, and ERJ, p. 9.

10 It is also interesting, even amusing to note that all the illustrations in which the author's face appears, flowing locks have been clumsily applied to either side. If Keshav Dev is "His Divine Grace Shri Shri 1008 Acharya Shri Keshav Dev Ji Maharaj," then one would think that this would be unnecessary!

11 DRN, pp. 35-38, and JBo, pp. 204-205. These forty are to be found in an unnamed "treatise in the National Library," DRN, p. 35. They are listed in English as in most cases neither the Indic nor the Thai translations are given.

12 Both of these works do present problems as well. In many instances, the renderings of the *mudras* are so poorly executed as to make them almost worthless. This, of course, is not the fault of the authors. In others, there are major anatomical errors including hands with five fingers! In still others, the obvious naivetŗ of the artist is most amusing, particularly in the apparent suppleness of some of the digits. Yet no attempt was made to clarify those "errors" or naive renderings. In addition, in both cases--i.e., LCS and GDe--a number of terms used to describe various *mudras* were confusing and, frankly, ill-used--e.g., "twisted" to denote the curled finger (bent or abducted at each knuckle). "Twisted" is an entirely different motion--i.e., it refers to rotating an object along its vertical axis, particularly when the base is secured. One twists a rope or piece of cloth, one may "twist" a finger, but a twisted finger is not a "curled" finger--i.e., one which is flexed or abducted at its knuckles. Also, a number of titles were transposed from one illustration to another creating some problems. Finally, there are numerous repeats of *mudras*, often under different names--e.g., the "*vajranjali mudra*" is repeated 59 times in form in LCS, and 51 times in GDe; bring the total number of different *mudras* down to a reasonable number. However, the task of coupling like *mudras* throughout the two volumes was a daunting and massive task. In addition the *mudras* presented in GDe are accompanied by excellent descriprion as to their use within the specific rite. However, the intorductory title are not always descriptive of the *mudras* true or generic name. A case in point: *Mudra* 1, begins with the title "*Kaji-i, Kia-chi-yi*, purification of the robes . . ." the description of the name-cum-use, but not the generic name which she further on identifies as "called 'fist of the lotus' . . . ." (Indic: *padma-mushti*). Therefore, the author, since this is a compilation, has choosen to use this first name/use title as the *mudra* title when no other identifier is found.

13 Foremost is KDe. This publication is obviously for

popular consumption. It is repetitive, in some cases contradictory, and the spelling errors and/or transcriptions are numerous, as noted in the text. Nonetheless, it presents the important thirty-two *Gayatri Mudras*.

Notes for: 'A,' pages 2-27

1 The Roman Numeral indicates a distinct variation. For example: the *anjali mudra* is illustrated and/or described in three different positions by different sources: *anjali mudra* I (BBh, p. 189), *anjali mudra II* (RSG, pp. 3 & 5), and *anjali mudra III* (AKG, pp. 20-21).

2 In the Theravada tradition there are three forms of the *abhaya mudra*: 1) the traditional form which is held in the right hand and denotes the appeasement "of the quarrels between the Kolyas and Shakyas," 2) held in the left hand denotes a warning to the sandalwood image not to revere the Lord Buddha, and 3) held in both hands which refers to the "calming of the waters." JBo, p. 203.

3 During the reign of Rama III, the king asked the Prince Patriarch Paramanujita Jinorasa (Paramanuchit Chinorot), son of Phra Buddha Yot Fa (Rama I), to review the sacred texts and note the principle events in the life of the Lord Buddha that were worthy of veneration. Forty events were compiled in addition to a number already in popular use. To these events appropriate *mudras* were assigned. The king then commissioned the forty postures (*mudras*) to be cast and placed within the *Rajakramanusarana Hall* of *Wat Phra Kaeo*--thirty three were cast and so deposited. In addition seven postures were assigned to the seven sites associated with the seven weeks following Enlightenment (DRN, p. 38)--i.e., 1] seated in meditation under a bodhi tree, 2] gazing, 3] on the jeweled walkway (surrounded by a jeweled mandala), 4] thinking out the *Abhidhamma* in the house of gems (surrounded by a jeweled mandala), 5] seated in meditation under a banyan tree, 6] sheltered by the Naga under the mucalinda tree, and 7] seated in meditation under the mimusops tree. Nine of these events/sites were assigned to astrological signs--i.e., #'s 6 to Jupiter, 6 (from the seven sites) to Saturn, 7 to the Sun, 14 to the Moon, 15 to Mercury, 20 to Rahu, 28 to Venus, 29 to Ketu, and 35 to Mars.

4 It is to be noted that in no other source does this *mudra* appear.

5 The various sources usually present these forty *mudras* in an English translation of the Thai terms. Parallel Sanskrit terms are not applied by the Thai. However, when ever possible the author has applied the appropriate Sanskrit vocabulary as purely "descriptive terms" for these *mudras*. In so doing, the right hand and then the left is "described." The phrase "This is a descriptive term" is utilized in these cases. See: OFr and ODD.

6 See note #5 above.

7 *Ibid.*

8 *Ibid.*

9 GDe, p. 38 entitles this mudra simply "Flames of [*Fudo*]*Acala*," and gives neither a Japanese nor Chinese transliteral equivalent, the term "*mudra*" is added by the author.

10 EDS, p. 42. This is confusing in that the illustration indicates the fingers pointing upward.

11 KDe, pp. 78-92, 107-108, being: *sumukham, samputam, vittam, visttam, dvimukham, trimukham, chaturmukham, panchamukham, sanmukham, adhomukham, vuapkanjali, saktam, yampasham, granthitam, chon-mukhmukham, pralambam, mustikam, matsayan, kurman, varahkam, singhakrant, mahakrant, mugdhram, palavam, surabhi, gyan, veragya, yoni, shankha, pankaj, linga* and *nirvan*.

12 The term adhishthana mudra is applied to this mudra as it appears and so named in LCS # 1.7 & 1.8, p. 58, although the specific combination is not given a Sanskrit name, with the exception that it is described as: "*Mudra* of the small three-pronged *vajra*" in both cases. The "small three-pronged *vajra*" is the form of the right hand, but does not include the left.

13 This form of beckoning is the polite form in Asia as opposed to the beckoning motion within the West in which the fingers and thumb are fisted, palm up, the index finger extended and repeatedly brought towards the palm and extended back out. This form of beckoning in Asia is considered extremely rude. Partially, because of the index finger which carries a potency of numerous derivations, and which is almost never used to point at or towards someone as it implies malevolent intent. This idea is seen in the tarjani mudra, a mudra of warning or menacing.

14 See note #5, above.

15 *Ibid.*

16 *Ibid.*

17 The name "*Ajanta*" indicates that this *mudra* is an adaptation of one to be found in the frescoes of the caves of *Ajanta*, as noted by EDS, p. 94.

18 TGR, Vol. II, part 1, p. 267, quoting *Abhinavagupta-charya*.

19 The *mudras* herein entitled, described and illustrated which are dedicated to the worship of *Tara* are to be found in SBe. The "assigned terms" are those *mudras* that are noted--e.g., "*ALOKE* "lamps", p. 148, and illustrated, p. 147, is given the title "*aloke mudra*" in this brief compilation. In most cases SBe does not include the Tibetan transliteral title, but identifies only with Sanskrit descriptive titles. In a smaller number of cases he does not include the Sanskrit or Tibetan transliteral title. In those instances the author has utilized the descriptive (title) included in the *mantra* for that specific *mudra*--e.g., SBe, p.347 (6 illustrations), "Fig. 41. The six gestures that generate the substitutes." Then on pp. 346-350 are listed brief ceremonial directions along with the

appropriate *mantra* and accompanying verses. The latter in English only. With the *mantra*: "*Om Svabhava-shuddham Sarva-dharmah Svabhava-shuddho Ham*," dedicated to "the purity of the *Dharma* realm," the 'title' "*Sarva-dharmah*" was utilized, somewhat arbitrarily, as the title for the *mudra*. The phrase: "This is an assigned term:" is utilized for the titles or names of these *mudras*.

20 SBe, pp. 148-150. "*OM Guru* and all *Tathagatas*: lamps; the gathering swelling ocean of clouds of offerings *HUM*."

21 EDS., p. 74.

22 *Ibid* The "Esoteric *Amida* is a form of the deity *Amida* (*Amitabha*) which assumes great importance in Japan.

23 Ibid.

24 *Ibid*.

25 *Ibid*.

26 *Ibid*.

27 *Ibid*.

28 MJS, p. 9, describes this *mudra* thusly: "'Bent', 'cupped hand', a *mudra* in which the fingers are separated and turned towards the palm." She further states that this *mudra* is common to the representation of the Lord *Shiva* in the *Tandava* form ("*Chaturatandava*"). RSG, p. 63, in his description of "*Siva -- Nrittamurtis*" lists "*Chaturam*" as one of the dancing forms. In the listing of the specific iconography he notes: "Another right hand is held in the *archita* pose (with the palm open and facing the visitor)(.)" In the Plate (144) one of the right hands is indeed "with the palm open and facing the visitor" but appears identical to *abhaya mudra*.

29 See note #5, above.

30 *Ibid*.

31 *Ibid*.

32 *Ibid*.

33 *Ibid*.

34 *Ibid*.

35 *Ibid*.

36 *Ibid*.

37 As EDS notes, p. 66, in the Christian tradition the left hand would have held the 'speech.' The right hand would have been raised as if making point. In addition, one of the attitudes of prayer, during the early Christian era, was to raise both hands, shoulder level, and parallel with the shoulders, both in the 'modified' *vitarka*-like *mudra*.

38 EDS, p. 69.

39 MJS, p. 9, who illustrates this *mudra* and describes it thusly: ". . . both hands are clasped together with fingers upwards and palms touching, and held near the chest." BBh, p. 189, also gives a similar description. In several Asian cultures--notably: Indian, Myanmar and Thailand--there are 'levels' in which this salutation pose is held. They are hierarchic levels--i.e., held at chest level to a person of lesser rank, at chin level to a person of similar rank, at forehead level to a person of greater rank, and above the head to a member of royalty or when offering *puja* to a deity.

40 ERJ II, p. 23; TGR, Vol I, p. 16; BBh, p. 189.

41 This would appear identical with the *namaskara mudra*, except it is to be noted that the position of that *mudra* is lower and frequently holding a small object--e.g., a *chintamani* jewel--between the palms.

42 Although in the *adhara mudra* the thumbs are separated from the fingers and splayed outward somewhat.

43 RSG, p. 3, defines this *mudra* in a position, in relation to the body, that is noteworthy as it implies supplication rather than salutation. It is also to be noted that this *mudra* is virtually identical to one of the pose assumed by Muslims during prayer.

44 AKG, p. 20, the illustration indicated that the hands, thus held, hold an image. The act of salutation is difficult to imagine. In several Asian cultures--e.g., India, Thailand, Myanmar and Malaysia--a form of formal salutation or greeting, especially where royalty are concerned, is to bring the hands together (as in *anjali mudra* I) over the head, but the palms are not open nor are the fingers splayed.

45 EDS, p. 80.

46 MSJ, p. 10, states that this *mudra* is "similar to the *pataka*(*hasta*)-*mudra*...." Her definition of the *pataka*(*hasta*)-*mudra* would present this form of the *arala mudra*. However, if the *pataka mudra* form as described by ACG and KVa is utilized another variation (*arala mudra III*) results.

47 The description of this *mudra* in ACG indicates an obvious difference or variation from that described by MJS, particularly in the orientation of the hand.

48 RSG, p. 63, is described as "palm open and facing the visitor." See also: *anchita mudra*, and note #5.

49 RSG, p 63, describes this *mudra* thusly: "the thumb and the other fingers are held so as to resemble a bow or crescent moon."

50 ACG, pp. 29, notes a number of additional "usages" for this *mudra*.

51 ACG, p. 44, lists this *mudra* amongst a number which he introduces by saying "according to a different book . . . ." He does not describe these *mudras*, merely names them.

52 *Ibid*.

53 See note #3 above.

54 ACG, p. 28, notes a number of additional "usages" for this *mudra*.

55 See note # 19, above.

56 SBe, p. 149. "*OM Guru* and all *Tathagatas*: accept this excellent, respectful, most respectful, and great oblation *HUM SVAHA*." The offering of water, ritually has ancient roots. In general, in Asia, when a guest arrives, particularly after a journey, water for the face and hands, or even a shower is politely offered. The feet of the Christ are washed and dried by the Magdalene. In the Muslim tradition, the devotee ritually bathes his face, hands and feet before every prayer.

57 GDe, pp. 22-23.

58 See note # 19, above.

59 SBe, p. 153. "We visualize all of space filled with the precious horse; we offer it, its color delightful as a peacock's throat, adorned with gold, swift as thought, circling the earth and returning within the morning."

60 ACG, pp. 41, notes a number of additional "usages" for this *mudra*.

61 *Ibid.*, p. 42.

62 ACG, p. 42, describes the *mudra* as: "*pataka* hands are shown with grace and with (movement of) the elbows." This description does have various interpretations, but with the "usage;" the form described above was chosen.

Notes for: 'B,' pages 28-41

1 ACG, p. 50, refers to this bird in English, the author has inserted the Indic equivalent.

2 See note # 19, in 'A,' p. 14, above.

3 SBe, p. 101. 'You summon, you absorb, you bind, you dissolve.'

4 EDS notes that the hands 'may' hold the *vajra* (right hand) and the *ghanta* (left hand) which would be similar to the *vajrahumkara mudra*.

5 It is to be noted that the sexual union is part of a Tantric ritual, referred to as *panchamakara* in which one of the five elements is ritual intercourse (Ind.: *maithuna* or *yuganaddha*). This is accomplished, not for physical gratification, but in the belief that the process is edifying in as much as it allows one to draw near to and glimpse the meaning of The Absolute One.

6 See note #3, in 'A,' p. 3, above. In addition, it is indicative of one of the many parallels between the Lord Buddha and Christ Jesus, in that after forty days in the wildernessm Jesus defeated Satan.

7 BCO, p. 215, referring to the latter descriptive meaning.

8 EDS, p. 41, presents a confusing drawing. Of the twelve drawings shown on this page, 1-8 and 10-12 are drawn from the point of view of the one holding the *mudra*. The drawing of #9 is drawn from the point of view of another person, other than the one holding the *mudra*.

9 EDS, p. 102.

10 EDS, p. 40.

11 EDS, p. 102.

12 GDe, p. 80, provides the name "*bon jiki(-)in*." This *mudra* is described as the "*mudra* of food." In addition there is a reference to an identical *mudra* "(no. 193)" (p. 62) which is called"*Fugen samaya*: and described as ". . . *samaya* of *Samanthabhadra*" and "wisdom superior to all wisdoms. . . ."

13 The Lord Brahmá, the member of the Hindu trinity (*trimurti*) as opposed to The Absolute One, *Brahma* (neuter).

14 See note #51, in 'A,' p. 22, above.

15 GDe, p. 79 entitles this *mudra* "*bu bosatsu*," the "*-in*" is added by the author. In addition, this is one of four *mudras* that are dedicated to "*Bodhisattvas* of the four offerings." See note #12 in "Introduction," p. xxii, above.

16 LCS, p. 213, entitles this *mudra* simply "*Buddha-lochani*," the term "*mudra*" is added by the author.

17 BCO, p. 206, and RSG, p. 5, both depict this *mudra*, while BBh, p. 44, refers to the *Tathagata*.

18 There appears to be some confusion in BCO with regard to this *mudra*. It is drawn on p. 206 with the label: *buddhashramana mudra*, and noted on p. 215, where it is referred to as the "aesthetics Gesture of Renunciation, also called Gesture Beyond Mercy." p. 187, referring to "*Buddha Kashyapa*," this gesture is shown and referred to in the text as "*Buddha Shramana* gesture of aesthetic renunciation, also called the Great Gesture of Nirvana, the State Beyond Mercy (Tib.: *Myang-hdas-Phyag-rgya*)." Again shown in Icons #101, 113, 119 & 129 (all Buddhas of Confession); where they are described as : "gesture of resignation" (p. 138) or "gesture...of renunciation" (p. 140).

19 See note #5, in 'A,' p. 3, above.

20 The depiction of this *mudra*, GDe, p. 414, "*Mudra* (*bukuin* [sic]) of *Nosai*" which is cited in the index as "*buku-in* 414." presents a problem. As with many of the illustrations in this tome, reproductions of the original, the drawing is faulty. The left hand is properly drawn and oriented but the "right" is not. Its illustration places the thumb on the outside of the hand!

21 GDe, p. 97 entitles this *mudra* "*butsu bu sammaya*," the "*-in*" is added by the author. See note #12 in "Introduction," p. xxii, above.

22 GDe, *loc. cit.*, the other two groups, within esoteric Buddhism, are the lotus (Ind.: *padma*) group and the *vajra* group.

Notes for: 'C,' pages 42-55

1 ACG, p. 49, refers to this animal in English, the author has inserted the Indic equivalent.

2 This *mudra*, GDe p. 298, is one of the eight *mudras* of *Pratisara* and as can be seen does not relate in form the *chakra mudra I*.

3 See note # 19, in 'A,' p. 14, above.

4 SBe, p. 153, The *mantra* is not translated, however, the accompanying verse is: "We visualize all of space filled with the precious wheel; we offer it, self-created from divine gold, its round nave radiating a thousand spokes to its most excellent rim, granting victory over all the most noble."

5 LCS, p. 215 entitles this *mudra* simply "*Chakravartin*," the term "*mudra*" is added by the author.

6 ACG illustrates this *mudra* in Plate XIV-A

7 This is an unusual *mudra* in that it implies direct physical assault--a physical assault in which a weapon or object is not involved. The representation of violent aggressive intent that is to be seen in the fierce deities of both the Buddhist and Hindu traditions is not unusual. However, in the case of these fierce deities the punishment or implied aggression is accomplished with a weapon or object which is an extension of the deity. Direct person to person, physical contact is obviated by the intervening 'weapon.' Within many Asian cultures, a threatening gesture may be accepted with or without a similar response. However, in anger or with aggressive intent, the physical touching--i.e., the touching of the other person with any part of ones body--is absolutely unacceptable without an equal or more aggressive response. Not to respond in such a manner would cause extreme 'loss of face' to the person which was 'touched.' Therefore, this mudra is most unusual in its implication.

8 MJS, p. 30, normally, the term "*hasta*" is utilized as being synonymous with "*mudra*." However, TGR, pp. 14-17, separates the two terms. "*hasta*" is used to describe eight poses: "the *varada*, the *abhaya*, the *kataka*, the *suchi*, the *tarjani*, the *katyavalambita*, the *danda* and the *vismaya*" (p. 14); while "*mudra* " describes five poses: *chin-mudra, vyakhyana-mudra, sandarshana-mudra, jnana-mudra* and *yoga-mudra* (pp. 16-17). RKP, pp. 6 f, recognizes 64 *mudras* that are to be found within the visual arts (two- and three-dimensional) and 108 *mudras* within Tantric practices. Therefore, the term "*chaturahasta mudra*" appears to contain a redundancy.

9 See also: *chatura mudra*.

10 RSG, p. 63, assigns this *mudra* to the *Chaturam* form of *Shiva-Nataraja*, and describes it as: ". . . the *catura* pose (palm outwards and hollowed into a semi-circle)." But its description is completely different from the *mudra* assigned to *Shiva-Nataraja* (*Chaturatandava*) by MJS identified as "*chaturahastamudra*," p. 30. See: *chaturahasta mudra*.

11 TGR, Vol. II, part 1, p. 267, referring to the description of: *Abhinavaguptacharya*

12 ACG, pp. 26-27, notes a number of additional "usages" for this *mudra*.

13 ACG, p. 42, notes a number of additional "usages" for this *mudra*.

14 GDe, p. 103, and LCS, p. 61, both present identical *mudras*. GDe (p. 103, #342) names the *mudra* "*kongo cho-(in)*. . . wall of *vajras*," and refers to the same in the Index as "*vajravali*," p. 508. Then on p. 106, GDe presents another illustrated *mudra* (#354) also given the English title "wall of *vajras*," but the Japanese term is "*kongo mo*," and the illustration is not the same as #342, but is a variation of: "#341 *ji ketsu*." LCS names it "*Vajra*-fencing, also called *catur-dig-bandha* 'fencing the four directions against evil forces.'"

15 See note #11, in 'A,' p. 6, above

16 The drawing reproduced in EDS, p. 102, is quite confusing as it is drawn as if seen by the one holding the *mudra*, opposite to the photograph shown in the "Pictorial Index" of the same.

17 GDe, p. 93, note 1, lists the twenty-eight *nakshatras* as: *Chitra, Svati, Vishakha, Anuradha, Jyeshtha, Mula, Purvashadha, Uttarashadha, Abhijit, Shravana, Dhanishtha, Shatabisha, Purva-bhadrapada, Uttara-bhadrapada, Revati, Asvini, Bharani, Krittika, Rohini, Mrigashirsha, Ardra, Punarvasu, Pushya, Ashlesha, Magha, Purva-phalguni, Uttara-phalguni*, and *Hasta*.

18 RSG, p. 3, uses the term *vyakhyana mudra* is as synonymous with *chin mudra*. On the other hand, BBh, p. 192, uses the term *vyakhyana mudra* is as synonymous with *dharmachakra mudra*.

19 It is to be noted that this appears to be a variation of *chin mudra I*. RSG, p. 3, describes this *mudra* thusly: "the tips of the thumb and forefinger touch each other to form a circle, while the other fingers are kept open. The palm faces outwards." This would appear to be identical to the description of TGR, p.p. 16-17. However, TGR refers the reader to Pl. V, fig. 15, facing p. 14, in which the palm indeed does face "to the front," but the fingers are pointed upwards, which again is identical to the illustration in HKS, p. 271, fig. 16. These two are identical to the *vitarka mudra* described by BBh, p. 199; RSG, p. 4 and illustrated on p. 9; AKG, p. 22 and illustrated on p. 23; ERJ II, p. 23; BCO, illustrated on p. 214; and MMR, p. 391. Therefore, the author has interpreted this *mudra* thusly: "the tips of the thumb and forefinger touch each other to form a circle, while the other fingers are kept open (and face downwards). The palm faces outwards."

20 GDe, p. 69, attributes this *mudra* to *Ratnasambhava* (Jap.: *Hocho Nyorai*) whose primary symbol is the *chintamani* jewel, and names the *mudra*: "*Nan butsu* . . . Buddha of the South."

21 GDe, p. 68 entitles this *mudra* "*cho kongo renge*," the "*-in*" is added by the author. See note #12 in "Introduction," p. xxii, above.

22 KDe, p. 84 spells this *mudra*"*chormukhookham*" and on p. 107 "*chonmukhmukham*." The latter spelling is used as those photographs of pp. 79-90 indicate frequent spelling errors from the reproduced drawings on pp . 107-108.

23 See note #11, in 'A,' p. 6, above

24 *Ibid*.

25 GDe, p. 66 entitles this *mudra* "*cho zai*," the "*-in*" is added by the author. See note #12 in "Introduction," p. xxii, above.

Notes for: 'D,' pages 56-64

1 GDe, p. 33 entitles this mudra "*dai kai*," the "*-in*" is added by the author. See note #12 in "Introduction," p. xxii, above.

2 The *dai ye-to no-in* (*mudra*) is nearly identical in form to the *mushofushi-in* (*mudra*).

3 It is similar to the *karana mudra* except that in the *damaru mudra*, the *damaru* is held.

4 As representative of husband and wife, the right hand (*mriga-shirsa mudra*) signifies the male, the husband; and the left hand, closed fisted (*shikhara mudra*) represents the female, the wife.

5 LCS, p. 152 entitles this *mudra* "*Bhagavan Dharani-Avalokiteshvara*," the "*mudra*" is added by the author.

6 EDS, p. 95, illustrates this *mudra*, but entitles it "*Temborin-in* (variant)." It is, to say the least, an extremely difficult *mudra* to form and hold physically.

7 LCS, p. 125 entitles this *mudra* "*dharma-pravartana*," the "*mudra*" is added by the author. It is further to be noted that this *mudra* is quite different from the *dharmachakra-mudra*, the traditional *mudra* for 'putting the Law into motion.'

8 MJS, p. 39, in describing the "*Dhenumudra*" presents a minor problem in saying "the fingers are placed together in imitation of a cow's udder." This would seem to indicate a combined *mudra*.

9 See note # 19, in 'A,' p. 14, above.

10 SBe, p. 150-151. "*OM Guru* and all *Tathagatas*: incense; the gathering swelling ocean of clouds of offerings *HUM*."

11 The term "*dhupa mudra*" is assigned this *mudra* as LCS, p. 186, # 3,192, identifies this gesture as: "Purification by incense."

12 See note #3, in 'A,' p. 3, above.

13 See note #5, in 'A,' p. 3, above.

14 See note #11, in 'A,' p. 6, above

Notes for: 'E,' page 65

1 See note #5, in 'A,' p. 3, above.

2 *Ibid.*

3 DRN, #22. p. 36. ODD, p.279 indicates an identical pose, however, it is entitled "looking back at the city of Vaisali." OFr, indicates a similar title, however the figure holds the *lolahasta-dhyana mudra* while looking over shoulder.

4 See note #5, in 'A,' p. 3, above.

Notes for: 'F,' page 66-67

1 GDe, p. 27 entitles this *mudra* "*fu ko*," the "*-in*" is added by the author. See note #12 in "Introduction," p. xxii, above.

2 EDS, p. 42.

3 GDe, p. 80 entitles this *mudra* "*fu ku-yo*," the "*-in*" is added by the author. See note #12 in "Introduction," p. xxii, above.

4 GDe, p. 35 entitles this *mudra* "*fu tsu ku yo*," the "-*in*" is added by the author. See note #12 in "Introduction," p. xxii, above.

Notes for: 'G,' pages 68-77

1 The thumbs may or may not be folded over the little fingers

2 HKS, p. 267, lists the *gajahasta*--along with the *kataka mudra*, *katiga mudra* and the *simha-karna mudra*--as a "purely artistic positions. . . ."

3 RSG, p. 63, inadvertently poses a huge conundrum. He describes the "*gajahasta* pose" as applied to the *Lalitam* form of the Lord Shiva's *Nrittamurtis* thusly: "*gajahasta* pose, (upper arm lifted up as high as the shoulder horizontally and the fore-arm held at right angles to the upper arm [author's note: so far so good!] and facing upwards) i.e., hand stretched right across the chest towards the other shoulder[.]" "And facing upwards!"--impossible if the forearm is at "right angles to the upper arm," but probable only if the forearm is not "at right angles to the upper arm." Finally, if the forearm was facing up, then the palm of that hand would also have to be facing upwards. It is to be noted that the important *Nataraja* form which, appears above the *Lalitam* form, merely lists the "*gajahasta* attitude" for the deity's left hand.

4 Whereas the *gaja*(*hasta*) *mudra* evokes the graceful curve of an elephant's trunk commensurate with a dance movement or pose, the *danda mudra* is characterized as being straight and stiff as a staff or stick (Indic: *danda*). ERJ II, p. p. 24, is the only source who assign an iconographic interpretation--i.e., " a sign of the greatest strength and power."

5 ACG, p. 42, notes a number of additional "usages" for this *mudra*.

6 See note # 19, in 'A,' p. 14, above. SBe, p. 148, spells this term: "*gandhe*."

7 Be, pp. 150-151. "*OM Guru* and all *Tathagatas*: perfumes; the gathering swelling ocean of clouds of offerings *HUM*."

8 EDS notes a number of variations of this *mudra*.

9 According to DRN, pp. 35-38; and JBo. pp. 204-205.

10 ACG, p. 49, refers to this animal in English, the author has inserted the Indic equivalent.

11 There are two other *vajra*-type *mudras* noted: the single point *vajra* (Jap.: *dókó*) and the three-pronged *vajra* (Jap.: *san-kḍ*).

12 EDS, pp. 38-40.

13 GDe, p. 61 entitles this *mudra* "*kongo baku*," the "-*in*" is added by the author. See note #12 in "Introduction," p. xxii, above.

14 This *mudra*, with variations, appears numerous times in GDe and LCS. It is noted in GDe, p. 46 as being the fist of anger (Jap: *ge-in*; Ind.: *krodha mudra, vajramushti mudra*) when singly presented. No name appears for the combined form except an introductory title: "*Kongo rin, Kin kang loen*." Therefore, *ge-in II* is rather arbitrarily utilized in this instance.

15 *Ibid*., referring to the *ge-in III*. No name appears for the combined form except an introductory title: "*jo fudo, Chheng pu tong*."

16 *Ibid*., referring to the *ge-in IV*. No name appears for the combined form except an introductory title: "*Go-san-ze, Hiang san shi*." And further down: "This mudra is formed by the 'fist of anger. . . ."

17 GDe, p. 85 entitles this *mudra* "*ge kai*," the "-*in*" is added by the author. See note #12 in "Introduction," p. xxii, above.

18 ACG, p. 49, refers to this animal in English, the author has inserted the Indic equivalent.

19 ACG, p. 49, refers to this animal in English, the author has inserted the Indic equivalent.

20 See note #11, in 'A,' p. 6, above

21 *Ibid*.

Notes for: 'H,' pages 78-86

1 GDe refers to this *mudra* when first presented as "*haku sho*," p. 7. The designation "-*in*'" (mudra) has been added by the author. See note #12 in "Introduction," p. xxii, above. There is no other designation other than "clapping" in either GDe, LCS or MiS.

2 ACG, Plate VII-C is identified as *hamsasya*, although the tips of the thumb and index finger join, forming a circle, identical to the *vitarka mudra*.

3 ACG, p. 36, notes a number of additional "usages" for this *mudra*.

4 ACG, pp. 26-27, notes a number of additional "usages" for this *mudra*.

5 EDS, p. 213, citing *Mochizuki, Bukkyó daijiten*; and *Oda Tokuno, Bukkyó daijiten*.

6 GDe and LCS refer to this *mudra* as: "*vajranjali mudra*."

7 ACG, p. 49, refers to this animal in English, the author has inserted the Indic equivalent.

8 See note #5, in 'A,' p. 3, above.

9 See note #3, in 'A,' p. 3, above.

10 The *hastasvastika mudra* is normally held crossed at the chest. However, for want of an adequate term, it is applied to this *mudra* as well.

11 See note #5, in 'A,' p. 3, above.

12 See note #3, in 'A,' p. 3, above.

13 The *hastasvastika mudra* is normally held crossed at the chest. However, for want of an adequate term, it is applied to this *mudra* as well. It is to be noted that the difference between this form and *hastasvastika mudra II* is in the position of the feet.

14 See note #5, in 'A,' p. 3, above.

15 See note #3, in 'A,' p. 3, above.

16 See note #13, above.

17 See note # 19, in 'A,' p. 14, above.

18 In the west, the form of the left hand would be considered as an obscene gesture known as "the finger" and translated as"fuck you!"

19 SBe, p. 153, the accompanying verse is: "We visualize all of space filled with the precious elephant; we offer we offer the six-tusked white elephant, the color of the moon, who quickly circles the ocean-girt earth, the divine circumference through the path of the earth."

20 Both the *Hayagriva mudra I* and *Hayagriva mudra II* are not repeated in GDe, nor are the two to be found in LCS. There are no other identifying term regarding these two *mudras* than the association with *Hayagriva*.

21 GDe, pp. 5 & 43, identifies this *mudra* as "*hi ko*." The "-*in*" has been added by the author. It is similar and related to the *kavacha mudra*. See note #12 in "Introduction," p. xxii, above.

22 See note # 19, in 'A,' p. 14, above.

23 SBe, p. 101. 'You summon, you absorb, you bind, you dissolve.'

24 This *mudra* is similar to the *ankusha mudra*. However, the *ankusha mudra's* index finger is more, but not completely, erect.

25 See note # 19, in 'A,' p. 14, above.

26 SBe, p. 101. 'You summon, you absorb, you bind, you dissolve.'

Notes for: 'I,' page 87-88

1 GDe, pp. 461 & 475, displays this *mudra* and attributes it to *Ishvara* (p. 461) and *Vishvakarma* (475), no other names are given.

2 GDe, p. 31 entitles this *mudra* simply "*Issai ho byo do kai go*," the term "*mudra*" is added by the author.

Notes for: 'J,' pages 89-97

1 See note # 19, in 'A,' p. 14, above.

2 SBe, p. 101. 'You summon, you absorb, you bind, you dissolve.'

3 GDe, p. 67 entitles this *mudra* "*jo renge*," the "*-in*" is added by the author. See note #12 in "Introduction," p. xxii, above.

4 See note # 19, in 'A,' p. 14, above.

5 SBe, p. 349, the translation is: "*OM*, Looking down with knowledge! Great gem, gathering of splendor spreading everywhere! Burn, Burn, blazing heart *HUM*!."

6 See note #5, in 'A,' p. 3, above.

7 *Ibid.*

8 *Ibid.*

9 *Ibid.*

10 *Ibid.*

11 MMR, p. 348. This *mudra* is similar in form to the Japanese *chi ken-in* (*mudra*) .

12 GDe, p. 37 entitles this *mudra* "*jo fudo*," the "*-in*" is added by the author. Since the *mudra* consists of both hands in the *funnu ken-in*, it is an apt *mudra* for the fierce *Achala*. See note #12 in "Introduction," p. xxii, above.

13 These denotations are assigned by EDS, pp. 85.

14 EDS, pp. 86-87, notes two forms of Type B but does not separate them into Variation 1 and Variation 2. This the author has done for sake of clarity.

15 *Ibid.*

16 *Ibid.* p. 87

17 GDe, p. 105 entitles this mudra "*jo zu ma ko ku*," the "*-in*" is added by the author. Additionally, GDe indicate that "the gesture is made with the left hand, of which the index, middle and ring fingers are straightened and represent a three-pronged *vajra/sen-ko* (sic)." The illustration indicates a variation of the *san ko-in* (*mudra*) in which the index, middle and ring fingers are not straight. See note #12 in "Introduction," p. xxii, above.

18 The illustration in GDe indicates a variation on the "three-pronged *vajra mudra*," and indeed, she identifies this *mudra* as noted in the above note, but with the first knuckles of the index, middle and ring finger flexed. For any finger to bend at its first knuckle requires that initially the participant in this *mudra* be "double jointed" or at least possess extreme control.

Notes for: 'K,' pages 98-125

1 ACG, p. 48, is not entirely clear. He states "*mukula* hands interlocked, extended and fingers waved." The above description is the interpretation of the author.

2 This *mudra* resembles one of the hand positions assumed by the Muslims during their prayers. In addition, it is also the position held by certain Christian denominations when receiving the Host during Holy Communion. In both cases, however, the palms are generally held parallel with the ground.

3 GDe, p. 61 entitles this *mudra* "*kai shin*," the "*-in*" is added by the author. See note #12 in "Introduction," p. xxii, above.

4 GDe merely entitles this *mudra* "*kaji ko sui*" the (-*in*) is added by the author. See note #12 in "Introduction," p. xxii, above.

5 ACG, p. 50, refers to this bird in English, the author has inserted the Indic equivalent.

6 See note # 19, in 'A,' p. 14, above.

7 SBe, pp. 156-157, the accompanying verse is: "May there be all good fortune by offering this holy object of good fortune (which sets the seal of delight on the heart of the most noble) pleasing as a peacock's neck, her carriage haughty, flashing like lightening as she holds the golden fish."

8 The reference to sexual union and this *mudra* is most interesting. It is a sign that is seen frequently in southern European countries--notably Italy, France and Spain. It denotes the same thing, as the sign is seen to mimic the external female sexual organs--i.e., the labia. In the Mediterranean area it is used to ward off the "evil eye."

9 ACG, p. 31, notes a number of additional "usages" for this *mudra*.

10 ACG, p. 50, refers to this bird in English, the author has inserted the Indic equivalent.

11 Within the Hindu tradition this *mudra* is frequently held by : *Shiva-Nataraja, Hayagriva* and *Yama*; and within the Buddhist tradition by: *Ekajata* and *Yama*.

12 ERJ, p. 8., additionally, this *mudra* is held by numerous fierce deities in both the *Chu Fo P'u-sa Sheng Hsiang Tsan* and the *sKu-brNyan brGya-phrag-gsum*. Here the *mudra* is employed against the enemies of religion and is seen as protective to the deity's devotee.

13 BBh, p. 211, in the "Index" indicates a single entry for "*Karana mudra*" in which he states: "correctly represented in XXV, d." Referring to Plate XXV, d., one sees the *mudra* held in the third left hand pointing to the side. However the same *mudra* is depicted in LCB, the *Chu Fo P'u-sa Sheng Hsiang Tsan Pantheon* #121, 123, 140, 143, 145, etc. in which the fingers point frequently upwards. However, it is also shown with the arm and hand in a downward position, as in #40, 44, 165, etc.

14 RSG, p. 7, identifies this pose as *karana mudra*. and displays it to the left of the traditionally formed *karana mudra* on the top of the page. It is related to the Japanese *Amida-butsu seppo-in* (*mudra*) *II* in form which is a variation of the *an-i-in* (*mudra*) (Ind.: *vitarka-mudrā*), it is also similar to the

damaru mudra or the *damaruhasta* (*mudra*). RSG describes neither the *karana mudra* nor the *damaru mudra* in his list of definitions.

15 ACG, p. 39, notes a number of additional "usages" for this *mudra*.

16 LCS, p. 213 entitles this *mudra* simply "*Karma-Akashagarbha*," the term "*mudra*" is added by the author.

17 ACG, p. 28-29, notes a number of additional "usages" for this *mudra*.

18 ACG, p. 28.

19 ACG, p. 28, describes this *mudra* as: "in the same hand (*ardhapataka*), the fore-finger and little finger are outspread." He then refers to TGR "1914, p. xxxi" (reprint 1993, pp. 14-15) who describes and illustrates the *kataka-hasta*, not the *kartari-mukha*. Also, an illustration (Plate VII-D) shows the "*Kartari mukha* or *mayura* hand" which is identical to the illustration of RSG, pp. 3 & 7, identified as the "*kartari-hasta*." The *mudra* illustrated in Plate XI-C is labeled "*katar mukha* (hand of an image in Madras Museum)."

20 HKS, p. 267, lists the *kataka*--along with the *gajahasta mudra*, *katiga mudra* and the *simha-karna mudra*--as a "purely artistic positions. . . ." This would appear to indicate that there is no meaning attached to them whatsoever. However, the terms have specific references to powerful and important animals and, therefore, cannot be merely dismissed as "purely artistic." Further, the *kataka mudra* is one that finds numerous variations, some of which simply do not relate to the others in form. See: **Figures 256-261**.

21 TGR, p. 15, describes this *mudra* as: "the tips of the fingers are loosely applied to the thumb so as to form a ring. . . " but illustrates it in Plate V, fig. 7, exactly as does RSG, p. 7 (right variation). See: *kataka mudra II*.

22 ACG, p. 40, notes a number of additional "usages" for this *mudra*, but fails to indicate what they are.

23 *Ibid*. There are a number of *mudras* which are similar--e.g., *kati mudra*, *katiga mudra* and *katyavalambita mudra*. The differences from one to the other is minimal, but enough to warrant separate depiction. See: **Figures 263-265**.

24 *Ibid*. This pose depicted in RSG is held rather high and noted to rest on the "loins" which is not the hip. It is held a bit higher and towards the front and may be confused with the *katihasta-mudra* which rest on the upper hip.

25 GDe, p. 3, #2, also names this *mudra* "*hokai sho*" ("the production of the World of *Dharma*") which is first employed in the *Garbhadhatu Mandala* rite.

26 GDe, p. 27 entitles this *mudra* "*ke bosatsu*," the "*-in*" is added by the author. In addition, this *mudra* is one of the four *mudras* of offerings and dedicated to the *Bodhisattva Vajrapushpa*. See note #12 in "Introduction," p. xxii, above.

27 GDe, pp. 38-39, 41, 43, 157 and 323; and LCS pp. 97. 134 and 186 refer to this and related *mudras* as "sword." LCS, pp. 210 and 222 entitles "*khadga mudra II*" as "*khadga-mudra*." The term , therefore, is also applied to the single-hand form by the author.

28 LCS, p. 222 entitles this *mudra* "*khadga-mudra*," while GDe, p. 38 entitles it either "drawing the sword" or "putting the sword back into the sheath."

29 The description given is based upon the illustration GDe, # 213, p. 68. However, her description is at variance with the illustration: "It is made by joining the hands in the form of making a 'sword', with the upright middle fingers pressed by the index fingers." The illustration simply does not represent this description. The following illustration, #214, p. 69 is identical, as noted by GDe, but with a different name. The variant name is not unusual.

30 See note # 19, in 'A,' p. 14, above.

31 SBe, p. 153, the accompanying verse is: "We visualize all of space filled with the precious general; we offer him, a hero with the strength of god; destroying the enemy, instantly accomplishing all the aims that move the mind of a champion."

32 ACG, p.41, describes the khatva mudra as: "the thumbs and forefingers of two *Catura* hands are free." If one reads the description of the *chatura mudra*, the form of this *mudra*, the *khatva mudra*, is singularly unclear, to say the least. On the other hand at the end of the description on p. 41 is "(Cf Plate XIV B)." Plate XIV B illustrates a *mudra* which could not be derived from two *chatura mudras* and is the one described above.

33 It is to be noted that the *kartari mudra*, a Hindu *mudra*, which is similar, possesses an opposite meaning--i.e., it denotes antagonism and death. See *kartari mudra*.

34 The source indicated the left hand: EDS, p. 71.

35 *Kilaka mudra I* is as described by ACG, p. 41, however, *kilaka mudra II* is identical to ones shown in GDe and LCS.

36 The term "*ko-in*" is drawn from GDe description of the "*Hi ko*" *mudra* ("putting on the armour"), p. 5.

37 GDe, p. 35 entitles this *mudra* "*dai rin-dan*."However, on p. 75 it is called "*kongo rin*" the "*-in*" is added by the author. See note #12 in "Introduction," p. xxii, above.

38 This *mudra* is first presented in GDe, p. 17, and entitled: *ko taku*, the (-in) is added by the author. See note #12 in "Introduction," p. xxii, above.

39 ACG, p. 49, refers to this animal in English, the author has inserted the Indic equivalent.

40 EDS does not offer an Indic equivalent. The term "*krodha*" (anger) is arbitrarily given by the author as it is frequently cited and displayed.

41 LCS, p. 109, # 2.145, illustrates this *mudra* and identifies it as: "*Vajradhupa bodhisattva*." On pp. 117 & 122, # 2.180 & # 2.199, the identical *mudra* is again represented, but without any title, then on p. 124, # 2.207, the same *mudra* is identified as "*Ksanti* 'patience.'"

42 BBh, p. 198, describes this *mudra*: "The two hands are joined palm to palm with fingers all stretched, the tips of which are turned downwards. . . ." AKG, pp. 22-23; ERJ, p. 9; and RSG, pp. 3 & 8, all describe and illustrate this *mudra*, but, the position as noted in *kshepana mudra I*.

43 EDS, p. 117,

44 ACG, p. 50, refers to this bird in English, the author has inserted the Indic equivalent.

45 See note # 19, in 'A,' p. 14, above.

46 SBe, p. 156, the accompanying verse is: "May there be all good fortune by offering this holy object of good fortune (which sets the seal of delight on the heart of the most noble) by this victorious pale-green maiden, learned in amorous melody, singing her deep-throated tones as she raises the banner."

47 KDe, pp. 85 & 108, spell this *mudra* "*kurmam*." Here, the final "m" is dropped for the sake of consistency.

48 See note #11, in 'A,' p. 6, above

49 HKS, p. 267, and illustrated on p. 271 (Plate III, #9), refers to this as "placing the *kurpara* by *Siva* on the head of a bull. . . ."

50 See note #5, in 'A,' p. 3, above.

51 ACG, p. 46, in reference to *Kuvera* states; "l. h. *Padma*, r. h. *Gada*." However, *gada mudra* is not described anywhere in that work. It may, on the other hand, be a single hand (Ind.: *asamyutta*) version of the combined (Ind.: *samyutta*) form of the same name, and, therefore, would be composed of the hand fisted, thumb on the inside and middle finger extended upwards.

Notes for: 'L,' pages 126-129

1 KVa, p. 137, lists "*Kangula*," an obvious misprint since the illustration, p. 136 #8, indicates the form that both ACG and MJS describe as *Langula*.

2 ACG, pp. 26-27, notes a number of additional "usages" for this *mudra*.

3 ACG, p. 42, notes a number of additional "usages" for this *mudra*.

4 See note #11, in 'A,' p. 6, above

5 GDe, p. 76 entitles this *mudra* as "*Mula-mahamudra* of *Locana*," the term "*-mudra*" is added to the deitiey's name only by the author.

6 HKS, p. 267.

7 See note #5, in 'A,' p. 3, above.

8 *Ibid.*

9 *Ibid.*

10 *Ibid.*

11 *Ibid.*

12 ODD, p.279, and DRN, p. 36, indicate *jnana-lolahasta mudra*, however, DRN entitles "the elephant glance." OFr, indicates a similar title as ODD, however the figure's hand position differs.

Notes for: 'M,' pages 130-144

1 LCS, p. 302 entitles this *mudra* merely "*Mahakala*," the term "*mudra*" is added by the author.

2 See note #11, in 'A,' p. 6, above

3 LCS, p. 213 entitles this *mudra* simply "*Maha-sthamaprapta*," the term "*mudra*" is added by the author.

4 GDe first presents this *mudra* on p. 396 and labels it "*Mula-mudra* of *Marici*." LCS first presents this *mudra* on p. 60, # 1.16 with the title "*maha-vajra-chakra*."The term(s) "*maha-vajra-chakra*" is applied to this *mudra* during the Eighteen Rites, but is not the generic name for this *mudra*.

5 ACG, p. 43, notes a number of additional "usages" for this *mudra*.

6 See note # 19, in 'A,' p. 14, above.

7 *Ibid.*

8 SBe, pp. 168-169, the translation is: "*OM* Diamond foundation *AH HUM*," and "*OM* Diamond outline *AH HUM*."

9 See note # 19, in 'A,' p. 14, above.

10 SBe, p. 153, the accompanying verse is: "We visualize all of space filled with the precious gem; we offer the green blazing turquoise, surpassing the brilliance of the sun, its eight portions of purity fulfilling all wishes."

11 GDe, p. 33 entitles this *mudra* "*ma no cho jo*," the "-*in*" is added by the author. See note #12 in "Introduction," p. xxii, above.

12 ACG, p. 49, refers to this animal in English, the author has inserted the Indic equivalent.

13 EDS provides no illustration of this *mudra*, but it is formed: "By separating the middle three fingers of the *kenjisshin-gassho*." There is no notation as to whether this "separating" is accomplished as described in this *mudra*-form, or as described in the following *mudra*-form. GDe, p. 14, # 37, illustrates the "*mifu renge gasho*" in which only the middle and ring fingers are separated. This has been labeled here as *mifu renge-in III*.

14 EDS, p. 42. Neither the description on p. 41, nor the drawing on p. 41, indicate whether the hands are brought together, back to back (which is an extremely awkward position), or if the back of the right hand is brought around to the left of the back of the left hand, crossing at the wrists.

15 ACG, pp. 33-34, notes a number of additional "usages" for this *mudra*. However, it is interesting that this *mudra* denotes "women and fear." In that one may perceive a diminution of the status of women.

16 KDe, pp. 87 and 108, spell this *mudra* "mugdhram" and "*mugdram*." respectively. The author suspects that what is meant here is "*mudgara*" (hammer) since the *mudra* illustrated resembles the same.

17 See note #11, in 'A,' p. 6, above

18 ACG, p. 49, refers to this animal in English, the author has inserted the Indic equivalent.

19 The *mushofushi-in* (*mudra*) is a *mudra* with a complex iconography. EDS states (p. 115) that "the erect fingers (middle, ring, and little) represents the Six Original Substances; the thumbs and the indexes, the four kinds of *Mandara*, etc." In addition, he notes that this *mudra* may be known by eight different names: *ritó-in* (principal *stupa*), *hen hokkai mushofushi-in*, *mushofushi tó-in* (ubiquitous *stupa*), *dai sotoba-in* (great *stupa*), *butsubu sotoba-in* (*stupa mudra* of the Buddha section), *Biroshana-in* (*Vairochana's* main attribute is the *stupa*), *Dainichi ken-in* and *Dai etó-in*. The *stupa* predominates iconically, and, indeed, the form of the *mudra* is *stupa*-like. The main or salient characteristics of this *mudra* are to be found in the shape of the index fingers as they touch the tips of the thumbs--i.e., bending at right angles at the second phalanges--and the arching middle fingers (as well as the ring and little fingers here in *mushofushi-in I*). Therefore, the term *stupa mudra*, or *mushofushi-in* is applied to other like forms found in either LCS and GDe where there is no other identification or titlegiven.

20 The *mushofushi-in* (*mudra*) *II* is noted in GDe, p. 131, as "*Mula-mahamudra* of *Locana*, no. 2," with no reference to "*stupa*" as is seen in the *mushofushi-in* (*mudra*) *I*. See: note 19 directly above.

21 GDe, pp. 132 & 144, presents this *mudra*, but without naming it. Rather, they are labeled "*Mudra* of *Ekaksara Cakrosnisa* (*Cakravartin*)" and "*Mula-mudra* of *Mahosnisa* (*Cakrosnisa*)." Since it appears to be a variation of the "*stupa* mudra," it is placed here as a variation of the *mushofushi-in* (*mudra*). See also: GDe identical *mudras* with different names such as: pp. 145, 149, 155, 158, 160, etc. See: note 19 above.

22 In the *kataka mudra*, the thumb touches the first phalanges of the index finger only and the fingers are not tightly fisted.

23 The *reng ken-in* one of four traditional fist-forms practiced by Japanese Buddhism.

24 See note #11, in 'A,' p. 6, above

25 ACG, p. 43, notes a number of additional "usages" for this *mudra*.

26 GDe, p. 210, illustrates a *mudra* which is identical to #6, but labels this illustration "*Mudra* of the *Sadaksara-sutra, myosenden-in*."

Notes for: 'N,' pages 145-155

1 EDS, p. 40.

2 Neither GDe nor LCS entitle this *mudra*. It is therefore, given the "*II*" designation as it is a variation on the *naibaku ken-in* (*mudra*) *I* and *III*.

3 *Ibid*. It is therefore, given the "*III*" designation as it is a variation on the *naibaku ken-in* (*mudra*) *I* and *II*.

4 See note # 19, in 'A,' p. 14, above.

5 SBe, p. 151, "*OM Guru* and all *Tathagatas*: food: the gathering swelling ocean of clouds of offering *HUM*."

6 ACG, p. 44, notes a number of additional "usages" for this *mudra*.

7 It is to be noted that this form of the *namaskara mudra* differs in its placement from that indicated in *namaskara mudra II*.

8 Although the *namaskara mudra* is known within the Hindu practice--i.e., the term is applied to a specific pose, MJS, p. 98--it appears that the term *anjali mudra* is generally applied to those related *mudra*-forms within the Hindu tradition and that *namaskara mudra* is applied to those similar or parallel *mudra*-forms within the Buddhist tradition. See *anjali mudra* above.

9 GDe, p. 44 entitles this *mudra* "*kan-nin*," the "*-in*" is added by the author. See note #12 in "Introduction," p. xxii, above.

10 LCS, p. 229 entitles this *mudra* simply "*Nayasutra*," the term "*mudra*" is added by the author.

11 The *Naya-sutra mudra I* and *II* may be identical, however, the drawings in LCS, p. 226, and GDe, p. 187, are such that the variation appears to be possible.

12 EDS, p. 40.

13 MJS, p. 102, it is assumed by the author that the phrase "in front of the eyes. . . ." is to be interpreted as: the opening formed by the thumb and little finger is brought up to the eye so as it may be seen through this opening.

14 See note # 19, in 'A,' p. 14, above.

15 SBe, pp. 154-156, the accompanying verse is: "May there be all good fortune by offering this holy object of good fortune (which sets the seal of delight on the heart of the most noble) by this shapely maiden, white as clouds on the horizon, enticingly holding her hands about the flask of treasure."

16 MJS, p. 102.

17 See note #5, in 'A,' p. 3, above.

18 *Ibid*.

19 See note #11, in 'A,' p. 6, above

20 ACG, p. 43, notes a number of additional "usages" for this *mudra*.

21 ACG, p. 42, notes a number of additional "usages" for this *mudra*.

22 ACG, *loc. cit.*, describes this *mudra* as: "*pataka* hands face upwards, turned over, (extended from) the shoulders to the buttocks." It is perceived that this description is the same as that noted above.

23 EDS, p. 102.

24 GDe, p. 79 entitles this *mudra* "*bu bosatsu*," and dedicates the *mudra* to the *Bodhisattva* of dance, *Vajranritya*.

25 Ibid., p. 28 entitles this *mudra* "*nyorai getsu*," the "-*in*" is added by the author. See note #12 in "Introduction," p. xxii, above.

26 *Ibid.*, p. 26 entitles this *mudra "nyorai hosso,"* the "-*in*" is added by the author. See note #12 in "Introduction," p. xxii, above.

27 *Ibid.*, p. 26 entitles this *mudra "nyorai saku,"* the "-*in*" is added by the author. See note #12 in "Introduction," p. xxii, above.

28 *Ibid.*, p. 26, states that this *mudra* is "a symbol of 'great compassion (*mahakaruna*) of *Buddha*.'"

29 *Ibid.*, p. 26 entitles this *mudra "nyorai shin,"* the "-*in*" is added by the author. See note #12 in "Introduction," p. xxii, above.

30 *Ibid.*, p. 27 entitles this *mudra "nyorai zo,"* the "-*in*" is added by the author. See note #12 in "Introduction," p. xxii, above.

Notes for: 'O,' page 156-157

1 EDS, p. 41.

Notes for: 'P,' pages 158-188

1 ACG, pp. 26-27, notes a number of additional "usages" for this *mudra*.

2 See note # 19, in 'A,' p. 14, above.

3 SBe, p. 156, the accompanying verse is: "May there be all good fortune by offering this holy object of good fortune (which sets the seal of delight on the heart of the most noble) by this sixteen-year-old maiden, blazing with azure-blue light, coquettishly holding the precious hundred-petaled lotus."

4 See note # 19, in 'A,' p. 14, above.

5 SBe, p. 149, "*OM Guru* and all *Tathagatas*: accept this great water for your feet. *HUM SVAHA*."

6 ACG, p. 42, notes a number of additional "usages" for this *mudra*.

7 See note #11, in 'A,' p. 6, above

8 GDe, p. 156 entitles this mudra "*Samaya-mudra* of *Pancha-guhya*," LCS, p. 246 entitles this mudra "*Samaya-mudra*."

9 See note #11, in 'A,' p. 6, above

10 See note #3, in 'A,' p. 3, above.

11 *Ibid.*

12 See note #3, in 'A,' p. 3, above. ODD, p. 679, #35 indicates the "walking" or "setting out to preach" posture, which is opposite in the *mudras* held by the hands from DRN, pp. 35-38; and JBo. pp. 204-205.

13 DRN., #14. p. 36.

14 OFr, p. 23, describes the situation as: "And then receiving the water in the almsbowl (20)." Facing this page, he presents position #20 which is different from that depicted in ODD, pp. 678-679 and described in JBo, p. 205, as well as DRN, p. 36.

15 According to DRN, pp. 35-38; and JBo. pp. 204-205.

16 *Ibid.*

17 DRN., #37. p. 37.

18 According to DRN, pp. 35-38; and JBo. pp. 204-205. OFr #8 depicts this mudra and refers to it as "dissuading *Mara*."

19 According to DRN, pp. 35-38; and JBo. pp. 204-205.

20 See note #3, in 'A,' p. 3, above This *mudra* is illustrated in ODD. p. 679 and OFr #26. It is in essence opposite to the *ahayavarada mudra*, in that the action is similar--i.e., the hand moves outward and then inward with emphasis on the outward movement--indicating the desire for the person to move away as noted in DRN, p. 37.

21 DRN, p. 37, describes this position as: "sitting with folded legs, the left hand on the knee and the right hand hanging at the level of the legs in a gesture of signaling someone to go away."

22 According to DRN, pp. 35-38; and JBo. pp. 204-205. See note #3, in 'A,' p. 3, above.

23 OFr does not indicate this position.

24 See note #3, in 'A,' p. 3, above.

25 According to DRN, pp. 35-38; and JBo. pp. 204-205. Although there are a number of standing *asanas*--e.g., ODD #s: 8, 11, 12, 21, 24, 27, 28, 31-35, 37, 39-44, 47. 49 50 & 52; OFr #s:4, 6, 7, 13, 17, 18, 21, 22, 27, 28 & 32--only ODD #34 is entitled as "standing *mudra*."

26 See note #3, in 'A,' p. 3, above.

27 DRN., #29. p. 37.

28 See note #3, in 'A,' p. 3, above.

29 *Ibid.*

30 ODD, p. 679, # 52.

31 See note #3, in 'A,' p. 3, above.

32 *Ibid.*

33 *Ibid.*

34 *Ibid.*

35 This, as well as a number of Thai *mudras*, possess titles which are lengthy in their description. The same is true of some of the more arcane Japanese *mudras*, as well. The title/terms of the "traditional" *mudras* are rather concise and, for the most part, abbreviated. The addition of new *mudras* to the various traditions generally demands longer descriptive titles.

36 See note #3, in 'A,' p. 3, above.

37 The *hastasvastika mudra* is normally held crossed at the chest. However, for want of an adequate term, it is applied to this *mudra* as well. It is to be noted that the difference between this form and *hastasvastika mudra II* and *III* is in the position of the feet.

38 See note #3, in 'A,' p. 3, above.
39 *Ibid.*
40 DRN., #6. p. 35, KIM. p. 5.
41 See note #3, in 'A,' p. 3, above.
42 DRN., #18. p. 36.
43 According to DRN, pp. 35-38; JBo. pp. 204-205; and ODD, p. 679, # 26. OFr, # 24 depicts this incident, but the *mudra* is different. He is shown seated in the European manner with his hands resting palm downward on his knees.
44 DRN., #18. p. 36.
45 OFr, p. 27, #24, indicates a *mudra* which is different from that described by DRN, pp. 35-38, JBo. pp. 204-205, and ODD, p. 679, # 26.
46 See note #3, in 'A,' p. 3, above.
47 See note #5, in 'A,' p. 3, above.
48 *Ibid.*
49 DRN., #13. p. 36; ODD, pp. 679-677 entitles this incident as "reflecting on world impermanency" and illustrates this pose in #44. OFr, p. 25, illus. #22 refers to removing "the shroud of the slave girl" and "pointing out analytical meditation arising from it." JBo, p. 204, names this pose as "contemplating the corpse (of the dead slave girl." DRN, JBo, OFr, and ODD all refer to the same story, varying the title and also the form.
50 See note #3, in 'A,' p. 3, above.
51 ODD, p. 679, # 35 which is identical to an illustration in JBo, p. 55, #38, entitled "Votive Tablet (*Pra Pim*)." However, DRN, #11. p. 36, and JBo, p. 204, # 11, indicate an opposite position for the hands, describing this posture as "the left hand hanging downward, the right raised in front of the breast." OFr, p. 20, indicates a similar posture to DRN and JBo, but names it "walking to *Kapilavatthu*."
52 *Ibid.*
53 *Ibid.*
54 DRN, #11. p. 36, and JBo, p. 204, # 11, indicate a position for the hands, describing this posture as "the left hand hanging downward, the right raised in front of the breast." OFr, p. 20, indicates a similar posture to DRN and JBo, but names it "walking to *Kapilavatthu*." ODD, p. 679, # 35 is opposite in the position of the hands.
55 See note #3, in 'A,' p. 3, above.
56 *Ibid.* According to DRN, pp. 35-38; and JBo. pp. 204-205.
57 See note #5, in 'A,' p. 3, above.
58 According to DRN, pp. 35-38; and JBo. pp. 204-205.
59 *Ibid.*, #35. p. 376.
60 See note #3, in 'A,' p. 3, above.
61 *Ibid.*
62 According to DRN, pp. 35-38; and JBo. pp. 204-205.
63 See note #5, in 'A,' p. 3, above.
64 *Ibid.*
65 See note #3, in 'A,' p. 3, above.
66 *Ibid.*
67 *Ibid.*
68 The *hastasvastika mudra* is normally held crossed at the chest. However, for want of an adequate term, it is applied to this *mudra* as well.
69 According to DRN, pp. 35-38; and JBo. pp. 204-205.
70 *Ibid.*
71 *Ibid.*
72 See note #3, in 'A,' p. 3, above.
73 See note #11, in 'A,' p. 6, above.
74 ACG, pp. 26-27, notes a number of additional "usages" for this *mudra*.
75 It is to be noted that the same form is called *abhaya-mudra* when associated with a deity as noted by: AKG, p. 20, BBh, p. 189, MJS, p. 1, RSG, p. 3, TGR, pp. 14-15, and HKS, p. 266. ACG, p. 29, equates the *pataka mudra* with the *abhaya mudra*; Plate VII-E, describes "Hands of a Dancing *Siva*, r.h. *Ardha-chandra* (for *pataka*), making *Abhaya mudra*." See: *abhaya mudra I.*
76 This description is at variance with ACG, pp. 26-27. See: *pataka-mudra I.*
77 See note #5, in 'A,' p. 3, above.
78 This *mudra* appears at various places within LCS (1.40, 3.70, 3.177, 3.222, 4,16) as well as GDe, pp. 15, 24, 122, 176 & 392). Both identify this *mudra* as "*patra*" (GDe p. 15; LCS 3.70). LCS 1.40 & 3.222 also states that in the "Eighteen Rites" an the "*Garbhadhatu Mandala*" is is called "*akshata*" as well..
79 It is obvious by the name that this *mudras* is a corollary to the asana known as *pralambapada*.
80 See note #11, in 'A,' p. 6, above.
81 See note # 19, in 'A,' p. 14, above.
82 SBe, p. 153, the accompanying verse is: "We visualize all of space filled with the precious minister; we offer him, his mind, his mind like a dagger, wise and prudent, guiding to all desires with his hidden store of subtlety, whose words must be heeded, having the eyes of a god."
83 GDe, p. 27 This *mudra* is one of the four *mudras* of offerings and dedicated to the *Bodhisattva Vajrapushpa*.
84 ACG, p. 40, notes a number of additional "usages" for this *mudra*.
85 See note # 19, in 'A,' p. 14, above.
86 SBe, p. 150, "*OM Guru* and all *Tathagatas*: flowers; the gathering swelling ocean of clouds of offerings *HUM*."

Notes for: 'R,' pages 189-196

1 The drawings in LCS, # 4.183, 4.186 and 4.187, pp.

261-261, are not entirely clear, as are a number of drawings in this tome.

2 This *mudra* is a variation on the *mushofushi-in* (*mudra*) (Ind.: *stupa mudra*). and is named "*Ratna-kalasa-mudra*," LCS, p. 254, # 4.159.

3 LCS, p. 247 entitles this *mudra* simply "*Ratnaprabha-Akashagarbha*," the term "*mudra*" is added by the author.

4 *Ibid*., p. 62, this *mudra* appears only in this rite and this volume.

5 GDe, p. 64 entitles this *mudra* "*renge-bu shu*," the "-in" is added by the author. See note #12 in "Introduction," p. xxii, above.

6 *Ibid*., p. 68 entitles this *mudra* "*ren renge*," the "-in" is added by the author. See note #12 in "Introduction," p. xxii, above.

7 ACG, p. 49, refers to this animal in English, the author has inserted the Indic equivalent.

Notes for: 'S,' pages 197-233

1 GDe, p. 215 entitles this *mudra* "*Mula-mudra* of *Sahasra-bhuja Avalokiteshvara mudra*."

2 GDe, p. 44, notes that this *mudra* symbolizes the Buddha's "victory over the demons." A symbolic meaning that is generally attributed to the *bhumisparsha mudra*.

3 GDe, p. 66 entitles this mudra "sai zai," the "-in" is added by the author. See note #12 in "Introduction," p. xxii, above.

4 See note # 19, in 'A,' p. 14, above.

5 SBe, p. 350, the translation is: "Homage to all the Buddhas! By the blazing light of the master over the evil spirits, a great assembly. *SVAHA*."

6 ACG, pp. 37, notes a number of additional "usages" for this *mudra*.

7 *Ibid*.

8 It is to be noted that EDS, p. 40, displays the *sanfuta gassho* (*mudra*) and equates it with the Indic *samputa mudra*. However, the form is considerably different.

9 See note #11, in 'A,' p. 6, above.

10 The illustration from KDe, p. 80. indicates that the fingers are not parallel to the ground, but point upwards about 15°.

11 EDS, p. 40.

12 ACG, p. 49, refers to this animal in English, the author has inserted the Indic equivalent.

13 GDe, p. 10, identifies this *mudra* by the Japanese title only, and further identifies it with the three-pronged *vajra* (*sanko*).

14 *Ibid*., p. 68 entitles this *mudra* "*sanko*," the "-in" is added by the author. See note #12 in "Introduction," p. xxii, above.

15 *Ibid*., p. 67 entitles this *mudra* "*sanko*," the "-in" is added by the author. See note #12 in "Introduction," p. xxii, above.

16 RSG, p. 3. Just what is meant is uncertain. None of the other sources mention this *mudra*.

17 ACG, p. 50, refers to this bird in English, the author has inserted the Indic equivalent.

18 TGR, Vol. II, part 1, pp. 289-290, identifies this *mudra* as it is applied to the deity *Vinadhara-Dakshinamurti*.

19 ACG, p. 33, notes a number of additional "usages" for this *mudra*.

20 See note # 19, in 'A,' p. 14, above.

21 SBe, p. 218

22 *Ibid*., p. 218, "Homage to all *Buddhas* and *Bodhisattvas*, and to their indestructible doctrine! O Blessed One!Great being seen by all the *Buddhas*! Do not hesitate, do not hesitate! Take! take this *torma*! *HUM HUM JA JA* Moving about everywhere *SVAHA*."

23 See note # 19, in 'A,' p. 14, above.

24 SBe, p. 346, the accompanying verse is: "From the white syllable 'A' of the gesture whose essence is the blessed *Shakyamuni* light radiated forth, cleansing the substance of the *torma* of the stain of holding it to be real: it becomes empty."

25 See note # 19, in 'A,' p. 14, above.

26 SBe, p. 348, the accompanying verse is: "Then from the yellow syllable '*TRAM*' of the gesture whose essence is the blessed *Ratnasambhava* light radiates forth, making the substance of the *torma* the five sense gratifications according to each one's desire."

27 See note # 19, in 'A,' p. 14, above.

28 SBe, p. 348, the accompanying verse is: "From the blue syllable '*KHAM*' of the gesture whose essence is the blessed *Vairochana* light radiates forth, making the substance of the *torma* an inexhaustible treasury pervading all the realms of space."

29 See note # 19, in 'A,' p. 14, above.

30 SBe, p. 151, "*OM Guru* and all *Tathagatas*: music: the gathering swelling ocean of clouds of offering *HUM*."

31 See note #11, in 'A,' p. 6, above

32 It is to be noted that this *mudra* is substantially different from the *shakatam mudra* noted by KDe. Further, ACG does not indicate the position of the hands.

33 LCS, p. 275 entitles this *mudra* simply "*Shakra*," the term "(*mudra*)" is added by the author.

34 LCS, p. 213 entitles this *mudra* simply "*Shakyamuni*," the term "(*mudra*)" is added by the author.

35 See note #11, in 'A,' p. 6, above

36 See note # 19, in 'A,' p. 14, above.

37 SBe, pp. 156-157, the accompanying verse is: "May there be all good fortune by offering this holy object of good fortune (which sets the seal of delight on the heart of the most noble) by this glorious maiden, the color of stainless emerald, seductively grasping the right-handed conch shell."

38 See note #11, in 'A,' p. 6, above
39 MJS, pp. 1 & 124.
40 ACG, p. 49, refers to this animal in English, the author has inserted the Indic equivalent.
41 See note #5, in 'A,' p. 3, above.
42 ACG, pp. 30-31, notes a number of additional "usages" for this *mudra*.
43 GDe, p. 105 entitles this *mudra* "*sho cha ro*," the "-in" is added by the author. Further, it is noted in GDe that this is a variation of the so *cha ro-in* (*mudra*). See note #12 in "Introduction," p. xxii, above.
44 See note # 19, in 'A,' p. 14, above.
45 SBe, p. 154, the accompanying verse is: "May there be all good fortune by offering this holy object of good fortune (which sets the seal of delight on the heart of the most noble) by this beautiful maiden, white as a conch shell, moonlight, proudly bearing aloft the glorious coiled knot."
46 ACG, p. 50, refers to this bird in English, the author has inserted the Indic equivalent.
47 The term *shuka* refers to a parrot and is associated with *Shri Kanchi Kamakshi* as well as the animal which draws *Kama's* chariot.
48 KDe, p. 51, spells this *mudra* as "*shoonya*."
49 ACG, p. 49, refers to this animal in English, the author has inserted the Indic equivalent.
50 There are a number of illustrations in LCS which represent ostensibly the same *mudra*, but none give the same title--i.e., *sima-bandha mudra*--if any: LCS, pp. 88,105, 106 and 137.
51 It is of interest to note that LCS, p. 61, offers as an alternative to *vajra-bandha*, the title *sima-bandha*. However, on p., the same title, *sima-bandha*, is given to a completely different form--i.e., *sima-bandha I*, as noted above.
52 ACG, p. 49, refers to this animal in English, the author has inserted the Indic equivalent.
53 HKS, p. 267, and illustrated on p. 269 (Plate I, #1), groups this mudra with the *kataka mudra* as being "purely artistic. . . ." This is somewhat erroneous since every *mudra* represents some thing or state.
54 HKS, p. 267, lists the *simhakarna mudra*--along with the *kataka mudra, katiga mudra* and the *gajahasta mudra*--as a "purely artistic positions. . . ."
55 See note #5, in 'A,' p. 3, above.
56 ACG, pp. 26-27, notes a number of additional "usages" for this *mudra*.
57 This *mudra* is identical to the *abhaya mudra III*. However in the *mudra III*, the figure is standing and in this *mudra* the figure is seated. In addition, KDe, p.86, spells this *mudra* "*shinghakrnt*," while on pp. 53 and 108 it is spelled: *singhakrant*."
58 See note #11, in 'A,' p. 6, above.
59 See note # 19, in 'A,' p. 14, above.
60 SBe, p. 156, the accompanying verse is: "May there be all good fortune by offering this holy object of good fortune (which sets the seal of delight on the heart of the most noble) by this long-eyed maiden, the color of powdered vermilion, shooting the arrow of her glance as she twirls the pearl umbrella."
61 ACG, pp. 34-35, notes a number of additional "usages" for this *mudra*.
62 See note # 19, in 'A,' p. 14, above.
63 SBe, p. 153, the accompanying verse is: "We visualize all of space filled with the precious queen; we offer her, as beautiful as an immortal maiden, delighting body and mind with her most excellent touch, bestowing the perfume of her skill, knowledge and eloquence."
64 BBh, p. 197. This description is rather confusing and as it is described, it appears to resemble the *mukula mudra*.
65 ACG, p. 32, notes a number of additional "usages" for this *mudra*.
66 This form of the *suchi mudra* resembles in no way the other three *suchi mudras* noted above. In addition the same form is noted in GDe as: "banner" (*dhvaja*) p. 62, and "food, *naivedya*" p. 80.
67 ACG, p. 43, notes a number of additional "usages" for this *mudra*.
68 The "summoning of sins" (*mudra*), LCS, p. 84, # 2.46, contains no other information than the English title. It is represented nowhere else in that study nor in GDe.
69 See note #11, in 'A,' p. 6, above
70 See note # 19, in 'A,' p. 14, above.
71 See note #11, in 'A,' p. 6, above
72 See note # 19, in 'A,' p. 14, above.
73 SBe, p. 155, the accompanying verse is: "May there be all good fortune by offering this holy object of good fortune (which sets the seal of delight on the heart of the most noble) by this slender bodied maiden, blazing with terrible jasmine light, gracefully carrying the golden wheel."
74 This *mudra*, as seen, presents a number of different hand and finger positions.
75 TGR, Vol 2, part 1, pp. 259-260 describes the elements of the *mudra* but does not indicate the placement of the hands in relation to the body except to say that the right hand should be kept near the navel.
76 ACG, p. 40, notes a number of additional "usages" for this *mudra*.
77 Ibid. Whether or not the hands are formed as indicated in the Figure 575, or "crossed" at the wrist is not clear.

Notes for: 'T,' pages 234-243

1 ACG, p. 42, notes a number of additional "usages" for this *mudra*.

2 *Ibid.*, p. 38, notes a number of additional "usages" for this *mudra.*

3 *Ibid.*

4 The sources which deal exclusively with Buddhist iconography indicate a horizontal direction for the *mudra*, whereas, those which deal exclusively with Hindu iconography indicate a vertical direction. The exception is: RSG, who treats both traditions and illustrates the 'Buddhist" horizontal direction, p. 8, although in his description he does not indicate direction, pp. 3-4; and BBh, p. 197, who appears to describe the vertical position.

5 See note #5, in 'A,' p. 3, above.

6 LCS, p. 84, #2.47, presents the identical *mudra* and merely entitles it "2.47 Breaking sins."

7 EDS, p. 42.

8 LCS, p. 112, #2.159, exhibits the mudra and states "*Vajratejas bodhisattva Karma-mandala Tejas-bodhisattva-mudra.*" Therefore, the above name is attached.

9 See note #5, in 'A,' p. 3, above.

10 See note # 19, in 'A,' p. 14, above.

11 AKG, p. 20, and refers to the victory (Ind.: *vijaya*) over the three worlds (Ind.: *triloka* aka *trilokya*).

12 BCO, p. 217.

13 See note #11, in 'A,' p. 6, above

14 ACG, pp. 27-28, notes a number of additional "usages" for this *mudra.*

15 RSG, p. 63.

16 MJS, p. 145.

17 BBh, pp. 147-148, describes the deity *Paramashva* who holds the tripitaka mudra; however, the illustration of this deity, Plate XXXIX, d., does not correspond with the description given by RSG, p. 63, as described in *tripitaka mudra I.*

18 This *mudra* is used in a number of other combined *mudras* with different titles--e.g., the *ko taku(-in)* (*mudra*).

Notes for: 'U,' pages 244-248

1 ACG, p. 41, indicates two *mudras* with the name "*Avahittha.*" The first is referred to Plate XI E which is entitled: "*udveshtitalapadma mudra.*" Therefore, the first "*Avahittha*" is perceived to be a misprint and is, indeed. "*udveshtitalapadma mudra.*"

2 *Ibid.*, p. 43, notes a number of additional "usages" for this *mudra.*

3 *Ibid.*, p. 50, refers to this bird in English, the author has inserted the Indic equivalent.

4 See note # 19, in 'A,' p. 14, above.

5 SBe, p. 152, the accompanying verse is: "We visualize all of space filled with with soft bedding, with turquoise knives, with soft hides, with pleasing garments for the joyful forests, with strong boots, with divine dwellings."

6 LCS, p. 171 entitles this *mudra* merely "*Upaya-paramita,*" the "*mudra*" is added by the author.

7 ACG, p. 38, notes a number of additional "usages" for this *mudra.*

8 *Ibid.*, p. 49, refers to this animal in English, the author has inserted the Indic equivalent.

9 *Ibid.*, p. 40, notes a number of additional "usages" for this *mudra.*

10 ERJ, p. 9.

Notes for: 'V,' pages 249-279

1 The *vajra mudra* presents a real conundrum. There are a number of different forms within Japanese iconography which refer to the *vajra*--e.g., *kongo* = *vajra, doko* = one point *vajra, goko* = five point *vajra* and *sanko* = three point *vajra.* EDS, p. 102, equates the *vajra mudra* with the *chi ken-in* (fist) which is nearly identical to the *tathagata* fist (Jap.: *nyorai ken-in*). He also parallels the *chi ken-in* (fist) with the *jnana mudra.* This *mudra*, GDe, p. 294, is related in form to the "exterior five-pronged vajra" (pp. 163, 206, etc.), the "inward five-pronged *vajra*" and the "exterior three-pronged *vajra*" (p. 359).

2 The term *vajra mudra* is applied to a number of different *mudra* in both LCS, p. 58, and GDe, p. 67, with differentiating their Sanskrit equivalents.

3 LCS, p. 247 entitles this *mudra* simply "*Vajra-Akashagarbha,*" the term "(*mudra*)" is added by the author.

4 See note # 19, in 'A,' p. 14, above.

5 SBe, pp. 159-164, "*OM AH* Lady of the diamond lamps *HUM.*"

6 See note # 19, in 'A,' p. 14, above.

7 SBe, p. 349, the accompanying verse is: "From the red syllable *'HRIH'* of the gesture whose essence is the blessed swirling nectar light radiates forth, making the substance of the *torma* the essence of the great nectar of knowledge."

8 LCS, p. 61, identifies this *mudra* as: "*vajra-bandha,* also called *sima-bandha.*" GDe, p. 103, calls it "*Ji ketsu, Ti kie,* consolidation of the ground" and equates this *mudra* with "the *mudra* of three-pronged *vajra / san-ko.*"

9 In the Japanese Buddhist (*Vajrayana, Mantrayana*) tradition the *vajranjali mudra* appears most important. In LCS and GDe the *vajranjali mudra* is by far the most prominent, appearing in LCS 59 times, and in GDe 51 times.

10 See note # 19, in 'A,' p. 14, above.

11 SBe, pp. 159-164, "*OM AH* Lady of the diamond vision *HUM.*"

12 See note # 19, in 'A,' p. 14, above.

13 SBe, *loc. cit.*, "*OM AH* Lady of the diamond mental events *HUM*."

14 See note # 19, in 'A,' p. 14, above.

15 SBe, *loc. cit.*, "*OM AH* Lady of the diamond incense *HUM*."

16 See note # 19, in 'A,' p. 14, above.

17 SBe, *loc. cit.*, "*OM AH* Lady of the diamond perfume *HUM*."

18 GDe, p. 83, does not specifically name this *mudra*. However, she does state: "*Bodhisattva* of Dance, *Vajragita*."

19 See note # 19, in 'A,' p. 14, above.

20 SBe, *loc. cit.*, "*OM AH* Lady of the diamond song *HUM*."

21 See note # 16 above.

22 SBe, *loc. cit.*, "*OM AH* Lady of the diamond laughter *HUM*."

23 LCS, p. 104, # 2.126, identifies this *mudra* as "*Vajrahetu bodhisattva*" only.

24 GDe, p. 91-92 entitles this *mudra* "*kongo-karuma bosatsu-in*" also called "*mudra* of *Bodhisattva Vajrakarma*." Its major variation from the *Vajrahumkara mudra I* is that this *mudra* does not possess either the *vajra* or *ghanta*.

25 See note # 19, in 'A,' p. 14, above.

26 This *mudra* resembles one of the positions assumed by Muslims during prayer.

27 SBe, pp. 159-164, "*OM AH* Lady of the diamond mime *HUM*."

28 See note # 19, in 'A,' p. 14, above.

29 *Ibid*.

30 SBe, *loc. cit.*, "*OM AH* Lady of the diamond drum *HUM*."

31 See note # 19, in 'A,' p. 14, above.

32 SBe, *loc. cit.*, "*OM AH* Lady of the diamond tabor *HUM*."

33 There appears to be some confusion with regards to thus *mudra*. GDe, p. 3, #1, the gesture is referred to as "fist of the lotus," while on p. 8, #16, the identical *mudra* is referred to as "the *vajra-fist* (*vajra-musti*, no.1)." Then, on p. 24, # 69, the clearly displayed *renge ken-in* (lotus fist) is referred to as "*vajra*-fist/*vajra-musti* (no. 16)." However, it is correctly labeled on p. 61, #188. LCS first displays this *mudra* as a combined form, p. 78. # 2,21 (unnamed), two combined *mudras* are names "*Vajramusti bodhisattva*" (p. 107, #2.133 & p. 115, #2.169) but neither display the *vajra-mushti*, rather they indicate the *renge ken-in*, and on p. 157, #3.77, a variation on the *naibaku ken-in* is called "*vajramusti*."

34 GDe first presents this *mudra* on p. 75, # 244 and labels it "*Kai mon*, opening the gates." The term(s) "*kai mon*" is applied to this *mudra* during the *Vajradhatu* rites, but is not the generic name for this *mudra*.

35 See note # 19, in 'A,' p. 14, above.

36 SBe, *loc. cit.*, "*OM AH* Lady of the diamond dance *HUM*."

37 See note # 19, in 'A,' p. 14, above.

38 SBe, *loc. cit.*, "*OM AH* Lady of the diamond flowers *HUM*."

39 See note # 19, in 'A,' p. 14, above.

40 SBe, *loc. cit.*, "*OM AH* Lady of the diamond taste *HUM*."

41 LCS, p. 111 entitles this *mudra* "*Vajrasattva bodhisattva*," the "*mudra*" is added by the author.

42 LCS, p. 202, refers to this *mudra* as: "Inner-bound-3 pronged-*vajra*-mudra."

43 See note # 19, in 'A,' p. 14, above.

44 SBe, *loc. cit.*, "*OM AH* Lady of the diamond touch *HUM*."

45 See note # 19, in 'A,' p. 14, above.

46 SBe, *loc. cit.*, "*OM AH* Lady of the diamond flute *HUM*."

47 See note # 19, in 'A,' p. 14, above.

48 SBe, *loc. cit.*, "*OM AH* Lady of the diamond lute *HUM*."

49 ACG, p. 49, refers to this animal in English, the author has inserted the Indic equivalent.

50 MJS, p. 153, also states that this is similar to the *anjali-mudra* and can be held with both hands.

51 *Ibid*., states that it is held only in the left hand.

52 See note #5, in 'A,' p. 3, above.

53 *Ibid*.

54 ACG, p. 41, states: "hands one upon the other (back to back), the thumbs and little fingers link." There is another possible variation, as noted in *Varaha mudra II*.

55 ACG, p. 41, the verbal description is such that this variation is a possibility.

56 ACG, p. 49, refers to this animal in English, the author has inserted the Indic equivalent.

57 As with virtually all the *Gayatri mudra* noted in KDe, pp. 79-90 and 107-108, there are numerous spelling transitions and differences. Here, *varahkam mudra* is spelled "*varhakam*," p. 86, and "*varahkam*," p. 108. In addition, the poses are reversed between the two and noted here as *varahkam mudra I* and *varahkam mudra II*.

58 See note #11, in 'A,' p. 6, above

59 *Ibid*.

60 KVa, p. 136, illus. 33, presents a real conundrum. The photo indicates the mudra being held in the left hand as the upper arm and part of the shoulder is visible. However, the hand has been rotated 180°, a physically impossible position!

61 GDe, p. 446, describes this *mudra* as: "*Mudra* of *Varsa* (rains) as a *Bodhisattva*." It is virtually identical, except for the separation of the hands to the *abhaya mudra III*.

62 The term "*vayu mudra*" is not found in GDe for this *mudra* (see: p. 4, #5, or on pp. 234, 235 & 308); neither is it so named in LCS (see: p. 241, #4.109 or p. 258, #4.177). However, the *mudra's* principle differentiation is the hooking of the index--i.e., the "wind (*vayu*)" fingers and such is noted by GDe, p. 4.

63 This *mudra* is specifically dedicated to the deity *Vayu*.

64 See note #11, in 'A,' p. 6, above.

65 ACG, p. 49, refers to this animal in English, the author has inserted the Indic equivalent.

66 See note #11, in 'A,' p. 6, above.

67 LCS represents this *mudra* in a number of locations--e.g., # 2.76, # 2.77, # 2.78, # 2.93;# 2.94; # 2.95, # 2.78, # 2.147, # 2.148 and # 2.149--however, in all cases the drawings are so poorly executed that a precise description is impossible. Therefore, this description is somewhat conjectural.

68 See note # 16 above.

69 SBe, p. 338.

70 LCS, p. 213 entitles this *mudra* simply "*Vinayaka,*" the term "(*mudra*)" is added by the author.

71 See note #11, in 'A,' p. 6, above

72 *Ibid.*

73 ACG, p. 49, refers to this animal in English, the author has inserted the Indic equivalent.

74 The confusion between the variant meanings (forms) of *vyakhyana mudra* is a conundrum. BBh and BCO both Buddhist iconographers see it as representing *dharmachakra mudra* (*vyakhyana mudra I*). AKG does not make this distinction. TGR and MJS who deal with Hindu iconography ascribe the term *vyakhyana mudra* as an alternative to chin *mudra* (*vyakhyana mudra II*), but EDS who deals with Japanese Buddhist iconography (*mudras*) equates it with *vitarka mudra* (*vyakhyana mudra III*).

75 HKS, p. 79.

Notes for: 'W,' page 280

1 JBo, illus. 124, pp. 165, indicates the right hand in the *abhaya mudra* and the left in the *lolahasta mudra*. OFr, p.20 & illus 21, indicates an image described as "Walking to *Kapilavatthu*." It is similar to the JBo, illus. 124, except the hand appears to be in the *jnana mudra*.

2 JBo, illus. 93, pp. 132, indicates the left hand in the *vitarka mudra*, while the right hand is in the *lolahasta mudra*.

Notes for: 'Y,' pages 281-284

1 LCS, p. 271 entitles this *mudra* simply "*Yama*," the term "*mudra*" is added by the author.

2 The two drawings, LCS, # 4.223 and 4.242, pp. 271 & 276, are so drawn that the position of the little finger is not entirely clear.

3 See note #11, in 'A,' p. 6, above

4 GDe, p. 92, displays a *mudra* entitled "*yo-cho jo-in*" and defines it as "*mudra* of invitation to the astral bodies." This *mudra* is identical to the "*ratna-ghata mudra*" displayed and named on p. 141.

5 MJS, p. 170, whether this *mudra* is held in one hand or two hands is not clear. However, the author feels that to hold this *mudra* in one hand and to form a triangle with the fingers is virtually impossible. Therefore, the illustration indicates that the *mudra* is held with two hands, forming a downward pointing triangle, a *yoni trikona*.

6 See note #11, in 'A,' p. 6, above

Notes for: 'Z,' page 285

1 There are a number of tantric, yogic and dramatic *mudras* in which some motion is an integral part of the *mudra*. Of course, it is impossible to depict that motion in two dimensional, static forms.

Bibliography

Agrawala, V.S. *Sparks from the Vedic Fire*. Varanasi: 1962.

Anderson, Leona M. *Vasantotsava: The Spring Festivals of India*. New Delhi: 1993.

Anuman Rajadhon, Phraya. *Life and Ritual of Old Siam*. New Haven: 1961

Asher, Frederick. *The Art of Eastern India, 300-800*. Minneapolis: 1980.

Avalon, Arthur (Sir John Woodroffe). *Shakta and Shakti*. 6 ed. New York: 1978.

Bahadur, S.P. *The Ramayana of Goswami Tulsidas*. Bombay: 1972.

Banerje, Jitendranath N. *The Development of Hindu Iconography*. 2nd ed., Calcutta: 1956.

__________. *Pauranic and Tantric Religion: Early Phase*. Calcutta: 1966.

Banerjee, P., et al. *Buddhist Iconography*. New Delhi: 1989.

Banerji, Sures Chandra. *A Glossary of Smriti Literature*. Calcutta:1963.

Bartlett, Norman. *Land of the Lotus Eaters*. New York: 1959.

Basche, James R. *Thailand; Land of the Free*. New York: 1971.

Batchelor, Stephen. *The Tibet Guide*. London: 1987.

Beek, Steve van. *The Arts of Thailand*. Hong Kong: 1985.

Beguin, G. *Forty-one Thang-kas from the Collection of His Holiness the Dalai Lama*. Paris: 1980.

__________. *Les arts du Nepal et du Tibet*: Paris, 1987

Bell, C. *The Religion of Tibet*. London: 1968.

Bernard, Theos. *Hindu Philosophy*. Bombay: 1989.

Beyer, Stephan. *The Cult of Tara: Magic and Ritual in Tibet*. Berkeley: 1973.

Bharati, Ahehananda. *The Tantric Tradition*. London: 1965.

Bhattacharya, B.C., *Indian Images*. Calcutta: 1921.

Bhattacharyya, Benoytosh, ed. *Guhyasameaja tantra or Tatheagataguhyaka*. Baroda: 1931.

__________. *The Indian Buddhist Iconography Mainly Based on the Seadhanamealea and other Cognate Tantric Texts of Rituals*. Calcutta: 1958.

__________. *An Introduction to Buddhist Esoterism*. London: 1932.

__________. ed. *Two Vajrayana Works*. Baroda: 1929.

Bhattacharyya, Dipak Chandra. *Studies in Buddhist Iconography*. New Delhi: 1978.

__________. *Iconology of Composite Images*. New Delhi: 1980.

__________. *Tantric Buddhist Iconographic Sources*. Delhi: 1974.

Bhattacharya, K. "Les religions brahmaniques dan l'ancien Cambodge, d'après l'épigraphie et l'iconographie," *Cahiers de l'École Française d'Extréme-Orient*; XLIX. Hanoi: 1961.

Bhattasali, N.K. *Iconography of Buddhist and Brahmanical Sculptures in the Dacca Museum*. Dacca:1929.

Bhishagranta, K.K. (ed. and trans). *Sushruta Samhita*. Varanasi: 1963.

Bijalwan, C. D. *Hindu Omens*. New Delhi: 1977.

Binyon, Laurence. *The Spirit of Man in Asian Art*. Cambridge: 1935.

Bodrogi, Tibor. *The Art of Indonesia*. Connecticut: 1972.

Boisselier, Jean. *The Heritage of Thai Sculpture*. Bangkok: 1975.

Boner, Alice. *Principles of Composition in Hindu Sculpture*. Leiden: 1962.

__________ and Sadasiva Rathsarma. *Silpa Prakasa Medieval Orissan Sanskrit Text on Temple Architecture* (trans.). s.l.: 1966.

Boribul Buribhand, Luang and Griswold, A.B. *Thai Images of the Buddha*. Bangkok: 1971.

Bowie, Theodore (ed.). *The Arts of Thailand*. Indiana University: 1960.

__________, Diskul, S., and Griswold, A.B. *The Sculpture of Thailand*. New York: 1972.

Bowring, John. *The Kingdom and the People of Siam*. Kuala Lumpur: 1969.

Buitenen, J.A.B. van, trans. & ed. *The Mahabharta: 1. The Book of the Beginning*. Chicago: 1973.

__________. *The Mahabharta: 2. The Book of the Assembly Hall, 3. The Book of the Forest*. Chicago: 1975.

__________. *The Mahabharta: 4. The Book of Virata, 5. The Book of the Effort*. Chicago: 1978.

Bunce, Fredrick W. *An Encyclopaedia of Buddhist Deities, Demigods, Godlings, Saints and Demons: With Special Focus on Iconographic Attributes*. 2 vols. New Delhi: 1994.

__________, *A Dictionary of Buddhist and Hindu Iconography--Illustrated--Objects, Devices, Concepts, Rites and Related Terms*. New Delhi: 1996.

__________. *An Encyclopaedia of Hindu Deities, Demigods, Godlings Demons and Heroes: With Special Focus on Iconographic Attributes*. New Delhi: 1999.

Cambell, Joseph. *The Masks of the God: Oriental Mythology*. New York: 1962.

Chad, E. and Yimsiri, K. *Thai Monumental Bronzes*. Bangkok: 1957.

Chandra, Lokesh. *Buddhist Iconography*. New Delhi:1991.

__________. "A Ninth Century Scroll of the Vajradhatu Mandala," *Indo-Asian Literatures* (Vol. 343). New Delhi: 1986.

__________ and Bunce Fredrick W. *360 Buddhas, Bodhisattvas and Other Deities: The "Chu Fo P'u-sa Sheng Hsiang Tsan" a Unique Pantheon*. New Delhi: 2002.

__________ and Sharada Rani. *Mudras in Japan: Symbolic Hand-postures in Japanese Mantrayana or the Esoteric Buddhism of the Shingon Denomination*. New Delhi: 1978.

Chattopadhyay, A. *Catalogue of Kanjur and Tanjur*. Caicutta: 1972.

Ch'en, Kenneth K.S. *Buddhism in China*. Princeton: 1964.

Chidbhavananda, Swami. *Facets of Brahman or Hindu Gods*. Tirupparaitturai: 1974.

Chopra, P.N., T.K. Ravindran, N. Subrahmanian. *History of South India*, 3 Vols. New Delhi: 1979.

Clark, Walter Eugene, *Two Lamaistic Pantheons*. New York: 1965.

The Committee for the Rattanakosin Bicentennial Celebration. *The Sights of Rattanakosin*. Bangkok: 1982.

Coomaraswamy, Ananda Kentish. *History of Indian and Indonesian Art*. New York: 1965.

__________. *The Mirror of Gesture*. New Delhi: 1997.

__________. *Yaksas*. 2 vol, repr. Washington: 1971.

__________. *The Transference of Nature in Indian Art*. repr. New York: 1956.

Copeland, Carolyn. *Thankas from the Koelz Collection*. Ann Arbor: 1980.Cornell University. *Bibliography of Thailand*. Ithaca: 1956.

Damrong Rajanubhab, H.R.H. Prince. "History of Siam prior to the Ayudhya Period," *Journal of the Siam Society*. XIII (2), Bangkok 1920.

__________. *Monuments of the Buddha in Siam*. Trans. Sulak Sivaraksa and A.B. Griswold with notes by Prince Subhadradis Diskul and A.B. Griswold. Bangkok: 1982.

Danielou, Alain. *Hindu Polytheism*. New York: 1964.

Das, Sarat Chandra. *A Tibetan-English Dictionary*. Calcutta: 1902.

David-Neel, A. *Magic and Mystery in Tibet*. New York: 1971.

Dayal, Har. *The Doctrine in Buddhist Sanskrit Literature*. Delhi: 1975.

de Bary, Wm. Theodore (ed.) et al. *Sources of Indian Tradition*, Vol. I. New York: 1958.

Devi, Gauri. *Esoteric Mudras of Japan: Mudras of the Garbhadhatu and Vajradhatu Mandalas, of Homa and Eighteen-step Tites, and of Main Buddhas and Bodhisattvas, Gods and Goddesses of Various Sutras and Tantras*. Delhi: 1999.

Dhanit Yupho. *Dharmachakra or the Wheel of the Law*. Bangkok: 1974.

Dimmitt, Cornelia and van Buitenen, J.A.B. *Classical Hindu Mythology: A Reader in Sanskrit Puranas*. Philadelphia:1978.

Dogra, Ramesh C. and Urmila. *A Dictionary of Hindu Names*. New Delhi: 1992.

Dowson, John. *A Classical Dictionary of Hindu Mythology*. London: 1928, repr. 1979.

Eck, Diana L. *Banaras, City of Light*. New York: 1982.

_________. *Darsan: Seeing the Divine Image in India*. Chambersburg: 1985.

Etiemble, trans. by James Hogarth. *Yuh Yu: An Essay on Eroticism and Love in Ancient China*. Geneva: 1970.

Evans-Wentz, W.Y. *The Tibetan Book of the Dead*. New York: 1973.

Fickle, Dorothy H. *The Life of the Buddha Murals in the Buddhaisawan Chapel*. Bangkok: 1979.

Fischer, Robert E. *Buddhist Art and Architecture*. New York: 1993.

Fischle, Willy H. *The Way to the Center: Symbols of Transformation in Tibetan Thankas*. London: 1982.

Five Hundred Gods of Narthang. c. 1810.

Fouchet, Max-Pol, trans. by Brian Rhys. *The Erotic Sculpture of India*. London: 1956

Frankfurter, O. "The Attitudes of the Buddha," *Journal of the Siam Society*. X/2, 1913, pp. 1-36.

Genoud, Charles. *Buddhist Wall Paintings of Ladakh*. Geneve: 1982.

Getty, Alice. *The Gods of Northern Buddhism: Their History, Iconography, and Progressive Evolution through the Northern Buddhist Countries*. Rutland, Vermont: 1962

Geshe Kelsang Gyatso. *Buddhism in the Tibetan Tradition*. London: 1984.

Gombrich, Richard Francis. *Precept and Practice: Traditional Buddhism in the Rural Highlands of Ceylon*. Oxford: 1971.

Gonda, Jan. *Aspects of Early Vishnuism*. Delhi: 1969.

Gordon, Antoinette K. *The Iconography of Tibetan Lamaism*. New Delhi: 1978.

Goswamy, B.N. and A.L. Dahmen-Dallapiccola. *An Early Document of Indian Art*. New Delhi: 1976.

Gredzens, David I. *Visions from the Top of the World*. Minneapolis: 1983.

Griswold, A.B., Lyins, E. and Diskul, S. *The Arts of Thailand: A Handbook*. Bloomington: 1960.

_________. *Dated Buddha Images of Northern Siam*. Ascuna, Switzerland: 1957.

_________. *Towards a History of Sukhodaya Art*. Bangkok: 1967.

Groslier, B. P. *The Art of Indochina: Including Thailand, Vietnam, Laos and Cambodia*. New York: 1962.

Grṃnwedel, Albert. *bSa-mbha-la I lan yig: Der Weg nach bSambhala*. Munchen: 1915.

_________. *Mythologie des Buddhismus in Tibet under Mongolei*. Leipzig:1900.

_________. *A review of the Collection of Lamaist Objects of Prince E. Ukhtomsky* (in Russian). St. Petersburg: 1905.

Guenther, H.V. *Tibetan Buddhism without Mystification*. Leiden: 1966.

_________. and C Thungpa. *The Dawn of Tantra*. Berkeley: 1975.

Gupte, Ramesh S. *Iconography of the Hindus, Buddhists and Jains*. Bombay: 1972.

Gyatsho, S. *Tibetan Mandalas: the Ngor Collection*. Tokyo: 1983.

Harshananda, Swami. *Hindu Gods and Goddesses*. Mylapore: 1981.

Hodgson, Brian H. *Essays on the Languages, Literature and Religion of Nepal and Tibet*. New Delhi: 1972.

_________. *Essays on the Languages, Literature and Religion of Nepal and Tibet together with further papers on the Geography, Ethnology and Commerce of these Countries*. Amsterdam: 1972.

Hoffman, H. *The Religion of Tibet*, trans. E. Fitzgerald. London: 1961.

Holt, Claire, *Art in Indonesia*. New York: 1967.

Hong Navanugrha, Nai. *Bronze Images of the Buddha*. Bangkok: 1927.

Hopkins, E.W. *Epic Mythology*. repr. Varanasi: 1968.

Humphreys, Christmas. *A Popular Dictionary of Buddhism*. New York: 1963.

_________. *Buddhism*. Baltimore: 1951.

"Indu" Inderjit. *Science of Symbols: Deeper View of Indian Deities*. New Delhi: 1977.

Jackson, David P. and Jackson, Janice A. *Tibetan Thangka Painting*. London: 1988.

Jagannathan, Shankunthala. *Hinduism, An Introduction*. Bombay: 1984.

Jansen, Eva Rudy. *The Book of Hindu Imagery: The Gods and Their Symbols*. Diever: 1993.

_________. *The Book of Buddhas*. Diever, Holland: 1993.

Jisl, Lumir. *Tibetan Art*. London: 1961.

Jospehson, Richard. *Swoyambu Historical Pictorial*. Kathmandu: 1985.

Karmay, H. *Early Sino-Tibetan Art*. Warminster: 1975.

Kelsang Gyatso. *Buddhism in the Tibetan Tradition*. London: 1984.

Kern, H. *Manual of Indian Buddhism*. New Delhi: 1974.

Keshav Dev (His Divine Grace Shri Shri 1008 Acharya Shri Keshav Dev Ji Maharaj). *Mudra Vigyan: A Way of Life*. Delhi:1996

Khanna & Co., J.B. Illustrations. Madras: n.d.

Kinsley, David. *Hindu Goddesses: Visions of the Divine Feminine in the Hindu Religious Tradition*. Berkeley: 1986.

Kishore, B.R. *Dances of India*. Delhi: n.d. (1988).

Kramrisch, S. *The Art of Nepal*. New York: 1964.

Lalou, M. *Iconographie des etoffes peintes d'apres le Manjusrimulakalpa*. Paris: 1930.

_________. *Repertoire du Tanjur d'apres le Catalogue de P. Cordier*. Paris: 1933.

_________. *Les religions du Tibet*. Paris: 1957.

Lauf, Detlef Ingo. *Tibetan Sacred Art; The Heritage of Tantra*. Berkeley: 1976.

_________. *Secret Revelations of Tibetan Thangkas*. Freiburg: 1976.

_________. *Secret Doctrines of the Tibetan Book of the Dead*. Boulder: 1977.

Lcan-skya Qutugtu Rol-pahi-rdo-rje. sKu-brnan-brgya-phrag-gsum or sKu-brnan-sum-brgya "Three-hundred Icons". 1736-1795.

Le May, Reginald. *A Concise History of Buddhist Art in Siam*. Tokyo: 1963.

_________. "Introduction to Study of Sculpture in Siam," *Burlington Magazine*. London: 1929.

Lessing, Ferdinamd D. *Yung-Ho-Kung: An Iconography of the Lamaist Cathedral in Peking*. Stockholm: 1942.

Liebert, G. *Iconographic Dictionary of the Indian Religions*. Leyden: 1976.

Liu, Lizhong. *Buddhist Art of the Tibetan Plateau*. Hong Kong: 1988.

Lurker, Manfred. *Dictionary of Gods and Goddesses, Devils and Demons*. London: 1987.

Malla, Kalayana, trans. by F.F. Arbuthnot & Richard F./ Burton. *Ananga Ranga: Stage of the Bodiless One, The Hindu Art of Love*. New York: 1964.

Mallmann, M.T. de. *Introduction a l'iconographie du tantrisme bouddhidtique*. Paris: 1975.

_________. *Etude iconographique sur Manjushri*. Paris: 1964.

Martin, E.O. *The Gods of India: Their History, Character and Worship*. Delhi: 1972.

Matics, K.I. *A History of Wat Phra Chetuphon and its Buddha Images*. Bangkok: 1979.

Minaev, I.P. (I.P. Minayeff). *Recherches sur le Bouddhisme*. Paris: 1894.

Mishra, Rambavan A. & Mishra, Lalbihasri. *Nityakarma Pujaprakasha*. Gorakhpur (UP): n.d.

Mitchell, A.G. *Hindu Gods and Goddesses*. London: 1982.

Mongolian Kanjur (Mon.: Monggol ganjur-un). 1717-1720.

Moor, Edward. *The Hindu Pantheon*. New Delhi: 1981 (repr.).

Mookerjee, Ajit. *Tantra Art*. s.l.: 1967.

_________. *Ritual Art of India*. London: 1985.

_________. *Kali, the Feminine Force.* New York: 1988.

_________ and Khanna, Madhu. *The Tantric Way: Art-Science-Ritual.* London: 1996.

Mulder, Jan Anton Niels. *Monks, Merit and Motivation.* De Kalb: 1973.

Narayan, R.K. *Gods, Demons and Others.* New Delhi: 1964.

Nebesky-Wojkowitz, Réne de. *Oracles and Demons of Tibet: The Cult and Iconography of the Tibetan Protective Deities.* New York: 1977.

Neven, A. *Lamaistic Art.* Brussels: 1975.

Newark Museum Association, *Catalogue of the Tibetan Collection and other Lamist Art*, vols. I-V, Newark, 1950.

_________. *Tibet, A Lost World*, Newark, 1978.

d'Oldenburg, S. "Materiaux pour l'iconographie bouddhique de Kharakhoto I," *Materiaux pour l'ethnographie de la Russie.* Tome 2. Sr. Petersburg: 1914, pp. 79-157.

Olschak, Blanche C. and Gesche Thupten Wangyal. *Mystic Art of Ancient Tibet.* Boston and London: 1988.

Olson, E. *Tantric Buddhist Art.* New York: 1974.

Oxford University Press. *Oxford-Duden Pictorial Thai and English Dictionary.* Oxford: 1993

Pal, Pratapaditya. *Tibetan Paintings: A Study of Tibetan Thankas Eleventhto Ninteenth Centuries.* Basel: 1984.

Pander, Eugene. *Das Pantheon des Tschangtscha Hutuktu.* Berlin: 1890.

Paothong Thongchua, Piriya Krairiksh and Pishnu Supanimit. *Art in Thailand Since 1932.* Bangkok: 1982.

Parmentier, H. *L'Art khmer primitif.* Paris: 1927.

Pathak, S.K., ed. *The Album of the Tibetan Art Collections.* Patna: 1986.

Paul, R.A. *The Tibetan Symbolic World.* Chicago: 1983.

Pawlin, Alfred. *Dhamma Vision.* Bangkok: 1984.

Paynes, Ernest Alexander. *The Saktas.* Calcutta: 1933.

Phrombhichitr, P. *Buddhist Art and Architecture.* Bangkok: 1952.

Pirya Krairiksh. *Art in Peninsular Thailand Prior to the 14th Century.* Bangkok: 1980.

_________. *Art Styles in Thailand.* Bangkok: 1977.

_________. *The Sacred Image: Sculpture from Thailand.* Cologne:1979.

_________. *Sculptures from Thailand.* Hong Kong:1982.

Pisit Charoenwongsa and Subhadradis, M.C. *Thailand.* Geneva: 1978.

Poduval, R. K. *Administrative Report of the Archeological Department.* Travancore State; 1107ME: 1930.

Poduval, R. V. *Kathakala and Diagram of Hand Poses.* Trivandrum: 1930.

Pratap Sinh Sah Dev, Shri (Maharaja of Nepal). *Purashcaryarnava*, repr. Delhi: n.d.

_________, (Pratapsinha Sahadeva). "Purashcaryarnavah: tantrasastranusari-vidhan-paddhati-niupanatmakah," *Encyclopaedia of Tantric Rituals*, repr. New Delhi: 1985.

Quaritch Wales, H.G. *Dvaravati: The Earliest Kingdom of Siam.* London: 1969.

Raghuvira and Lokesh Chandra. *A New Tibeto-Mongol Pantheon*, Vol. I-XX. New Delhi: 1961-72.

Rajanubhab, Prince Damrong. *Monuments of Buddha in Siam.* Bangkok: 1973.

Rajawaramuni, Phra (Prayuth Payuthto). *Dictionary of Buddhism (Brief Dictionary of Buddhist Dharma).* Bangkok: P.S. 2528 (1985).

Rajesh, A. P.. *Hindu Tantra Shastra.* New Delhi: n.d.

Rao, T.A. Gopinatha. *Elements of Hindu Iconography*, 4 vols. Madras: 1914-16; repr. Delhi: 1993.

Rapson, E.J., et al (eds.). *The Cambridge History of India*, 6 Vols. Delhi: 1955.

Rawson, Phillip S. *The Art of Southeast Asia.* New York: 1967.

_________. *The Art of Tantra.* New York: 1978.

_________. *Indian Sculpture.* London: 1966.

_________. *Erotic Art of the East.* New York: 1968.

Ray, N.-R. *Introduction to the Study of Therevada Buddhism in Burma*. Calcutta: 1946.

Reynolds, Valrae. *Tibet, A Lost World*. New York: 1978.

Reynolds, V., Heller, A. and Gyatso, J. *Catalogue of the Newark Museum Tibetan Collection, III, Sculpture and Painting*. Newark: 1986.

Rhie, Marylin M. and Thurman, Robert A.F. Wisdom and Compassion: *The Sacred Art of Tibet*. New York: 1991.

__________. *From the Land of Snows: Buddhist Art of Tibet*. Amherst, Mass.: 1984.

Roerich, George N. *Tibetan Paintings*. Paris: 1925.

__________. *Blue Annals*. New Delhi: 1988.

Rowland, Benjamin. *The Art and Architecture of India: Hindu, Buddhist, Jain*. Baltimore: 1967.

Rubissow, Helen. *Art of Asia*. New York: 1954.

Salmony, M. *Sculpture in Siam*. London: 1925.

Saran, Prem. *Tantra, Hedonism in Indian Culture*. New Delhi: 1998.

Saraswati, S.K. *A Survey of Indian Sculpture*. Calcutta: 1957.

Sarkar, H. *Some Contributions of India to the Ancient Civilization of Indonesia and Malaysia*. Calcutta: 1970.

__________. *Studies in Early Buddhist Architecture of India*. Delhi: 1966.

Saso, Michael. *Homa Rites and Mandala Meditation in Tendai Buddhism*. New Delhi: 1991.

Sastri, H. Krishna. *South-Indian Images of Gods and Goddesses*. (reprint) New Delhi:1986.

Saunders, E. Dale. *Mudra: A study of Symbolic Gestures in Japanese Buddhist Sculpture*. New York: 1960.

Schlagintweit, Emil. *Le bouddhisme au Tibet*. Paris: 1881.

__________. *Buddhism in Tibet*. sl: nd.

Sharma, B.N. *Iconographic Parallelism in India and Nepal*. Hyderabad: 1975.

Sharma, R.C. *The Splendour of Mathura: Art and Museum*. New Delhi: 1994.

Sastri, H. Krishna. *South-Indian Images of Gods and Goddesses*. New Delhi: 1986

Shastri, Hera Prasad. *A Descriptive Catalogue of Sanskrit Manuscripts in the Government Collection under the care of the Asiatic Society of Bengal*. Calcutta: 1917.

Sherring, M. A. *Banaras, The Sacred City of the Hindus*. (London: 1868) repr. Delhi: 1990.

Sierksma, F. *Tibet's Terrifying Deities*. Tokyo: 1966.

Silpa Bhirasri. *Thai Buddhist Art (Architecture)*. 5th ed. Bangkok: 1979.

Singh, Dharam Vir. *Hinduism, An Introduction*. Jaipur: 1991.

Singh, M. *Himalayan Art*. New York: 1968.

Sivaramamurti, C. *The Art of India*. New York: 1977.

__________. *Le Stupa de Barobudur*. Paris: 1960.

Sjamsuddin, R., et. al. (eds.). *East Java: The Glorious Century*. s.l. (The Regional Government of East Java): 1991.

Smith, Ronald Bishop. *Siam; The History of the Thais*. Bethesda: 1966.

Snellgrove, David L. *Indo-Tibetan Buddhism*, vols. I-II. Boston: 1987.

__________. *Four Lamas of Dolpo*. Cambridge: 1967.

__________. *The Image of the Buddha*. Tokyo: 1978.

__________. *Buddhist Himalaya*. Oxford: 1957.

Sonami, H. and Tachikawa, M., eds. *Tibetan Mandalas: The Ngor Collection*, 2 vols. Tokyo: 1983.

Sta(h)el-Holstein, A. F. von (ed.), *Der Karmapradeipa*. Halle: 1900.

__________. *The Keapcyapaparivarta*. Shanghai: 1926.

Stern, P. *L'Art du Champa et son evolution*. Toulouse: 1942.

Stratton, Carol and Scott, M. McN. *The Art of Sukhothai: Thailand's Golden Age*. Singapore: 1987.

Stutley, M. and J. *A Dictionary of Hinduism*. London: 1977.

Suong Wattanavrangkul. *Outstanding Sculpture of Buddhist and Hindu Gods from Private Collections in Thailand*. Bangkok: B.E. 2518 (1975 A.D.).

Subhadradis Diskul, M.C. *Art in Thailand: A Brief History*. Bangkok: 1981.

_________ (ed.). *The Art of Srivijaya*. Kuala Lumpur: 1980.

_________. *Sukhothai Art*. Bangkok: B.E. 2252 (1978 A.D.).

Surveyor, Suna K. *Immortal Tales from Kalidasa*. Bombay: 1988.

Sutthi, (Phra) Suradej. *Translation of Thai pang* (mudras): Bangkok, 22 August 2000.

Tajima, Ryujun. *Les deux grands mandalas et la doctrine de l'esoterisme Shingon*. Tokyo: 1959.

Tambish, S. J. *Buddhism and the Spirit Cults of North-east Thailand*. Cambridge: 1970.

Terwiel, B. J. *Monks and Magic*. Bangkok: 1975.

Tewari, S.P. *Hindu Iconography*. New Delhi: 1979.

Thapar, D.R. *Icons in Bronze*. London:1961.

Tibet House Museum, *Catalogue of the Inaugural Exhibition*. New Delhi: 1965.

Thapar, D.R. *Icons in Bronze*. London:1961.

Tucci, Giuseppi. *The Religions of Tibet*. Berkeley: 1980.

_________. *The Theory and Practice of the Mandala*. London: 1961.

_________. *Tibetan Painted Scrolls*. Rome: 1949.

_________. *Indo Tibetica*, vols. I-II. New Delhi: 1988.

_________. *Indo Tibetica*, vols. I-IV. ed. L. Chandra. trans. U.M. Vesçi. New Delhi: 1988-89.

_________. *Rati-Lílá: An Interpretation of the Tantric Imagery of the Temples of Nepal*. Geneva:1969

Tulku, T. *Sacred Art of Tibet*. Berkeley: 1972.

Van Beek, Steve and Tettoni, Luca Invernizzi. *The Arts of Thailand*. Hong Kong: 1986.

Vatsyayan, Kapila. *Buddhist Iconography*. New Delhi: 1989.

_________. *The Square and the Circle of the Indian Arts*. New Delhi: 1983.

_________. *Indian Classical Dance*. New Delhi: 1974 (2nd reprint: 1997).

Vettam Mani. *Puranic Encyclopaedia*. Delhi: 1975.

Vira, Raghu and Chandra, Lokesh, eds. *A New Tibeto-Mongolian Pantheon*. New Delhi: 1961.

Visser, M. W. de. *Ancient Buddhism in Japan*. London: 1935.

Vogel, J. P. *The Influences of Indian* Art. s.l.: 1925.

von Schroeder, Ulrich. *Indo-Tibetan Bronzes*. Hong Kong: 1981.

Waddell, L.A. *The Buddhism of Tibet or Lamaism*. Cambridge: 1958.

Wales, H. G. Q. *Dvaravati; The Earliest Kingdom of Siam*. London: 1969.

Wattanavrangkul, Snong. *Outstanding Sculptures of Bhudhist (sic) and Hindu Gods From Private Collections in Thailand*. s.l. (Bangkok?): 1975.

Watts, Michael. *Thailand*. Oxford: 1986

Wayman, A. *The Buddhist Tantras*. New York: 1973.

Wells, Kenneth E. *Thai Buddhism: Its Rites and Activities*. Bangkok: 1975.

White, Joyce. *Discovery of a Lost Bronze Age: Ban Chiang*. University of Pennsylvania and the Smithsonian Institution: 1982.

Whitfield, Roderick. *The Art of Central Asia*, Vols I-III. Tokyo: 1982, 1983, 1985.

Wilkins, W. J. *Hindu Mythology, Vedic and Puranic*. New Delhi: 1991.

Williams, C.A.S. *Outlines of Chinese Symbolism and Art Motives*. New York: 1976.

Zimmer, H. *Artistic Form and Yoga in the Sacred Images of India*. Princeton: 1984.

_________, ed. by J. Campbell. *The Art of Indian Asia*, 2 vols. New York:1955.

Zwalf, W. *Heritage of Tibet*. London: 1981.

_________, ed. *Buddhism, Art and Faith*. London: 1985.

Appendix A
Descriptive Terms' Designations

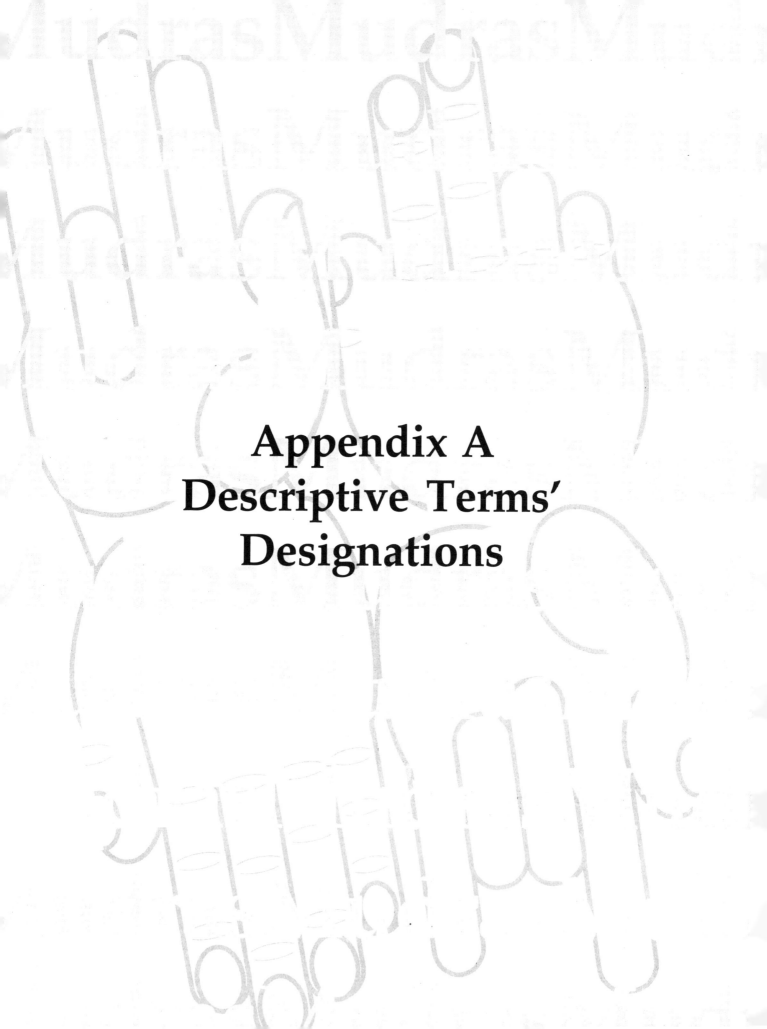

Descriptive Term Designations

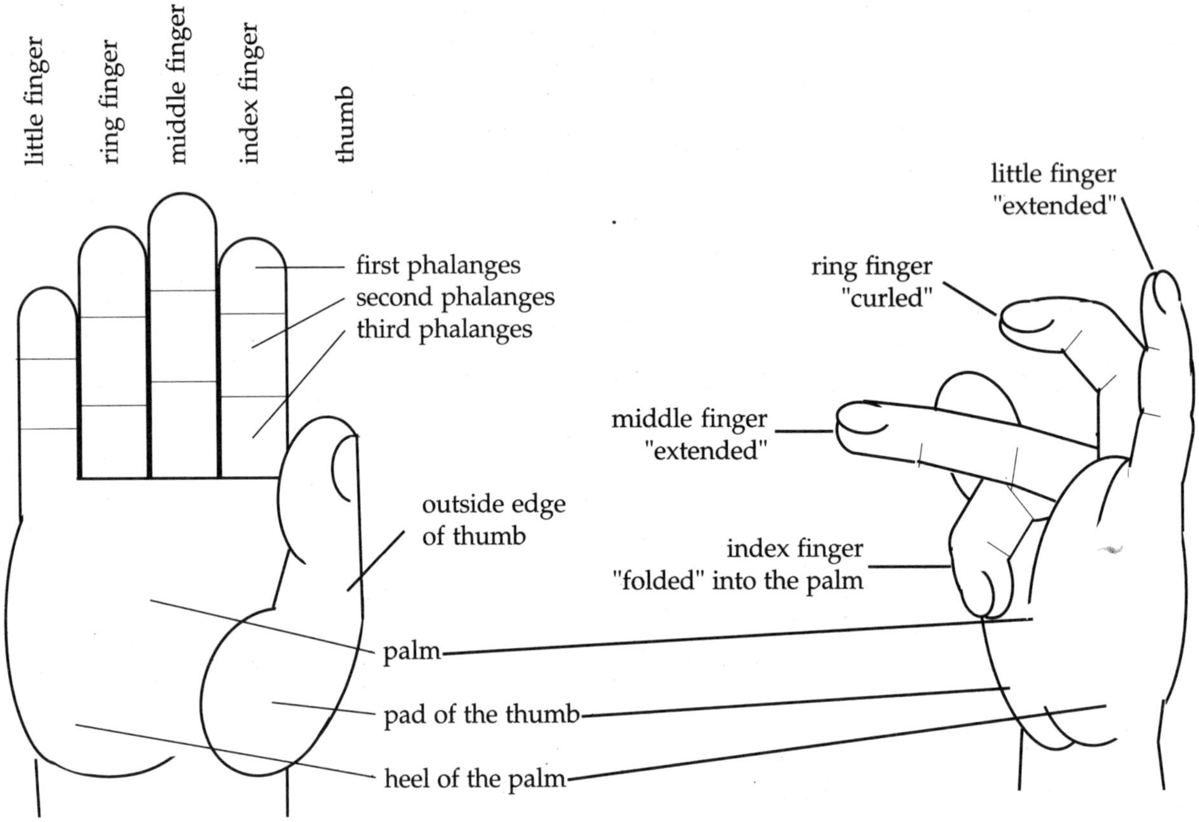

little finger
ring finger
middle finger
index finger
thumb
first phalanges
second phalanges
third phalanges
outside edge of thumb
palm
pad of the thumb
heel of the palm
little finger "extended"
ring finger "curled"
middle finger "extended"
index finger "folded" into the palm

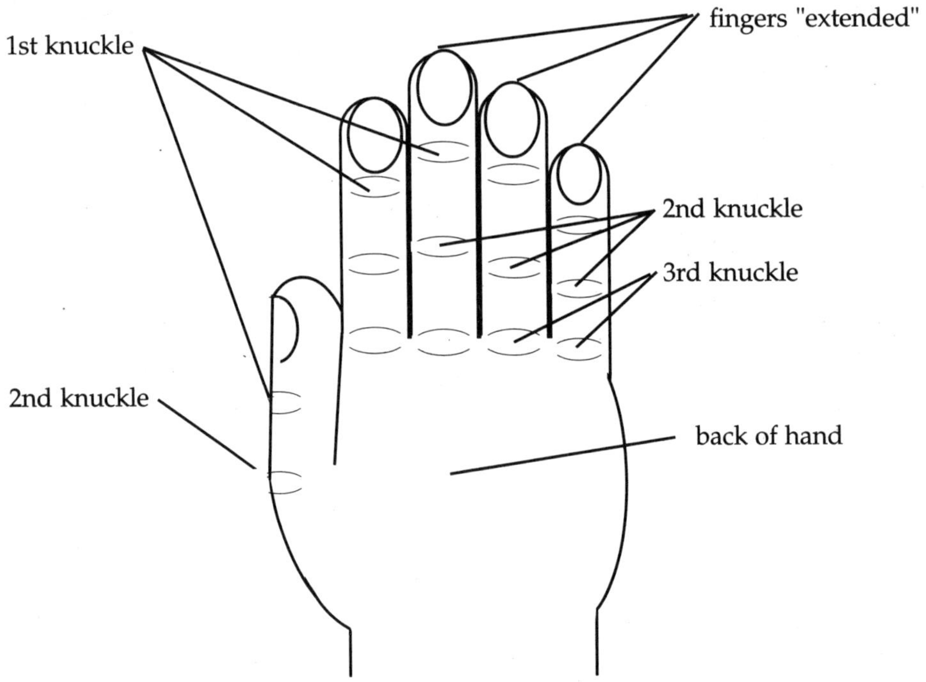

1st knuckle
fingers "extended"
2nd knuckle
3rd knuckle
2nd knuckle
back of hand

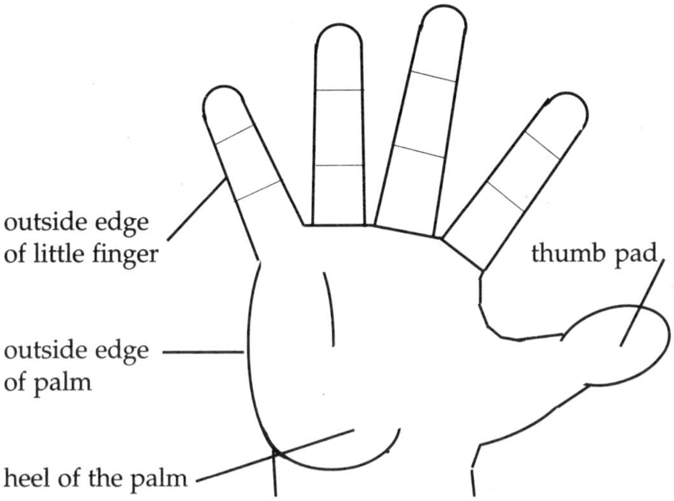

fingers and thumb
"splayed"

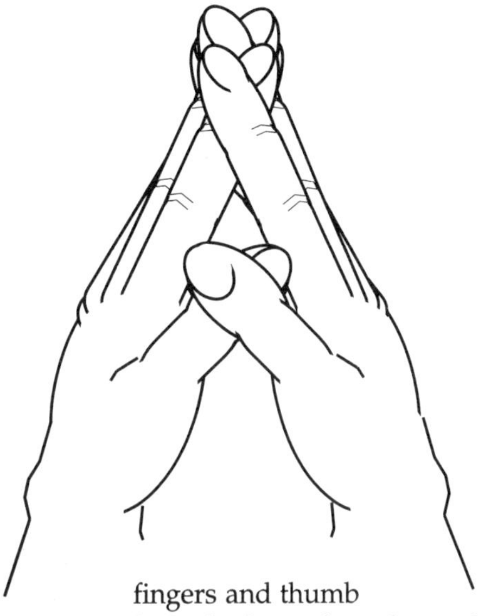

fingers and thumb
"interlaced" on the "outside at the tips"

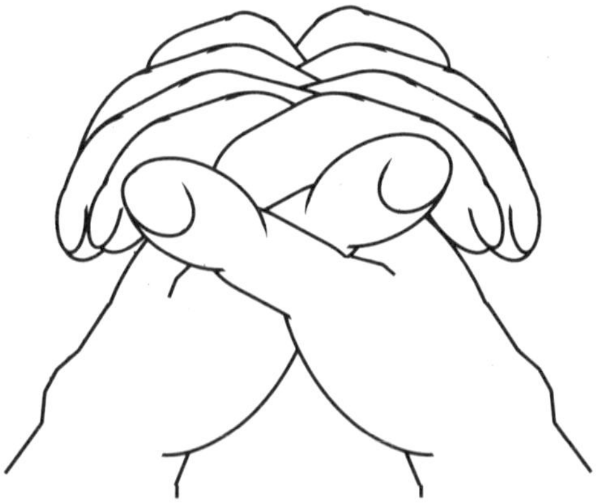

fingers and thumb
"interlaced" on the "outside"

fingers and thumb
"interlaced" on the "inside"

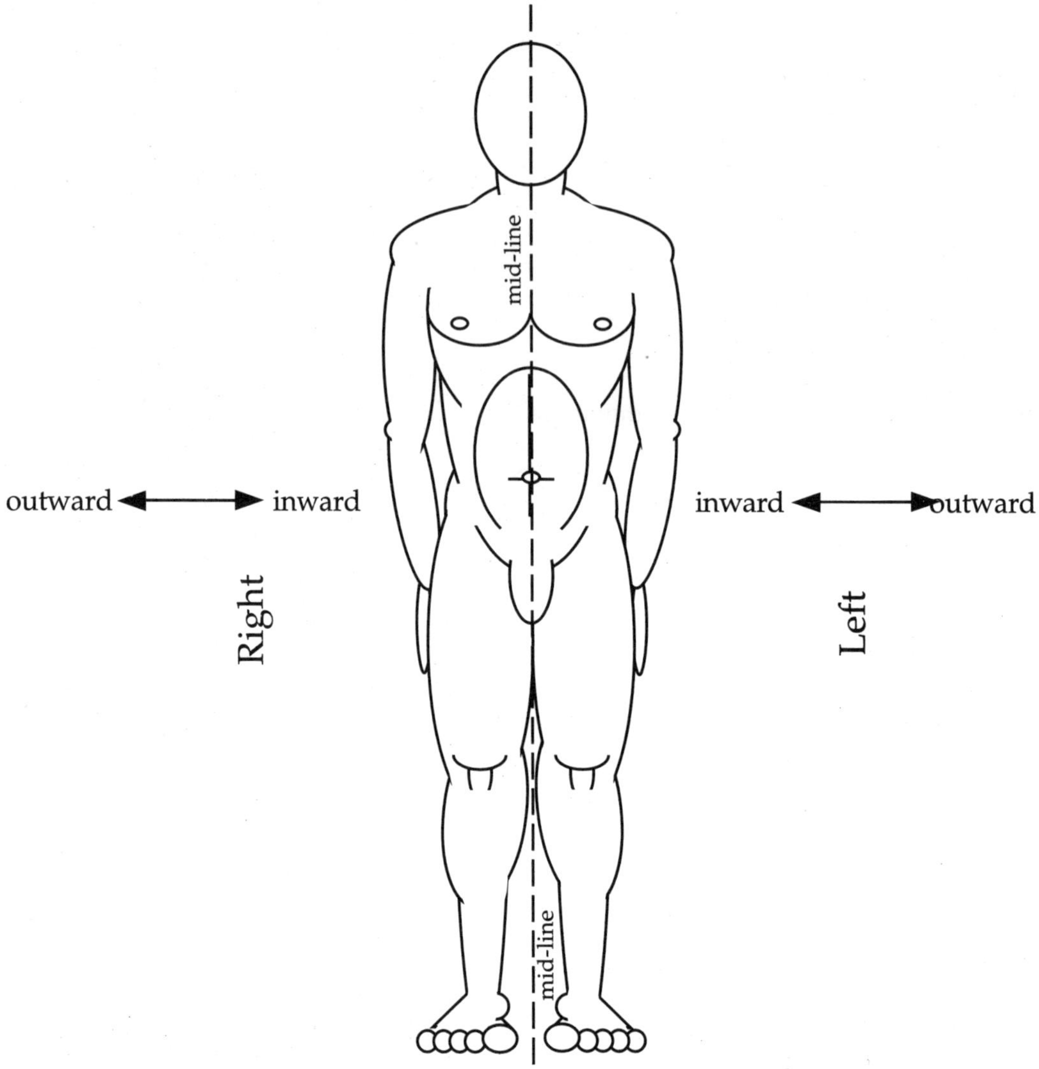
mid-line
outward
inward
inward
outward
Right
Left
mid-line

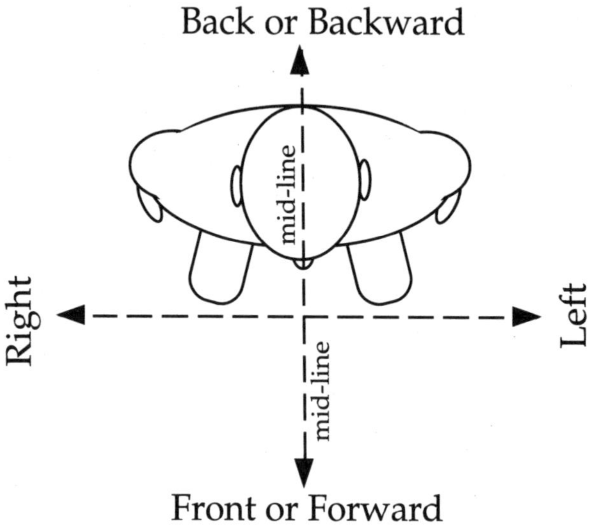
Back or Backward
mid-line
Right
Left
mid-line
Front or Forward

Appendix B
Thai Postures of the Lord Buddha

About the Thai Postures of the Lord Buddha

For centuries the various *mudras* and *asanas* assigned to the Lord Buddha had been established and accepted throughout the Buddhist world, particularly amongst the orthodox Theravadists. New *mudras* and/or *asanas* would appear from time to time either to be accepted or neglected or relegated to oblivion as heretical. In many cases, the iconography had been so firmly established that to tamper with it, particularly in widely accepted events--i.e., the subduing of the evil one, Mara--was not to be accepted. As accepting and inclusive as Buddhism is of other faiths and the practising of other rites within its faith's structure--e.g., the Nats of Burma--there were a number of areas considered to be well within the heterodox and bordering on heresy--e.g., the theology of the Mahayanists. Yet, new postures did appear from time to time, new *mudras*, especially combined forms (Ind.: samyutta), held by both hands, which became popular.

The Chakri King, Rama III (Phra Nangklao) before and after his ascension to the throne was interested in the images of the Lord Buddha. As king they would adorn his capitol as an act of kingly merit by the casting of images. The first two reigns of the Chakri Dynasty had been absorbed with the transfer of the many images both great and small from the ruined, former capitol, Ayutthaya, to Bangkok, as well as from other areas throughout the realm. Not only did this amassing of images in the royal capitol aid in establishing its legitimacy of the city and the dynasty, it was an act of regal merit. That meritorious work had been largely completed by the ascension of Phra Nangklao as Rama III to the kingship.

King, Rama III, requested of the Prince Patriarch Paramanujita Jinorasa (Somtej Phra Paramanujit), the son of the first Chakri, King, Rama I (Phra Buddha Yot Fa), to search the sacred texts and assemble a list of acceptable events and postures from the life of the Lord Buddha that might lend themselves to images. This he did and composed a text now preserved in the National Library, Bangkok. Not only as an act of faith and merit, by ordaining new and re-ordaining old forms, Rama III would also be establishing an iconography that would be purely Chakri.

The Prince Patriarch researched, studied, conferred and compiled a list of forty postures along with descriptive passages based upon the life of the Lord Buddha as found in the sacred texts. The forty postures[1] are: 1) Performing austerities, 2) Accepting a rice gruel offering, 3) Floating a salver, 4) Accepting an offering of grass, 5) Subduing Mara, 6) Meditation sitting, 7) Standing meditation, 8) Walking Meditation, 9) Making four bowls into one, 10) Partaking of Myrobalam, 11) Walking out to preach, 12) Bestowing Ordination, 13) Pointing to a corpse, 14) Calming the Seas, 15) Holding an alms-bowl, 16) Eating, 17) Offering the relics of his hair, 18) Travelling by boat, 19) Calming the relatives, 20) Accepting offerings from the beasts (elephant and monkey), 21) Restraining Phra Kaenchan (sandalwood image), 22) Looking back to Vaisali (the elephant glance), 23) Reflecting on impending death, 24) Accepting a bowl of water from Ananda, 25) Bathing, 26) Standing leaves for a mat, 27) Gandhara Buddha image, 28) Reflecting, 29) Adamantine posture, 30) Contemplating aging, 31) Imprinting his footprints, 32) Expounding the constituent elements, 33) Accepting a mango, 34) Expelling Phra Wakkli. 35) Reclining, Entering Parinirvana, 36) Eating of rice gruel, 37) Dissuading Mara, 38) Threading a needle, 39) Indicating the principal disciples, and 40) Disclosing the three worlds. The king then commissioned the forty postures to be cast and placed within the *Rajakramanusarana Hall* of *Wat Phra Kaeo*. Ultimately only thirty three images were cast and so deposited.

A number of these images had been and were to become hallmarks of Thai images of the Lord Buddha--e.g., *pang maravichai* (subduing Mara), *pang ham-samut* (Calming the Seas), *pang harm-marn* (restraining or Dissuading Mara), and *pang parinippharn* (Reclining, Entering Parinirvana)--and a few only to be seen in Thailand.

The following table indicates fifty-eight postures. The left column (#1-56) are the titles taken from ODD, p. 678, which correspond to the illustrations on the following page (p. 679). The nect column (second from left) lists the thirty-four images represented in OFr, while the second from right column indicates the forty postures listed in DRN.

Fifty-eight Thai Postures of the Lord Buddha

Taken from the *Oxford-Duden Pictorial Thai and English Dictionary*; O. Frankfurter, *The Attitudes of the Buddha*; and Damrong Rajanubhah, *Monuments of the Buddha in Siam*.

	Oxford-Duden[2]	Frankfurter[3]	P. Damrong Rajanubhab[4]	Thai equivalent
1.	Queen Maya giving birth to the Buddha[5]		p. 3, no number	***not represented***
2.	The Great Departure	***not represented***	***not represented***	
3.	Cutting His topknot	***not represented***	***not represented***	
4.	Undergoing austerities[6]	p. 4, #1	p. 35, #1	
5.	Accepting an offering of honey-sweetened rice[7]	p. 5, #2	p. 35, #2	
6.	Partaking of honey-sweetened rice[8]	***not represented***	p. 37, #36	
7.	Floating a salver against the current[9]	p. 6, #3	p. 35, #3	
8.	Accepting an offering of grass leaves for a sitting mat[10]	p. 7, #4	p. 35, #4	
9.	Meditation (sitting)[11]	***not represented***	p. 35, #6	
10.	Subduing Mara (Adamantine Pose)[12]	p. 8, #5	p. 35, #5, p. 37, #29	
11.	(Standing meditation) Looking at the Bodhi tree in gratefulness[13]	p. 9, #6	p. 35, #7	
12.	Walking Meditation with an aureole around his head[14]	p. 10, #7, "on the jeweled walkway"	p. 35, #8	
13.	Seated Buddha image with an aureole around the body	***not represented***	***not represented***	
14.	Dissuading Mara[15]	p. 11, #8	p. 37, #37	
15.	Seated Buddha image protected by seven-headed naga (Muchalinda)[16]	p. 12, #9	***not represented***	
16.	Partaking of a myrobalan nut[17]	p. 13, #10	p. 36, #10	pang chan samor
17.	Miracle of merging the four alms bowls of the four guardians of the earth into one[18]	p. 14, #11	p. 36, #9	

Fifty-eight Thai Postures of the Lord Buddha

Oxford-Duden		Frankfurter	P. Damrong Rajanubhab	Thai equivalent
18.	Offering his locks to the two merchants[19]	p. 15, #12	p. 36, #17	
19.	Accepting dried, sweetened rice balls	*not represented*	*not represented*	
20.	Giving the First Sermon	*not represented*	*not represented*	
21.	Reflecting[20]	p. 16, #13	p. 37, #28	
22.	Ordaining the Bhikkhu (disciple)[21]	p. 17, #14	p. 36, #12 ". . . ordination by saying *'hi bhikkhu.'*"	
23.	Partaking of a meal[22]	*not represented*	p. 36, #16	
24.	Pacifying the Ocean[23]	*not represented*	p. 36, #14	
25.	Indicating the principal disciples[24]	p. 18, #15	p. 37, #39	
26.	Boarding a boat[25]	p .27 #24	p. 36, #18	
27.	Performing a miracle	*not represented*	*not represented*	
28.	Holding an alms-bowl[26]	p. 21, #18	p. 36, #15	
29.	Accepting an offering of a mango[27]	p. 22, #19	p. 37, #33	
30.	Performing a series of double miracles	*not represented*	*not represented*	
31.	Descending from the Tavatimsa Heaven[28]	p. 24, #21	*not represented*	
32.	Disclosing the three worlds[29]	*not represented*	p. 38, #40	
33.	Persuading the relatives not to quarrel[30]	*not represented*	p. 36, #19	
34.	Standing leaves for a sitting mat[31]	*not represented*	p. 37, #26 "standing"	
35.	Walking, setting out to preach[32]	p. 20, #17, "walking to Kapilavatthu	p. 36, #11	
36.	Sitting in *vajrasana* (cross-legged posture)	*not represented*	*not represented*	
37.	Bathing in rain water[33]	p. 30, #27	p. 37, #25	
38.	Expelling Phra Wakkli[34]	p. 29, #26, "Vakkali"	p. 37, #34	
39.	Giving pardon or Dispelling fear	*not represented*	*not represented*	
40.	Giving Blessing	*not represented*	*not represented*	
41.	Salvation of Sinners	*not represented*	*not represented*	

Fifty-eight Thai Postures of the Lord Buddha

Oxford-Duden	Frankfurter	P. Damrong Rajanubhab	Thai equivalent
42. Gandhara Buddha image, Requesting the rain[35]	p. 32, #29	p. 37, #27	
43. Pointing to a corpse[36]	*not represented*	p. 36, #13	
44. Reflecting on world impermancy[37]	p. 25, #22	*not represented*	
45. Threading a needle[38]	p. 26, #23	p. 37, #38	
46. Putting on a monastic robe	*not represented*	*not represented*	
47. Imprinting his footprints[39]	p. 31, #28	p. 37, #31	
48. Accepting offerings from an elephant and a monkey[40]	p. 28, #25, "in the Palelayaka Forest"	p. 36, #20	
49. Urging Phra Kaenchan (the sandalwood image)[41]	*not represented*	p. 36, #21	
50. Converting King Maha Chompoo	*not represented*	*not represented*	
51. Contemplating the truth of aging[42]	p. 33, #30	p. 37, #30	
52. Looking back at the city of Vaisali[43]	p. 35, #32	p. 36, #22 elephant glance	
53. Demonstrating majestic signs and miracles	*not represented*	*not represented*	
54. Announcing his approaching death[44]	p. 34, #31	p. 36, #23	
55. Accepting a bowl of water from Phra Ananda[45]	p. 23, #20, Ananda is not noted	p. 37, #24	
56. Reclining, Entering Parinirvana[46]	p. following #32 (P. 36?)	p. 37, #35	
57. *not represented*	p. 19, #16, "guarding against the cold"[47]	*not represented*	
58. *not represented*		p. 37, #32 "Expounding on constituent elements"[48]	

Notes on Thai Postures of the Lord Buddha

[1] The titles are taken from ODD, p. 678.

[2] *Ibid.*

[3] Referring to OFr, pp. 1-35+.

[4] Referring to DRN, pp. 35-38, and JBo, pp. 204-205.

[5] Both ODD, p. 179, #1, and OFr, p. 3 and illustration facing with no number, are similar in form. It is to be noted that throughout OFr, only the pages upon which text appears are paginated (verso). The facing pages (recto) are not paginated.

[6] Both ODD, p. 279, #4 and OFr facing p. 4, #1 are virtually identical

[7] ODD, p. 279, #5, and OFr facing p. 5, #2, differ somewhat, The Bodily posture is identical, however, ODD indicates right hand resting on knee, palm up, while the left rests upon the thigh, palm down. OFr presents the figure holding a large shallow salver in both hands, resting on the knees.

[8] ODD, p. 279, #6, and DRN, p. 37, # 36 are virtually identical in representation and description of the same.

[9] ODD, p. 279, #7, and OFr facing p. 6, #3, and DRN, p. 35, #3 are quite similar. The only variation is seen in ODD #7 in which the right hand holds a small salver which is absent in OFr #3.

[10] ODD, p. 279, #8, and OFr facing p. 7, #4, and DRN, p. 35, #4 are virtually identical.

[11] ODD, p. 279, #9, and DRN, p. 35, # 6 are identical in representation and description of the same.

[12] ODD, p. 279, #10, and OFr facing p. 8, #5, and DRN, p. 35, #4 are alike.

[13] ODD, p. 279, #11, and DRN, p. 35, # 7 are identical in representation and description, OFr facing p. 9, #6, displays the figure standing in *samabhangasana*, and the hands, rather "crossed over the thighs" (DRN, p. 35), are held in *dhyana mudra*.

[14] ODD, p. 279, #12, and OFr facing p. 10, #7, and DRN, p. 35, #8, present essentially the same position, although OFr, #7 is so drawn as not to show "the left foot raised" (DRN, p. 35). In addition DRN entitles this "on the jeweled walkway," while ODD and OFr calls this pose "walking meditation."

[15] ODD, p. 279, #14, which shows the Buddha seated in *virasana*, right hand raised to chest level holding the *vitarka mudra* and left hand resting in lap with palm upwards (*dhyana mudra*). This position is identified as "Dissuading Mara." OFr, #8 is similar, but with one important difference--i.e., the right hand holds the *abhaya mudra*. DRN, p. 37, #37 ("restraining Mara) describes a similar pose, and JBo, p. 203, discusses "the three (standing) *abhaya mudras*" to which he adds the fourth, "the restraining of Mara." Below ODD image #14, on p. 279, is displayed image #20 which is entitled "giving the first sermon." Here the image is represented with the *vitarka mudra* in the right hand. Since the *vitarka mudra* is a teaching pose, it would seem that ODD, images #14 and #20 had been transposed.

[16] ODD, p. 279, #15, and OFr facing p. 12, #9, present a similar situation. However, ODD, #15, indicates the Lord Buddha as sitting upon the coils of the serpent, while OFr, #9 indicates the body enclosed in the coils of Muchalinda. DRN, pp. 35-38, does not mention this pose. "Buddha Protected by Naga" had been an iconographic image long employed in Thailand, certainly long before the Chakri Dynasty. DRN, Figure 7, illustrates such an image from the "Labapuri style" (Lopburi) and JBo, p. 102, Plate 67, illustrates the Buddha of Grahi from the Srivijaya School, however, important as it is historically and iconographically, it is not to be found in the list of forty.

[17] ODD, p. 279, #16, OFr facing p. 13, #10, and DRN, p. 36, #10, present essentially the same image.

[18] ODD, p. 279, #17, OFr facing p. 14, #11, and DRN, p. 36, #9, are identical in representation and description.

[19] ODD, p. 279, #18, OFr facing p. 15, #12, and DRN, p. 36, #17, represent comparable poses.

[20] ODD, p. 279, #21, OFr facing p. 16, #13, and DRN, p. 37, #28, are identical.

[21] ODD, p. 279, #22, and OFr facing p. 17, #14, display nearly similar poses in which the right hand is similar to *abhaya mudra* with fingers folded slightly towards the palm (OFr), and held out to the right with palm downward and fingers extended (ODD #22). However, only OFr #14 truly corresponds to DRN #12, which states "right hand beckoning."

[22] ODD, p. 279, #23, and DRN, p. 36, #16, represent virtually the same position.

[23] ODD, p. 279, #24, and DRN, p. 36, #14, represent identical positions.

[24] ODD, p. 279, #25, OFr facing p. 18, #15, and DRN, p. 37, #39, refer to the same action, however, ODD indicates the right hand points upward with the palm rotated towards the body. This is not the *tarjani mudra* of warning as in that *mudra* the

palm faces outward, or away from the body. The pointing of the finger upwards in this situation is puzzling.

25 ODD, p. 279, #26, OFr facing p. 27, #24, and DRN, p. 36, #18 all refer to the same situation. However, only ODD and DRN display and describe the same position. OFr indicates the same *asana*, but both hands rest, palm downward on the knees.

26 ODD, p. 279, #28, OFr facing p. 21, #18, and DRN, p. 36, #15, are all the same.

27 ODD, p. 279, #29, and DRN, p. 37, #33, are identical. OFr facing p. 22, #19, indicates the left hand resting in the lap (dhyana mudra) an not with "the left hand on the knee. . . ." (DRN, p. 37).

28 ODD, p. 279, #31 ("Descending from Tavatimsa Heaven" in which the hands are both held at waist level in *vitarka mudra* [teaching or expounding]) bears no resemblance to OFr facing p. 24, #21, in which the hands are held shoulder level, to the side, and hands extended upwards with palms facing away from the body. Since this is not on of the forty postures noted by DRN, it is difficult to say which is accurate. Further, neither bear resemblance to the fragment of the same subject from Wat Trapang Thong Lang, Sukhothai.

29 ODD, p. 279, #32, and DRN, p. 38, #40, exhibit and describe the same posture.

30 ODD, p. 279, #33, and DRN, p. 36, #19, are identical in presentation and description.

31 ODD, p. 279, #34, and DRN, p. 37, #26, are identical although the titles differ somewhat.

32 DRN, p. 37, #11, and OFr, p. 20, #17 are identical in description and presentation. However, ODD, p. 279, #35, is reversed in all aspects. Could this be a printing error?

33 ODD, p. 279, #37, OFr, p. 30, #27, and DRN, p. 37, #25, are all similar.

34 ODD, p. 279, #38, and OFr, p. 29, #26, present identical postures. However, they do not correspond to DRN, p. 37, #34, which is described as "left hand on the knee and right hand hanging at the level of the legs in a gesture signaling someone to move away."

35 ODD, p. 279, #42, and DRN, p. 37, #27, are virtually identical in representation and description. However, OFr, p. 32, #29, is significantly different. The right hand is held in a pose similar to the *simha-mukha mudra* or the *karana mudra*, while the left rests, palm upwards on the knee in a similar *mudra*.

36 ODD, p. 279, #43, and DRN, p. 36, #13 bear no resemblance to each other, although they have similar titles.

37 ODD, p. 279, #44, and OFr, p. 25, #22 are identical.

38 ODD, p. 279, #45, OFr, p. 26, #23, and DRN, p. 37, #38, all represent the same event with minor variations.

39 Neither ODD, p. 279, #47, nor OFr, p. 31, #28, are similar. ODD indicates the figure standing with arms hanging to the side, OFr indicates a standing figure with right hand against chest and left arm hanging to the side. DRN, p. 37, #31, describes a position in which the figure is standing in which "the hands crossed at the thighs."

40 ODD, p. 279, #48, and OFr, p. 28, #25, are identical, but they both differ from DRN, p. 36, #20, in that both hands are resting on the knee, palm upwards. DRN states that the "left hand palm downward in the lap."

41 ODD, p. 279, #49, and DRN, p. 36, #21, indicate and describe the same posture. It is to be noted that it is opposite to the posture (DRN) #33, "persuading the relatives not to quarrel."

42 ODD, P. 279, #51, OFr, p. 33, #30, and DRN, p. 37, #30 are identical.

43 ODD, p. 279, #52 and DRN, p. 36, #22, present and describe the same pose. OFr, p. 35, #32 indicates a variation in the position of the hands--i.e., the right hangs to the side and the left is held in front as if in *dhyana mudra*.

44 ODD, p. 279, #54 and DRN, p. 36, #23, display and describe the same position. OFr, p. 34, #32, indicates a variation in the placement and pose of the left hand, in that it rests, palm upward in the lap.

45 ODD, p. 279, #55 and DRN, p. 37, #24, are identical in presentation and description. OFr, p. 23, #20, again indicates a variation, in that both hands hold the bowl to the right.

46 ODD, p. 279, #56, OFr (page following #32 [p.36?] with no number) and DRN, p. 37, #35, are all identical.

47 OFr, p. 19, #16, Indicates a posture which is not represented in either ODD or DRN. The description indicates the Lord Buddha garbed "to guard against the cold." The illustration indicates a seated figure with a robe clutched in crossed hands at chest level.

48 DRN, p. 37, #32, is not represented in either ODD or OFr.

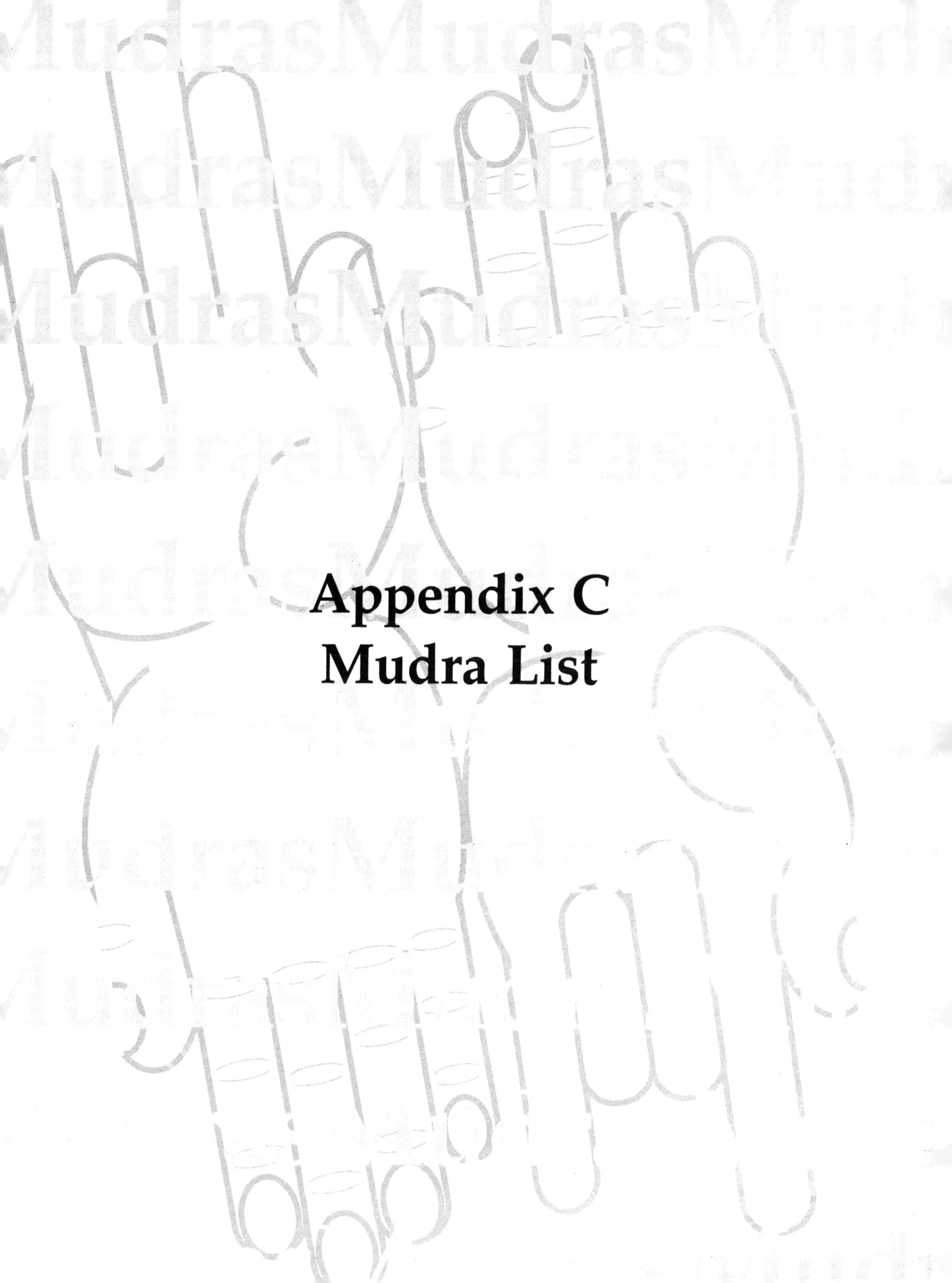

Appendix C
Mudra List

Mudra List

-- A --

abhaya mudra I
abhaya mudra II
abhaya mudra III
abhaya mudra IV
abhaya-abhaya mudra
abhaya-dhyana mudra
abhaya-katyavalambita mudra
abhaya-lolahasta mudra I
abhayamdada mudra
abhisheka mudra
abhisheka-guhya mudra
abhisheka(na) mudra
accepting the bundle of grass mudra
accepting the rice-gruel offering mudra
Achala-agni mudra
adamantine posture
adara gassho (mudra) I
adara gassho (mudra) II
adhara mudra I
adhara mudra II
adho-mukham mudra
adhishthana mudra
adho-mushti-mukula mudra
agni-chakra mudra
agni-chakra-shamana mudra I
agni-chakra-shamana mudra II
agni-jvala mudra
agni-shala mudra
agraja mudra
ahayavarada mudra
ahayavarada-dhyana mudra
ahayavarada-kataka mudra
ahayavarada-jnana mudra
ahvana mudra
aja-mukha mudra
Ajánta temborin-in (mudra)
akasha-jala mudra
akka-in (mudra)
akshata mudra
ala-padma mudra
alapallava mudra
alinga mudra
alingana mudra
aloke mudra
amalaka mudra
Ambarisha mudra
Amida-butsu seppo-in (mudra) I
Amida-butsu seppo-in (mudra) II
Amida-butsu seppo-in (mudra) III
Amida-butsu seppo-in (mudra) IV
Amida-butsu seppo-in (mudra) V
Amida-butsu seppo-in (mudra) VI
anchita mudra
anchita-ahayavarada mudra
anchita-anchita mudra I
anchita-anchita mudra II
anchita-dhyana mudra
anchita-katyavalambita mudra
anchita-lolahasta mudra
anchita-nidratahasta mudra I
anchita-nidratahasta mudra II
Angarakha mudra
an-i-in (mudra)
an-i-shoshu-in (mudra)
anjali mudra I
anjali mudra II
anjali mudra III
anjalikarma mudra
ankusha mudra
an-shan-yin (mudra)
anuchitta mudra
anuja mudra
an-wei she-ch'u-yin (mudra)

an-wei-yin (mudra)
anzan-in (mudra)
apan mudra
apan-vayu mudra
arala mudra I
arala mudra II
arala mudra III
arala-kataka-mukha mudra
archita mudra
ardhachandra mudra I
ardhachandra mudra II
ardha-chatura mudra
ardha-mukha mudra
ardha-mukula mudra
ardhanjali mudra
ardhanjali-dhyana mudra
ardha-pataka mudra
ardha-rechita mudra
argham mudra
argha mudra
Arjuna mudra I
arjuna mudra II
ashcharya mudra
ashoka mudra
ashta-dala-padma mudra
ashva-ratna mudra
ashvattha mudra
avahana mudra
avahani mudra
avahittha mudra
aviddha-vakra mudra

-- B --

bahya-bandha mudra
baka mudra
baku jo in (mudra)
Balaramavatara mudra
BAM mudra
bana mudra
basara-un-kongo-in (mudra) I
basara-un-kongo-in (mudra) II
bathing mudra
bdud-rtsi thabs-sbyor phyag-rgya (mudra)
bestowing ordination mudra
Bhagiratha mudra
bhartri mudra
bhartri-bhratri mudra
bhasparsha mudra
bherunda mudra
Bhima mudra
Bhimarathi mudra
bhinnanjali mudra
bhramara mudra
bhuddhashramana mudra
bhumi-bandha mudra
bhumishparsha mudra
bhumishparshana mudra
bhumisparsha mudra
bhusparsha mudra
bhutadamara mudra
bihararieisata gassho (mudra)
Biroshana-in (mudra)
biroshananyoraidaimyochi-in (mudra)
boda gassho (mudra)
bodaiindodaiichichi-in (mudra)
bodhashri mudra
bon jiki-in (mudra)
Brahma mudra
Brahmana mudra
brahmokta-shuktunda mudra
Brihaspati mudra
bu bosatsu-in (mudra)
Buddhalochani mudra
buddhapatra mudra
buddhashramana mudra I
buddhashramana mudra II
buddhashramana-dhyana mudra
Budha mudra
buku-in (mudra)
bu mo-in (mudra)
buppatsu-in (mudra)
butsu bu sammaya-in (mudra)
butsubu sotoba-in (mudra)

bu zo-in (mudra)
bya-lding phyag-rgya (mudra)

-- C --

calling down the rain mudra
carrying the alms bowl mudra
chaga mudra
chakra mudra I
chakra mudra II
chakra-ratna mudra
chakravaka mudra
chakravartin mudra
chakshur mudra
champaka mudra
Chandra mudra
chandrakala mudra I
chandrakala mudra II
chandra-mriga mudra
chapetadana mudra
chaturahasta mudra
chatura mudra I
chatura mudra II
chatura mudra III
chaturashra mudra
chatur-dig-bandha mudra
chatur-mukham mudra
chhu tshong mo khiu keu-yin (mudra)
chih-ch'ṃan-yin (mudra)
chi ken-in (mudra) I
chi ken-in (mudra) II
chiku cho sho-in (mudra)
chin mudra I
chin mudra II
chin-kang ho-chang (mudra)
chintamani mudra I
chintamani mudra II
chintamani mudra III
chintamani mudra IV
chintamani mudra V
chitta mudra
chitta-guhya mudra
cho butsu fu-in (mudra)
cho kongo renge-in (mudra)
cho nen ju-in (mudra)
chonmukhmukham mudra I
chonmukhmukham mudra II
choosing the chief disciples mudra
chos-dbying rnam-dag phyag-rgya (mudra)
cho zai-in (mudra)
chuan-fa-lun-yin (mudra)
chuan-yṃeh-lo-hung chin-kang-yin (mudra)
ch'u-ti-yin (mudra)
contemplating the approach of his death mudra
contemplating the corpse mudra

-- D --

dai kai-in (mudra)
dai sotoba-in (mudra)
dai ye-to no-in (mudra)
damaru mudra
damaruhasta (mudra)
dampati mudra
dana mudra
danda mudra
danda[hasta] mudra
dbang-sgyur 'khor-lo'i phyag-rgya (mudra)
Dharani-Avalokiteshvara mudra
dharmachakra mudra
dharmachakra-pravartana mudra
dharmachakra-pravartana-bodhisattva-varga-mudra
dharma-pravartana mudra
Dharmaraja mudra
dhenu mudra I
dhenu mudra II
Dhritarashtra mudra
dhupa mudra I
dhupa mudra II
dhupa mudra III
dhyana mudra I
dhyan(a) mudra II

dhyanahasta mudra
dhyana-nidratahasta mudra
diamond fist (mudra)
Dilipa mudra
dipa mudra
discoursing on the decrepitude of old age mudra
dola(hasta) mudra
dola mudra
dvi-mukham mudra
dvirada mudra

-- E --

eating the myrobalan fruit mudra
eating the rice gruel mudra
elephant glance mudra
expounding the constituent elements mudra

-- F --

fo-puo-yin (mudra)
fu ko-in (mudra)
fukushu gassho (mudra)
fu ku-yo-in (mudra)
funnu ken-in (mudra)
fu tsu ku yo-in (mudra)

-- G --

gada mudra
Gaganaganja mudra I
Gaganaganja mudra II
gaja mudra
gaja(hasta) mudra
gajadanta mudra
gandha mudra I
gandha mudra II
gandha mudra III
gandharan temborin-in (mudra)
gandhararattha mudra
gandharva-raja mudra
Ganga mudra
gardabha mudra
garuda mudra
garuda-paksha mudra
gazing at the bodhi tree mudra
ge baku goko (gassho) mudra
gebaku ken-in (mudra) I
gebaku ken-in (mudra) II
gebaku ken-in (mudra) III
ge-in (mudra) I
ge-in (mudra) II
ge-in (mudra) III
ge-in (mudra) IV
ge kai-in (mudra)
ghanta mudra
ghanta-vadana mudra
girika mudra
go buku-in (mudra)
godhika mudra
go-san-ze (mudra)
granthitam mudra
gshegs-gsol phyag-rgya (mudra)
gyan mudra

-- H --

hachiu-in (mudra)
haku sho-in (mudra) I
haku sho-in (mudra) II
hamsa mudra
hamsa-paksha mudra I
hamsa-paksha mudra II
hamsasya mudra I
hamsasya mudra II
hanjakugoshochaku gassho (mudra)
hansi mudra
haranama gassho (mudra)
harina mudra I
harina mudra II
Harishchandra mudra
hastasvastika mudra I
hastasvastika mudra II

hastasvastika mudra III
hastasvastika mudra IV
hasti-ratna mudra
Hayagriva mudra I
Hayagriva mudra II
hemanta mudra
hen hokkai mushofushi-in (mudra)
hi ko-in (mudra)
hintala mudra
HOH mudra
hokai sho-in (mudra)
honzon bu jo no-in (mudra)
hora no-in (mudra)
hridayaya (mudra)

-- I --

Indra mudra
in the Palelayaka forest mudra
ishtaprada mudra
Ishvara mudra
issai ho byo do kai go (mudra)

-- J --

JAH mudra
jambu mudra
jigs-med phyag-rgya
ji ketsu-in (mudra)
jo kongo-in (mudra)
jo renge-in (mudra)
jnanam mudra
jnana mudra I
jnana mudra II
jnana-avalokite mudra
jnana-jnana mudra I
jnana-jnana mudra II
jnana-lolahasta mudra I
jnana-lolahasta mudra II
jnana-mushti mudra
jnana-nidratahasta mudra
jnana-shri mudra
jnyana mudra
jo fudo-in (mudra)
jo-in (mudra) I
jo-in (mudra) II
jo-in (mudra) III
jo-in (mudra) IV
jo-in (mudra) V
jo-in (mudra) VI
jo-in (mudra) VII
jo-in (mudra) VIII
jo zu ma ko ku-in (mudra)
ju-ni kushi ji shin-in (mudra)
jyeshta-bhratri mudra

-- K --

kacchapa mudra
kadali mudra
kai mon-in (mudra)
ka-in (mudra)
kai shin-in (mudra)
kaji ko sui-in (mudra)
kaka mudra
Kalkiavatara mudra
kamala mudra
kamjayi mudra
kanaka-matsya mudra
kandanjali mudra
kanishtha-bhratri mudra
kanjo-in (mudra)
kanshukuden-in (mudra)
kapittha mudra I
kapittha mudra II
kapittha mudra III
kapota mudra I
kapota mudra II
karana mudra I
karana mudra II
karihasta (mudra)
karkata mudra
Karma-Akashagarbha mudra

kartari (hasta) mudra
kartari-danda mudra
kartari-mukha mudra I
kartari-mukha mudra II
kartari-mukha mudra III
kartari-svastika mudra
Karttivirya mudra
kashyapa mudra
kataka mudra I
kataka mudra II
kataka mudra III
kataka mudra IV
kataka mudra V
kataka mudra VI
kataka-mukha mudra
kataka-vardhana mudra
kati mudra
katiga mudra
katisamsthita mudra
katyavalambita mudra
kavacha mudra I
kavacha mudra II
kavachaya (mudra)
Kaveri mudra
kaya-kavacha mudra
kayen sho-in (mudra)
ke bosatsu-in (mudra)
ke man-in (mudra)
kengo baku-in mudra
kenji(sshin)-gassho (mudra)
kenjisshin-gassho (mudra)
kenro kongo ken-in (mudra)
kesha-bandha mudra
ketaki mudra
Ketu mudra
khadga mudra I
khadga mudra II
khadga mudra III
khadga mudra IV
khadga-mukula mudra
khadga-ratna mudra
khadira mudra
khanda-chatura mudra
khanda-mukula mudra
khatva mudra
kia-yin (mudra)
kichijo-in (mudra)
kilaka mudra
kimbei-in (mudra)
kimyo-gassho (mudra)
ko-in (mudra)
kongo baku-in (mudra)
kongo cho-in (mudra)
kongo-gassho (mudra)
kongo-karuma bosatsu-in (mudra)
kongo-ken-in (mudra) I
kongo-ken-in (mudra) II
kongo ken-in (mudra) III
kongo mo-in (mudra)
kongo rin-in (mudra)
ko taku(-in) (mudra)
krishna-mriga mudra
Krishnavatara mudra
Krishnaveri mudra
krodha mudra
kshanti mudra
Kshattriya mudra
kshepana mudra I
kshepana mudra II
Kshitigarbha mudra
kuan butsu kai ye-in (mudra)
kuan-ting-yin mudra
kuken (mudra)
kukkuta mudra
kumma(n)ra gassho (mudra)
kunda-dhvaja mudra
kurma mudra I
kurma mudra II
kurma mudra III
Kurmavatara mudra
kurpara mudra I
kurpara mudra II
kurpara-kurpara mudra
kuruvaka mudra

kushala mudra
Kuvera mudra

-- L --

Lakshmi mudra
lakucha mudra
lalita mudra
langula mudra
lata mudra
lina mudra
lina-karkata mudra
linalapadma mudra
linga mudra
Lochana mudra
lolahasta (mudra)
lolahasta-abhaya mudra I
lolahasta-abhaya mudra II
lolahasta-dhyana mudra
lolahasta-lolahasta mudra II
lolahasta-vitarka mudra
looking back at the city of Vaisali mudra

-- M --

madhya-pataka mudra
Maha-Akashagarbha mudra
maha-bana mudra
maha-jnana-khadga mudra
Mahakala mudra
maha-karma mudra
mahakrant mudra
mahakrantam mudra
maha-nabhi mudra
maha-samaya mudra
Mahasthamaprapta
maha-vajra-chakra mudra
makara mudra
making the four alms bowls into one mudra
making a gift of hair mudra
making the venerable Vakkali move away mudra
ma-mo-mdos mudra(s)
mandala mudra
mandara mudra
mani-ratna mudra
Manmatha mudra
ma no cho jo-in (mudra)
manwichai (mudra)
maravijaya mudra
marishitenhobyo-in (mudra)
marjara mudra
matri mudra
matsya mudra
Matsyavatara mudra
mayura mudra
meditating mudra
mi be renge gassho (mudra)
mifu renge-gassho (mudra)
mifu renge-in (mudra) I
mifu renge-in (mudra) II
mifu renge-in (mudra) III
miharita gassho (mudra)
Milarepa's mudra
mragi mudra
mrigashirsha mudra I
mrigashirsha mudra II
Mrit-Sanjivani mudra
mudgaram mudra
mugdhram mudra
mukha mudra
mukula mudra
mula-guhya mudra
mu no sho shu-go-in (mudra)
mushaka mudra
mushofushi-in (mudra) I
mushofushi-in (mudra) II
mushofushi-in (mudra) III
mushofushi to-in (mudra)
mushti mudra
mushtikam mudra
mushti-mriga mudra
mushti-svastika mudra
myosenden-in (mudra)

-- N --

naga mudra
naga-bandha mudra
Nahusha mudra
naibaku ken-in (mudra) I
naibaku ken-in (mudra) II
naibaku ken-in (mudra) III
Nairriti mudra
naivedye mudra
Nakula mudra
Nala mudra
nalini-padmakosha mudra
namaskara mudra I
namaskara mudra II
nananda mudra
nan kan-nin-in (mudra)
narangi mudra
Narasimhavatara mudra
Narmada mudra
Naya-sutra mudra I
Naya-sutra mudra II
nebina gassho (mudra)
netra mudra I
netra mudra II
netratroyaiya (mudra)
nidhi-ghata mudra
nidratahasta (mudra)
nidratahasta-vitarka mudra
nidratahasta-nidratahasta mudra
nimbasala mudra
nirvan(a) mudra
nishedha mudra
nitamba mudra
niwa-in (mudra)
nometsumumyokokuan-in mudra
nritya mudra
nyo-i-shu-in (mudra)
nyorai cho-in (mudra)
nyorai getsu-in (mudra)
nyorai hosso-in (mudra)
nyorai ken-in (mudra)
nyorai saku-in (mudra)
nyorai shin-in (mudra)
nyorai zo-in (mudra)

-- O --

ongyo-in (mudra) I
ongyo-in (mudra) II
on the jeweled walkway mudra
ottanasha gassho (mudra)

-- P --

padma mudra I
padma mudra II
padmahasta (mudra)
padmakosha mudra
padma-kunjara mudra
padma-mushti (mudra)
padmanjali mudra
padyam mudra
paksha-pradyota mudra
paksha-vanchita mudra
palasa mudra
pallava mudra
pallavam mudra
panasa mudra
Pancha-guhya mudra
pancha-mukham mudra
pancha-nayana mudra
Panchoshnisha mudra
pang chan-samor
pang chong-krom-keaw
pang ham-phra-kaen-chan
pang ham-samut
pang hamyat
pang harm-marn
pang khabphrawakkali
pang khor-phon
pang lila I
pang lila II

pang loy-tard
pang maravichai
pang nakawalok I
pang nakawalok II
pang palelai
pang parinippharn
pang pattakit
pang perdlok
pang phraditthanroy-phrabuddhabatr
pang phra-keit-tatu
pang phra-nang
pang phrasarnbhatr
pang phratabreakhanan I
pang phratabreakhanan II
pang phratarn-ehibhikkhu
pang phratopyun
pang plong-aryusangkharn
pang plong-kammathan
pang prongahyuksankhan
pang rab-pholmamuang
pang ram-pueng
pang sanghlupnammamuangduaibaht
pang sawoimathupayas
pang sedetphutthadannernpai
pang s(h)aiyas
pang song-nam-phon
pang song-picharanacharatham
pang sonkhem
pang sung-rabmathupayas
pang sung-rabyaka
pang tavainetr
pang thong-tang-etatakkasatarn
pang tukkarakiriya
pang uhm-bhatr
pankajam mudra
pankaj mudra
Papanasini mudra
Parashuramavatara mudra
pardisha-mukula mudra
parijata mudra
partaking of food mudra
Parvati mudra
pasha mudra I
pasha mudra II
pasha mudra III
pashatarjani mudra
pataka mudra I
pataka mudra II
pataka-dhyana mudra
patali mudra
patra mudra
performing austerities mudra
phat (mudra)
pitri mudra
porcupine deer mudra
pothi mudra
pralambam mudra
pranama mudra
pran mudra
prasada mudra
pravartita mudra
pravartitahasta (mudra)
prithvi mudra
puga mudra
pu mu-yin (mudra)
puna mudra
purn-gyan mudra
punnaga mudra
Purukutsa mudra
Pururavas mudra
purusha-ratna mudra
pushpa-mala mudra I
pushpa-mala mudra II
pushpanjali (mudra)
pushpa mudra
pushpaputa mudra
pushpe mudra

-- R --

Ragaraja Mula-mudra
Ragavajra mudra
Raghuramavatara mudra
Rahu mudra

rasala mudra
ratna-ghata mudra
ratna mudra I
ratna mudra II
ratna-kalasha mudra
Ratnaprabha-Akashagarbha mudra
ratna-vahana mudra
Ravana mudra
receiving the mango mudra
receiving the offering of water mudra
rechita mudra
reclining mudra
reflecting mudra
reflecting on worldly impermanence mudra
rei-in (mudra)
rekha mudra
renge-bu shu-in (mudra)
renge ken-in (mudra)
renge-no-in (mudra)
ren renge-in (mudra)
restraining Mara mudra
restraining the kinsmen mudra
restraining the sandalwood image mudra
restraining the waters mudra
revealing the three worlds mudra
rgya-chen shugs-ldan phyag-rgya (mudra)
rin-chen sgrom-bu'i phyag-rgya (mudra)
rishabha mudra
rito-in (mudra)
rupa mudra

-- S --

Sachittotpada-Bodhisattva mudra
sadung-man (mudra)
Sagara mudra
Sahadeva mudra
Sahasra-bhuja Avalokiteshvara mudra
sai butsu-in (mudra)
sai fuku sho ma-in (mudra)
sa-in (mudra)
sai zai-in (mudra)
saku-in (mudra)
samadhi mudra
samanta-buddhanam mudra
samdamsa mudra I
samdamsa mudra II
samdamsa-mukula mudra
samputa mudra I
samputa mudra II
samputam mudra
samputanjali mudra
samyama mudra
samyama-nayaka mudra
sandarshana mudra
sanfuta gassho (mudra)
sanjali mudra
sankaisaisho-in (mudra)
sankirna mudra
sankirna-makara mudra
san-ko-cho-in (mudra)
san-ko-in (mudra) I
san-ko-in (mudra) II
santi mudra
sapatni mudra
sarasa mudra
Sarasvati mudra I
Sarasvati mudra II
sarpakara mudra
sarpa mudra
sarpashirsha mudra
sarva-buddha-bodhisattvanam mudra
sarva-dharmah mudra
sarvarajendra mudra
sarva-tathagata-avalokite mudra
sarva-tathagatebhyo mudra
sashu-gassho (mudra)
segan-in (mudra)
segan-semui-in (mudra)
sems-ma rdo-rje-ma'i phyag-rgya (mudra)
semui-in (mudra)
se-ten cho sho no-in (mudra)
setting the dish afloat mudra
shabda mudra I

shabda mudra II
Shaibya mudra
shakata mudra I
shakata mudra II
Shakra mudra
Shakyamuni (mudra)
Shambhu mudra
Shanaischara mudra
shami mudra
shankha mudra I
shankha mudra II
shankha mudra III
shankha mudra IV
shankha mudra V
shankha-varta mudra
Shanmukha mudra
shan-mukham mudra
shantida mudra
sharad mudra
Sharasvati mudra
Sharayu mudra
shashanka mudra
shayana mudra
Shibi mudra
shih-wu-wei-yin
shih-yṃan-yin (mudra)
shikhara mudra
shikhayai (mudra)
shimshapa mudra
shirasi (mudra)
shirsha mudra
Shiva-linga mudra
shizaige ken-in (mudra)
sho cha ro-in (mudra)
sho ko-in (mudra)
shri-vatsya mudra
Shudra mudra
shuka mudra
shukatunda mudra
shukatundaka mudra
Shukra mudra
shumi sen ho-in (mudra)
shunya mudra
shvan mudra
sh̉vashri mudra
shvashura mudra
sima-bandha mudra I
sima-bandha mudra II
simha mudra
simhakarna mudra I
simhakarna mudra II
simhakarna-simhakarna mudra
simhakrantam mudra
simha-mukha mudra
sindkuvara mudra
singhakrant mudra
sitatapatra mudra
snusha mudra
so cha ro-in mudra
so ko shu-go-in (mudra)
sokuchi-in (mudra) I
sokuchi-in (mudra) II
sola-padma mudra
stamping his footprint in the ground mudra
standing mudra
sthirabodhi mudra
stri mudra
stri-ratna mudra
stupa mudra
suchi mudra I
suchi mudra II
suchi mudra III
suchi mudra IV
suchi-viddha mudra
suchyasya mudra
sukri mudra
Sumeru mudra
summoning sins (mudra)
sumukham mudra
supratishtha mudra
surabhi mudra I
surabhi mudra II
Surya mudra I
Surya mudra II

sutra mudra
suvarna-chakra mudra
]Suvarnamukhi mudra
svakuchagraha mudra
svastika mudra I
svastika mudra II
svastika mudra III
svastika mudra IV
svastika mudra V
swastika mudra

-- T --

tai-ken-in (mudra)
tala-mukha mudra
tala-pataka mudra
tala-simha mudra
tamrachuda mudra I
tamrachuda mudra II
tarjani mudra I
tarjani mudra II
tarjani (II)-dhyana mudra
tarjanipasha mudra
tarpana mudra
Tathagata-damshtra mudra
tathagata-kukshi mudra
tathagata-mushti (mudra)
tathagata-vachana mudra
tattva mudra
teiriei gassho (mudra)
tejas-bodhisattva mudra
temborin-in (mudra)
temborin-in mudra II
threading the needle mudra
Tibetan temborin-in (mudra)
tilaka mudra
ting-yin (mudra)
to myo-in (mudra)
torma mudra
Trailokyavijaya mudra I
Trailokyavijaya mudra II
traveling by boat mudra
trijnana mudra
tri-mukham mudra
trintrini mudra
tripitaka mudra I
tripitaka mudra II
tripitaka mudra III
tripitaka mudra IV
trisharana mudra
trishula mudra I
trishula mudra II
trishula mudra III
Tungabhadra mudra

-- U --

uddhrita mudra
udveshtitalapadma mudra
udvritta mudra
ulbana mudra
uluka mudra
unmukhonmukham mudra
Upakeshini mudra
uparatna mudra
Upaya-paramita mudra
urnanabha mudra
urusamsthita mudra
ushnisha mudra
ushtra mudra
ut-pal kha-bye-ba'i phyag-rgya (mudra)
utsanga mudra
uttanaja mudra
uttarabodhi mudra
utthana-vanchita mudra

-- V --

vairagyam mudra
vaishnava mudra
Vaishravana mudra
Vaishya mudra

vajra mudra I
vajra mudra II
vajra mudra III
vajra mudra IV
Vajra-Akashagarbha mudra
vajra-aloke mudra
vajra-amrita-kundali mudra
vajra-anjalikarma mudra
vajra-bandha mudra
vajranjali mudra
vajra-darshe mudra
vajra-dharme mudra
vajra-dhupe mudra
vajra-gandhe mudra
vajra-gita mudra
vajra-gite mudra
vajra-hasye mudra
Vajrahetu mudra
vajrahumkara mudra I
vajrahumkara mudra II
vajrahunkara mudra
vajra-jala mudra
vajra-jvala mudra
vajrakarma mudra
vajra-kashyapa mudra I
vajra-kashyapa mudra II
Vajrakula (mudra)
vajra-lasye mudra
vajra-mala mudra
vajra-manas mudra
vajra-mridamge mudra
vajra-muraje mudra
vajra-mushti II
vajra-mushti III
vajra-mushti (kai mon) mudra
vajra-nritye mudra
vajrapataka mudra
vajra-pushpe mudra
vajra-rasye mudra
Vajrasattva mudra
vajra-shri mudra
vajra-shrinkhala mudra
vajra-sparshe mudra
vajra-suchi mudra
vajravali mudra
vajra-vamshe mudra
vajra-vine mudra
vakula mudra
Vamanavatara mudra
vanara mudra
vandana mudra I
vandana mudra II
vandani mudra
vara mudra
varada mudra
varada-dhyana mudra I
varada-dhyana mudra II
varaha mudra I
varaha mudra II
varaha mudra III
varahakam mudra
varahkam mudra I
varahkam mudra II
Vara-kaya-samaya-mudra
vardhamana mudra
vardhamanaka mudra
vardhamana mudra
varsha mudra
Varuna mudra
varun(a) mudra
vasanta mudra
vata mudra
vayan mudra
vayu mudra I
vayu mudra II
Vayu mudra III
veragya mudra
Vetravati mudra
vhalo mudra
viapkanjali mudra
vidya mudra
Vijneshvara mudra

vikasitapadma mudra
vilva mudra
Vinayaka mudra
viparita mudra
viparyasta mudra
viprakirna mudra
Virudhaka mudra I
Virudhaka mudra II
Virya-paramita mudra
Vishnu mudra
vismaya mudra I
vismaya mudra II
vismaya-vitarka mudra
vistritam mudra
visttam mudra
vitarka mudra
vitatam mudra
vittam mudra
vyaghra mudra
vyaghra mudra II
vyakhyana mudra I
vyakhyana mudra II
vyakhyana mudra III
vyala mudra
vyali mudra
vyapkanjali mudra

-- W --

wai-fu ch'ṃan-yin (mudra)
walking mudra
womb (fist mudra)
wu-so-pu-chih-yin (mudra)

-- Y --

Yaksha mudra
Yakshini mudra
Yama mudra I
Yama mudra II
yampasham mudra
Yamuna mudra
Yayati mudra
ye-shes skar-mda'i phyag-rgya (mudra)
yin-hsing-yin mudra
yo-cho jo-in (mudra)
yoni mudra I
yoni mudra II
yoni mudra III
yoga mudra

-- Z --

zen-in (mudra)
zu ko-in (mudra)

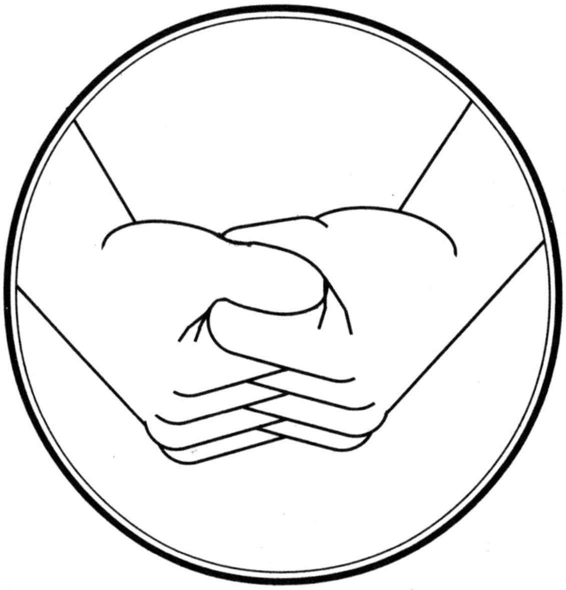

Acknowledgements

Acknowledgements

No work such as this can be accomplished alone. There are a number of people I wish to thank who have aided in this endeavour.

First I would like to thank Suradej Sutthi, Bangkok, for his supplying me with the English tranliterations of the Thai titles noted in the *Oxford-Duden Pictorial Thai and English Dictionary* and O. Frankfurter, "The Attitudes of the Buddha," *The Journal of the Siam Society*, vol. X, Part 2, with the following exceptions: *Oxford-Duden Pictorial Thai and English Dictionary* #6, 23, 32, 33, 34, 35, 54 & 55; as well as O. Frankfurter, "The Attitudes of the Buddha," #17 & 20, to whom I thank: Mr. Benjamin Sukanjanajtee, Second Secretary, Cultural and Information Affairs, Royal Embassy of Thailand, Kuala Lumpur, for his time and kind assistance. I thank Dr. Lokesh Chandra for allowing a xerox copy of the publication: Lokesh Chandra and Sharada Rani, *Mudras in Japan*, now out of print. Pertaining to that publication, I thank Susheel K. Mittal for the lengthy photocopying and having that copy bound for my convenience.

In addition, I would like to acknowledge, again, the various sources from which I compiled the descriptions of the various mudras. Each is noted within the appropriate entry; but, particularly the following: Chandra, Lokesh and Sharada Rani. *Mudras in Japan: Symbolic Hand-postures in Japanese Mantrayana or the Esoteric Buddhism of the Shingon Denomination*. New Delhi: 1978; Coomaraswamy, Ananda Kentish. *The Mirror of Gesture*. New Delhi: 1997; Devi, Gauri. *Esoteric Mudras of Japan: Mudras of the Garbhadhatu and Vajradhatu Mandalas, of Homa and Eighteen-step Tites, and of Main Buddhas and Bodhisattvas, Gods and Goddesses of Various Sutras and Tantras*. Delhi: 1999; Gupte, Ramesh S. *Iconography of the Hindus, Buddhists and Jains*. Bombay: 1972; Gopinatha Rao, T.A. *Elements of Hindu Iconography*, 4 vols. Madras: 1914-16; repr. Delhi: 1993; and Saunders, E. Dale. *Mudra: A study of Symbolic Gestures in Japanese Buddhist Sculpture*. New York: 1960.